Programming and Engineering Computing with MATLAB 2022

AF882290

Huei-Huang Lee

Department of Engineering Science
National Cheng Kung University, Taiwan

SDC
PUBLICATIONS

SDC Publications
P.O. Box 1334
Mission, KS 66222
913-262-2664
www.SDCpublications.com
Publisher: Stephen Schroff

ISBN-13: 978-1-63057-546-5

ISBN-10: 1-63057-546-1

Printed and bound in the United States of America.

Contents

List of Tables

Preface

Use of the Book

This book is developed mainly for junior undergraduate engineering students who have no programming experience, completely new to MATLAB. It may be used in courses such as Computers in Engineering, or others that use MATLAB as a software platform. It also can be used as a self-study book for learning MATLAB.

Features of the Book

Case studies and examples are the core of the book. We believe that the best way to learn MATLAB is to study programs written by experienced programmers and that these example programs determine the quality of a book. The examples in this book are carefully designed to teach students MATLAB programming as well as to inspire their problem-solving potential. Many are designed to solve a class of problems, instead of a particular problem.

Learning by doing is the teaching approach: students are guided to tackle a problem using MATLAB statements first and then the statements are explained line by line. If the meanings of a statement are obvious, further explanation may not be necessary at all. We believe that this is the most **efficient** and **pain-free** way of learning MATLAB. This approach, together with the extensive use of ordered **textboxes**, **figures**, and **tables**, largely reduces the size of the book, while providing desirable **readability** and **comprehensiveness**.

Junior-college-level engineering problems are used. **Background knowledge** for these engineering problems is illustrated as thoroughly as possible.

Reference materials outside the book can be found mostly either in the **MATLAB on-line help** or in **Wikipedia**, their exact locations always pointed out. The idea is that the reference materials should be immediately available for the students; they don't need to go to the library searching for reference books or journal papers. **Cross references** inside the book always come with the **page numbers** to facilitate the reading.

To Students: How to Work with the Book

Chapter 1 introduces MATLAB programming environment and overviews MATLAB functionalities. Chapters 2-9 discuss basic MATLAB functionalities in a progressive and comprehensive way. Chapters 10-13 give advanced topics that are useful in the college years. Each chapter consists of sections, each covering a topic and providing one or more examples. Related MATLAB functions are tabulated at the end of a section. Additional exercise problems are appended at the end of Chapters 2-9.

Examples in a section are presented in a consistent way. An example is usually described first, followed by a MATLAB script. In many cases, the explanation is not even needed, since, as you type and execute the commands, you'll appreciate the concepts that the example intends to convey. Text/graphics output, sometimes input as well, is presented. The rest of the text is to explain the statements of the script.

Although providing all program files (see SDC Publications Website, next page), we hope that you type each statement yourself, since as you type you are acquainting yourself with the MATLAB language. Often, you mistype and take lots of time to fix the mistakes. However, fixing errors is a precious experience of the learning process. Further, whenever possible, execute the statements one at a time (If necessary, using debugging mode; see Section 1.11) and watch the outcome of each statement, i.e., the text/graphic output on the screen.

One of the objectives of this book is to familiarize you with MATLAB on-line documentation, to ensure your continuing growth of MATLAB programming techniques even after the completion of this book. Therefore, consult the MATLAB on-line documentation as often as possible. In this book, we expect you to look up the on-line documentation yourself, whenever a new function is encountered.

To Instructors: How I Use the Book

The book is designed to be like a workbook. Each chapter should be able to be completed in 1-2 weeks. Each week in the classroom, I briefly introduce the materials and, after the classroom hours, let the students work with the book themselves on computers. I also create a weekly on-line discussion forum and let the students post their results, questions, comments, extra work, and so forth. I rate each student's post with a score of 0-5. The accumulated score becomes the grade for the week. I also participate in the discussion and record students' questions that are worth further illustration in the classroom. This teaching model has proved to be efficient and my students love it.

Download the Program Files

There are no supporting files needed for this book. You type, save, and run each example program, and observe the outcome of the program. However, if you really hate typing, all the program files are available for free download from the SDC publications website. Another reason we provide these program files is that we suggest you open a program on your MATLAB desktop when you read the text explaining the program. By doing so, you don't have to flip the pages back-and-forth when you read the text, which is sometimes annoying and distracting.

Author's Webpage

You also can download the program files from the following webpage:

http://lab.es.ncku.edu.tw/hhlee/Site/MATLAB2022.html

Notations

To efficiently present the material, the writing of this book is not always done in a traditional format. Chapters and sections are numbered in a traditional way, e.g., Chapter 1, Section 1.2, etc. Textboxes in a section are ordered with numbers enclosed by square brackets (e.g., [3]). We may refer to the third textbox in Section 1.2 as "1.2[3]." When referring to a textbox from the same section, we drop the section identifier; for the foregoing example, we simply write "[3]." Equations are numbered in a similar way, except that lower-case letters enclosed by round brackets (parentheses) are used to identify the equations. For example, "1.2(a)" refers to the first equation in Section 1.2. These notations are summarized as follows:

[1], [2], ...	A number enclosed by brackets is used to identify a textbox.
(a), (b), ...	A lower-case letter enclosed by round brackets is used to identify an equation.
Reference	References are italicized.
Workspace	Boldface is used to highlight words, especially MATLAB keywords.
Round-cornered textbox	A round-cornered textbox indicates that mouse or keyboard actions are needed.
Sharp-cornered textbox	A sharp-cornered textbox is for commentary, no mouse or keyboard actions needed.
→, ←, ↓, ↑, ↘, ↙, ↗, ↖	An arrow is used to point to the location of the next textbox.
↵	This symbol is used to indicate that the next textbox is on the next page.
#	This symbol is used to indicate that it is the last textbox of a section/subsection.

Huei-Huang Lee

Associate Professor
Department of Engineering Science
National Cheng Kung University, Taiwan
e-mail: hhlee@mail.ncku.edu.tw
webpage: http://lab.es.ncku.edu.tw/hhlee

Chapter 1

Getting Started, Desktop Environment, and Overview

This chapter introduces MATLAB desktop environment and gives you an overview of the MATLAB functionalities. Each section either introduces a topic that will be detailed in the future chapters or presents features of the MATLAB desktop environment that will be useful throughout the book. The introduction of the topics provides an overview of MATLAB. If you feel it is difficult to fully comprehend, don't worry, we'll give you the details in the future chapters. Now, fasten your seat belt and enjoy the learning experience...

1.1 Start and Quit MATLAB

[1] In this section, I'll guide you to start and quit MATLAB and also to browse its graphical user interface (GUI), called the **MATLAB desktop**.

About Textboxes

In this book, textboxes within a section/subsection (e.g., Section 1.1) are ordered with numbers enclosed by square brackets ([]). When you read the text, please follow the order of the textboxes. An arrow is used at the end of a textbox (e.g., see [1-10]) to locate the next textbox. The symbol ↵ is used to indicate that the next textbox is on the next page (e.g., [11]). The symbol # is used to indicate that it is the last textbox of a section/subsection (e.g., [21], next page). A round-cornered textbox (e.g., [2, 5, 11]) is to indicate that mouse or keyboard **actions** are needed in that step. A sharp-cornered textbox (e.g., [1, 3-4, 6-10]) is used for commentary only, no mouse or keyboard actions needed. ↙

(macOS) (Windows)

[2] To start MATLAB, double-click MATLAB icon. →

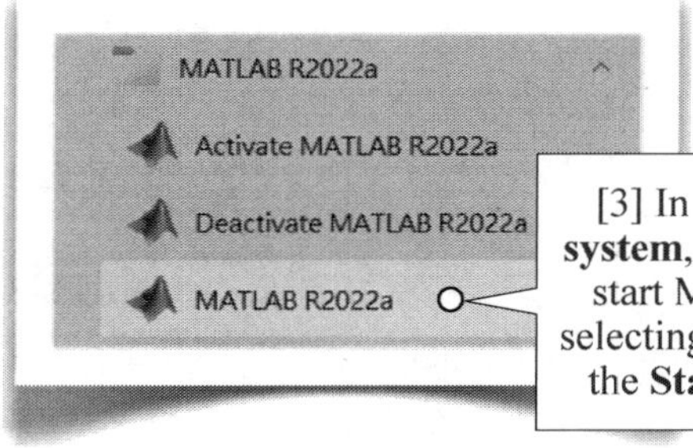

[3] In a **Windows system**, you may also start MATLAB by selecting an icon from the **Start menu**. ↓

[4] The MATLAB **desktop** appears in its default layout. ←

[5] If your desktop layout is not like this, pull-down-select **Layout>Default**. ←

[6] This is the path of the **Current Folder** where you access your files. You may change the **Current Folder** by clicking the small triangles. ↓

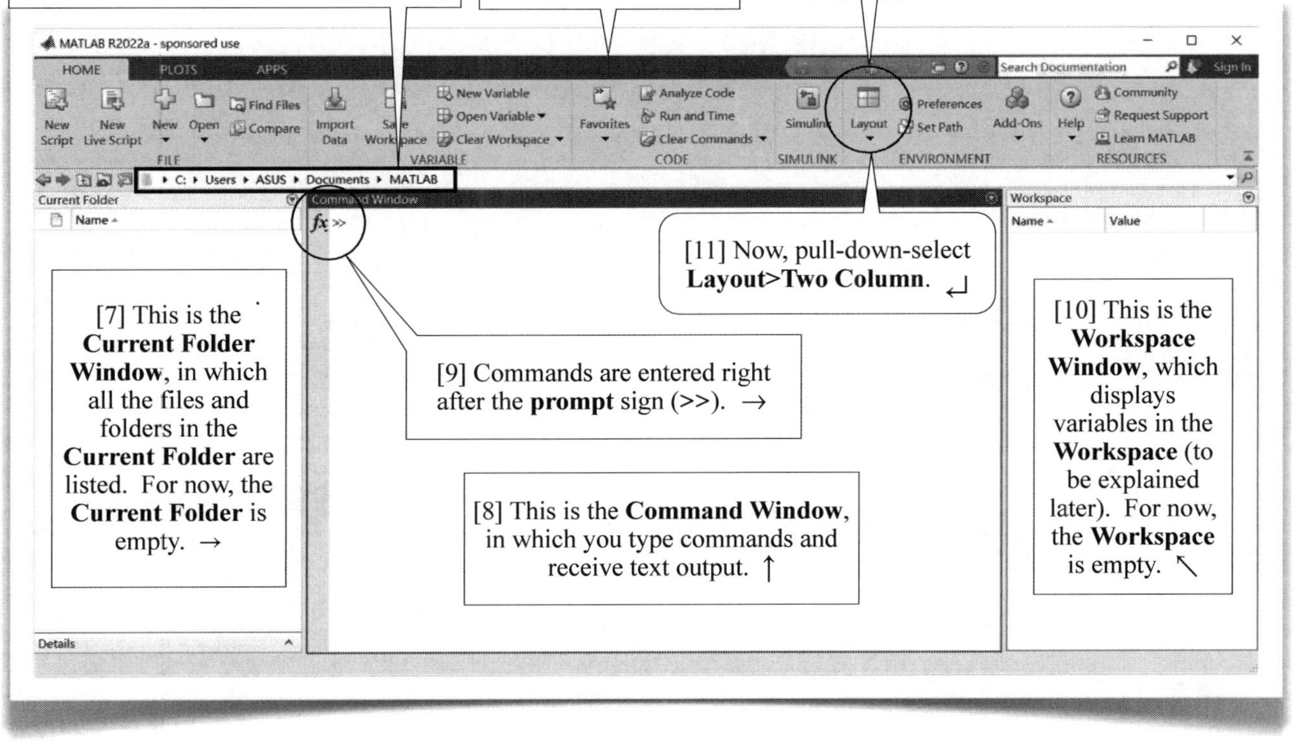

[7] This is the **Current Folder Window**, in which all the files and folders in the **Current Folder** are listed. For now, the **Current Folder** is empty. →

[8] This is the **Command Window**, in which you type commands and receive text output. ↑

[9] Commands are entered right after the **prompt** sign (>>). →

[10] This is the **Workspace Window**, which displays variables in the **Workspace** (to be explained later). For now, the **Workspace** is empty. ↖

[11] Now, pull-down-select **Layout>Two Column**. ↵

[12] The desktop changes to a **Two Column** layout. Throughout this book, we'll stick to the **Two Column** layout. ↘

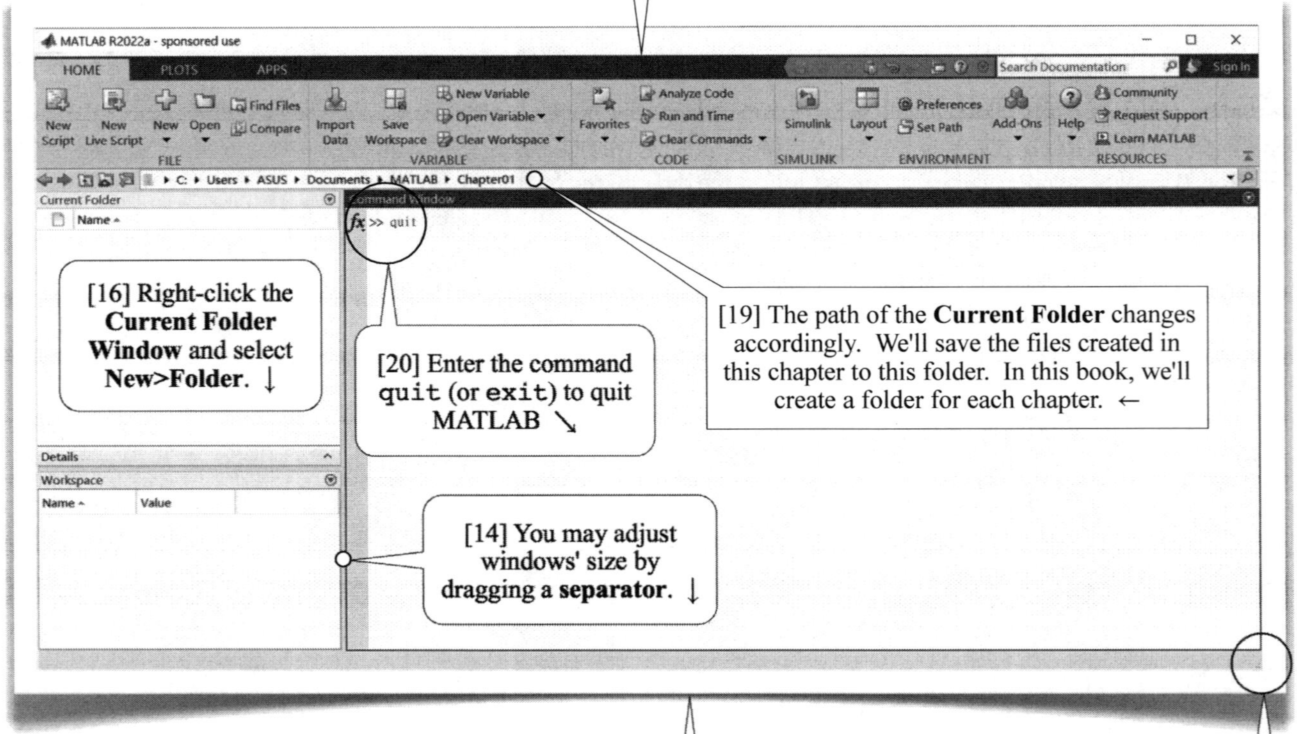

[16] Right-click the **Current Folder Window** and select **New>Folder**. ↓

[20] Enter the command `quit` (or `exit`) to quit MATLAB ↘

[19] The path of the **Current Folder** changes accordingly. We'll save the files created in this chapter to this folder. In this book, we'll create a folder for each chapter. ←

[14] You may adjust windows' size by dragging a **separator**. ↓

[15] The desktop layout will be preserved next time you start MATLAB again; i.e., the change of the layout is permanent until you change it again. ↖

[13] You may adjust the overall desktop size by dragging the lower-right corner. ↖

[17] Type **Chapter01** (and press **Enter**) as the name of the new folder. ↓

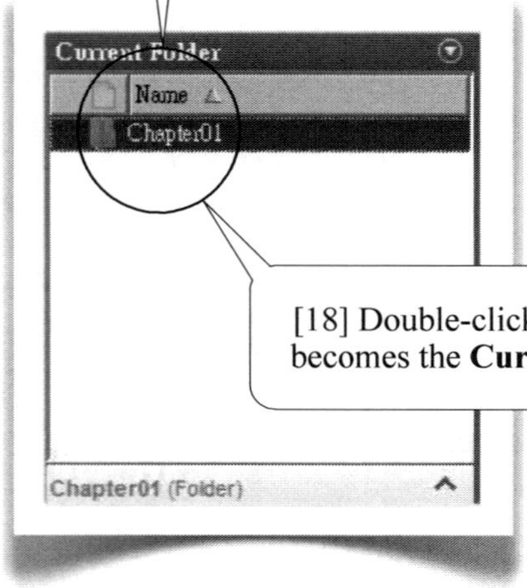

[18] Double-click **Chapter01**. It becomes the **Current Folder**. ↗

[21] You may also quit MATLAB by clicking the **Close** button of the window. #

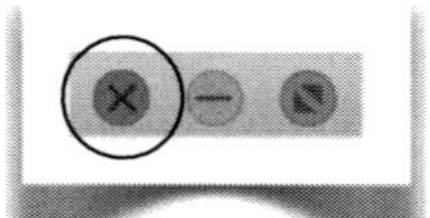

(macOS)

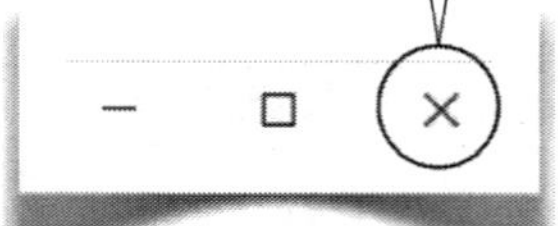

(Windows)

1.2 Entering Commands

[1] Entering commands in the **Command Window** is a way to get things done with MATLAB. A command in MATLAB is also called a **statement**. In this section, we'll learn how to use MATLAB as a calculator by entering **assignment statements** to calculate the position of a ball thrown in space. The following simple problem will be used throughout this chapter to demonstrate many features of MATLAB.

Problem Description

Consider that a ball is thrown in space [2-5]. The position (x, y) of the ball at time $t = 1$ sec is

$$x = (v_0 \cos\theta)t = (5 \text{ m/s})(\cos 45^\circ)(1 \text{ s}) = 3.5355 \text{ m} \quad \text{(a)}$$

$$y = (v_0 \sin\theta)t - \frac{1}{2}gt^2 = (5 \text{ m/s})(\sin 45^\circ)(1 \text{ s}) - \frac{1}{2}(9.81 \text{ m/s}^2)(1 \text{ s})^2 = -1.3695 \text{ m} \quad \text{(b)}$$

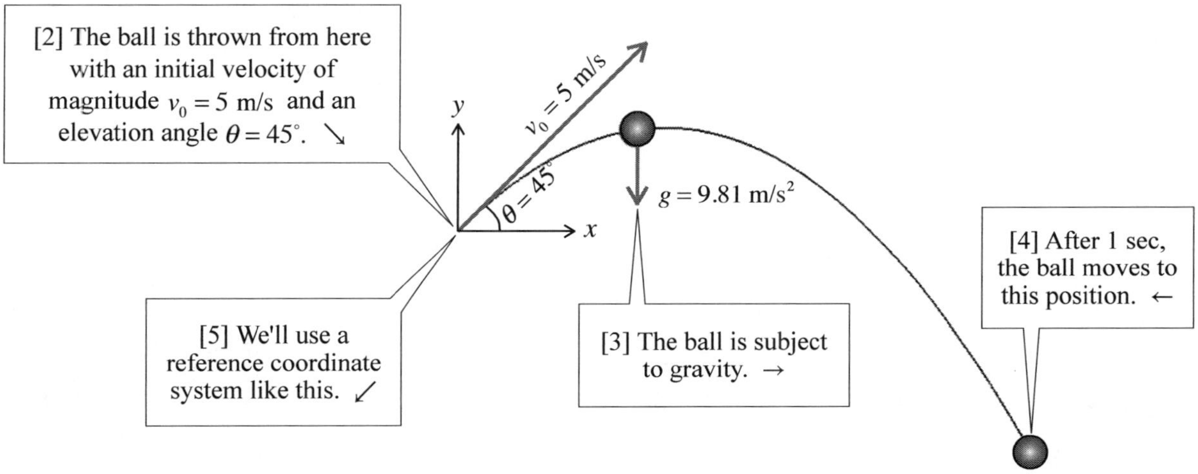

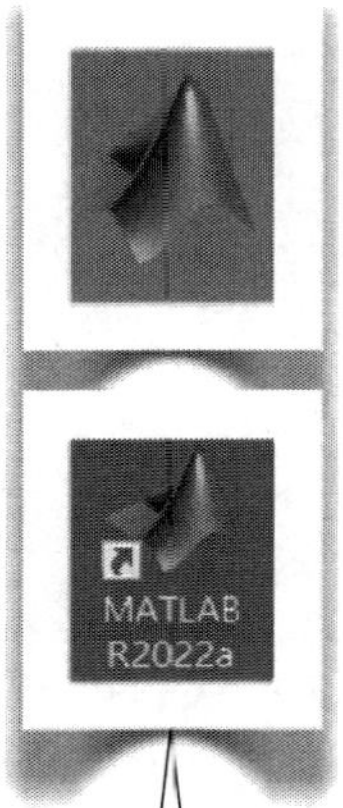

[6] Start MATLAB. →

[7] Enter the following commands one after another and watch the text output on your **Command Window** (see [8], next page, for the **Command Window** output).

```
>> v0 = 5
>> theta = pi/4
>> g = 9.81
>> t = 1
>> x = v0*cos(theta)*t
>> y = v0*sin(theta)*t-g*t^2/2
```

In the first command, a variable `v0` is created in the **Workspace** and a value `5` is assigned to the variable.

In the second command, another variable `theta` is created and the value `pi` (which is a built-in constant with a value of 3.141592653589793) is divided by 4 and assigned to the variable. The third and fourth commands are self-explained.

In the fifth command, x-position is calculated using Eq. (a). And in the sixth command, y-position is calculated using Eq. (b). Note that `cos` and `sin` are MATLAB built-in functions; each takes radius as angular unit. ↵

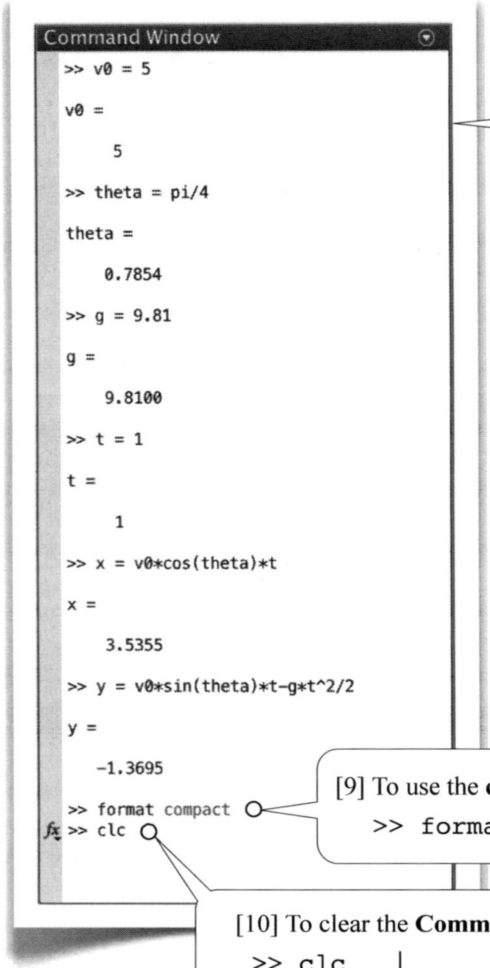

[8] Your **Command Window** should look like this. Note that an extra blank line is inserted between two text lines. That's because **loose** output format was used by default. ↙

[9] To use the **compact** format, type

```
>> format compact
```
↓

[10] To clear the **Command Window**, type

```
>> clc
```
↓

[11] The variables with their values are stored in a portion of your computer memory, called the **Workspace**. The **Workspace Window** lists each variable's name and other information. ↑

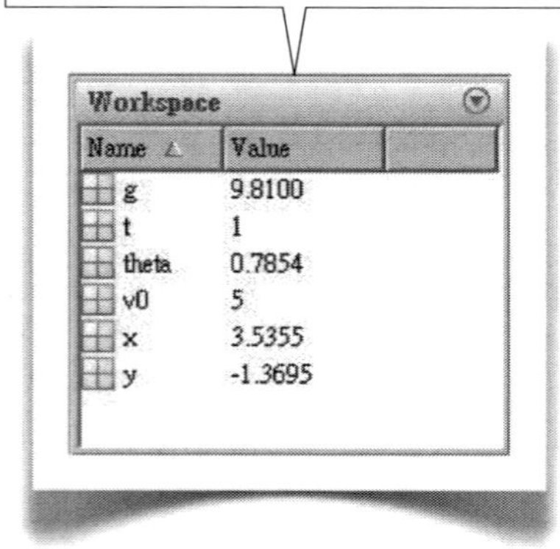

[12] To clear the **Workspace**, type

```
>> clear
```

Now all the variables are deleted from the **Workspace**. ↘

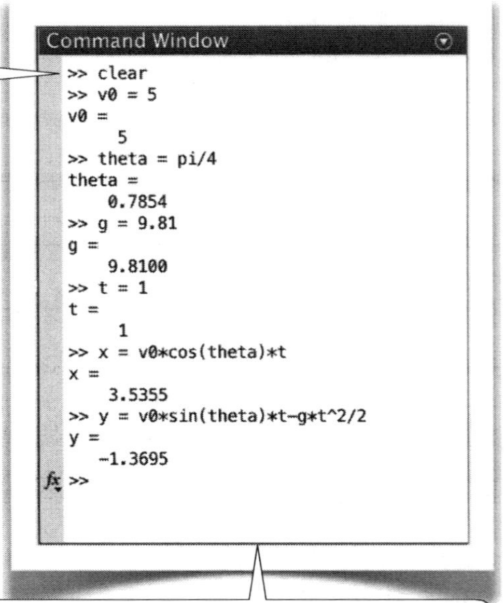

[13] With **compact** output format [9], enter the commands in [7] again. The extra blank lines mentioned in [8] are removed. In this book, we'll always use **compact** format [9] to save space. We'll discuss the output format in detail in 2.3b[3], page 76. ↙

Assignment Statements

[14] As mentioned, each command you entered is also called a **statement**. All the statements in [7] (last page) are **assignment statements**, which have a syntax like this

```
variable = expression
```

The `expression` is evaluated and the value is stored in the `variable`. If the variable does not exist yet, MATLAB creates one. The rules for a variable name are summarized in Table 1.2, page 16.

An expression is a syntactic combination of data, functions, operators, and special characters (see 2.11a[1], page 105). **Expressions** are the most frequent building blocks in a MATLAB program; we'll discuss them in Chapter 2. ↵

If you make a mistake...

[15] To demonstrate the correction of a mistake, please enter the following incorrect command:

```
>> y = v0*sin(theta)*t-g^2*t/2
y =
    -44.5825
```

Now, in your keyboard, press the **up-arrow** key (↑). ↘

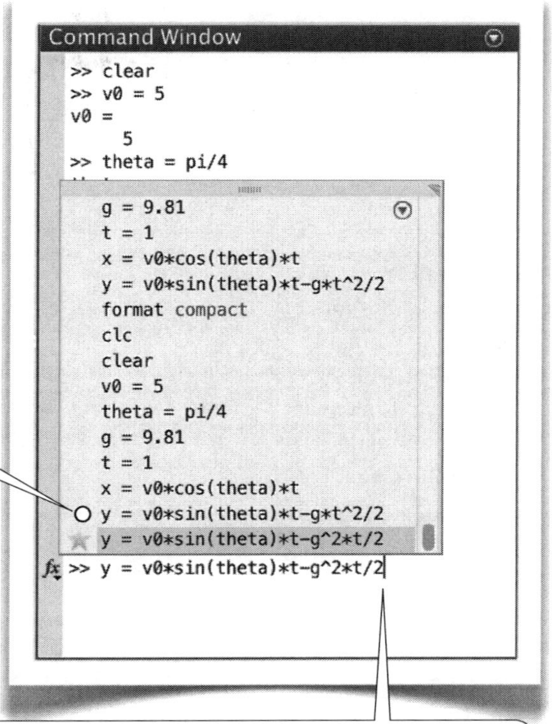

[17] Or click a command in the list, such as this correct command, to replace the current command. ↓

[18] After correcting the command, press the **Enter** key,

```
>> y = v0*sin(theta)*t-g*t^2/2
y =
    -1.3695
```

↙

[16] The pressing of the **up-arrow** key (↑) opens a **Command History Window**, which records the commands you've entered. The last command reappears after the **prompt** (>>). You may edit the incorrect command by moving the cursor and typing... ↖

On-line Documentation

[19] Click the **Help** button to open an on-line documentation window [20], with which you may look up the details of a command or a function. ↓

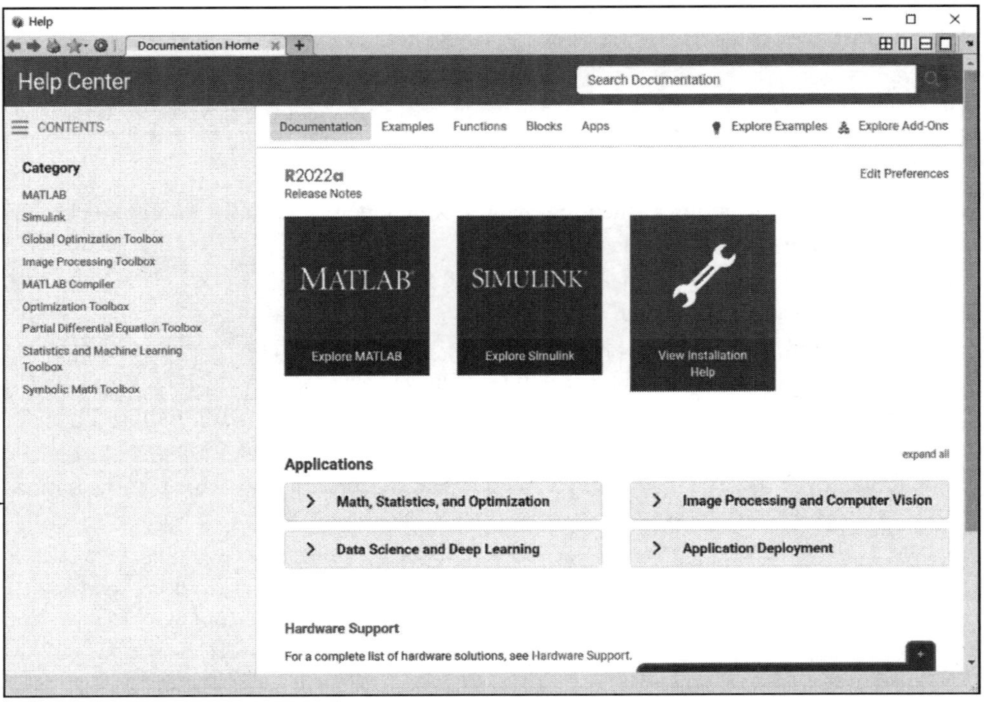

[20] The on-line documentation window. ↵

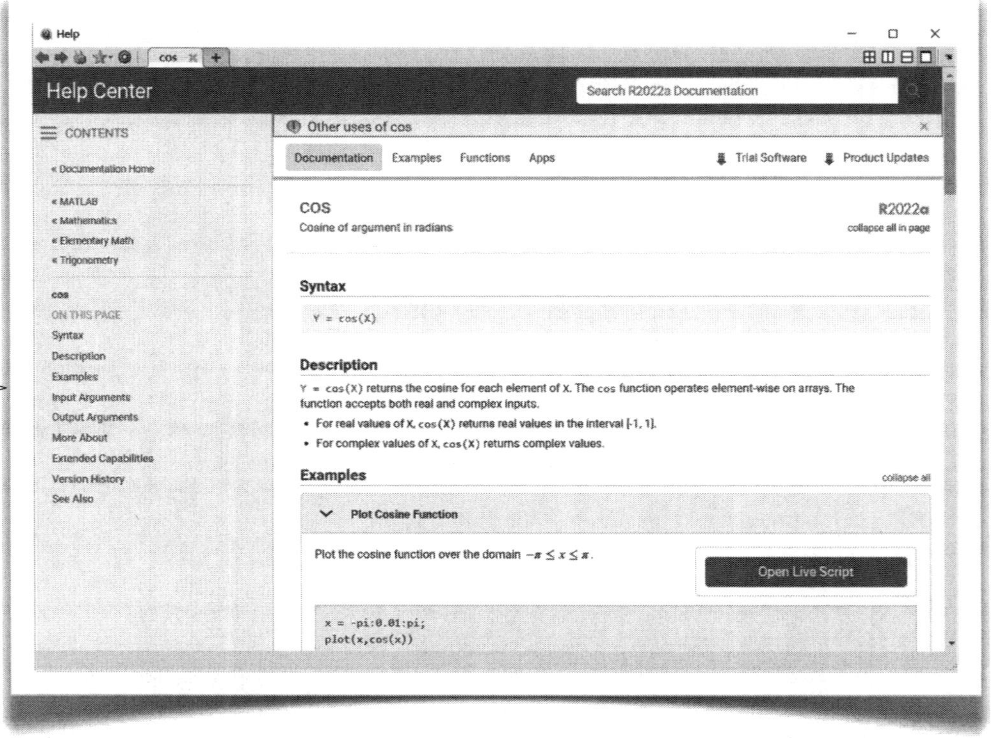

[21] Another way to display an on-line documentation for a command or a function is by typing its name in the **Command Window**; e.g.,

```
>> doc cos ↓
```

[22] Consult the on-line documentation whenever necessary, as often as possible. I expect you to look up the on-line documentation whenever a new command or a new function is encountered. Outside the MATLAB desktop, you can access on-line documentation from the website

```
http://www.mathworks.com/help/matlab/
```

#

Table 1.2 Rules for Variable Names

Variable names are examples of identifier names, which include **variable names** and **function names**. The following are the rules for an identifier name:

- A name contains only letters (A-Z, a-z), digits (0-9), and underscore (_).
- A name must begin with a letter.
- The maximum length of a name is 63. (*Type* >> `namelengthmax` *to obtain this number.*)
- A name is case-sensitive; i.e., there is a difference between uppercase and lowercase letters.
- It is legal, but not recommended, to use a built-in function name as a user-defined name. In that case, the built-in function is temporarily "invisible."
- The following MATLAB keywords cannot be used as names: (*Type* >> `iskeyword` *to obtain this list.*)

break	case	catch	classdef	continue	else	elseif
end	for	function	global	if	otherwise	parfor
persistent	return	spmd	switch	try	while	

1.3 Array Expressions

[1] The name MATLAB stands for **matrix laboratory**, since MATLAB treats all data as matrices. This often makes computations very efficient and sometimes facilitates the programming tasks. In this book, we'll guide you to get used to this matrix approach.

A matrix is an array of numbers organized in *m* rows and *n* columns, called an *m*-by-*n* matrix. In 1.2[7] (page 13), all data are scalar; they can be viewed as one-by-one matrices. Similarly, a row vector of *n* elements can be viewed as a 1-by-*n* matrix, and a column vector of *n* elements can be viewed as an *n*-by-1 matrix.

In terms of **dimensionality**, a matrix can be called a two-dimensional array, a vector (either a row vector or a column vector) can be called a one-dimensional array, and a scalar can be called a zero-dimensional array. With MATLAB, it is possible to create three-dimensional arrays, four-dimensional arrays, etc.

In this section, we'll calculate the position of the ball (as described in Section 1.2) at various time points, using expressions involving one-dimensional arrays. ↓

[2] The following commands calculate the position of the ball at 0, 0.2, 0.4, 0.6, 0.8, and 1.0 seconds. Your **Command Window** and **Workspace Window** should look like [3] and [4], respectively. ↓

```
>> v0 = 5;
>> theta = pi/4;
>> g = 9.81;
>> t = [0, 0.2, 0.4, 0.6, 0.8, 1]
>> x = v0*cos(theta)*t
>> y = v0*sin(theta)*t-g*t.^2/2
```

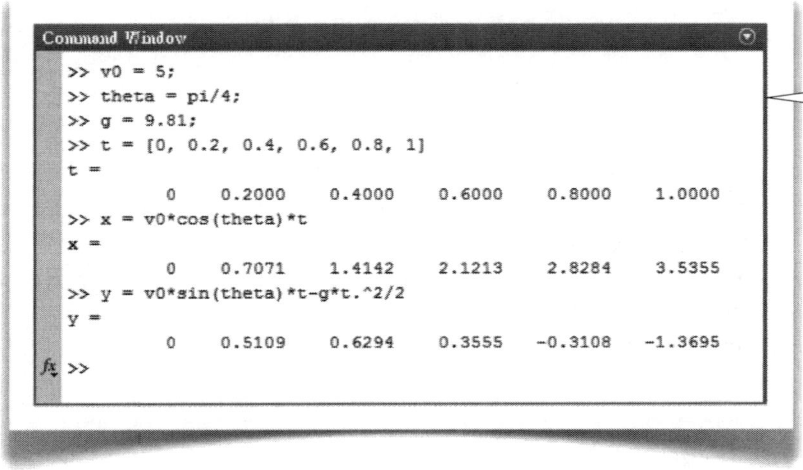

[3] Your **Command Window** looks like this. Remember, we assume that compact format is used (1.2[9, 13], page 14). ↓

[4] And your **Workspace Window** looks like this. ↙

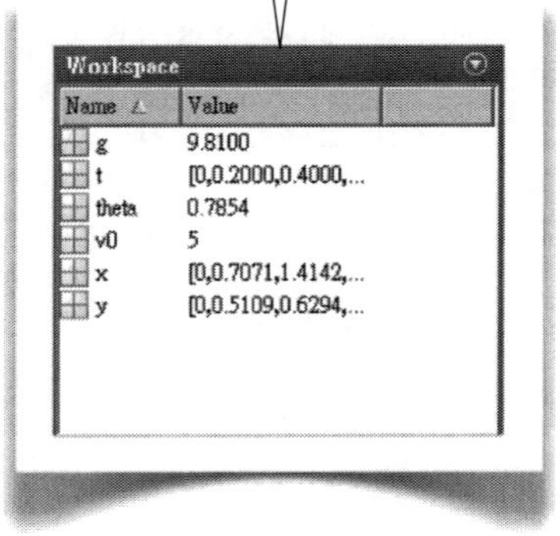

Use semicolons (;) to suppress output

[5] By default, the resulting value of a command is displayed in the **Command Window**. It is sometimes not desirable or even annoying. You may use a semicolon (**;**) to suppress the output of the result. When a statement ends with a semicolon, the text output is suppressed.

In [2], we suppressed the output for the first three statements because they involve no calculations. ↵

[6] The 4th statement

```
>> t = [0, 0.2, 0.4, 0.6, 0.8, 1]
```

creates a **row vector**, a **one-dimensional array**, of 6 elements representing 6 time points. The commas can be omitted; i.e., this statement can be rewritten as

```
>> t = [0 0.2 0.4 0.6 0.8 1]
```

There are shortcuts to create the same array; for example (please try them yourself),

```
>> t = [0:0.2:1]
>> t = 0:0.2:1
```

The syntax for the last command is

```
variable = start:increment:end
```

If the *increment* is omitted, it defaults to one. For example, `-1:4` generates a row vector `[-1 0 1 2 3 4]`. Note that, when you use the colon (`:`) to generate a vector, the square brackets `[ ]` can be omitted. ↓

[7] In the 5th statement

```
>> x = v0*cos(theta)*t
```

each element of `t` is multiplied by the scalar `v0*cos(theta)`. The result is a row vector of 6 elements, the same length of `t`, representing the *x*-positions at times stored in `t`. A row vector `x` of 6 elements is then created, and the results are assigned to `x`. ↓

[8] In the 6th statement

```
>> y = v0*sin(theta)*t-g*t.^2/2
```

the result of the first item of the right-hand side (i.e., `v0*sin(theta)*t`) is a **row vector** of 6 elements (similar to [7]). For the second item

```
g*t.^2/2
```

each element of `t` is squared (`.^2`), multiplied by the scalar `g`, and divided by `2`. The result is also a **row vector** of 6 elements. Two row vectors are then operated and the result is assigned to another row vector `y`.

Without a dot (`.`) before the exponentiation operator (`^`), `t^2` would be interpreted as `t*t` and would be erroneous because two matrices can be multiplied only when they have the same inner dimensions (2.8a[5], page 94). The operator `.^` is called an element-wise exponentiation operator (2.8a[6-7], pages 95-96; also see Table 2.8, page 92). ↓

Summary

[9] One-dimensional arrays are called **vectors**, which can be either **row vectors** or column vectors. Two-dimensional arrays are called **matrices**. As demonstrated in [7-8], array operations are very powerful features of MATLAB. We'll introduce more array operations in Chapter 2.

Remember that this chapter is to provide a big, yet incomplete, picture of MATLAB functionalities. If you have difficulties comprehending some statements, don't worry, we'll give you the details and more in the future chapters. #

1.4 Data Visualization: Line Plots

1.4a 2D Line Plots

[1] The best way to present your data is in graphics form. MATLAB has a rich repertoire of graphics capabilities from which you can choose to present your data. In this section, I'll show you that a trajectory of the ball (as described in Section 1.2) can be plotted with a few simple commands. ↓

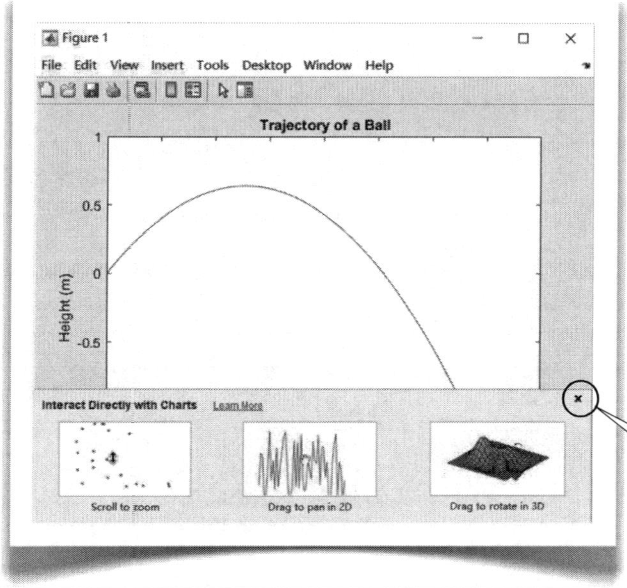

[2] The following commands draw a trajectory of a ball as shown in [3]. ↓

```
>> clear, clc
>> v0 = 5; theta = pi/4; g = 9.81;
>> t = 0:0.02:1;
>> x = v0*cos(theta)*t;
>> y = v0*sin(theta)*t-g*t.^2/2;
>> plot(x, y)
>> title('Trajectory of a Ball')
>> xlabel('Distance (m)')
>> ylabel('Height (m)')
```

[3] You see a **Figure Window** (**Figure 1**) created in the screen and a **line plot** produced in the window. If you see a window like this, click to close it. ↓

A command line may have multiple commands

[4] Multiple commands can be typed in a single command line, as demonstrated in the first two lines in [2]. Either commas (`,`) or semicolons (`;`) can be used to separate commands in a line; the difference is that the semicolon (`;`) suppresses the output while the comma (`,`) does not.

In programming practice, saving space is usually not the main purpose of typing multiple commands in a single line. Rather, the main purpose is to group similar commands together, improving readability and maintainability. ↓

[5] In the first line

```
>> clear, clc
```

the comma (`,`) is used to separate commands in a command line. Since `clear` and `clc` (see 1.2[17], page 15) do not produce any text output, the following three lines have the same effects:

```
>> clear, clc
>> clear; clc
>> clear; clc;
```

I suggest that you always include a `clear` to clear the **Workspace** and a `clc` to clear the **Command Window**. Clearing the **Workspace** is especially important because it prevents you from accidentally using a variable in the **Workspace** simply because you mistakenly type that variable name. ↵

[6] In the 2nd line

```
>> v0 = 5; theta = pi/4; g = 9.81;
```

the semicolons (`;`) not only separate commands in a command line but also suppress output on the **Command Window**. ↓

[7] The 3rd line

```
>> t = 0:0.02:1;
```

creates a row vector containing numbers from 0 to 1, each increasing 0.02, totaling 51 elements (see the syntax in 1.3[6], page 18). MATLAB creates curves by connecting data points with straight lines. Therefore, to draw a smooth curve, we need enough time points. The semicolon at the end of the command line suppresses output on the **Command Window**. Without the semicolon, it would list 51 numbers as shown in [8], which is annoying.

The 4th and 5th lines have been analyzed in 1.3[7-8] (page 18), except that the vectors **x** and **y** now have 51 elements, rather than 6 elements. →

```
>> t = 0:0.02:1
t =
  Columns 1 through 5
         0    0.0200    0.0400    0.0600    0.0800
  Columns 6 through 10
    0.1000    0.1200    0.1400    0.1600    0.1800
  Columns 11 through 15
    0.2000    0.2200    0.2400    0.2600    0.2800
  Columns 16 through 20
    0.3000    0.3200    0.3400    0.3600    0.3800
  Columns 21 through 25
    0.4000    0.4200    0.4400    0.4600    0.4800
  Columns 26 through 30
    0.5000    0.5200    0.5400    0.5600    0.5800
  Columns 31 through 35
    0.6000    0.6200    0.6400    0.6600    0.6800
  Columns 36 through 40
    0.7000    0.7200    0.7400    0.7600    0.7800
  Columns 41 through 45
    0.8000    0.8200    0.8400    0.8600    0.8800
  Columns 46 through 50
    0.9000    0.9200    0.9400    0.9600    0.9800
  Column 51
    1.0000
```

[8] Without the semicolon to suppress the output, the **Command Window** would be like this. ↙

[9] The 6th line

```
>> plot(x, y)
```

produces the trajectory curve shown in [3], last page. The curve is produced by connecting the following data points with straight line segments:

$$(x(i),\ y(i)),\ i = 1,\ 2,\ \ldots\ n$$

where $n = 51$ in this case. The **axis limits** (0 to 4 for x-axis and -1.5 to 1 for y-axis in [3]) are automatically chosen by MATLAB. We'll show you how to change the axis limits later.

The 7th line

```
>> title('Trajectory of a Ball')
```

adds a title to the plot, as shown in [3]. The last two lines add labels for the x-axis and the y-axis, respectively. #

1.4b 3D Line Plots

3-D Line Plots

[1] The function `plot3(x,y,z)` produces a curve in the 3-D space. The curve is produced by connecting the following data points with straight line segments:

$$(x(i),\ y(i),\ z(i)),\ i = 1,\ 2,\ \ldots n$$

As an example, the following commands draw a spiral curve shown in [2].

```
>> clear, clc, close
>> theta = 0:pi/100:8*pi;
>> x = cos(theta);
>> y = sin(theta);
>> z = theta/(8*pi);
>> plot3(x, y, z)
```

Note that the `close` command in the first line closes the "current" **Figure Window** (i.e., 1.4a[3], page 19). ↙

[3] Click to close the **Figure Window**. ↓

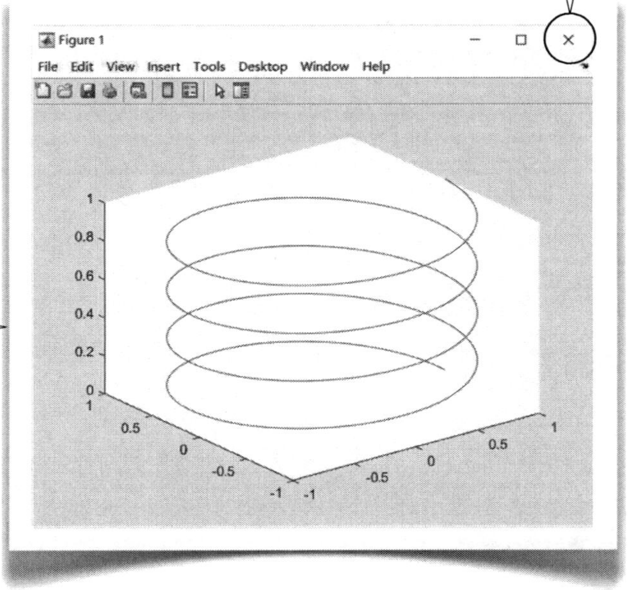

[2] The `plot3` (6th line) command creates a new **Figure Window** and plots a 3-D curve. ↗

Summary

[4] This section demonstrates that, with simple graphics commands, data can be graphically visualized. We'll discuss details and more of data visualization in Chapter 5. #

1.5 MATLAB Scripts

[1] When the number of statements (commands) to accomplish a task is getting large, typing in the **Command Window** becomes impractical. If you make a mistake, then you may have to retype everything. A more practical way is to save the statements in a text file, and then execute the statements. If there is an error, you correct it and execute the file again. A collection of statements in a text file is called a **script** (or a **program**) and the file is called a **script file**. In this section, we'll learn how to use the **MATLAB Script Editor** to accomplish the task in the last section. ←

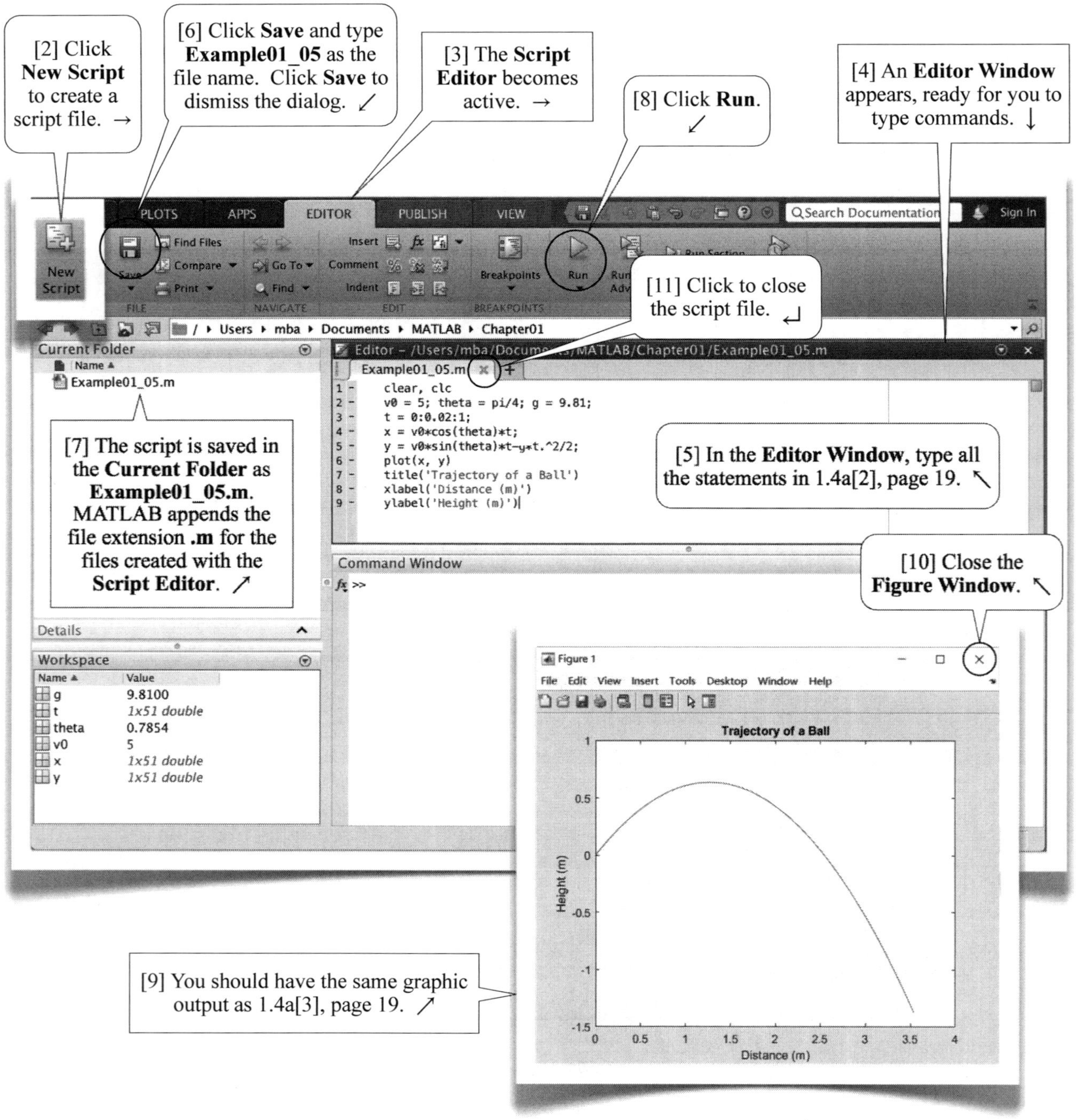

User-Defined Commands

[12] Other than clicking **Run** (see [8], last page), another way to run a program is typing its name in the Command Window:

```
>> Example01_05
```

In other words, the script becomes a user-defined command; the command even can be used in another script, just like any MATLAB built-in commands.

It is possible to create a user-defined command so that we can pass arguments. We'll discuss this in Section 3.5. ↙

[13] To demonstrate some more features of the **Script Editor**, let's open the file again. In the **Current Folder** window, double-click to open the script file. ↙

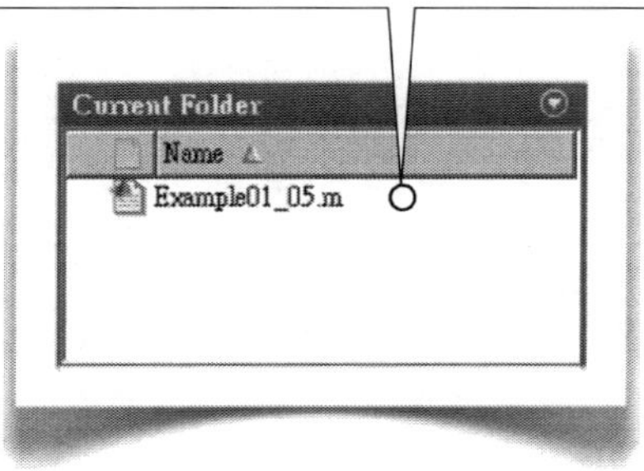

[14] The **Script Editor** implicitly checks the syntax for each statement. To illustrate this feature, now delete the semicolon at the end of line 3; it becomes

```
t = 0:0.02:1
```
↓

[18] Close the **Editor Window** (without saving the file). This closes all the opened script files. ↵

[16] An orange-color bar (a warning) and a red-color bar (an error) appear here. Move your mouse over the orange-color bar. A **warning** message appears suggesting that you terminate this statement with a semicolon to suppress the output. Now, correct the command by adding a semicolon to make this orange-color bar disappear. ↓

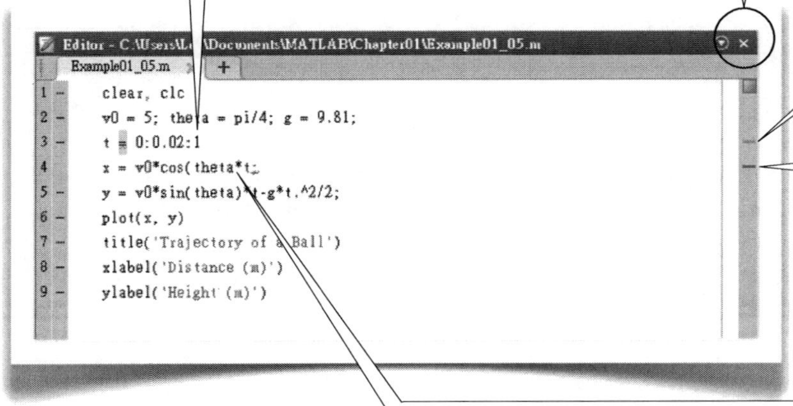

[17] Move your mouse over the red-color bar. An **error** message appears saying that the syntax is invalid. Add a right-parenthesis to correct the error, removing the red-color bar. ↖

[15] Also, remove the right parenthesis in line 4; it becomes

```
x = v0*cos(theta*t;
```
↗

Adding Comments in a Script

[19] It is a good programming habit to document your scripts with comments. It enhances the readability of your scripts not only for other people but also for yourself, particularly after a long period of time. Any text after a percent sign (%) is green-colored and regarded as comments and ignored by MATLAB (see [20] for an example).

In this book, to make a program concise, we usually don't add comments in the program, but remember, as a good programming style, you should always document your programs with comments so that your programs are as readable as possible. ↓

[20] An example of script documented with comments. Note that, in the **Script Editor**, comments are displayed in green color. ↓

```
% This is a program to calculate
% and plot the trajectory of a ball

clear, clc % clear Workspace and Command Window

% Initial speed v0, m/s
% Elevation angle theta, radians
% Gravitational acceleration g, m/s^2
v0 = 5; theta = pi/4; g = 9.81;

t = 0:0.02:1; % The time ranges from 0 sec to 1 sec
x = v0*cos(theta)*t; % x-coordinates
y = v0*sin(theta)*t-g*t.^2/2; % y-coordinates

% Plot the trajectory
plot(x, y)
title('Trajectory of a Ball')
xlabel('Distance (m)')
ylabel('Height (m)')
```

Summary

[21] The syntax checking demonstrated in [14-17] (last page) is useful. You should always make sure all the statements are syntactically valid. And, remember, always document your programs with comments.

This section demonstrates the use of the **MATLAB Script Editor** to write scripts (programs). You could use any text editor (such as **Notepad** in a Windows system, or **TextEdit** in a Macintosh system) to write MATLAB scripts (**.m** files). However, the **MATLAB Script Editor** provides many features over a plain text editor, facilitating this task. MATLAB R2016a announced a new script editor, called **Live Editor**. We'll introduce the **Live Editor** in Section 1.8. #

1.6 Data Visualization: Surface Plots

[1] In Section 1.4a, we demonstrate that a 2-D line plot can be used to represent a function $y = f(x)$. Now, surface plots can be used to represent a function of two independent variables, $z = f(x,y)$. Let **x**, **y**, **z** be *m*-by-*n* matrices, then the function `surf(x,y,z)` generates a surface mesh in which the grid lines intersect at the following $m \times n$ points

$$(x(i,j),\ y(i,j),\ z(i,j)),\ i = 1,\ 2,\ \dots m;\ j = 1,\ 2,\ \dots n$$

Each patch of the mesh is then colored according to its height.

To create a surface plot $z = f(x,y)$, we usually define a rectangular grid using *x* and *y* and then calculate the *z*-values according to $z = f(x,y)$. In this way, *x* is a *m*-by-*n* matrix of identical rows, and *y* is a *m*-by-*n* matrix of identical columns. We will demonstrate this idea in the following example.

Trajectory Surface

In Section 1.4a, we learned how to draw a trajectory curve. Different elevation angles will generate different trajectory curves. Collection of these curves forms a **trajectory surface**. In this section, we want to create a trajectory surface (see [3], next page). We also draw a ground plane ([4], next page). The intersection between the trajectory surface and the ground plane is where the ball hits the ground.

The trajectory surface is expressed as $z = f(x,\theta)$, where *x* is the horizontal distance, θ is the elevation angle, and *z* is the height. To express the height this way, we may solve Eq. 1.2(a) (page 13) for the time *t*

$$t = \frac{x}{v_0 \cos\theta} \qquad \text{(a)}$$

and substitute the time *t* into Eq. 1.2(b)

$$y = (v_0 \sin\theta)t - \frac{1}{2}gt^2 = x\tan\theta - \frac{1}{2}g\left(\frac{x}{v_0\cos\theta}\right)^2 \qquad \text{(b)}$$ ↓

Example01_06.m: Trajectory Surface

[2] Create a new script (1.5[2], page 22), type the following commands (the number before each line is added by the author and is not part of the command), save as Example01_06.m (1.5[6]), and run the script (1.5[8]). The graphic output is shown in [3-5] (next page). We'll explain these lines in [8-17], pages 26-28. ↵

```
clear, clc, close all
v0 = 5; g = 9.81;
x = 0:0.1:3; n = length(x);
theta = pi/8:pi/100:3*pi/8; m = length(theta);
X = repmat(x, m, 1);
Theta = repmat(theta', 1, n);
Z = X.*tan(Theta)-0.5*g*(X./(v0*cos(Theta))).^2;
surf(X, Theta, Z)
hold on
Z = zeros(m, n);
surf(X, Theta, Z)
xlabel('Distance, m')
ylabel('Angle, radian')
zlabel('Height, m')
colorbar
axis vis3d
```

[5] The intersection between the trajectory surface and the ground plane is where the ball hits the ground. ↙

[3] This program plots a "trajectory surface," a combination of the trajectory curves of various elevation angles. →

[4] This is the ground plane, where the height is zero. ↑

[6] To view from different angles, move your mouse over the plot (to reveal this toolbar), click **Rotate 3D**, and left-click-drag the graph. ↙

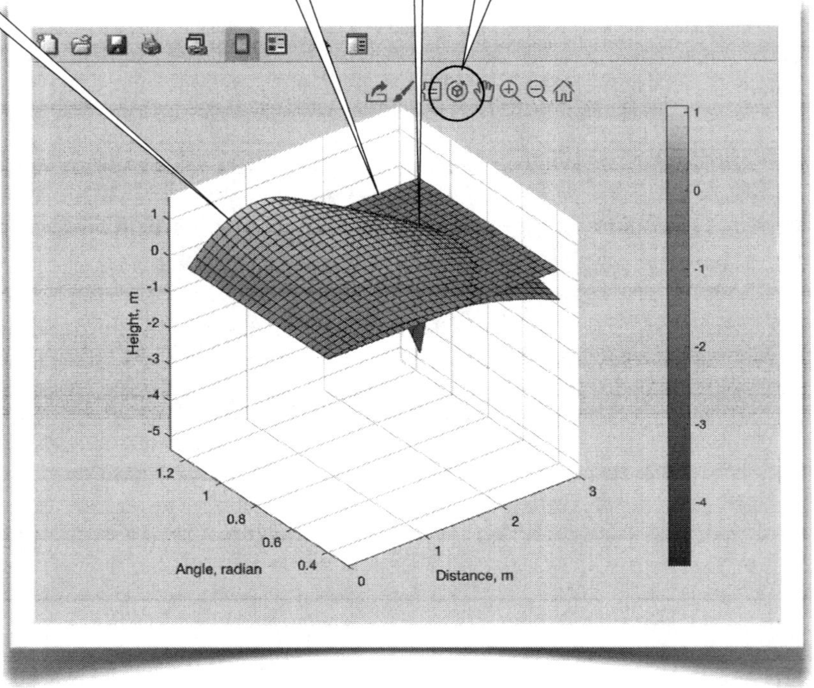

[7] This is the **Workspace** after the execution of the program. By default, MATLAB stores all numerical data as `double` type, double-precision floating-point (Section 2.3). →

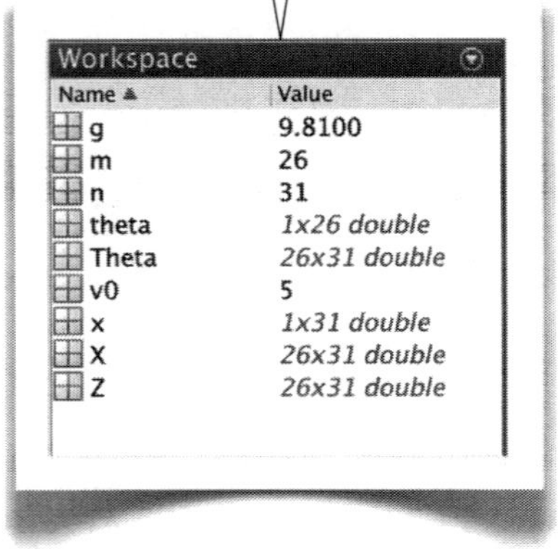

[8] In line 1, the command

```
close all
```

closes all existing **Figure Windows**. If there is no **Figure Window**, this command has no effects. This line is a short hand for the following line

```
close('all')
```

When the input parameters of a function are characters, the parentheses and the quotation marks can be omitted (also see [15], page 28).

As a good programming habit, always do these "housekeeping" tasks (clear the **Workspace**, the **Command Window**, and all **Figure Windows**) at the beginning of a program, to ensure that you start with a "clean" environment.

Line 2

```
v0 = 5; g = 9.81;
```

creates and initializes the initial speed `v0` (5 m/s) and the gravitational acceleration `g` (9.81 m/s^2). ↵

[9] In line 3, the command

```
x = 0:0.1:3;
```

creates a row vector containing numbers from 0 to 3, each increasing 0.1, representing 31 time points. The command

```
n = length(n);
```

stores the length of `x` in the variable `n` (which is 31, see [7], last page). The built-in function `length` outputs the number of elements of a vector. For a matrix, it outputs the larger dimension. For example, for a 2-by-3 matrix `A`, `length(A)` outputs 3. To obtain both dimensions, use the function `size`. Thus, `size(A)` outputs a vector `[2 3]`.

In line 4, the commands

```
theta = pi/8:pi/100:3*pi/8;
```

create a row vector of 26 elements. The elevation angle `theta` ranges from `pi/8` to `3*pi/8`, each increasing `pi/100`. The command

```
m = length(theta);
```

stores the length of `theta` in the variable `m` (which is 26, see [7]). ↓

[10] In line 5

```
X = repmat(x, m, 1);
```

the built-in function `repmat` is read "replicate matrix," and `repmat(A, r, s)` replicates `A` matrix `r` times in row direction (i.e., downward) and `s` times in column direction (i.e., rightward). Thus, `repmat(x, m, 1)` replicates `x` (which is a 31-element row vector) in row-direction (downward) 26 times. The result `X` is a 26-by-51 matrix; its 26 rows are identical. The matrix `X` will be used in lines 7 and 8. ↓

[11] In line 6,

```
Theta = repmat(theta', 1, n);
```

the notation `theta'` means the transpose of the vector `theta`; it's a short hand of `transpose(theta)`. Since `theta` is a 1-by-26 row vector, the transpose of `theta` is a 26-by-1 column vector.

This command replicates the column vector `theta'` in column direction (rightward) 51 times. The result `Theta` is a 26-by-31 matrix; its 31 columns are identical.

In MATLAB, the variable names are **case sensitive**; the variables `Theta` and `theta` are different. In this book, to facilitate the reading, the variable names for matrices usually start with upper-case letters, while the variable names for vectors or scalars usually start with lower-case letters. ↓

[12] Line 7

```
Z = X.*tan(Theta)-0.5*g*(X./(v0*cos(Theta))).^2;
```

calculates the heights of the ball according to Eq. (b), page 25. It uses element-wise multiplication (`.*`), element-wise division (`./`), and element-wise exponentiation (`.^`). The result `Z` is a 26-by-31 matrix. Line 7 demonstrates the power of using array expressions (Section 1.3).

Lines 5 and 6 are typical procedure to prepare matrices used in array expressions (such as lines 7); lines 5 and 6 can be replaced by the following statement (2.12d[3], page 111):

```
[X Theta] = meshgrid(x, theta);
```

Try to rerun the program with this replacement. ↓

[13] Line 8

```
surf(X, Theta, Z)
```

generates a surface according to the method described in [1], page 25. Note that the three matrices have the same sizes. Each patch of the surface is colored according to its *z*-value. The *z*-values are mapped to a **colormap**. We'll show this **colormap** in line 15. ↓

[14] Line 9

```
hold on
```

prevents the existing graphs being erased due to subsequent plotting commands (e.g., `surf` in line 11). With this command, subsequent graphs will be added to the existing graphs. Try to rerun the program without this line and see the difference. Note that this line is shorthand for `hold('on')`. ↓

[15] In line 10

```
Z = zeros(m, n);
```

the function `zeros(m, n)` outputs an `m`-by-`n` matrix with all-zero values. Here, `Z`, a 26-by-31 matrix, will be used in the next line to plot the ground plane. ↓

[16] Line 11

```
surf(X, Theta, Z)
```

plots a ground plane.

Lines 12-14 add labels in three axes, respectively.

Line 15 displays a colorbar in the figure (page 26). The **colorbar** contains colors in the default **colormap**. ↓

[17] Line 16

```
axis vis3d
```

freezes the aspect ratio among three axes. Without this line, when you rotate the view ([6], page 26), the aspect ratio would be adjusted to fit into the entire window. The rotation of the view would not be smooth. Try to rerun the program without this line and see the visual difference. #

1.7 Symbolic Mathematics

[1] The distance the ball hits the ground is called the **range** of the ball-throwing [2]. To calculate the range, we may solve Eq. 1.2(b) (page 13) for the time t at $y = 0$,

$$y = (v_0 \sin\theta)t - \frac{1}{2}gt^2 = 0 \qquad \text{(a)}$$

$$t = \frac{2v_0 \sin\theta}{g} \qquad \text{(b)}$$

and substitute the time t into Eq. 1.2(a), page 13,

$$x = (v_0 \cos\theta)t = \frac{2v_0^2 \cos\theta \sin\theta}{g} = \frac{v_0^2 \sin 2\theta}{g} \qquad \text{(c)}$$

We may write the range R as a function of the elevation angle θ:

$$R(\theta) = \frac{v_0^2 \sin 2\theta}{g} \qquad \text{(d)}$$

In this section, we'll demonstrate the **symbolic mathematics** by performing the above mathematical manipulations. →

[2] The horizontal distance where the ball hits the ground is the range of the ball-throwing (see 1.6[5], page 26). ↙

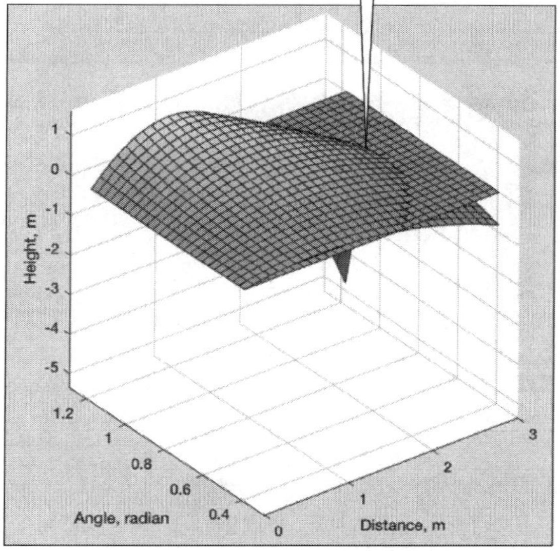

Example01_07.m: Ball-Throwing Ranges

[3] Create a new script, type the following commands, save as Example01_07.m, and run the script. →

```
clear, clc, close all
syms v0 theta g t
x = v0*cos(theta)*t
y = v0*sin(theta)*t-g*t^2/2
solutions = solve(y, t)
t0 = solutions(2)
range = subs(x, t, t0)
range = simplify(range)
range = subs(range, [v0, g], [5, 9.81])
fplot(range, [pi/8, 3*pi/8])
title('Range as Function of Angle')
xlabel('Elevation angle (degrees)')
ylabel('Range (m)')
```

[4] The program plots the range as a function of the elevation angle. ↵

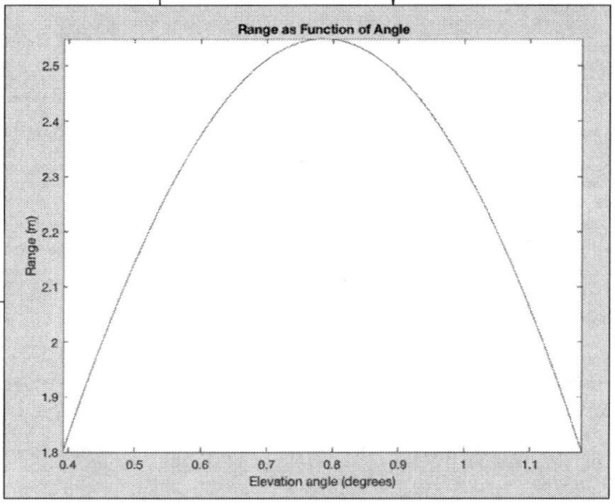

[5] After running Example01_07.m, the output on the **Command Window** looks like this. Note that the number in the beginning of each line is added by the author. Remember, we assume that compact format is used (1.2[9, 13], page 14) ↓

```
14   x =
15   t*v0*cos(theta)
16   y =
17   t*v0*sin(theta) - (g*t^2)/2
18   solutions =
19                       0
20   (2*v0*sin(theta))/g
21   t0 =
22   (2*v0*sin(theta))/g
23   range =
24   (2*v0^2*cos(theta)*sin(theta))/g
25   range =
26   (v0^2*sin(2*theta))/g
27   range =
28   (2500*sin(2*theta))/981
```

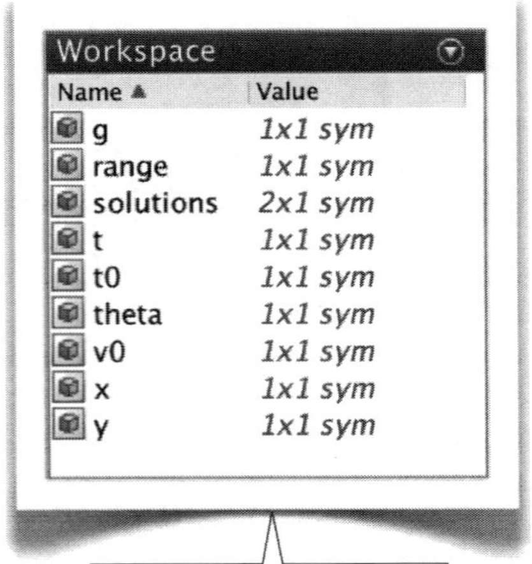

[6] The **Workspace** looks like this. ↓

About Example01_07.m

[7] Line 2

```
syms v0 theta g t
```

declares that `v0`, `theta`, `g`, and `t` are symbolic variables (the type is **sym**, see [6]). Each symbolic variable has to be declared before being used. Remember that this is shorthand for the following statement:

```
syms('v0', 'theta', 'g', 't')
```

Line 3

```
x = v0*cos(theta)*t
```

creates a symbolic expression using the symbolic variables `v0`, `theta`, and `t`. The symbolic expression is then assigned to `x`, which is automatically of type **sym** (see [6] and lines 14-15]). Similarly, line 4

```
y = v0*sin(theta)*t-g*t^2/2
```

creates another symbolic expression and assigns it to the symbolic variable `y` (see lines 16-17).

Line 5

```
solutions = solve(y, t)
```

solves the equation `y = 0` for `t` symbolically. The equation has two solutions, stored in `solutions` as a column vector (see lines 18-20 and [6]). Note that the first solution (line 19) is zero and the second solution (line 20) is consistent with Eq. (b), last page. ↵

About Example01_07.m (Continued)

[8] Line 6

```
t0 = solutions(2)
```

retrieves the second element of vector `solutions` (lines 21-22). Since the variable `solutions` is a 2-by-1 matrix, this statement can also be written as

```
t0 = solutions(2,1)
```

As a rule, when the size of the last dimension is one, the last index can be omitted (also see 1.9[23], page 37).

Line 7

```
range = subs(x, t, t0)
```

substitutes the symbol `t` in `x` (which is `v0*cos(theta)*t`) with `t0` (which is `2*v0*sin(theta)/g`). That is, $x = x(t_0)$. The result is shown in lines 23-24, which can be further simplified, by recognizing that

$$2\cos\theta\sin\theta \equiv \sin 2\theta$$

This is done in line 8,

```
range = simplify(range)
```

And the result is shown in lines 25-26, which is consistent with Eq. (d).

To plot the range as a function of the angle θ, we now use specific numeric values of the initial velocity `v0` and gravitational acceleration `g`. Line 9

```
range = subs(range, [v0, g], [5, 9.81])
```

substitutes the initial velocity `v0` with the number 5 and the gravitational acceleration `g` with 9.81. The output is shown in lines 27-28.

Function `fplot`

In line 10,

```
fplot(range, [pi/8, 3*pi/8])
```

the function `fplot` is used to plot a function when its symbolic form is known. The second argument of `fplot` specifies the interval of the independent variable.

Details and More

We'll discuss details and more of symbolic mathematics, including the function `fplot`, in Chapter 9. #

1.8 Live Script

[1] MATLAB R2016a announced a new script editor, called **Live Editor**; its corresponding script is called the **Live Script**, and the script file extension is **.mlx**. (Rather than **.m** for the "plane" script introduced in Section 1.5). It provides many features (*Help>MATLAB>Programming Scripts and Functions>Live Scripts*). One of them is that it outputs textbook-quality equations when using Symbolic Mathematics.

The following steps [2-7] take you to visit the **Live Editor**. ↙

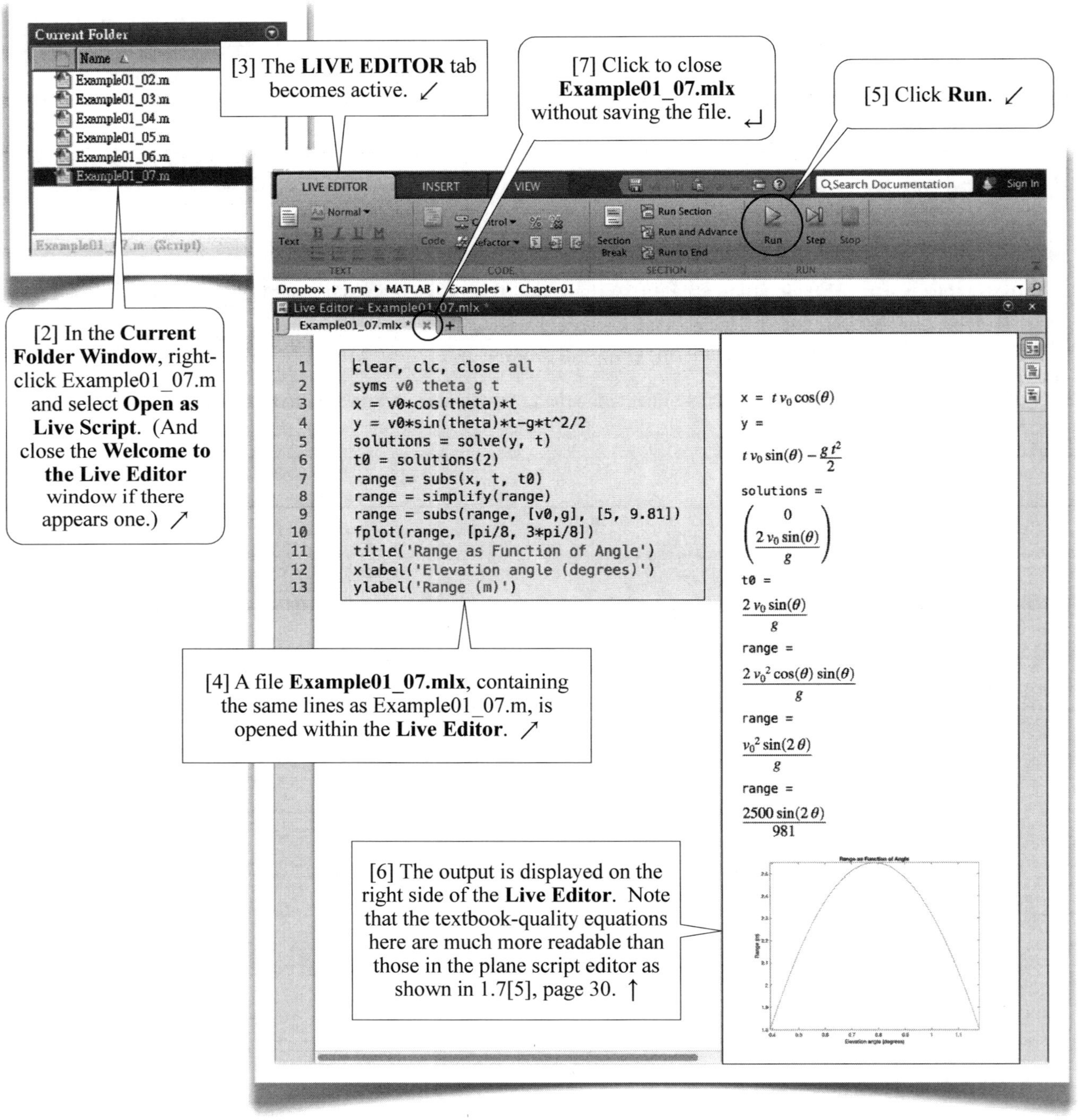

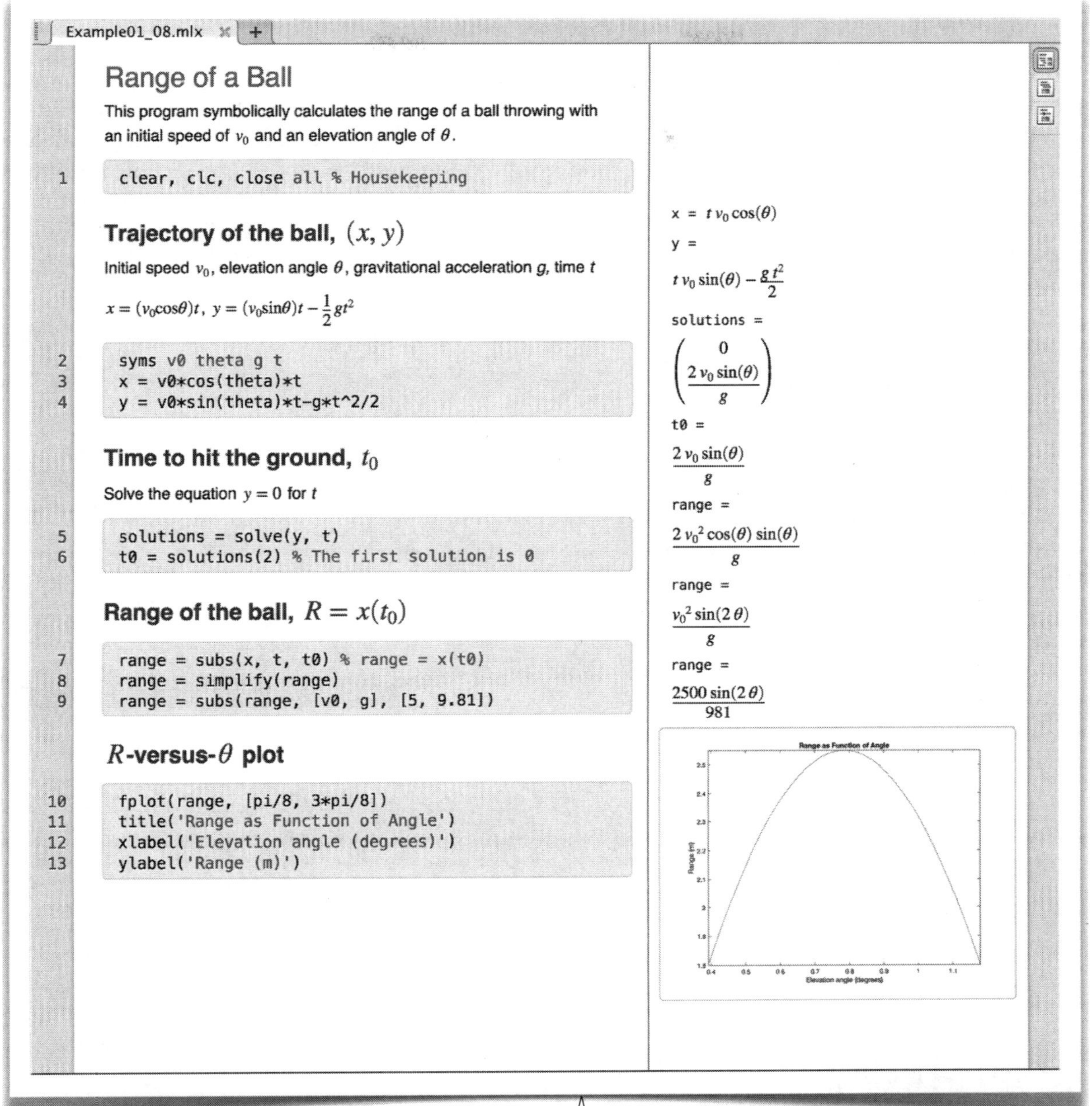

[8] Another feature of the **Live Editor** is that it allows formatted text and equations embedded within a program. Note that the program statements are highlighted with gray background. This is an example created by the author, based on Example01_07.m. ↓

Scripts in this book can be executed in either editor

[9] In this book, we save all the scripts using the traditional plane **Script Editor**, i.e., all scripts end with an extension **.m**. The scripts are written in a way that they also can be opened as **Live Scripts** ([2], last page) and executed under **Live Editor**. They, of course, can be saved as **.mlx** files. In short, all the scripts in this book can be executed with MATLAB 2018a or later versions in either the plane **Script Editor** or the **Live Editor**. It is suggested that you be familiar with both the plane **Script Editor** and the **Live Editor**. #

1.9 Screen Text Input/Output

[1] The program in Section 1.5 calculates the trajectory with a specific initial velocity (5 m/s) and a specific elevation angle (45 degrees). To maximize the usefulness of the program, you should allow the program to calculate the trajectory with any values of velocity and elevation angle. This section shows you how to input data by typing from the keyboard.

As mentioned in Section 1.4, you should present data in graphics form whenever it is possible. If you want to output your data in text form, you should tabulate the data in an easy-to-read fashion. This section also shows you how to display data on the screen. ↓

Example01_09.m: Trajectory Table

[2] Create a new file, type the following commands, save as Example01_09.m, and run the script. Enter 5 for the initial velocity and 45 for the elevation angle (see [3]). ↓

```
1   clear, clc
2   v0 = input('Enter initial speed (m/s): ');
3   theta = input('Enter elevation angle (degrees): ');
4   theta = theta*pi/180;
5   g = 9.81;
6   t = 0:0.1:1;
7   x = v0*cos(theta)*t;
8   y = v0*sin(theta)*t-g*t.^2/2;
9   Table = [t', x', y'];
10  disp(' ')
11  disp('   time (s)      x (m)      y (m)')
12  disp(Table)
```

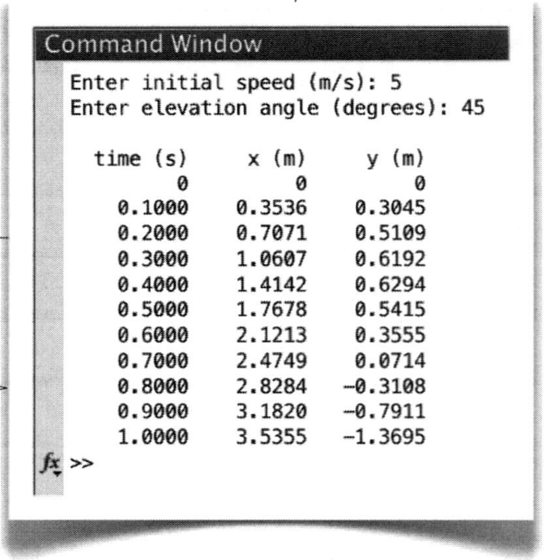

[3] In the **Command Window**, enter 5 for the initial velocity and 45 for the elevation angle. This program outputs a table of trajectory like this. ↙

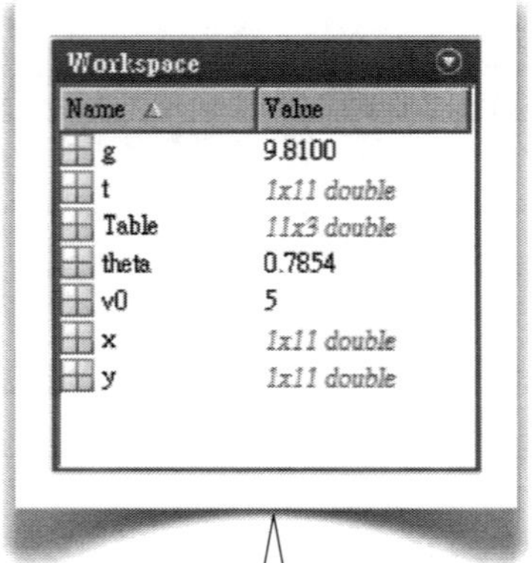

[4] This is the **Workspace** after the execution of the program. →

[5] Line 2 displays the following text

`Enter initial speed (m/s):`

on the **Command Window** and waits until the user enters a number from the keyboard. It reads the number and assigns the number to the variable `v0`.

Similarly, line 3 displays the following text

`Enter elevation angle (degrees):`

and waits until the user enters a number from the keyboard. It reads the number and assigns it to the variable `theta`. ↵

[6] Line 4

```
theta = theta*pi/180;
```

converts the angle unit from degrees to radians; the functions `cos` and `sin` always assume radians as the unit. The result is assigned to the variable `theta` itself.

Lines 5-8 calculate *x*- and *y*-coordinates at various time points. Note that `t`, `x`, `y` are row vectors of 11 elements (see [4]). ↓

[7] Line 9,

```
Table = [t', x', y'];
```

creates a matrix `Table` using `t'` (remember that the apostrophe means transposition) as its first column, `x'` as the second column, and `y'` as the third column. The result `Table` is an 11-by-3 matrix (see [4]).

Recall that commas (`,`) are used to separate elements in a row, while semicolons (;) are used to separate rows in a matrix. In general, data separated by commas (`,`) become columns of a matrix. Similarly, data separated by semicolons (`;`) become rows of a matrix.

Another way to write this statement is:

```
Table = [t; x; y]';
```

You should try this by yourself. →

[8] Line 10

```
disp(' ')
```

displays a space character (`' '`) and moves the cursor to the next line. The purpose of this statement is to insert a blank line before the heading of the trajectory table (see [3]). Similarly, line 11 displays the heading (again, see [3]) and moves the cursor to the next line.

Line 12 displays the contents of `Table`, which is an 11-by-3 matrix, and moves the cursor to the next line. Note that it displays each row of the matrix with a line.

Function `disp`

The function `disp` displays a data of any type. In line 10, the data is a single character (space). A single character must be quoted with two single quotation marks. In line 11, the data is a vector of characters. Multiple characters quoted with two single quotation marks is treated as a vector of characters, also called a **string**. We'll discuss more about characters and strings in Chapter 2.

In line 12, the data is a matrix; `disp` displays the matrix one row at a line. Note that each number is displayed with four digits (by default) after the decimal point.

Using `disp` to display data in the screen seems easy but is often not flexible enough. For example, displaying the time with four digits after the decimal point seems unnecessary; one digit should be enough. ↓

Function `fprintf`

[9] The function `fprintf` provides more controls in formatting the output data. Assume that we want to output the time with one digit after the decimal point and the coordinate with three digits after the decimal point. Append the following two statements to Example01_09.m ([2], last page) and rerun the program (see [10], next page, for the output):

```
13  fprintf('\n  time (s)     x (m)      y (m)\n')
14  fprintf('%10.1f %9.3f %9.3f\n', Table')
```

Line 13 prints a blank line and a heading on the **Command Window**. The `\n` is a special character called the **newline character**. It moves the "printing head" down to the beginning of the next line; it in effect prints a blank line.

Line 14 prints the elements of `Table'` according to **format specifications** (Table 7.1a, page 280), the first input argument of `fprintf`. In this case, three **formats** are specified: `%10.1f`, `%9.3f`, and `%9.3f`. Each **format specifier** starts with a percent sign (`%`) and ends with a letter. Here, `f` specifies a **fixed-point format**, fixed number of digits after decimal point. In-between are two numbers separated by a decimal point. The first number specifies the total printing width and the second number specifies the number of digits after the decimal point.

Since there are only three format specifiers, each time three numbers are retrieved "linearly" (explained in [11-22]) from the array `Table'` and printed according to the three **format specifiers**. The first two numbers are followed by a space, respectively, and the third number is followed by a newline character, i.e., ready to print on the next line. This repeats until all the numbers in `Table'` are used up. The output is shown in [10], next page.

We'll discuss more on screen text input/output in Section 7.1. ↵

```
time (s)      x (m)      y (m)
     0.0      0.000      0.000
     0.1      0.354      0.305
     0.2      0.707      0.511
     0.3      1.061      0.619
     0.4      1.414      0.629
     0.5      1.768      0.542
     0.6      2.121      0.356
     0.7      2.475      0.071
     0.8      2.828     -0.311
     0.9      3.182     -0.791
     1.0      3.536     -1.369
```

[10] Lines 13 and 14 produce a new trajectory table in which the time has one digit after the decimal point and the coordinate has three digits after the decimal point. ↓

How are the elements of a matrix ordered in the memory?

[11] In our computer memory, the elements of a matrix are stored linearly in column-wise fashion: 1st column, 2nd column, 3rd column, and so forth. To illustrate this concept, let's examine the contents of the 11-by-3 matrix `Table`. ←

[12] In **Workspace**, double-click the variable `Table`. →

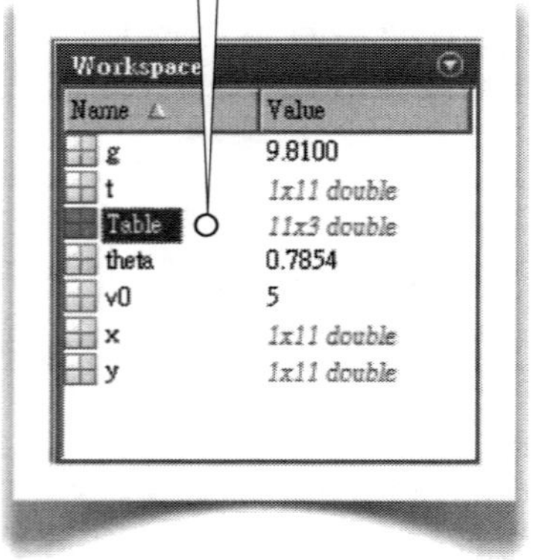

[15] This is the 13th element of the matrix. ↓

[13] A spread sheet similar to that in **Microsoft Excel** is opened, showing the elements of `Table`. You actually can edit the numbers in this spread sheet. ↙

[17] Click to close the spread sheet. ↵

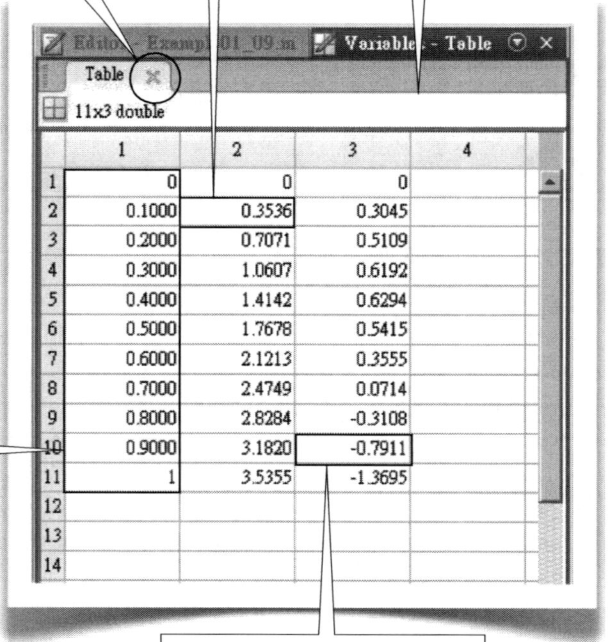

[14] Elements in a matrix are stored column-wise in the computer memory. Thus, these are the first 11 elements of the matrix. ↑

[16] And this is the 32nd element of the matrix. ↖

Back to Line 14: How are the Data Printed?

[18] Line 14 prints the contents of `Table'` (rather than `Table`). To familiarize you with the linear nature of the matrix, let's use `Table'` as another example to examine the order of its elements. Now, create a matrix `Table1` which is a copy of `Table'`:

```
>> Table1 = Table'
```

Note that `Table1` is 3-by-11 matrix. Now, open the new matrix as shown in [19]. ↓

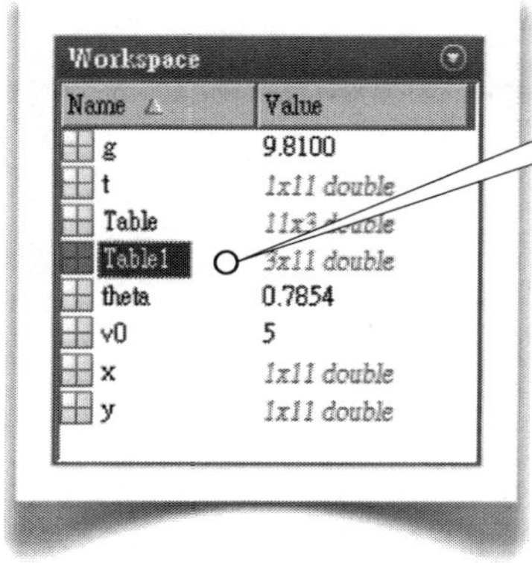

[19] In **Workspace**, double-click the variable `Table1`. ↓

[20] These are the first 3 elements of `Table'`. Since line 14 has only 3 format specifiers,

`%10.1f %9.3f %9.3f\n`

these 3 numbers are printed according to the three format specifiers (see [10], last page). And then a newline character is printed, i.e., ready to print on the next line. ↓

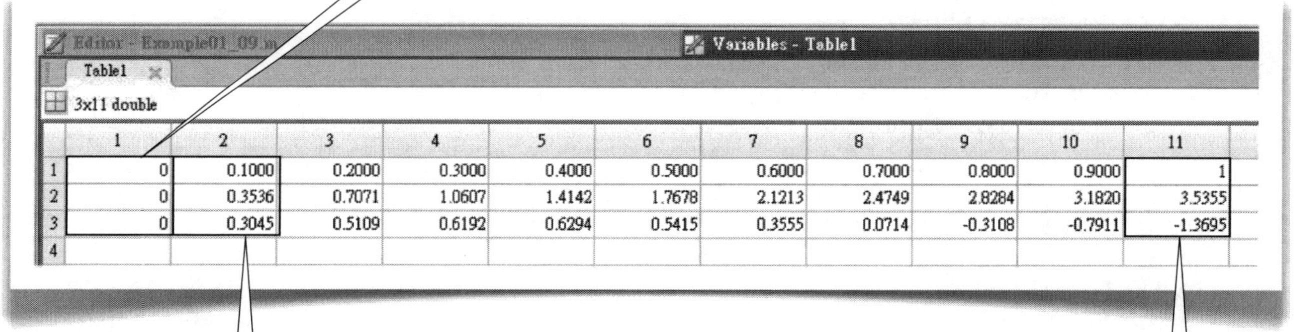

	1	2	3	4	5	6	7	8	9	10	11
1	0	0.1000	0.2000	0.3000	0.4000	0.5000	0.6000	0.7000	0.8000	0.9000	1
2	0	0.3536	0.7071	1.0607	1.4142	1.7678	2.1213	2.4749	2.8284	3.1820	3.5355
3	0	0.3045	0.5109	0.6192	0.6294	0.5415	0.3555	0.0714	-0.3108	-0.7911	-1.3695
4											

[21] These are the second 3 elements of `Table'`. Again, these 3 numbers are printed according to the three format specifiers (see [10], last page). And the printing head jumps to the next line. →

[22] Finally, the last 3 elements are printed (see [10]), and the printing head jumps to the next line. ↓

Indexing to a Matrix: Subscript Indexing and Linear Indexing

[23] Suppose we want to retrieve the element in the 10th row, 3rd column of `Table` (see [16], last page) and assign it to a variable `height`; we may use **subscript indexing**:

```
height = Table(10,3)
```

or **linear indexing**:

```
height = Table(32)
```

In line 14, it actually accesses the elements of `Table'` using linear indexing. In many situations, the linear indexing provides a convenient way to access the elements of a matrix. #

1.10 Text File Input/Output

[1] In the last section, we demonstrated the input of text from a keyboard and the output of text to a computer screen. Sometimes, we want the program to write the text in a file so that later we can open the file and examine the text. Sometimes, we even want the program to read text from a file (rather than the keyboard). In this section, we'll demonstrate the output of text to a file and the input of text from a file. ↓

Example01_10.m: Text File I/O

[2] Create a new script, type the following commands, save as Example01_10.m, and run the script. This program demonstrates input/output of a text file. ↓

```
1   clear, clc
2   v0 = 5; theta = pi/4; g = 9.81;
3   t = 0:0.1:1;
4   x = v0*cos(theta)*t;
5   y = v0*sin(theta)*t-g*t.^2/2;
6   Table = [t; x; y];
7   % Write to a file
8   file = fopen('Datafile01_10.dat', 'w');
9   fprintf(file, '   Time (s)      x (m)      y (m)\n');
10  fprintf(file, '%10.1f %9.3f %9.3f\n', Table);
11  fclose(file);
12  % Read from the file
13  clear
14  file = fopen('Datafile01_10.dat', 'r');
15  fscanf(file, '   Time (s)      x (m)      y (m)\n');
16  Table = fscanf(file, '%f %f %f\n', [3,11]);
17  fclose(file);
18  % Print on the screen
19  fprintf('   Time (s)      x (m)      y (m)\n');
20  fprintf('%10.1f %9.3f %9.3f\n', Table);
```

[3] This program prints a table of trajectory, the same as that in 1.9[10] (page 36), on a file **Datafil01_10.dat** (lines 8-11). Then, the Workspace is cleared (line 13), and finally the data in the file are read back (lines 14-17) and printed on the screen (lines 19-20). This is what printed on **Command Window**. ↵

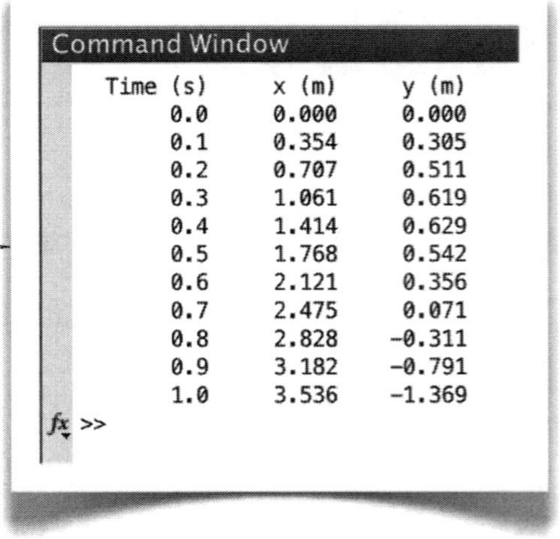

[4] Lines 8-11 create a file **Datafile01_10.dat** in the **Current Folder**. Now, right-click the file and select **Open as Text**. →

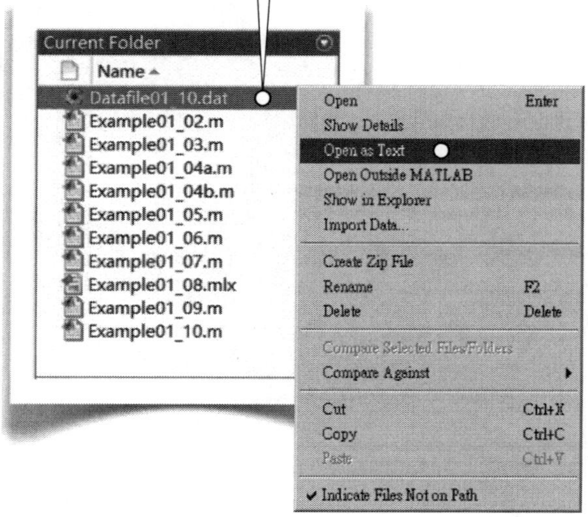

[5] The file **Datafile01_10.dat** is opened as an editable text file. It can be edited with any text editors (1.5[21], page 24). →

[6] Click to close the text file. ↓

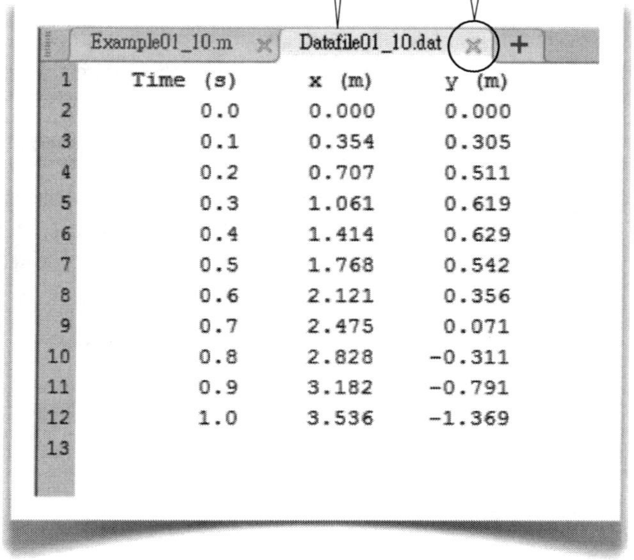

[7] You should be able to read lines 1-5 by yourself.

Line 6

```
Table = [t; x; y];
```

creates a 3-by-11 matrix by concatenating three 11-element row vectors `t`, `x`, and `y`.

Lines 7, 12, 18 are comment lines. Remember that any text after % is ignored by MATLAB. ↓

[8] Line 8

```
file = fopen('Datafile01_10.dat', 'w');
```

opens a file **Datafile01_10.dat** and outputs a **file identifier**, which is assigned to the variable `file`. The **file access type** `'w'` specifies that the file is opened for writing (reading is always permitted) and the existing contents, if any, are discarded (overwritten). If **Datafile01_10.dat** doesn't exist, one is created.

When a file is opened, you may think of it as a "pipe" that is created to connect the program and file. By enabling reading, the pipe allows the data to "flow" from the file to the program. Similarly, by enabling writing, the pipe allows the data to "flow" from the program to the file.

Lines 9-10

```
fprintf(file, '  Time (s)     x (m)     y (m)\n');
fprintf(file, '%10.1f %9.3f %9.3f\n', Table);
```

are similar to lines 13-14 in 1.9[9], page 35, except that the **file identifier**, as the first input argument of `fprintf`, is used to direct the output to the file (instead of the screen). Also note that, in 1.9[9], `Table` is an 11-by-3 matrix and has to be transposed to make the order correct. Here, `Table` is a 3-by-11 matrix; it does not need to be transposed.

Line 11 closes the file, removing the "pipe" and the writing and reading are disabled. ↵

[9] Line 13 clears the **Workspace**; we want to assure that the data from now on are indeed read from the file. Line 14 opens the file again for reading only. The **file access type** `'r'` specifies a read-only type (writing is prohibited).

Line 15

```
fscanf(file, '    Time (s)        x (m)       y (m)\n');
```

reads texts from the file (see the contents in [5]) according to the **format specification**, which says: read the characters

```
'    Time (s)        x (m)       y (m)\n'
```

It in effect moves the "reading head" from the beginning to the second line of the file.

Line 16

```
Table = fscanf(file, '%f %f %f\n', [3,11]);
```

repeatedly reads three numbers and a newline character each time, assigning the numbers to `Table` linearly. The variable `Table` is treated as a 3-by-11 matrix, specified in the third input argument. Without specifying dimensions, the variable `Table` would assume a column vector of 33 elements. You may try this by yourself.

We'll discuss more on text file input/output in Section 7.2. #

1.11 Debug Your Programs

Running Programs in Blocks (Sections)

[1] As your program is getting lengthy, you may want to organize the program in blocks, run the program one block at a time, and examine variables at each stage to make sure everything is okay. Using `%%`, you can divide a program into **blocks** (also called **sections**). After the execution of a block, you can examine the changes of the **Current Folder** and the **Workspace**. You also can examine the value of a variable by typing its name on the **Command Window**. This is a simple way of debugging your program: finding the erratic statements and correcting them. This simple idea is demonstrated in steps [2-10]. A more powerful way of debugging a program is illustrated in the next page. ↙

[4] Delete **Datafile01_10.dat** by right-click-selecting **Delete**. ↓

[7] Click **Run and Advance**. This executes a **block** and advances to the next **block**. ↙

[3] Pull-down-select **Save>Save as...** and save the file as Example01_11.m. ↗

[9] Click **Run and Advance** three more times to complete the execution of the program. ←

[10] Close the program. ↵

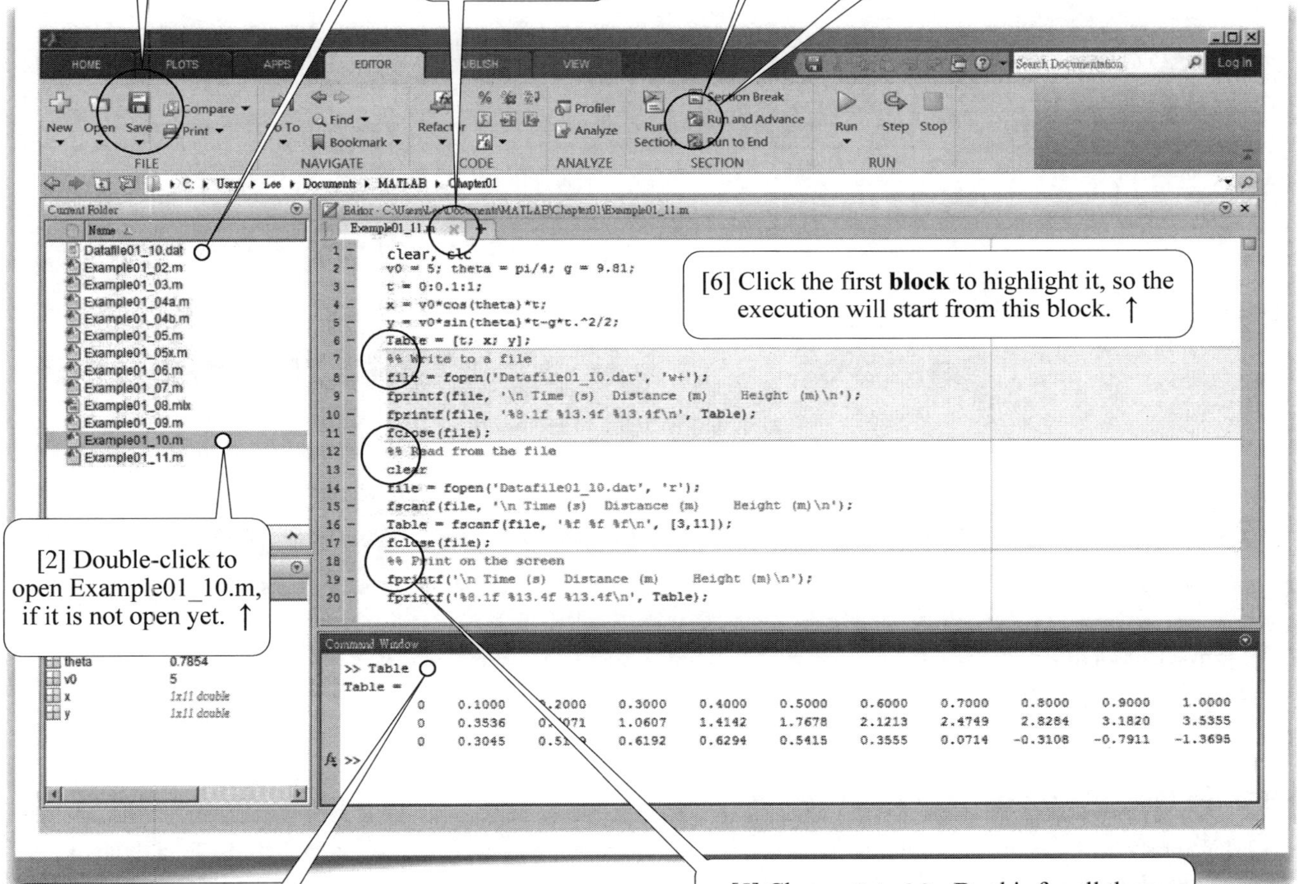

[6] Click the first **block** to highlight it, so the execution will start from this block. ↑

[2] Double-click to open Example01_10.m, if it is not open yet. ↑

[8] Type `Table` to examine its contents. ↗

[5] Change `%` to `%%`. Do this for all three comment lines. By doing this, the program is divided into 4 **blocks** (or **sections**). ↑

Running Programs with Break Points

[11] A more powerful way of debugging your programs is to set **break points**. After clicking **Run**, the execution will stop at a break point, and you can examine variables by typing variable names in the **Commands Window**. This idea is demonstrated in steps [12-22]. ↓

[14] If a program is too long to be contained in the **Editor Window**, a small bar appears here; you may drag the small bar to split the window into two. ←

[13] Delete **Datafile01_10.dat** by right-click-selecting **Delete**. ↗

[15] Click here (line 8). A break point (red marker) is set here. →

[16] Click **Run**. MATLAB is now in **debug mode**. ↓

[22] Click **Quit Debugging**. ↓

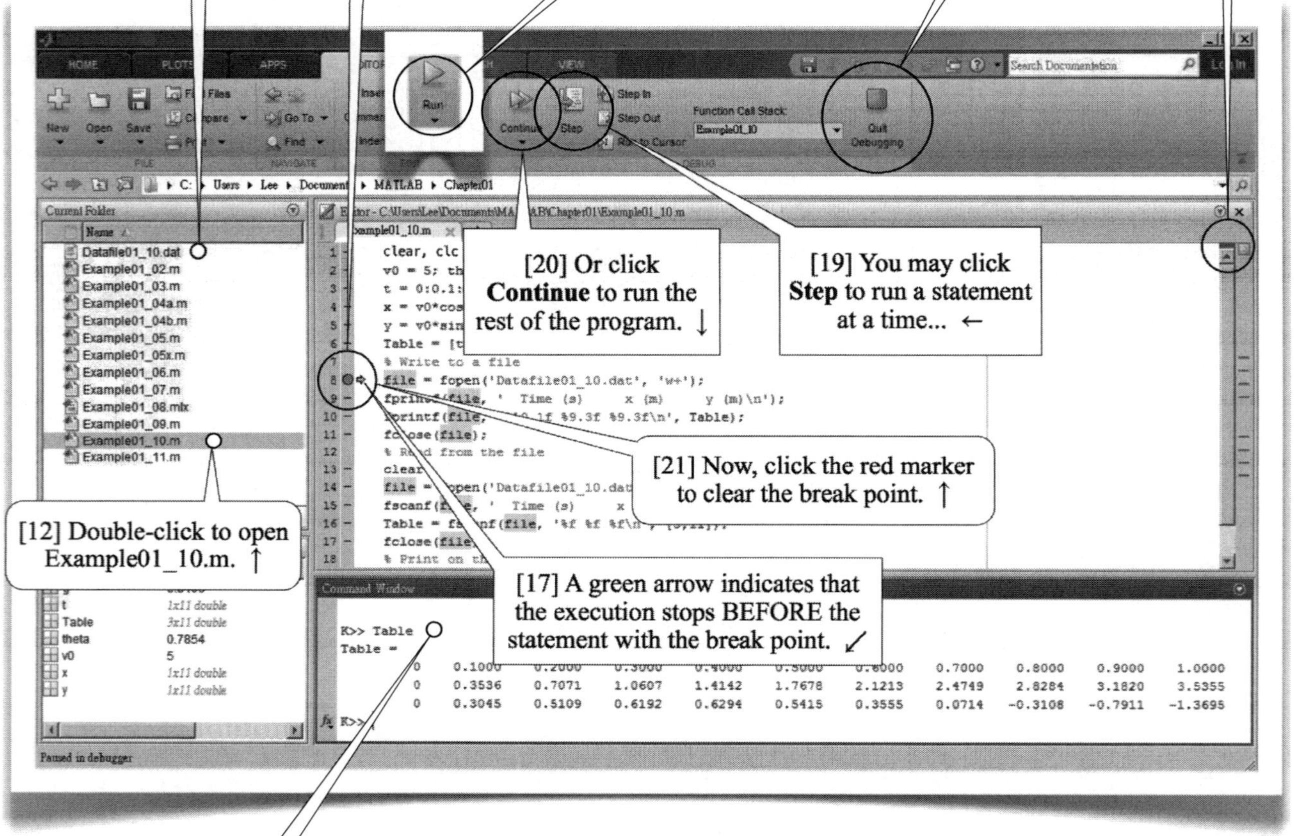

[20] Or click **Continue** to run the rest of the program. ↓

[19] You may click **Step** to run a statement at a time... ←

[21] Now, click the red marker to clear the break point. ↑

[12] Double-click to open Example01_10.m. ↑

[17] A green arrow indicates that the execution stops BEFORE the statement with the break point. ↙

[18] Type `Table` to examine its contents. ↗

Other Useful Debugging Features

[23] You may set up as many **break points** as you want. Remember that the execution stops right BEFORE the line with a **break point**. Another useful debugging feature is **Run to Cursor** (the button next to the **Step** button [19]); it enables you to run the program to the line where you've positioned the cursor. Another way of examining variable values in **debug mode** is to position the cursor to the variable; its current value appears in a "datatip" box. ↵

Evaluate Selection

[24] By highlighting a series of statements and right-selecting **Evaluate Selection in Command Window**, the statements are executed. This provides a flexible way of running your program. Note that the highlighting statements are not necessary inside the **Script Editor**; it could be anywhere as long as MATLAB is running. For example, you may execute statements in the MATLAB **help** window. ↓

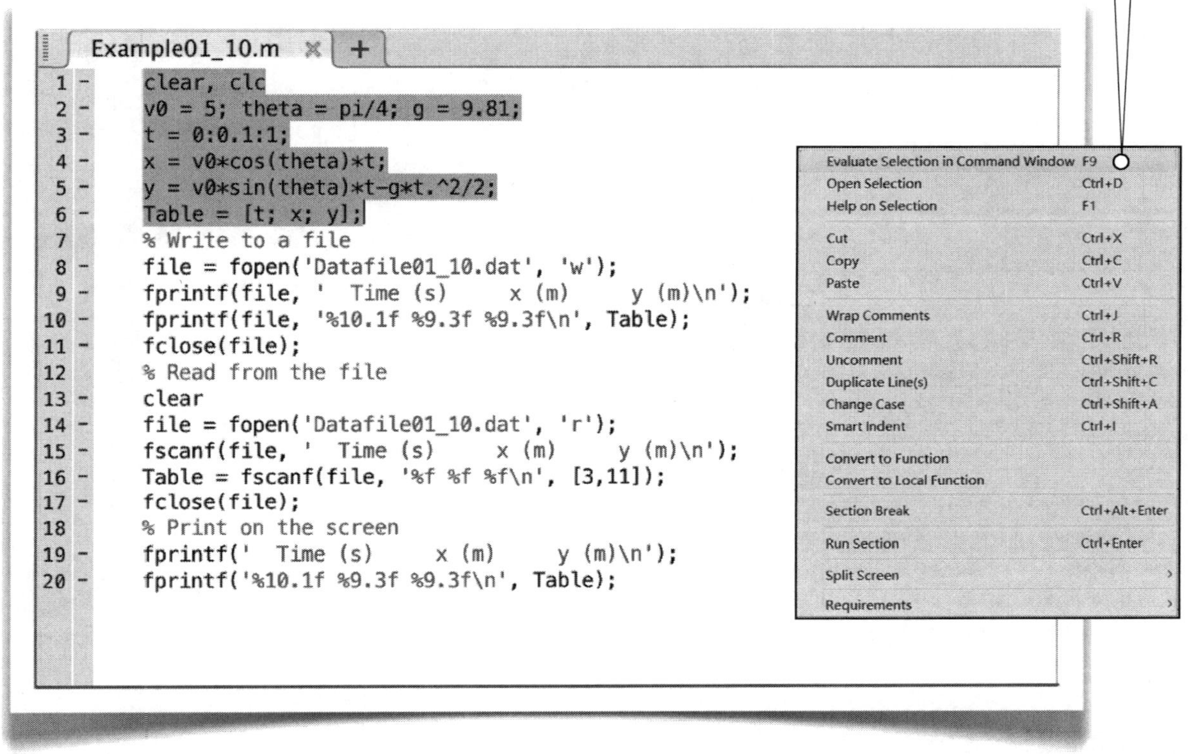

Execute One Statement at a Time

[25] Whenever possible, we suggest that you execute an example program one line at a time and observe the outcome of each line. To do this, you may enter the commands one after another, or you may save the commands in a script file, then select a statement (multiple statements are allowed) and right-click-select Evaluate Selection. If you really hate typing, all script files are available for free download from SDC Publications (see SDC Publications Website in **Preface**, page 9) or from the author's webpage (see Author's Webpage in **Preface**, page 9).

Open a Program when Reading the Textbook

Another reason we provide these script files is that we suggest that you open a script on your MATLAB desktop when you read the textbook. By doing so, you don't have to flip the pages of the textbook back-and-forth when you read the text, which is sometimes annoying and distracting.

Debug with Live Script Editor

We've demonstrated the debugging capabilities of the the plane Script Editor. The **Live Script Editor** has similar capabilities. Open a script as a **Live Script** (see 1.8[2], page 32) and explore these debugging capabilities yourself. #

1.12 Binary File Input/Output

[1] Data stored in a file can be in text form (as demonstrated in Section 10) or in binary form (to be demonstrated in this section). Text data can be read by human eyes, while binary data are usually not for human eyes. In general, the binary form is more efficient (in terms of computer memory and processing time) than the text form. Therefore, if data are not to be read by human eyes, binary input/output should be used. ↓

Example01_12.m: Binary File I/O

[2] Create a new script, type the following commands, save as Example01_12.m, and run the script. This program demonstrates input/output of a binary file. →

```
1   clear, clc
2   v0 = 5; theta = pi/4; g = 9.81;
3   t = 0:0.1:1;
4   x = v0*cos(theta)*t;
5   y = v0*sin(theta)*t-g*t.^2/2;
6   Table = [t; x; y];
7   % Write to a file
8   save('Datafile01_12');
9   % Read from the file
10  clear
11  load('Datafile01_12');
12  % Print on the screen
13  fprintf('   Time (s)     x (m)     y (m)\n');
14  fprintf('%10.1f %9.3f %9.3f\n', Table);
```

[3] This is the output on the screen (lines 13-14). ↓

```
Command Window
   Time (s)     x (m)     y (m)
       0.0     0.000     0.000
       0.1     0.354     0.305
       0.2     0.707     0.511
       0.3     1.061     0.619
       0.4     1.414     0.629
       0.5     1.768     0.542
       0.6     2.121     0.356
       0.7     2.475     0.071
       0.8     2.828    -0.311
       0.9     3.182    -0.791
       1.0     3.536    -1.369
>>
```

About Example01_12.m

[4] This program generates a table of trajectory, `Table`, as usual (lines 2-6). Using the function `save`, line 8 saves all the variables in the **Workspace** to a file **Datafile01_12.mat**. It saves not only the values of variables but also the variables' names, types, dimensions, etc. By default, MATLAB appends an extension **.mat** for the file name. Line 10 clears the **Workspace** to make sure that the data from now on are indeed loaded from the file.

Line 11 loads the variables in the file **Datafile01_12.mat** to the **Workspace**, including their values, names, types, dimensions, etc. Note that, by default, MATLAB assumes an extension **.mat** for the file name.

Finally, the table of trajectory is printed on the screen (lines 13-14; also see [3]). ↓

Summary

[5] This program demonstrates how variables can be saved in a binary file and loaded from a binary file to the **Workspace**. The functions `save` and `load` process the data in binary form (also called the unformatted form). Comparing with the text form (or formatted form) demonstrated in Section 1.10, the binary form is more efficient, both in computing time and in storage. In general, if data are not to be read by human eyes, binary input/output should be used. We'll discuss more on binary file input/output in Section 7.3 and on MAT-files (files with a **.mat** extension) in Section 7.4. #

1.13 Images and Sounds

[1] MATLAB provides many functions for image/sound processing. This section shows you some basic functions, such as reading an image/sound file, displaying the image on the screen, and playing the sound file (assuming you have a speaker connected to your computer). ↓

Example01_13.m: Images and Sounds

[2] This program displays an image [4], plays a song, and plots the audio signals of the song [5]. ↓

```
1  clear, clc
2  Photo = imread('peppers.png');
3  image(Photo)
4  axis image
5  load handel
6  sound(y, Fs)
7  figure
8  plot(y)
```

[4] Lines 2-4 produce this figure. ↓

Execute One Statement at a Time

[3] Remember, whenever possible, we suggest that you execute an example program one command at a time and observe the outcome of each command. You may enter the commands one after another, or you may save the commands in a script file, then select a statement (or multiple statements) and right-click-select **Evaluate Selection** (1.11[24-25], page 43). If you really hate typing the commands, all the program files are available for free download from the SDC publications website (see SDC Publications Website in **Preface**, page 9) or the author's webpage (see Author's Webpage in **Preface**, page 9). ↗

[5] Lines 7-8 produce this figure. (This figure is at the same position of the figure in [4]. You need to drag this figure aside to reveal the figure in [4].) ↙

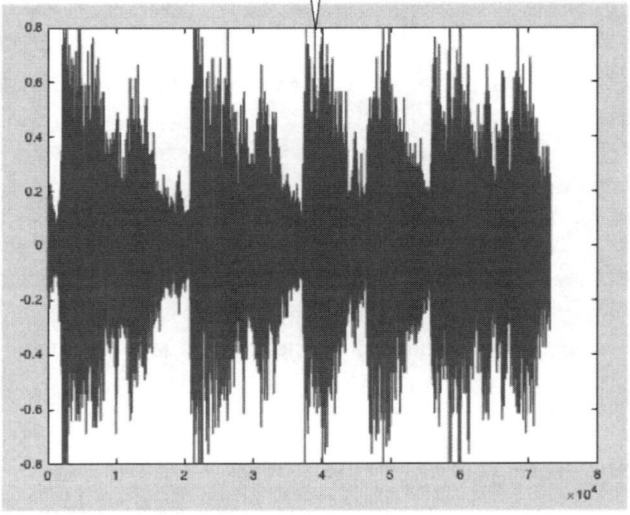

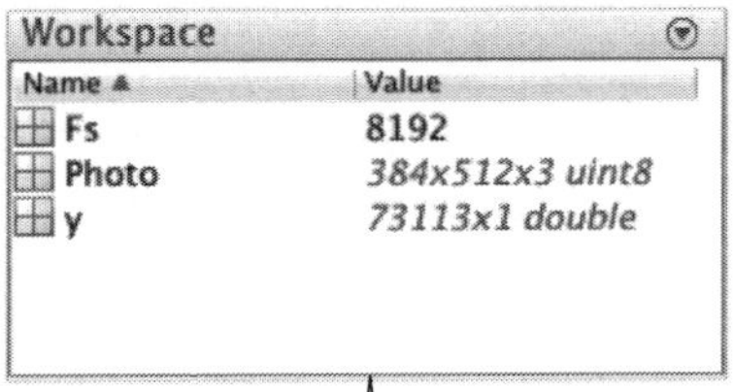

[6] This is the **Workspace** after the execution of the program. ↵

Location of the MATLAB Demo Files

[7] Line 2 reads an image data file **peppers.png** and stores the data in the variable `photo`, which is a 384-by-512-by-3 array of type `uint8` (see [6], last page, and Table 2.1, page 71). This image file is one of the MATLAB demo files. To see the location of the file **peppers.png**, type

```
>> which peppers.png
```

The response should be like this

```
MatlabPath\toolbox\matlab\imagesci\peppers.png
```

where *`MatlabPath`* is the path of your MATLAB installation. The image has 384-by-512 pixels; each pixel is described by three `uint8` numbers (0-255; see Table 2.1, page 71), representing the RGB (red, green, and blue) intensities.

Search Path

MATLAB functions that work with files always accept the full paths to those files as input. If you do not specify the full path, then MATLAB looks for files in the **Current Folder** first, and then in folders on the **search path**. The command `path` can be used to view or change the **search path**.

```
>> path
```

(*For details and more, type* >> `doc path`) ↓

[8] Line 3 displays the image on a **Figure Window** [4]. Line 4 sets the same length for the data units along *x*-axis and *y*-axis and fits the axes box tightly around the data. This is a standard procedure for displaying an image on a **Figure Window**; without this command, the image is usually twisted. Try it yourself. ↓

[9] Line 5 loads a data file **handel.mat**. This is a MATLAB demo sound file stored in the folder

```
MatlabPath/toolbox/matlab/audiovideo
```

which is in the **Search Path** (see [7]). Remember the location of the file can be retrieved by using the command `which` (see [7]).

Recall that a **.mat** file stores not only data but also variable names and dimensions. This sound file consists of `y` and `Fs` (see [6], last page); `y` is a column vector containing the audio signals and `Fs` is a scalar specifying the frequency in hertz.

Line 6 plays the audio signals `y` with the frequency `Fs`, which is Handel's *Messiah*. Of course, we assume that your computer has a speaker. ↓

[10] Line 7 creates a new **Figure Window** (it overlaps the existing **Figure Window** [4]) and line 8 plots the audio signals `y` on the newly created **Figure Window** [5]. With only one argument, the function `plot` plots the data `y` versus the index of each value; i.e., this statement is equivalent to `plot(x, y)`, where

```
x = [1, 2, 3, ..., length(y)]
```

Details and More

Chapter 6 will discuss details and more on images, animations, audios, and videos. #

1.14 Flow Controls

[1] All the programs so far are executed statement-by-statement sequentially. A flow control statement (such as `for`-statement, `if`-statement, `switch`-statement, `while`-statement, etc.) alters the execution sequence. This section demonstrates the use of a `for`-loop to control the execution flow. ↓

Example01_14.m: For-Loops

[2] Create a new script, type the following commands, save as Example01_14.m, and run the script. ↙

```
1   clear, clc
2   v0 = 5; theta = pi/4; g = 9.81;
3   fprintf('  Time (s)     x (m)     y (m)\n');
4   for t = 0:0.1:1
5       x = v0*cos(theta)*t;
6       y = v0*sin(theta)*t-g*t.^2/2;
7       fprintf('%10.1f %9.3f %9.3f\n', t, x, y)
8   end
```

```
Command Window
  Time (s)     x (m)     y (m)
       0.0     0.000     0.000
       0.1     0.354     0.305
       0.2     0.707     0.511
       0.3     1.061     0.619
       0.4     1.414     0.629
       0.5     1.768     0.542
       0.6     2.121     0.356
       0.7     2.475     0.071
       0.8     2.828    -0.311
       0.9     3.182    -0.791
       1.0     3.536    -1.369
>>
```

[3] This is the output on the screen. →

For-Loop

[4] Line 4 starts a `for`-loop and line 8 ends the `for`-loop. In-between is the **body** of the `for`-loop, which can be one or more statements. The indentation of the **body** (lines 5-7) is not required; it is a recommended style for better readability.

A syntax for the `for`-statement (line 4) is

`for` *`variable`* `=` *`row-vector`*

The statements inside a `for`-loop (here, lines 5-7) are repeatedly executed, each time the *`variable`* assumes a value sequentially in the *`row-vector`*. The loop breaks (i.e., the execution jumps out of the `for`-loop) when all values are used up.

Inside the `for`-loop, lines 5 and 6 calculate the coordinates `x` and `y` and line 7 prints the values of `t`, `x`, and `y` according to the specified formats (`%10.1f`, `%9.3f`, `%9.3f` and a newline character). Upon the finish of the `for`-loop, the output on the screen is as usual [3].

An advantage of this implementation is that it uses very little memory: it uses two `doubles` to store the coordinates, while in the previous implementations they use two vectors of `doubles` to store the coordinates.

Details and More

There are other flow-control statements. We'll discuss more flow control statements in Sections 1-4, Chapter 3. #

1.15 User-Defined Functions

1.5a Subfunctions (Local Functions)

[1] This section demonstrates a way of creating user-defined functions. A function-call alters the execution flow, therefore providing a flow-control mechanism. The real power of using user-defined functions is to modularize a program, i.e., dividing a long program into manageable units of functions. The rules for a user-defined function name are the same as those for a variable name, given in Table 1.2, page 16. ↓

Example01_15a.m: Subfunctions (Local Functions)

[2] Create a program like this, save as Example01_15a.m, and run the program. This program demonstrates the creation and use of user-defined functions. ↓

```
1   clear, clc, global g
2   v0 = 5; theta = pi/4; g = 9.81;
3   t = 0:0.1:1;
4   [distance, height] = generateTable(v0, theta, t);
5   printTable(t, distance, height);
6
7   function [x, y] = generateTable(v0, angle, time)
8   global g
9   x = v0*cos(angle)*time;
10  y = v0*sin(angle)*time-g*time.^2/2;
11  end
12
13  function printTable(t, x, y)
14  fprintf('  Time (s)     x (m)      y (m)\n');
15  for k = 1:length(t)
16      fprintf('%10.1f %9.3f %9.3f\n', t(k), x(k), y(k))
17  end
18  end
```

Main Program and Functions

[3] There is a **main program** (lines 1-5) and two **user-defined functions** (lines 7-11, and lines 13-18) in this program file. The main program must be placed before any user-defined functions. The execution of the program starts from the first statement of the main program and ends at the statement right before a function-statement (line 7).

The two user-defined functions are called **subfunctions**, also called **local functions**. The syntax of the function-statements (lines 7 and 13) is

`function` *`output-arguments`* `=` *`name`*`(`*`input-arguments`*`)`

The *`input-arguments`* is a list of variables separated by commas. The *`output-arguments`* is a row vector of variables. Either the *`output-arguments`* or *`input-arguments`* may be absent or may be a single variable; in that case the square brackets in the *`output-arguments`* are not needed.

According to the MATLAB syntax rules, closing a subfunction with an `end` statement (lines 11 and 18) is not always necessary. However, as a good programming style and for better readability, I strongly suggest that you always close a function with an `end` statement. ↵

Each function has its own Workspace

[4] Each function has its own **Workspace**; i.e., variables in a function are local to that function; across functions, variables with the same name are independent to each other (unless it is declared as `global`, see [5]). A `clear` statement at the beginning of a user-defined function is usually not necessary. ↓

Global Variables

[5] Lines 1 and 8 declare that `g` is a **global** variable; i.e., it is "visible" in both the main program and the function `trajectory`. Using global variables is a way to communicate among functions (and the main program). Note that the variable `g` cannot be "seen" in the function `printTable` (lines 13-18), since it is not declared as a `global` in that function. ↓

Function `generateTable`

[6] The function `generateTable` (lines 7-11) takes three variables (`v0`, `angle`, and `time`) as input arguments, calculates the trajectory, and outputs `x` and `y` coordinates. ↓

Function `printTable`

[7] The function `printTable` (lines 13-18) takes three variables (`t`, `x`, and `y`) as input arguments, and prints the trajectory table as usual [8]. It does not have any output arguments. ↓

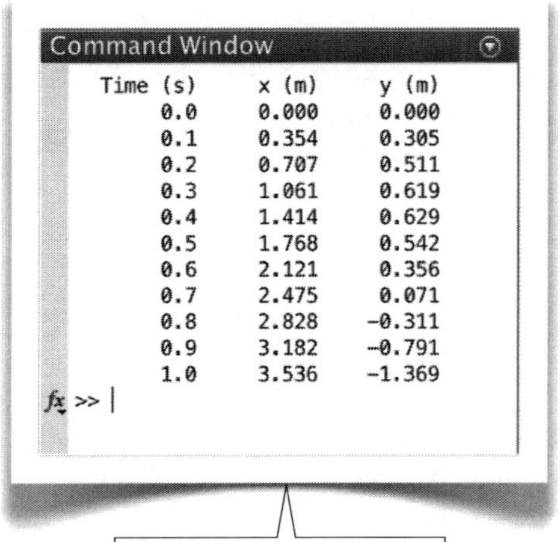

[8] This is the output on the screen. ↗

Main Program

[9] The main program (lines 1-5) sets up variables (lines 1-3), calls the function `generateTable` (line 4) to calculate `distance` and `height`, and then calls the function `printTable` (line 5) to print the trajectory table [8].

In line 4, the function call of `generateTable` causes the execution transfer to line 7. The values of the variables `v0`, `theta`, and `t` (line 4) are copied to the input arguments `v0`, `angle`, and `time` (line 7), respectively. At the end of function `generateTable` (line 11), the execution returns to the main program (line 4) and the values of the output variables `x`, and `y` (line 7) of the function are copied to the variables `distance`, and `height` (line 4), respectively, in the main program. ↓

Blank Lines

[10] Blank lines (lines 6, 12) can be inserted anywhere in the program for better readability. ↓

Subfunctions are local to the program file

[11] Subfunctions are local to the program file to which they belong; therefore, they are also called **local functions**. Their names are not visible from other files; i.e., they cannot be called from other program files. ↓

User-Defined Commands

[12] As mentioned (1.5[12], page 23), a program like Example01_15a.m can be treated as a user-defined command. You can invoke a program by its name in the **Command Window**, in a plane **Script**, or in a **Live Script**; for example:

```
>> Example01_15a
```

With the plane **Script Editor**, if there is no main program, the first user-defined function serves as the main program (this feature is not supported when using the **Live Editor**); in that case, the first user-defined function is also called a **main function**. This feature makes it possible to create a user-defined command with input arguments. Example01_15b.m, next page, demonstrates this feature. #

1.15b Programs with Input Arguments

Example01_15b.m: A Program with Input Arguments

[1] Create a program like this, save as Example01_15b.m, and run the program by typing (see [2])

```
>> Example01_15b(5, pi/4)
```

This program demonstrates the creation of a user-defined command with input arguments, here, `v0` and `theta`. Note that the dimmed statements are copied from Example01_15a.m. ↓

```
function Example01_15b(v0, theta)
global g
g = 9.81;
t = 0:0.1:1;
[distance, height] = generateTable(v0, theta, t);
printTable(t, distance, height);
end

function [x, y] = generateTable(v0, angle, time)
global g
x = v0*cos(angle)*time;
y = v0*sin(angle)*time-g*time.^2/2;
end

function printTable(t, x, y)
fprintf('   Time (s)      x (m)      y (m)\n');
for k = 1:length(t)
    fprintf('%10.1f %9.3f %9.3f\n', t(k), x(k), y(k))
end
end
```

```
>> Example01_15b(5, pi/4)
   Time (s)      x (m)      y (m)
       0.0      0.000      0.000
       0.1      0.354      0.305
       0.2      0.707      0.511
       0.3      1.061      0.619
       0.4      1.414      0.629
       0.5      1.768      0.542
       0.6      2.121      0.356
       0.7      2.475      0.071
       0.8      2.828     -0.311
       0.9      3.182     -0.791
       1.0      3.536     -1.369
>>
```

[2] To provide input arguments, you cannot just click the **Run** button. You need to type in the **Command Window**, in a plane **Script**, or in a **Live Script**. ↓

Details and More

[3] As your programs become large and complicated, you need to organize a program into files, each containing several functions. The more you learn programming techniques, the better you know how to organize your programs.

We'll discuss details and more on user-defined functions and program files in Chapter 3. #

1.16 Cell Arrays

[1] An ordinary **array** (vector, matrix, three-dimensional array, etc.; see Section 1.3) contains elements of the **same type** (e.g., `double`). The elements themselves can be an array, but they must have the same dimensional sizes. A **cell array** removes these restrictions. A cell array can contain elements of different types or/and different dimensional sizes. This section demonstrates the creation of a cell array that contains all information describing the trajectory of a thrown ball, including the initial speed, elevation angle, time points, *x*-coordinates, and *y*-coordinates. The first two elements of the cell array are scalars, while the last three elements are vectors. ↓

[3] This is the output. ↓

```
Command Window
Initial velocity = 5 m/s
Elevation angle = 45 degrees

  Time (s)      x (m)      y (m)
       0.0      0.000      0.000
       0.1      0.354      0.305
       0.2      0.707      0.511
       0.3      1.061      0.619
       0.4      1.414      0.629
       0.5      1.768      0.542
       0.6      2.121      0.356
       0.7      2.475      0.071
       0.8      2.828     -0.311
       0.9      3.182     -0.791
       1.0      3.536     -1.369
fx >>
```

Example01_16.m: Cell Arrays

[2] Create a program like this and run the program.
This program demonstrates the creation and use of **cell arrays**. ↑

```
1   clear, clc
2   v0 = 5; theta = pi/4; g = 9.81;
3   t = 0:0.1:1;
4   x = v0*cos(theta)*t;
5   y = v0*sin(theta)*t-g*t.^2/2;
6   Trajectory = {v0, theta, t, x, y};
7   printTrajectory(Trajectory)
8
9   function printTrajectory(Traj)
10  fprintf('Initial velocity = %.0f m/s\n', Traj{1})
11  fprintf('Elevation angle = %.0f degrees\n\n', Traj{2}*180/pi)
12  fprintf('  Time (s)      x (m)      y (m)\n');
13  for k = 1:length(Traj{3})
14      fprintf('%10.1f %9.3f %9.3f\n', Traj{3}(k), Traj{4}(k), Traj{5}(k))
15  end
16  end
```

The Main Program

[4] This program consists of a main program (lines 1-7) and a function `printTrajectory` (lines 9-16). Lines 1-5 calculate the trajectory as usual. Line 6

```
Trajectory = {v0, theta, t, x, y};
```

creates a 5-element **cell array**. Note that curly brackets (braces, {}) are used to create **cell arrays**, while square brackets ([]) are used to create ordinary arrays. Line 7

```
printTrajectory(Trajectory)
```

calls the function `printTrajectory`. The contents of `Trajectory` are copied to the input argument `Traj` (line 9) of the function `printTrajectory`. ↵

Function `printTrajectory`

[5] The function `printTrajectory` (lines 9-16) takes an input argument `Traj`, a cell array containing the trajectory information, and prints a table of trajectory (see [3], last page). In lines 10 and 11, the **format specifier**

```
%.0f
```

specifies that no digits (`.0`) are printed after the decimal point (the decimal point is thus removed). The absence of the total width signifies a minimum printing width.

Access the Elements of a Cell Array

The curly brackets `{}` can be used to access the values of a cell array. This is demonstrated in lines 10-11 and 13-14. In line 14, the curly bracket `{}` is used to index to an element of the cell array, while the round brackets `()` are used to index to an element of an ordinary array. For example, `Traj{5}` refers to the array `y`, while `Traj{5}(k)` refers to the kth element of the array `y`. ↓

Two-Dimensional Cell Arrays

[6] Creation of a cell array is similar to the creation of an ordinary array, except that curly brackets (braces, `{}`) are used instead of square brackets (`[]`). Like the ordinary arrays, semicolons can be used to create two-dimensional cell arrays; for example,

```
C = {'Velocity', 5; 'Angle', pi/4}
```

creates a 2-by-2 cell array; the screen output is

```
C =
    'Velocity'    [     5]
    'Angle'       [0.7854]
```

The four elements of the cell array `C` are referred to as `C{1,1}`, `C{2,1}`, `C{1,2}`, and `C{2,2}`.

Details and More

Cell arrays are heavily used. One of the uses of cell arrays is to represent an array of variable-length characters. We'll discuss details and more in Chapter 4. #

1.17 Structures

[1] A cell array can contain elements of different types, different dimensional sizes. You access the elements by indices. Like a cell array, a **structure** can contain elements of different types, different dimensional sizes. However, you access the elements by **names** (instead of indices). In this fashion, you don't have to know the order of the elements, and it often enhances the readability. This section demonstrates the creation of a structure that contains all information describing the trajectory of a thrown ball, including the initial speed, elevation angle, time points, *x*-coordinates, and *y*-coordinates. ↓

[3] This is the output. ↓

```
Command Window
Initial velocity = 5 m/s
Elevation angle = 45 degrees

  Time (s)     x (m)     y (m)
       0.0     0.000     0.000
       0.1     0.354     0.305
       0.2     0.707     0.511
       0.3     1.061     0.619
       0.4     1.414     0.629
       0.5     1.768     0.542
       0.6     2.121     0.356
       0.7     2.475     0.071
       0.8     2.828    -0.311
       0.9     3.182    -0.791
       1.0     3.536    -1.369
fx >>
```

Example01_17.m: Structures

[2] Create a program like this and run the program.
This program demonstrates the creation and use of **structures**. ↑

```
 1  clear, clc
 2  v0 = 5; theta = pi/4; g = 9.81;
 3  t = 0:0.1:1;
 4  x = v0*cos(theta)*t;
 5  y = v0*sin(theta)*t-g*t.^2/2;
 6  Trajectory.velocity = v0;
 7  Trajectory.angle = theta;
 8  Trajectory.time = t;
 9  Trajectory.distance = x;
10  Trajectory.height = y;
11  printTrajectory(Trajectory)
12
13  function printTrajectory(Traj)
14  fprintf('Initial velocity = %.0f m/s\n', Traj.velocity)
15  fprintf('Elevation angle = %.0f degrees\n\n', Traj.angle*180/pi)
16  fprintf('  Time (s)     x (m)     y (m)\n');
17  for k = 1:length(Traj.time)
18      fprintf('%10.1f %9.3f %9.3f\n', ...
19          Traj.time(k), Traj.distance(k), Traj.height(k))
20  end
21  end
```

The Main Program

[4] This program consists of a main program (lines 1-11) and a function `printTrajectory` (lines 13-21). Lines 1-5 calculate the trajectory as usual. A **structure** contains one or more **named fields**, which may be different in type and in dimensional sizes. Lines 6-10 demonstrate a way of creating a **structure** of 5 fields (`velocity`, `angle`, `time`, `distance`, and `height`). The 5 fields are assigned `v0`, `theta`, `t`, `x`, and `y`, respectively. Line 11 calls the function `printTrajectory`. The contents of `Trajectory` are copied to the input argument `Traj` (line 13) of the function `printTrajectory`. ↵

Access the Elements of a Structure

[5] As mentioned, to access the elements of a structure, we use its field names. This is demonstrated in lines 6-10, 14-15, 17, and 19. In line19, `Traj.height` refers to an entire array, while `Traj.height(k)` refers to the kth element of the array.

Continuation of a Statement

In line 18, an ellipsis (`...`) is used to continue a statement to the next line; i.e., in this case, lines 18 and 19 are treated as a single statement.

Details and More

It is possible to create an array of **structures**, called a **structure array**, in which all elements of the array are **structures** of the same fields. **Structures** are heavily used. We'll discuss details and more on **structures** in Chapter 4. #

1.18 Graphical User Interfaces (GUI)

[1] A program, also called an **app** (short for application), needs a user interface, which involves taking input from the user and giving output to the user. So far, all the user interfaces we created are text-based. In general, a graphics-based user interface is more intuitive and more user-friendly than a text-based one.

MATLAB provides three ways to build **apps** with graphical user interfaces: **Programmatic Approach**, **GUIDE**, and **App Designer**.

With **Programmatic Approach**, you use MATLAB functions to create a **Figure Window** and place interactive components in the **Figure Window**, programmatically, without the assist of other interactive tools such as **GUIDE** or **App Designer**.

GUIDE (Graphical User Interface Development Environment) provides an interactive environment to assist in the creation of the **Figure Window** and the interactive components.

The **App Designer**, new in R2016a, a major enhancement to **GUIDE**, has a larger set of interactive components and a more intuitive way of building apps.

This section demonstrates the use of **Programmatic Approach** to build a ball-throwing **app**.

In sections 1.19 and 1.20, **GUIDE** and **App Designer**, respectively, are used to build the same **app**.

Chapter 8 will discuss details and more on GUI designs. →

Example01_18.m: GUI

[2] Create a program like this and run the program. This program creates a GUI as shown in [3-6], next page. ↵

```
clear, clc
global g velocityBox angleBox
g = 9.81;
figure('Position', [30,70,500,400])
axes('Units', 'pixels', ...
    'Position', [50,80,250,250])
axis([0, 10, 0, 10])
xlabel('Distance (m)'), ylabel('Height (m)')
title('Trajectory of a Ball')

uicontrol('Style', 'text', ...
    'String', 'Initial velocity (m/s)', ...
    'Position', [330,300,150,20])
velocityBox = uicontrol('Style', 'edit', ...
    'String', '5', ...
    'Position', [363,280,80,20]);
uicontrol('Style', 'text', ...
    'String', 'Elevation angle (deg)', ...
    'Position', [330,240,150,20])
angleBox = uicontrol('Style', 'edit', ...
    'String', '45', ...
    'Position', [363,220,80,20]);
uicontrol('Style', 'pushbutton', ...
    'String', 'Throw', ...
    'Position', [363,150,80,30], ...
    'Callback', @pushbuttonCallback)

function pushbuttonCallback(pushButton, ~)
global g velocityBox angleBox
v0 = str2double(velocityBox.String);
theta = str2double(angleBox.String)*pi/180;
t1 = 2*v0*sin(theta)/g;
t = 0:0.01:t1;
x = v0*cos(theta)*t;
y = v0*sin(theta)*t-g*t.^2/2;
hold on
comet(x, y)
end
```

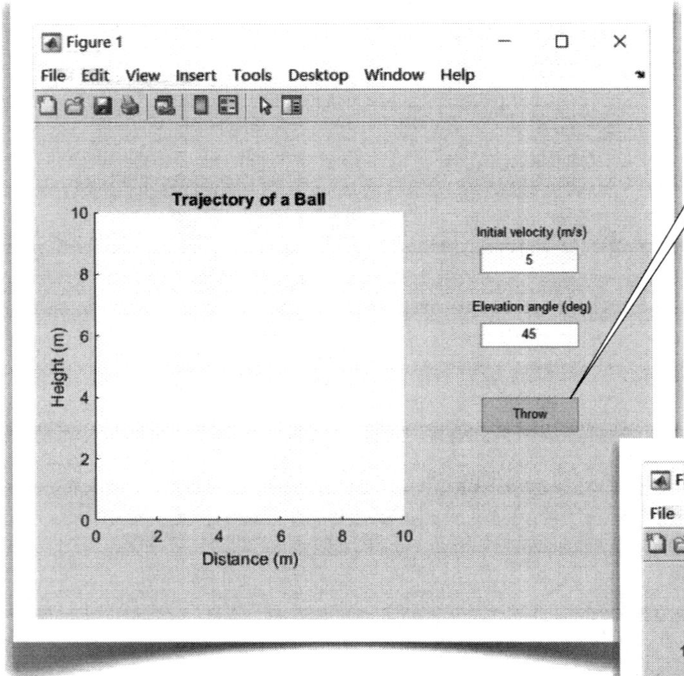

[3] Click **Throw** to produce a trajectory for the default initial velocity and elevation angle. ↙

[6] To quit the program, click **Close**. ↓

[5] This GUI has five **UI control objects**: two **static text objects**, two **editable text boxes**, and a push-button. ↑

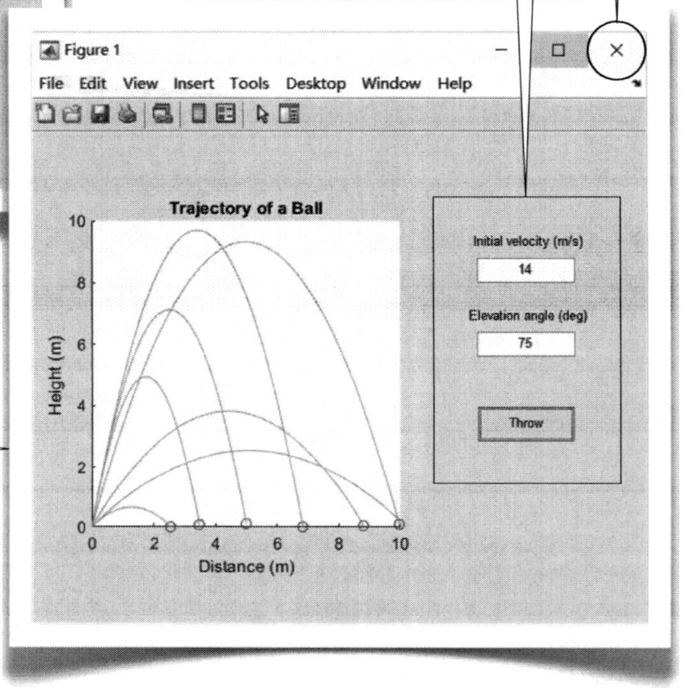

[4] Try other input values. These trajectories are produced by the following initial velocities and elevation angles: (5 m/s, 45 deg), (10 m/s, 45 deg), (10 m/s, 60 deg), (10 m/s, 80 deg), (12 m/s, 80 deg), (14 m/s, 80 deg), (14 m/s, 75 deg). ↗

What is this program doing?

[7] This program creates a GUI as shown in [3-6], in which the user inputs two numbers (the initial velocity and the elevation angle) and then clicks the **Throw** button [3] to start the animation of a ball along its trajectory until it hits the ground.

The main program (lines 1-26) sets up the GUI and then waits for a **callback** from a **UI control object**.

There are five **UI control objects** [5] defined in lines 11-26, respectively: two **static text objects**, two **editable text boxes**, and a **push-button**.

For each UI control object, we may specify one or more **callback functions**; each can be triggered by an **event**, e.g., a push-down in a push-button object or a change of value in an editable text object.

In this case, we only specify a **callback function** (lines 28-38; also see line 26) for the push-button. A click of the push-button causes a call of the callback function; i.e., whenever the push-button is clicked, the function `pushbuttonCallback` (lines 28-38) is executed once.

The callback function `pushbuttonCallback` retrieves the values in the two editable text boxes (lines 30-31), calculates the trajectory (lines 32-35), and animates the trajectory using the built-in function `comet` (line 37). ↵

Variables Passed to a Callback Function

[8] A callback function is not called directly from any statement of your program. It is called from a UI management system, which passes two variables to the callback function. The first variable (`pushButton` in line 28) is a **handle** to a **structure** data (Section 1.17) containing properties of the **UI control object** that triggers the callback, in this case, the push-button. The second variable (~ in line 28) is not used for the current version of MATLAB. It is reserved for use in the future versions of MATLAB. The tilde (~) in line 28 is used as a placeholder for an unused argument.

In our case, the handle `pushButton` (line 28) points to a **structure** data describing the push-button. For example

```
pushButton.BackgroundColor
```

stores the background color of the push-button. You may change the background color, e.g., by inserting the following statement anywhere in function `pushbuttonCallback`, running the program, and clicking **Throw** button.

```
pushButton.BackgroundColor='red';
```

The handle `pushButton` is not used in our program.

Global Variables

When a variable is declared as `global` in several functions, these functions share a single copy of that variable (1.15[5], page 49). Any change of value to that variable, in any function that declares it as global, becomes effective in other functions that declare it as global. Using global variables is a way to comunicate information among functions.

In our program, three variables are declared `global` in the main program and the function `pushbuttonCallback` (lines 2 and 29). Doing so, we in effect pass the three variables from the main program to the function `pushbuttonCallback`. The variables `velocityBox` (see lines 2, 14, and 29-30) and `angleBox` (see lines 2, 20, 29, and 31) are handles to the two editable text boxes, respectively.

Figure Windows

Line 4 creates a **Figure Window** with position at $x = 30$ pixels and $y = 70$ pixels, width 500 pixels, and height 400 pixels. The position is relative to the origin at the lower-left corner of your computer screen.

Axes Objects

Lines 5-6 create an **axes object** with position at $x = 50$ pixels and $y = 80$ pixels, width 250 pixels, and height 250 pixels. The position is relative to the origin at the lower-left corner of the **Figure Window**. The pixels are not the default units for the function `axes`; therefore, we need to specify the pixels as the units (line 5) if we want to specify the position in pixels. Line 7 specifies the axis limits: 0 to 10 data units (here, meters) for both horizontal-axis and vertical-axis.

UI Control Objects

Lines 11-26 create five **UI control objects** (see [5], last page): two **static text objects**, two **editable text boxes**, and a **push-button**. MATLAB provides many UI control objects that allow you to design sophisticated graphical user interfaces. #

1.19 GUIDE

[1] This section demonstrates the use of **GUIDE** (Graphical User Interface Development Environment) to create an app that has the same functionality as the one created in the last section. ↓

[2] To start **GUIDE**, on **Command Window**, type ↘

```
>> guide
```

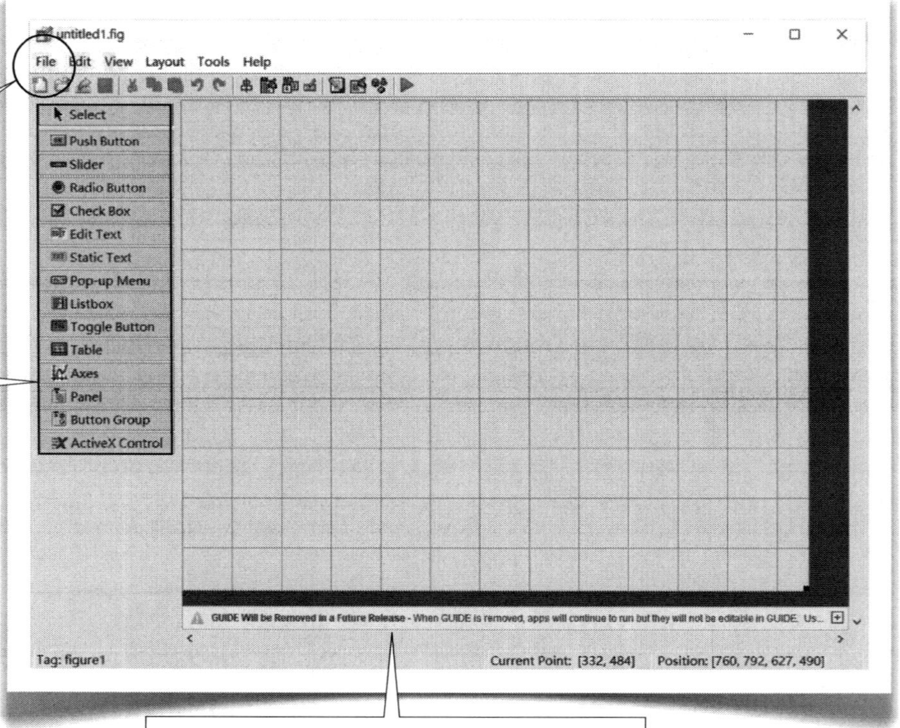

[4] Pull-down-select **File>Preferences...** ↓

[6] Step [5] is to make sure that, for clarity, the objects' names are shown next to the icons. ↵

[3] A warning message says that the GUIDE will be removed in a future release. ↖

[5] Make sure **Show names in component palette** is checked and click **OK**. ↑

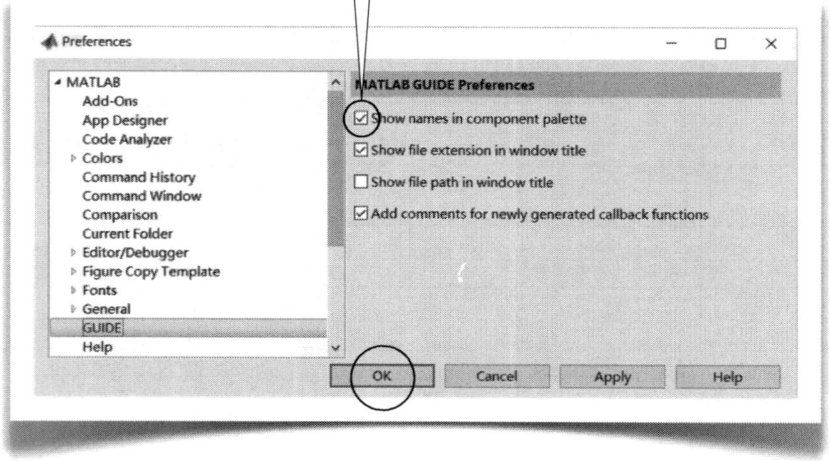

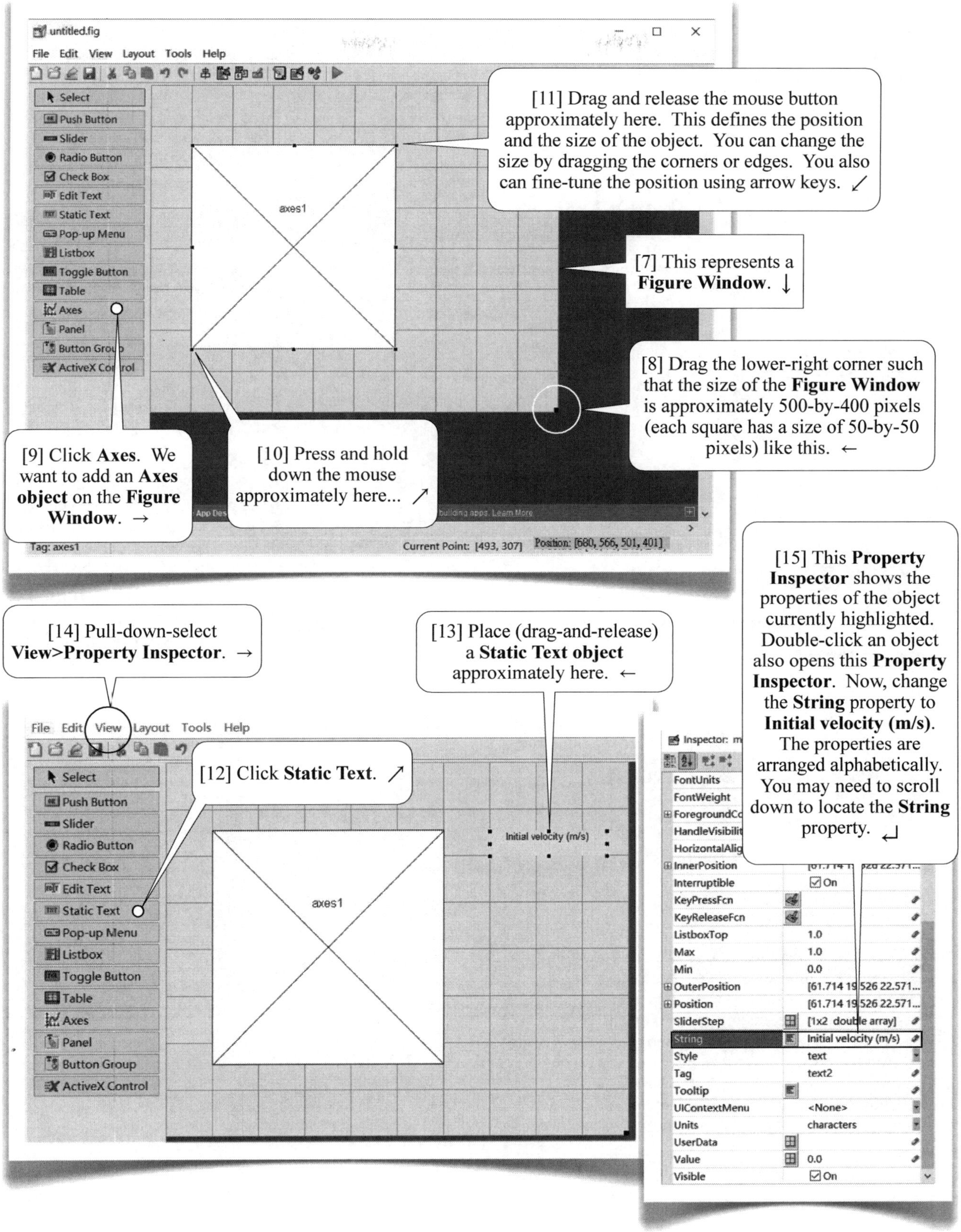
[7] This represents a Figure Window. ↓
[8] Drag the lower-right corner such that the size of the Figure Window is approximately 500-by-400 pixels (each square has a size of 50-by-50 pixels) like this. ←
[9] Click Axes. We want to add an Axes object on the Figure Window. →
[10] Press and hold down the mouse approximately here... ↗
[11] Drag and release the mouse button approximately here. This defines the position and the size of the object. You can change the size by dragging the corners or edges. You also can fine-tune the position using arrow keys. ↙
[12] Click Static Text. ↗
[13] Place (drag-and-release) a Static Text object approximately here. ←
[14] Pull-down-select View>Property Inspector. →
[15] This Property Inspector shows the properties of the object currently highlighted. Double-click an object also opens this Property Inspector. Now, change the String property to Initial velocity (m/s). The properties are arranged alphabetically. You may need to scroll down to locate the String property. ↵
untitled.fig
axes1
Initial velocity (m/s)
Tag: axes1
Current Point: [493, 307]
Position: [680, 566, 501, 401]

[22] Click **Push Button**. ↘

[16, 20] Click **Edit Text**. ↘

[18] Click **Static Text**. ↘

[28] Click to close the GUIDE. If you want to edit this GUI later, see [37], page 62. ↲

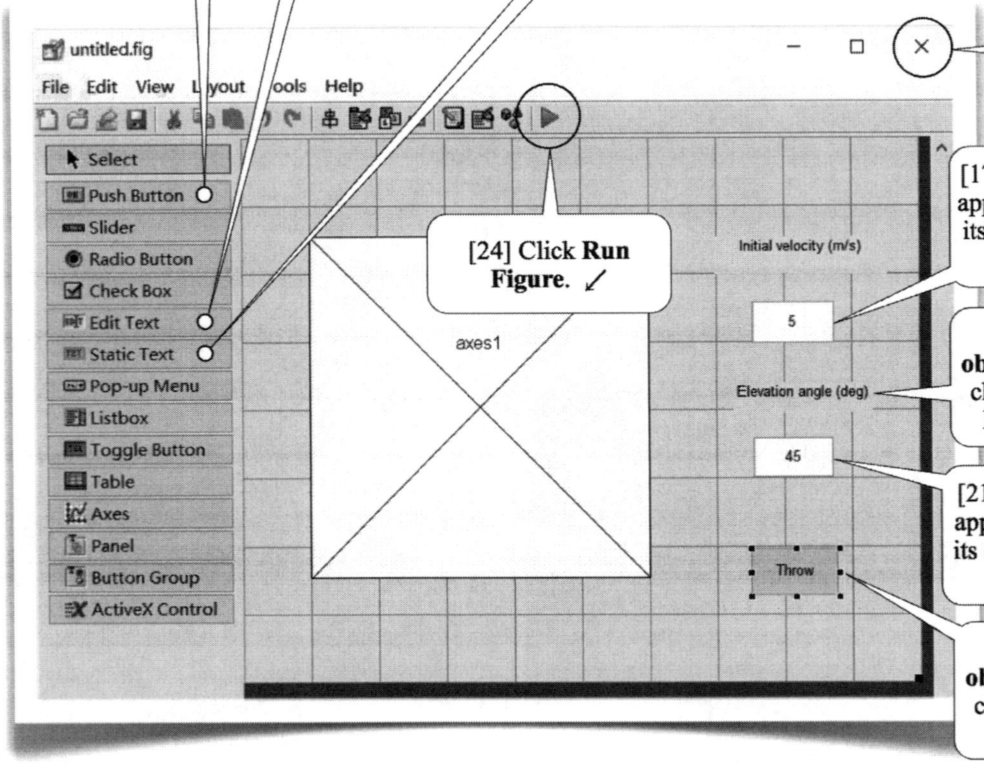

[24] Click **Run Figure**. ↙

[17] Place an **Edit Text object** approximately here and change its **String** property to **5** (as the default value). ↖

[19] Place a **Static Text object** approximately here and change its **String** property to **Elevation angle (deg)**. ↖

[21] Place an **Edit Text object** approximately here and change its **String** property to **45** (as the default value). ↖

[23] Place a **Push Button object** approximately here and change its **String** property to **Throw**. ↖

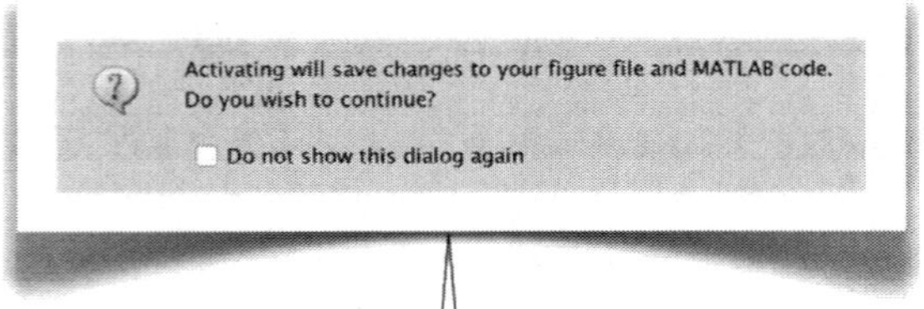

[25] Click **Yes** in response to this message. A **Save As** window appears. Type **Example01_19** as the file name and click **Save**. Two files are created in the Current Folder: **Example01_19.fig** and **Example01_19.m**. The former defines the GUI (as shown in [26-27]) and the latter is a program in which we will add statements, for example, defining the callback actions. →

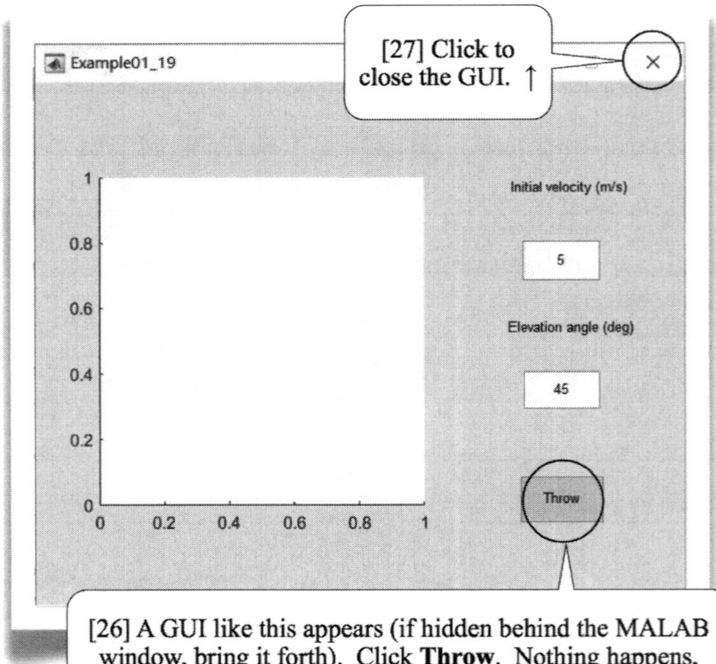

[27] Click to close the GUI. ↑

[26] A GUI like this appears (if hidden behind the MALAB window, bring it forth). Click **Throw**. Nothing happens, because we haven't defined the callback actions yet. ↑

```
% --- Executes just before Example01_19 is made visible.
function Example01_19_OpeningFcn(hObject, eventdata, handles, varargin)
% This function has no output args, see OutputFcn.
% hObject    handle to figure
% eventdata  reserved - to be defined in a future version of MATLAB
% handles    structure with handles and user data (see GUIDATA)
% varargin   command line arguments to Example01_19 (see VARARGIN)

% Choose default command line output for Example01_19
handles.output = hObject;

% Update handles structure
guidata(hObject, handles);

% UIWAIT makes Example01_19 wait for user response (see UIRESUME)
% uiwait(handles.figure1);
axis([0, 10, 0, 10])
xlabel('Distance (m)'), ylabel('Height (m)')
title('Trajectory of a Ball')
```

[29] A program Example01_19.m is automatically opened in the **Editor Window**. ↓

[30] Locate the function `Example01_19_OpeningFcn` (which is the second function in the file) and append these statements (which set up an initial **Axes**) at the end of the function like this. This function will be executed before the GUI appears. ↓

```
% --- Executes during object creation, after setting all properties.
function edit1_CreateFcn(hObject, eventdata, handles)
% hObject    handle to edit1 (see GCBO)
% eventdata  reserved - to be defined in a future version of MATLAB
% handles    empty - handles not created until after all CreateFcns called

% Hint: edit controls usually have a white background on Windows.
%       See ISPC and COMPUTER.
if ispc && isequal(get(hObject,'BackgroundColor'), get(0,'defaultUicontrolBackgroundColor'))
    set(hObject,'BackgroundColor','white');
end
global velocityBox
velocityBox = hObject;
```

[31] Locate the function `edit1_CreateFcn` and append these statements (in which `velocityBox` is a handle to the first **Edit Text Object**) at the end of the function like this. This function will be executed when the first **Edit Text object** is created. ↓

```
% --- Executes during object creation, after setting all properties.
function edit2_CreateFcn(hObject, eventdata, handles)
% hObject    handle to edit2 (see GCBO)
% eventdata  reserved - to be defined in a future version of MATLAB
% handles    empty - handles not created until after all CreateFcns called

% Hint: edit controls usually have a white background on Windows.
%       See ISPC and COMPUTER.
if ispc && isequal(get(hObject,'BackgroundColor'), get(0,'defaultUicontrolBackgroundColor'))
    set(hObject,'BackgroundColor','white');
end
global angleBox
angleBox = hObject;
```

[32] Locate the function `edit2_CreateFcn` and append these statements (in which `angleBox` is a handle to the second **Edit Text Object**) at the end of the function like this. This function will be executed when the second **Edit Text object** is created. ↵

```
% --- Executes on button press in pushbutton1.
function pushbutton1_Callback(hObject, eventdata, handles)
% hObject    handle to pushbutton1 (see GCBO)
% eventdata  reserved - to be defined in a future version of MATLAB
% handles    structure with handles and user data (see GUIDATA)
global velocityBox angleBox
g = 9.81;
v0 = str2double(velocityBox.String);
theta = str2double(angleBox.String)*pi/180;
t1 = 2*v0*sin(theta)/g;
t = 0:0.01:t1;
x = v0*cos(theta)*t;
y = v0*sin(theta)*t-g*t.^2/2;
hold on
comet(x, y)
```

[33] Locate the function **pushbutton1_Callback** (which is the last function of the file) and append these statements (which calculate and animate the trajectory) at the end of function like this. This function will be executed whenever the **Push-Button object** is pushed down. ↙

[34] Click **Run**. ↓

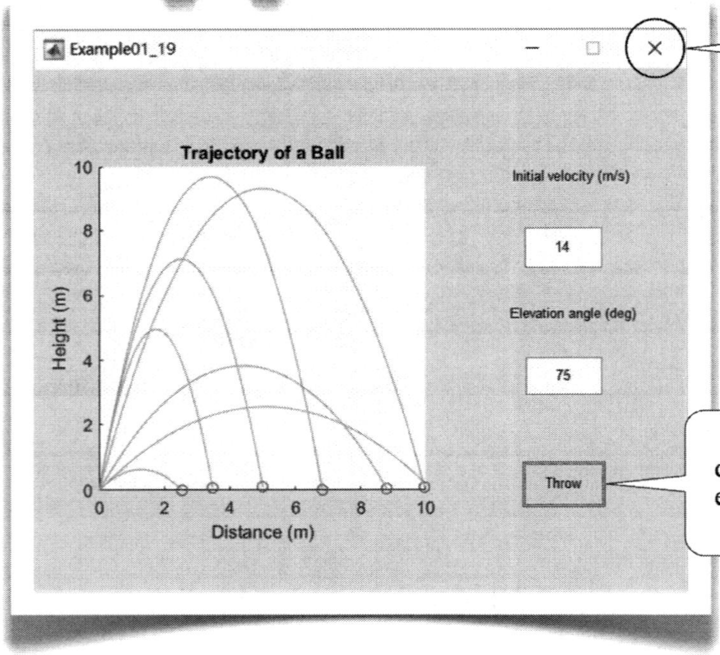

[36] Click to quit the program. ↓

[35] Click **Throw** and try different initial velocities and elevation angles (e.g., use the data in 1.18[4], page 56). ↑

Edit GUI

[37] Designing a GUI is usually an iterative process: you design an initial GUI, test, modify, test, modify, and so forth. You can edit this GUI by right-clicking the file **Example01_19.fig** and select **Open in GUIDE**, or by typing

```
>> guide Example01_19
```

#

1.20 App Designer

[1] Introduced in R2016a, **App Designer** provides more interactive components and a more intuitive way of building apps (see *Help>MATLAB>App Building>App Designer*) than **GUIDE**. This section demonstrates the use of **App Designer** to create an **app** that has the same functionality as the ones created in the last two sections. →

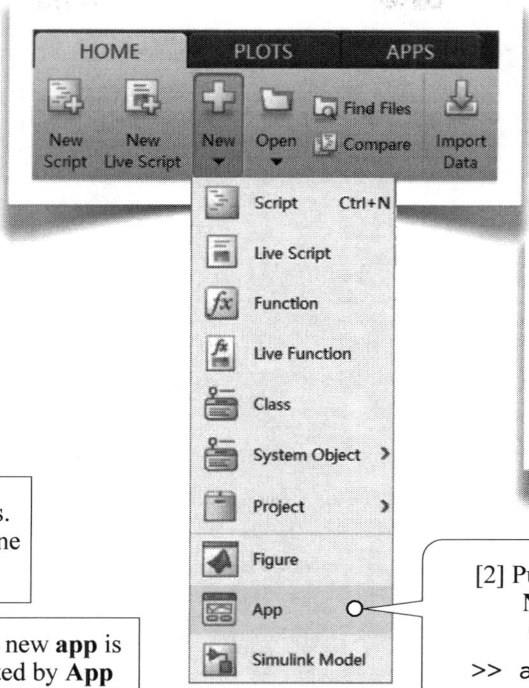

[2] Pull-down-select **New>App**. Or type ↑

```
>> appdesigner
```

[3] In the **MATLAB App Designer** window, click **Blank App**. ↙

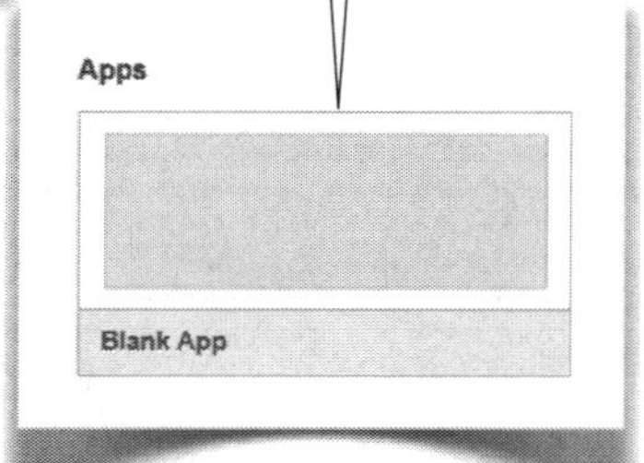

[4] An **App Designer** window appears. The entire app-building task will be done within this environment. ↓

[5] The default name for the new **app** is **app1.mlapp**. An **app** created by **App Designer** has a file extension **.mlapp**. ↓

[6] You may switch between **Design View** and **Code View**. The **Design View** lets you arrange components in a **Figure**, while the **Code View** lets you work on functions (e.g., callback functions). Initially, we're in **Design View**. ↓

[9] The **Component Browser** displays the names of existing components. A component with the name **app.UIFigure** (e.g., [7]) is preexisting. Click the name (or the **Figure** [7]) to highlight it. ↓

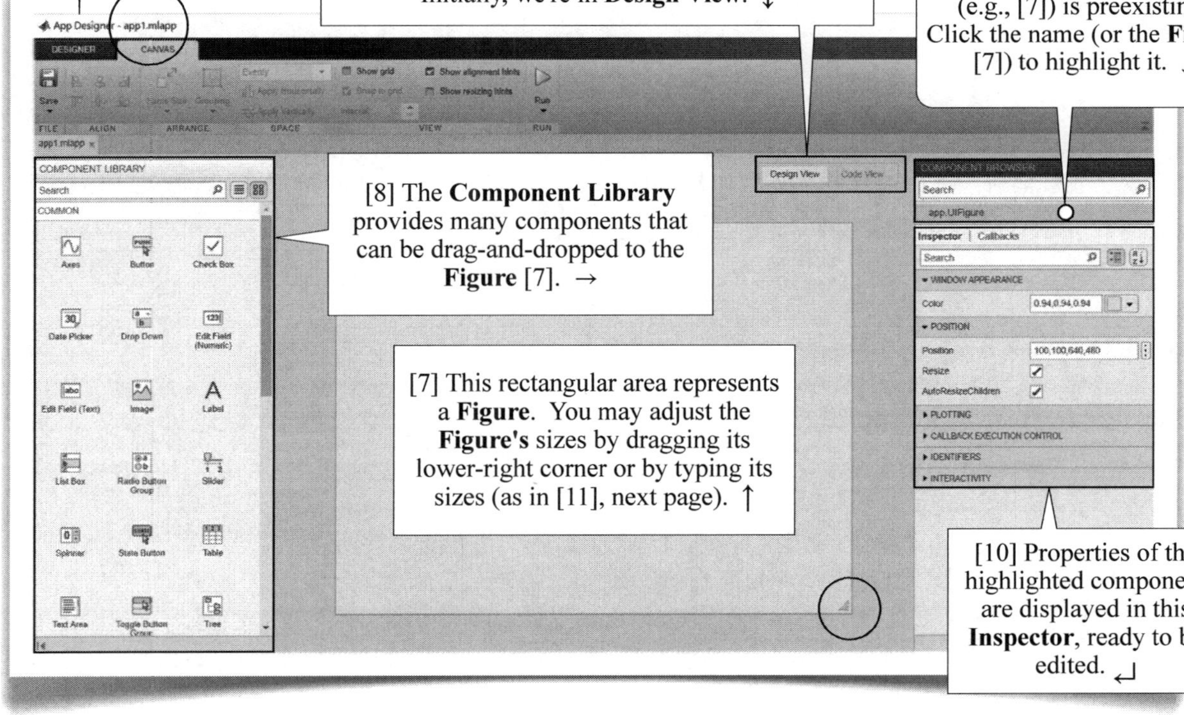

[8] The **Component Library** provides many components that can be drag-and-dropped to the **Figure** [7]. →

[7] This rectangular area represents a **Figure**. You may adjust the **Figure's** sizes by dragging its lower-right corner or by typing its sizes (as in [11], next page). ↑

[10] Properties of the highlighted component are displayed in this **Inspector**, ready to be edited. ↵

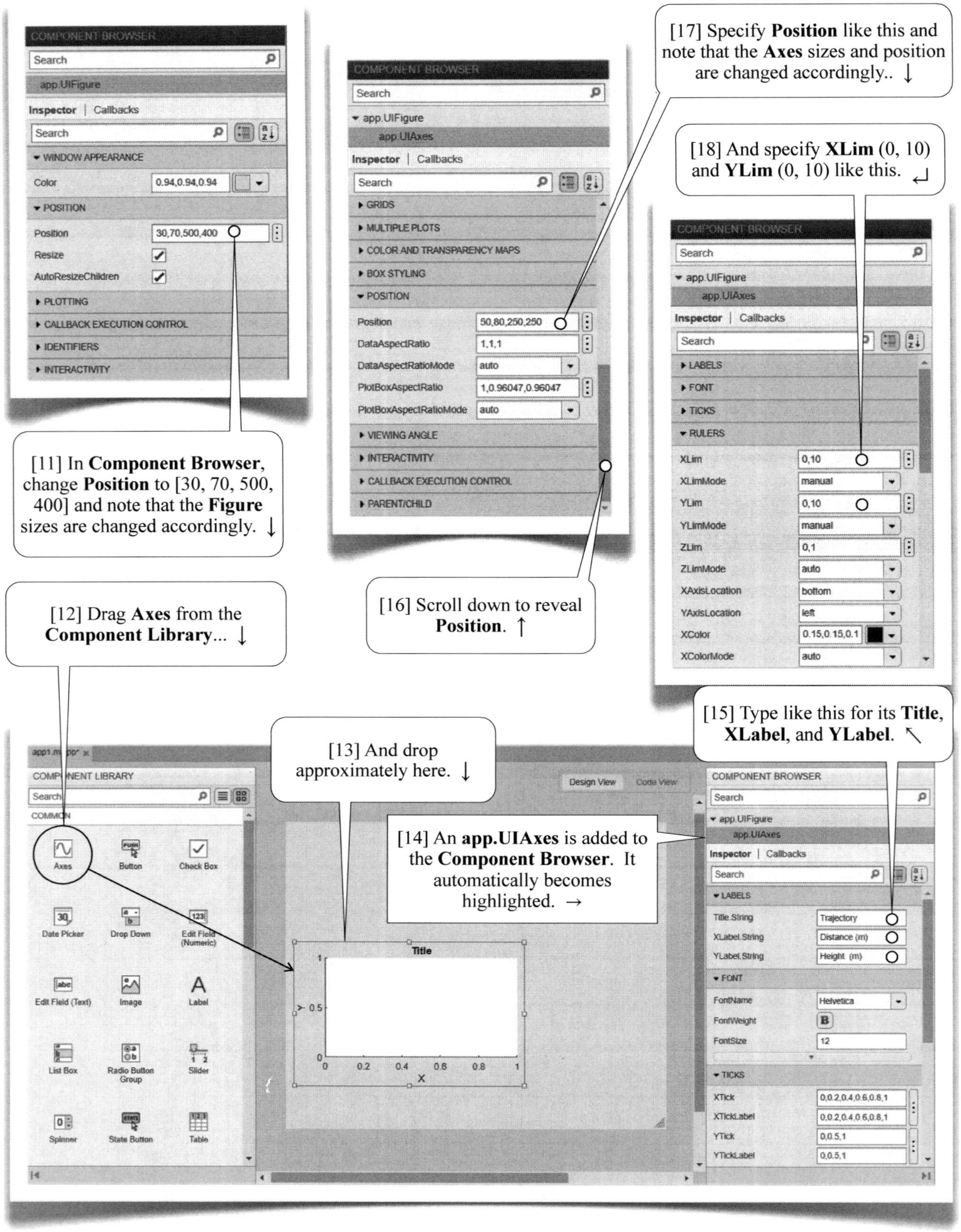
[11] In Component Browser, change Position to [30, 70, 500, 400] and note that the Figure sizes are changed accordingly. ↓
[12] Drag Axes from the Component Library... ↓
[13] And drop approximately here. ↓
[14] An app.UIAxes is added to the Component Browser. It automatically becomes highlighted. →
[15] Type like this for its Title, XLabel, and YLabel. ↖
[16] Scroll down to reveal Position. ↑
[17] Specify Position like this and note that the Axes sizes and position are changed accordingly.. ↓
[18] And specify XLim (0, 10) and YLim (0, 10) like this. ↲
COMPONENT BROWSER
app.UIFigure
app.UIAxes
Inspector | Callbacks
Position
30,70,500,400
50,80,250,250
XLim
0,10
YLim
0,10
COMPONENT LIBRARY
Axes
Button
Check Box
Date Picker
Drop Down
Edit Field (Numeric)
Edit Field (Text)
Image
Label
List Box
Radio Button Group
Slider
Spinner
State Button
Table
Design View
Code View
Title.String
Trajectory
XLabel.String
Distance (m)
YLabel.String
Height (m)

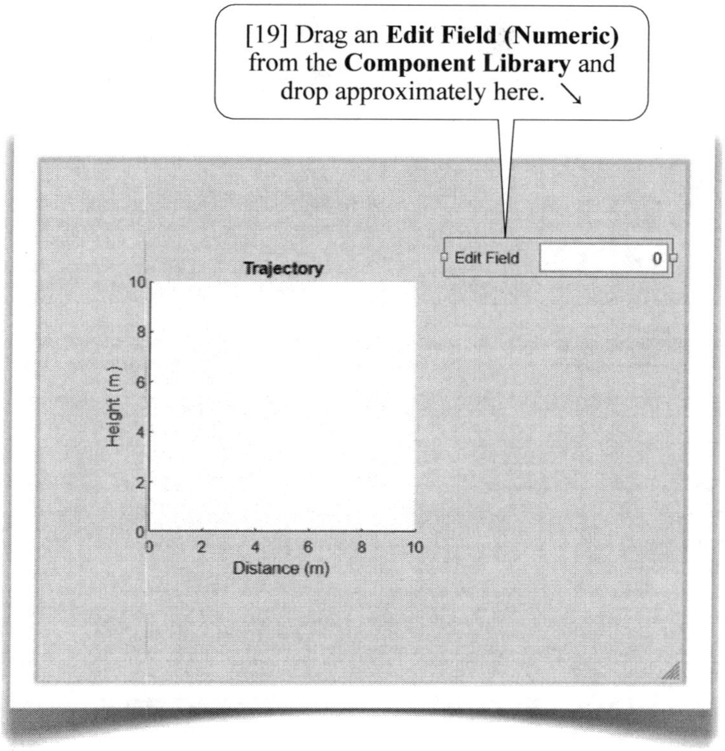
[19] Drag an **Edit Field (Numeric)** from the **Component Library** and drop approximately here. ↘
Edit Field
0
Trajectory
Height (m)
Distance (m)

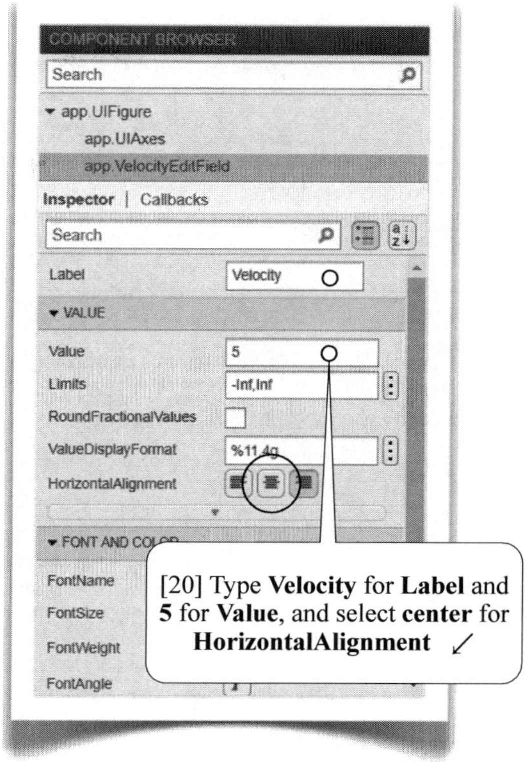
COMPONENT BROWSER
Search
app.UIFigure
app.UIAxes
app.VelocityEditField
Inspector | Callbacks
Label
Velocity
VALUE
Value
5
Limits
-Inf,Inf
RoundFractionalValues
ValueDisplayFormat
%11.4g
HorizontalAlignment
FONT AND COLOR
FontName
FontSize
FontWeight
FontAngle
[20] Type **Velocity** for **Label** and **5** for **Value**, and select **center** for **HorizontalAlignment** ↙

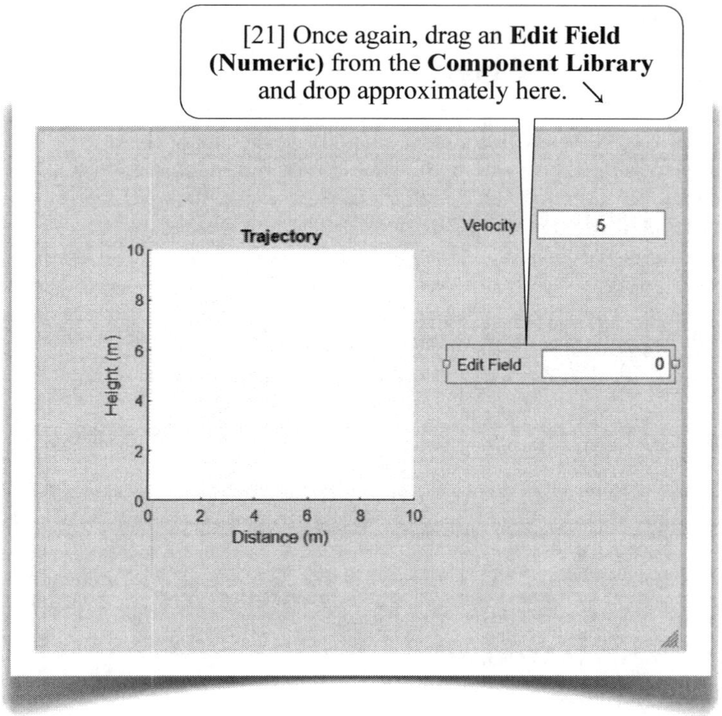
[21] Once again, drag an **Edit Field (Numeric)** from the **Component Library** and drop approximately here. ↘
Velocity
5
Edit Field
0
Trajectory
Height (m)
Distance (m)

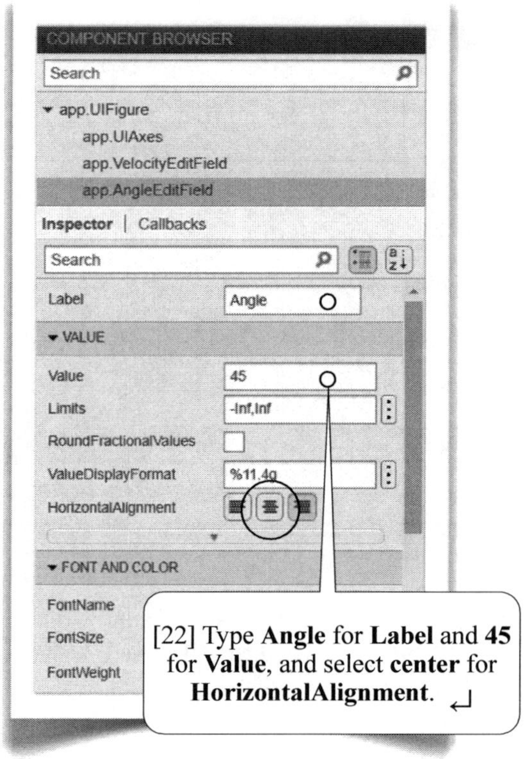
COMPONENT BROWSER
Search
app.UIFigure
app.UIAxes
app.VelocityEditField
app.AngleEditField
Inspector | Callbacks
Label
Angle
VALUE
Value
45
Limits
-Inf,Inf
RoundFractionalValues
ValueDisplayFormat
%11.4g
HorizontalAlignment
FONT AND COLOR
FontName
FontSize
FontWeight
[22] Type **Angle** for **Label** and **45** for **Value**, and select **center** for **HorizontalAlignment**. ↵

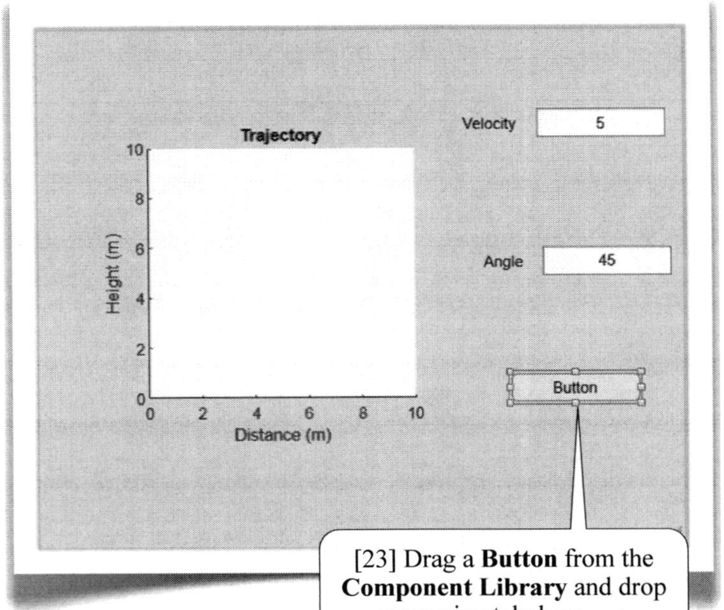

[23] Drag a **Button** from the **Component Library** and drop approximately here. →

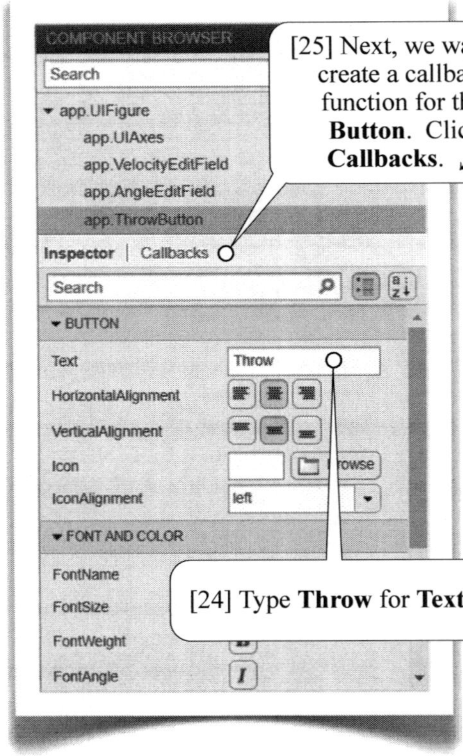

[25] Next, we want to create a callback function for this **Button**. Click **Callbacks**. ↙

[24] Type **Throw** for **Text**. ↑

[26] Pull-down-select **<add ButtonPushedFcn callback>**. ↘

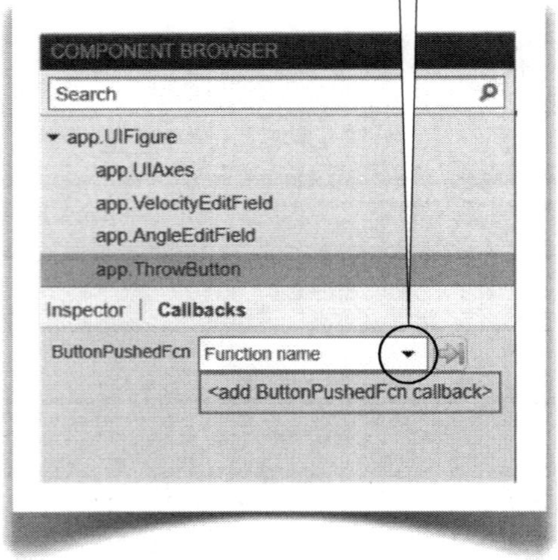

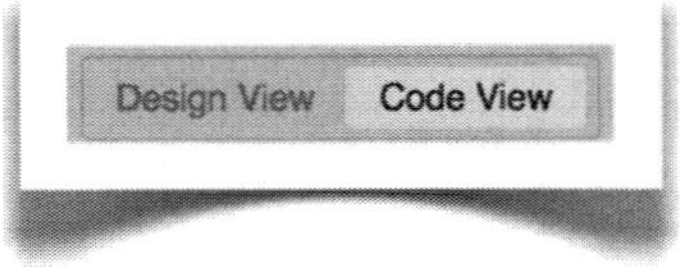

[27] The **Code View** becomes activated and the cursor resides at a place suggesting where you should type the statements for the callback function, `ThrowButtonPushed`, which will be executed whenever the **Throw** button [23] is pushed. ↙

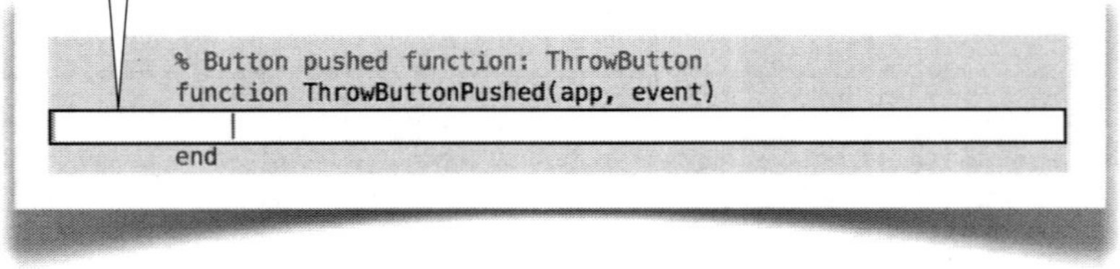

[28] Now, type the statements like this. ↵

```
% Button pushed function: ThrowButton
function ThrowButtonPushed(app, event)
    g = 9.81;
    v0 = app.VelocityEditField.Value;
    theta = app.AngleEditField.Value*pi/180;
    t1 = 2*v0*sin(theta)/g;
    t = 0:0.01:t1;
    x = v0*cos(theta)*t;
    y = v0*sin(theta)*t-g*t.^2/2;
    hold(app.UIAxes, 'on')
    comet(app.UIAxes, x, y)
end
```

[29] Click **Save**, and type **Example01_20** as the name. An **Example01_20.mlapp** is created in the **Current Folder**. →

[30] Click **Run**. ↓

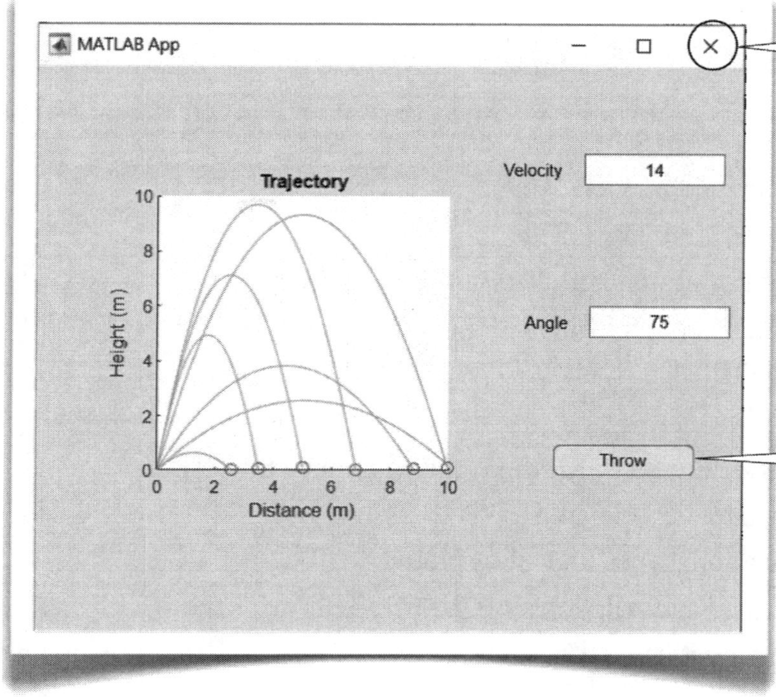

[32] Click to quit the **app**. ↓

[31] Click **Throw** and try different initial velocities and elevation angles (e.g., use the data in 1.18[4], page 56). ↑

[33] Click to quit **App Designer**. ↙

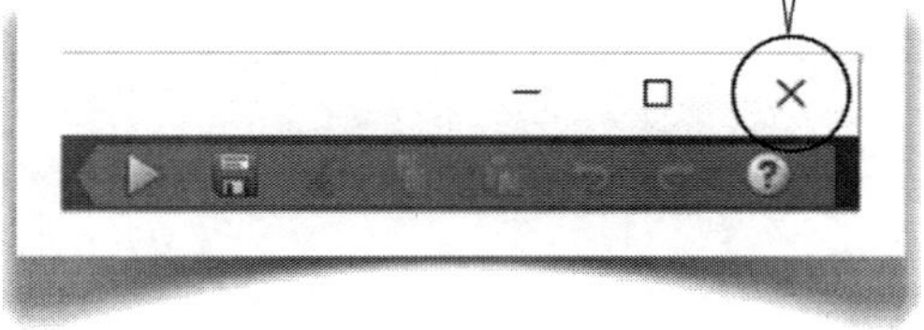

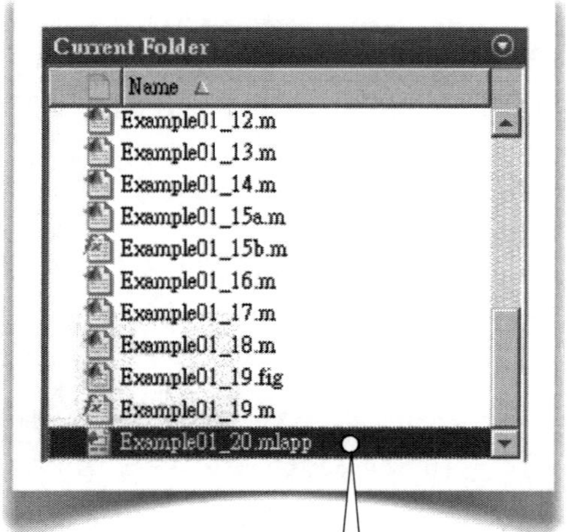

[34] To run the **app** again, right-click-select **Run** (or double-click it). To modify the **app**, right-click-select **Open**. →

Three Ways to Build a GUI

[35] We've introduced three ways (Sections 1.18, 1.19, and 1.20) to build a GUI. For a small program, I personally prefer the programmatic approach (Section 1.18); for a medium to large-scaled program, the newest introduced **App Designer** is usually recommended (Section 1.20). In Chapter 8, we'll discuss GUI design in more detail. #

Chapter 2

Data Types, Operators, and Expressions

An expression is a syntactic combination of **numbers**, **variables**, **operators**, and **functions**. An expression always results in a **value**. The right-hand side of an assignment statement is always an expression. You may notice that most of the statements we demonstrated in Chapter 1 are assignment statements. It is fair to say that expressions are the most important building block of a program.

2.1 Unsigned Integers

[1] The figure below shows the classification of the 12 **basic data types** (highlighted with shaded boxes) in MATLAB. We called them "basic" since they are implemented in a computer's hardware level; all other data types (e.g., **array**, **cell array**, **structure**, etc.) in MATLAB are implemented in some software levels on the top of these basic data types. By default, MATLAB assumes `double` for all numbers. For example,

```
a = 75
```

where the number 75 is treated as a `double`; therefore a variable `a` of the type `double` is created to store the number. To create a number of a type other than `double`, you must explicitly use a data type conversion function; e.g.,

```
b = int8(75)
```

where the right-hand-side is an `int8`; therefore, a variable `b` of the type `int8` is created to store the number. You may verify the types (or called **classes**) of the variables `a` and `b` by typing the command `whos`,

```
>> whos
  Name      Size      Bytes     Class
  a         1x1           8     double
  b         1x1           1     int8
```

This information can be displayed in the **Workspace Window** (see [2-3], next page). Note that 8 bytes of the memory are needed to store a `double`, while only 1 byte (8 bits) is needed to store an `int8`. But how? Starting from this section, we'll provide some exercises through which you will not only learn how these basic data are stored in the memory (i.e., how they are represented with 0s and 1s) but also learn some useful programming techniques. ↵

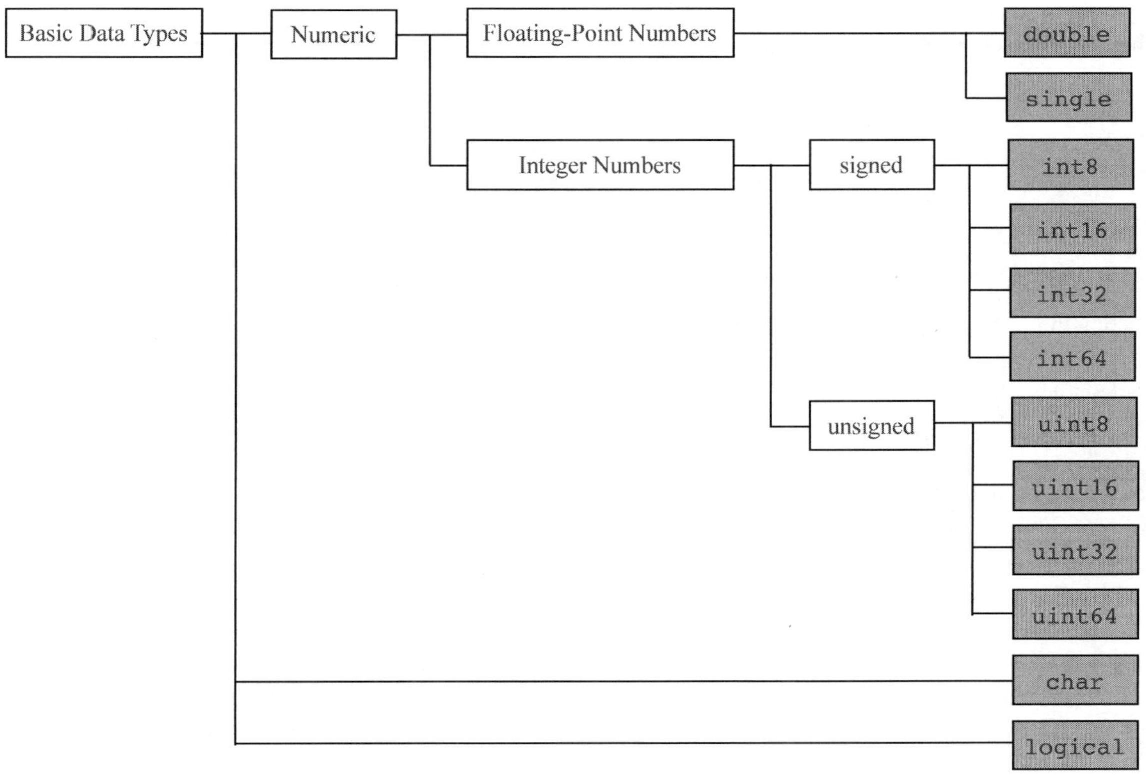

[2] Additional information of the variables in the **Workspace** can be displayed by pulling down this button and selecting **Choose Columns**. For the rest of the book, we set up the **Workspace Window** like this. ←

[3] This symbol indicates a numeric type, either a scalar or an array. ↓

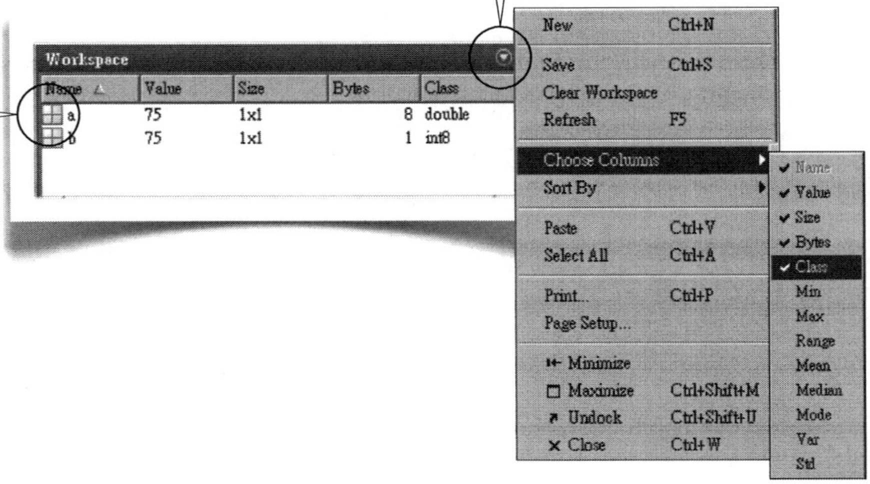

Unsigned Integers

[4] Computer representation of unsigned integers is straightforward. For example, the decimal number 75 is represented by a binary number 01001011. A binary number can be converted to a decimal number by treating 1 at the nth digit as 2^{n-1}. Thus, the binary number 01001011 is converted to a decimal number 75 as following:

$$(0\times 2^7+1\times 2^6+0\times 2^5+0\times 2^4+1\times 2^3+0\times 2^2+1\times 2^1+1\times 2^0)_{10}=75_{10}$$

On the other hand, the decimal number 75 can be converted into the binary number by successive divisions of 2:

75	divided by 2 is	37,	remainder 1
37	divided by 2 is	18,	remainder 1
18	divided by 2 is	9,	remainder 0
9	divided by 2 is	4,	remainder 1
4	divided by 2 is	2,	remainder 0
2	divided by 2 is	1,	remainder 0
1	divided by 2 is	0,	remainder 1

After collecting the remainders bottom-up, you have the binary number 1001011 (which is equal to 01001011).

In general, a binary number $b_{n-1}b_{n-2}\ldots b_1b_0$ (where each of b_{n-1}, b_{n-2}, ... , b_1, and b_0 is a binary digit (bit), either 0 or 1) is converted into a decimal number by

$$(b_{n-1}\times 2^{n-1}+b_{n-2}\times 2^{n-2}+\ldots+b_1\times 2^1+b_0\times 2^0)_{10}\equiv\left(\sum_{k=0}^{n-1}b_k\times 2^k\right)_{10}$$

Obviously, the minimum value an unsigned integer can represent is zero; i.e., *an unsigned integer cannot represent a negative number*. The maximum value an unsigned integer can represent depends on how many binary digits (bits) it uses. For example, the maximum value for an 8-bit unsigned integer (`uint8`) is

$$(11111111)_2=(2^8-1)_{10}=255_{10}$$

In general, when n bits are used, the maximum value an unsigned integer can represent is $(2^n-1)_{10}$.

Table 2.1 (next page) lists information about the four unsigned integer types in MATLAB, including their conversion functions, their minimum/maximum values, and the functions to find these minimum/maximum values. ↵

Example02_01.m: Unsigned Integers

[5] These statements demonstrate the concepts given in the last page. A **Command Window** session is shown in [6]. ↓

```
1  clear
2  d = 75
3  u = uint8(d)
4  bits = dec2bin(u)
5  number = bin2dec(bits)
```

[6] This is a **Command Window** session of Example02_01.m. ↓

```
6   >> clear
7   >> d = 75
8   d =
9        75
10  >> u = uint8(d)
11  u =
12    uint8
13     75
14  >> bits = dec2bin(u)
15  bits =
16      '1001011'
17  >> number = bin2dec(bits)
18  number =
19       75
```

About Example02_01.m

[7] In line 2, the number 75 is treated as a `double` by default; therefore, a variable `d` of the type `double` is created to store the number. A 64-bit **floating-point** representation, to be discussed in Section 2.3, is used for `double` data.

In line 3, the function `uint8` converts the number `d` to an 8-bit unsigned integer format (without altering the value 75), and a variable `u` of the type `uint8` is created to store the number.

In line 4, the function `dec2bin` converts the decimal number `u` to a character string `bits` representing binary number. The bit pattern in lines 15-16 is consistent with that in [4], last page. Note that, in line 16, leading zeros are not present. In line 5, the function `bin2dec` converts the character string `bits` back to the decimal number 75 (see lines 18-19). Both the functions `dec2bin` and `bin2dec` convert numbers using the procedure described in [4], last page. #

Table 2.1 Unsigned Integer Numbers

Conversion Function	Function to find the minimum value	Minimum value	Function to find the maximum value	Maximum value
`uint8`	`intmin('uint8')`	0	`intmax('uint8')`	255
`uint16`	`intmin('uint16')`	0	`intmax('uint16')`	65535
`uint32`	`intmin('uint32')`	0	`intmax('uint32')`	4294967295
`uint64`	`intmin('uint64')`	0	`intmax('uint64')`	18446744073709551615

Details and More: Help>MATLAB>Language Fundamentals>Data Types>Numeric Types

2.2 Signed Integers

[1] With 8 bits, the positive integer 75 is represented by 01001011. How to represent the negative integer -75? A simple idea is to use a bit as the "sign bit." For example, we might use the leftmost bit as the sign bit: 0 for positive and 1 for negative. Thus, if 01001011 represents +75, then 11001011 represents -75. A problem of this representation is that both 00000000 and 10000000 represent the same number, zero. Another problem is that two numbers with the opposite signs can not be added in a simple way; e.g., 01001011 + 11001011 = 00010100, which is not correct; adding -75 to 75 should result in zero.

One's Complement Representation

Another idea is to use one's complement representation. It also uses a sign bit as before: 0 for positive and 1 for negative. If the sign bit indicates that it is a negative number, then its complement pattern (i.e., converting 0s to 1s and 1s to 0s) is interpreted as its absolute value. For example, since the leftmost bit of 10110100 indicates that it is a negative number, its complement pattern 01001011 (75_{10}) is interpreted as its absolute value. Thus, the bit pattern 10110100 is interpreted as -75. Many early computers used this method (*Wikipedia> One's Complement*). One of the previous problems still exists with this approach: both 00000000 and 11111111 represent the same number, zero.

Two's Complement Representation

Modern computers use **two's complement representation**. It also uses a sign bit as before. If the sign bit indicates that it is a negative number, then its two's complement pattern (i.e., adding one to its complement pattern) is used to represent its absolute value. For example, since the leftmost bit of 10110101 indicates that it is a negative number, we take its complement (01001010), add one (01001011, which has a decimal value of 75), and interpret the bit pattern 10110101 as -75. Thus, 00000000 represents zero, and 11111111 represents -1. Table 2.2a gives some examples of unsigned/signed representation. ↵

Table 2.2a Unsigned/Signed Representation

Bit pattern	Unsigned value	Signed value
`000`	0	0
`001`	1	1
`010`	2	2
`011`	3	3
`100`	4	-4
`101`	5	-3
`110`	6	-2
`111`	7	-1
`00000000`	0	0
`11111111`	255	-1
`01111111`	127	127
`10000000`	128	-128

Details and More: Wikipedia>Two's complement

Table 2.2b Signed Integer Numbers

Conversion Function	Function to find the minimum value	Minimum value	Function to find the maximum value	Maximum value
`int8`	`intmin('int8')`	-128	`intmax('int8')`	127
`int16`	`intmin('int16')`	-32768	`intmax('int16')`	32767
`int32`	`intmin('int32')`	-2147483648	`intmax('int32')`	2147483647
`int64`	`intmin('int64')`	-9223372036854775808	`intmax('int64')`	9223372036854775807

Details and More: Help>MATLAB>Language Fundamentals>Data Types>Numeric Types

Minimum/Maximum Values

[2] From Table 2.2a (last page), with 8 bits, the minimum signed value is 10000000 (-128_{10}) and the maximum value is 01111111 (127_{10}). In general, when n-bits are used, the minimum value is -2^{n-1} and the maximum value is $2^{n-1}-1$. Table 2.2b (last page) lists information about the four signed integer types in MATLAB, including their conversion functions, their minimum/maximum values, and the functions to find these minimum/maximum values. ↓

Example02_02.m: Signed Integers

[3] These statements demonstrate some concepts about signed integers. A **Command Window** session is shown in [4]. →

```
1   clear
2   d = 200
3   u = uint8(d)
4   bits = dec2bin(u)
5   t = int8(u)
6   s = typecast(u, 'int8')
7   a = int16(u)
8   bits = dec2bin(a)
```

```
9   >> clear
10  >> d = 200
11  d =
12     200
13  >> u = uint8(d)
14  u =
15    uint8
16     200
17  >> bits = dec2bin(u)
18  bits =
19      '11001000'
20  >> t = int8(u)
21  t =
22    int8
23     127
24  >> s = typecast(u, 'int8')
25  s =
26    int8
27     -56
28  >> a = int16(u)
29  a =
30    int16
31     200
32  >> bits = dec2bin(a)
33  bits =
34      '11001000'
```

[4] This is a **Command Window** session of Example02_02.m. ↓

About Example02_02.m

[5] Lines 1-3 are similar to those in Example02_01.m, page 71. Now, the variable u, an 8-bit unsigned integer, has a value of 200, which has a bit pattern 11001000, confirmed in line 4 (also see line 19).

In line 5, the value 200 is converted to an `int8`; however, since the maximum value of an `int8` is 127 (see Table 2.2b, last page), the value is "overflown" and only the maximum value (127) is stored in an `int8`. Therefore, the variable `t` has a value of 127 (see lines 21-23).

In line 6, the function `typecast` preserves the bit pattern of the unsigned value 200 (11001000) while changing its type to `int8`. Now, the bit pattern is interpreted as a value of -56 (see lines 25-27), using two's complement representation: Since the leftmost bit of 11001000 indicates that it is a negative number, we take its complement (00110111), add one (00111000, which has a decimal value of 56), and interpret the bit pattern 10110101 as -56.

To store the value 200 in a signed integer, we need at least an `int16`. Line 7 successfully converts the value 200 to an `int16` and stores it in the variable `a` (also see lines 29-31); line 8 confirms that the bit pattern of `u` is preserved in `a` (also see lines 33-34). #

2.3 Floating-Point Numbers

2.3a Floating-Point Numbers

[1] Your computer uses floating-point representation to store real numbers. MATLAB has two types of floating-point numbers: double precision (`double`) and single precision (`single`); a `double` uses 8 bytes (64 bits) of memory while a `single` uses 4 bytes (32 bits). As mentioned, `double` is the default data type and, therefore, is the most extensively used data type. Table 2.3a (next page) lists information about the two floating-point types, including their conversion functions, their minimum/maximum values, and the functions to find these minimum/maximum values.

Floating-Point Representation

The figure below (*source: https://en.wikipedia.org/wiki/File:IEEE_754_Double_Floating_Point_Format.svg, by Codekaizen*) shows an example bit pattern of a double-precision floating-point number. It uses 64 bits in computer memory: 1 bit (the 63rd bit) for the sign, 11 bits (the 52nd-62nd bits) for the exponent, and 52 bits (the 0th-51st bits) for the fraction. The 64-bit pattern is interpreted as a value of

$$(-1)^{sign}(1.b_{51}b_{50}\cdots b_0)_2\times 2^{exponent-1023}$$

Thus, the bit pattern below is interpreted as

$$+(1.11)_2\times 2^{1027-1023}=(2^0+2^{-1}+2^{-2})\times 2^4=1.75\times 16=(28)_{10}$$

↓

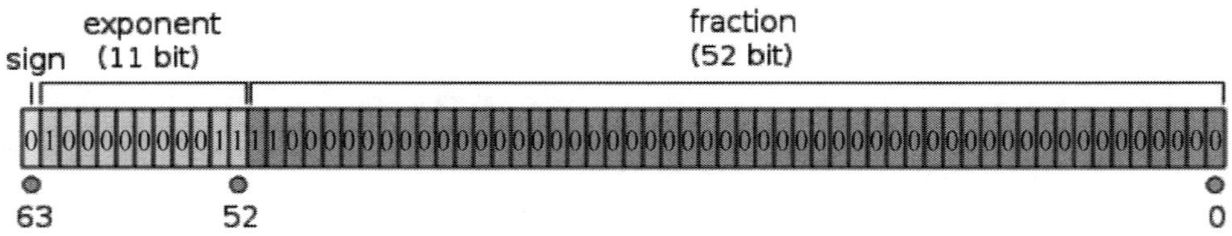

Fractional Binary Numbers

[2] For those who are not familiar with the binary numbers, here is another example. A decimal number 258.369 is interpreted as

$$(258.369)_{10}=2\times 10^2+5\times 10^1+8\times 10^0+3\times 10^{-1}+6\times 10^{-2}+9\times 10^{-3}$$

Similarly, a binary number 1101.01101 can be interpreted as

$$\begin{aligned}(1101.01101)_2&=1\times 2^3+1\times 2^2+0\times 2^1+1\times 2^0+0\times 2^{-1}+1\times 2^{-2}+1\times 2^{-3}+0\times 2^{-4}+1\times 2^{-5}\\&=8+4+0+1+0+0.25+0.125+0+0.03125\\&=(13.40625)_{10}\end{aligned}$$

↲

Example02_03a.m: Floating-Point Numbers

[3] These statements confirm that the decimal number 28 is indeed represented by the bit pattern in [1], last page. A **Command Window** session is shown in [4].

```
1   clear
2   d = 28
3   a = typecast(d, 'uint64')
4   b = dec2bin(a, 64)
```

Line 2 creates a double-precision floating-point number 28 and stores it in the variable `d`. The bit pattern should be like the one in [1], last page.

In line 3, the function `typecast` preserves the 64-bit pattern while changing its type to `uint64`. Now, the bit pattern is interpreted as a value of 4628574517030027264 (see line 12), which can be calculated by

$$2^{62} + 2^{53} + 2^{52} + 2^{51} + 2^{50} = 4628574517030027264$$

Line 4 demonstrates another way (than using `bitget` and `fliplr`) to display the bit pattern. The function `dec2bin(a,64)` retrieves the bit pattern from an integer number `a` and outputs the bit pattern in a text form (i.e., a string, to be introduced in the next section). The result is shown in line 15, the same as the one in [1], last page. ↓

```
5   >> clear
6   >> d = 28
7   d =
8       28
9   >> a = typecast(d, 'uint64')
10  a =
11    uint64
12     4628574517030027264
13  >> b = dec2bin(a, 64)
14  b =
15      '0100000000111100000000000000000000000000000000000000000000000000'
16  >>
```

[4] This is a **Command Window** session of Example02_03a.m. #

Table 2.3a Floating-Point Numbers

Conversion Function	Function to find the minimum value	Minimum value	Function to find the maximum value	Maximum value
`double`	`realmin('double')`	2.2251e-308	`realmax('double')`	1.7977e+308
`single`	`realmin('single')`	1.1755e-38	`realmax('single')`	3.4028e+38

Details and More: Help>MATLAB>Language Fundamentals>Data Types>Numeric Types

2.3b Significant Digits of Floating-Point Numbers

Example02_03b.m: Significant Digits of Floating-Point Numbers

[1] These statements explore the number of significant digits of floating-point numbers. A **Command Window** session is shown in [2], next page. →

```
1  clear
2  format short
3  format compact
4  a = 1234.5678901234567890 1234
5  fprintf('%.20f\n', a)
6  format long
7  a
8  b = single(a)
9  fprintf('%.20f\n', b)
```

```
10  >> clear
11  >> format short
12  >> format compact
13  >> a = 1234.56789012345678901234
14  a =
15     1.2346e+03
16  >> fprintf('%.20f\n', a)
17  1234.56789012345689116046
18  >> format long
19  >> a
20  a =
21       1.234567890123457e+03
22  >> b = single(a)
23  b =
24    single
25     1.2345679e+03
26  >> fprintf('%.20f\n', b)
27  1234.56787109375000000000
```

[2] This is a **Command Window** session of Example02_03b.m. ↓

Screen Output Format

[3] Lines 2, 3, and 6 set **Command Window** output display format. The syntax is

`format` *`style`*

The `short` (line 2) sets the display of fixed-decimal format 4 digits after the decimal point, the `long` (line 6) 15 digits after the decimal point. The `compact` (line 3) suppresses blank lines to make the output lines compact (also see 1.2[9-10], page 14). The opposite of `compact` is `loose` (default), which adds blank lines to make the output lines more readable. In this book, we always use `compact` style to save space.

Table 2.3b (next page) lists available format styles. Remember, you may always consult the on-line documentation whenever a new command is encountered. For example:

```
>> doc format
```

Double Precision Floating-Point Numbers

In line 4, we assign a number of 24 significant figures to the variable `a` of `double`. We will see that, due to the limited storage space (64 bits), not all the figures can be stored in the variable `a`. The number is displayed (line 15) in short format, i.e., 4 digits after the decimal point. Note that, in displaying the number, it is rounded to the last digit.

In line 5, we attempt to print the number with 20 digits after the decimal point. The result (line 17) shows that only the first 16 digits are the same as what was assigned to the variable `a`. The extra digits are lost due to the limited storage space. We conclude that *a double-precision floating point number has 16 significant digits*.

With long format (line 6), the number is displayed with 15 digits after the decimal point (lines 7, 21). Note that, again, in displaying the number, it has been rounded to the last digit. ↵

Single-Precision Floating-Point Numbers

[4] Line 8 converts the value stored in the variable `a` (which is of type `double`, 64-bit long) to a single-precision floating-point number (32-bit long). The output (line 25) shows that it reduces to 8 significant digits, due to the shorter storage space. The extra digits are discarded during the conversion. This is also confirmed with line 9; its output in line 27 is accurate up to the 8th digits. We conclude that *a single-precision floating point number has 8 significant digits*. #

Table 2.3b Numeric Output Format

Function	Description or Example
`format compact`	Suppress blank lines
`format loose`	Add blank lines
`format short`	3.1416
`format long`	3.141592653589793
`format shortE`	3.1416e+00
`format longE`	3.141592653589793e+00
`format shortG`	`short` or `shortE`
`format longG`	`long` or `longE`
`format shortEng`	Exponent is a multiple of 3
`format longEng`	Exponent is a multiple of 3
`format +`	Display the sign (+/-)
`format bank`	Currency format; 3.14
`format hex`	400921fb54442d18
`format rat`	Rational; 355/133

Details and More: >> doc format

2.4 Characters and Strings

2.4a Characters and Strings

ASCII Codes

[1] In MATLAB, a **character** is represented using single quotes; e.g., `'A'`, `'b'`, etc. Internally, MATLAB uses 2 bytes (16 bits) to store a character according to **ASCII Code** (see *Wikipedia>ASCII*, also see 2.4b, page 80). An ASCII code is a number representing a character, either printable or non-printable. The ASCII codes of the characters `'A'`, `'B'`, and `'C'` are 65, 66, and 67, respectively. A character can be converted to a numeric value according to **ASCII Codes**. For example, since `'A'` is internally represented by an ASCII code 65, `double('A')` results in a number 65.

The most frequently used non-printable character is the **newline** character (1.9[9], page 35). MATLAB uses `'\n'` to represent the newline character.

The notation such as `'ABC'` is used to represent a row vector of characters; i.e., it is equivalent to `['A', 'B', 'C']`. A row vector of characters is also called a **string**. ↓

Example02_04a.m: Characters

[2] These statements demonstrate some concepts about **characters** and **strings**. A **Command Window** session is shown in [3] and the **Workspace** is shown in [4-5], next page. →

```
clear
a = 'A'
b = a + 1
char(65)
char('A' + 2)
c = ['A', 'B', 'C']
d = ['AB', 'C']
e = ['A', 66, 67]
f = 'ABC'
f(1)
f(2)
f(3)
```

```
>> clear
>> a = 'A'
a =
    'A'
>> b = a + 1
b =
    66
>> char(65)
ans =
    'A'
>> char('A' + 2)
ans =
    'C'
>> c = ['A', 'B', 'C']
c =
    'ABC'
>> d = ['AB', 'C']
d =
    'ABC'
>> e = ['A', 66, 67]
e =
    'ABC'
>> f = 'ABC'
f =
    'ABC'
>> f(1)
ans =
    'A'
>> f(2)
ans =
    'B'
>> f(3)
ans =
    'C'
```

[3] This is a **Command Window** session of Example02_04a.m. ↵

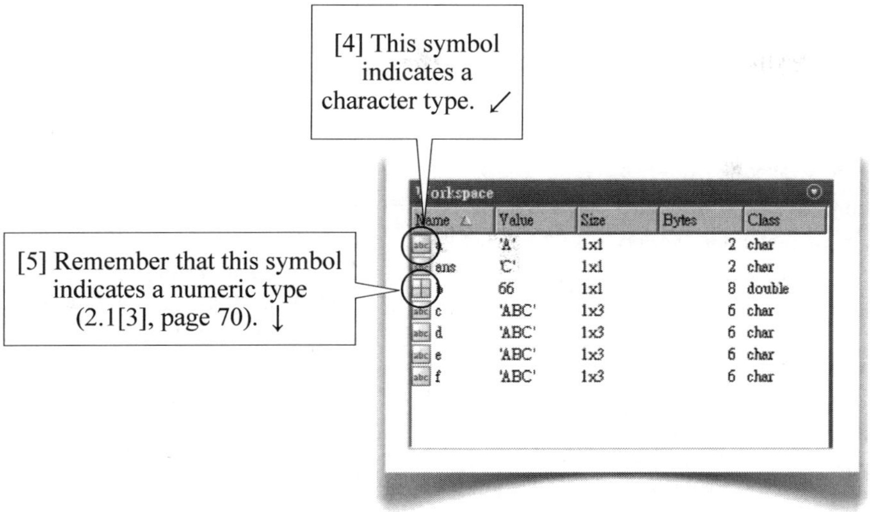

About Example02_4a.m

[6] In line 2, a character `A` is assigned to a variable `a`, which is of type `char` (line 16).

In line 3, since + (plus) is a numeric operator, MATLAB converts the variable `a` to a numeric value, 65, and then adds 1. The result is 66 and the variable `b` is of numeric type, a `double` (line 19).

In line 4, the numeric value 65 is converted to a `char`, using the function `char`. The result is the character `'A'` (line 22).

In line 5, again, since + (plus) is a numeric operator, MATLAB converts the character `'A'` to a numeric value, 65, and then adds 2. The result is 67, which, after converting to `char` type, is the character `'C'` (line 25).

Numeric Operations Involving Characters

A numeric operator (+, -, etc.) always operates on numeric values, and the result is a numeric value. If a numeric operation involves characters, the characters are converted to numeric values according to ASCII codes.

We'll introduce numerical operations in Section 2.7 and Section 2.8 and string manipulations in Section 2.10.

String: Row Vector of Characters

Line 6 creates a row vector of three characters `'A'`, `'B'`, and `'C'`. It is displayed as `'ABC'` (line 28). A row vector of character is also called a **string**. The variable `c` is a **string**.

Line 7 seemingly creates a row vector of two elements. However, since `'AB'` itself is a row vector of two characters, the result is a row vector of three characters `'ABC'` (line 31). There is no difference between variables `c` and `d`; both are strings of three characters `'ABC'`.

In line 8, since an array must have elements of the same data type and since there is a character in the array, MATLAB converts the number 66 and 67 to characters according to ASCII Codes. The result is a row vector of three characters `'ABC'`. There is no difference between variables `c`, `d`, and `e`.

Line 9 demonstrates an easy way to create a vector of characters, a string. There is no difference between the variables `c`, `d`, `e`, and `f`. They are all vectors of three characters `ABC`, confirmed in lines 10-12.

The Variable `ans`

In lines 4-5 and 10-12, there are no variables to store the result of the expressions. Whenever there is no variable to store the resulting value of an expression, MATLAB always uses the variable `ans` (short for **answer**) to store that value (also see lines 21, 24, 39, 42, 45). #

2.4b ASCII Codes

Example02_04b.m: ASCII Codes

[1] MATLAB stores characters according to ASCII Code. ASCII codes 32-126 represent printable characters on a standard keyboard. This example prints a table of characters corresponding to the ASCII Codes 32-126 (see the output in [2]). →

```
 1  clear
 2  fprintf('     0 1 2 3 4 5 6 7 8 9\n')
 3  for row = 3:12
 4      fprintf('%2d   ', row)
 5      for column = 0:9
 6          code = row*10+column;
 7          if (code < 32) || (code > 126)
 8             fprintf('  ')
 9          else
10             fprintf('%c ', code)
11          end
12      end
13      fprintf('\n')
14  end
```

```
     0 1 2 3 4 5 6 7 8 9
 3           ! " # $ % & '
 4   ( ) * + , - . / 0 1
 5   2 3 4 5 6 7 8 9 : ;
 6   < = > ? @ A B C D E
 7   F G H I J K L M N O
 8   P Q R S T U V W X Y
 9   Z [ \ ] ^ _ ` a b c
10   d e f g h i j k l m
11   n o p q r s t u v w
12   x y z { | } ~
```

[2] This is the output of Example02_04b.m. Note that ASCII Code 32 corresponds to the space character. ↓

About Example02_4b.m

[3] Line 2 prints a heading of column numbers and a newline character, moving the cursor to the next line.

Each pass of the outer `for`-loop (lines 3-14) prints a row on the screen; the row numbers are designated as 3, 4, ... 12 for each pass. In the beginning of the loop (line 4), the row number is printed. Then 10 characters are printed using an inner `for`-loop (lines 5-12). At the end of the outer for-loop, a newline character is printed (line 13), moving the cursor to the next line.

Each pass of the inner `for`-loop (lines 5-12) prints a character aligning with the column number. Line 6 generates an ASCII code using the row-number and column-number; for example, the ASCII code corresponds to row-number 4 and column-number 5 is 45. If an ASCII code is less than 32 or larger than 126 (line 7) then two spaces are printed (line 8), otherwise the ASCII code is printed as a character followed by a space (line 10).

The expression `(code < 32) || (code > 126)` in the `if`-statement (line 7) is a logical expression. We'll introduce logical data in Section 2.5 and logical expressions in Section 2.9.

In line 10, the format specifier `%c` requires a character data, therefore `code` (a `double`) is converted to a character according to the ASCII Code. #

2.5 Logical Data

Logical Values: `true` and `false`

[1] The only logical values are `true` and `false`. MATLAB uses one byte (8 bits) to store a logical value. When a logical value is converted to a number, `true` becomes 1 and `false` becomes 0. When a numeric value is converted to a logical value, any non-zero number becomes `true` and zero becomes `false`. ↓

Example02_05.m: Logical Data Type

[2] These statements demonstrate some concepts about **logical** data. A **Command Window** session and the **Workspace** is shown in [3-4], respectively. ↘

```
clear
a = true
b = false
c = 6 > 5
d = 6 < 5
e = (6 > 5)*10
f = false*10+true*2
g = (6 > 5) & (6 < 5)
h = (6 > 5) | (6 < 5)
k = logical(5)
m = 5 | 0
n = (-2) & 'A'
```

[4] This symbol indicates a logical type. ↵

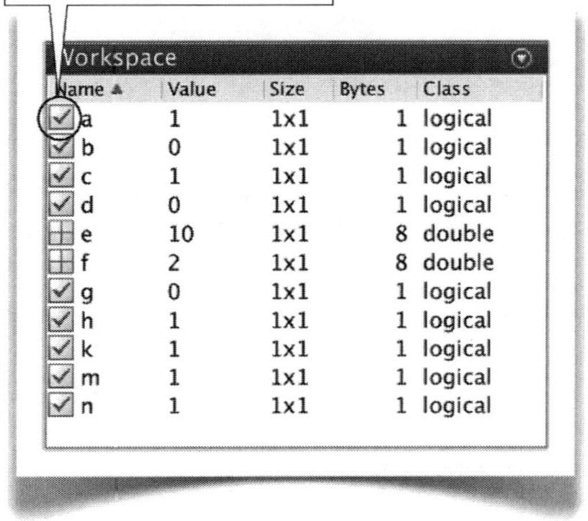

Name ▲	Value	Size	Bytes	Class
a	1	1x1	1	logical
b	0	1x1	1	logical
c	1	1x1	1	logical
d	0	1x1	1	logical
e	10	1x1	8	double
f	2	1x1	8	double
g	0	1x1	1	logical
h	1	1x1	1	logical
k	1	1x1	1	logical
m	1	1x1	1	logical
n	1	1x1	1	logical

```
>> clear
>> a = true
a =
  logical
   1
>> b = false
b =
  logical
   0
>> c = 6 > 5
c =
  logical
   1
>> d = 6 < 5
d =
  logical
   0
>> e = (6 > 5)*10
e =
    10
>> f = false*10+true*2
f =
     2
>> g = (6 > 5) & (6 < 5)
g =
  logical
   0
>> h = (6 > 5) | (6 < 5)
h =
  logical
   1
>> k = logical(5)
k =
  logical
   1
>> m = 5 | 0
m =
  logical
   1
>> n = (-2) & 'A'
n =
  logical
   1
```

[3] This is a **Command Window** session of Example02_05.m. ←

About Example02_05.m

[5] Line 2 assigns `true` to a variable `a`, which is then of type `logical` (line 16). When displayed on the **Command Window**, `true` is always displayed as 1 (line 17).

Line 3 assigns `false` to a variable `b`. When displayed on the **Command Window**, `false` is always displayed as 0 (line 21).

Relational Operators

A relational operator (>, <, etc., to be introduced in Section 2.9) always operates on two numeric values, and the result is a logical value.

In line 4, the number 6 and the number 5 are operated using the logical operator >. The result of `6 > 5` is `true` and is assigned to `c`, which is of type `logical` and displayed as 1 (lines 24-25).

In line 5, the number 6 and the number 5 are operated using the logical operator <. The result of `6 < 5` is `false` and is assigned to `d`, which is of type `logical` and displayed as 0 (lines 28-29).

Numeric Operations Involving Logical Values

A numeric operator (+, –, etc., to be introduced in Section 2.8) always operates on numeric values, and the result is a numeric value. If a numeric operator involves logical values, the logical values are converted to numeric values: `true` becomes 1 and `false` becomes 0.

In line 6, the result of `6 > 5` is a logical value `true`, which is to be multiplied by the number 10. Since the multiplication (`*`) is a numeric operator, MATLAB converts `true` to the number 1, and the result is 10 (line 32), which is a `double` number. When a `double` number is output to the **Command Window**, its type is not shown; remember that `double` is the default data type.

In line 7, again, since the multiplication (`*`) and the addition (`+`) are numeric operators, MATLAB converts `false` to 0 and `true` to 1, and the result is 2 (line 35), which is a `double` number.

Logical Operators

A logical operator (AND, OR, etc.) always operates on logical values, and the result is a logical value. If a logical operation involves numeric values, the numeric values are converted to logical values (non-zero values become `true` and zero becomes `false`).

MATLAB uses the symbol `&` for logical AND and the symbol `|` for logical OR. Table 2.5a (next page) lists the rules for logical `AND` (`&`). Table 2.5b (next page) lists the rules for logical `OR` (`|`).

In line 8, the result of `6 > 5` is `true` and the result of `6 < 5` is `false`. The result of logical AND (`&`) operation for a `true` and a `false` is `false` (lines 38-39).

In line 9, the result of local OR (`|`) operation for a `true` and a `false` is `true` (lines 42-43).

We'll introduce relational and logical operators in Section 2.9.

Conversion to Logical Data Type

Line 10 converts a numeric value 5 to logical data type. The result is `true` (lines 46-47). When converted to a logical value, any non-zero number becomes `true` and the zero becomes `false`. A `true` is displayed as 1 and a `false` is displayed as zero.

In line 11, since `|` (OR) is a logical operator, MATLAB converts the numbers 5 and 0 to logical values `true` and `false`, respectively. The result is `true` (lines 50-51).

In line 12, again, since `&` (AND) is a logical operator, MATLAB converts both the number `-2` and the character `'A'` to logical values `true`. The result is `true` (lines 54-55). ↵

Avoid Using `i`, `j`, and the letter `l` as Variable Names

[6] In MATLAB, both letters `i` and `j` are used to represent the constant $\sqrt{-1}$. If you use them as variable names, they are overridden by the values assigned to them and no longer represent $\sqrt{-1}$. In this book, we'll avoid using them as variable names.

The letter `l` is often confused with the number `1`. In this book, we'll also avoid using it as a variable name. #

Table 2.5a Rules of Logical `and` (`&`)

AND (&)	true	false
true	true	false
false	false	false

Table 2.5b Rules of Logical `or` (`|`)

OR (|)	true	false
true	true	true
false	true	false

2.6 Arrays

2.6a Arrays Creations

All Data Are Treated as Arrays

[1] MATLAB treats all data as arrays. A zero-dimensional array (1×1) is called a scalar. A one-dimensional array is called a **vector**, either a row vector ($1 \times c$) or a column vector ($r \times 1$). A two-dimensional array ($r \times c$) is called a **matrix**. A three-dimensional array ($r \times c \times p$) may be called a **three-dimensional array** or **three-dimensional matrix**. It is possible to create four or more dimensional arrays; in practice, however, they are seldom used. The first dimension is called the **row dimension**, the second dimension is called the **column dimension**, and the third dimension is called the **page dimension**. ↓

Example02_06a.m

[2] Type the following commands (also see [3]). ↘

```
 1  clear
 2  a = 5
 3  b = [5]
 4  c = 5*ones(1,1)
 5  D = ones(2, 3)
 6  e = [1, 2, 3, 4, 5]
 7  f = [1 2 3 4 5]
 8  g = [1:5]
 9  h = 1:5
10  k = 1:1:5
11  m = linspace(1, 5, 5)
```

```
12  >> clear
13  >> a = 5
14  a =
15       5
16  >> b = [5]
17  b =
18       5
19  >> c = 5*ones(1,1)
20  c =
21       5
22  >> D = ones(2, 3)
23  D =
24       1     1     1
25       1     1     1
26  >> e = [1, 2, 3, 4, 5]
27  e =
28       1     2     3     4     5
29  >> f = [1 2 3 4 5]
30  f =
31       1     2     3     4     5
32  >> g = [1:5]
33  g =
34       1     2     3     4     5
35  >> h = 1:5
36  h =
37       1     2     3     4     5
38  >> k = 1:1:5
39  k =
40       1     2     3     4     5
41  >> m = linspace(1, 5, 5)
42  m =
43       1     2     3     4     5
```

[3] This is a **Command Window** session of Example02_06a.m. ←

Scalar

[4] Lines 2-4 show three ways to create the same scalar. Line 2 creates a single value 5. Line 3 creates a vector of one element, i.e., a scalar. Line 4 creates a 1x1 matrix (see an explanation below for the function `ones`). The variables `a`, `b`, and `c` are all **scalars**; they are all equal; there is no difference among these three variables.

Function `ones`

The function `ones` (lines 4-5) creates an array of all ones with specified dimension sizes. The syntax is

```
ones(sz1, sz2, ..., szN)
```

where `sz1` is the size of the first dimension (row dimension), `sz2` is the size of the second dimension (column dimension), and so forth. The function `ones` is one of the array creation functions. Table 2.6a (page 88) lists some array creation functions. ↵

Row Vectors

[5] Lines 6-11 show many ways to create the same row vector. Line 6 creates a row vector using the square brackets ([ ]). Commas are used to separate elements in a row. The commas can be omitted (line 7).

Line 8 creates a row vector using the colon notation (`:`). The square brackets can be omitted (line 9). In a more general form, an increment number can be inserted between the starting number and the ending number (line 10; also see 1.3[6], page 18). The function `linspace` (line 11) creates a row vector of linearly spaced numbers. The syntax is

```
linspace(start, end, n)
```

where *n* is the total number of elements. If *n* is omitted, its default is 100.

There is no difference among the variables `e`, `f`, `g`, `h`, `k`, and `m`. #

2.6b Arrays Indexing

Example02_06b.m

[1] Type the following commands (also see [2]). ↘

```
1   clear
2   a = zeros(1,5)
3   a(1,5) = 8
4   a(5) = 9
5   a([1, 2, 4]) = [8, 7, 6]
6   a(1:4) = [2, 3, 4, 5]
7   [rows, cols] = size(a)
8   len = length(a)
9   b = a
10  c = a(1:5)
11  d = a(3:5)
12  e = a(3:length(a))
13  f = a(3:end)
14  f(5) = 10
```

[3] Line 2 creates a 1-by-5 array (i.e., a row vector) of all zeros. Remember that there are two ways to access an element of an array: **subscript indexing** and **linear indexing** (1.9[23], page 37). Line 3 uses subscript indexing, while line 4 uses linear indexing. For a vector (row vector or column vector), we usually use linear indexing.

Line 5 assigns three values to the 1st, 2nd, and 4th elements of the array `a`; i.e., line 5 is equivalent to

```
a(1) = 8, a(2) = 7, a(4) = 6
```

Line 6, since `1:4` means `[1,2,3,4]`, assigns four values to the 1st-4th elements of the array `a`. ↵

```
15  >> clear
16  >> a = zeros(1,5)
17  a =
18       0     0     0     0     0
19  >> a(1,5) = 8
20  a =
21       0     0     0     0     8
22  >> a(5) = 9
23  a =
14       0     0     0     0     9
25  >> a([1, 2, 4]) = [8, 7, 6]
26  a =
27       8     7     0     6     9
28  >> a(1:4) = [2, 3, 4, 5]
29  a =
30       2     3     4     5     9
31  >> [rows, cols] = size(a)
32  rows =
33       1
34  cols =
35       5
36  >> len = length(a)
37  len =
38       5
39  >> b = a
40  b =
41       2     3     4     5     9
42  >> c = a(1:5)
43  c =
44       2     3     4     5     9
45  >> d = a(3:5)
46  d =
47       4     5     9
48  >> e = a(3:length(a))
49  e =
50       4     5     9
51  >> f = a(3:end)
52  f =
53       4     5     9
54  >> f(5) = 10
55  f =
56      4     5     9     0    10
```

[2] This is a **Command Window** session of Example02_06b.m. ←

Size and Length of an Array

[4] The function `size` (line 7) outputs dimensional sizes of an array. In line 7, `size(a)` outputs two values: number of rows and number of columns; and a two-element vector is used to receive the output values.

The length of an array is the maximum dimension size of the array; i.e.,

`length(a) ≡ max(size(a))`

In this case, the length of the array `a` is 5 (line 8; also see lines 36-38, last page). ↓

[5] Line 9 assigns the entire array `a` to a variable `b`, which becomes the same sizes and contents as the array `a`. Line 10 uses another way to assign all the values of the array `a` to a variable. The variables `a`, `b`, and `c` are the same in sizes and contents.

Lines 11-13 demonstrate three ways to assign the 3rd, 4th, and 5th elements of the array `a` to a variable. The variables `d`, `e`, and `f` are the same in sizes and contents. Note that, in line 13, the keyword `end` means the **last index** of the underlying array.

Line 14 attempts to assign a value to the 5th element of the array `f`, which is a row vector of length 3. MATLAB expands the array `f` to a row vector of length 5 to accommodate the value and pads zeros for the unused elements; `f` now is a row vector of length 5. #

2.6c Colon: Entire Column/Row

Example02_06c.m

[1] Type the following commands (also see [2]). →

```
clear
a = [1, 2; 3, 4; 5, 6]
b = 1:6
c = reshape(b, 3, 2)
d = reshape(b, 2, 3)
e = d'
c(:,3) = [7, 8, 9]
c(4,:) = [10, 11, 12]
c(4,:) = []
c(:,2:3) = []
```

```
>> clear
>> a = [1, 2; 3, 4; 5, 6]
a =
     1     2
     3     4
     5     6
>> b = 1:6
b =
     1     2     3     4     5     6
>> c = reshape(b, 3, 2)
c =
     1     4
     2     5
     3     6
>> d = reshape(b, 2, 3)
d =
     1     3     5
     2     4     6
>> e = d'
e =
     1     2
     3     4
     5     6
>> c(:,3) = [7, 8, 9]
c =
     1     4     7
     2     5     8
     3     6     9
>> c(4,:) = [10, 11, 12]
c =
     1     4     7
     2     5     8
     3     6     9
    10    11    12
>> c(4,:) = []
c =
     1     4     7
     2     5     8
     3     6     9
>> c(:,2:3) = []
c =
     1
     2
     3
```

[2] This is a **Command Window** session of Example02_06c.m. ↵

Function `reshape`

[3] Line 2 creates a 3-by-2 matrix. Line 3 creates a row vector of 6 elements. Line 4 reshapes the vector `b` into a 3-by-2 matrix. The reshaping doesn't alter the order of the elements stored in the array (see 1.9[11-16], page 36); it alters dimensionality and dimension sizes. Note that `c` is different from `a` (see lines 14-16 and 22-24). To obtain a matrix the same as `a` from the vector `b`, we reshape `b` into a 2-by-3 matrix (line 5) and then transpose it (line 6). Now `e` is the same as `a` (lines 31-33).

Colon: The Entire Column/Row

Line 7 assigns 3 elements to the third column of `c`. Note that `[7, 8, 9]` is automatically transposed, becoming a column. Line 8 assigns 3 elements to the fourth row of `c`.

The colon (:) represents the entire column when placed at the row (first) index and represents the entire row when placed at the column (second) index.

Empty Data

Line 9 sets the fourth row of `c` to be empty, i.e., deleting the entire row. Line 10 sets the 2nd-3rd columns to be empty, i.e., deleting the 2nd-3rd columns.

The `[ ]` represents an empty data. #

2.6d Concatenation and Flipping

Example02_06d.m

[1] Type the following commands (also see [2]). →

```
 1  clear
 2  a = reshape(1:6, 3, 2)
 3  b = [7; 8; 9]
 4  c = horzcat(a, b)
 5  d = [a, b]
 6  e = b'
 7  f = vertcat(d, e)
 8  g = [d; e]
 9  h = fliplr(c)
10  k = flipud(c)
```

```
11  >> clear
12  >> a = reshape(1:6, 3, 2)
13  a =
14       1     4
15       2     5
16       3     6
17  >> b = [7; 8; 9]
18  b =
19       7
20       8
21       9
22  >> c = horzcat(a, b)
23  c =
24       1     4     7
25       2     5     8
26       3     6     9
27  >> d = [a, b]
28  d =
29       1     4     7
30       2     5     8
31       3     6     9
32  >> e = b'
33  e =
34       7     8     9
35  >> f = vertcat(d, e)
36  f =
37       1     4     7
38       2     5     8
39       3     6     9
40       7     8     9
41  >> g = [d; e]
42  g =
43       1     4     7
44       2     5     8
45       3     6     9
46       7     8     9
47  >> h = fliplr(c)
48  h =
49       7     4     1
50       8     5     2
51       9     6     3
52  >> k = flipud(c)
53  k =
54       3     6     9
55       2     5     8
56       1     4     7
```

[2] This is a **Command Window** session of Example02_06d.m. ↵

Concatenation of Arrays

[3] Line 2 creates a 3-by-2 matrix `a` by reshaping the vector `[1:6]`: the first 3 elements become the first column, and the second 3 elements become the second column. Line 3 creates a column vector `b` of 3 elements.

Using function `horzcat`, line 4 concatenates `a` and `b` horizontally to create a 3-by-3 matrix `c`. Line 5 demonstrates a more convenient way to do the same job, using a comma (`,`) to concatenate arrays horizontally.

Line 6 transposes (see 1.6[12], page 27) the column vector `b` to create a row vector `e` of 3 elements.

Using the function `vertcat`, line 7 concatenates `d` and `e` vertically to create a 4-by-3 matrix `f`. Line 8 demonstrates a more convenient way to do the same job, using a semicolon (`;`) to concatenate arrays vertically.

Flipping Matrices

Using the function `fliplr` (flip left-side right), line 9 flips the matrix `c` horizontally. Using the function `flipud` (flip upside down), line 10 flips the matrix `c` vertically.

Functions for array replication, concatenation, flipping, and reshaping are summarized in Table 2.6b.

More Array Operations

We'll introduce arithmetic operations for numeric data, including arrays and scalars, in the next two sections. #

Table 2.6a Array Creation Functions

Function	Description
`zeros(n,m)`	Create an n-by-m matrix of all zeros
`ones(n,m)`	Create an n-by-m matrix of all ones
`eye(n)`	Create an n-by-n identity matrix
`diag(v)`	Create a square diagonal matrix with v on the diagonal
`rand(n,m)`	Create an n-by-m matrix of uniformly distributed random numbers in the interval (0,1)
`randn(n,m)`	Create an n-by-m matrix of random numbers from the standard normal distribution
`linspace(a,b,n)`	Create a row vector of n linearly spaced numbers from a to b
`[X,Y] = meshgrid(x,y)`	Create a 2-D grid coordinates based on the coordinates in vectors x and y.
Details and More: Help>MATLAB>Language Fundamentals>Matrices and Arrays	

Table 2.6b Array Replication, Concatenation, Flipping, and Reshaping

Function	Description
`repmat(a,n,m)`	Replicate array a n times in row-dimension and m times in column-dimension
`horzcat(a,b,...)`	Concatenate arrays horizontally
`vertcat(a,b,...)`	Concatenate arrays vertically
`flipud(A)`	Flip an array upside down
`fliplr(A)`	Flip an array left-side right
`reshape(A,n,m)`	Reshape an array to an n-by-m matrix
Details and More: Help>MATLAB>Language Fundamentals>Matrices and Arrays	

2.7 Sums, Products, Minima, and Maxima

[1] This section introduces some frequently used functions that calculate the sum, product, minima, and maxima of an array. These functions are summarized in Table 2.7. ↓

Example02_07.m

[2] Type the following commands (also see [3]). ↘

```
clear
a = 1:5
b = sum(a)
c = cumsum(a)
d = prod(a)
e = cumprod(a)
f = diff(a)
A = reshape(1:9, 3, 3)
g = sum(A)
B = cumsum(A)
h = prod(A)
C = cumprod(A)
D = diff(A)
p = min(a)
q = max(a)
r = min(A)
s = max(A)
```

Table 2.7
Sums, Products, Minima, and Maxima

Function	Description
`sum(A)`	Sum of array elements
`cumsum(A)`	Cumulative sum
`diff(A)`	Differences between adjacent elements
`prod(A)`	Product of array elements
`cumprod(A)`	Cumulative product
`min(A)`	Minimum
`max(A)`	Maximum

```
>> clear
>> a = 1:5
a =
       1      2      3      4      5
>> b = sum(a)
b =
      15
>> c = cumsum(a)
c =
       1      3      6     10     15
>> d = prod(a)
d =
     120
>> e = cumprod(a)
e =
       1      2      6     24    120
>> f = diff(a)
f =
       1      1      1      1
>> A = reshape(1:9, 3, 3)
A =
       1      4      7
       2      5      8
       3      6      9
>> g = sum(A)
g =
       6     15     24
>> B = cumsum(A)
B =
       1      4      7
       3      9     15
       6     15     24
>> h = prod(A)
h =
       6    120    504
>> C = cumprod(A)
C =
       1      4      7
       2     20     56
       6    120    504
>> D = diff(A)
D =
       1      1      1
       1      1      1
```

[3] This is a **Command Window** session of Example02_07.m (continued at [4], next page). ↵

```
62  >> p = min(a)
63  p =
64        1
65  >> q = max(a)
66  q =
67        5
68  >> r = min(A)
69  r =
70        1     4     7
71  >> s = max(A)
72  s =
73        3     6     9
```

[4] This is a **Command Window** session of Example02_07.m (Continued). →

Sums and Products of Vectors

[5] Let a_i, $i = 1, 2, \ldots, n$, be the elements of a vector **a** (either row vector or column vector). When applied to a vector, the function `sum` (line 3) outputs a scalar b, where

$$b = a_1 + a_2 + \ \ldots \ + a_n$$

In this example (line 24),

$$b = 1 + 2 + 3 + 4 + 5 = 15$$

When applied to a vector, the function `cumsum` (cumulative sum; line 4) outputs a vector **c** of n elements, where

$$c_1 = a_1 \text{ and } c_i = c_{i-1} + a_i;\ i = 2, 3, \ldots, n$$

In this example (line 27),

$$c_1 = a_1 = 1$$
$$c_2 = c_1 + 2 = 3$$
$$c_3 = c_2 + 3 = 6$$
$$c_4 = c_3 + 4 = 10$$
$$c_5 = c_4 + 5 = 15$$

When applied to a vector, function `prod` (line 5) outputs a scalar d,

$$d = a_1 \times a_2 \times \ \ldots \ \times a_n$$

In this example (line 30),

$$d = 1 \times 2 \times 3 \times 4 \times 5 = 120$$

When applied to a vector, the function `cumprod` (cumulative product; line 6) outputs a vector **e** of n elements, where

$$e_1 = a_1 \text{ and } e_i = e_{i-1} \times a_i;\ i = 2, 3, \ldots, n$$

In this example (line 33),

$$e_1 = a_1 = 1$$
$$e_2 = e_1 \times 2 = 2$$
$$e_3 = e_2 \times 3 = 6$$
$$e_4 = e_3 \times 4 = 24$$
$$e_5 = e_4 \times 5 = 120$$

When applied to a vector, the function `diff` (line 7) outputs a vector **f** of n-1 (not n) elements, where

$$f_i = a_{i+1} - a_i;\ i = 1, 2, \ldots, n-1$$

In this example (line 36),

$$f_1 = 2 - 1 = 1$$
$$f_2 = 3 - 2 = 1$$
$$f_3 = 4 - 3 = 1$$
$$f_4 = 5 - 4 = 1$$

↵

Sums and Products of Matrices

[6] Let A_{ij}, $i = 1, 2, \ldots, n$, $j = 1, 2, \ldots, m$ be the elements of an $n \times m$ matrix **A**. When applied to a matrix, the function `sum` (line 9) outputs a row vector **g**, where g_j is the sum of the jth column of the matrix **A**; i.e.,

$$g_j = A_{1j} + A_{2j} + \ldots + A_{nj};\ j = 1, 2, \ldots, m$$

In this example (line 44),

$$g_1 = 1 + 2 + 3 = 6$$
$$g_2 = 4 + 5 + 6 = 15$$
$$g_3 = 7 + 8 + 9 = 24$$

Note that the summing is along the **first dimension** (i.e., the row dimension); this rule also applies to the functions `cumsum`, `prod`, and `cumprod` and also applies to three-dimensional arrays.

When applied to a matrix, the function `cumsum` (line 10) outputs an $n \times m$ matrix **B**, where

$$B_{1j} = A_{1j} \text{ and } B_{ij} = B_{(i-1)j} + A_{ij};\ i = 2, 3, \ldots, n;\ j = 1, 2, \ldots, m$$

In this example (lines 47-49),

$$B_{11} = A_{11} = 1 \qquad B_{12} = A_{12} = 4 \qquad B_{13} = A_{13} = 7$$
$$B_{21} = B_{11} + 2 = 3 \qquad B_{22} = B_{12} + 5 = 9 \qquad B_{23} = B_{13} + 8 = 15$$
$$B_{31} = B_{21} + 3 = 6 \qquad B_{32} = B_{22} + 6 = 15 \qquad B_{33} = B_{23} + 9 = 24$$

When applied to a matrix, the function `prod` (line 11) outputs a row vector **h**,

$$h_j = A_{1j} \times A_{2j} \times \ldots \times A_{nj};\ j = 1, 2, \ldots, m$$

In this example (line 52),

$$h_1 = 1 \times 2 \times 3 = 6$$
$$h_2 = 4 \times 5 \times 6 = 120$$
$$h_3 = 7 \times 8 \times 9 = 504$$

When applied to a matrix, the function `cumprod` (line 12) outputs an $n \times m$ matrix **C**, where

$$C_{1j} = A_{1j} \text{ and } C_{ij} = C_{(i-1)j} \times A_{ij};\ i = 2, 3, \ldots, n;\ j = 1, 2, \ldots, m$$

In this example (lines 55-57),

$$C_{11} = A_{11} = 1 \qquad C_{12} = A_{12} = 4 \qquad C_{13} = A_{13} = 7$$
$$C_{21} = C_{11} \times 2 = 2 \qquad C_{22} = C_{12} \times 5 = 20 \qquad C_{23} = C_{13} \times 8 = 56$$
$$C_{31} = C_{21} \times 3 = 6 \qquad C_{32} = C_{22} \times 6 = 120 \qquad C_{33} = C_{23} \times 9 = 504$$

When applied to a matrix, the function `diff` (line 13) outputs an $(n-1) \times m$ (not $n \times m$) matrix **D**, where

$$D_{ij} = A_{(i+1)j} - A_{ij};\ i = 1, 2, \ldots, n-1;\ j = 1, 2, \ldots, m$$

In this example (lines 60-61),

$$D_{11} = 2 - 1 = 1 \qquad D_{12} = 5 - 4 = 1 \qquad D_{13} = 8 - 7 = 1$$
$$D_{21} = 3 - 2 = 1 \qquad D_{22} = 6 - 5 = 1 \qquad D_{23} = 9 - 8 = 1$$

Minima and Maxima

The output of the functions `min` or `max` for a vector are scalars (lines 14-15, 64, 67).

The output of the functions `min` or `max` for an $n \times m$ matrix is a row vector of m elements (lines 16-17, 70, 73), in which each element is the minimum/maximum of the corresponding column. #

2.8 Arithmetic Operators

2.8a Matrix Operations

[1] An arithmetic operator operates on one (unary operator) or two (binary operator) numeric data and the result is also a numeric data. If any of the operands is not a numeric data, it is converted to a numeric data. Table 2.8 lists some of the frequently used arithmetic operators.

Precedence Level of Operators

The precedence level of operators determines the order in which MATLAB evaluates an operation. We attach to each operator a precedence number as shown in Tables 2.8 (and Tables 2.9a, 2.9b in page 99); *the lower number has higher precedence*. For operators with the same precedence level, the evaluation is from left to right. The parentheses `()` has highest precedence level (1), while the assignment = has lowest precedence level (13).

Names of Operators

An operator is actually a short hand of a function name. For example, `5+6` is internally evaluated using the function call

```
>> plus(3,5)
ans =
     8
```

This feature is useful when creating classes and their associate operators. In Section 4.9, we'll demonstrate the creation of a class of polynomial, for which we'll implement the addition and subtraction of polynomials using the operators + and `-`. →

Example02_08a.m

[2] These statements demonstrate some arithmetic operations on **matrices** (see the **Command Window** session in [3-4], next page). ↵

```
clear
A = reshape(1:6, 2, 3)
B = reshape(7:12, 2, 3)
C = A+B
D = A-B
E = B'
F = A*E
a = [3, 6]
b = a/F
c = b*F
G = F^2
H = A.*B
K = A./B
M = A.^2
P = A+10
Q = A-10
R = A*1.5
S = A/2
```

Table 2.8 Arithmetic Operators

Operator	Name	Description	Precedence level
+	plus	Addition	6
-	minus	Subtraction	6
*	mtimes	Multiplication	5
/	mrdivide	Division	5
^	mpower	Exponentiation	2
.*	times	Element-wise multiplication	5
./	rdivide	Element-wise division	5
.^	power	Element-wise exponentiation	2
-	uminus	Unary minus	4
+	uplus	Unary plus	4

Details and More:
Help>MATLAB>Language Fundamentals>Operators and Elementary Operations>Operator Precedence
Help>MATLAB>Language Fundamentals>Operators and Elementary Operations>Arithmetic

```
>> clear
>> A = reshape(1:6, 2, 3)
A =
     1     3     5
     2     4     6
>> B = reshape(7:12, 2, 3)
B =
     7     9    11
     8    10    12
>> C = A+B
C =
     8    12    16
    10    14    18
>> D = A-B
D =
    -6    -6    -6
    -6    -6    -6
>> E = B'
E =
     7     8
     9    10
    11    12
>> F = A*E
F =
    89    98
   116   128
>> a = [3, 6]
a =
     3     6
>> b = a/F
b =
  -13.0000   10.0000
>> c = b*F
c =
     3     6
>> G = F^2
G =
       19289       21266
       25172       27752
>> H = A.*B
H =
     7    27    55
    16    40    72
>> K = A./B
K =
    0.1429    0.3333    0.4545
    0.2500    0.4000    0.5000
>> M = A.^2
M =
     1     9    25
     4    16    36
```

[3] A **Command Window** session of Example02_08a.m (continued at [4]). ↓

```
>> P = A+10
P =
    11    13    15
    12    14    16
>> Q = A-10
Q =
    -9    -7    -5
    -8    -6    -4
>> R = A*1.5
R =
    1.5000    4.5000    7.5000
    3.0000    6.0000    9.0000
>> S = A/2
S =
    0.5000    1.5000    2.5000
    1.0000    2.0000    3.0000
```

[4] A **Command Window** session of Example02_08a.m (Continued). ↵

Addition of Matrices

[5] Let A_{ij}, $i=1, 2, \ldots, n; j=1, 2, \ldots, m$ be the elements of an $n \times m$ matrix **A**, and B_{ij}, $i=1, 2, \ldots, n; j=1, 2, \ldots, m$ be the elements of another $n \times m$ matrix **B**. The addition (line 4) of the two matrices is an $n \times m$ matrix **C**,

$$C_{ij} = A_{ij} + B_{ij}$$
$$i=1, 2, \ldots, n; j=1, 2, \ldots, m$$

In this example (lines 30-31),

$$C_{11} = 1+7 = 8 \quad C_{12} = 3+9 = 12 \quad C_{13} = 5+11 = 16$$
$$C_{21} = 2+8 = 10 \quad C_{22} = 4+10 = 14 \quad C_{23} = 6+12 = 18$$

Subtraction of Matrices

The subtraction (line 5) of **B** from **A** is an $n \times m$ matrix **D**,

$$D_{ij} = A_{ij} - B_{ij}$$
$$i=1, 2, \ldots, n; j=1, 2, \ldots, m$$

In this example (lines 34-35),

$$D_{11} = 1-7 = -6 \quad D_{12} = 3-9 = -6 \quad D_{13} = 5-11 = -6$$
$$D_{21} = 2-8 = -6 \quad D_{22} = 4-10 = -6 \quad D_{23} = 6-12 = -6$$

Transpose of Matrices

The transpose (line 6; also see 1.6[12], page 27) of **B** is an $m \times n$ matrix **E**,

$$E_{ij} = B_{ji}$$
$$i=1, 2, \ldots, m; j=1, 2, \ldots, n$$

In this example (lines 38-40)

$$E_{11} = B_{11} = 7 \quad E_{12} = B_{21} = 8$$
$$E_{21} = B_{12} = 9 \quad E_{22} = B_{22} = 10$$
$$E_{31} = B_{13} = 11 \quad E_{32} = B_{23} = 12$$

Multiplication of Matrices

The multiplication (line 7) of an $n \times m$ matrix **A** by an $m \times p$ matrix **E** is an $n \times p$ matrix **F**

$$F_{ij} = \sum_{k=1}^{m} A_{ik} \times E_{kj}$$
$$i=1, 2, \ldots, n; j=1, 2, \ldots, p$$

In this example (lines 43-44), $n = 2$, $m = 3$, and $p = 2$, and the result is a 2×2 matrix:

$$F_{11} = 1\times7 + 3\times9 + 5\times11 = 89$$
$$F_{21} = 2\times7 + 4\times9 + 6\times11 = 116$$
$$F_{12} = 1\times8 + 3\times10 + 5\times12 = 98$$
$$F_{22} = 2\times8 + 4\times10 + 6\times12 = 128$$

Note that two matrices can be multiplied only if the two matrices have the same **inner dimension size**. ↵

Division of Matrices

[6] The division (line 9) of an $r \times m$ matrix **a** by an $m \times m$ matrix **F** (i.e., **a/F**) is an $r \times m$ matrix **b**; they are related by

$$\mathbf{b}_{r\times m} \times \mathbf{F}_{m\times m} = \mathbf{a}_{r\times m}$$

In this example (line 50), $r = 1$ and $m = 2$, and the result is a 1×2 row vector **b**,

$$\mathbf{b} = [\ -13 \quad 10\ ]$$

since it satisfies (see lines 10 and 53)

$$\begin{bmatrix} -13 & 10 \end{bmatrix} \times \begin{bmatrix} 89 & 98 \\ 116 & 128 \end{bmatrix} = \begin{bmatrix} 3 & 6 \end{bmatrix}$$

Note that **a** and **F** must have the same **column size** and, in the above example, **F** is a square matrix and the resulting matrix **b** has the same dimension sizes as **a**. In general, **F** is not necessarily a square matrix. If **F** is not a square matrix, then **a/F** will output a least-squares solution **b** of the system of equations $\mathbf{b}\times\mathbf{F} = \mathbf{a}$ (see line 8 in page 97, for example).

Exponentiation of Square Matrices

The exponentiation of a square matrix is the repeated multiplication of the matrix itself. For example (line 11)

$$\mathbf{F}\,\hat{}\,2 \equiv \mathbf{F}\times\mathbf{F}$$

In this example (lines 56-57)

$$\mathbf{F}\,\hat{}\,2 = \begin{bmatrix} 89 & 98 \\ 116 & 128 \end{bmatrix} \times \begin{bmatrix} 89 & 98 \\ 116 & 128 \end{bmatrix}$$
$$= \begin{bmatrix} 19289 & 21266 \\ 25172 & 27752 \end{bmatrix}$$

Element-Wise Multiplication of Matrices

The element-wise multiplication (`.*` in line 12) operates on two $n\times m$ matrices of the same sizes **A** and **B**, and the result is a matrix **H** of the same size,

$$H_{ij} = A_{ij} \times B_{ij}$$
$$i = 1,\ 2,\ \ldots,\ n;\ j = 1,\ 2,\ \ldots,\ m$$

In this example (lines 60-61)

$$H_{11} = 1\times 7 = 7 \quad H_{12} = 3\times 9 = 27 \quad H_{13} = 5\times 11 = 55$$
$$H_{21} = 2\times 8 = 16 \quad H_{22} = 4\times 10 = 40 \quad H_{23} = 6\times 12 = 72$$

Element-Wise Division of Matrices

The element-wise division (`./` in line 13) also operates on two $n\times m$ matrices of the same sizes **A** and **B**, and the result is a matrix **K** of the same size,

$$K_{ij} = A_{ij} / B_{ij}$$
$$i = 1,\ 2,\ \ldots,\ n;\ j = 1,\ 2,\ \ldots,\ m$$

In this example (lines 64-65)

$$K_{11} = 1/7 \quad K_{12} = 3/9 = 1/3 \quad K_{13} = 5/11$$
$$K_{21} = 2/8 = 0.25 \quad K_{22} = 4/10 = 0.4 \quad K_{23} = 6/12 = 0.5$$

↵

Element-Wise Exponentiation of Matrices

[7] The element-wise exponentiation (line 14) operates on an $n \times m$ matrix **A** and a scalar q, and the result is an $n \times m$ matrix **M**,

$$M_{ij} = \left(A_{ij}\right)^q$$
$$i = 1,\ 2,\ \ldots,\ n;\ j = 1,\ 2,\ \ldots,\ m$$

In this example (lines 68-69)

$$M_{11} = 1^2 = 1 \quad M_{12} = 3^2 = 9 \quad M_{13} = 5^2 = 25$$
$$M_{21} = 2^2 = 4 \quad M_{22} = 4^2 = 16 \quad M_{23} = 6^2 = 36$$

Operations Between a Matrix and a Scalar

Let @ be one of the operators `+`, `-`, `*`, `/`, `.*`, `./`, or `.^`, and s be a scalar, then **A**@s is an $n \times m$ matrix **V**, where

$$V_{ij} = A_{ij} @ s$$
$$i = 1,\ 2,\ \ldots,\ n;\ j = 1,\ 2,\ \ldots,\ m$$

and s@**A** is also an $n \times m$ matrix **W**, where

$$W_{ij} = s @ A_{ij}$$
$$i = 1,\ 2,\ \ldots,\ n;\ j = 1,\ 2,\ \ldots,\ m$$

For example (lines 15-18)

$$\mathbf{A} + 10 = \begin{bmatrix} 1+10 & 3+10 & 5+10 \\ 2+10 & 4+10 & 6+10 \end{bmatrix}$$

$$\mathbf{A} - 10 = \begin{bmatrix} 1-10 & 3-10 & 5-10 \\ 2-10 & 4-10 & 6-10 \end{bmatrix}$$

$$\mathbf{A} \times 1.5 = \begin{bmatrix} 1\times 1.5 & 3\times 1.5 & 5\times 1.5 \\ 2\times 1.5 & 4\times 1.5 & 6\times 1.5 \end{bmatrix}$$

$$\mathbf{A}/2 = \begin{bmatrix} 1/2 & 3/2 & 5/2 \\ 2/2 & 4/2 & 6/2 \end{bmatrix}$$

In other words, an operation **A**@s or s@**A** can be thought of as an element-wise operation in which the scalar s is expanded such that it has the same sizes as the matrix **A** and each element has the same value s. For example

$$\mathbf{A} + 10 = \begin{bmatrix} 1 & 3 & 5 \\ 2 & 4 & 6 \end{bmatrix} + \begin{bmatrix} 10 & 10 & 10 \\ 10 & 10 & 10 \end{bmatrix}$$

$$\mathbf{A} \times 1.5 = \begin{bmatrix} 1 & 3 & 5 \\ 2 & 4 & 6 \end{bmatrix} .* \begin{bmatrix} 1.5 & 1.5 & 1.5 \\ 1.5 & 1.5 & 1.5 \end{bmatrix}$$

#

2.8b Vector Operations

Example02_08b.m

[1] These statements demonstrate some arithmetic operations on **vectors** (also see [2]). Remember that a vector is a special case of matrices. Thus operations on vectors are special cases of those on matrices. ↓

```
1   clear
2   a = 1:4
3   b = 5:8
4   c = a+b
5   d = a-b
6   e = a*(b')
7   f = (a')*b
8   g = a/b
9   h = a.*b
10  k = a./b
11  m = a.^2
```

[2] This is a **Command Window** session of Example02_08b.m. ↓

```
12  >> clear
13  >> a = 1:4
14  a =
15       1     2     3     4
16  >> b = 5:8
17  b =
18       5     6     7     8
19  >> c = a+b
20  c =
21       6     8    10    12
22  >> d = a-b
23  d =
24      -4    -4    -4    -4
25  >> e = a*(b')
26  e =
27      70
28  >> f = (a')*b
29  f =
30       5     6     7     8
31      10    12    14    16
32      15    18    21    24
33      20    24    28    32
34  >> g = a/b
35  g =
36      0.4023
37  >> h = a.*b
38  h =
39       5    12    21    32
40  >> k = a./b
41  k =
42      0.2000    0.3333    0.4286    0.5000
43  >> m = a.^2
44  m =
45       1     4     9    16
```

Arithmetic Operators for Vectors

[3] A vector is a special matrix, in which either the row-size or the column-size is equal to one. Thus, all the rules of the arithmetic operations for matrices apply to those for vectors.

Division (/) by a Non-Square Matrix

In line 8, since `b` is not a square matrix, `g` is not an exact solution of `g*b = a`. Instead, `g` is the least-squares solution of the equation `g*b = a` (*for details and more:* `>> doc /`). In general, if `a` is an $r \times m$ matrix and `b` is a $t \times m$ matrix, then the result `g` of slash operator (`/`) is an $r \times t$ matrix.

In this case `a` is a 1×4 matrix and `b` is also a 1×4 matrix; therefore, the result `g` must be a 1×1 matrix, i.e., a scalar. MATLAB seeks the least-squares solution for the system of 4 equations:

$$g \times [\ 5 \quad 6 \quad 7 \quad 8\ ] = [\ 1 \quad 2 \quad 3 \quad 4\ ]$$

and the least-squares solution is $g = 0.4023$ (line 36). #

2.8c Scalar Operations

Example02_08c.m

[1] These statements demonstrate some arithmetic operations on **scalars** (also see [2]). Remember that a scalar is a special case of matrices. Thus operations on scalars are special cases of those on matrices. ↓

```
clear
a = 6
b = 4
c = a+b
d = a-b
e = a*b
f = a/b
g = a^2
h = a.*b
k = a./b
m = a.^2
```

[2] This is a **Command Window** session of Example02_08c.m. ↓

```
>> clear
>> a = 6
a =
     6
>> b = 4
b =
     4
>> c = a+b
c =
    10
>> d = a-b
d =
     2
>> e = a*b
e =
    24
>> f = a/b
f =
    1.5000
>> g = a^2
g =
    36
>> h = a.*b
h =
    24
>> k = a./b
k =
    1.5000
>> m = a.^2
m =
    36
```

Arithmetic Operators for Scalars

[3] A scalar is a 1x1 matrix. Thus, all the rules of the arithmetic operations for matrices can apply to those for scalars.

Note that, in cases of scalar operations, there is no difference between operators with or without a dot (**.**); i.e., for scalar operations, * is the same as **.***, / is the same as **./**, and ^ is the same as **.^**. #

2.9 Relational and Logical Operators

Relational Operators

[1] A relational operator (Table 2.9a; also see 2.5[5], page 82) always operates on two numeric data (scalars, vectors, or matrices); the result is a logical data. If any of the operands is not a numeric data, it is converted to a numeric data.

As a rule, the two operands **A** and **B** must have the same sizes, and the result is a logical data of the same sizes (except `isequal`, which results in a single logical value). However, when one of the operands is a scalar, e.g., **A** > *s*, where *s* is a scalar and **A** is a matrix, the scalar is expanded such that it has the same size as the matrix **A** and each element has the same value *s* (also see 2.8a[7], page 96).

Logical Operators

A logical operator (Table 2.9b; also see 2.5[5], page 82) operates on one or two logical data (scalars, vectors, or matrices), and the result is a logical data of the same sizes. If any of the operands is not a logical data, it is converted to a logical data: a non-zero value is converted to a `true` and a zero is converted to a `false`. ↓

Table 2.9a Relational Operators

Operator	Description	Precedence level
`==`	Equal to	8
`~=`	Not equal to	8
`>`	Greater than	8
`<`	Less than	8
`>=`	Greater than or equal to	8
`<=`	Less than or equal to	8
`isequal`	Determine array equality	

Details and More: Help>MATLAB>Language Fundamentals>Operators and Elementary Operations>Relational Operations

Table 2.9b Logical Operators

Operator	Description	Precedence level
`&`	Logical AND	9
`|`	Logical OR	10
`~`	Logical NOT	4
`&&`	Logical AND (short-circuit)	11
`||`	Logical OR (short-circuit)	12

Details andMore: Help>MATLAB>Language Fundamentals>Operators and Elementary Operations>Logical Operations

Example02_09.m

[2] These statements demonstrate some relational and logical operations (also see [3-4], next page). ↵

```
clear
A = [5,0,-1; 3,10,2; 0,-4,8]
Map = (A > 6)
location = find(Map)
list = A(location)
list2 = A(find(A>6))
list3 = A(find(A>0 & A<=8 & A~=3))
list4 = A(A>0 & A<=8 & A~=3)
~A
~~A
isequal(A, ~~A)
```

```
12  >> clear
13  >> A = [5,0,-1; 3,10,2; 0,-4,8]
14  A =
15       5     0    -1
16       3    10     2
17       0    -4     8
18  >> Map = (A > 6)
19  Map =
20    3×3 logical array
21     0   0   0
22     0   1   0
23     0   0   1
24  >> location = find(Map)
25  location =
26       5
27       9
28  >> list = A(location)
29  list =
30      10
31       8
32  >> list2 = A(find(A>6))
33  list2 =
34      10
35       8
36  >> list3 = A(find(A>0 & A<=8 & A~=3))
37  list3 =
38       5
39       2
40       8
41  >> list4 = A(A>0 & A<=8 & A~=3)
42  list4 =
43       5
44       2
45       8
46  >> ~A
47  ans =
48   3×3 logical array
49     0   1   0
50     0   0   0
51     1   0   0
52  >> ~~A
53  ans =
54    3×3 logical array
55     1   0   1
56     1   1   1
57     0   1   1
58  >> isequal(A, ~~A)
59  ans =
60   logical
61    0
```

[3] This is a **Command Window** session of Example02_09.m. ↗

Workspace

Name ▲	Value	Size	Bytes	Class
A	[5,0,−1;3,10,...	3x3	72	double
ans	0	1x1	1	logical
list	[10;8]	2x1	16	double
list2	[10;8]	2x1	16	double
list3	[5;2;8]	3x1	24	double
list4	[5;2;8]	3x1	24	double
location	[5;9]	2x1	16	double
Map	*3x3 logical*	3x3	9	logical

[4] The **Workspace**. ↓

About Example02_09.m

[5] In line 3, the expression `A > 6` results in a logical-value matrix the same size as `A` (lines 20-23). The logical matrix can be thought of as a "map" indicating the locations of the elements that are greater than 6. Note that the parentheses in line 3 are not needed, since the assignment (=) has lowest precedence (2.8a[1], page 92). We sometimes add redundant parentheses to enhance the readability, avoiding confusion.

Function `find`

The function `find` (line 4) takes a **logical array** as input argument and outputs a **column vector** of numbers that are the **linear indices** (1.9[23], page 37) of the elements with the value `true` in the array.

Here (line 4), the 5th and 9th elements (in linear indexing) of `Map` have the value `true`, so it outputs a column vector consisting of 5 and 9 (lines 26-27).

In line 5, the vector `location` is used to access the array `A`; the result is a column vector containing the numbers in `A(5)` and `A(9)` (lines 30-31).

If we are concerned only with the numbers themselves (not the locations), then the commands in lines 3-5 can be combined, as shown in line 6, resulting in the same two values (lines 34-35).

Using function `find` with a logical expression as the input argument allows us to find the elements in an array that meet specific conditions. Suppose we want to find the numbers in the array `A` that are positive, less than or equal to 8, but not equal to 3; we may write the statement as shown in line 7, and the result is in lines 38-40. ↵

Logical Indexing

[6] In line 6, we are finding the elements in `A` such that they are greater than 6. This task can be accomplished by means of **logical indexing**:

```
>> A(A>6)
```

The result is the same as line 6. In other words, the logical matrix `Map` can be viewed as an **indexing matrix**, and

```
>> A(Map)
```

outputs all the elements `A(i,j)` for which their corresponding `Map(i,j)` is true.

Similarly, using the logical indexing, line 7 can be simplified as follows:

```
>> list3 = A(A>0 & A<=8 & A~=3)
```

In other words, the function `find` in lines 6 and 7 can be removed. This is demonstrated in line 8 and lines 43-45.

Logical NOT (~)

The logical NOT (~) reverses logical values: `true` becomes `false`, and `false` becomes `true`. If we apply it on a numerical array (line 9), a nonzero value becomes `false` and a zero value becomes `true` (lines 49-51). If we apply the logical NOT again on the previous result (line 10), the outcome is of course a logical array. Here, we want to show that for a numerical array, in general,

$$(\sim\sim A) \neq A$$

This is demonstrated in lines 11 and 59-61. The function `isequal` (line 11) compares two arrays and outputs `true` if they are equal in size and contents, otherwise outputs `false`.

Short-Circuit Logical AND (&&) and OR (||)

Let *`expr1`* and *`expr2`* be two logical expressions. The result of *`expr1&&expr2`* is the same as *`expr1&expr2`*, but the former is more efficient (i.e., less computing time). Similarly, the result of *`expr1||expr2`* is the same as *`expr1|expr2`*, but the former is more efficient. The operators `&&` and `||` are called short-circuit logical operators (see Table 2.9b, page 99).

In *`expr1&&expr2`*, *`expr2`* is evaluated only if the result is not fully determined by *`expr1`*. For example, if *`expr1`* equals `false`, then the entire expression evaluates to `false`, regardless of the value of *`expr2`*. Under these circumstances, there is no need to evaluate *`expr2`* because the result is already known.

Similarly, in *`expr1||expr2`*, *`expr2`* is evaluated only if the result is not fully determined by *`expr1`*. For example, if *`expr1`* equals `true`, then the entire expression evaluates to `true`, regardless of the value of *`expr2`*. Under these circumstances, there is no need to evaluate *`expr2`* because the result is already known. #

2.10 String Manipulations

2.10a String Manipulations

[1] A row vector of characters is also called a **string**. Single quotes are used to represent strings; e.g., `'ABC'` represents a row vector of three characters (2.4a[1]. page 78). Table 2.10 (page 104) summarizes some useful functions for string manipulations. ↓

Example02_10a.m: String Manipulations

[2] Type and run the following statements, which demonstrate some string manipulations. Input your name and age as shown in [3]. ↓

```
clear
a = 'Hello,';
b = 'world!';
c = [a, ' ', b];
disp(c)
name = input('What is your name? ', 's');
years = input('What is your age? ');
disp(['Hello, ', name, '! You are ', num2str(years), ' years old.'])
str = sprintf('Pi = %.8f', pi);
disp(str)
Names1 = [
    'David  '
    'John   '
    'Stephen'];
Names2 = char('David', 'John', 'Stephen');
if isequal(Names1, Names2)
    disp('The two lists are equal.')
end
name = deblank(Names1(2,:));
disp(['The name ', name, ' has ', num2str(length(name)), ' characters.'])
```

```
>> Example02_10a
Hello, world!
What is your name? Lee
What is your age? 60
Hello, Lee! You are 60 years old.
Pi = 3.14159265
The two lists are equal.
The name John has 4 characters.
>>
```

[3] This is a test run of Example02_10a.m. ↵

About Example02_10a.m

[4] Remember that a string is a row vector of characters. The most convenient way to concatenate strings is using square brackets as shown in line 4; `c` is now a row vector of 13 characters.

The function `disp` displays a data of any type (lines 5 and 22). A newline character (`\n`) is automatically output at the end of the display. On the other hand, you need to append newline characters when using the function `fprintf` if you want the cursor to move to the next line.

Line 6 requests a data input from the screen. With the `'s'` as the second argument, the input data will be read as a string, and you don't have to include the single quotes for the string (line 23). Without the `'s'` as the second argument, you would have to use the single quotes (`''`) to input a string, otherwise the data will be read as a `double` (lines 7 and 24).

The function `sprintf` (line 9) is the same as `fprintf` except that it writes to a string (rather than to the screen). Here, we write the value of π with 8 digits after the decimal point in a string and then assign to the string `str` (line 9) and display the string (lines 10 and 26).

In lines 11-14, a single statement continues for 4 lines, without using ellipses (`...`). A newline character between a pair of square brackets is treated as a semicolon plus an ellipsis. Thus, this statement (lines 11-14) creates 3 rows of strings; it is a 3-by-7 matrix of `char`. Note that rows of a matrix must have the same length. That's why we pad the first two strings with trailing blanks (lines 12-13) to make the lengths of the three strings equal.

Another way to create a column of strings (i.e., a matrix of `char`) is using the function `char`. Line 15 creates a column of strings exactly the same as that in lines 11-14. The function `char` automatically pads the strings with trailing blanks so that the three strings have the same length.

Lines 16-18 and 27 confirm the equality of the two matrices.

The function `deblank` (line 19) removes trailing blanks from a string. `Names1(2,:)` refers to the entire 2nd row (i.e., the string `'John   '`). After removing the trailing blanks, four characters remain in the string (lines 20 and 28). #

2.10b Example: A Simple Calculator

Example02_10b.m: A Simple Calculator

[1] This program uses function `eval` to create a simple calculator. Type and run the program, and see a test run in [2], next page. ↵

```
clear
disp('A Simple Calculator')
while true
    expr = input('Enter an expression (or quit): ', 's');
    if strcmp(expr,'quit')
        break
    end
    disp([expr, ' = ', num2str(eval(expr))])
end
```

[2] This is a test run of the program Example02_8b.m. #

```
>> Example02_10b
A Simple Calculator
Enter an expression (or quit): 3+5
3+5 = 8
Enter an expression (or quit): sin(pi/4) + (2 + 2.1^2)*3
sin(pi/4) + (2 + 2.1^2)*3 = 19.9371
Enter an expression (or quit): quit
>>
```

Table 2.10 String Manipulations

Function	Description
`A = char(a,b,...)`	Convert the strings to a matrix of rows of the strings, padding blanks
`disp(X)`	Display value of variable
`x = input(prompt,'s')`	Request user input
`s = sprintf(format,a,b,...)`	Write formatted data to a string
`s = num2str(x)`	Convert number to string
`x = str2num(s)`	Convert string to number
`x = str2double(s)`	Convert string to double precision value
`x = eval(exp)`	Evaluate a MATLAB expression
`s = deblank(str)`	Remove trailing blanks from a string
`s = strtrim(str)`	Remove leading and trailing blanks from a string
`tf = strcmp(s1,s2)`	Compare two strings (case sensitive)
`tf = strcmpi(s1,s2)`	Compare two strings (case insensitive)

Details and More:
Help>MATLAB>Language Fundamentals>Data Types>Characters and Strings; Data Type Conversion

2.11 Expressions

2.11a Example: Law of Sines

[1] An expression is a syntactic combination of **data** (constants or variables; scalars, vectors, matrices, etc.), **functions** (built-in or user-defined), **operators** (arithmetic, relational, or logical), and **special characters** (see Table 2.11a, page 107). An expression always results in a **value** of certain type, depending on the operators.

Table 2.11b (page 107) lists some frequently used math functions. ↓

Example: Law of Sines

[2] The law of sines for an arbitrary triangle states that (see *Wikipedia>Trigonometry*):

$$\frac{a}{\sin\alpha} = \frac{b}{\sin\beta} = \frac{c}{\sin\gamma} = \frac{abc}{2A} = 2R \qquad \text{(a)}$$

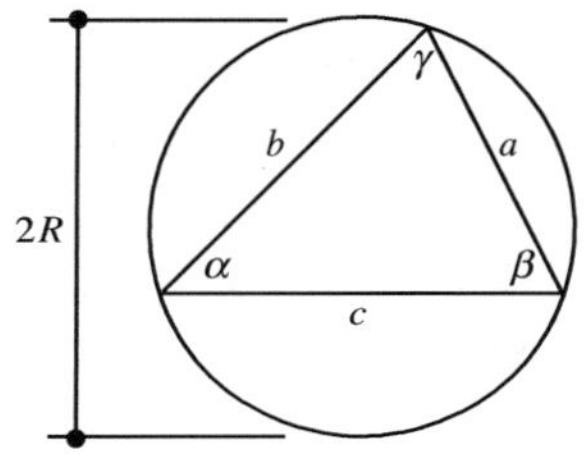

where α, β, and γ are the three angles of a triangle; *a*, *b*, and *c* are the lengths of the sides opposite to the respective angles; *A* is the area of the triangle; *R* is the radius of the circumscribed circle of the triangle:

$$R = \frac{abc}{\sqrt{(a+b+c)(a-b+c)(b-c+a)(c-a+b)}} \qquad \text{(b)}$$

Knowing *a*, *b*, and *c*, then α, β, γ,and *A* can be calculated as follows:

$$\alpha = \sin^{-1}\frac{a}{2R},\ \beta = \sin^{-1}\frac{b}{2R},\ \gamma = \sin^{-1}\frac{c}{2R} \qquad \text{(c)}$$

$$A = \frac{abc}{4R} \text{ or } A = \frac{1}{2}bc\sin\alpha \qquad \text{(d)}$$ ↓

Example02_11a.m: Law of Sines

[3] This script calculates the angles α, β, γ of a triangle and its area *A*, given three sides $a = 5$, $b = 6$, and $c = 7$. ↵

```
clear
a = 5;
b = 6;
c = 7;
R = a*b*c/sqrt((a+b+c)*(a-b+c)*(b-c+a)*(c-a+b))
alpha = asind(a/(2*R))
beta = asind(b/(2*R))
gamma = asind(c/(2*R))
sumAngle = alpha + beta + gamma
A1 = a*b*c/(4*R)
A2 = b*c*sind(alpha)/2
```

```
12  >> Example02_11a
13  R =
14       3.5722
15  alpha =
16     44.4153
17  beta =
18     57.1217
19  gamma =
20     78.4630
21  sumAngle =
22     180
23  A1 =
24     14.6969
25  A2 =
26     14.6969
27  >>
```

[4] This is the screen output of Example02_11a.m. →

About Example02_11a.m

[5] Function `sind` (line 11) is the same as the function `sin` in 1.2[7] (page 13) except that `sind` assumes degrees (instead of radians) as the unit of the input argument. Similarly, the function `asind` (lines 6-8), inverse sine function, outputs an angle in degrees (the function `asin` outputs an angle in radians).

Line 5 calculates the radius of the circumscribed circle according to Eq. (b), its output in lines 13-14.

Lines 6-8 calculate the three angles according to equations in (c), their outputs are in lines 15-20.

Line 9 confirms that the sum of the three angles is indeed 180 degrees (line 22).

Lines 10-11 calculate the area of the triangle using two different formulas in [2], and they indeed have the same values (lines 23-26). #

2.11b Example: Law of Cosines

Example02_11b.m: Law of Cosines

[1] The law of cosines states that (see *Wikipedia>Trigonometry*, with the same notations in 2.11a[2], last page):

$$a^2 = b^2 + c^2 - 2bc\cos\alpha \quad \text{or} \quad \alpha = \cos^{-1}\frac{b^2 + c^2 - a^2}{2bc} \tag{a}$$

With $a = 5$, $b = 6$, $c = 7$, the angle α, β, and γ can be calculated as follows:

```
clear
a = 5; b = 6; c = 7;
alpha = acosd((b^2+c^2-a^2)/(2*b*c))
beta = acosd((c^2+a^2-b^2)/(2*c*a))
gamma = acosd((a^2+b^2-c^2)/(2*a*b))
```

↓

[2] This is the screen output of Example02_11b.m. The outputs are consistent with those in 2.11a[4]. #

```
>> Example02_11b
alpha =
   44.4153
beta =
   57.1217
gamma =
   78.4630
>>
```

Table 2.11a
Special Characters

Special characters	Description
`[ ]`	Brackets
`{ }`	Braces
`( )`	Parentheses
`'`	Matrix transpose
`.`	Field access
`...`	Continuation
`,`	Comma
`;`	Semicolon
`:`	Colon
`@`	Function handle

Details and More:
Help>MATLAB>Language Fundamentals>Operators and Elementary Operations>MATLAB Operators and Special Characters

Table 2.11b
Elementary Math Functions

Function	Description
`sin(x)`	Sine (in radians)
`sind(x)`	Sine (in degrees)
`asin(x)`	Inverse sine (in radians)
`asind(x)`	Inverse sine (in degrees)
`cos(x)`	Cosine (in radians)
`cosd(x)`	Cosine (in degrees)
`acos(x)`	Inverse cosine (in radians)
`acosd(x)`	Inverse cosine (in degrees)
`tan(x)`	Tangent (in radians)
`tand(x)`	Tangent (in degrees)
`atan(x)`	Inverse tangent (in radians)
`atand(x)`	Inverse tangent (in degrees)
`atan2(y,x)`	Four-quadrant inverse tangent (radians)
`atan2d(y,x)`	Four-quadrant inverse tangent (degrees)
`abs(x)`	Absolute value
`sqrt(x)`	Square root
`exp(x)`	Exponential (base *e*)
`log(x)`	Logarithm (base *e*)
`log10(x)`	Logarithm (base 10)
`factorial(n)`	Factorial
`sign(x)`	Sign of a number
`rem(a,b)`	Remainder after division
`mod(a,m)`	Modulo operation

Details and More:
Help>MATLAB>Mathematics>Elementary Math

2.12 Example: Function Approximation

2.12a Scalar Expressions

Taylor Series

[1] At the hardware level, your computer can only perform simple arithmetic calculations such as addition, subtraction, multiplication, division, etc. Evaluation of a function value such as $\sin(\pi/4)$ is usually carried out with software or firmware. But how? In this section, we use sin(x) as an example to demonstrate the idea. This section also guides you to familiarize yourself with the way of thinking when using matrix expressions.

The sine function can be approximated using a Taylor series (Section 9.6 gives more detail on the Taylor series):

$$\sin x = x - \frac{x^3}{3!} + \frac{x^5}{5!} - \frac{x^7}{7!} + \ldots \qquad \text{(a)}$$

The more terms, the more accurate the approximation. ↙

Example02_12a.m: Scalar Expressions

[2] This script evaluates $\sin(\pi/4)$ using the Taylor series in Eq. (a). The screen output is shown in [3]. →

```
1   clear
2   x = pi/4;
3   term1 = x;
4   term2 = -x^3/(3*2);
5   term3 = x^5/(5*4*3*2);
6   term4 = -x^7/(7*6*5*4*3*2);
7   format long
8   sinx =term1+term2+term3+term4
9   exact = sin(x)
10  error = (sinx-exact)/exact
```

```
11  sinx =
12     0.707106469575178
13  exact =
14     0.707106781186547
15  error =
16      -4.406850247592559e-07
```

[3] This is the screen output. ↓

About Example02_12a.m

[4] We used 4 terms to calculate the function value sin(x) (lines 2-8, 11-12). Line 9 calculates the function values using the built-in function `sin` (line 14), which is used as a baseline for comparison. Line 10 calculates the error of the approximation (line 16). We conclude that, with merely four terms, the program calculates a function value to the accuracy of an order of 10^{-7}. #

2.12b Use of For-Loop

[1] In theory, an infinite number of terms of polynomials is required to achieve the exact value of sin(x). We need a general representation of these terms. We may rewrite the Taylor series in Eq. 2.12a(a) as follows:

$$\sin x = \sum_{k=1}^{\infty} (-1)^{k-1} \frac{x^{2k-1}}{(2k-1)!} \qquad \text{(a)}$$

We now use a `for`-loop (Sections 1.14, 3.4) to calculate $\sin(\pi/4)$. ↵

Example02_12b.m: Use of For-Loop

[2] Type and run this program. The screen output is the same as 2.12a[3], last page. ↓

```
1   clear
2   x = pi/4; n = 4; sinx = 0;
3   for k = 1:n
4       sinx = sinx + ((-1)^(k-1))*(x^(2*k-1))/factorial(2*k-1);
5   end
6   format long
7   sinx
8   exact = sin(x)
9   error = (sinx-exact)/exact
```

About Example02_12b.m

[3] In line 2, the variable `sinx` is initialized to zero. The statement within the `for`-loop (line 4) runs four passes. In each pass, the variable `k` is assigned 1, 2, 3, and 4, respectively; a term is calculated according to the formula in Eq. (a) and added to the variable `sinx`. At the completion of the `for`-loop, `sinx` has the function value; the output is the same as 2.12a[3], last page. To increase the accuracy of the value, you may simply increase the number of items (see [4], for example). ↓

[4] This is the screen output when 6 items are used (i.e., change to `n = 6` in line 2). Note that the error reduces to an order of 10^{-12}. #

```
sinx =
   0.707106781179619
exact =
   0.707106781186547
error =
    -9.797690960678494e-12
```

2.12c Vector Expressions

Example02_12c.m: Vector Expressions

[1] This script produces the same outputs as 2.12a[3], last page, using a vector expression (line 4) in place of the `for`-loop used in Example02_12b.m. ↵

```
1   clear
2   x = pi/4; n = 4; k = 1:n;
3   format long
4   sinx = sum(((-1).^(k-1)).*(x.^(2*k-1))./factorial(2*k-1))
5   exact = sin(x)
6   error = (sinx-exact)/exact
```

About Example02_12c.m

[2] In line 2, the variable `k` is created as a row vector of four elements; `k = [1,2,3,4]`. The `for`-loop in Example02_12b.m is now replaced by a vector expression (line 4), which uses the function `sum` and element-wise operators (`.^`, `.*`, and `./`). To help you understand the statement in line 4, we break it into several steps:

```
step1 = k-1
step2 = (-1).^step1
step3 = 2*k-1
step4 = x.^step3
step5 = step2.*step4
step6 = factorial(step3)
step7 = step5./step6
step8 = sum(step7)
sinx = step8
```

Using `k = [1,2,3,4]`, following the descriptions of element-wise operations (2.8a[6-7], pages 95-96) and the function `sum` for vectors (2.7[5], page 90), we may further elaborate these steps as follows:

```
step1 = [0,1,2,3]
Step2 = (-1).^[0,1,2,3] ≡ [1,-1,1,-1]
step3 = [1,3,5,7]
step4 = x.^[1,3,5,7] ≡ [x,x^3,x^5,x^7]
step5 = [1,-1,1,-1].*[x,x^3,x^5,x^7] ≡ [x,-x^3,x^5,-x^7]
step6 = factorial([1,3,5,7]) ≡ [1,6,120,5040]
step7 = [x,-x^3,x^5,-x^7]./[1,6,120,5040] ≡ [x,-x^3/6,x^5/120,-x^7/5040]
step8 = x-x^3/6+x^5/120-x^7/5040
sinx = x-x^3/6+x^5/120-x^7/5040
```

Substituting `x` with `pi/4`, we have `sinx = 0.707106469575178`. #

2.12d Matrix Expressions

Example02_12d.m: Matrix Expressions

[1] This script calculates sin(x) for various x values and produces a graph as shown in [2], next page. A matrix expression (line 6) is used in this script. ↵

```
1   clear
2   x = linspace(0,pi/2,20);
3   n = 4;
4   k = 1:n;
5   [X, K] = meshgrid(x, k);
6   sinx = sum(((-1).^(K-1)).*(X .^ (2*K-1))./factorial(2*K-1));
7   plot(x*180/pi, sinx, 'o', x*180/pi, sin(x))
8   title('Approximation of sin(x)')
9   xlabel('x (deg)')
10  ylabel('sin(x) (dimensionless)')
11  legend('Approximation', 'Exact', 'Location', 'southeast')
```

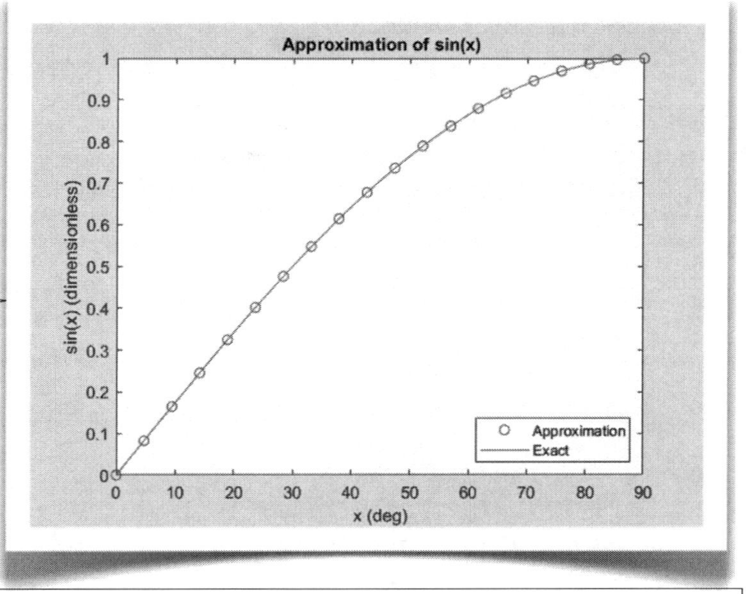

[2] Example02_12d.m plots an approximation of sin(x) using 4-term Taylor series for various x values (circular marks); it also plots a solid curve representing the exact function values. ↓

Function `meshgrid`

[3] Line 2 creates a row vector of 20 x-values using the function `linspace` (2.6a[5], page 85). Line 4 creates a row vector of four integers.

Line 5 generates 2-D grid coordinates `X` and `K` based on the coordinates in the row vectors `x` and `k`; the sizes of `X` and `K` are also based on the sizes of `x` and `k`. If the length of `x` is `nx` and the length of `k` is `nk`, then both `X` and `K` are `nk`-by-`nx` matrices; each row of `X` is a copy of `x`, and each column of `K` is a copy of `k'`. In other words, line 5 is equivalent to the following statements:

```
nx = length(x); nk = length(k);
X = repmat(x, nk, 1);
K = repmat(k', 1, nx);
```

where the function `repmat` was used in lines 5-6 of Example01_06.m (page 25) and explained in 1.6[11-12] (pages 26-27). Actually, lines 5-6 of Example01_06.m can be replaced by the following statement (try it yourself):

```
[Time, Theta] = meshgrid(time, theta)
```

In line 5 of Example02_12d.m, last page, both `X` and `K` are matrices. X contains angle values varying along column-direction while keeping constant in row-direction. `K` contains item-numbers (1, 2, 3, and 4) varying along row-direction while keeping constant in column-direction. Please verify this yourself.

Matrix Expression (Line 6)

Analysis of line 6 is similar to line 4 of Example02_12c (see 2.12c[2], last page). However, now we're dealing with matrices. The argument of the function `sum` is now a 4-by-20 matrix, each column corresponding to an angle value, each row corresponding to a `k` value. The function `sum` sums up the four values in each column (2.7[6], page 91), resulting in a row vector of 20 values, which are plotted as circular marks in [2].

Plotting Marks and Curve

Line 7 plots the 20 values with circular marks, along with the exact function values, by default, using a solid line. Line 11 adds legends (Section 5.7) on the lower-right corner of the graphic area. #

2.12e Multiple Curves

Example02_12e.m: Multiple Curves

[1] This script plots four approximated curves and an exact curve of sin(x) as shown in [2], the four approximated curves corresponding to the Taylor series of 1, 2, 3, and 4 items, respectively. ↓

```
1   clear
2   x = linspace(0,pi/2,20);
3   n = 4;
4   k = 1:n;
5   [X, K] = meshgrid(x, k);
6   sinx = cumsum(((-1).^(K-1)).*(X .^ (2*K-1))./factorial(2*K-1));
7   plot(x*180/pi, sinx(1,:), '+-', ...
8        x*180/pi, sinx(2,:), 'x-', ...
9        x*180/pi, sinx(3,:), '*', ...
10       x*180/pi, sinx(4,:), 'o', ...
11       x*180/pi, sin(x))
12  title('Approximation of sin(x)')
13  xlabel('x (deg)')
14  ylabel('sin(x) (dimensionless)')
15  legend('1 term', '2 terms', '3 terms', '4 terms', 'Exact', ...
16         'Location', 'southeast')
```

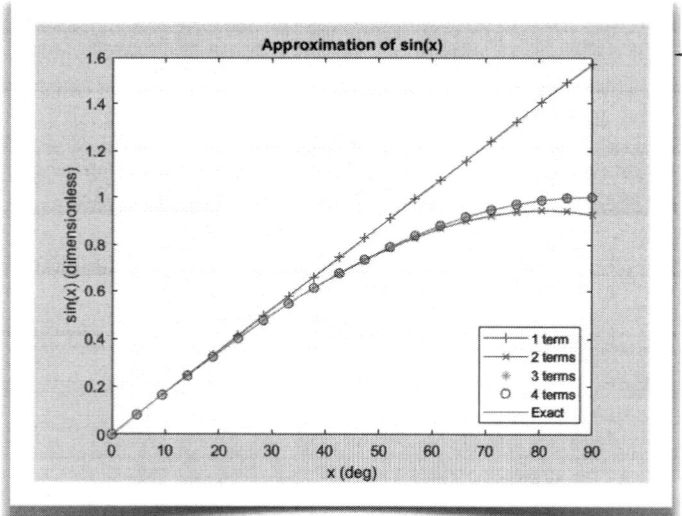

[2] Example02_12e.m plots four approximated curves and an exact curve of sin(x), for comparison. ↓

About Example02_12e.m

[3] Line 6 looks like line 6 in Example02_12d.m except that the function `cumsum` (2.7[6], page 91) is used in place of `sum`. The function `cumsum` calculates the cumulative sums of the four values in each column, resulting in a 4-by-20 matrix, the kth row representing the approximated function values when `k` terms are added up. Lines 7-11 plot the four approximated curves, each a row of the function values, and the exact curve. ↓

Line Styles and Marker Types

[4] In line 7, the notation `'+-'` means a plus **marker** and a solid **line style**. Similarly, in line 8, `'x-'` means a cross marker and a solid line style. Table 5.5a (page 226) lists various line styles and marker types.

Legend

Lines 15-16 add a **Legend** (Section 5.7) on the "southeast" (i.e., the lower-right) of the **Axes**. #

2.13 Example: Series Solution of a Laplace Equation

Laplace Equations

[1] Laplace equations have many applications (see *Wikipedia>Laplace's equation* or any Engineering Mathematics textbooks). Consider a Laplace equation in a two-dimensional, cartesian coordinate system:

$$\frac{\partial^2 \phi}{\partial x^2} + \frac{\partial^2 \phi}{\partial y^2} = 0$$

subject to the boundary conditions $\phi(x,0) = \phi(x,1) = \phi(1,y) = 0$ and $\phi(0,y) = y(1-y)$, where $0 \le x \le 1$ and $0 \le y \le 1$.

A series solution of the equation is

$$\phi(x,y) = 4\sum_{k=1}^{\infty} \frac{1-\cos(k\pi)}{(k\pi)^3} e^{-k\pi x} \sin(k\pi y) \qquad \text{(a)}$$

You may verify the solution by substituting it into the equation and the boundary conditions. ↓

Example02_13.m: Series Solution of a Laplace Equation

[2] This script calculates the solution $\phi(x,y)$ according to Eq. (a) and plots a three-dimensional surface $\phi = \phi(x,y)$ [3]. ↓

```
clear
k = 1:20;
x = linspace(0,1,30);
y = linspace(0,1,40);
[X,Y,K]  = meshgrid(x, y, k);
Phi = sum(4*(1-cos(K*pi))./(K*pi).^3.*exp(-K.*X*pi).*sin(K.*Y*pi), 3);
surf(x, y, Phi)
xlabel('\itx')
ylabel('\ity')
zlabel('\phi(\itx\rm,\ity\rm)')
```

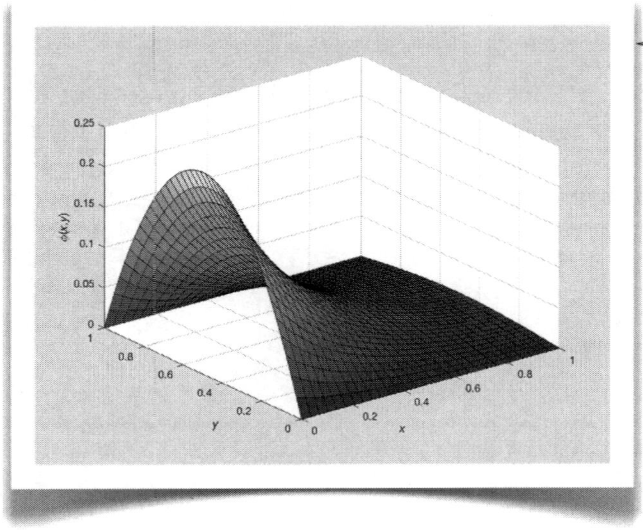

[3] This program plots a surface representing the solution Eq. (a) of a Laplace equation. ↓

[4] **Workspace.** ↵

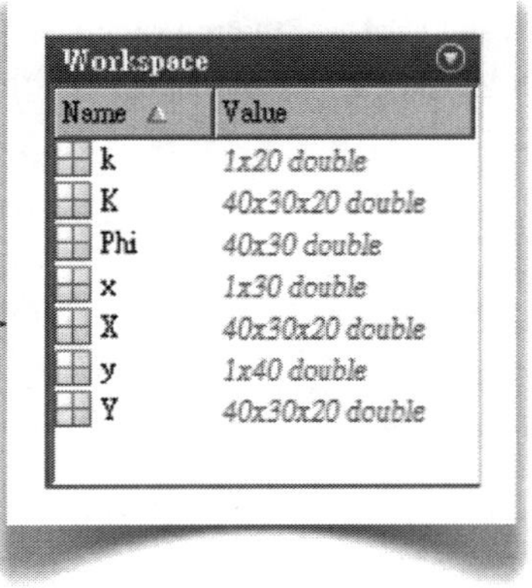

3-D Grid Coordinates Created with `meshgrid`

[5] Line 5 generates 3-D grid coordinates `X`, `Y`, and `K` defined by the row vectors `x`, `y`, and `k`. If the lengths of `x`, `y`, and `k` are `nx`, `ny`, and `nk`, respectively, then `X`, `Y`, and `K` have sizes `ny`-by-`nx`-by-`nk` (see [4], last page). This statement is equivalent to the following statements:

```
nx = length(x); ny = length(y); nk = length(k);
X = repmat(x, ny, 1, nk);
Y = repmat(y', 1, nx, nk);
K = repmat(reshape(k,1,1,nk), ny, nx, 1);
```

The function `reshape` in the last statement reshapes the vector `k` to a $1\times1\times nk$ vector, which is called a **page-vector** (remember that a $1\times m$ matrix is a **row-vector**, and an $m\times1$ matrix is a **column-vector**). Note that `X` varies in column-dimension while keeping constant in both row-dimension and page-dimension; `Y` varies in row-dimension while keeping constant in both column-dimension and page-dimension; `K` varies in page-dimension while keeping constant in both row-dimension and column-dimension.

3-D Array Expressions (Line 6)

While the expression in line 6 of Example02_12d.m (page 110) is a matrix expression, the expression in line 6, last page, is a 3D extension of matrix expressions.

Remember, by default, function `sum` sums up the values along the first dimension (i.e., the row-dimension, see 2.7[6], page 91); however, you may specify the dimension along which the summing is performed. Here, in line 6, the second argument of the function `sum` specifies that the summing is along the third-dimension (i.e., the page-dimension), resulting in a 40-by-30 matrix.

Function `surf`

In line 9 of Example01_06.m (page 25), the function `surf` takes three matrices as input arguments. Here, in line 7 (last page) the first two input arguments are row vectors. Line 7 is equivalent to the following statements

```
nx = length(x); ny = length(y);
X = repmat(x, ny, 1);
Y = repmat(y', 1, nx);
surf(X, Y, Phi);
```

Greek Letters and Math Symbols

Lines 8-10 add label texts to the plot. Here, to display the Greek letter ϕ, the character sequence `\phi` is used (line 10).

The character sequence `\it` (italicize) is used to signal the beginning of a series of italicized characters, and `\rm` is used to signal the removing of the italicization.

The character sequence for frequently used Greek letters and math symbols is listed in Table 5.6a (page 229). #

2.14 Example: Deflection of Beams

Simply Supported Beams

[1] Consider a simply supported beam subject to a force F (see [2], *source: https://en.wikipedia.org/wiki/File:Simple_beam_with_offset_load.svg, by Hermanoere*). The beam has a cross section of width w and height h, and a Young's modulus E. The deflection y of the beam as a function of x is (*Reference: W. C. Young, Roark's Formula for Stress & Strain, 6th ed, p. 100*)

$$y = -\theta x + \frac{Rx^3}{6EI} - \frac{F}{6EI} < x - a >^3$$

where

$$\theta = \frac{Fa}{6EIL}(2L-a)(L-a),\ R = \frac{F}{L}(L-a),\ I = \frac{wh^3}{12}$$

$$< x - a >^3 = \begin{cases} 0, \text{ if } x \le a \\ (x-a)^3, \text{ if } x > a \end{cases}$$

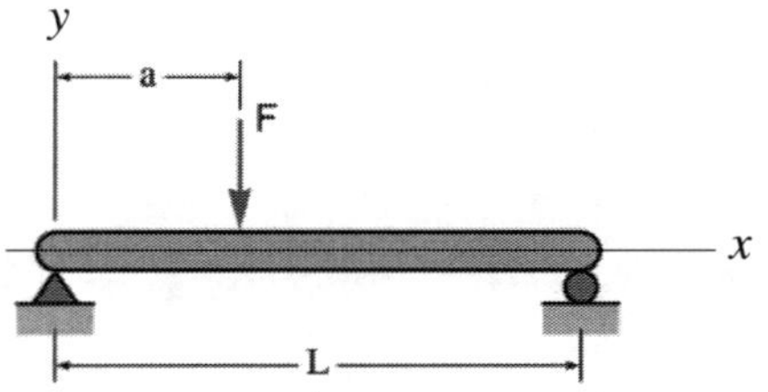

[2] This is the simply supported beam considered in this section. ↓

Physical meanings of these quantities are as follows: θ is the clockwise rotational angle of the beam at the left end; R is the reaction force on the beam at the left end; I is the area moment of inertia of the cross section.

In this section, we'll plot a deflection curve and find the maximum deflection and its corresponding location, using the following parameters:

$w = 0.1$ m, $h = 0.1$ m, $L = 8$ m, $E = 210$ GPa, $F = 3000$ N, $a = L/4$ →

Example02_14.m: Deflection of Beams

[3] This script produces a graphic output shown in [4] (next page) and a text output shown in [5] (next page). ↵

```
clear
w = 0.1;
h = 0.1;
L = 8;
E = 210e9;
F = 3000;
a = L/4;
I = w*h^3/12;
R = F/L*(L-a);
theta = F*a/(6*E*I*L)*(2*L-a)*(L-a);
x = linspace(0,L,100);
y = -theta*x+R*x.^3/(6*E*I)-F/(6*E*I)*((x>a).*((x-a).^3));
plot(x,y*1000)
title('Deflection of a Simply Supported Beam')
xlabel('x (m)'); ylabel('Deflection (mm)')
y = -y;
[ymax, index] = max(y);
fprintf('Maximum deflection %.2f mm at x = %.2f m\n', ymax*1000, x(index))
```

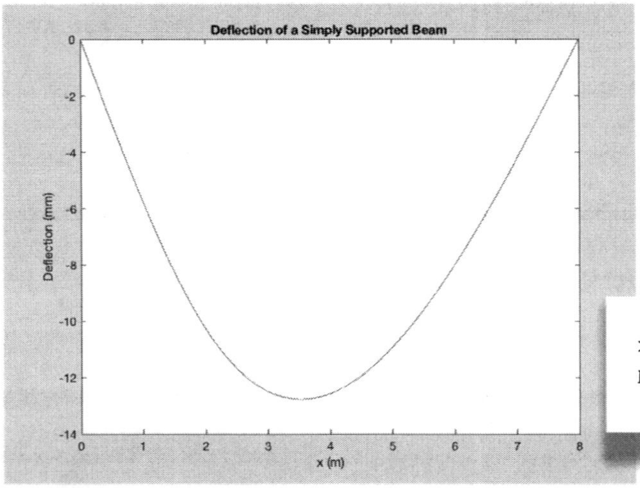

[4] This program plots a curve representing the deflection of the simply supported beam in [1-2], last page. ↓

```
>> Example02_14
Maximum deflection 12.78 mm at x = 3.56 m
```

[5] Text output of the program. ↓

Logical Operators in Numeric Expressions

[6] The function

$$< x - a >^3 \; = \begin{cases} 0, \text{ if } x \le a \\ (x-a)^3, \text{ if } x > a \end{cases}$$

is implemented (see line 12) using a logical operator

```
(x>a).*((x-a).^3)
```

Remember that, in a numeric expression, `true` is converted to 1 and `false` is converted to 0. ↓

[7] This is the solution output by a program using finite element methods; the maximum deflection (12.783 mm) is consistent with the value in [5]. #

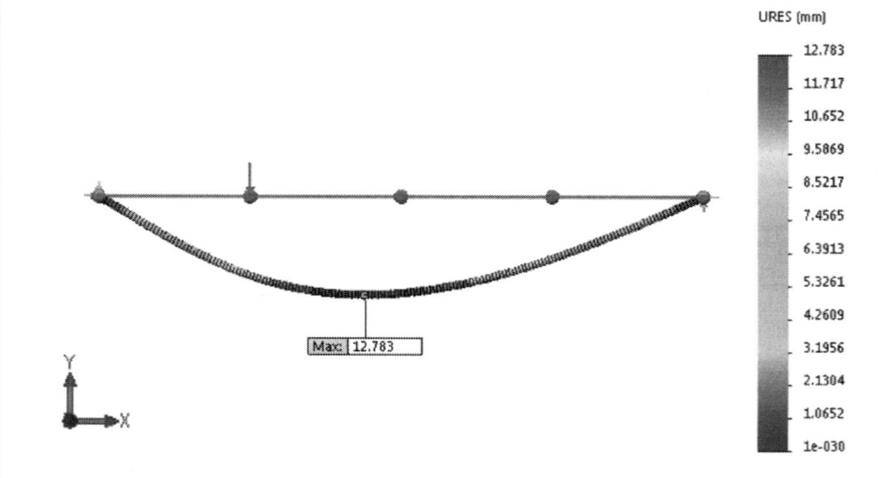

2.15 Example: Vibrations of Supported Machines

2.15a Undamped Free Vibrations

Free Vibrations of a Supported Machine

[1] The figure shown in [2] (*source: https://commons.wikimedia.org/wiki/File:Mass_spring_damper.svg, by Pbroks13*) represents a machine supported by a layer of elastic, energy-absorbing material. In the figure, m is the mass of the machine; k is the spring constant of the support; i.e., $F_s = -kx$, where F_s is the elastic force acting on the machine and x is the displacement of the machine; c is the damping constant; i.e., $F_d = -c\dot{x}$, where F_d is the damping force acting on the machine and $\dot{x}$ is the velocity of the machine. (*Reference: Wikipedia>Damping.*)

Imagine that you lift the machine upward a distance δ from its static equilibrium position and then release. The machine would vibrate up-and-down. It is called a **free vibration**, since no external forces are involved.

To derive the governing equation, consider that the machine moves with a displacement x and a velocity $\dot{x}$. The machine is subject to an elastic force $F_s = -kx$ and a damping force $F_d = -c\dot{x}$. Newton's second law states that the resultant force acting on the machine is equal to the multiplication of the mass m and its acceleration $\ddot{x}$. We have $-kx - c\dot{x} = m\ddot{x}$, or

$$m\ddot{x} + c\dot{x} + kx = 0$$

with the initial conditions (ICs)

$$x(0) = \delta, \ \dot{x}(0) = 0$$

→

[2] In this section, we use this mass-spring-damper model to represent a machine supported by a layer of elastic, energy-absorbing material. ↓

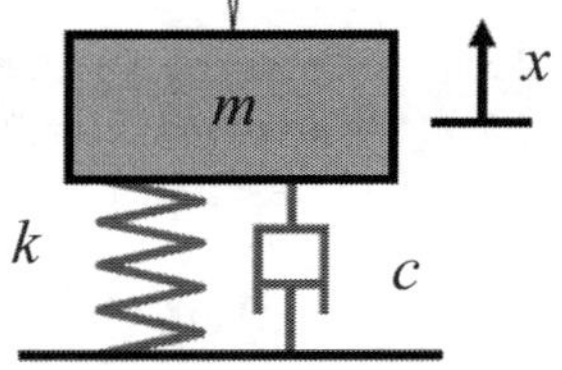

Undamped Free Vibrations

[3] First, we neglect the damping effects of the supporting material, i.e., $c = 0$. The equation reduces to

$$m\ddot{x} + kx = 0, \ \text{ICs: } x(0) = \delta, \ \dot{x}(0) = 0 \quad \text{(a)}$$

The solution for Eq. (a) is

$$x(t) = \delta \cos \omega t \quad \text{(b)}$$

where ω (with SI unit rad/s) is the natural frequency of the undamped system,

$$\omega = \sqrt{\frac{k}{m}} \quad \text{(c)}$$

You may verify the solution (b) by substituting it to Eq. (a).

The natural period (with SI unit s) is then

$$T = \frac{2\pi}{\omega} \quad \text{(d)}$$

Example02_15a.m ([4], next page) calculates and plots the solution, using the following parameters

$$m = 1 \text{ kg}, \ k = 100 \text{ N/m}, \ \delta = 0.2 \text{ m}$$

Note that these values are arbitrarily chosen for instructional purposes; they may not be practical in the real-world. ↵

[5] This is the output of Example02_15a.m. Without damping effects, the machine vibrates forever; i.e., the amplitudes never fade away. #

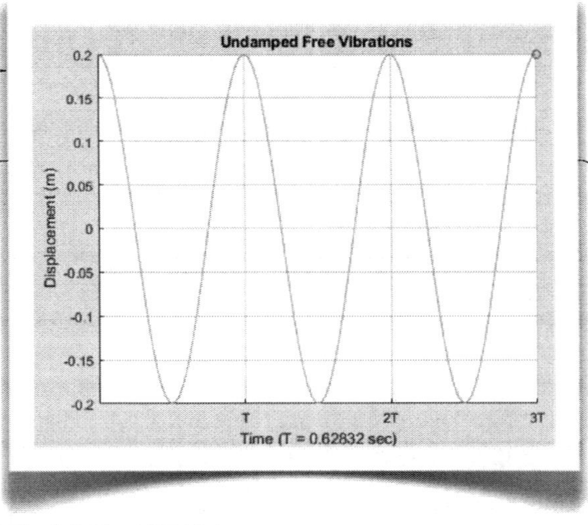

Example02_15a.m: Undamped Free Vibrations

[4] This program calculates and plots the solution $x(t)$ in Eqs. (b, c), last page. The graphic output is shown in [5]. ↑

```
clear
m = 1; k = 100; delta = 0.2;
omega = sqrt(k/m);
T = 2*pi/omega;
t = linspace(0, 3*T, 100);
x = delta*cos(omega*t);
axes('XTick', T:T:3*T, 'XTickLabel', {'T','2T','3T'});
axis([0, 3*T, -0.2, 0.2])
grid on
hold on
comet(t, x)
title('Undamped Free Vibrations')
xlabel(['Time (T = ', num2str(T), ' sec)'])
ylabel('Displacement (m)')
```

2.15b Damped Free Vibrations

[1] Now we include the damping effects of the supporting material and assume $c = 1\ \text{N/(m/s)}$. The equation becomes

$$m\ddot{x} + c\dot{x} + kx = 0,\quad \text{ICs: } x(0) = \delta,\ \dot{x}(0) = 0 \tag{a}$$

There exists a critical damping $c_c = 2m\omega$ such that when $c > c_c$, the machine doesn't oscillate and it is called an **over-damped** case. When $c < c_c$, the machine oscillates and it is called an **under-damped** case. When $c = c_c$, the machine also doesn't oscillate and it is called a **critically-damped** case. In our case,

$$\omega = \sqrt{\frac{k}{m}} = \sqrt{\frac{100\,\text{N/m}}{1\text{ kg}}} = 10\ \text{rad/s}$$

$$c_c = 2m\omega = 2(1\text{ kg})(10\text{ rad/s}) = 20\ \text{N/(m/s)}$$

Since $c < c_c$, the system is an under-damped case. The solution for the under-damped case is

$$x(t) = \delta e^{-\frac{ct}{2m}}\left(\cos\omega_d t + \frac{c}{2m\omega_d}\sin\omega_d t\right) \tag{b}$$

where ω_d (with SI unit rad/s) is the natural frequency of the damped system,

$$\omega_d = \omega\sqrt{1 - \left(\frac{c}{c_c}\right)^2} \tag{c}$$

where c/c_c is called the **damping ratio**. In our case $c/c_c = 0.05$. Note that, for small damping ratios, $\omega_d \approx \omega$. ↵

[3] The output of Example02_15b.m. Due to the inclusion of the damping effects, the vibrations gradually fade away. #

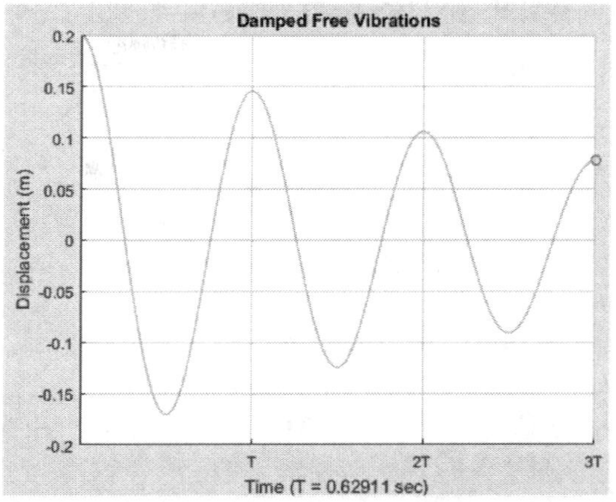

Example02_15b.m: Damped Free Vibrations

[2] This program calculates and plots the solution *x*(*t*) in Eqs. (b, c), last page. The graphic output is shown in [3]. ↑

```
clear
m = 1; k = 100; c = 1; delta = 0.2;
omega = sqrt(k/m);
cC = 2*m*omega;
omegaD = omega*sqrt(1-(c/cC)^2);
T = 2*pi/omegaD;
t = linspace(0, 3*T, 100);
x = delta*exp(-c*t/(2*m)).*(cos(omegaD*t)+c/(2*m*omegaD)*sin(omegaD*t));
axes('XTick', T:T:3*T, 'XTickLabel', {'T','2T','3T'});
axis([0, 3*T, -0.2, 0.2])
grid on
hold on
comet(t, x)
title('Damped Free Vibrations')
xlabel(['Time (T = ', num2str(T), ' sec)'])
ylabel('Displacement (m)')
```

2.15c Harmonically Forced Vibrations

[1] Now, imagine that there is a rotating part in the machine and, due to eccentric rotations, the rotating part generates an up-and-down harmonic force $F\sin\omega_f t$ on the support, where ω_f is the angular frequency of the rotating part and F is the centrifugal forces due to the eccentric rotations. We assume $F = 2$ N and $\omega_f = 2\pi$ rad/s (i.e., 1 Hz). Adding this force to Newton's second law, we have the equation

$$m\ddot{x} + c\dot{x} + kx = F\sin\omega_f t \tag{a}$$

The solution of Eq. (a) is a superposition of two parts: First, the free vibrations caused by the initial conditions. This part will eventually vanish due to the damping effects, as shown in 2.15b[3], and is called the **transient response**. Second, the vibrations caused by the harmonic forces. This part remains even after the transient vibrations vanish and is called the **steady-state response**, described by

$$x(t) = x_m \sin(\omega_f t - \varphi) \tag{b}$$

where x_m is the amplitude and φ is the **phase angle** (see *Wikipedia>Phase (wave)*) of the vibrations,

$$x_m = \frac{F/k}{\sqrt{\left[1-(\omega_f/\omega)^2\right]^2 + \left[2(c/c_c)(\omega_f/\omega)\right]^2}} \tag{c}$$

$$\varphi = \tan^{-1}\frac{2(c/c_c)(\omega_f/\omega)}{1-(\omega_f/\omega)^2} \tag{d}$$

↵

Example02_15c.m: Forced Vibrations

[2] This program plots the steady-state response *x*(*t*) in Eqs. (b, c, d), last page. The graphic output is shown in [3]. ↓

```
clear
% System parameters
m = 1; k = 100; c = 1;
f = 2; omegaF = 2*pi;

% System response
omega = sqrt(k/m);
cC = 2*m*omega;
rC = c/cC;
rW = omegaF/omega;
xm = (f/k)/sqrt((1-rW^2)^2+(2*rC*rW)^2);
phi = atan((2*rC*rW)/(1-rW^2));
T = 2*pi/omegaF;
t = linspace(0, 3*T, 100);
x = xm*sin(omegaF*t-phi);

% Graphic output
axes('XTick', T:T:3*T, 'XTickLabel', {'T','2T','3T'});
axis([0, 3*T, -0.2, 0.2])
grid on
hold on
comet(t, x)
title('Harmonically Forced Vibrations')
xlabel(['Time (T = ', num2str(T), ' sec)'])
ylabel('Displacement (m)')
text(T,-0.1,['Amplitude = ', num2str(xm*1000), ' mm'])
text(T,-0.12,['Phase angle = ', num2str(phi*180/pi), ' degrees'])
```

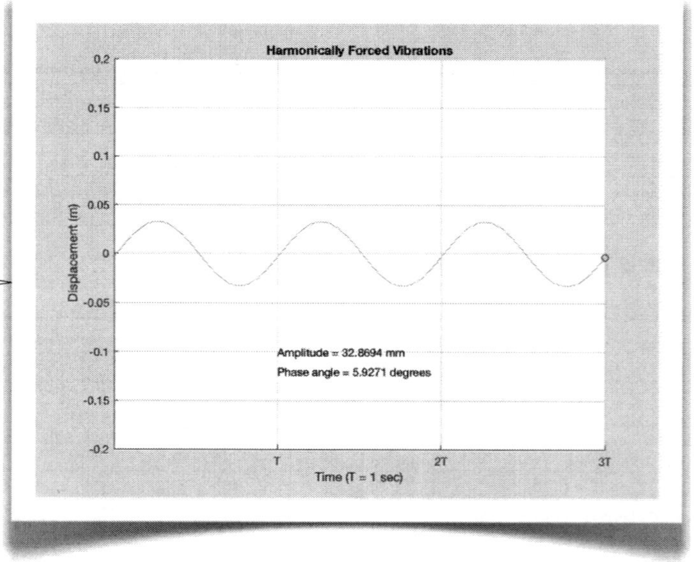

[3] The output of Example02_15c.m. #

2.16 Additional Exercise Problems

Problem02_01: Moment of Inertia of an Area

Write a script to calculate the moments of inertia (*Wikipedia>Second moment of area*) I_x and I_y of a Z-shape area shown below. Check your results with the following data: $I_x = 4{,}190{,}040$ mm^4 and $I_y = 2{,}756{,}960$ mm^4. A hand-calculation procedure is listed in the table below, in which the Z-shape area is divided into three rectangles; their area properties are calculated separately and then totaled.

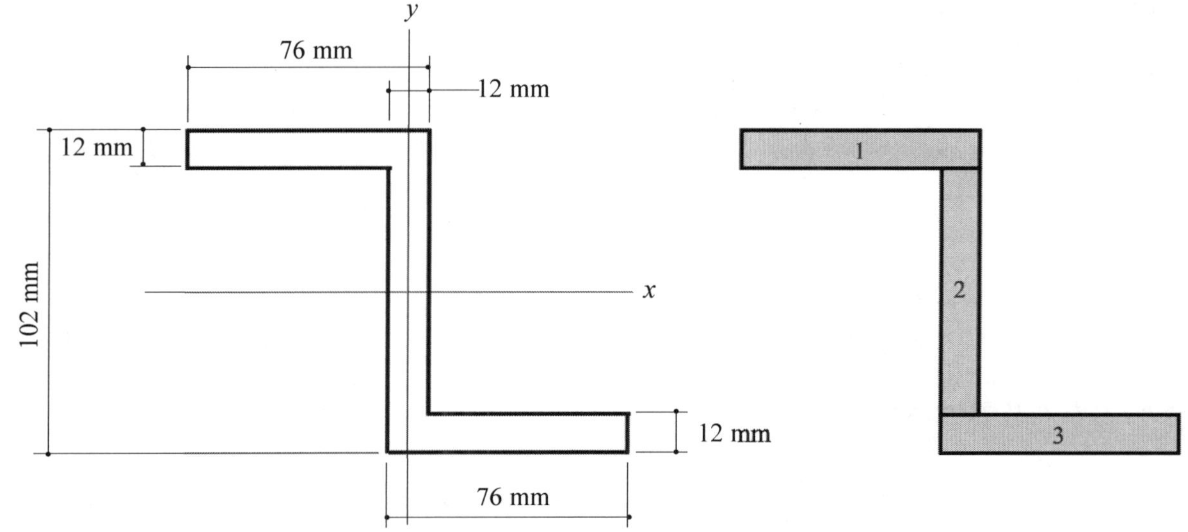

Rectangle	b mm	h mm	$\bar{x}$ mm	$\bar{y}$ mm	$\bar{I}_x$ mm^4	$\bar{I}_y$ mm^4	A mm^2	$A\bar{y}^2$ mm^4	$A\bar{x}^2$ mm^4	I_x mm^4	I_y mm^4
1	76	12	-32	45	10944	438976	912	1846800	933888	1857744	1372864
2	12	78	0	0	474552	11232	936	0	0	474552	11232
3	76	12	32	-45	10944	438976	912	1846800	933888	1857744	1372864
Total							2760			4190040	2756960
Notes: $\bar{I}_x = bh^3/12$, $\bar{I}_y = hb^3/12$, $A = bh$, $I_x = \bar{I}_x + A\bar{y}^2$, $I_y = \bar{I}_y + A\bar{x}^2$											

Problem02_02: Binomial Coefficient

The binomial coefficient (*Wikipedia>Binomial coefficient*) is given by

$$C_x^n = \frac{n!}{x!(n-x)!}$$

where both n and x are integer number and $x \le n$. Write a script that allows the user to input the values of n and x, calculates C_x^n, and reports the result.

Use the following data to verify your program: $C_3^{10} = 120$, $C_{10}^{15} = 3003$, and $C_4^{100} = 3{,}921{,}225$.

Problem02_03: Binomial Distribution

The binomial distribution (*Wikipedia>Binomial distribution*) is given by

$$f(x) = C_x^n p^x (1-p)^{n-x},\ x = 0,\ 1,\ 2,\ \ldots,\ n$$

where p is a real number ($0 < p < 1$) and C_x^n is given in Problem02_02, last page. Write a script that allows the user to input the values of n and p, and produces a binomial distribution curve.

Use $n = 100$ and $p = 0.5$ to verify your program, which produces a binomial distribution curve as shown to the right.

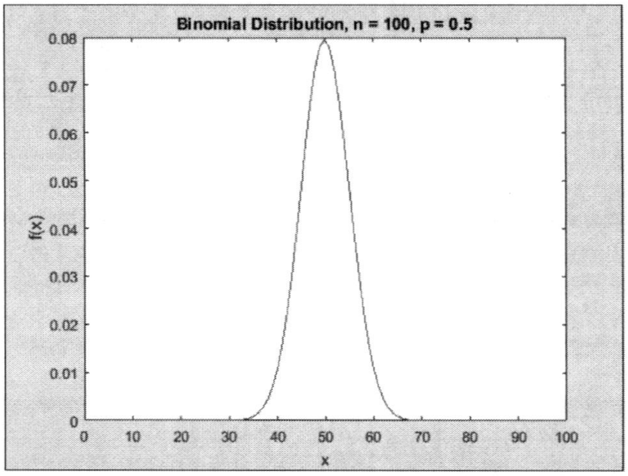

Problem02_04: Thermal Stresses in a Pipe

The radial stress σ_r and hoop stress σ_h in a long pipe due to a temperature T_a at its inner surface of radius a and a temperature T_b at its outer surface of radius b are, respectively, (*A. H. Burr and J. B. Cheatham, Mechanical Analysis and Design, 2nd ed., Prentice Hall, p. 496.*)

$$\sigma_r = \frac{\alpha E(T_a - T_b)}{2(1-\nu)\ln(b/a)}\left[\frac{a^2}{b^2-a^2}\left(\frac{b^2}{r^2}-1\right)\ln(b/a) - \ln(b/r)\right]$$

$$\sigma_h = \frac{\alpha E(T_a - T_b)}{2(1-\nu)\ln(b/a)}\left[1 - \frac{a^2}{b^2-a^2}\left(\frac{b^2}{r^2}+1\right)\ln(b/a) - \ln(b/r)\right]$$

where r is the radial coordinate of the pipe (originated at the center), E is the Young's modulus, ν is the Poisson's ratio, and α is the coefficient of thermal expansion.

Write a script that allows the user to input the values of a, b, T_a and T_b, and generates a σ_r-versus-r curve and a σ_h-versus-r curve as shown to the right, which uses the following data: $a = 6$ mm, $b = 12$ mm, $T_a = 260^\circ C$, $T_b = 150^\circ C$, $E = 206$ GPa, $\nu = 0.3$, $\alpha = 2 \times 10^{-5}\ /^\circ$C.

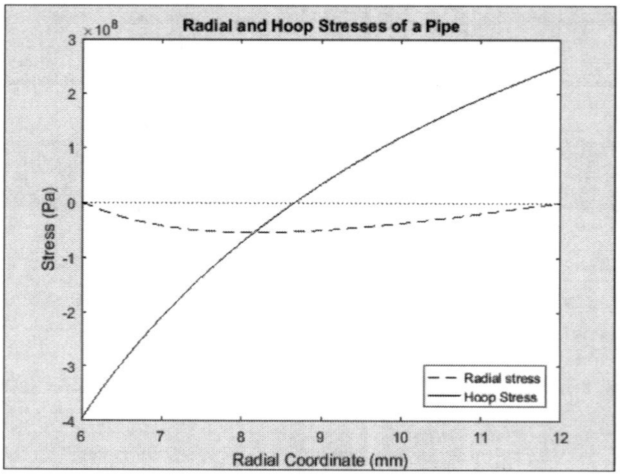

Problem02_05: Displacement of a Piston

The displacement p of the piston shown in 6.3[3-7] (page 261) is given by

$$p = a\cos\theta + \sqrt{b^2 - a\sin\theta}$$

Write a script to plot the displacement p as a function of angle θ (in degrees; $0 \le \theta \le 360^\circ$) when $a = 1.1$ and $b = 2.7$.

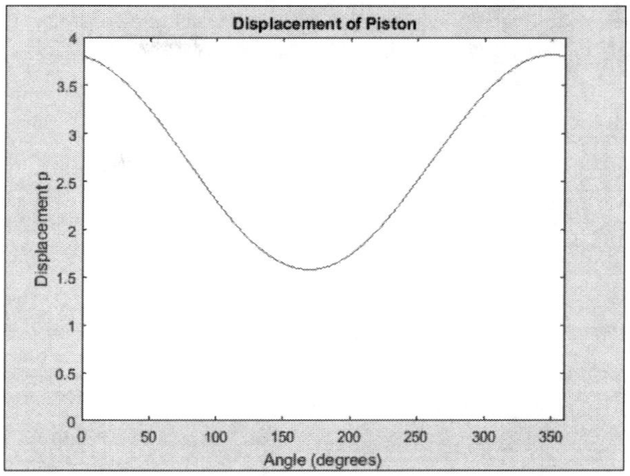

Problem02_06: Calculation of π

The ratio of a circle's circumference to its diameter, π, can be approximated by the following formula:

$$\pi = \sum_{k=0}^{n} \left(\frac{4}{8k+1} - \frac{2}{8k+4} - \frac{1}{8k+5} - \frac{1}{8k+6} \right) \left(\frac{1}{16} \right)^k$$

Write a script that allows the user to input the value of n, and outputs the calculated value of π.

Problem02_07

Write a script to generate a mesh, using `mesh(x,y,z)`, defined by

$$z(x,y) = \frac{32}{3\pi} \sum_{k=0}^{50} \frac{\sin(k\pi/4)}{k^2} \sin(k\pi x)\cos(k\pi y)$$

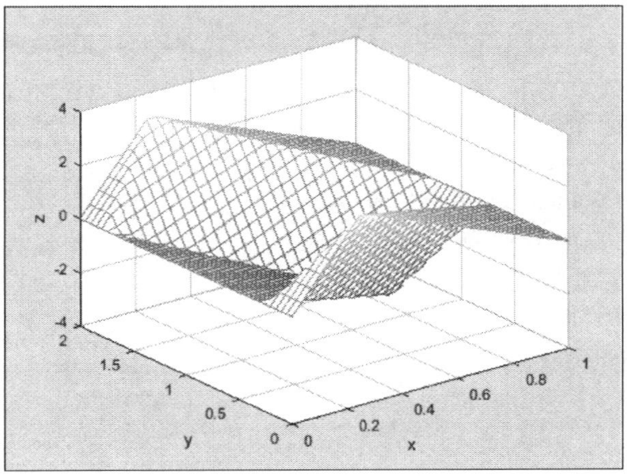

Chapter 3

Flow Controls, Functions, and Programs

A program may consist of one or more program files; one of them is the main program file. Each program file may consist of a main program and functions. If a program file starts with a function, it is called a main function; other functions are called subfunctions, nested functions, or anonymous functions. Subfunctions are local to the program file to which they belong, while nested functions and anonymous functions are local to the function to which they belong. Execution of a program starts from the main program (or main function) of the main program file.

3.1 If-Blocks

Syntax and Semantics: if-Blocks

[1] The syntax for an `if`-block is

```
if logical-expr1
    statements1
elseif logical-expr2
    statements2
...
    ...
else
    statements3
end
```

An `if`-block begins with an `if`-statement and closes with an `end` statement. The `elseif` and `else` blocks are optional. An if-block may include multiple `elseif` blocks, but may include only one `else` block.

In the `if`-block, *`logical-expr1`* is evaluated. If the value is `true`, *`statements1`* (which can be single or multiple statements) is executed. Otherwise, *`logical-expr2`* is evaluated, and so on. Finally, if none of the logical expressions are `true`, *`statements3`* is executed. ↓

Example03_01.m: If-Blocks

```
clear
n1 = input('Enter a number: ');
n2 = input('Enter another number: ');
disp('Test #1')
string = 'At least one is non-positive';
if n1>0 && n2>0
    string = 'Both are positive';
end
disp(string)

disp('Test #2')
if n1>0 && n2>0
    disp('Both are positive.')
else
    disp('At least one is non-positive.')
end

disp('Test #3')
if n1>0 && n2>0
    disp('Both are positive.')
elseif n1==0 || n2 == 0
    disp('At least one is zero.')
else
    disp('At least one is negative.')
end

disp('Test #4')
if n1>0 && n2>0
    disp('Both are positive.')
elseif n1==0 || n2 == 0
    disp('At least one is zero.')
elseif n1*n2 < 0
    disp('They have opposite signs.')
else
    disp('Both are negative')
end

disp('Test #5')
a = [n1, n2];
if all(a>0)
    disp('Both are positive')
elseif any(a>0)
    disp('One of them is positive.')
else
    disp('None of them is positive.')
end
```

[2] This program demonstrates the use of `if`-blocks. It requests two numbers and reports the nature of the two numbers. See [3] (next page) for an input/output session. ↵

```
>> Example03_01
Enter a number: 5
Enter another number: -2
Test #1
At least one is non-positive
Test #2
At least one is non-positive.
Test #3
At least one is negative.
Test #4
They have opposite signs.
Test #5
One of them is positive.
>>
```

[3] A test-run of Example03_01.m. ↓

Functions `any` and `all`

[4] The function `any` and `all` (lines 40 and 42) can be used to test a logical array. For a logical array `g`, the function `any(g)` outputs `true` if any of the elements are `true`, otherwise it outputs `false`; the function `all(g)` outputs `true` if all of the elements are `true`, otherwise it outputs `false`. ↓

Multiple Statements in a Single Line

[5] Separated by commas (`,`) or semicolons (`;`), multiple statements can be written in a single line. This is also true for an `if`-block. For example:

```
n = input('Enter a number: ');
if n>0, disp('Positive!'), end
```

The comma after the `if` statement can be omitted, but the comma after an executable statement (here, `disp`) cannot be omitted:

```
n = input('Enter a number: ');
if n>0 disp('Positive!'), end
```

Another example:

```
n = input('Enter a number: ');
if n>0 disp('Positive!'), else, disp('Non-positive!'), end
```

The comma after the `else` can be omitted:

```
n = input('Enter a number: ');
if n>0 disp('Positive!'), else disp('Non-positive!'), end
```

The comma after an `elseif` also can be omitted, for example

```
n = input('Enter a number: ');
if n>0 disp('+'), elseif n==0 disp('0'), else disp('-'), end
```

The purpose of these demonstrations is to show some grammatical concepts, not to encourage you to write these ways. I suggest that you always write an `if`-block in a structured block, as demonstrated in [2], last page. #

3.2 Switch-Blocks

3.2a Syntax and Semantics

[1] The syntax for a `switch`-block is

```
switch expr
    case expr1
        statements1
    case expr2
        statements2
    ...
        ...
    otherwise
        statements3
end
```

A `switch`-block begins with a `switch`-statement and closes with an `end` statement. The `otherwise` block is optional. The result of *`expr`* must be a numeric scalar or a string. The *`expr1`*, *`expr2`*, ... are usually numeric scalars, or strings.

When *`expr`*, *`expr1`*, `expr2`, ... are numeric scalars, the `switch`-block is equivalent to the following `if`-block:

```
if expr == expr1
    statements1
elseif expr == expr2
     statements2
...
    ...
else
    statements3
end
```

When *`expr`*, *`expr1`*, `expr2`, ... are strings, the `switch`-block is equivalent to the following `if`-block:

```
if strcmp(expr,expr1)
    statements1
elseif strcmp(expr,expr2)
     statements2
...
    ...
else
    statements3
end
```

↗

Example03_02a.m: Pizza Menu

[2] Type and run this program. See [3] for an input/output. ↓

```
clear
fprintf(['Cheese\n' ...
    'Mushroom\n' ...
    'Sausage\n' ...
    'Pineapple\n'])
choice = input('Choose a pizza: ', 's');
choice = lower(strtrim(choice));
switch choice
    case 'cheese'
        disp('Cheese pizza $3.99')
    case 'mushroom'
        disp('Mushroom pizza $3.66')
    case 'sausage'
        disp('Sausage pizza $4.22')
    case 'pineapple'
        disp('Pineapple pizza $2.99')
    otherwise
        disp('Sorry?')
end
```

```
Cheese
Mushroom
Sausage
Pineapple
Choose a pizza: pineapple
Pineapple pizza $2.99
```

[3] A test-run of Example03_02a.m. You choose a pizza and the program tells you its price. ↵

About Example03_02a.m

[4] Lines 2-5 list a text-based menu on the screen; they could have been written in a single line like this:

```
fprintf('Cheese\nMushroom\nSausage\nPineapple\n')
```

However, it would be hard to read. Note that to split a string into several lines (line 2-5), you need to close the string with a single quote and then open the string at the next line.

In line 7, the user's input string is processed this way: the leading and trailing blanks are removed using `strtrim` and any uppercase characters are converted to lowercase using the function `lower`. #

3.2b Example: A Graphical Pizza Menu

Example03_02b.m: Pizza Menu

[1] Type and run this program. See [2-3] for an input/output. →

```
 1  clear
 2  choice = menu('Choose a pizza', ...
 3      'Cheese', 'Mushroom', 'Sausage', 'Pineapple');
 4  switch choice
 5      case 1
 6          disp('Cheese pizza $3.99')
 7      case 2
 8          disp('Mushroom pizza $3.66')
 9      case 3
10          disp('Sausage pizza $4.22')
11      case 4
12          disp('Pineapple pizza $2.99')
13  end
```

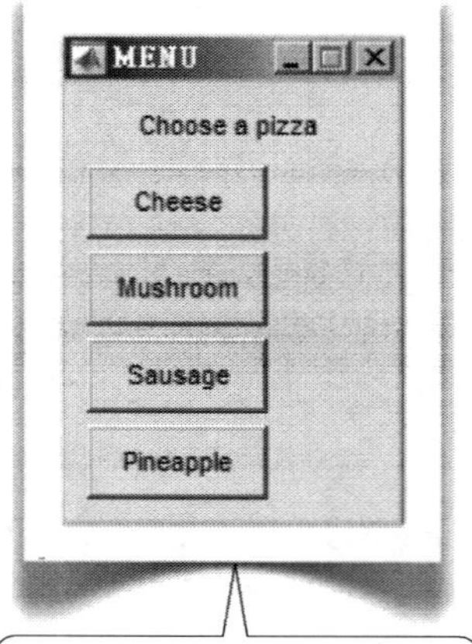

[2] A **menu** is displayed on the screen. Click a button, e.g., **Pineapple**. ↓

[3] A price displays on the **Command Window**. ↓

```
Pineapple pizza $2.99
```

About Example03_02b.m

[4] The function `menu` (lines 2-3) displays a graphics-based menu [2] on the screen, waiting for your clicking. After you click a button, the function returns an integer number indicating the ordinal number of the button.

In this example, the `otherwise` block is not present because the output value from the function `menu` is always 1, 2, 3, or 4.

A small imperfection of either program in this section is that you can ask the price only once. If you want to ask another pizza's price, you have to re-run the program. We'll fix this problem using a `while`-loop, in the next section. #

3.3 While-Loops

3.3a Syntax and Semantics

[1] The syntax for a `while`-loop is

```
while logical-expr
    statements
end
```

A `while`-loop begins with a `while`-statement and closes with an `end` statement. The `while`-loop is equivalent to the following `if`-block:

```
if logical-expr
    statements
    jump to the if-statement
end
```

First, *`logical-expr`* is evaluated. If it is `true`, the *`statements`* is executed and then the execution flow jumps to the `if`-statement and *`logical-expr`* is evaluated again, and so forth. The `while`-loop breaks (jumps out of the loop) when the *`logical-expr`* is `false`. ↓

Example03_03a.m: Pizza Menu

[2] Type and run this program. See [3-4] for an input/output. ↘

```
clear
choice = 0;
while choice ~= 5
    choice = menu('Choose a pizza', ...
        'Cheese', 'Mushroom', 'Sausage', 'Pineapple', 'Quit');
    switch choice
        case 1
            disp('Cheese pizza $3.99')
        case 2
            disp('Mushroom pizza $3.66')
        case 3
            disp('Sausage pizza $4.22')
        case 4
            disp('Pineapple pizza $2.99')
        case 5
            disp('Bye!')
    end
end
```

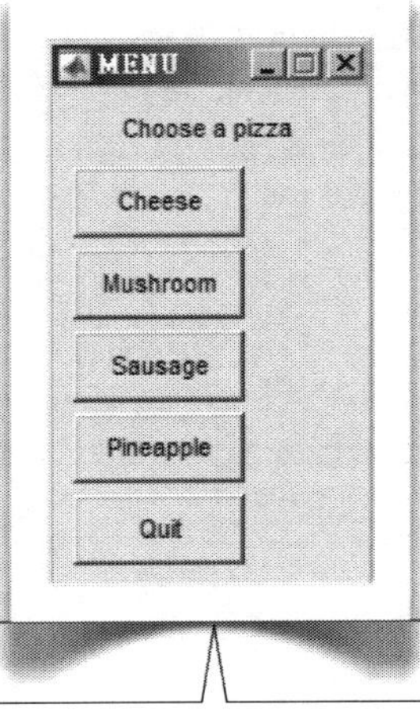

[3] A **menu** is displayed on the screen. Now you can click as many times as you want. When you're satisfied, click **Quit**. ←

```
Sausage pizza $4.22
Mushroom pizza $3.66
Cheese pizza $3.99
Pineapple pizza $2.99
Bye!
```

[4] The prices displayed on the **Command Window**. #

3.3b Forever-True While-Loops

Example03_03b.m: Pizza Menu

[1] Program Example03_03a.m can be slightly modified using a "forever-true `while`-loop" (lines 2-18) and a `break`-statement (line 16). I personally prefer this style to that in Example03_03a.m. ↓

```
 1  clear
 2  while 1
 3      choice = menu('Choose a pizza', ...
 4          'Cheese', 'Mushroom', 'Sausage', 'Pineapple', 'Quit');
 5      switch choice
 6          case 1
 7              disp('Cheese pizza $3.99')
 8          case 2
 9              disp('Mushroom pizza $3.66')
10          case 3
11              disp('Sausage pizza $4.22')
12          case 4
13              disp('Pineapple pizza $2.99')
14          case 5
15              disp('Bye!')
16              break;
17      end
18  end
```

`Break` Statement

[2] A `break`-statement (line 16) terminates (aborts) a `while`-loop (or a `for`-loop, next section); i.e., in this case, the execution flow jumps OUT of the `end`-statement in line 18; in our case, the program stops. A `continue`-statement is similar but different from a `break`-statement. The `continue`-statement instructs the execution flow jump TO the `end`-statement of a `while`-loop or a `for`-loop; in our case, it would jump to the end-statement in line 18 and continue the next pass (See >> *doc continue*). #

3.4 For-Loops

3.4a Syntax and Semantics

[1] A syntax for a `for`-loop is

```
for index = values
    statements
end
```

where *`values`* is usually a row-vector, but it can be an array of any dimension.

A `for`-loop begins with a `for`-statement and closes with an `end`-statement. If the *`values`* is a row-vector, then the above `for`-loop is equivalent to the following `while`-loop:

```
k = 1; n = length(values);
while k <= n
    index = values(k)
    statements
    k = k + 1;
end
```

That is, in each pass of the `for`-loop, an element of *`values`* is used as *`index`* until all the elements are used up.

If the *`values`* is a matrix, then the `for`-loop is equivalent to the following `while`-loop:

```
k = 1; [nr, nc] = size(values);
while k <= nc
    index = values(:,k)
    statements
    k = k + 1;
end
```

Note that the *`index`* is a column-vector now. ↓

Example03_04a.m: For-Loops

[2] The program Example02_13.m (page 113) is rewritten using a `for`-loop as follows. Type and test-run the program. The output is the same as before (2.13[3], page 113); this program uses less memory space (you may compare [3], next page, with 2.13[4], page 113) but may take more computing time. ↵

```
clear
x = linspace(0,1,30);
y = linspace(0,1,40);
[X,Y]  = meshgrid(x, y);
Phi = zeros(40,30);
for k = 1:20
    Phi = Phi+4*(1-cos(k*pi))/(k*pi)^3*exp(-k*X*pi).*sin(k*Y*pi);
end
surf(x, y, Phi)
xlabel('\itx')
ylabel('\ity')
zlabel('\phi(\itx\rm,\ity\rm)')
```

[3] The **Workspace**. ↓

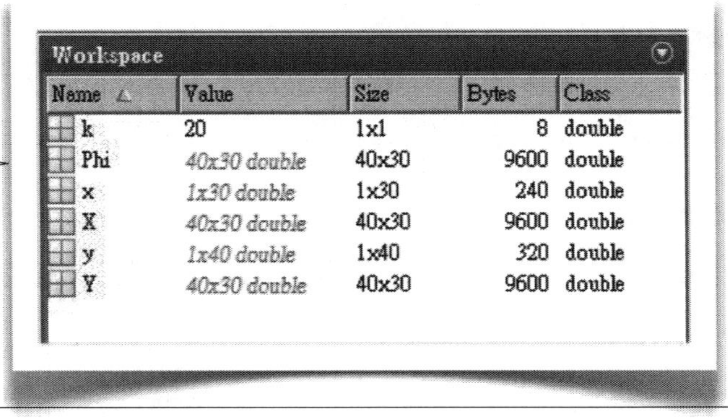

Name	Value	Size	Bytes	Class
k	20	1x1	8	double
Phi	40x30 double	40x30	9600	double
x	1x30 double	1x30	240	double
X	40x30 double	40x30	9600	double
y	1x40 double	1x40	320	double
Y	40x30 double	40x30	9600	double

About Example03_04a.m

[4] Line 4 creates two matrices `X` and `Y`, instead of three three-dimensional arrays as in line 5 of Example02_13.m, page 113, saving a large amount of memory space.

Lines 5-8 replace line 6 of Example02_13.m. Note that the use of element-wise operators in Example02_13.m (`.*`, `./`, and `.^`) becomes unnecessary and ordinary operators (`*`, `/`, and `^`) can be used instead.

The two programs have the same output. As demonstrated here, using `for`-loops reduces the amount of memory. The two matrices `X` and `Y` need 19.2 kB (40x30x2x8 bytes) of memory, while the three 3-D arrays `X`, `Y`, and `K` in Example02_13.m need 576 kB (40x30x20x3x8), 30 times the memory! However, using built-in array operation capabilities (Example02_13.m) is usually faster. We'll discuss this further in 3.4b[2], next page. #

3.4b Nested For-Loops

Example03_04b.m: Nested For-Loops

[1] The *`statements`* inside a `for`-loop (3.4a[1], last page) may include other `for`-loops, called **nested loops**. Type and run the following program. There are 3 layers of `for`-loops. The expression in lines 9-10 is now a scalar expression. The output is the same as before (2.13[3], page 113); the **Workspace** is the same as 3.4a[3] (this page) except that additional two variables (`i` and `j`) are added to the **Workspace**. ↵

```
 1  clear
 2  x = linspace(0,1,30);
 3  y = linspace(0,1,40);
 4  [X,Y]  = meshgrid(x, y);
 5  Phi = zeros(40,30);
 6  for i = 1:40
 7      for j = 1:30
 8          for k = 1:20
 9              Phi(i,j) = Phi(i,j)+4*(1-cos(k*pi))/(k*pi)^3 ...
10                  *exp(-k*X(i,j)*pi)*sin(k*Y(i,j)*pi);
11          end
12      end
13  end
14  surf(x, y, Phi)
15  xlabel('\itx')
16  ylabel('\ity')
17  zlabel('\phi(\itx\rm,\ity\rm)')
```

Measuring Time: Functions `tic` and `toc`

[2] To measure the time needed to execute a portion of a program, we may insert the function `tic` (which starts a stopwatch) before the portion and insert the function `toc` (which stops the stopwatch) after the portion. MATLAB will report on the **Command Window** the **elapsed time** (in seconds) to execute the portion of the program. For example, insert the functions `tic` and `toc` in the program Example03_04b.m as follows:

```
tic
for i = 1:40
    for j = 1:30
        for k = 1:20
            Phi(i,j) = Phi(i,j)+4*(1-cos(k*pi))/(k*pi)^3 ...
                *exp(-k*X(i,j)*pi)*sin(k*Y(i,j)*pi);
        end
    end
end
toc
```

To compare with program Example02_13.m, we also insert functions `tic` and `toc` as follows

```
tic
Phi = sum(4*(1-cos(K*pi))./(K*pi).^3.*exp(-K.*X*pi).*sin(K.*Y*pi), 3);
toc
```

It leaves you to confirm that, as mentioned in 3.4a[4], last page, using built-in array operation capabilities (Example02_13.m, page 113) is usually more efficient in terms of computing time than using `for`-loops (Example03_04a.m or Example03_04b.m). Further, programs using built-in array operation capabilities can be easily adapted to a parallel computing environment. #

3.5 User-Defined Functions

3.5a Syntax and Semantics

Example03_05a.m: User-Defined Functions

[1] Type the following program, which calculates the period and the response of a damped free vibration system based on the formula in Eqs. (b, c), page 118; click **Save** button (1.5[6], page 22) and accept the default file name Example03_05a, which is the same as the function name (line 1). You must accept the default name; the file name must match the main function name in a program file. MATLAB saves the file as Example03_05a.m.

You cannot run this function by clicking the **Run** button (1.5[8], page 22). You must "call" the function and provide its input arguments from the **Command Window** (as demonstrated in [2]), from a **script** (or from a **Live Script**). ↓

```
1   function [T, x] = Example03_05a(m, k, c, delta, t)
2   % Under-damped free vibrations of a mass-spring-damper system
3   % Input Arguments:
4   %       m = Mass, a scalar, SI unit: kg
5   %       k = Spring constant, a scalar, SI unit: N/m
6   %       c = Damping constant, a scalar, SI unit: N/(m/s)
7   %       delta = Initial displacement, a scalar, SI unit: m
8   %       t = Time, a row vector, SI unit: s
9   % Output Arguments:
10  %       T = Period, a scalar, SI unit: s
11  %       x = Displacement, a row vector of the same length of t, SI unit: m
12  % On Error, it prints a message and returns:
13  %       T = 0, a scalar
14  %       x = 0, a scalar
15  omega = sqrt(k/m);
16  cC = 2*m*omega;
17  if c>= cC
18      disp('Not an under-damped system!')
19      T = 0; x = 0;
20      return;
21  end
22  omegaD = omega*sqrt(1-(c/cC)^2);
23  T = 2*pi/omegaD;
24  x = delta*exp(-c*t/(2*m)).*(cos(omegaD*t)+c/(2*m*omegaD)*sin(omegaD*t));
25  end
```

Use of Example03_05a

[2] On the **Command Window**, type the following commands. ↵

```
26  >> doc Example03_05a
27  >> time = linspace(0,5,100);
28  >> [period, response] = Example03_05a(1, 100, 1, 0.2, time);
29  >> plot(time, response)
30  >> Example03_05a(1, 100, 1, 0.2, time)
31  ans =
32      0.6291
```

Example03_05a - MATLAB File Help View code for Example03_05a

Example03_05a

```
Under-damped free vibrations of a mass-spring-damper system
Input Arguments:
    m = Mass, a scalar, SI unit: kg
    k = Spring constant, a scalar, SI unit: N/m
    c = Damping constant, a scalar, SI unit: N/(m/s)
    delta = Initial displacement, a scalar, SI unit: m
    t = Time, a row vector, SI unit: s
Output Arguments:
    T = Period, a scalar, SI unit: s
    x = Displacement, a row vector of the same length of t, SI unit: m
On Error, it prints a message and returns:
    T = 0, a scalar
    x = 0, a scalar
```

[3] Line 26 displays a **Help Window**, listing the **comments** below the first line, the function definition (i.e., lines 2-14). ↓

[4] Line 29 outputs a curve essentially the same as that in 2.15b[3], page 119. ↙

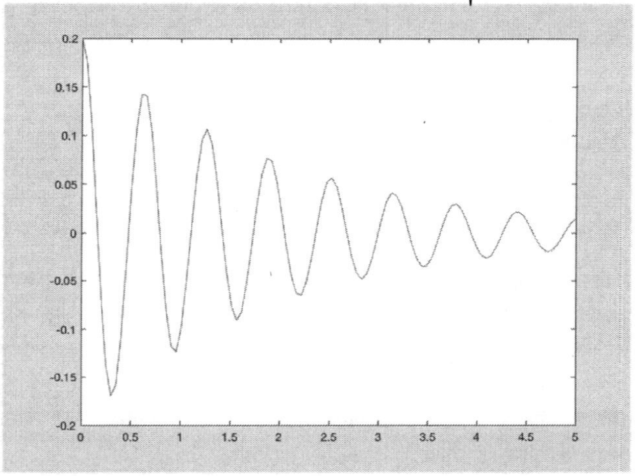

Search Path

[5] When you call a function (line 28) or want to display its on-line help (line 26), MATLAB looks for the file in the **Current Folder** first, and, if not found, then looks for those folders that are in the **search path** (1.13[7], page 46). Remember that the command `path` can be used to view or change the **search path**. ↓

Syntax and Semantics: `function` Definitions

[6] The syntax for a `function` definition is

```
function [output-args] = name(input-args)
    comments
    statements
end
```

The naming convention for functions follows the rules for variable names (see Table 1.2, page 16). All elements other than the keyword `function` and the *`name`* are optional. If the keyword `end` is omitted, the function definition closes at the end of the file or another function definition statement is encountered. As a good programming style, I strongly suggest that you always close a function with an `end`-statement. If *comments* is omitted, the on-line documentation for the function (see [3]) is no longer available. For a function with no output arguments, *`output-args`* and the equal sign (=) are omitted. If there is only one output argument, the square brackets may be omitted. Multiple input arguments must be separated by commas. If there are no input arguments, the parentheses may be omitted. You sometimes want to define a function with no statements (e.g., a placeholder); in that case, *`statements`* may be omitted. ↵

Close a Function with/without `end` Statements

[7] As mentioned in [6], last page, a function can be closed with or without an `end` statement. However, to avoid confusion, it is illegal to use both conventions in a program file. That is, if one of the functions in a program file is closed with an `end` statement, all the other functions in that file MUST be closed with `end` statements. ↓

Input/Output Arguments

[8] In line 28, the function **Example03_05a** is called, and the values `1`, `100`, 1, `0.2`, and `time` are copied to the input arguments `m`, `k`, `c`, `delta`, and `t` (line 1). At the completion of the function, the values `T` and `x` in line 1 are copied to `period` and `response` in line 28.

A function uses its own **Workspace** (therefore, a `clear` statement at the beginning of a function is not necessary); it cannot "see" the variables outside the function and vice versa. Using input/output arguments is a way to pass values into or out of the function. As mentioned in 1.15[5] (page 49) and 1.18[8] (page 57), using `global` variables is another way to pass values into or out of a function.

Lines 30-32 demonstrate that, if there are no variables to accept the output arguments of a function, MATLAB stores the value of the FIRST output argument in the variable `ans`. #

3.5b Example: Use of Example03_05a

Example03_05b.m: Damped Free Vibrations

[1] Type, save, and run the following program, which is based on Example02_15b.m (page 119); it demonstrates the use of the function Example03_05a (lines 4 and 6). The output is the same as 2.15b[3], page 119. ↓

```
1   clear
2   mass = 1; spring = 100; damper = 1; delta = 0.2;
3   time = 0;
4   T = Example03_05a(mass, spring, damper, delta, time);
5   time = linspace(0, 3*T, 100);
6   [T, response] = Example03_05a(mass, spring, damper, delta, time);
7   axes('XTick', T:T:3*T, 'XTickLabel', {'T','2T','3T'});
8   axis([0, 3*T, -0.2, 0.2])
9   grid on
10  hold on
11  comet(time, response)
12  title('Damped Free Vibrations')
13  xlabel(['Time (T = ', num2str(T), ' sec)'])
14  ylabel('Displacement (m)')
```

Purposes of Using Functions: Modularization and Abstraction

[2] Two of the benefits of using functions are modularization and abstraction. The function **Example03_05a** is used twice, in lines 4 and 6. In line 4, the function is called to evaluate the period, so the time span can be determined (line 5). In line 6, the function is called again to calculate the response. When using the function **Example03_05a**, you don't need to know the details of the function. All you have to know is the input and output arguments. Note that, in line 4, since only one variable `T` is used to store the output, the first output argument is copied to the variable `T`. #

3.6 Subfunctions

3.6a Subfunctions (Local Functions)

[1] We've introduced **subfunctions** in Section 1.15, as illustrated in Example01_15a.m (page 48), in which we defined two subfunctions. The part before the two subfunctions is the **main program**. Subfunctions are local to the file, not seen outside the file; therefore, they are also called **local functions**. The main program can be called from outside the file as long as the program file is in the **Current Folder** or in the **search path**. ↓

Example03_06a.m: Damped Free Vibrations

[2] In the following program, lines 1-14 are copied from Example03_05b.m (last page), and lines 16-27 are copied from Example03_05a.m (page 134) with the comments removed; the function name Example03_05a is changed to UDFV (under-damped free vibrations) as shown in lines 4, 6, and 16. The output is the same as 2.15b[3], page 119.

```
1   clear
2   mass = 1; spring = 100; damper = 1; delta = 0.2;
3   time = 0;
4   T = UDFV(mass, spring, damper, delta, time);
5   time = linspace(0, 3*T, 100);
6   [T, response] = UDFV(mass, spring, damper, delta, time);
7   axes('XTick', T:T:3*T, 'XTickLabel', {'T','2T','3T'});
8   axis([0, 3*T, -0.2, 0.2])
9   grid on
10  hold on
11  comet(time, response)
12  title('Damped Free Vibrations')
13  xlabel(['Time (T = ', num2str(T), ' sec)'])
14  ylabel('Displacement (m)')
15
16  function [T, x] = UDFV(m, k, c, delta, t)
17  omega = sqrt(k/m);
18  cC = 2*m*omega;
19  if c>= cC
20      disp('Not an under-damped system!')
21      T = 0; x = 0;
22      return;
23  end
24  omegaD = omega*sqrt(1-(c/cC)^2);
25  T = 2*pi/omegaD;
26  x = delta*exp(-c*t/(2*m)).*(cos(omegaD*t)+c/(2*m*omegaD)*sin(omegaD*t));
27  end
```

Lines 1-14 are the main program, while the function UDFV (lines 16-27) is a subfunction. Since the main program doesn't have any input arguments, it can be called by clicking the **Run** button (1.5[8], page 22). #

3.6b Incompatibilities with Earlier Versions

[1] As mentioned in 1.8[9], page 33, all the scripts in this book can be executed with 2018a or later versions in either **Script Editor** or **Live Editor**. If you are using an earlier version, please be aware of the following incompatibilities.

Script Editor in Earlier Versions

Example03_06a.m cannot be executed with **Script Editor** in 2016a or earlier versions, unless you rewrite the main program as a function, as shown in Example03_06b.m [2], which is made by removing the `clear`-statement (since a function has its own **Workspace**, the `clear`-statement becomes unnecessary) and inserting lines 1 and 15 into Example03_06a.m. The function Example03_06b (lines 1-15) is called a **main function** (instead of a **main program**). Starting from 2016b, **Script Editor** allows both forms (Example03_06a.m and Example03_06b.m).

Live Editor in Earlier Versions

Live Editor has been available since MATLAB 2016a. However, **Live Editor** doesn't support **local functions** until 2016b; which means Example03_06a.m cannot be opened as a **Live Script** with 2016a or earlier versions. Further, **Live Editor** doesn't support the idea of **main functions** until 2018a; which means Example03_06b.m cannot be opened as a **Live Function** with 2017b or earlier versions. ↓

Example03_06b.m: MATLAB 2016a or Earlier Versions

[2] This program can be executed in all versions of MATLAB. The output is the same as that in 2.15b[3], page 119. To run it with a **Live Editor** in MATLAB 2018a, right-click the file and choose **Open as Live Function**, and type Example03_06b on the command window. #

```
 1  function Example03_06b
 2  mass = 1; spring = 100; damper = 1; delta = 0.2;
 3  time = 0;
 4  T = UDFV(mass, spring, damper, delta, time);
 5  time = linspace(0, 3*T, 100);
 6  [T, response] = UDFV(mass, spring, damper, delta, time);
 7  axes('XTick', T:T:3*T, 'XTickLabel', {'T','2T','3T'});
 8  axis([0, 3*T, -0.2, 0.2])
 9  grid on
10  hold on
11  comet(time, response)
12  title('Damped Free Vibrations')
13  xlabel(['Time (T = ', num2str(T), ' sec)'])
14  ylabel('Displacement (m)')
15  end
16
17  function [T, x] = UDFV(m, k, c, delta, t)
18  omega = sqrt(k/m);
19  cC = 2*m*omega;
20  if c>= cC
21      disp('Not an under-damped system!')
22      T = 0; x = 0;
23      return;
24  end
25  omegaD = omega*sqrt(1-(c/cC)^2);
26  T = 2*pi/omegaD;
27  x = delta*exp(-c*t/(2*m)).*(cos(omegaD*t)+c/(2*m*omegaD)*sin(omegaD*t));
28  end
```

3.7 Nested Functions

Example03_07.m: Ball-Throwing

[1] Create a new file, copy all the lines in Example01_18.m (page 55), and make the following changes: delete lines 1, 2, and 29 in Example01_18.m; insert lines 1 and 37 so that the main program becomes a function; indent all the lines of the function `pushbuttonCallback` (lines 27-36) as shown to emphasize that it is a **nested function** (this step is not really necessary, but it is a good programming style). Save as Example03_07.m, and run the program. The resulting GUI is the same as that in 1.18[3-6], page 56. ↵

```
1   function Example03_07
2   g = 9.81;
3   figure('Position', [30,70,500,400])
4   axes('Units', 'pixels', ...
5       'Position', [50,80,250,250])
6   axis([0, 10, 0, 10])
7   xlabel('Distance (m)'), ylabel('Height (m)')
8   title('Trajectory of a Ball')
9
10  uicontrol('Style', 'text', ...
11      'String', 'Initial velocity (m/s)', ...
12      'Position', [330,300,150,20])
13  velocityBox = uicontrol('Style', 'edit', ...
14      'String', '5', ...
15      'Position', [363,280,80,20]);
16  uicontrol('Style', 'text', ...
17      'String', 'Elevation angle (deg)', ...
18      'Position', [330,240,150,20])
19  angleBox = uicontrol('Style', 'edit', ...
20      'String', '45', ...
21      'Position', [363,220,80,20]);
22  uicontrol('Style', 'pushbutton', ...
23      'String', 'Throw', ...
24      'Position', [363,150,80,30], ...
25      'Callback', @pushbuttonCallback)
26
27      function pushbuttonCallback(pushButton, ~)
28          v0 = str2double(velocityBox.String);
29          theta = str2double(angleBox.String)*pi/180;
30          t1 = 2*v0*sin(theta)/g;
31          t = 0:0.01:t1;
32          x = v0*cos(theta)*t;
33          y = v0*sin(theta)*t-g*t.^2/2;
34          hold on
35          comet(x, y)
36      end
37  end
```

Nested Functions

[2] A **nested function** (lines 27-36) is a function within a parent function. Here, the nested function `pushbuttonCallback` (lines 27-36) is defined within the parent function `Example03_07` (lines 1-37). A nested function is local to its parent function; i.e., it can be called only from the parent function. A unique feature of a nested function is that all the variables in the parent function are visible to the nested function, but the variables in the nested function are not visible to the parent function. Thus, the `global` statements in Example01_18.m become unnecessary; that's why we deleted them. It becomes a standard practice to use nested functions to implement callback functions, as demonstrated in Example03_07.m. Also note that the parent of a nested function must be a function and must not be a main program.

Live Function

To execute the program with **Live Editor**, right-click the file Example03_07.m and select **Open as Live Function**. The file will be opened as Example03_07.mlx [3]. The function Example03_07 then can be called from **Command Window**, **Script Editor**, or **Live Editor**. ↓

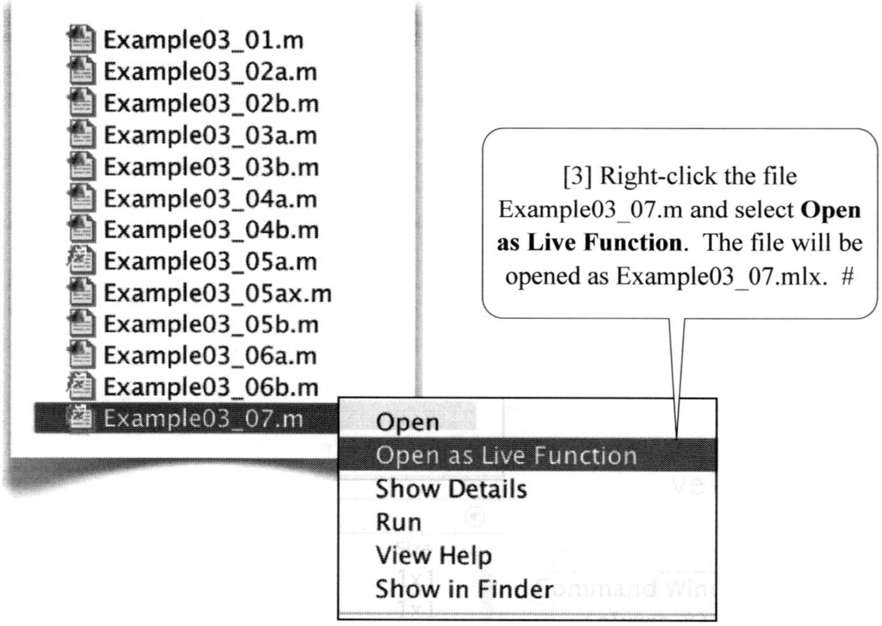

3.8 Function Handles

3.8a Function Handles

[1] A **handle** is also called a **pointer**; *see Wikipedia>Pointer (computer programming)*. The value of a handle is the address of a data or a function. Conceptually, we say that the **handle** points to the data or the function. If a handle stores the address of a data, the handle is called a **data handle**. If the handle stores the address of a function, it is called a **function handle**.

To retrieve the address of a function, we use the notation @. An example is shown in line 26 of Example01_18.m (page 55), in which the address of the function `pushbuttonCallback` is passed to the function `uicontrol`, so the `pushbutton` object knows where to find the callback function whenever it is pushed. ↓

Example03_08a.m: Finding Zeros

[2] Create and run the following program, which finds zeros of the function $f(x) = e^{-4x} \cos 3\pi x$, i.e., solving the equation $e^{-4x} \cos 3\pi x = 0$. ↓

```
clear
handle = @oscillation;
x1 = fzero(handle, 0.2)
x2 = fzero(handle, 0.5)
x3 = fzero(handle, 0.8)

function fx = oscillation(x)
fx = exp(-4*x)*cos(3*pi*x);
end
```

[3] Output of Example03_08a.m. ↓

```
x1 =
    0.1667
x2 =
    0.5000
x3 =
    0.8333
```

Function `fzero`

[4] Many MATLAB functions require a function handle as an input argument. The function `fzero` is an example; its syntax is like this

`x = fzero(`*`handle`*`, `*`x0`*`)`

It finds `x` (a scalar) such that the value of a function at `x` is zero. The input argument *`handle`* is a handle to the function. The input argument *`x0`* can be a scalar or a two-element vector. For a scalar, `fzero` finds a solution near *`x0`*. For a two-element vector `[a,b]`, `fzero` finds a solution in the interval between `a` and `b`. ↵

About Example03_08a.m

[5] This program finds zeros of the function $f(x) = e^{-4x} \cos 3\pi x$, i.e., it solves the nonlinear equation

$$e^{-4x} \cos 3\pi x = 0 \quad \text{(a)}$$

A preliminary study (see [6]) shows that the left-hand side of Eq. (a) has zero values near $x = 0.2$, 0.5, and 0.8. The graph [6] is plotted using the following commands:

```
>> x = linspace(0,1,100);
>> fx = exp(-4*x).*cos(3*pi*x);
>> plot(x,fx, [0,1], [0,0])
```

Lines 7-9 define the left-hand side of Eq. (a). Line 2 retrieves the address of the function and assigns to `handle`, which has a data type of `function_handle` (see [7]). Lines 3-5 find the solutions near $x = 0.2$, 0.5, and 0.8, respectively. ↓

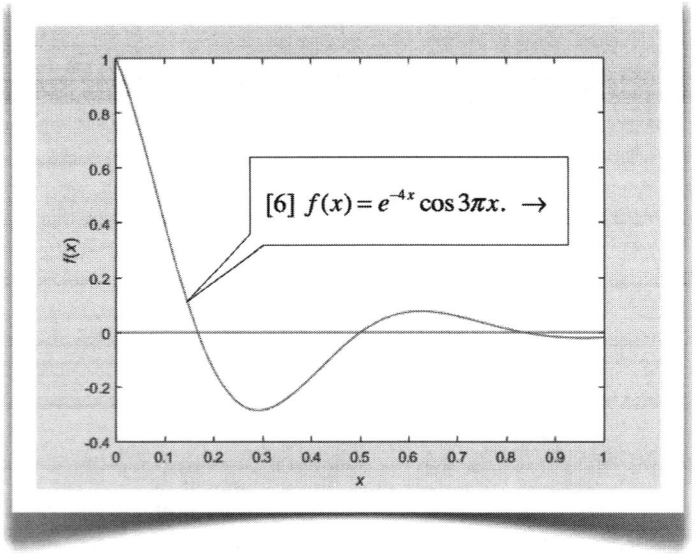

[6] $f(x) = e^{-4x} \cos 3\pi x$. →

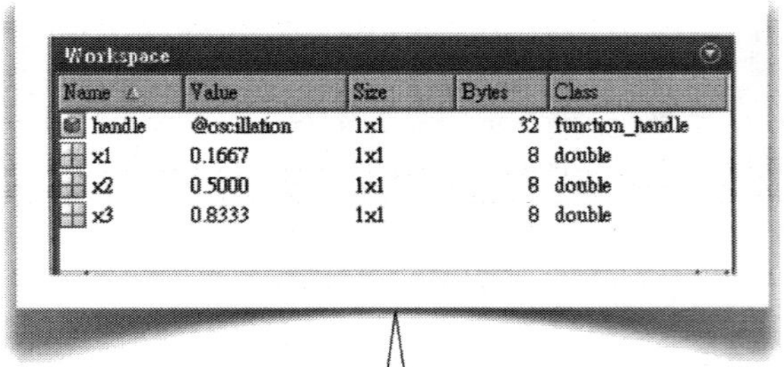

[7] The variable `handle` has a type (class) of `function_handle`. #

Table 3.8 Function Handles	
Function	Description
handle = @function	Retrieve function handle
handle(...)	Evaluate function value
Details and More: Help>MATLAB>Language Fundamentals>Data Types>Function Handles	

3.8b An Implementation of Function `fzero`

Example03_08b.m: Finding Zeros

[1] The following program contains a simple implementation of the function `fzero` (lines 11-24). Create a new file, copy all the lines in Example03_08a.m (page 141), make changes in lines 3 and 4 as shown, add a function `fzero` (lines 11-24), and run the program. The output is shown in [2]. ↓

```
1   clear
2   handle = @oscillation;
3   x1 = fzero(handle, 0.1)
4   x2 = fzero(handle, 0.4)
5   x3 = fzero(handle, 0.8)
6
7   function fx = oscillation(x)
8   fx = exp(-4*x)*cos(3*pi*x);
9   end
10
11  function x = fzero(handle, x0)
12  tolerance = 1.0e-6;
13  step = 0.01;
14  x = x0;
15  s1 = sign(handle(x));
16  while step/x > tolerance
17      if s1 == sign(handle(x+step))
18          x = x+step;
19      else
20          step = step/2;
21      end
22  end
23  disp('Simplified version')
24  end
```

```
Simplified version
x1 =
    0.1667
Simplified version
x2 =
    0.5000
Simplified version
x3 =
    0.8333
```

[2] Output of Example03_08b.m. ↓

About Example03_08b.m

[3] Instead of using the built-in function `fzero`, we now write our version of `fzero`, which will be somehow different from the built-in one. Starting with a point *x*0, the built-in function `fzero` finds a solution which may be GREATER or LESS than *x*0, while our simplified version finds a solution that is always GREATER than *x*0. That's why we need to change the starting points in lines 3 and 4. Also note that, because of the existence of the user-defined function `fzero`, the built-in function `fzero` is temporarily invisible (see Section 3.10).

The algorithm is simple: starting from an initial value *x*0, it scans increasingly along *x*-axis to find a solution. If there exists a solution between *x* and *x*1, then the function values *f*(*x*) and *f*(*x*1) have different signs. Further, if *x* and *x*1 are close enough (within a tolerance), than *x* may be regarded as a solution with certain accuracy.

It sets up a `tolerance` (line 12) and a `step` (line 13; the difference between *x* and *x*1), starts with *x*0 (line 14) and records the sign of *f*(*x*) (line 15), and then enters a `while`-loop (lines 16-22). Inside the `while`-loop, if *f*(*x*) and *f*(*x*1) have the same signs (line 17), then *x* is increased by `step` (line 18); otherwise `step` is halved (line 20). The loop iterates until `step/x` is not greater than `tolerance` (line 16).

Note that, in lines 15 and 17, the function handle `handle` is used as if it is a function name. The purpose of line 23 is to make sure that our version of function (not the built-in one) is indeed used. #

3.9 Anonymous Functions

3.9a Syntax and Semantics

Example03_09a.m: Anonymous Functions

[1] This script demonstrates the use of anonymous functions. It solves the nonlinear equation $e^{-4x}\cos 3\pi x = 0$ near 0.2, 0.5, and 0.8 (the same as those in 3.8a[2], page 141). It also evaluates the function values $f(x) = e^{-4x}\cos 3\pi x$ at 0.2, 0.5, and 0.8. The output is shown in [2].

```
1  clear
2  fun = @(x) exp(-4*x)*cos(3*pi*x);
3  x1 = fzero(fun, 0.2)
4  x2 = fzero(fun, 0.5)
5  x3 = fzero(fun, 0.8)
6  fx1 = fun(0.2)
7  fx2 = fun(0.5)
8  fx3 = fun(0.8)
```

Note that, in this program, we use the built-in function `fzero`, not the user-defined function `fzero` in lines 11-24 of Example03_08b.m, last page. →

```
x1 =
    0.1667
x2 =
    0.5000
x3 =
    0.8333
fx1 =
   -0.1389
fx2 =
  -2.4861e-17
fx3 =
    0.0126
```

[2] The output of Example03_09a.m. ←

Syntax and Semantics: Anonymous Functions

[3] Line 2 defines an anonymous function. An anonymous function is not defined in the way described in 3.5a[6] (page 135); rather, it is associated with a variable whose data type is **function handle**. Anonymous functions can accept input arguments as described before. A limitation of anonymous functions is that they can contain only a **single statement**; the result of the statement is the output of the function. The syntax for an anonymous function is

```
handle = @(input-args) statement
```

To call the function, you use the variable *`handle`* in place of a function name; i.e.,

```
handle(input-args)
```

↓

Visibility of Variables

[4] An anonymous function can use previously defined variables. For example, Example03_09a.m could be rewritten as follows. #

```
clear, a = 4; b = 3;
fun = @(x) exp(-a*x)*cos(b*pi*x);
x1 = fzero(fun, 0.2)
x2 = fzero(fun, 0.5)
x3 = fzero(fun, 0.8)
fx1 = fun(0.2)
fx2 = fun(0.5)
fx3 = fun(0.8)
```

3.9b Example: Symmetrical Two-Spring System

Symmetrical Two-Spring System

[1] The figure to the right shows a symmetrical two-spring system. The system is subject to a force F and the springs are initially in a horizontal position. We want to determine the displacement x as shown in the figure.

The elongation ΔL of each spring is

$$\Delta L = \sqrt{L^2 + x^2} - L$$

Applying Newton's first law in the vertical direction ($\sum F = 0$) at the node where the force F applies, we have the equilibrium equation among the two spring forces and the external force as follows:

$$2k\left(\sqrt{L^2 + x^2} - L\right)\frac{x}{\sqrt{L^2 + x^2}} - F = 0 \qquad \text{(a)}$$

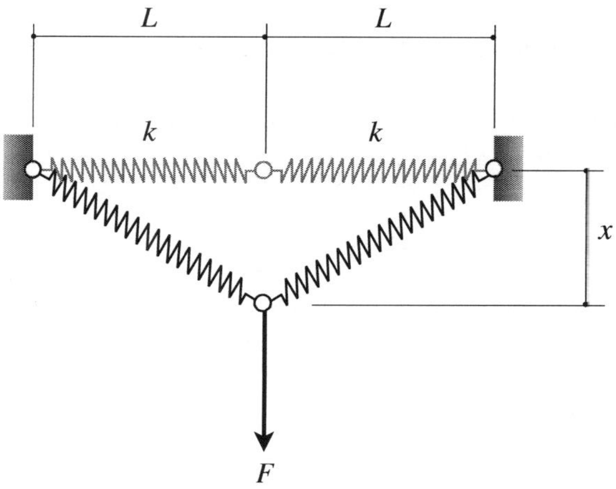

Example03_09b.m solves Eq. (a) for x, assuming $k = 6.8$ N/cm, $L = 12$ cm, and $F = 9.2$ N. ↓

Example03_09b.m: Symmetrical Two-Spring System

[2] Create a new file, type the following lines, and run the program.

```
1   clear
2   k = 6.8; L = 12; F = 9.2;
3   equation = @(x) 2*k*(sqrt(L^2+x^2)-L)*x/sqrt(L^2+x^2)-F;
4   fzero(equation, 0)
```

Note that, in this program, we use the built-in function `fzero`, not the user-defined function `fzero` in defined lines 11-24 of Example03_08b.m, page 143. ↓

```
x =
    6.1485
```

[3] The output of Example03_09b.m. Note that we arbitrarily choose zero as an initial value (line 4). #

3.10 Function Precedence Order

Function Precedence Order

[1] In Example03_08b.m (page 143), we demonstrated that when a user-defined function (`fzero`) has the same name as a built-in function, the user-defined function has higher precedence than the built-in one; i.e., the user-defined function overrides the built-in function; the built-in function is temporarily invisible.

Table 3.10 lists the precedence order for variables/functions that have the same name. With the same name, a variable has higher precedence order than functions. This is demonstrated in Example03_10.m below. ↙

Example03_10.m

[2] On the **Command Window**, execute the following commands. The output is shown in [3]. →

```
1   clear
2   a = sin(1)
3   sin = 3:5;
4   b = sin(1)
5   clear
6   c = sin(1)
```

```
7   >> clear
8   >> a = sin(1)
9   a =
10       0.8415
11  >> sin = 3:5;
12  >> b = sin(1)
13  b =
14       3
15  >> clear
16  >> c = sin(1)
17  c =
18       0.8415
```

[3] The output of Example03_10.m. ↓

[4] In line 2, the only variable or function with the name `sin` that MATLAB recognizes is the built-in function `sin`, which is therefore used, and the result is 0.8415 (line 10).

In line 3, a variable named `sin` is created as a row vector `[3,4,5]`. Now the built-in function `sin` becomes "invisible," since the precedence order of a variable is higher than a function (see Table 3.10). Therefore, in line 4, `sin(1)` is interpreted as the first element of the row vector `sin`, and the result is 3 (line 14).

Line 5 clears all the variables; the variable `sin` is removed from the memory. Therefore, in line 6, when `sin` is referred to again, it is interpreted as the built-in function `sin`, and the result is 0.8415 (line 18). #

Table 3.10 Variable/Function Precedence Order

Description	Precedence level
Variables	1
Nested functions	3
Subfunction (local functions)	4
Functions in current folder	9
Functions in the search path	10

Details and More:
Help>MATLAB>Programming Scripts and Functions>Functions>Function Basics>Function Precedence Order

3.11 Program Files

Main Program File

[1] In 3.5a, the two **program files** Example03_05b.m (page 136) and Example03_05a.m (page 134) constitute a program. The execution starts from the first executable statement of Example03_05b.m; therefore it is called a **main program file**. The execution of a program always starts from the **main program** of a **main program file**.

Program Files

A program may consist of several **program files**; one of them is the **main program file**, of which the execution starts from the first executable statement. Each program file may contain several functions, including subfunctions, nested functions, and anonymous functions. The part before user-defined function is the main program. If there is no main program, then the first function of a program file is called the main function. Main programs or main functions can be called from outside of the file. A subfunction is local to a program file; i.e., it can be called only from the functions in that program file. Nested functions and anonymous functions are local to their parent functions. ↓

Example03_11.m: Damped Free Vibrations

[2] This program is a modified version of Example03_05b.m. This program file and the program file Example03_05a.m constitute a program. Run the program, using the following input data (see [3], next page): m = 1 kg, k = 100 N/m, c = 1 N/(m/s), and delta = 0.2 m; the graphics output should be the same as 2.15b[3], page 119. ↵

```
clear
[mass, spring, damper, delta] = askProperties;
time = 0;
T = Example03_05a(mass, spring, damper, delta, time);
time = linspace(0, 3*T, 100);
[T, response] = Example03_05a(mass, spring, damper, delta, time);
plotDisplacement(T, time, response)

function [m, k, c, delta] = askProperties
m = input('Enter the mass (kg): ');
k = input('Enter the spring constant (N/m): ');
c = input('Enter the damper constant (N/(m/s)): ');
delta = input('Enter the initial displacement (m): ');
end

function plotDisplacement(T, time, response)
axes('XTick', T:T:3*T, 'XTickLabel', {'T','2T','3T'});
axis([0, 3*T, -0.2, 0.2])
grid on
hold on
comet(time, response)
title('Damped Free Vibrations')
xlabel(['Time (T = ', num2str(T), ' sec)'])
ylabel('Displacement (m)')
end
```

[3] A test-run of Example03_11.m. ↓

```
>> Example03_11
Enter the mass (kg): 1
Enter the spring constant (N/m): 100
Enter the damper constant (N/(m/s)): 1
Enter the initial displacement (m): 0.2
>>
```

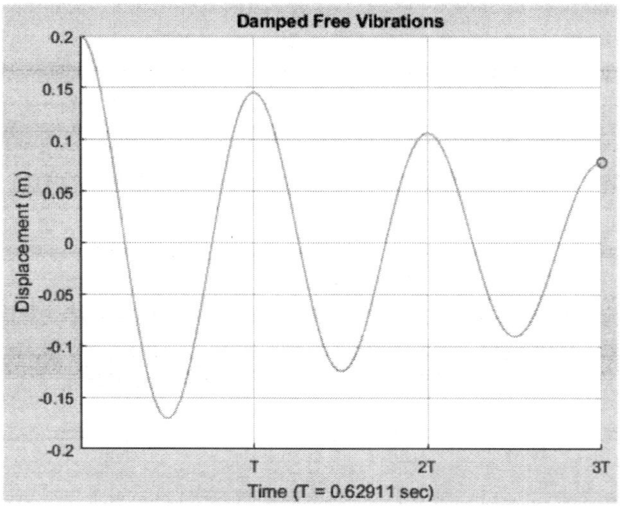

About Example03_11.m

[4] This program consists of two program files: Example03_11.m (last page) and Example03_05a.m (page 134); Example03_11.m is the main program file.

Example03_05a.m consists of a single user-defined function, which also serves as the main function; i.e., it can be called from other program files. Note that the main function name must be the same as the file name (with the file name extension **.m** removed).

Example03_11.m consists of a main program (lines 1-7) and two user-defined functions: `askProperties` (lines 9-14) and `plotDisplacement` (lines 16-25). The two functions are local to the file Example03_11.m; i.e., they can be called only from Example03_11.m. #

3.12 Example: Deflection of Beams

Example03_12.m: Deflection of Beams

[1] The following program calculates the deflection at the center of a simply supported beam subject to a uniform load q (SI unit: N/m) as shown in [2] (*Figure source: https://commons.wikimedia.org/wiki/File:Simple_beam_with_uniform_distributed_load.svg, by Hermanoere*). It uses the formulas in 2.14[1] (page 115). The uniform load q can be thought of as n evenly spaced concentrated forces $F = qL/n$, with a spacing of L/n. If n is large enough (e.g., $n = 1000$), we'll obtain a solution close to the theoretical solution. We assume $q = 500$ N/m and the same properties for the beam as those in 2.14, $w = 0.1$ m, $h = 0.1$ m, $L = 8$ m, $E = 210$ GPa. ↙

```
1   w = 0.1; h = 0.1; L = 8; E = 210e9; q = 500;
2   n = 1000; F = q*L/n;
3   delta = 0;
4   for k = 1:n
5       a = (L/n)*k;
6       delta = delta + deflection(w, h, L, E, F, a, L/2);
7   end
8   fprintf('Deflection at center is %.4f mm\n', delta*1000)
9
10  function delta = deflection(w, h, L, E, F, a, x)
11  I = w*h^3/12;
12  R = F/L*(L-a);
13  theta = F*a/(6*E*I*L)*(2*L-a)*(L-a);
14  delta = theta*x-R*x.^3/(6*E*I)+F/(6*E*I)*((x>a).*((x-a).^3));
15  end
```

[2] This is the simply supported beam considered in this section. →

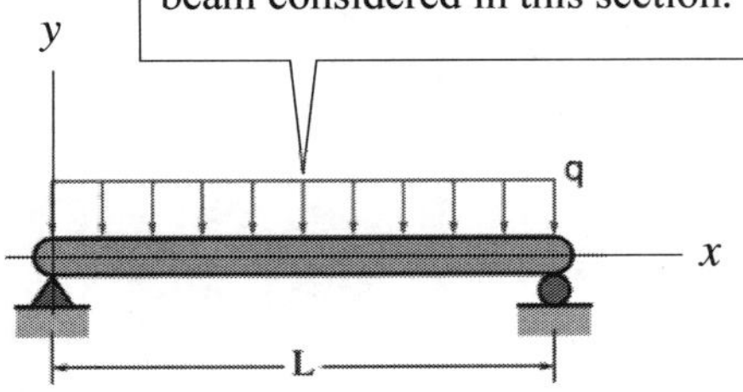


```
Deflection at center is 15.2381 mm
```

[3] The output of Example03_12.m. ↓

About Example03_12.m

[4] Using the formulas in 2.14[1] (page 115), the function `deflection` (lines 10-15) calculates the deflection at location x to the left end of the beam due to a force F applied at a distance a to the left end.

Lines 3-7 calculate the total deflection due to the n concentrated forces. In line 6, the deflection due to a concentrated force is calculated by calling the function `deflection` and accumulated. Line 8 reports the result [3].

↵

Verification of the Result

[5] The result [3], last page, can be verified using a well-know formula; see *Wikipedia>Deflection (engineering)*:

$$\delta = \frac{5qL^4}{384EI}$$

which can be easily calculated with the following commands:

```
>> w = 0.1; h = 0.1; L = 8;
>> E = 210e9; q = 500;
>> I = w*h^3/12;
>> delta = 5*q*L^4/(384*E*I)*1000
delta =
   15.2381
```

Arbitrary Loads

This section demonstrates the calculation of deflection for a particular case of loads. The same idea can be used to calculate the deflection of a simply supported beam subject to any concentrated and/or distributed loads. #

3.13 Example: Sorting and Searching

[1] Imagine that you're storing thousands of customers' data according to the alphabetical order of the customers' names. Storing data in a particular order is to facilitate searching. Another example is a dictionary. Tens of thousands (or even millions) of words, with their definitions, are stored in alphabetical order, so the searching of a word will be easier. In this section, we use a vector of numbers to demonstrate the ideas of sorting and searching. ↓

Example03_13.m: Sorting and Searching

[2] This program performs sorting and searching of numbers (continued at [3], next page). Before looking into the statements, test-run the program as shown in [4], next page. ↵

```
a = []; n = 0;
disp('1. Input numbers and sort')
disp('2. Display the list')
disp('3. Search')
disp('4. Save')
disp('5. Load')
disp('6. Quit')
while 1
    task = input('Enter a task number: ');
    switch task
        case 1
            while 1
                string = input('Enter a number (or stop): ', 's');
                if strcmpi(string, 'stop')
                    break;
                else
                    n = n+1;
                    a(n) = str2num(string);
                end
            end
            a = sort(a);
        case 2
            disp(a)
        case 3
            key = input('Enter a key number: ');
            found = search(a, key);
            if found
                disp(['Index = ', num2str(found)])
            else
                disp('Not found!')
            end
        case 4
            save('Datafile03_13', 'a')
        case 5
            load('Datafile03_13')
            n = length(a);
        case 6
            break
    end
end
```

[3] Example03_13.m (Continued) ↓

```
42  function out = sort(a)
43  n = length(a);
44  for i = n-1:-1:1
45      for j = 1:i
46          if a(j) > a(j+1)
47              tmp = a(j);
48              a(j) = a(j+1);
49              a(j+1) = tmp;
50          end
51      end
52  end
53  out = a;
54  end
55
56  function found = search(a, key)
57  n = length(a);
58  low = 1;
59  high = n;
60  found = 0;
61  while low <= high && ~found
62      mid = floor((low+high)/2);
63      if key == a(mid)
64          found = mid;
65      elseif key < a(mid)
66          high = mid-1;
67      else
68          low = mid+1;
69      end
70  end
71  end
```

```
72   >> Example03_13
73   1. Input numbers and sort
74   2. Display the list
75   3. Search
76   4. Save
77   5. Load
78   6. Quit
79   Enter a task number: 1
80   Enter a number (or stop): 6
81   Enter a number (or stop): 9
82   Enter a number (or stop): 3
83   Enter a number (or stop): 5
84   Enter a number (or stop): 1
85   Enter a number (or stop): 7
86   Enter a number (or stop): stop
87   Enter a task number: 2
88        1     3     5     6     7     9
89   Enter a task number: 3
90   Enter a key number: 6
91   Index = 4
92   Enter a task number: 4
93   Enter a task number: 6
94   >> Example03_13
95   1. Input numbers and sort
96   2. Display the list
97   3. Search
98   4. Save
99   5. Load
100  6. Quit
101  Enter a task number: 5
102  Enter a task number: 2
103       1     3     5     6     7     9
104  Enter a task number: 6
105  >>
```

A Test-Run of Example03_13.m

[4] Before you look into the statements of a program, always study the functionalities of the program first. You may just test-run the program, using some examples.

Start to run the program (line 72). It displays a menu of 6 tasks to be chosen (lines 73-78).

Task 1 (line 79) requests the input of a series of numbers; you input numbers one after another (lines 80-85) until you enter a `stop` (line 86). The numbers are then sorted and stored in a list in ascending order. Task 2 (line 87) displays the list of numbers (line 88). Note that the numbers are in ascending order. Task 3 (line 89) searches a key number in the list. It requests the input of the key number (line 90), searches the key number in the list, and then displays the index in the list (line 91). Task 4 (line 92) saves the list in a file. Task 6 (line 93) quits the program.

Re-start the program again (lines 94-100). Task 5 (line 101) loads the list from the file. Lines 102-103 display the list. Line 104 quits the program. ↵

About Example03_13.m

[5] The program consists of a main program (lines 1-40) and two user-defined functions (lines 42-71). The function `sort` (lines 42-54) sorts a list `a` of numbers in ascending order and outputs the sorted list `out`. The function `search` (lines 56-71) searches a key number `key` in the list `a` and outputs the index number `found`; if `key` is not found in the list, it outputs a zero.

Bubble Sort

Function `sort` (lines 42-54) overrides the built-in function `sort` (see on-line help: >> *`doc sort`*). Using a **bubble sort algorithm** (*Wikipedia>Bubble sort*), our version sorts a vector of numbers `a` in an ascending order and outputs the sorted vector `out`. The bubble sort algorithm is also called a **sinking sort algorithm**. The idea is as follows. It steps through the vector (lines 45-51), compares each pair of adjacent numbers (line 46), and swaps them (lines 47-49) if they are not in ascending order. After the first pass of the outer `for`-loop (lines 44-52), the largest number "sinks" down to the bottom of the vector; i.e., the smaller numbers "bubble" up toward the top. The pass through the vector is repeated (lines 44-52) until the vector is sorted out.

Binary Search

Using a **binary search algorithm** (*Wikipedia>binary search algorithm*), function `search` (lines 56-71) finds a number `key` in a vector `a` and outputs the location in the vector or outputs zero if the number is not found. The binary search algorithm is also called a half-interval search **algorithm**. The idea is as follows. It begins by comparing `key` with the value of the middle element of the vector `a` (line 62). If `key` is equal to the middle element's value (line 63), then the location is returned (line 64) and the search is complete. If `key` is less than the middle element's value (line 65), then the search continues on the first half of the vector (line 66). If `key` is greater than the middle element's value (line 67), then the search continues on the second half of the vector (line 68). This process continues, eliminating half of the elements and comparing `key` with the value of the middle element of the remaining elements, until `key` is either found (and its location is returned), or until the entire vector has been searched (and a zero value is returned).

The Main Program

The main program (lines 1-40) implements a text-based user-interface. It displays a menu of 6 tasks (lines 2-7) for the user to choose. Within a `while`-loop (lines 8-40), it requests the input of a task number (line 9) and switches to a `case`-block accordingly (lines 10-39).

For task case 1 (input numbers and sort), it uses a `while`-loop (lines 12-20) to accept numbers (line 13) and adds the numbers to the end of the vector (lines 17-18). Note that the input data is always treated as a string (`'s'` in line 13) to allow the input of a number or a string `stop`. The loop breaks (line 15) when a string `stop` is input by the user (line 14). We use `strcmpi` (instead of `strcmp`) to allow non-lowercase characters. Finally, it uses the function `sort` to sort the vector (line 21).

For task case 2 (display the list), it uses the built-in function `disp` to display the contents of the vector (line 23).

For task case 3 (search), it reads a `key` from the user (line 25) and calls the function `search` to find `key` (line 26). If found (line 27), the location is displayed (line 28); otherwise a "Not found!" message is displayed (lines 29-30).

For task case 4 (save), it uses the built-in function `save` to save the vector (line 33) in a file `Datafile03_13`.

For task case 5 (load), it uses the built-in function `load` to load the vector (line 35) from the file `Datafile03_13` and calculates the length of the vector (line 36).

For task case 6 (quit), it breaks the `while`-loop (line 38), jumping out of the `while`-loop, and quits the program.

Graphical User Interface

In Section 8.5, we'll build a graphical user interface (GUI) for this program. #

3.14 Example: Statically Determinate Trusses (Version 1.0)

Statically Determinate Planar Trusses

[1] Member forces of a statically determinate truss (*Wikipedia>Truss*) can be calculated using static equilibrium equations alone. For a planar truss, that (the statically determinate truss) means (1) the truss is supported at two positions, in which one is a hinged support and the other is a roller support (or the truss is supported at three positions of roller supports, not all of them sliding in the same direction); (2) The number of members m and the number of nodes n have a relationship

$$m+3=2n \tag{a}$$

The left-hand side ($m + 3$) is the number of forces to be found (m member forces and 3 reaction forces); the right-hand side is the number of static equilibrium equations that can be established (two equations for each nodes).

For example, consider a 3-bar truss problem shown below, where $m=3$ and $n=3$. Let F_1, F_2, and F_3 be three member forces (positive signs for tensile forces) and R_1, R_2, and R_3 be three reaction forces from the supports to the truss (the signs follow the reference coordinate system x-y).

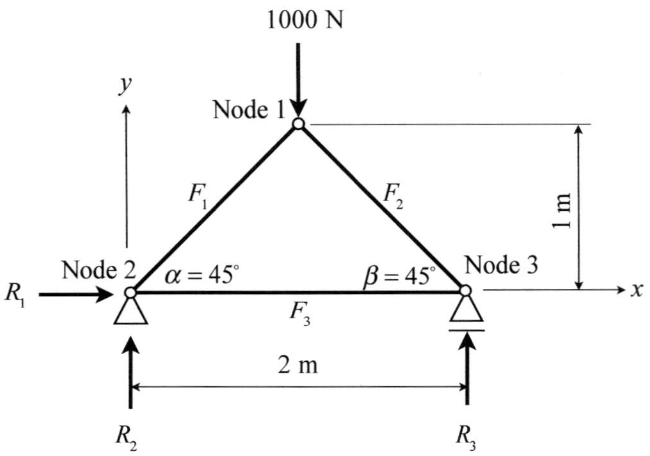

At node 1, the two equilibrium equations are

$$-F_1\cos\alpha+F_2\cos\beta=0$$
$$-F_1\sin\alpha-F_2\sin\beta-1000=0$$

At node 2, the two equilibrium equations are

$$F_1\cos\alpha+F_3+R_1=0$$
$$F_1\sin\alpha+R_2=0$$

At node 3, the two equilibrium equations are

$$-F_2\cos\beta-F_3=0$$
$$F_2\sin\beta+R_3=0$$

Substitute $\alpha=\beta=45^\circ$ into the equations. In a matrix form, the 6 equations above can be written as

$$\begin{bmatrix} -0.7071 & 0.7071 & 0 & 0 & 0 & 0 \\ -0.7071 & -0.7071 & 0 & 0 & 0 & 0 \\ 0.7071 & 0 & 1 & 1 & 0 & 0 \\ 0.7071 & 0 & 0 & 0 & 1 & 0 \\ 0 & -0.7071 & -1 & 0 & 0 & 0 \\ 0 & 0.7071 & 0 & 0 & 0 & 1 \end{bmatrix} \begin{pmatrix} F_1 \\ F_2 \\ F_3 \\ R_1 \\ R_2 \\ R_3 \end{pmatrix} = \begin{pmatrix} 0 \\ 1000 \\ 0 \\ 0 \\ 0 \\ 0 \end{pmatrix} \tag{b}$$

Note that the matrix in Eq. (b) has $2n$ rows and $m+3$ columns. And since $m+3=2n$, it is a square matrix. ↵

[2] The system of equations in Eq. (b) can be easily solved with the following MATLAB commands:

```
>> a = sqrt(2)/2;
>> A = [-a  a  0  0  0  0;
        -a -a  0  0  0  0;
         a  0  1  1  0  0;
         a  0  0  0  1  0;
         0 -a -1  0  0  0;
         0  a  0  0  0  1];
>> b = [0, 1000, 0, 0, 0, 0]';
>> x = A\b
x =
  -707.1068
  -707.1068
   500.0000
          0
   500.0000
   500.0000
```

We have $F_1 = F_2 = -707.1068$ N, $F_3 = 500$ N, $R_1 = 0$, and $R_2 = R_3 = 500$ N.

The last command (`x = A\b`) solves a system of linear equations `A*x = b`. Note that `b` is a column vector. The matrices `A` and `b` have the same number of rows. We'll give you more details about this **left divide operator** (or **backslash operator**) in Sections 9.7 and 10.3. ↓

Incremental Development of a Program

[3] In this section and Sections 3.15, 4.4, 6.8, and 8.8, we'll incrementally develop a program that can solve all the statically determinate planar truss problems.

In this section, we'll develop a function `solveTruss` (lines 8-59, next page) that solves any statically determinate planar truss problems, provided that the data to describe the truss are given. The truss is described with two numeric **matrices**, `Nodes` and `Members`. As a demonstration, this function is used to solve the 3-bar truss problem.

In Section 3.15, a text-based user-interface will be developed, so it can read any set of data representing a statically determinate planar truss problem from the user and solve it. In this stage, the function `solveTruss` and the matrix form of the truss data, `Nodes` and `Members`, remain unchanged.

In Section 4.4, the truss data, `Nodes` and `Members`, are redesigned by using **structure arrays** (instead of numeric **matrices**). The entire program, including the function `solveTruss`, needs to be rewritten accordingly.

In Section 6.8, a function `plotTruss` is added to allow the plotting of the truss on a **Figure Window**.

In Section 8.8, we'll replace the text-based user-interface with a graphical user-interface (GUI). ↓

Example03_14.m: Truss 1.0

[4] This program solves the 3-bar truss problem described in [1], last page. (Continued at [5], next page.) ↵

```
1   clear, Nodes = [
2       1, 1, 0, 0, 0, -1000;
3       0, 0, 1, 1, 0,     0;
4       2, 0, 0, 1, 0,     0];
5   Members = [1, 2; 1, 3; 2, 3];
6   [Nodes, Members] = solveTruss(Nodes, Members)
7
```

[5] Example03_14.m (Continued). The output is shown in [6-7], next page. ↵

```
function [outNodes, outMembers] = solveTruss(Nodes, Members)
n = size(Nodes,1); m = size(Members,1);
if (m+3) < 2*n
    disp('Unstable!')
    outNodes = 0; outMembers = 0; return
elseif (m+3) > 2*n
    disp('Statically indeterminate!')
    outNodes = 0; outMembers = 0; return
end
A = zeros(2*n, 2*n); loads = zeros(2*n,1); nsupport = 0;
for i = 1:n
    for j = 1:m
        if Members(j,1) == i || Members(j,2) == i
            if Members(j,1) == i
                n1 = i; n2 = Members(j,2);
            elseif Members(j,2) == i
                n1 = i; n2 = Members(j,1);
            end
            x1 = Nodes(n1,1); y1 = Nodes(n1,2);
            x2 = Nodes(n2,1); y2 = Nodes(n2,2);
            L = sqrt((x2-x1)^2+(y2-y1)^2);
            A(2*i-1,j) = (x2-x1)/L;
            A(2*i,  j) = (y2-y1)/L;
        end
    end
    if (Nodes(i,3) == 1)
        nsupport = nsupport+1;
        A(2*i-1,m+nsupport) = 1;
    end
    if (Nodes(i,4) == 1)
        nsupport = nsupport+1;
        A(2*i, m+nsupport) = 1;
    end
    loads(2*i-1) = -Nodes(i,5);
    loads(2*i)   = -Nodes(i,6);
end
forces = A\loads;
Members(:,3) = forces(1:m);
nsupport = 0;
for i = 1:n
    if (Nodes(i,3) == 1)
        nsupport = nsupport+1;
        Nodes(i,7) = forces(m+nsupport);
    end
    if (Nodes(i,4) == 1)
        nsupport = nsupport+1;
        Nodes(i,8) = forces(m+nsupport);
    end
end
outNodes = Nodes; outMembers = Members;
disp('Solved successfully.')
end
```

```
>> Example03_14
Solved successfully.
Nodes =
     1     1     0     0     0  -1000     0     0
     0     0     1     1     0      0     0   500
     2     0     0     1     0      0     0   500
Members =
    1.0000    2.0000  -707.1068
    1.0000    3.0000  -707.1068
    2.0000    3.0000   500.0000
>>
```

[7] These are three reaction forces. ↓

[6] These are three member forces. →

Truss Data: `Nodes` and `Members`

[8] A truss is described by two matrices, `Nodes` and `Members`. Table 3.14a and Table 3.14b list the data in the two matrices, respectively, for the 3-bar truss described in [1], page 154. The row-dimensional size of `Nodes` is the total number of nodes *n* (3 nodes in this case), while the row-dimensional size of `Members` is the total number of members *m* (3 members in this case). `Nodes` is an *n*-by-8 matrix and `Members` is an *m*-by-3 matrix.

Each node is described by its coordinates (*x* and *y*), support conditions (*supportx* and *supporty*), loads (*loadx* and *loady*), and reaction forces (*reactionx* and *reactiony*). The first six data (*x*, *y*, *supportx*, *supporty*, *loadx*, *loady*) are prepared in the main program (lines 1-4), while the last two data (*reactionx*, *reactiony*) are calculated in the function `solveTruss` (lines 8-59). For support conditions (*supportx* and *supporty*), 0 means the direction is not supported (i.e., free) and 1 means the direction is supported (i.e., constrained).

Each member is described by its two connecting nodes (*node1* and *node2*) and its member force (*force*). The first two data (*node1*, *node2*) are prepared in the main program (line 5), while the last data (*force*) are calculated in the function `solveTruss` (line 8-59). ↵

Table 3.14a Nodal Data for 3-Bar Truss

node	*x*	*y*	*supportx*	*supporty*	*loadx*	*loady*	*reactionx*	*reactiony*
1	1	1	0	0	0	-1000	0	0
2	0	0	1	1	0	0	0	500
3	2	0	0	1	0	0	0	500

Table 3.14b Member Data for 3-Bar Truss

member	*node1*	*node2*	*force*
1	1	2	-707.11
2	1	3	-707.11
3	2	3	500

Function `solveTruss`

[9] The function `solveTruss` (lines 8-59) calculates the member forces (*force* in Table 3.14b) and the reaction forces (*reactionx* and *reactiony* in Table 3.14a).

First (lines 9-16), it makes sure that the truss is indeed statically determinate (i.e., $m+3=2n$; see Eq. (a), page 154). If it is not, i.e., unstable (line 10) or statically indeterminate (line 13), the function simply displays a message (lines 11, 14) and returns zeros for both output arguments (lines 12, 15).

Second (lines 17-43), it establishes a system of linear equations, like the one in Eq. (b), page 154,

```
A*forces = loads
```
(c)

where `A` is a $2n \times (m+3)$ square matrix (remember, for statically determinate truss, $2n = m+3$), `forces` is a column vector of size $(m+3)$ and `loads` is a column vector of size $2n$.

Third (line 44), Eq. (c) is solved for the member forces (the first *m* elements of `forces`) and the reaction forces (the last 3 elements of `forces`) by using the **left divide operator** (see [2], page 155).

Finally (lines 45-59), the member forces and the reaction forces are saved in the variables `Members` and `Nodes`.

Further Improvement of the Program

In the next section, we'll add a text-based user-interface for the program, so, by reading truss data from the user, the program can solve various statically determinate planar truss programs. And we'll use the new program to solve the 3-bar truss problem described in this section and a 21-bar truss. We'll build a graphical user-interface for this program in Section 8.8. #

3.15 Example: Statically Determinate Trusses (Version 2.0)

Example03_15.m: Truss 2.0

[1] This is an improved version of Example03_14.m. It implements a text-based user-interface, allowing the user to define a statically determinate truss. We'll use this program to solve two truss problems: the 3-bar truss problem (page 154) is solved in [6] (page 164), and a 21-bar truss problem ([7], page 165) is solved in [8-11] (pages 165-167).

```
clear
Nodes = []; Members = [];
disp(' 1. Input nodal coordinates')
disp(' 2. Input connecting nodes of members')
disp(' 3. Input three supports')
disp(' 4. Input loads')
disp(' 5. Print truss')
disp(' 6. Solve truss')
disp(' 7. Print results')
disp(' 8. Save data')
disp(' 9. Load data')
disp('10. Quit')
while 1
    task = input('Enter the task number: ');
    switch task
        case 1
            Nodes = inputNodes(Nodes);
        case 2
            Members = inputMembers(Members);
        case 3
            Nodes = inputSupports(Nodes);
        case 4
            Nodes = inputLoads(Nodes);
        case 5
            printTruss(Nodes, Members)
        case 6
            [Nodes, Members] = solveTruss(Nodes, Members);
        case 7
            printResults(Nodes, Members)
        case 8
            saveAll(Nodes, Members)
        case 9
            [Nodes, Members] = loadAll;
        case 10
            break
    end
end
```

(Continued at [2] on the next page.) ↵

[2] Example03_15.m (Continued)

```
function output = inputNodes(Nodes)
while 1
    data = input('Enter [node, x, y] or 0 to stop: ');
    if data(1) == 0
        break
    else
        Nodes(data(1),1:2) = data(2:3);
    end
end
output = Nodes;
end

function output = inputMembers(Members)
m = 0;
while 1
    data = input('Enter [node1, node2] or 0 to stop: ');
    if data(1) == 0
        break
    else
        m = m+1;
        Members(m,1:2) = data;
    end
end
output = Members;
end

function output = inputSupports(Nodes)
Nodes(:,3:4) = 0;
for k = 1:3
    data = input('Enter [node, dir] (dir: ''x'' or ''y''): ');
    if data(2) == 'x'
        Nodes(data(1),3) = 1;
    elseif data(2) == 'y'
        Nodes(data(1),4) = 1;
    end
end
output = Nodes;
end

function output = inputLoads(Nodes)
Nodes(:,5:6) = 0;
while 1
    data = input('Enter [node, load-x, load-y] or 0 to stop: ');
    if data(1) == 0
        break
    else
        Nodes(data(1),5:6) = data(2:3);
    end
end
output = Nodes;
end
```

(Continued at [3], next page.) ↵

[3] Example03_15.m (Continued)

```
function printTruss(Nodes, Members)
if (size(Nodes,2)<6 || size(Members,2)<2)
    disp('Truss data not complete'); return
end
fprintf('\nNodal Data\n')
fprintf('Node         x        y Support-x  Support-y   Load-x   Load-y\n')
for k = 1:size(Nodes,1)
    fprintf('%4.0f%9.2f%9.2f%11.0f%11.0f%9.0f%9.0f\n', k, Nodes(k, 1:6))
end
fprintf('\nMember Data\n')
fprintf('Member  Node1    Node2\n')
for k = 1:size(Members,1)
    fprintf('%4.0f%9.0f%9.0f\n', k, Members(k, 1:2))
end
end

function printResults(Nodes, Members)
if (size(Nodes,2)<8 || size(Members,2)<3)
    disp('Results not available!'), return
end
fprintf('\nReaction Forces\n')
fprintf('Node  Reaction-x  Reaction-y\n')
for k = 1:size(Nodes,1)
    fprintf('%4.0f%12.2f%12.2f\n', k, Nodes(k, 7:8))
end
fprintf('\nMember Forces\n')
fprintf('Member     Force\n')
for k = 1:size(Members,1)
    fprintf('%4.0f%12.2f\n', k, Members(k, 3))
end
end

function saveAll(Nodes, Members)
fileName = input('Enter file name (default Datafile): ', 's');
if isempty(fileName)
    fileName = 'Datafile';
end
save(fileName, 'Nodes', 'Members')
end

function [Nodes, Members] = loadAll
fileName = input('Enter file name (default Datafile): ', 's');
if isempty(fileName)
    fileName = 'Datafile';
end
load(fileName)
end

```

(Continued at [4], next page.) ↵

[4] Example03_15.m (Continued) ↵

```
function [outNodes, outMembers] = solveTruss(Nodes, Members)
n = size(Nodes,1); m = size(Members,1);
if (m+3) < 2*n
    disp('Unstable!')
    outNodes = 0; outMembers = 0; return
elseif (m+3) > 2*n
    disp('Statically indeterminate!')
    outNodes = 0; outMembers = 0; return
end
A = zeros(2*n, 2*n); loads = zeros(2*n,1); nsupport = 0;
for i = 1:n
    for j = 1:m
        if Members(j,1) == i || Members(j,2) == i
            if Members(j,1) == i
                n1 = i; n2 = Members(j,2);
            elseif Members(j,2) == i
                n1 = i; n2 = Members(j,1);
            end
            x1 = Nodes(n1,1); y1 = Nodes(n1,2);
            x2 = Nodes(n2,1); y2 = Nodes(n2,2);
            L = sqrt((x2-x1)^2+(y2-y1)^2);
            A(2*i-1,j) = (x2-x1)/L;
            A(2*i,  j) = (y2-y1)/L;
        end
    end
    if (Nodes(i,3) == 1)
        nsupport = nsupport+1;
        A(2*i-1,m+nsupport) = 1;
    end
    if (Nodes(i,4) == 1)
        nsupport = nsupport+1;
        A(2*i, m+nsupport) = 1;
    end
    loads(2*i-1) = -Nodes(i,5);
    loads(2*i)   = -Nodes(i,6);
end
forces = A\loads;
Members(:,3) = forces(1:m);
nsupport = 0;
for i = 1:n
    if (Nodes(i,3) == 1)
        nsupport = nsupport+1;
        Nodes(i,7) = forces(m+nsupport);
    end
    if (Nodes(i,4) == 1)
        nsupport = nsupport+1;
        Nodes(i,8) = forces(m+nsupport);
    end
end
outNodes = Nodes; outMembers = Members;
disp('Solved successfully.')
end
```

Main Program

[5] The main program (lines 1-37, page 159) displays a menu of 10 tasks (lines 3-12). A `while`-loop (lines 13-37) is used to request a task number and execute the task that accomplishes a part of the truss analysis. According to the user's choice (line 14), it calls a function (lines 15-36). The rest of the program is to implement these functions (the functions in lines 17, 19, 21, 23, 25, 29, 31, and 33). The function `solveTruss` used in line 27 is simply a copy from the lines 8-59 of Example03_14.m (page 156; also see lines 139-190, last page).

Function `inputNodes`

Function `inputNodes` (lines 39-49, page 160) requests nodal coordinates from the user (line 41) and stores them in the variable `Nodes` (line 45), which is then output to the caller (line 48). The user must repeatedly type the coordinates in MATLAB's vector format (i.e., enclosed with square brackets; e.g., `[3 2 0]`) or `0` to terminate the input. For an illegal format of input (e.g., entering `3`), the function `input` (line 41) would crash and report an error message.

Function `inputMembers`

Function `inputMembers` (lines 51-63, page 160) requests two connecting nodes for each member from the user (line 54) and stores them in the variable `Members` (line 59), which is then output to the caller (line 62). The user must repeatedly type the two nodal numbers in MATLAB's vector format (i.e., enclosed with square brackets; e.g., `[1 2]`) or `0` to terminate the input. For an illegal format of input, the function `input` would crash and report an error message.

Function `inputSupports`

Function `inputSupports` (lines 65-76, page 160) requests three support positions (node number) and directions (`'x'` or `'y'`) from the user (line 68) and stores them in the variable `Nodes` (lines 69-73), which is then output to the caller (line 75). Note that, in line 68, inside a pair of apostrophes (single quotes), two consecutive apostrophes are treated as a single apostrophe.

Function `inputLoads`

Function `inputLoads` (lines 78-89, page 160) requests each load's position (node number) and its *x*-component and *y*-component from the user (line 81) and stores them in the variable `Nodes` (line 85), which is then output to the caller (line 88).

Functions `printTruss` and `printResults`

Function `printTruss` (lines 91-105, page 161) prints the input data. Function `printResults` (lines 107-121, page 161) prints the calculated results.

Functions `saveAll` and `loadAll`

Function `saveAll` (lines 123-129, page 161) saves variables `Nodes` and `Members` in a file specified by the user (line 124). If the user simply presses the **Enter** key, a default file name `Datafile` is assumed (lines 125-127). Function `loadAll` (lines 131-137, page 161) reads variables, `Nodes` and `Members`, from a file specified by the user; the default file name is `Datafile` (lines 133-135).

Function `solveTruss`

Function `solveTruss` (lines 139-190, last page) is a copy from lines 8-59 of Example03_14.m, page 156. ↵

```
>> Example03_15
 1. Input nodal coordinates
 2. Input connecting nodes of members
 3. Input three supports
 4. Input loads
 5. Print truss
 6. Solve truss
 7. Print results
 8. Save data
 9. Load data
10. Quit
Enter the task number: 1
Enter [node, x, y] or 0 to stop: [1 1 1]
Enter [node, x, y] or 0 to stop: [2 0 0]
Enter [node, x, y] or 0 to stop: [3 2 0]
Enter [node, x, y] or 0 to stop: 0
Enter the task number: 2
Enter [node1, node2] or 0 to stop: [1 2]
Enter [node1, node2] or 0 to stop: [1 3]
Enter [node1, node2] or 0 to stop: [2 3]
Enter [node1, node2] or 0 to stop: 0
Enter the task number: 3
Enter [node, dir] (dir: 'x' or 'y'): [2 'x']
Enter [node, dir] (dir: 'x' or 'y'): [2 'y']
Enter [node, dir] (dir: 'x' or 'y'): [3 'y']
Enter the task number: 4
Enter [node, load-x, load-y] or 0 to stop: [1 0 -1000]
Enter [node, load-x, load-y] or 0 to stop: 0
Enter the task number: 5

Nodal Data
Node        x        y  Support-x  Support-y    Load-x    Load-y
   1     1.00     1.00          0          0         0     -1000
   2     0.00     0.00          1          1         0         0
   3     2.00     0.00          0          1         0         0

Member Data
Member  Node1    Node2
   1        1        2
   2        1        3
   3        2        3
Enter the task number: 6
Solved successfully.
Enter the task number: 7

Reaction Forces
Node  Reaction-x  Reaction-y
   1        0.00        0.00
   2        0.00      500.00
   3        0.00      500.00

Member Forces
Member      Force
   1      -707.11
   2      -707.11
   3       500.00
Enter the task number: 8
Enter file name (default Datafile): Datafile03_15a
Enter the task number: 10
>>
```

[6] Now, use Example03_15.m to solve the 3-bar truss problem, page 154; the input data are listed in the shaded areas of Table 3.14a and Table 3.14b, page 157. This is the screen input/output. Input data are **boldfaced**. ↵

[7] As a second example, consider a 21-bar statically determinate planar truss. ↘

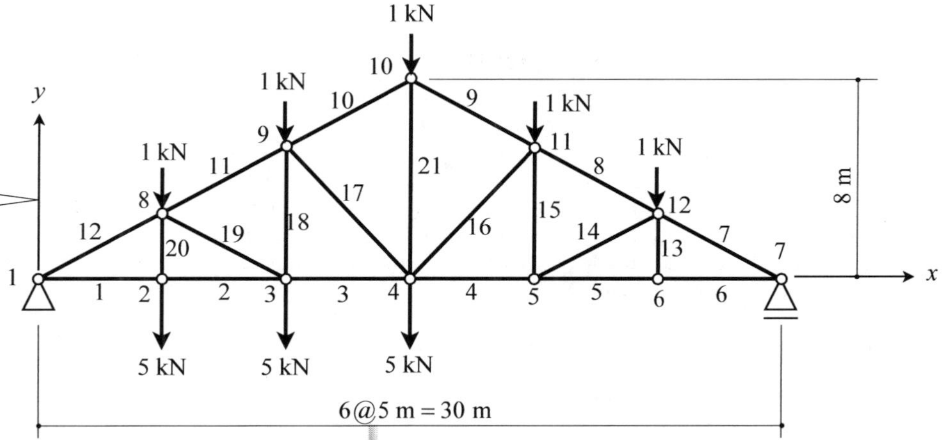


```
>> Example03_15
 1. Input nodal coordinates
 2. Input connecting nodes of members
 3. Input three supports
 4. Input loads
 5. Print truss
 6. Solve truss
 7. Print results
 8. Save data
 9. Load data
10. Quit
Enter the task number: 1
Enter [node, x, y] or 0 to stop: [1 0 0]
Enter [node, x, y] or 0 to stop: [2 5 0]
Enter [node, x, y] or 0 to stop: [3 10 0]
Enter [node, x, y] or 0 to stop: [4 15 0]
Enter [node, x, y] or 0 to stop: [5 20 0]
Enter [node, x, y] or 0 to stop: [6 25 0]
Enter [node, x, y] or 0 to stop: [7 30 0]
Enter [node, x, y] or 0 to stop: [8 5 8/3]
Enter [node, x, y] or 0 to stop: [9 10 8*2/3]
Enter [node, x, y] or 0 to stop: [10 15 8]
Enter [node, x, y] or 0 to stop: [11 20 8*2/3]
Enter [node, x, y] or 0 to stop: [12 25 8/3]
Enter [node, x, y] or 0 to stop: 0
Enter the task number: 2
Enter [node1, node2] or 0 to stop: [1 2]
Enter [node1, node2] or 0 to stop: [2 3]
Enter [node1, node2] or 0 to stop: [3 4]
Enter [node1, node2] or 0 to stop: [4 5]
Enter [node1, node2] or 0 to stop: [5 6]
Enter [node1, node2] or 0 to stop: [6 7]
Enter [node1, node2] or 0 to stop: [7 12]
Enter [node1, node2] or 0 to stop: [12 11]
Enter [node1, node2] or 0 to stop: [11 10]
Enter [node1, node2] or 0 to stop: [10 9]
Enter [node1, node2] or 0 to stop: [9 8]
Enter [node1, node2] or 0 to stop: [8 1]
Enter [node1, node2] or 0 to stop: [12 6]
Enter [node1, node2] or 0 to stop: [12 5]
Enter [node1, node2] or 0 to stop: [11 5]
Enter [node1, node2] or 0 to stop: [11 4]
Enter [node1, node2] or 0 to stop: [9 4]
Enter [node1, node2] or 0 to stop: [9 3]
Enter [node1, node2] or 0 to stop: [8 3]
Enter [node1, node2] or 0 to stop: [8 2]
Enter [node1, node2] or 0 to stop: [10 4]
Enter [node1, node2] or 0 to stop: 0
```

[8] Use Example03_15.m to solve the 21-bar truss problem [7]; the input data are listed in the shaded areas of Table 3.15a and Table 3.15b, page 168. This is the screen input/output. Input data are **boldfaced**. (Continued at [9], next page.) ↵

```
Enter the task number: 3
Enter [node, dir] (dir: 'x' or 'y'): [1 'x']
Enter [node, dir] (dir: 'x' or 'y'): [1 'y']
Enter [node, dir] (dir: 'x' or 'y'): [7 'y']
Enter the task number: 4
Enter [node, load-x, load-y] or 0 to stop: [2 0 -5000]
Enter [node, load-x, load-y] or 0 to stop: [3 0 -5000]
Enter [node, load-x, load-y] or 0 to stop: [4 0 -5000]
Enter [node, load-x, load-y] or 0 to stop: [8 0 -1000]
Enter [node, load-x, load-y] or 0 to stop: [9 0 -1000]
Enter [node, load-x, load-y] or 0 to stop: [10 0 -1000]
Enter [node, load-x, load-y] or 0 to stop: [11 0 -1000]
Enter [node, load-x, load-y] or 0 to stop: [12 0 -1000]
Enter [node, load-x, load-y] or 0 to stop: 0
Enter the task number: 5

Nodal Data
Node        x        y  Support-x  Support-y   Load-x   Load-y
   1     0.00     0.00          1          1        0        0
   2     5.00     0.00          0          0        0    -5000
   3    10.00     0.00          0          0        0    -5000
   4    15.00     0.00          0          0        0    -5000
   5    20.00     0.00          0          0        0        0
   6    25.00     0.00          0          0        0        0
   7    30.00     0.00          0          1        0        0
   8     5.00     2.67          0          0        0    -1000
   9    10.00     5.33          0          0        0    -1000
  10    15.00     8.00          0          0        0    -1000
  11    20.00     5.33          0          0        0    -1000
  12    25.00     2.67          0          0        0    -1000

Member Data
Member  Node1    Node2
   1        1        2
   2        2        3
   3        3        4
   4        4        5
   5        5        6
   6        6        7
   7        7       12
   8       12       11
   9       11       10
  10       10        9
  11        9        8
  12        8        1
  13       12        6
  14       12        5
  15       11        5
  16       11        4
  17        9        4
  18        9        3
  19        8        3
  20        8        2
  21       10        4
Enter the task number: 6
Solved successfully.
```

[9] Solving the 21-bar truss problem (Continued). (Continued at [10], next page.) ↵

```
Enter the task number: 7

Reaction Forces
Node  Reaction-x  Reaction-y
   1        0.00    12500.00
   2        0.00        0.00
   3        0.00        0.00
   4        0.00        0.00
   5        0.00        0.00
   6        0.00        0.00
   7        0.00     7500.00
   8        0.00        0.00
   9        0.00        0.00
  10        0.00        0.00
  11        0.00        0.00
  12        0.00        0.00

Member Forces
Member       Force
   1      23437.50
   2      23437.50
   3      17812.50
   4      13125.00
   5      14062.50
   6      14062.50
   7     -15937.50
   8     -14875.00
   9     -13812.50
  10     -13812.50
  11     -20187.50
  12     -26562.50
  13          0.00
  14      -1062.50
  15        500.00
  16      -1370.73
  17      -8224.39
  18       8000.00
  19      -6375.00
  20       5000.00
  21      12000.00
Enter the task number: 8
Enter file name (default Datafile): Datafile03_15b
Enter the task number: 10
>>
```

[10] Solving the 21-bar truss problem (Continued). ↓

[11] Calculated member forces. ↓

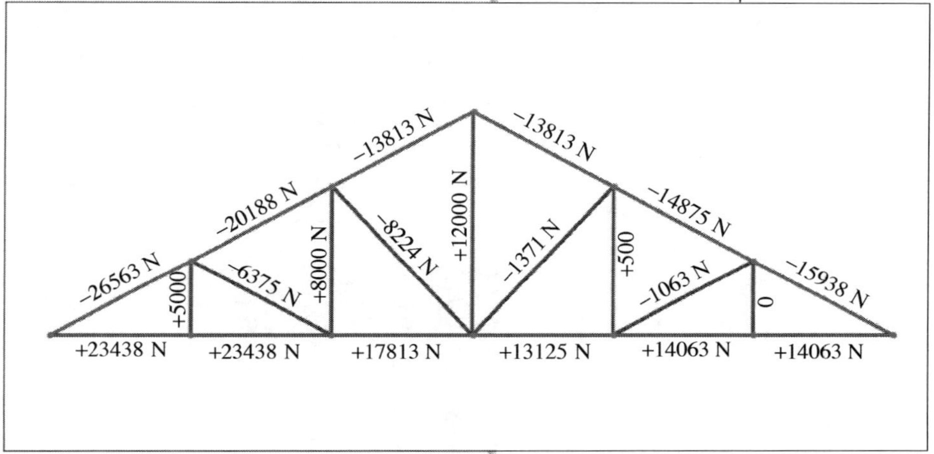

Further Improvement of the Program

[12] The program Example03_15.m can be improved in at least two aspects: the data representation and the user interface. We stored all the data in two matrices, `Nodes` and `Members`. A problem of using matrices is that you need to know which column stores what data. Using **structure** array (Section 1.17) may ease this problem. We'll discuss **structure** data in Section 4.3 and present a modified version in Section 4.4, which uses **structure** arrays to store nodal and member data.

In this program, we implemented a text-based user interface. A more intuitive and appealing way is using a graphical user interface (GUI), such as one presented in Sections 1.18, 1.19, and 1.20. We'll discuss the GUI in more detail in Chapter 8 and present a GUI for this program in Section 8.8. #

Table 3.15a Nodal Data for the 21-Bar Truss

node	*x*	*y*	*supportx*	*supporty*	*loadx*	*loady*	*reactionx*	*reactiony*
1	0	0	1	1	0	0	0	12500
2	5	0	0	0	0	-5000	0	0
3	10	0	0	0	0	-5000	0	0
4	15	0	0	0	0	-5000	0	0
5	20	0	0	0	0	0	0	0
6	25	0	0	0	0	0	0	0
7	30	0	0	1	0	0	0	7500
8	5	2.6667	0	0	0	-1000	0	0
9	10	5.3333	0	0	0	-1000	0	0
10	15	8	0	0	0	-1000	0	0
11	20	5.3333	0	0	0	-1000	0	0
12	25	2.6667	0	0	0	-1000	0	0

Table 3.15b Member Data for the 21-Bar Truss

member	*node1*	*node2*	*force*
1	1	2	23437.5
2	2	3	23437.5
3	3	4	17812.5
4	4	5	13125
5	5	6	14062.5
6	6	7	14062.5
7	7	12	-15937.5
8	12	11	-14875
9	11	10	-13812.5
10	10	9	-13812.5
11	9	8	-20187.5
12	8	1	-26562.5
13	12	6	0
14	12	5	-1062.5
15	11	5	500
16	11	4	-1370.73
17	9	4	-8224.39
18	9	3	8000
19	8	3	-6375
20	8	2	5000
21	10	4	12000

3.16 Additional Exercise Problems

Problem03_01: For-Loops and While-Loops

A `for`-loop is equivalent to a `while`-loop as mentioned in 3.4a[1], page 131. As an exercise, rewrite Example03_04b.m (page 132), using `while`-loops instead of the `for`-loops. In general, if using a `for`-loop can accomplish a task, then you should use a `for`-loop rather than using a `while`-loop, due to readability considerations.

Problem03_02: Switch-Blocks and If-Blocks

A `switch`-block is equivalent to an `if`-block as mentioned in 3.2a[1], page 127. As an exercise, rewrite Example03_03b.m (page 130), using an `if`-block instead of the `switch`-block. In general, if using a `switch`-block can accomplish a task, then you should use a `switch`-block rather than using an `if`-block, due to readability considerations.

Problem03_03: Functions

We mentioned, in 3.5b[2] (page 136), that the purpose of using functions is modularization and abstraction. In this exercise, we use a short program to illustrate the ideas. This program is so short that you may not be able to appreciate the ideas of modularization and abstraction. However, as a program becomes large, these ideas are useful.

Consider Problem02_03 (page 122) again, and generate the same graphic output as before. This time, organize the program into a main function and three subfunctions. This is the main function:

```
clear
[n,p] = getData;
x = 0:n;
fx = Binomial(p, n, x);
drawCurve(x, fx, p, n)
end
```

You are asked to implement the three subfunctions: `getData`, `Binomial`, and `drawCurve`. Function `getData` allows the user to input the values of `n` and `p`. Function `Binomial` calculates $f(x)$ of the binomial distribution (see Problem02_03, page 122). Function `drawCurve` produces the graphic output.

Problem03_04: Function `fzero`

Use the MATLAB built-in function `fzero` to find a value x that satisfies

$$x = \left(1 + \frac{1}{x}\right)^x$$

Chapter 4

Cell Arrays, Structures, Tables, and User-Defined Classes

A data type is also called a **class**. The built-in classes we've discussed in Chapter 3 include numeric classes (**double**, **int32**, etc), **character**, **logical**, and **function handle**. **Cell array** and **structure** mentioned in Chapter 1 are also built-in classes. A class is defined by a set of lower-level **data** and **operations** on the data. For example, the class **double** has a binary data representation shown in 2.3[1] (page 74) and its operations include plus, minus, times, etc. It is possible to create **user-defined classes**. In a user-defined class, the data are called the **properties**, and the operations are called the **methods**.

4.1 Cell Arrays

4.1a Cell Arrays Containing Strings of Different Lengths

[1] As mentioned in 1.16[1] (page 51), a cell array can contain elements of different types, different dimensional sizes. An application of cell arrays is to create an array of strings of different lengths. Many MATLAB built-in functions use cell arrays; therefore, you need to know the concepts behind the cell array. ↓

Example04_01a.m

[2] These commands demonstrate some important concepts about ordinary arrays and cell arrays. A screen output is shown in [5], next page. Schematic diagrams of the array b (or c) and d are shown in [3-4]; they are further explained in [6], next page. ↓

```
clear
a = ['David', 'John', 'Stephen']
b = ['David  '; 'John   '; 'Stephen']
size(b)
c = char('David', 'John', 'Stephen')
size(c)
d = {'David', 'John', 'Stephen'}
d(1)
d{1}
d{1}(1)
d{3}(7)
```

[3] A schematic diagram of the array b (or c). ↓

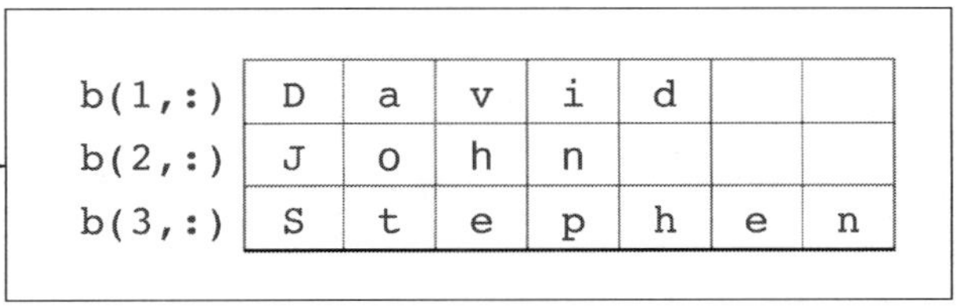

[4] A schematic diagram of the cell array d. ↵

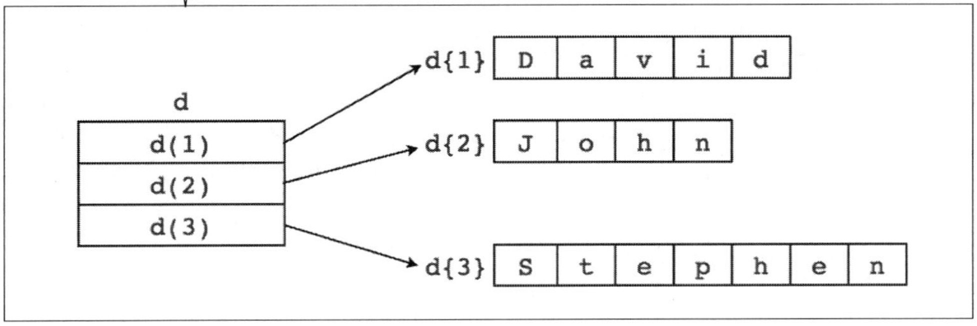

```
12   >> clear
13   >> a = ['David', 'John', 'Stephen']
14   a =
15       'DavidJohnStephen'
16   >> b = ['David  '; 'John   '; 'Stephen']
17   b =
18     3×7 char array
19       'David  '
20       'John   '
21       'Stephen'
22   >> size(b)
23   ans =
24        3     7
25   >> c = char('David', 'John', 'Stephen')
26   c =
27     3×7 char array
28       'David  '
29       'John   '
30       'Stephen'
31   >> size(c)
32   ans =
33        3     7
34   >> d = {'David', 'John', 'Stephen'}
35   d =
36     1×3 cell array
37       {'David'}    {'John'}    {'Stephen'}
38   >> d(1)
39   ans =
40     1×1 cell array
41       {'David'}
42   >> d{1}
43   ans =
44       'David'
45   >> d{1}(1)
46   ans =
47       'D'
48   >> d{3}(7)
49   ans =
50       'n'
```

[5] The output of Example04_01a.m. →

Ordinary Arrays

[6] Remember that a string such as `'David'` is a row vector of characters. Line 2 concatenates 3 strings into one string, using commas (`,`). The result is a row vector of 16 characters (line 15).

To concatenate the three strings in column-direction, you need to pad the shorter strings with trailing blanks because the three strings must be the same length (lines 3, 18-21). It is a 3-by-7 matrix of characters (lines 4, 24; also see [3], last page). Remember that, to concatenate row vectors into a matrix, the row vectors must have the same length. The following command would cause an output of error message saying "Dimensions of matrices being concatenated are not consistent."

```
>> e = ['David';'John';'Stephen']
```

The same result of line 3 can be achieved by using the function `char`, which automatically pads the strings with trailing blanks (lines 5-6, 27-30, 33). Contents of `b` and `c` are the same (see [3], last page).

Cell Arrays

A cell array can contain elements of different types, different dimensional sizes. In particular, a cell array can store strings of different lengths (lines 7, 36-37). Note that a pair of curly braces (`{}`, line 7) are used for creating a cell array.

A cell array is actually an array of pointers (see *Wikipedia>Pointer (computer programming)*); also see 3.8a[1], page 141). Each element of the cell array is an address pointing to a data, which can be a scalar, a vector, a matrix, or even a cell array; they do not necessarily have the same sizes.

Thus, `d(1)` (line 8) is a **pointer** (or called a **cell**, line 40) pointing to the string `'David'` (line 41; also see [4], last page).

The notation `d{k}` (line 9) refers to the **contents** to which the pointer `d(k)` points. In this case, `d{1}` is the string `'David'` (lines 44). Therefore, `d{1}(1)` (line 10) is the character `'D'` (line 47), and `d{3}(7)` (line 11) is the character `'n'` (line 50). #

4.1b Multi-Dimensional Cell Arrays

Example04_01b.m

[1] Like an ordinary array, a cell array may be multi-dimensional, as demonstrated in the following commands. The text output is shown in [2] and the graphic output is in [3]. ↓

```
1   clear
2   a = 45;
3   b = 'David';
4   c = [1, 2, 3];
5   d = [4, 5; 6, 7];
6   e = {a, b; c, d}
7   disp(e)
8   celldisp(e)
9   cellplot(e)
10  e{1,1}
11  e{2,1}(2)
12  e{1,2}(1)
13  e{2,2}(2,1)
```

[2] The text output of Example04_01b.m. ↓

```
14   >> clear
15   >> a = 45;
16   >> b = 'David';
17   >> c = [1, 2, 3];
18   >> d = [4, 5; 6, 7];
19   >> e = {a, b; c, d}
20   e =
21     2×2 cell array
22       {[        45]}     {'David'    }
23       {1×3 double}      {2×2 double}
24   >> disp(e)
25       [          45]     'David'
26       [1×3 double]      [2×2 double]
27   >> celldisp(e)
28   e{1,1} =
29       45
30   e{2,1} =
31        1      2      3
32   e{1,2} =
33   David
34   e{2,2} =
35        4      5
36        6      7
37   >> cellplot(e)
38   >> e{1,1}
39   ans =
40       45
41   >> e{2,1}(2)
42   ans =
43        2
44   >> e{1,2}(1)
45   ans =
46       'D'
47   >> e{2,2}(2,1)
48   ans =
49        6
```

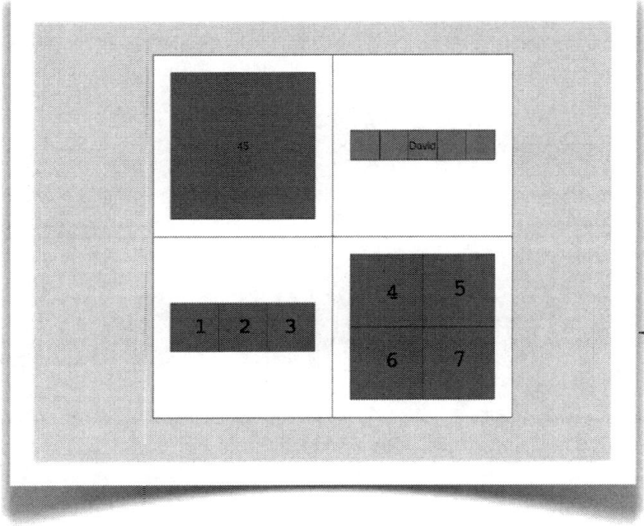

[3] The function `cellplot` (line 9) displays a structure diagram of a cell array. Note that some of the numbers in the diagram are added by the author for clarity. ↵

Two-dimensional Cell Arrays

[4] Line 6 creates a 2-by-2 cell array, using semicolons to separate the rows. Remember that a cell array itself is an array of **pointers**; lines 22-23 display these pointers. The function `disp(e)` (line 7) displays the contents of the four pointers (lines 25-26). The function `celldisp(e)` (line 8) displays the **contents** of the cell array `e` in a more detailed fashion (lines 28-36).

The function `cellplot(e)` (line 9) displays a diagram ([3], last page) showing the structure of `e`.

With these concepts in mind, it is easy to understand the facts that `e{1,1}` is 45 (lines 10, 40), `e{2,1}(2)` is 2 (lines 11, 43), `e{1,2}(1)` is the character `'D'` (lines 12, 46), and `e{2,2}(2,1)` is 6 (lines 13, 49). #

Table 4.1 Cell Arrays

Function	Description
`c = cell(n,m)`	Create an n-by-m cell array
`celldisp(c)`	Display cell array contents
`cellplot(c)`	Graphically display cell array
`c = struct2cell(s)`	Convert structure to cell array
`c = table2cell(t)`	Convert table to cell array
`s = cell2struct(c)`	Convert cell array to structure
`t = cell2table(c)`	Convert table to structure

Details and More: Help>MATLAB>Language Fundamentals>Data Types>Cell Arrays

4.2 Functions of Variable-Length Arguments

4.2a Variable-Length Input Arguments

Example04_02a.m: Variable-Length Input Arguments

[1] MATLAB allows the creation of functions of variable-length arguments. The following program includes a function `area` (lines 8-40) that allows variable-length input arguments; it calculates the area of a circle, square, rectangle, or triangle, according to its first input argument. Lines 2-6 are examples of using this function; the output is shown in [2], next page. ↵

```
1   clear
2   p = area('circle', 5)
3   q = area('square', 6)
4   s = area('rectangle', 7, 8)
5   t = area('triangle', 'bh', 9, 10)
6   u = area('triangle', 'abc', 5, 6, 7)
7
8   function output = area(varargin)
9   output = 0;
10  switch varargin{1}
11      case 'circle'
12          if nargin == 2
13              r = varargin{2};
14              output = pi*r^2;
15          end
16      case 'square'
17          if nargin == 2
18              a = varargin{2};
19              output = a^2;
20          end
21      case 'rectangle'
22          if nargin == 3
23              b = varargin{2};
24              h = varargin{3};
25              output = b*h;
26          end
27      case 'triangle'
28          if strcmp(varargin{2},'bh') && nargin == 4
29              b = varargin{3};
30              h = varargin{4};
31              output = b*h/2;
32          elseif strcmp(varargin{2}, 'abc') && nargin == 5
33              a = varargin{3};
34              b = varargin{4};
35              c = varargin{5};
36              R = a*b*c/sqrt((a+b+c)*(a-b+c)*(b-c+a)*(c-a+b));
37              output = a*b*c/(4*R);
38          end
39  end
40  end
```

[2] Output of Example04_02a.m. Note that p is the area of a circle, q is the area of a square, s is the area of a rectangle, and t and u are areas of two triangles, respectively. ↓

```
p =
   78.5398
q =
    36
s =
    56
t =
    45
u =
   14.6969
```

Built-In Variables varargin and nargin

[3] MATLAB provides two built-in variables `varargin` and `nargin` (in MATLAB, all built-in "variables" are actually functions) that allow the implementation of functions of variable-length input arguments. The variable `varargin` (used in lines 8, 10, 13, 18, 23-24, 28-30, and 32-35) is a **cell array**, of which each element points to an input argument provided by the calling function. The variable `nargin` (used in lines 12, 17, 22, 28, and 32) stores the number of input arguments. For example, line 6 causes the execution transfer to the function `area` (line 8), within which the variable `nargin` has value 5 and the variable `varargin` is a cell array of 5 elements: `'triangle'`, `'abc'`, 5, 6, and 7. To confirm this, set up a break point (Section 1.11) at line 6, run the program, step in (click the **Step In** button) to the function `area`, and examine the variables `nargin` and `varargin` as follows:

```
K>> nargin
ans =
     5
K>> varargin
varargin =
  1×5 cell array
    'triangle'    'abc'    [5]    [6]    [7]
```

Function area

The function `area` (lines 8-40) calculates the area of a shape which can be a circle, square, rectangle, or triangle. The shape is determined by the first input argument, a string. If it is a circle (lines 11), then the second argument is taken as the radius (line 13) and the area is calculated (line 14). If it is a square (line 16), then the second argument is taken as the length of the sides (line 18). If it is a rectangle (line 21), then the second and third arguments (lines 23-24) are taken as the lengths of the base and the height, respectively.

If it is a triangle (line 27), then the calling function may provide the lengths of the base and the height, or the lengths of three sides, depending on the second input argument: If `'bh'` is specified in the second input argument (line 28), the third and fourth input arguments (lines 29-30) are taken as the lengths of the base and the height, respectively; If `'abc'` is specified in the second input argument (line 32), the third, fourth, and fifth input arguments (lines 33-35) are taken as the lengths of the three sides, respectively. The area of the triangle with three sides is calculated according to the formulas in 2.11a[2], page 105.

In all the cases, if the number of input arguments is not correct, the function returns zero (line 9), indicating that an error is encountered. #

4.2b Variable-Length Input/Ouput Arguments

Example04_02b.m: Variable-Length Input/Output Arguments

[1] The following program includes a function `properties` (lines 9-38) that not only allows variable-length input arguments but also allows variable-length output arguments. It, in addition to calculating the area of a shape, can also calculate the moment of inertia of the shape (*Wikipedia>Second moment of area*), according to the number of output arguments provided by the calling function. See [2], next page, for an output. ↵

```
 1  clear
 2  Ac = properties('circle', 5)
 3  As = properties('square', 6)
 4  Ar = properties('rectangle', 7, 8)
 5  [Ac, Ic] = properties('circle', 5)
 6  [As, Is] = properties('square', 6)
 7  [Ar, Ir] = properties('rectangle', 7, 8)
 8
 9  function varargout = properties(varargin)
10  varargout{1} = 0;
11  switch varargin{1}
12      case 'circle'
13          if nargin == 2
14              r = varargin{2};
15              varargout{1} = pi*r^2;
16              if nargout == 2
17                  varargout{2} = pi*r^4/4;
18              end
19          end
20      case 'square'
21          if nargin == 2
22              a = varargin{2};
23              varargout{1} = a^2;
24              if nargout == 2
25                  varargout{2} = a^4/12;
26              end
27          end
28      case 'rectangle'
29          if nargin == 3
30              b = varargin{2};
31              h = varargin{3};
32              varargout{1} = b*h;
33              if nargout == 2
34                  varargout{2} = b*h^3/12;
35              end
36          end
37  end
38  end
```

```
Ac =
    78.5398
As =
     36
Ar =
     56
Ac =
    78.5398
Ic =
  490.8739
As =
     36
Is =
    108
Ar =
     56
Ir =
  298.6667
```

[2] The output of Example04_02b.m. →

Built-In Variables `varargout` and `nargout`

[3] MATLAB provides two built-in variables `varargout` and `nargout` that allow the implementation of functions of variable-length output arguments. The variable `varargout` (used in lines 9-10, 15, 17, 23, 25, 32, and 34) is a **cell array**, of which each element points to an output argument provided by the calling statement. The variable `nargout` (used in lines 16, 24, and 33) stores the number of output arguments in the calling statement.

Function `properties`

The function `properties` (lines 9-38), in addition to calculating the area of a shape, may also calculate the moment of inertia of the shape (*Wikipedia>Second moment of area*), according to the number of output arguments provided by the calling statement. If one output argument is provided (e.g., lines 2-4), then only the area is calculated and output. If two output arguments are provided (e.g., line 5-7), then both area and the moment of inertia are calculated and output.

In line 15, a value of `pi*r^2` is first stored somewhere in the memory, and the address is assigned to the first element of the cell array `varargout`. Line 15 can be written in an alternative way:

```
varargout(1) = {pi*r^2};
```

Please try it yourself. Lines 17, 23, 25, 32, and 34 may be written in a similar way.

Note that if no output argument is provided, it is treated as if one output argument is provided. #

Table 4.2 Functions of Variable-Length Arguments

Function	Description
`varargin`	Cell array containing the list of input arguments
`nargin`	Number of input arguments
`varargout`	Cell array containing the list of output arguments
`nargout`	Number of output arguments

Details and More: Help>MATLAB>Programming Scripts and Functions>Functions>Input and Output Arguments

4.3 Structures

Structures

[1] In Table 3.14a (page 157), nodal data are stored in an $n \times 8$ matrix, where n is the number of nodes. An obvious problem of this data representation is that all elements have to be the same type. A logical data might be more suitable to describe the support conditions (*supportx* and *supporty*). Another problem is that a table such as Table 3.14a has to be maintained to keep track of the fact that, for example, the loads are stored in the 5th and 6th columns. Using **structure** arrays will avoid these problems.

Elements of a **structure** data are referred to by **field** names (instead of by indices in a matrix or a cell array). Like the elements of a cell array, the fields of a **structure** can have different data types, lengths. Therefore, a structure data can be thought of as a cell array in which each element has a field name. ↓

Example04_03.m

[2] The following commands demonstrate creations and manipulations of **structures**.
A screen output is shown in [3-4]. ↓

```
clear
node.x = 1;
node.y = 1;
node.supportx = 0;
node.supporty = 0;
node.loadx = 0;
node.loady = -1000;
disp(node)
clear
node = struct('x',1,'y',1,'supportx',0,'supporty',0,'loadx',0,'loady',-1000)
Nodes(1) = node
Nodes(2) = struct('x',0,'y',0,'supportx',1,'supporty',1,'loadx',0,'loady',0);
Nodes(3) = struct('x',2,'y',0,'supportx',0,'supporty',1,'loadx',0,'loady',0);
disp(Nodes)
Nodes(1).x = 5.6;
disp(Nodes(1))
disp(node)
fieldnames(Nodes)
```

[3] A screen output of Example04_03.m (Continued at [4], next page). ↵

```
>> clear
>> node.x = 1;
>> node.y = 1;
>> node.supportx = 0;
>> node.supporty = 0;
>> node.loadx = 0;
>> node.loady = -1000;
>> disp(node)
           x: 1
           y: 1
    supportx: 0
    supporty: 0
       loadx: 0
       loady: -1000
```

```
>> clear
>> node = struct('x',1,'y',1,'supportx',0,'supporty',0,'loadx',0,'loady',-1000)
node =
  struct with fields:

         x: 1
         y: 1
  supportx: 0
  supporty: 0
     loadx: 0
     loady: -1000
>> Nodes(1) = node
Nodes =
  struct with fields:

         x: 1
         y: 1
  supportx: 0
  supporty: 0
     loadx: 0
     loady: -1000
>> Nodes(2) = struct('x',0,'y',0,'supportx',1,'supporty',1,'loadx',0,'loady',0);
>> Nodes(3) = struct('x',2,'y',0,'supportx',0,'supporty',1,'loadx',0,'loady',0);
>> disp(Nodes)
  1×3 struct array with fields:
    x
    y
    supportx
    supporty
    loadx
    loady
>> Nodes(1).x = 5.6;
>> disp(Nodes(1))
         x: 5.6000
         y: 1
  supportx: 0
  supporty: 0
     loadx: 0
     loady: -1000
>> disp(node)
         x: 1
         y: 1
  supportx: 0
  supporty: 0
     loadx: 0
     loady: -1000
>> fieldnames(Nodes)
ans =
  6×1 cell array
    {'x'       }
    {'y'       }
    {'supportx'}
    {'supporty'}
    {'loadx'   }
    {'loady'   }
```

[4] Screen output of Example04_03.m (Continued). ↵

About Example04_03.m

[5] In lines 20-25, we create a **structure** (`node`), which has six fields: `x`, `y`, `supportx`, `supporty`, `loadx`, and `loady` (see Table 3.14a, page 157). Lines 26-32 display `node`. Line 34 demonstrates an equivalent way of creating the same **structure** data (lines 35-43). As mentioned in [1], last page, a **structure** such as `node` can be thought of as a cell array of six elements, each having a field name.

In line 44, the entire structure data `node` is copied to the first element of an array `Nodes`, which is now a 1-by-1 structure array, i.e., a "scalar" **structure**, and is the same as `node` (lines 45-53).

Line 54 creates a second element and line 55 creates a third element for the **structure array** `Nodes`. When displaying a **structure array** (line 56), only its dimension (1-by-3) and field names are shown (lines 57-63).

Line 64 assigns a value to `Nodes(1).x`. Lines 65-71 display the contents of `Nodes(1)`, which are different from the contents of `node` (line 72-78). We show these to emphasize that, in line 44, the contents of `node` are duplicated and become the contents of `Nodes(1)`. Changes of `Nodes(1)` do not affect the contents of `node`; they are two independent data. To understand why we emphasize this, try these commands:

```
>> f = figure
>> f.Color = [0, 0, 1]
```

The first command creates a figure window (see line 7 of Example01_13.m, page 45) and returns a handle `f`. The handle `f` points to a **structure** data that describes the figure window; its background color by default is [0.94, 0.94, 0.94], a gray color. In the second command, we change the background color to [0, 0, 1], a blue color. The internal structure data is actually modified, and the background color changes to the blue color.

This confusion comes from the fact that, in MATLAB, the same syntax is used for accessing a field data using either a **structure** or **structure handle**. Therefore, be aware of whether a function returns a **structure** or a **handle**.

In line 79, the function `fieldnames` is used to retrieve the **field names** of the **structure array** `Nodes`. It outputs a cell array containing the field names (lines 81-87). #

Table 4.3 Structures

Function	Description
`s = struct(field,v)`	Create structure, equivalent to `s.field = v`
`s = rmfield(s,field)`	Remove fields from structure
`names = fieldnames(s)`	Return a cell array of strings containing the names of the fields in a structure
`s = cell2struct(c)`	Convert cell array to structure
`s = table2struct(t)`	Convert table to structure
`c = struct2cell(s)`	Convert structure to cell
`t = struct2table(s)`	Convert structure to table

Details and More: Help>MATLAB>Language Fundamentals>Data Types>Structures

4.4 Example: Statically Determinate Trusses (Version 3.0)

Example04_04.m: Truss 3.0

[1] This is a modification of the program Example03_15.m by replacing the **matrices** `Nodes` and `Members` with two structure arrays. The purpose of the modification is to enhance the readability of the program. Now, open Example03_15.m and save as Example04_04.m and modify the program as described in [2-11]. ↓

```
 1  clear
 2  Nodes = struct; Members = struct;
 3      disp(' 1. Input nodal coordinates')
 4      disp(' 2. Input connecting nodes of members')
 5      disp(' 3. Input three supports')
 6      disp(' 4. Input loads')
 7      disp(' 5. Print truss')
 8      disp(' 6. Solve truss')
 9      disp(' 7. Print results')
10      disp(' 8. Save data')
11      disp(' 9. Load data')
12      disp('10. Quit')
13  while 1
14      task = input('Enter the task number: ');
15      switch task
16          case 1
17              Nodes = inputNodes(Nodes);
18          case 2
19              Members = inputMembers(Members);
20          case 3
21              Nodes = inputSupports(Nodes);
22          case 4
23              Nodes = inputLoads(Nodes);
24          case 5
25              printTruss(Nodes, Members)
26          case 6
27              [Nodes, Members] = solveTruss(Nodes, Members);
28          case 7
29              printResults(Nodes, Members)
30          case 8
31              saveAll(Nodes, Members)
32          case 9
33              [Nodes, Members] = loadAll;
34          case 10
35              break
36      end
37  end
38
```

[2] Modify the main program (lines 1-38) as shown in line 2. Line 2 creates two scalar (1-by-1) **structures** with no fields. ↵

```
39  function output = inputNodes(Nodes)
40  while 1
41      data = input('Enter [node, x, y] or 0 to stop: ');
42      if data(1) == 0
43          break
44      else
45          Nodes(data(1)).x = data(2);
46          Nodes(data(1)).y = data(3);
47      end
48  end
49  output = Nodes;
50  end
51
52  function output = inputMembers(Members)
53  m = 0;
54  while 1
55      data = input('Enter [node1, node2] or 0 to stop: ');
56      if data(1) == 0
57          break
58      else
59          m = m+1;
60          Members(m).node1 = data(1);
61          Members(m).node2 = data(2);
62      end
63  end
64  output = Members;
65  end
66
67  function output = inputSupports(Nodes)
68  for i = 1:size(Nodes,2)
69      Nodes(i).supportx = 0;
70      Nodes(i).supporty = 0;
71  end
72  for k = 1:3
73      data = input('Enter [node, dir] (dir: ''x'' or ''y''): ');
74      if data(2) == 'x'
75          Nodes(data(1)).supportx = 1;
76      elseif data(2) == 'y'
77          Nodes(data(1)).supporty = 1;
78      end
79  end
80  output = Nodes;
81  end
82
```

[3] Modify the function `inputNodes` (lines 39-50) as shown in lines 45-46. ↓

[4] Modify the function `inputMembers` (lines 52-65) as shown in lines 60-61. ↓

[5] Modify the function `inputSupports` (lines 67-81) as shown in lines 68-71, 75, and 77. Note that `size(Nodes,2)` in line 68 outputs the number of nodes *n*. The variable `Nodes` is a 1-by-*n* structure array. The function `size(Nodes,2)` may be replaced by `length(Nodes)`. ↵

[6] Modify the function `inputLoads` (lines 83-98) as shown in lines 84-87 and 93-94. ↓

```
83   function output = inputLoads(Nodes)
84   for i = 1:size(Nodes,2)
85       Nodes(i).loadx = 0;
86       Nodes(i).loady = 0;
87   end
88   while 1
89       data = input('Enter [node, load-x, load-y] or 0 to stop: ');
90       if data(1) == 0
91           break
92       else
93           Nodes(data(1)).loadx = data(2);
94           Nodes(data(1)).loady = data(3);
95       end
96   end
97   output = Nodes;
98   end
99
100  function printTruss(Nodes, Members)
101  if (size(fieldnames(Nodes),1)<6 || size(fieldnames(Members),1)<2)
102      disp('Truss data not complete'); return
103  end
104  fprintf('\nNodal Data\n')
105  fprintf('Node        x         y  Support-x  Support-y   Load-x   Load-y\n')
106  for k = 1:size(Nodes,2)
107      fprintf('%4.0f%9.2f%9.2f%11.0f%11.0f%9.0f%9.0f\n', ...
108          k, Nodes(k).x, Nodes(k).y, ...
109          Nodes(k).supportx, Nodes(k).supporty, ...
110          Nodes(k).loadx, Nodes(k).loady)
111  end
112  fprintf('\nMember Data\n')
113  fprintf('Member  Node1    Node2\n')
114  for k = 1:size(Members,2)
115      fprintf('%4.0f%9.0f%9.0f\n', k, Members(k).node1, Members(k).node2)
116  end
117  end
118
```

[7] Modify the function `printTruss` (lines 100-117) as shown in lines 101, 106-110, and 114-115. ↵

[8] Modify the function `printResults` (lines 119-133) as shown in lines 120, 125-126, and 130-131. ↓

```
119   function printResults(Nodes, Members)
120   if (size(fieldnames(Nodes),1)<8 || size(fieldnames(Members),1)<3)
121       disp('Results not available!'), return
122   end
123   fprintf('\nReaction Forces\n')
124   fprintf('Node  Reaction-x  Reaction-y\n')
125   for k = 1:size(Nodes,2)
126       fprintf('%4.0f%12.2f%12.2f\n', k, Nodes(k).reactionx, Nodes(k).reactiony)
127   end
128   fprintf('\nMember Forces\n')
129   fprintf('Member     Force\n')
130   for k = 1:size(Members,2)
131       fprintf('%4.0f%12.2f\n', k, Members(k).force)
132   end
133   end
134
135   function saveAll(Nodes, Members)
136   fileName = input('Enter file name (default Datafile): ', 's');
137   if isempty(fileName)
138       fileName = 'Datafile';
139   end
140   save(fileName, 'Nodes', 'Members')
141   end
142
143   function [Nodes, Members] = loadAll
144   fileName = input('Enter file name (default Datafile): ', 's');
145   if isempty(fileName)
146       fileName = 'Datafile';
147   end
148   load(fileName)
149   end
150
151   function [outNodes, outMembers] = solveTruss(Nodes, Members)
152   n = size(Nodes,2); m = size(Members,2);
153   if (m+3) < 2*n
154       disp('Unstable!')
155       outNodes = 0; outMembers = 0; return
156   elseif (m+3) > 2*n
157       disp('Statically indeterminate!')
158       outNodes = 0; outMembers = 0; return
159   end
```

[9] The function `saveAll` (lines 135-141) need not be modified. ↓

[10] The function `loadAll` (lines 143-149) need not be modified. ↓

[11] Modify the function `solveTruss` (lines 151-206) as shown in the lines highlighted. ↵

```
A = zeros(2*n, 2*n); loads = zeros(2*n,1); nsupport = 0;
for i = 1:n
    for j = 1:m
        if Members(j).node1 == i || Members(j).node2 == i
            if Members(j).node1 == i
                n1 = i; n2 = Members(j).node2;
            elseif Members(j).node2 == i
                n1 = i; n2 = Members(j).node1;
            end
            x1 = Nodes(n1).x; y1 = Nodes(n1).y;
            x2 = Nodes(n2).x; y2 = Nodes(n2).y;
            L = sqrt((x2-x1)^2+(y2-y1)^2);
            A(2*i-1,j) = (x2-x1)/L;
            A(2*i,   j) = (y2-y1)/L;
        end
    end
    if (Nodes(i).supportx == 1)
        nsupport = nsupport+1;
        A(2*i-1,m+nsupport) = 1;
    end
    if (Nodes(i).supporty == 1)
        nsupport = nsupport+1;
        A(2*i, m+nsupport) = 1;
    end
    loads(2*i-1) = -Nodes(i).loadx;
    loads(2*i)   = -Nodes(i).loady;
end
forces = A\loads;
for j = 1:m
    Members(j).force = forces(j);
end
nsupport = 0;
for i = 1:n
    Nodes(i).reactionx = 0;
    Nodes(i).reactiony = 0;
    if (Nodes(i).supportx == 1)
        nsupport = nsupport+1;
        Nodes(i).reactionx = forces(m+nsupport);
    end
    if (Nodes(i).supporty == 1)
        nsupport = nsupport+1;
        Nodes(i).reactiony = forces(m+nsupport);
    end
end
outNodes = Nodes; outMembers = Members;
disp('Solved successfully.')
end
```

Run the Program

[12] Now test-run the new version using the two example problems in 3.14[1] (page 154) and 3.15[7] (page 165). The screen input/output are the same as those shown in 3.15[6] (page 164) and 3.15[8-10] (pages 165-167), respectively. #

4.5 Tables

[1] A **table** looks like an ordinary two-dimensional array (i.e., matrix) except that each column has a field name and the columns may be of different data types. A **table** can also be viewed as a **structure**, in which each field is a column vector. If you ever heard of a **relational database** system (see *Wikipedia>Relational database*), the **table** is MATLAB's implementation of the **relational model**. ↓

Example04_05.m

[2] The following commands demonstrate the creation and manipulation of **tables**.
A screen output is shown in [3-4]. ↵

```
clear
x = [1, 0, 2]'; y = [1, 0, 0]';
supportx = [0, 1, 0]'; supporty = [0, 1, 1]';
loadx = [0, 0, 0]'; loady = [-1000, 0, 0]';
Nodes = table(x, y, supportx, supporty, loadx, loady)
Nodes.Properties
Nodes.Properties.RowNames = {'top', 'left', 'right'};
disp(Nodes)
size(Nodes)
Nodes = sortrows(Nodes, {'x', 'y'})
node = Nodes(2,:)
Nodes(4,:) = array2table([2, 2, 0, 0, 100, 200]);
Nodes.Properties.RowNames{4} = 'node4';
Nodes(5,:) = cell2table({0, 2, 0, 0, 0, 0});
n = struct('x', 1.5, 'y', 0.5, ...
    'supportx', 0, 'supporty', 0, 'loadx', 0, 'loady',0);
Nodes = [Nodes; struct2table(n)];
Nodes(6,5) = array2table(300);
class(Nodes(6,5))
Nodes.loady(6) = 150;
class(Nodes.loadx(6))
disp(Nodes)
Nodes(4:6,:) = [];
disp(Nodes)
Nodes(1:3,:) = [];
size(Nodes)
```

```
>> clear
>> x = [1, 0, 2]'; y = [1, 0, 0]';
>> supportx = [0, 1, 0]'; supporty = [0, 1, 1]';
>> loadx = [0, 0, 0]'; loady = [-1000, 0, 0]';
>> Nodes = table(x, y, supportx, supporty, loadx, loady)
Nodes =
  3×6 table
    x    y    supportx    supporty    loadx    loady
    _    _    ________    ________    _____    _____
    1    1    0           0           0        -1000
    0    0    1           1           0            0
    2    0    0           1           0            0
>> Nodes.Properties
ans =
  TableProperties with properties:
             Description: ''
                UserData: []
          DimensionNames: {'Row'  'Variables'}
           VariableNames: {'x'  'y'  'supportx'  'supporty'  'loadx'  'loady'}
    VariableDescriptions: {}
           VariableUnits: {}
      VariableContinuity: []
                RowNames: {}
>> Nodes.Properties.RowNames = {'top', 'left', 'right'};
>> disp(Nodes)
             x    y    supportx    supporty    loadx    loady
             _    _    ________    ________    _____    _____
    top      1    1    0           0           0        -1000
    left     0    0    1           1           0            0
    right    2    0    0           1           0            0
>> size(Nodes)
ans =
     3     6
>> Nodes = sortrows(Nodes, {'x', 'y'})
Nodes =
  3×6 table
             x    y    supportx    supporty    loadx    loady
             _    _    ________    ________    _____    _____
    left     0    0    1           1           0            0
    top      1    1    0           0           0        -1000
    right    2    0    0           1           0            0
>> node = Nodes(2,:)
node =
  1×6 table
           x    y    supportx    supporty    loadx    loady
           _    _    ________    ________    _____    _____
    top    1    1    0           0           0        -1000
```

[3] A screen output of Example04_05.m (Continued at [4], next page). ↵

[4] Screen output of Example04_05.m (Continued). ↓

```
74   >> Nodes(4,:) = array2table([2, 2, 0, 0, 100, 200]);
75   >> Nodes.Properties.RowNames{4} = 'node4';
76   >> Nodes(5,:) = cell2table({0, 2, 0, 0, 0, 0});
77   >> n = struct('x', 1.5, 'y', 0.5, ...
78          'supportx', 0, 'supporty', 0, 'loadx', 0, 'loady',0);
79   >> Nodes = [Nodes; struct2table(n)];
80   >> Nodes(6,5) = array2table(300);
81   >> class(Nodes(6,5))
82   ans =
83          'table'
84   >> Nodes.loady(6) = 150;
85   >> class(Nodes.loadx(6))
86   ans =
87          'double'
88   >> disp(Nodes)
89                   x       y     supportx    supporty    loadx    loady
90                  ___     ___    ________    ________    _____    _____
91          left      0       0    1           1               0        0
92          top       1       1    0           0               0    -1000
93          right     2       0    0           1               0        0
94          node4     2       2    0           0             100      200
95          Row5      0       2    0           0               0        0
96          Row6    1.5     0.5    0           0             300      150
97   >> Nodes(4:6,:) = [];
98   >> disp(Nodes)
99                   x    y    supportx    supporty    loadx    loady
100                  _    _    ________    ________    _____    _____
101         left     0    0    1           1           0            0
102         top      1    1    0           0           0        -1000
103         right    2    0    0           1           0            0
104  >> Nodes(1:3,:) = [];
105  >> size(Nodes)
106  ans =
107         0     6
```

Creation of Tables

[5] Line 5 demonstrates the use of the function `table` to create a **table**. We're creating a **table** using the data shown in Table 3.14a, page 157. Using the function `table`, line 5 creates a **table** from six variables; these variables must be column vectors of the same length (but may be different types). Note that each variable is transposed (lines 2-4) so it becomes a column vector. Lines 32-38 show that `Nodes` is a 3-by-6 **table**: 3 rows and 6 fields. By default, function `table` takes the names of input variables as the field names.

Properties of Table

A **table** variable such as `Nodes` has a property field, storing its properties, which can be listed as shown in lines 6 and 40-49. The `Nodes.Properties` (line 6) itself is a structure (lines 41-49), of which each field can be modified. For example, line 7 sets up names for the rows. Lines 8 and 52-56 show that `Nodes` is a 3-by-6 **table**; each column has a name (`x`, `y`, `supportx`, `supporty`, `loadx`, and `loady`) and each row also has a name (`top`, `left`, and `right`). The size (3-by-6) is also confirmed in lines 9 and 58-59. ↵

Manipulation of Rows

[6] Line 10 sorts the rows of the **table**, by default, in ascending order based on the column `x` as the primary key and the column `y` as the secondary key, resulting in a table shown in lines 61-67.

Line 11 demonstrates a way to retrieve a row of a table. Note that the result is of type **table** (lines 69-73).

Lines 12-17 demonstrate various ways to add a row to a **table**. In line 12, a row is created as an array and converted to a one-row **table** (using the function `array2table`), and it is assigned to `Nodes` as its 4th row. Line 13 specifies a name for the new row; remember that the field `RowNames` is a cell array (see line 49). In line 14, a row is created as a cell array and converted to a one-row **table** (using the function `cell2table`), and it is assigned to `Nodes` as its 5th row. In lines 15-16, a row is created as a **structure** of the same field names (column names) as the **table**. In line 17, the **structure** is then converted to a one-row **table** (using the function `struct2table`), and it is concatenated to `Nodes` as its 6th row. Note that the concatenation using square brackets and semicolons is the same as that for ordinary arrays.

Access Elements

There are two ways to refer to an element of a **table**. First, it is treated as a two-dimensional table, and an element can be accessed using two indices (line 18). In this way, the number 300 has to be converted to a **table** in order to be assigned to `Nodes(6,5)`, since `Nodes(6,5)` is of type **table**. This is confirmed in lines 19 and 82-83. The second way is to treat the **table** as a **structure** of arrays, in which each field is a column vector. In line 20, `Nodes.loady` is a column vector and `Nodes.loady(6)` is the 6th element of the column vector. In this way, there is no need to convert a number, since `Nodes.loady(6)` is of type `double`. This is confirmed in lines 21 and 86-87.

After adding three rows, the **table** now has six rows (lines 22 and 89-96).

Line 23 demonstrates a way of removing rows from a **table**. After removing three rows (line 23) from `Nodes`, the **table** has three rows left (lines 24 and 99-103). Line 25 removes the last three rows from the **table**. It becomes a 0-by-6 **table** (lines 26 and 106-107). #

Table 4.5 Tables

Function	Description
`t = table(v1,v2,...)`	Create table from variables
`t = array2table(a)`	Convert array to table
`t = cell2table(c)`	Convert cell array to table
`t = struct2table(s)`	Convert structure to table
`a = table2array(t)`	Convert table to array
`c = table2cell(t)`	Convert table to cell
`s = table2struct(t)`	Convert table to structure
`t = sortrows(t)`	Sort rows of array or table
`T.Properties`	Properties of table T

Details and More: Help>MATLAB>Language Fundamentals>Data Types>Tables

4.6 Conversion of Cell Arrays

Example: Polymer Database

[1] The table below lists the names and properties of some polymers. In this section, we want to demonstrate the creation of a **cell array** storing the polymer data below and demonstrate the conversion of the **cell array** to a **structure array** and to a **table**. In Sections 4.7 and 4.8, we'll use the same information below to demonstrate the creation and the conversion of a **structure array** and a **table**, respectively. ↓

Name	Abbreviation	Melting Temperature (°C)	Crystallization Temperature (°C)	Density (g/cm^3)
Polyethylene	PE	135	56	0.96
Polypropylene	PP	171	86	0.95
Polyoxymethylene	POM	180	90	1.42
Polyethylene terephthalate	PET	266	158	1.38

Example04_06.m: Polymer Database

[2] This script first creates a **cell array** to store the information (lines 2-5), then converts the **cell array** to a **structure array** using the function `cell2struct` (lines 9-10), and finally converts the **cell array** to a **table** using the function `cell2table` (line 14). In each stage, it displays PET's name and melting temperature (lines 6-7, 11-12, and 15-18) to demonstrate the access of data. ↵

```
1   clear
2   Polymer_Cell = {'Polyethylene',               'PE',  135,  56, 0.96;
3                   'Polypropylene',              'PP',  171,  86, 0.95;
4                   'Polyoxymethylene',           'POM', 180,  90, 1.42;
5                   'Polyethylene terephthalate', 'PET', 266, 158, 1.38};
6   PET_Name = Polymer_Cell{4,1}
7   PET_Melting = Polymer_Cell{4,3}
8
9   Field = {'Name', 'Abbreviation', 'Melting', 'Crystallization', 'Density'};
10  Polymer_Structure = cell2struct(Polymer_Cell, Field, 2);
11  PET_Name = Polymer_Structure(4).Name
12  PET_Melting = Polymer_Structure(4).Melting
13
14  Polymer_Table = cell2table(Polymer_Cell, 'VariableNames', Field);
15  PET_Name = Polymer_Table.Name(4)
16  PET_Melting = Polymer_Table.Melting(4)
17  PET_Name = Polymer_Table(4,1)
18  PET_Melting = Polymer_Table(4,3)
```

```
>> clear
>> Polymer_Cell = {'Polyethylene',                 'PE',  135,  56, 0.96;
                   'Polypropylene',                'PP',  171,  86, 0.95;
                   'Polyoxymethylene',             'POM', 180,  90, 1.42;
                   'Polyethylene terephthalate', 'PET', 266, 158, 1.38};
>> PET_Name = Polymer_Cell{4,1}
PET_Name =
    'Polyethylene terephthalate'
>> PET_Melting = Polymer_Cell{4,3}
PET_Melting =
   266
>>
>> Field = {'Name', 'Abbreviation', 'Melting', 'Crystallization', 'Density'};
>> Polymer_Structure = cell2struct(Polymer_Cell, Field, 2);
>> PET_Name = Polymer_Structure(4).Name
PET_Name =
    'Polyethylene terephthalate'
>> PET_Melting = Polymer_Structure(4).Melting
PET_Melting =
   266
>>
>> Polymer_Table = cell2table(Polymer_Cell, 'VariableNames', Field);
>> PET_Name = Polymer_Table.Name(4)
PET_Name =
  1x1 cell array
    {'Polyethylene terephthalate'}
>> PET_Melting = Polymer_Table.Melting(4)
PET_Melting =
   266
>> PET_Name = Polymer_Table(4,1)
PET_Name =
  table
              Name
    ____________________________
    'Polyethylene terephthalate'
>> PET_Melting = Polymer_Table(4,3)
PET_Melting =
  table
    Melting
    _______
    266
```

[3] The output of Example04_06.m. →

[4] The **Workspace**. ↵

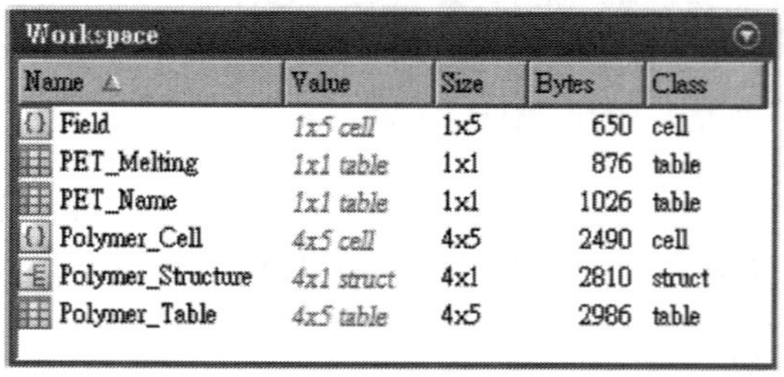

About Example04_06.m

[5] Lines 2-5 create a 4-by-5, two-dimensional **cell array** and store the information listed in [1], page 191. Note that, like an ordinary array, rows of a cell array are separated by semicolons and elements within a row are separated by commas. In general, for a two-dimensional **cell array**, elements in a row or in a column are not necessarily the same type. However, in our case, elements in a column have the same type (but the strings in a column do not have the same length).

To demonstrate the access of an element in a **cell array**, line 6 retrieves PET's name (lines 25-26), and line 7 retrieves PET's melting temperature (lines 28-29).

Line 10 converts the **cell array** into a **structure array**, using the function `cell2struct`. The variable `Field`, a **cell array** prepared in line 9, storing the field names, is input to `cell2struct` as an argument. The third input argument of `cell2struct` specifies that the second dimension (i.e., column dimension) of the **cell array** is to be used as fields in creating the **structure array**. In this case, using the first dimension (i.e., row dimension) would result in an error. Line 11 retrieves PET's name (lines 34-35), and Line 12 retrieves PET's melting temperature (lines 37-38).

Line 14 converts the **cell array** into a **table**, using the function `cell2table`. The variable `Field` is used again as an input argument to specify the field names. Line 15 retrieves PET's name (lines 42-44), and Line 16 retrieves PET's melting temperature (lines 46-47). Line 17 uses indexing method to retrieve PET's name (lines 49-53), and Line 18 retrieves PET's melting temperature (lines 55-59). Note that, with indexing method, the result is of type **table** (see [4], last page). #

4.7 Conversion of Structure Arrays

Polymer Database Revisit

[1] In this section, we demonstrate the creation of a **structure array** storing the polymer data listed in 4.6[1] (page 191) and demonstrate the conversion of the **structure array** to a **cell array** and to a **table**. ↓

Example04_07.m: Polymer Database

[2] This script creates a **structure array** storing the polymer data (lines 2-21), converts the **structure array** to a **cell array** using the function `struct2cell` (line 25), and converts the **structure array** to a **table** using the function `struct2table` (line 30). In each stage, it displays PET's name and melting temperature (lines 22-23, 27-28, and 31-34) to demonstrate the access of data. ↵

```
 1  clear
 2  Polymer_Structure = [struct('Name', 'Polyethylene',                 ...
 3                              'Abbreviation', 'PE',                    ...
 4                              'Melting', 135,                          ...
 5                              'Crystallization', 56,                   ...
 6                              'Density', 0.96);
 7                       struct('Name', 'Polypropylene',                 ...
 8                              'Abbreviation', 'PP',                    ...
 9                              'Melting', 171,                          ...
10                              'Crystallization', 86,                   ...
11                              'Density', 0.95);
12                       struct('Name', 'Polyoxymethylene',              ...
13                              'Abbreviation', 'POM',                   ...
14                              'Melting', 180,                          ...
15                              'Crystallization', 90,                   ...
16                              'Density', 1.42);
17                       struct('Name', 'Polyethylene terephthalate',    ...
18                              'Abbreviation', 'PET',                   ...
19                              'Melting', 266,                          ...
20                              'Crystallization', 158',                 ...
21                              'Density', 1.38)];
22  PET_Name = Polymer_Structure(4).Name
23  PET_Melting = Polymer_Structure(4).Melting
24
25  Polymer_Cell = struct2cell(Polymer_Structure);
26  Polymer_Cell = Polymer_Cell';
27  PET_Name = Polymer_Cell{4,1}
28  PET_Melting = Polymer_Cell{4,3}
29
30  Polymer_Table = struct2table(Polymer_Structure);
31  PET_Name = Polymer_Table.Name(4)
32  PET_Melting = Polymer_Table.Melting(4)
33  PET_Name = Polymer_Table(4,1)
34  PET_Melting = Polymer_Table(4,3)
```

```
>> clear
>> Polymer_Structure = [struct('Name', 'Polyethylene',                   ...
                               'Abbreviation', 'PE',                    ...
                               'Melting', 135,                          ...
                               'Crystallization', 56,                   ...
                               'Density', 0.96);                        ...
                        struct('Name', 'Polypropylene',                 ...
                               'Abbreviation', 'PP',                    ...
                               'Melting', 171,                          ...
                               'Crystallization', 86,                   ...
                               'Density', 0.95);                        ...
                        struct('Name', 'Polyoxymethylene',              ...
                               'Abbreviation', 'POM',                   ...
                               'Melting', 180,                          ...
                               'Crystallization', 90,                   ...
                               'Density', 1.42);                        ...
                        struct('Name', 'Polyethylene terephthalate',    ...
                               'Abbreviation', 'PET',                   ...
                               'Melting', 266,                          ...
                               'Crystallization', 158',                 ...
                               'Density', 1.38)];
>> PET_Name = Polymer_Structure(4).Name
PET_Name =
    'Polyethylene terephthalate'
>> PET_Melting = Polymer_Structure(4).Melting
PET_Melting =
   266
>>
>> Polymer_Cell = struct2cell(Polymer_Structure);
>> Polymer_Cell = Polymer_Cell';
>> PET_Name = Polymer_Cell{4,1}
PET_Name =
    'Polyethylene terephthalate'
>> PET_Melting = Polymer_Cell{4,3}
PET_Melting =
   266
>>
>> Polymer_Table = struct2table(Polymer_Structure);
>> PET_Name = Polymer_Table.Name(4)
PET_Name =
  1x1 cell array
    {'Polyethylene terephthalate'}
>> PET_Melting = Polymer_Table.Melting(4)
PET_Melting =
   266
>> PET_Name = Polymer_Table(4,1)
PET_Name =
  table
                Name
    ____________________________
    'Polyethylene terephthalate'
>> PET_Melting = Polymer_Table(4,3)
PET_Melting =
  table
    Melting
    _______
    266
```

[3] This is the output of Example04_07.m. ↵

[4] The **Workspace**. ↓

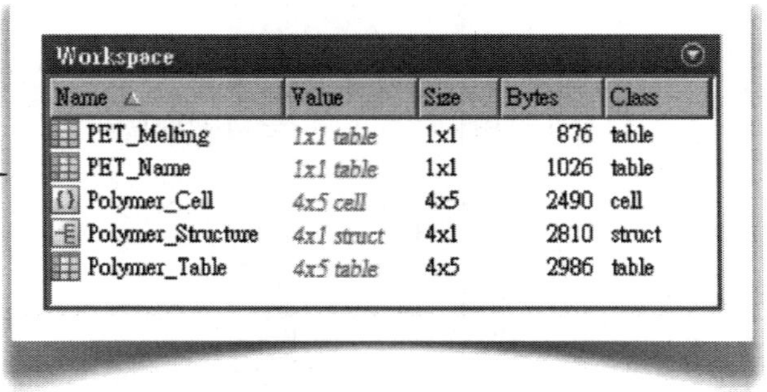

Name	Value	Size	Bytes	Class
PET_Melting	1x1 table	1x1	876	table
PET_Name	1x1 table	1x1	1026	table
Polymer_Cell	4x5 cell	4x5	2490	cell
Polymer_Structure	4x1 struct	4x1	2810	struct
Polymer_Table	4x5 table	4x5	2986	table

About Example04_07.m

[5] Lines 2-21 create an array of four **structures** (i.e., a **structure array**) and store the polymer data listed in the table in 4.6[1], page 191. Note that we separate the four **structures** using semicolons (lines 6, 11, and 16), creating a 4-by-1 **structure array** (see [4]).

To demonstrate the access of an element in the **structure array**, line 22 retrieves PET's name (lines 57-58), and line 23 retrieves PET's melting temperature (lines 60-61).

Line 25 converts the **structure array** into a **cell array**, using the function `struct2cell`, which converts the 5-field, 4-row **structure array** into a 5-by-4 **cell array**. Line 26 transposes the cell array, so it becomes a 4-by-5 **cell array** (see [4]). Line 27 retrieves PET's name (lines 66-67), and Line 28 retrieves PET's melting temperature (lines 69-70).

Line 30 converts the **structure array** into a **table**, using the function `struct2table`, retaining the same field names as the **structure array**. Line 31 retrieves PET's name (lines 74-76), and line 32 retrieves PET's melting temperature (lines 78-79). Line 33 uses indexing method to retrieve PET's name (lines 81-85), and line 34 retrieves PET's melting temperature (lines 87-91). Note that, with indexing method, the result is of type **table** (see [4]). #

4.8 Conversion of Tables

Polymer Database Revisit

[1] In this section, we demonstrate the creation of a **table** storing the polymer data listed in 4.6[1] (page 191) and demonstrate the conversion of the **table** to a **structure array** and to a **cell array**. ↓

Example04_08.m: Polymer Database

[2] This script creates a **table** storing the polymer data (lines 2-8), converts the **table** to a **cell array** using the function `table2cell` (line 14), and converts the **table** to a **structure array** using the function `table2struct` (line 18). In each stage, it displays PET's name and melting temperature (lines 9-12, 15-16, and 19-20) to demonstrate the access of data. ↓

```
 1  clear
 2  Name = {'Polyethylene', 'Polypropylene', 'Polyoxymethylene', ...
 3          'Polyethylene terephthalate'}';
 4  Abbreviation = {'PE', 'PP', 'POM', 'PET'}';
 5  Melting = [135, 171, 180, 266]';
 6  Crystallization = [56, 86, 90, 1585]';
 7  Density = [0.96, 0.95, 1.42, 1.38]';
 8  Polymer_Table = table(Name,Abbreviation,Melting,Crystallization,Density);
 9  PET_Name = Polymer_Table.Name(4)
10  PET_Melting = Polymer_Table.Melting(4)
11  PET_Name = Polymer_Table(4,1)
12  PET_Melting = Polymer_Table(4,3)
13
14  Polymer_Cell = table2cell(Polymer_Table);
15  PET_Name = Polymer_Cell{4,1}
16  PET_Melting = Polymer_Cell{4,3}
17
18  Polymer_Structure = table2struct(Polymer_Table);
19  PET_Name = Polymer_Structure(4).Name
20  PET_Melting = Polymer_Structure(4).Melting
```

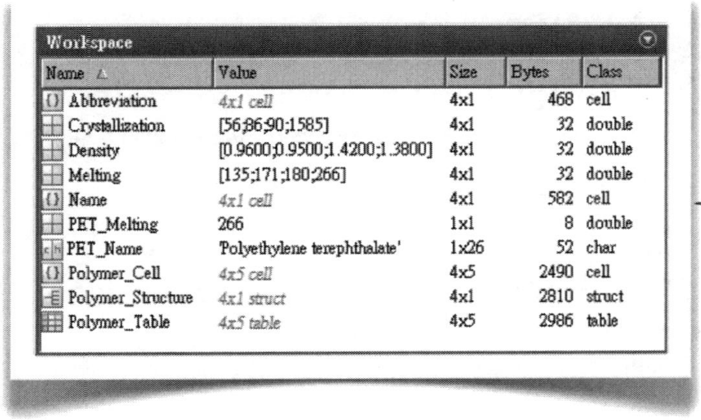
Workspace

Name	Value	Size	Bytes	Class
Abbreviation	4x1 cell	4x1	468	cell
Crystallization	[56;86;90;1585]	4x1	32	double
Density	[0.9600;0.9500;1.4200;1.3800]	4x1	32	double
Melting	[135;171;180;266]	4x1	32	double
Name	4x1 cell	4x1	582	cell
PET_Melting	266	1x1	8	double
PET_Name	'Polyethylene terephthalate'	1x26	52	char
Polymer_Cell	4x5 cell	4x5	2490	cell
Polymer_Structure	4x1 struct	4x1	2810	struct
Polymer_Table	4x5 table	4x5	2986	table

[3] The **Workspace**. ↵

```
>> clear
>> Name = {'Polyethylene', 'Polypropylene', 'Polyoxymethylene', ...
           'Polyethylene terephthalate'}';
>> Abbreviation = {'PE', 'PP', 'POM', 'PET'}';
>> Melting = [135, 171, 180, 266]';
>> Crystallization = [56, 86, 90, 1585]';
>> Density = [0.96, 0.95, 1.42, 1.38]';
>> Polymer_Table = table(Name,Abbreviation,Melting,Crystallization,Density);
>> PET_Name = Polymer_Table.Name(4)
PET_Name =
  1x1 cell array
    {'Polyethylene terephthalate'}
>> PET_Melting = Polymer_Table.Melting(4)
PET_Melting =
   266
>> PET_Name = Polymer_Table(4,1)
PET_Name =
  table
                 Name
    ____________________________
    'Polyethylene terephthalate'
>> PET_Melting = Polymer_Table(4,3)
PET_Melting =
  table
    Melting
    _______
    266
>>
>> Polymer_Cell = table2cell(Polymer_Table);
>> PET_Name = Polymer_Cell{4,1}
PET_Name =
    'Polyethylene terephthalate'
>> PET_Melting = Polymer_Cell{4,3}
PET_Melting =
   266
>>
>> Polymer_Structure = table2struct(Polymer_Table);
>> PET_Name = Polymer_Structure(4).Name
PET_Name =
    'Polyethylene terephthalate'
>> PET_Melting = Polymer_Structure(4).Melting
PET_Melting =
   266
```

[4] The output of Example04_08.m. ↵

About Example04_08.m

[5] Lines 2-3 create a **cell array** `Name` containing polymers' names. Line 4 creates a **cell array** `Abbreviation` containing polymers' abbreviations. Line 5 creates an (ordinary) array `Melting` containing polymer's melting temperatures. Line 6 creates an array `Crystallization` containing polymer's crystallization temperatures. Line 7 creates an array `Density` containing polymer's densities. Note that each of the above arrays was transposed, so that it becomes a column array. Line 8 uses the above five variables to create a 4-by-5 **table** (see [3], page 197). By default, the variable names are used as field names.

To demonstrate the access of an element in the **table**, line 9 retrieves PET's name (lines 30-32), and line 10 retrieves PET's melting temperature (lines 34-35). Line 11 uses indexing method to retrieve PET's name (lines 37-41), and line 12 uses indexing method to retrieve PET's melting temperature (lines 43-47).

Line 14 converts the **table** into a **cell array**, using the function `table2cell`. The 4-by-5 **table** is converted into a 4-by-5 **cell array** (see [3]). Line 15 retrieves PET's name (lines 51-52), and line 16 retrieves PET's melting temperature (lines 54-55).

Line 18 converts the **table** into a **structure array**, using the function `table2struct`, retaining the same field names. Line 19 retrieves PET's name (lines 59-60), and line 20 retrieves PET's melting temperature (lines 62-63). #

4.9 User-Defined Classes

[1] In this section, we'll demonstrate the creation of a class (data type) representing polynomials. A row vector is used to represent a polynomial; the coefficients of the polynomial are stored in the row vector. We'll define operators (such as plus, minus, etc.) that operate on a polynomial or two polynomials. ↓

Poly.m

[2] Type the following statements and save in the **Current Folder** as **Poly.m** (the file name must be consistent with the class name, specified in line 1). The class Poly is an implementation of the polynomial (*Wikipedia>Polynomial*), including its representing data structure and some operations on the polynomial. This is a simple demonstration of user-defined class. We'll show you the application of this class in [4], next page. (Continued at [3], next page.) ↵

```
1  classdef Poly
2      properties
3          coef = zeros(1,99);
4      end
5      methods
6          function p = Poly(varargin)
7              for k = 1:nargin
8                  p.coef(nargin-k+1) = varargin{k};
9              end
10         end
11         function disp(p)
12             for k = 99:-1:3
13                 if p.coef(k)
14                     fprintf('%+fx^%d', p.coef(k), k-1);
15                 end
16             end
17             if p.coef(2)
18                 fprintf('%+fx', p.coef(2));
19             end
20             fprintf('%+f\n', p.coef(1))
21         end
22         function p = plus(p1, p2)
23             p = Poly;
24             p.coef = p1.coef+p2.coef;
25         end
26         function p = minus(p1, p2)
27             p = Poly;
28             p.coef = p1.coef-p2.coef;
29         end
30         function p = uminus(p1)
31             p = Poly;
32             p.coef = -p1.coef;
33         end
```

[3] Poly.m (Continued) ↓

```
34          function p = uplus(p1)
35              p = Poly;
36              p.coef = p1.coef;
37          end
38          function p = mtimes(p1, p2)
39              p = Poly;
40              for i = 1:99
41                  for j = 1:99
42                      if p1.coef(i) && p2.coef(j)
43                          p.coef(i+j-1) = p.coef(i+j-1)+p1.coef(i)*p2.coef(j);
44                      end
45                  end
46              end
47          end
48          function output = value(p, x)
49              output = zeros(1,length(x));
50              for k = 1:99
51                  if p.coef(k)
52                      output = output + p.coef(k)*x.^(k-1);
53                  end
54              end
55          end
56      end
57  end
```

```
58  >> clear
59  >> a = Poly(3,2,1)
60  a =
61  +3.000000x^2+2.000000x+1.000000
62  >> b = Poly(5,6)
63  b =
64  +5.000000x+6.000000
65  >> c = Poly(8)
66  c =
67  +8.000000
68  >> d = a+b
69  d =
70  +3.000000x^2+7.000000x+7.000000
71  >> e = -a-b*(-c+a)
72  e =
73  -15.000000x^3-31.000000x^2+21.000000x+41.000000
74  >> value(e, 2.5)
75  ans =
76   -334.6250
77  >> x = linspace(-3,3);
78  >> y = value(e,x);
79  >> plot(x,y)
```

Example04_09.m

[4] To demonstrate the use of the new **class**, type these commands and watch the output. Line 79 produces a figure shown in [5], next page. ↵

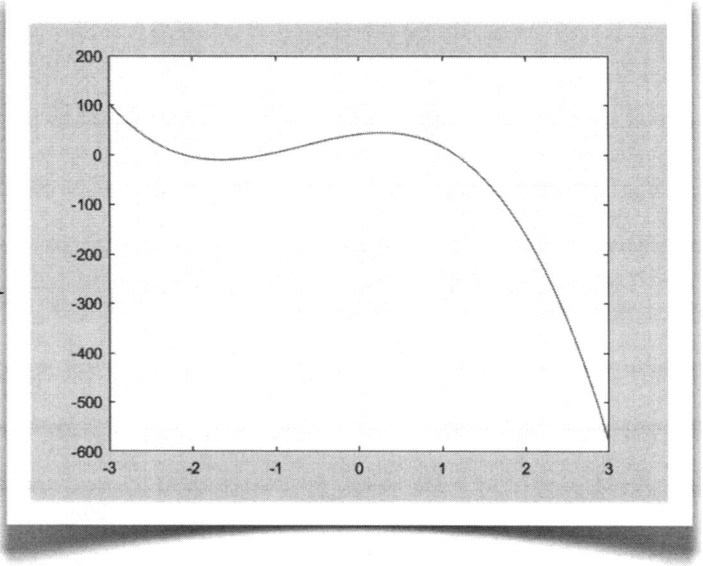

[5] Line 79 produces a figure like this. ↓

About Example04_09.m

[6] Lines 59-61 create a polynomial of degree 2,

$$a = 3x^2 + 2x + 1$$

Lines 62-64 create a polynomial of degree 1,

$$b = 5x + 6$$

Lines 65-67 create a polynomial of degree 0, i.e., a constant,

$$c = 8$$

Creation of polynomials is implemented in lines 6-10; it automatically calls the function `disp`, defined in lines 11-21.

Lines 68-70 demonstrate the addition of two polynomials. Lines 71-73 demonstrate a more involved polynomial expression. Note that, in line 71, the first minus is a unary operator (implemented in lines 30-33), while the second minus is a binary operator (implemented in lines 26-29; also see Table 2.8, page 92); the third minus is also a unary operator; the plus is a binary operator, implemented in lines 22-25.

In line 74, the function `value` (implemented in lines 48-55) accepts a `Poly` and a `double` *x* as input arguments and returns the function value of the polynomial at *x* (lines 75-76). The function can accept an array *x* and returns an array of the same size. This is demonstrated in lines 77-78. Line 79 plots a curve of the function (see [5])

$$y = -15x^3 - 31x^2 + 21x + 41$$

→

About Poly.m

[7] The definition of the class `Poly` (lines 1-57) consists of a **properties** section (lines 2-4), which defines a data structure representing a polynomial, and a **methods** section (lines 5-56), which defines operations on the polynomials.

In the **properties** section (lines 2-4), we use a row vector to represent a polynomial, in which the kth element stores the coefficient of the term of degree *k*-1. Note that our implementation allows a maximum of 99 terms (line 3) in a polynomial.

In the **methods** section (lines 5-56), we define 8 operations on polynomials: creation of a polynomial (lines 6-10), display of a polynomial (line 11-21), addition of two polynomials (lines 22-25), subtraction of two polynomials (lines 26-29), unary minus of a polynomial (lines 30-33), unary plus of a polynomial (lines 34-37), multiplication of two polynomials (lines 38-47), and the function value calculation of a polynomial (lines 48-55). Note that we don't need to implement the multiplication of a polynomial with a constant number, since a constant number can be treated as a polynomial of degree zero.

Lines 6-10 implement how an object of `Poly` is created, using variable-length input arguments (Section 4.2). The user inputs the coefficients of a polynomial (e.g., lines 59, 62, and 65), from higher-order terms to lower, which are then stored in the array `coef`.

Lines 11-21 implement how an object of `Poly` is displayed (see lines 61, 64, 67, 70, and 73). ↵

Object-Oriented Programming

[8] The concepts and techniques introduced in this section constitute the so called **object-oriented programming** paradigm. For details and more, please see *Help>MATLAB> Advanced Software Development>Object-Oriented Programming*.

In this paradigm, an instance of a class is called an **object**, which is nothing but what we used to call a **data**. For example, `a`, `b`, `c`, `d`, and `e` in [4] are **objects** of class `Poly`. ↓

Differentiation and Integration of a Polynomial

[9] You may implement the differentiation and integration of a polynomial by adding the following two functions into the **methods** section of the class `Poly`:

```
function p = diff(p1)
    p = Poly;
    for k = 2:99
        if p1.coef(k)
            p.coef(k-1) = p1.coef(k)*(k-1);
        end
    end
end
function p = int(p1)
    p = Poly;
    for k = 1:99
        if p1.coef(k)
            p.coef(k+1) = p1.coef(k)/k;
        end
    end
end
```

And you may test-run the new version of `Poly` by continuing the commands in Example04_09.m ([4], page 201):

```
>> f = int(e)
f =
-3.750000x^4-10.333333x^3+10.500000x^2+41.000000x+0.000000
>> g = diff(f)
g =
-15.000000x^3-31.000000x^2+21.000000x+41.000000
```

↓

Overload Functions

[10] In 2.7[2] (page 89) we used a built-in function `diff` (lines 7 and 13) to calculate the differences between adjacent elements of an array. The function `diff` in [9] (this page) is said to **overload** the functions of the same name. Similarly, the functions `disp`, `plus`, `minus`, `uminus`, `uplus`, `mtimes` in Poly.m (pages 200-201) are overloading functions (also see Table 2.8, page 92).

When multiple functions of the same name exist, MATLAB uses **class** names to determine which version of function to use. You can think the "full name" of a function is the combination of the function name and its class name. For example, the "full name" of `disp` and `plus` in Poly.m is `disp_Poly` and `plus_Poly`, respectively.

For details and more, see *Help>MATLAB>Advanced Software Development>Object-Oriented Programming>Class Definition>Methods>Overload Functions in Class Definitions*. #

4.10 Additional Exercise Problems

Problem04_01: Cell Arrays

The table below lists names, chemical symbols, atomic numbers, and atomic masses of some chemical elements. Create a **cell array** to store these data, convert the **cell array** to a **structure array**, and then convert the **cell array** to a **table**. In each stage, retrieve helium's atomic mass (4.003).

Name	Symbol	Atomic Number	Atomic Mass
Carbon	C	6	12.011
Helium	He	2	4.003
Hydrogen	H	1	1.008
Nitrogen	N	7	14.007
Oxygen	O	8	15.999

Problem04_02: Structure Arrays

Create a **structure array** to store the data in Problem04_01, convert the **structure array** to a **cell array**, and then convert the **structure array** to a **table**. In each stage, retrieve helium's atomic mass (4.003).

Problem04_03: Tables

Create a **table** to store the data in Problem04_01, convert the **table** to a **cell array**, and then convert the **table** to a **structure array**. In each stage, retrieve helium's atomic mass (4.003).

Problem04_04: Add Rows to Existing Cell Arrays

Add the following two chemical elements into the **cell array** created in Program04_01. Retrieve sodium's atomic mass (22.990).

Name	Symbol	Atomic Number	Atomic Mass
Sodium	Na	11	22.990
Chlorine	Cl	17	35.453

Problem04_05: Add Rows to Existing Structure Arrays

Add the two elements in Problem04_04 into the **structure array** created in Program04_02. Retrieve sodium's atomic mass (22.990).

Problem04_06: Add Rows to Existing Tables

Add the two elements in Problem04_04 into the **table** created in Program04_03. Sort the rows of the **table** in ascending order based on the atomic numbers. Retrieve sodium's atomic mass (22.990).

Problem04_07: Implement Function `plot` for the Class `Poly`

Add a function `plot` to the class `Poly` (see Poly.m, pages 200-201). The function has an interface like this

```
function plot(p, a, b)
```

where `p` is of class `Poly`, and `a` and `b` are two real numbers. It plots a polynomial function with the range from `a` to `b`. For example,

```
>> plot(Poly(3,2,1), -3, 3)
```

produces a plot as shown right.

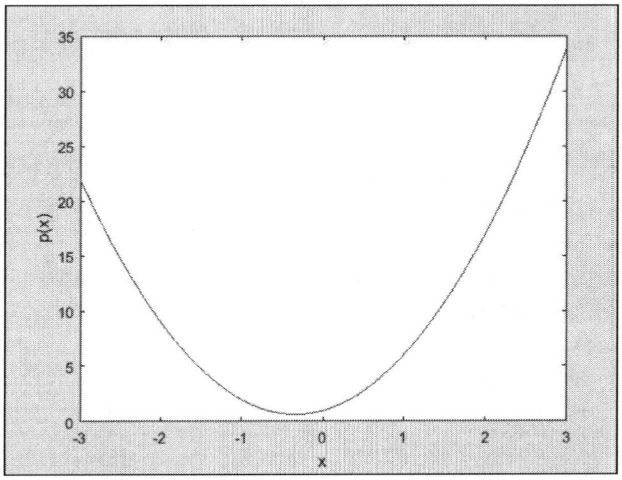

Chapter 5

Data Visualization: Plots

Visual perception is the most efficient way of understanding data. MATLAB provides many forms of plots to aid engineers in presenting their data in various visual forms. Familiarizing yourself with these plotting techniques will facilitate your presentation of data.

5.1 Graphics Objects and Parent-Children Relationship

5.1a Graphics Objects and Parent-Children Relationship

[1] The GUI created in 1.18[4-5] (page 56; see a copy below) consists of many graphics objects; they form a parent-children relationship shown below. The **Figure** is on the top of the parent-children hierarchy. (We'll show that more than one **Figure** can be created under a **Root** object; the **Root** is actually the "ancestor" of all graphics objects.) Under the **Figure**, we've created 6 graphics objects: an **Axes**, two **Static Texts**, two **Edit Texts**, and a **Push Button**. And under the **Axes**, 7 **Line** objects (the trajectories) were created. This section introduces some basic concepts about graphics objects and their parent-children relationship. ↓

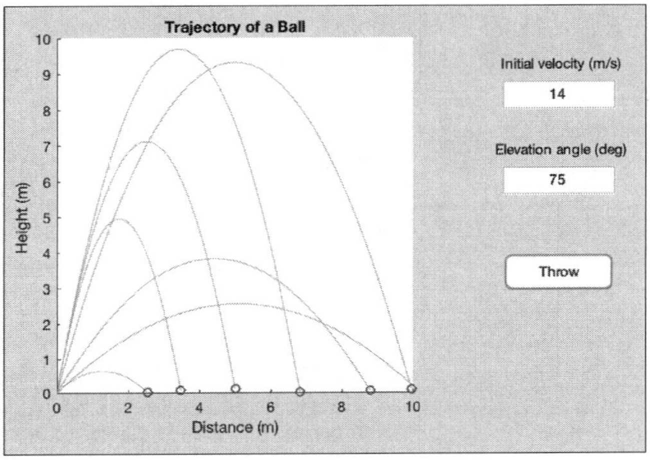

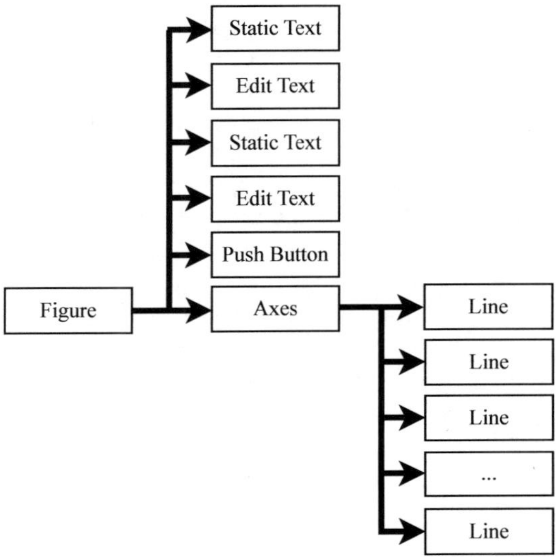

Example05_01a.m

[2] The following commands create some graphics objects and demonstrate the parent-children relationship among these graphic objects. →

```
1   clear
2   x = linspace(0,2*pi);
3   y = sin(x);
4   hCurve = plot(x,y);
5   hCurve.Parent
6   hAxes = hCurve.Parent;
7   hAxes.Parent
8   hFigure = hAxes.Parent;
9   hFigure.Parent
10  hRoot = hFigure.Parent;
11  hRoot.Parent
12  hRoot.Children
13  hFigure.Children
14  hAxes.Children
15  hCurve.Children
16  delete(hCurve)
17  delete(hAxes)
18  delete(hFigure)
```

[3] Line 4 produces a sine curve. ↵

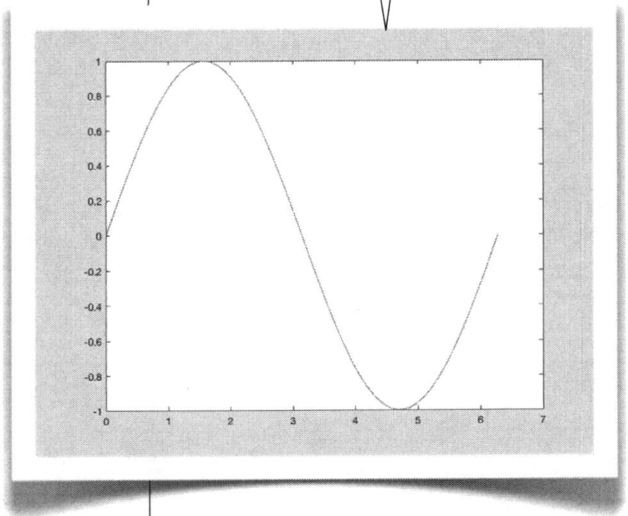

```
19  >> clear
20  >> x = linspace(0,2*pi);
21  >> y = sin(x);
22  >> hCurve = plot(x,y);
23  >> hCurve.Parent
24  ans =
25    Axes with properties:
26
27               XLim: [0 7]
28               YLim: [-1 1]
29             XScale: 'linear'
30             YScale: 'linear'
31      GridLineStyle: '-'
32           Position: [0.1300 0.1100 0.7750 0.8150]
33              Units: 'normalized'
34
35    Show all properties
36  >> hAxes = hCurve.Parent;
37  >> hAxes.Parent
38  ans =
39    Figure (1) with properties:
40
41        Number: 1
42          Name: ''
43         Color: [0.9400 0.9400 0.9400]
44      Position: [1000 918 560 420]
45         Units: 'pixels'
46
47    Show all properties
48  >> hFigure = hAxes.Parent;
49  >> hFigure.Parent
50  ans =
51    Graphics Root with properties:
52
53            CurrentFigure: [1×1 Figure]
54      ScreenPixelsPerInch: 72
55               ScreenSize: [1 1 2560 1440]
56         MonitorPositions: [1 1 2560 1440]
57                    Units: 'pixels'
58
59    Show all properties
60  >> hRoot = hFigure.Parent;
61  >> hRoot.Parent
62  ans =
63    0×0 empty GraphicsPlaceholder array.
```

[4] This is a **Command Window** session of Example05_01a.m.

In line 4, the function `plot` produces a sine curve (see [3], last page) and returns a handle of the curve. The curve is a **Line** object. The handle `hCurve` now points to the **Line** object.

When the **Line** object is created in line 4, a **Figure** object and an **Axes** object are automatically created. Together with a preexisting **Root** object, these four objects form a parent-children relationship as shown in [5], next page. The rest of the commands here reiterate this relationship.

Each graphics object has a set of **properties**, two of which are **Parent** and **Children**. Line 5 shows a way to access the **Line** object's parent, which is the **Axes** object. Lines 24-33 output a short list of the **Axes's** properties. If you click the hyperlink at the end of the properties (line 35), a complete list of the **Axes's** properties will be listed.

After the execution of line 6, the handle `hAxes` now points to the **Axes** object.

The **Axes's** parent is a **Figure** object (lines 7 and 38-47), and in line 8 we use a handle `hFigure` to point to the **Figure** object.

The **Figure's** parent is a **Root** object (lines 9 and 50-59), and in line 10 we use a handle `hRoot` to point to the **Root** object.

Lines 11 and 62-63 demonstrate that the **Root** object has no parent; a **Root** is the ancestor of all other graphics objects. (Continued at [6], next page.) ↵

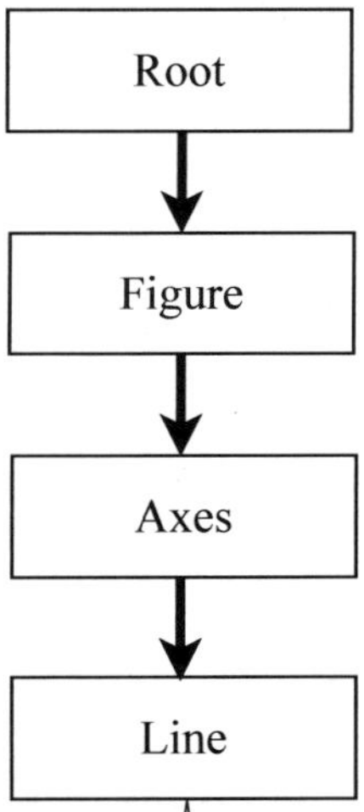

[5] Four graphics objects created in line 22 of Example05_01a.m form a parent-children relationship like this. ↓

```
64  >> hRoot.Children
65  ans =
66    Figure (1) with properties:
67
68        Number: 1
69          Name: ''
70         Color: [0.9400 0.9400 0.9400]
71      Position: [1000 918 560 420]
72         Units: 'pixels'
73
74    Show all properties
75  >> hFigure.Children
76  ans =
77    Axes with properties:
78
79              XLim: [0 7]
80              YLim: [-1 1]
81            XScale: 'linear'
82            YScale: 'linear'
83     GridLineStyle: '-'
84          Position: [0.1300 0.1100 0.7750 0.8150]
85             Units: 'normalized'
86
87    Show all properties
88  >> hAxes.Children
89  ans =
90    Line with properties:
91
92                Color: [0 0.4470 0.7410]
93            LineStyle: '-'
94            LineWidth: 0.5000
95               Marker: 'none'
96           MarkerSize: 6
97      MarkerFaceColor: 'none'
98                XData: [1×100 double]
99                YData: [1×100 double]
100               ZData: [1×0 double]
101
102   Show all properties
103 >> hCurve.Children
104 ans =
105   0×0 empty GraphicsPlaceholder array.
106 >> delete(hCurve)
107 >> delete(hAxes)
108 >> delete(hFigure)
```

[6] (Continued) Lines 12 and 65-74 show that the **Root's** only child is the **Figure**; lines 13 and 76-87 show that the **Figure's** only child is the **Axes**; lines 14 and 89-102 show that the **Axes's** only child is the **Line**; lines 15 and 104-105 show that the **Line** has no child for the time being.

Lines 16-18 demonstrate the deletion of the three graphics objects; the deletion order is from children to parents. If you delete a parent object, the children (and grandchildren) would be deleted automatically. #

5.1b Creation and Deletion of Objects

Example05_01b.m

[1] In Example05_01a.m, when a **Line** is created, a **Figure** and an **Axes** are automatically created. It is possible to create **Figures** and **Axes** manually. The following commands demonstrate manual creation of a **Figure** and an **Axes** before creation of three **Line** objects as children of the **Axes**. →

```
1   clear
2   x = linspace(0,2*pi);
3   figure
4   axes('XLim', [0,2*pi], 'YLim', [-1,1])
5   hold on
6   plot(x, sin(x), x, cos(x))
7   plot([0,2*pi],[0,0])
8   hAxes = gca;
9   hCurve = hAxes.Children
10  delete(hCurve(1))
11  delete(hCurve(2))
12  delete(hAxes)
13  delete(gcf)
```

```
14  >> clear
15  >> x = linspace(0,2*pi);
16  >> figure
17  >> axes('XLim', [0,2*pi], 'YLim', [-1,1])
18  >> hold on
19  >> plot(x, sin(x), x, cos(x))
20  >> plot([0,2*pi],[0,0])
21  >> hAxes = gca;
22  >> hCurve = hAxes.Children
23  hCurve =
24    3×1 Line array:
25
26    Line
27    Line
28    Line
29  >> delete(hCurve(1))
30  >> delete(hCurve(2))
31  >> delete(hAxes)
32  >> delete(gcf)
```

[2] This is a **Command Window** session of Example05_01b.m.

Line 3 creates an empty **Figure**. Line 4 creates an **Axes** object with its axis limits specified: `[0-2*pi]` for *x*-axis and `[-1,1]` for *y*-axis. Line 6 creates two **Line** objects: a sine curve and a cosine curve. Note that, without the command `hold on` (line 5), the axis limits would be recalculated by the `plot` function in line 6 (you should try this yourself). Line 7 creates another **Line**, a straight line, by connecting two points: (0,0) and $(2\pi, 0)$. Remember that the command

```
plot([x1 x2], [y1 y2])
```

connects two points (x_1, y_1) and (x_2, y_2) with a straight line. Now the graphics objects and their parent-children relationship look like [3-4], next page.

In line 8, the built-in function `gca` (get current axes) returns a handle to the **Axes**.

After execution of line 9, `hCurve` stores a 3-by-1 column vector of handles (lines 23-28). The **Axes** has three children.

Lines 10-11 delete two **Line** objects. Line 12 deletes the **Axes**; the last **Line** is also deleted automatically. Line 13 deletes the **Figure** by using the built-in function `gcf` to get the current figure. `gcf` returns a handle to the current **Figure**. ↵

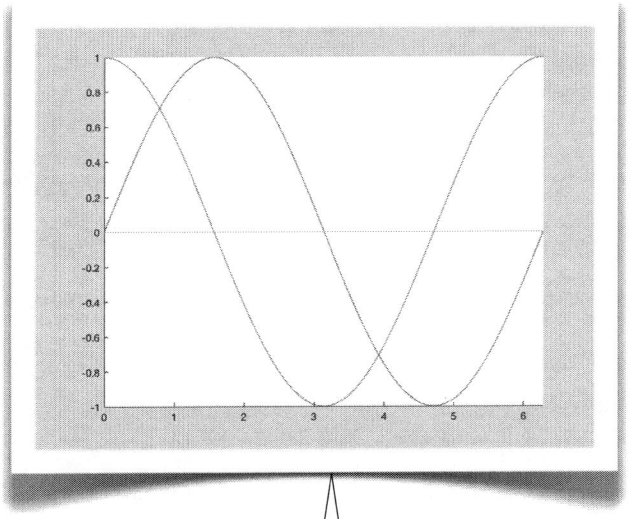

[3] The graphics objects created in Example05_01b.m. →

[4] The graphics objects created in Example05_01b.m and their parent-children relationship. #

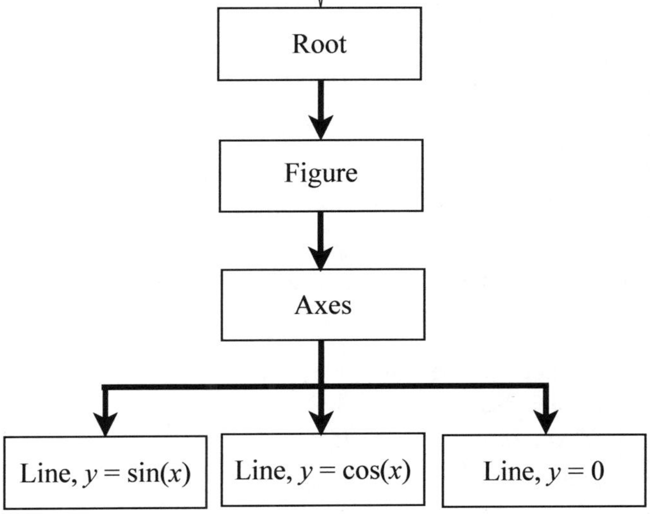

Table 5.1 Graphics Objects

Function	Description
`hf = figure`	Create figure window
`ha = axes`	Create axes object
`hr = groot`	Get handle of root object
`hf = gcf`	Get handle of current figure
`ha = gca`	Get handle of current axes
`ho = gco`	Get handle of current object
`v = get(h,property)`	Get graphics object properties
`set(h,name,value)`	Set graphics object properties
`delete(h)`	Delete objects

Details and More: Help>MATLAB>Graphics>Graphics Objects

5.2 Graphics Objects Properties

[1] The function `get` can be used to retrieve the properties of a graphics object. You may also refer to the properties with the dot operator. For example, create a **Line** handle `hCurve` by entering

```
>> clear
>> x = linspace(0, 2*pi);
>> hCurve = plot(x, sin(x));
```

then either of the following commands

```
>> get(hCurve, 'LineWidth')
>> hCurve.LineWidth
```

outputs the line width (by default, 0.5) of the **Line** object. With the function `get`, property names are not case-sensitive, and you may abbreviate them to as few letters as to make them unique; for example

```
>> get(hCurve, 'linew')
```

also outputs the line width. However, when using the dot operator, property names are case-sensitive, and abbreviations are not allowed.

There are several ways to modify properties of a graphics object. First, you can use the dot operator (`.`) and the assignment (=); for example:

```
>> hCurve.LineWidth = 2
```

which changes the line width to 2 units. This is equivalent to using the built-in function `set`, as follows:

```
>> set(hCurve, 'LineWidth', 2)
```

With the function `get`, property names are not case-sensitive, and abbreviations are allowed.

Second, you may open a **Property Inspector** window [2] by typing:

```
>> inspect(hCurve)
```

and change the values.

Third, you may open a **Property Editor** from a pull-down menu in the **Figure Window** (see [3]), or by typing

```
>> propedit
```

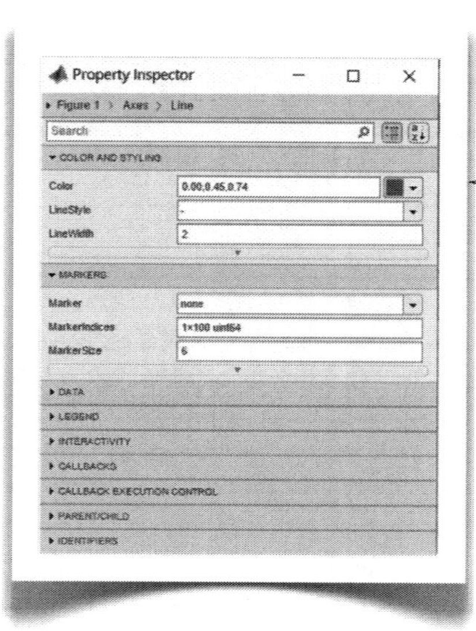

[2] **Property Inspector**. ↓

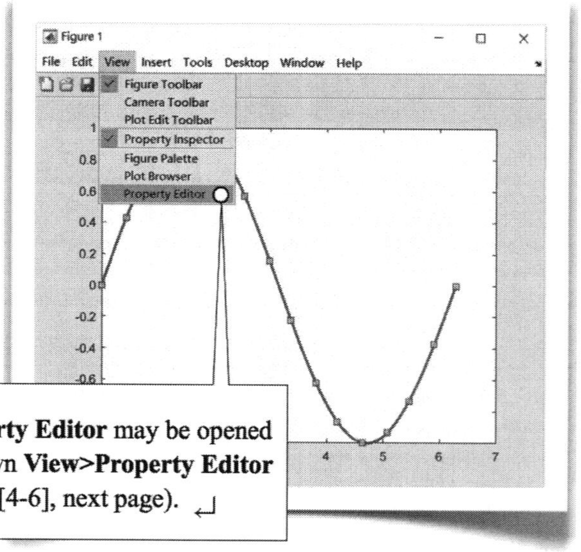

[3] The **Property Editor** may be opened by pulling-down **View>Property Editor** (also see [4-6], next page).

[4] In the **Property Editor**, you may modify the properties of a selected (highlighted) graphics object. ↙

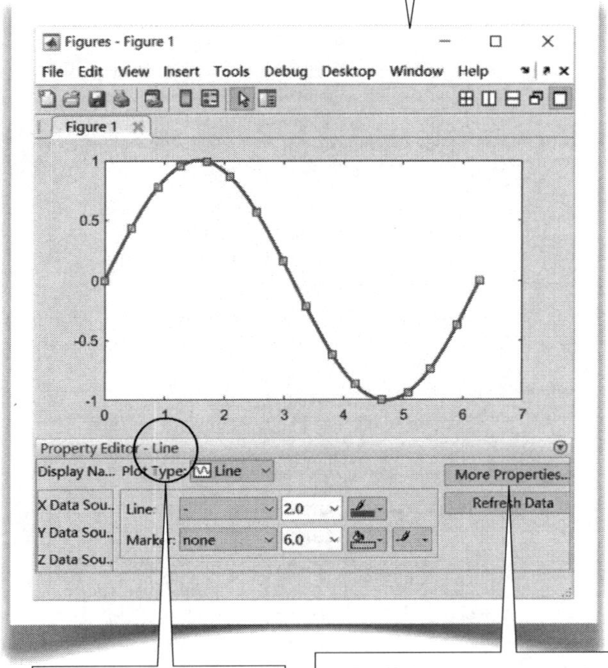

[5] This shows the selected object. ↑

[6] Click **More Properties** to open a **Property Inspector** [2] if it is not opened. ↓

[7] The command

```
>> get(hCurve)
```

outputs all properties of the **Line** (see [8]).

Remember the function `groot` (Table 5.1, page 211) outputs a handle of the **Root**; therefore, the command

```
>> get(groot)
```

outputs all properties of the **Root** (see [9]).

Similarly, the functions `gcf` and `gca` output handles of current **Figure** and current **Axes**, respectively; therefore, the commands

```
>> get(gcf)
>> get(gca)
```

output all properties of the **Figure** (see [10], next page) and **Axes** (see [11-13], pages 214-215), respectively. ↗

[8] Output of `get(hCurve)`. ↓

```
              Alphamap: [1x64 double]
   AlignVertexCenters: 'off'
            Annotation: [1x1 ...]
         BeingDeleted: 'off'
           BusyAction: 'queue'
        ButtonDownFcn: ''
             Children: []
             Clipping: 'on'
                Color: [0 0.4470 0.7410]
            CreateFcn: ''
            DeleteFcn: ''
          DisplayName: ''
     HandleVisibility: 'on'
              HitTest: 'on'
        Interruptible: 'on'
            LineStyle: '-'
            LineWidth: 0.5000
               Marker: 'none'
      MarkerEdgeColor: 'auto'
      MarkerFaceColor: 'none'
           MarkerSize: 6
               Parent: [1x1 Axes]
        PickableParts: 'visible'
             Selected: 'off'
   SelectionHighlight: 'on'
                  Tag: ''
                 Type: 'line'
        UIContextMenu: []
             UserData: []
              Visible: 'on'
                XData: [1x100 double]
            XDataMode: 'manual'
          XDataSource: ''
                YData: [1x100 double]
          YDataSource: ''
                ZData: [1x0 double]
          ZDataSource: ''
```

[9] Output of `get(groot)`. ↵

```
       CallbackObject: [0×0 GraphicsPlaceholder]
             Children: [0×0 GraphicsPlaceholder]
        CurrentFigure: [0×0 GraphicsPlaceholder]
   FixedWidthFontName: 'Courier New'
     HandleVisibility: 'on'
     MonitorPositions: [1 1 2560 1440]
               Parent: [0×0 GraphicsPlaceholder]
      PointerLocation: [2232 543]
          ScreenDepth: 32
 ScreenPixelsPerInch: 72
           ScreenSize: [1 1 2560 1440]
    ShowHiddenHandles: 'off'
                  Tag: ''
                 Type: 'root'
                Units: 'pixels'
             UserData: []
```

[10] Output of `get(gcf)`. →

```
              Alphamap: [1x64 double]
          BeingDeleted: 'off'
            BusyAction: 'queue'
         ButtonDownFcn: ''
              Children: [1x1 Axes]
              Clipping: 'on'
       CloseRequestFcn: 'closereq'
                 Color: [0.94 0.94 0.94]
              Colormap: [64x3 double]
             CreateFcn: ''
           CurrentAxes: [1x1 Axes]
      CurrentCharacter: ''
         CurrentObject: []
          CurrentPoint: [0 0]
             DeleteFcn: ''
          DockControls: 'on'
              FileName: ''
     GraphicsSmoothing: 'on'
      HandleVisibility: 'on'
         IntegerHandle: 'on'
         Interruptible: 'on'
        InvertHardcopy: 'on'
           KeyPressFcn: ''
         KeyReleaseFcn: ''
               MenuBar: 'figure'
                  Name: ''
              NextPlot: 'add'
                Number: 1
           NumberTitle: 'on'
      PaperOrientation: 'portrait'
         PaperPosition: [0.2500 2.5000 8 6]
     PaperPositionMode: 'manual'
             PaperSize: [8.5000 11]
             PaperType: 'usletter'
            PaperUnits: 'inches'
                Parent: [1x1 Root]
               Pointer: 'arrow'
     PointerShapeCData: [16x16 double]
   PointerShapeHotSpot: [1 1]
              Position: [520 378 560 420]
              Renderer: 'opengl'
          RendererMode: 'auto'
                Resize: 'on'
         SelectionType: 'normal'
        SizeChangedFcn: ''
                   Tag: ''
               ToolBar: 'auto'
                  Type: 'figure'
         UIContextMenu: []
                 Units: 'pixels'
              UserData: []
               Visible: 'on'
   WindowButtonDownFcn: ''
 WindowButtonMotionFcn: ''
     WindowButtonUpFcn: ''
     WindowKeyPressFcn: ''
   WindowKeyReleaseFcn: ''
  WindowScrollWheelFcn: ''
           WindowStyle: 'normal'
```

[11] Output of `get(gca)` (Continued on next page). ↵

```
                     ALim: [0 1]
                 ALimMode: 'auto'
   ActivePositionProperty: 'outerposition'
        AmbientLightColor: [1 1 1]
             BeingDeleted: 'off'
                      Box: 'on'
                 BoxStyle: 'back'
               BusyAction: 'queue'
            ButtonDownFcn: ''
                     CLim: [0 1]
                 CLimMode: 'auto'
           CameraPosition: [3.5000 0 17.3205]
       CameraPositionMode: 'auto'
             CameraTarget: [3.5000 0 0]
         CameraTargetMode: 'auto'
           CameraUpVector: [0 1 0]
       CameraUpVectorMode: 'auto'
          CameraViewAngle: 6.6086
      CameraViewAngleMode: 'auto'
                 Children: [1x1 Line]
                 Clipping: 'on'
            ClippingStyle: '3dbox'
                    Color: [1 1 1]
               ColorOrder: [7x3 double]
          ColorOrderIndex: 2
                CreateFcn: ''
             CurrentPoint: [2x3 double]
          DataAspectRatio: [3.5000 1 1]
      DataAspectRatioMode: 'auto'
                DeleteFcn: ''
                FontAngle: 'normal'
                 FontName: 'Helvetica'
                 FontSize: 10
            FontSmoothing: 'on'
                FontUnits: 'points'
               FontWeight: 'normal'
                GridAlpha: 0.1500
            GridAlphaMode: 'auto'
                GridColor: [0.15 0.15 0.15]
            GridColorMode: 'auto'
            GridLineStyle: '-'
         HandleVisibility: 'on'
                  HitTest: 'on'
            Interruptible: 'on'
  LabelFontSizeMultiplier: 1.1000
                    Layer: 'bottom'
           LineStyleOrder: '-'
      LineStyleOrderIndex: 1
                LineWidth: 0.5000
           MinorGridAlpha: 0.2500
       MinorGridAlphaMode: 'auto'
           MinorGridColor: [0.10 0.10 0.10]
       MinorGridColorMode: 'auto'
       MinorGridLineStyle: ':'
                 NextPlot: 'replace'
            OuterPosition: [0 0 1 1]
                   Parent: [1x1 Figure]
```

[12] Output of `get(gca)` (Continued). ↘

```
            PickableParts: 'visible'
       PlotBoxAspectRatio: [1 0.7903 0.7903]
   PlotBoxAspectRatioMode: 'auto'
                 Position: [0.1300 0.1100 0.7750 0.8150]
               Projection: 'orthographic'
                 Selected: 'off'
       SelectionHighlight: 'on'
               SortMethod: 'childorder'
                      Tag: ''
                  TickDir: 'in'
              TickDirMode: 'auto'
     TickLabelInterpreter: 'tex'
               TickLength: [0.0100 0.0250]
               TightInset: [0.0506 0.0532 0.0071 0.0202]
                    Title: [1x1 Text]
  TitleFontSizeMultiplier: 1.1000
          TitleFontWeight: 'bold'
                     Type: 'axes'
            UIContextMenu: []
                    Units: 'normalized'
                 UserData: []
                     View: [0 90]
                  Visible: 'on'
            XAxisLocation: 'bottom'
                   XColor: [0.1500 0.1500 0.1500]
               XColorMode: 'auto'
                     XDir: 'normal'
                    XGrid: 'off'
                   XLabel: [1x1 Text]
                     XLim: [0 7]
                 XLimMode: 'auto'
               XMinorGrid: 'off'
               XMinorTick: 'off'
                   XScale: 'linear'
                    XTick: [0 1 2 3 4 5 6 7]
               XTickLabel: {8x1 cell}
           XTickLabelMode: 'auto'
       XTickLabelRotation: 0
                XTickMode: 'auto'
            YAxisLocation: 'left'
                   YColor: [0.1500 0.1500 0.1500]
               YColorMode: 'auto'
                     YDir: 'normal'
                    YGrid: 'off'
                   YLabel: [1x1 Text]
                     YLim: [-1 1]
                 YLimMode: 'auto'
               YMinorGrid: 'off'
               YMinorTick: 'off'
                   YScale: 'linear'
                    YTick: [-1 -0.8 -0.6 -0.4 -0.2 0 0.2 0.4 0.6 0.8 1]
               YTickLabel: {11x1 cell}
           YTickLabelMode: 'auto'
       YTickLabelRotation: 0
                YTickMode: 'auto'
                   ZColor: [0.1500 0.1500 0.1500]
               ZColorMode: 'auto'
```

[13] Output of `get(gca)` (Continued). #

```
                     ZDir: 'normal'
                    ZGrid: 'off'
                   ZLabel: [1x1 Text]
                     ZLim: [-1 1]
                 ZLimMode: 'auto'
               ZMinorGrid: 'off'
               ZMinorTick: 'off'
                   ZScale: 'linear'
                    ZTick: [-1 0 1]
               ZTickLabel: ''
           ZTickLabelMode: 'auto'
       ZTickLabelRotation: 0
                ZTickMode: 'auto'
```

Details and More

Help>MATLAB>Graphics> Graphics Objects

5.3 Figure Objects

Example05_03.m: Figures

[1] The following commands demonstrate some important properties of a **Figure** object. Carefully observe the outcome of each command. ↓

```
 1  clear
 2  scrsz = get(groot, 'ScreenSize');
 3  h1 = figure;
 4      h1.Position = [20, 60, scrsz(3)/4, scrsz(4)/3];
 5      h1.Name = 'Bottom-left Figure Window';
 6  h2 = figure;
 7      h2.Visible = 'off';
 8      h2.Units = 'normalized';
 9      h2.Position = [0.1, 0.2, 0.3, 0.4];
10      h2.Visible = 'on';
11      h2.Color = [0.8, 0.8, 0.8];
12      h2.Name = 'A Window of Gray Background';
13      h2.NumberTitle = 'off';
14      h2.ToolBar = 'none';
15      h2.MenuBar = 'none';
16  delete(h1)
17  delete(h2)
```

About Example05_03.m

[2] In line 2, the built-in function `groot` returns a handle to the **root** object, and the function `get` is used to retrieve the screen size, which is a row vector of four elements: [*left*, *bottom*, *width*, *height*], with default units pixels (see the `ScreenSize` and `Units` properties in 5.2[9], page 213).

Line 3 creates a **Figure** object. Line 4 sets the position and size of the **Figure**, specified as [*left*, *bottom*, *width*, *height*]. Line 5 sets the title of the **Figure** (see the `Position` and `Name` properties in 5.2[10], page 214; also see Table 5.3, next page). The **Figure** now looks like [3], next page.

Line 6 creates a second **Figure** object. Line 7 makes the figure object invisible. Line 8 sets the units normalized: 0-1 for both *width* and *height*. Line 9 sets the position and size using the normalized units. Line 10 makes the figure object visible. Line 11 sets the background color to a gray. The color is described by 3 numbers (0-1) representing red, green, and blue intensities (thus, [0 0 0] is black and [1 1 1] is white). Line 13 turns off the display of the title number (in this case, "Figure 2"). Line 14 removes the toolbar and line 15 removes the menu bar. The **Figure** now looks like [4], next page.

Lines 16-17 delete the two **Figure** objects. ↵

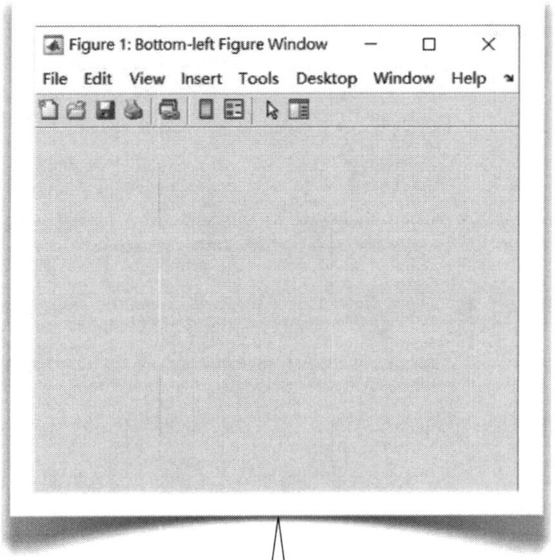

[3] Lines 3-5 create a **Figure** like this. →

[4] Lines 6-15 create a **Figure** like this. #

Table 5.3 Figure Properties

Properties	Description
`Color`	Background color
`MenuBar`	Menu bar display
`ToolBar`	Toolbar display
`Name`	Title
`NumberTitle`	Display of title number
`Position`	Position and size of drawable area
`Units`	Units of measurement (pixels)
`Visible`	Figure window visibility
`Resize`	Resize mode (on)

Details and More:
Help>MATLAB>Graphics> Graphics Objects>Graphics Object Properties>Top-Level Object>Figure Properties

5.4 Axes Objects

5.4a Axes Properties

Example05_04a.m: Axes Properties

[1] An **Axes** object includes an x-axis, a y-axis (or two y-axes; see 5.4b[3], page 219), their tick marks and labels, etc. The following commands demonstrate some important properties of **Axes** objects. Observe the outcome of each command. ↓

```
 1  clear
 2  h = axes;
 3      xlabel('Time (sec)');
 4      ylabel('Displacement (mm)');
 5      title('Displacement vs. Time');
 6      axis([0, 20, 0, 10000]);
 7      grid on
 8      box on
 9      h.YScale = 'log';
10      h.XTick = [0, 5, 10, 15, 20];
11      h.XTickLabel = {'0','T','2T','3T','4T'};
12      h.FontSize = 11;
13  delete(h)
14  delete(gcf)
```

About Example05_04a.m

[2] Line 2 creates an **Axes** object; its parent object, a **Figure**, is automatically created. Lines 3-5 add axis labels and a title to the **Axes**. Line 6 sets the axes limits: 0-20 for the x-axis, and 0-1000 for the y-axis. Line 7 turns the grid on. Line 8 displays an axes box outline. Line 9 sets logarithmic scale for the y-axis. Line 10 sets tick mark locations at 0, 5, 10, 15, and 20 (in data units). Line 11 sets the tick mark labels (at the tick mark locations) as 0, T, 2T, 3T, and 4T. Line 12 changes the font size to 11 points (the default is 10 points). The **Figure** now looks like [3].

Line 13 deletes the **Axes** object, and line 14 deletes the **Figure** object. Note that line 13 is not really necessary, since line 14 alone would automatically delete the **Axes** as well. →

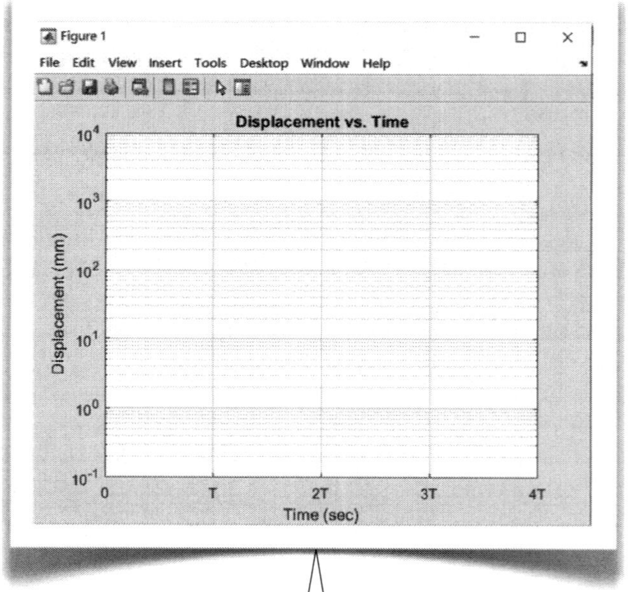

[3] Lines 2-12 create a **Figure** like this. #

5.4b Two *y*-Axes in an **Axes** Object: `yyaxis`

Example05_04b.m: Two *y*-Axes in an **Axes** Object

[1] The following commands demonstrate two *y*-axes in an **Axes** object. ↓

```
1   clear
2   t = linspace(0,0.1); w = 50;
3   y = sin(w*t);
4   v = w*cos(w*t);
5   yyaxis left
6   hLine1 = plot(t, y);
7   xlabel('Time (sec)')
8   ylabel('Displacement (mm)')
9   yyaxis right
10  hLine2 = plot(t, v);
11  ylabel('Velocity (mm/s)')
12  delete(hLine1)
13  delete(hLine2)
14  delete(gca)
15  delete(gcf)
```

About Example05_04b.m

[2] Line 3 creates a vector **y** representing the displacement of a simple harmonic motion (SHM, *Wikipedia>Simple harmonic motion*) of angular frequency **w** (rad/s). Line 4 creates a vector representing the velocity of the SHM. Note that the displacement ranges from -1 to 1, while the velocity ranges from -50 to 50. Now we want to plot a displacement-versus-time curve and a velocity-versus-time curve in the same **Axes**. The left *y*-axis will be used for the displacement, while the right *y*-axis will be used for the velocity.

Line 5 activates the left *y*-axis (this is the default axis; therefore, this statement may be removed); subsequent graphics commands will target the left side. Line 6 plots the displacement curve (using the left *y*-axis) and stores the **Line** handle in `hLine1`. Lines 7-8 label the axes.

Line 9 activates the right *y*-axis; subsequent graphics commands will target the right side. Line 10 plots the velocity curve (using the right *y*-axis) and stores the **Line** handle in `hLine2`. Line 11 labels the right *y*-axis. The **Figure** now looks like [3].

Lines 12-15 delete all graphics objects. Note that lines 12-14 are not really necessary, since deletion of the **Figure** in line 15 alone would automatically delete all its children and grandchildren. We delete them one-by-one from bottom up just for instructional purposes. →

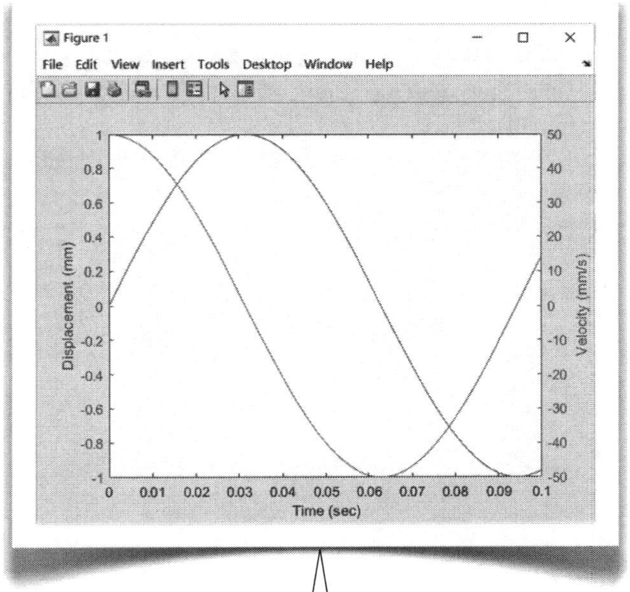

[3] Lines 2-11 create a **Figure** like this. #

5.4c Scaling of Axes

Example05_04c.m: Scaling of Axes

[1] The following commands demonstrate some additional **Axes** options. ↓

```
1   clear
2   t = linspace(0,2*pi);
3   plot(cos(t), sin(t))
4   axis equal
5   limits = axis;
6   axis square
7   axis([limits(1),limits(2),limits(1), limits(2)])
8   delete(gca)
9   delete(gcf)
```

About Example05_04c.m

[2] Line 3 creates a circle shown in [3]. By default, MATLAB fits a curve into the drawable area of the **Axes** and therefore the circle becomes distorted and looks like an ellipse.

Line 4 sets the unit spacing on both axes to be equal; it in effect restores the circularity of the circle [4]. In line 5, the function `axis` with no input arguments outputs the axes limits, a row vector of four numbers `[xmin xmax ymin ymax]`, which is then saved in the variable `limits`. Later in line 7, the *x*-limits are used for both axes.

Line 6 sets the axes box to become a square (see [5], next page). Now both *x*-limits and *y*-limits become `[-1,1]`. The circle looks too congested in a drawing area.

Line 7 sets both the *x*-limits and the *y*-limits to the old *x*-limits stored in line 5 (see [6], next page). This is for a better visual effect.

Line 8 deletes the **Axes** object, and line 9 deletes the **Figure** object; note that line 9 alone would delete the **Axes** as well. ↓

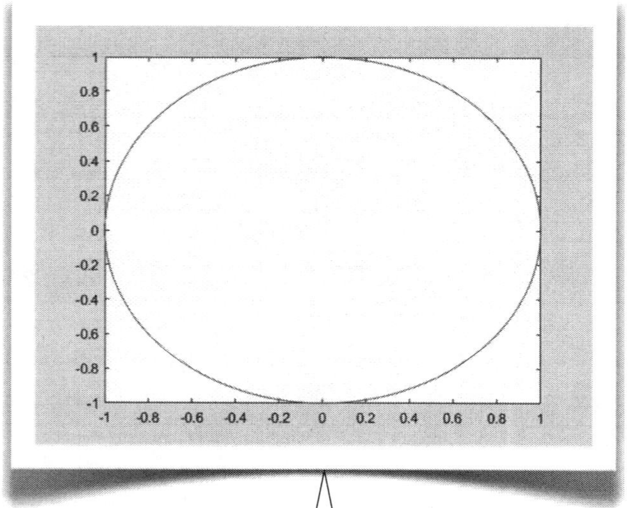

[3] Line 3 creates a circle like this. →

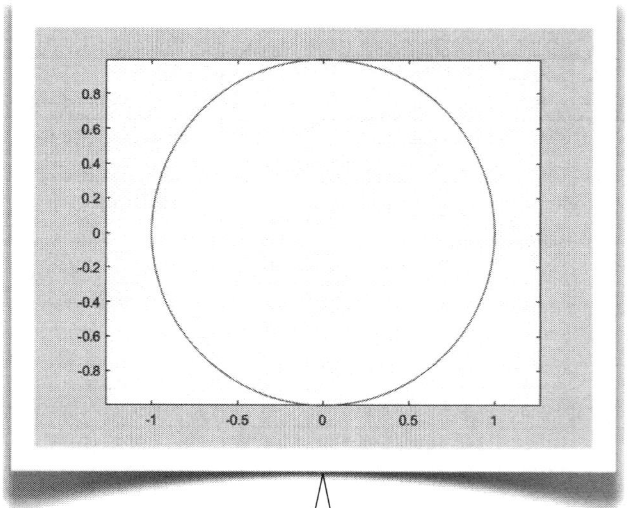

[4] Line 4 restores the circularity of the circle. ↵

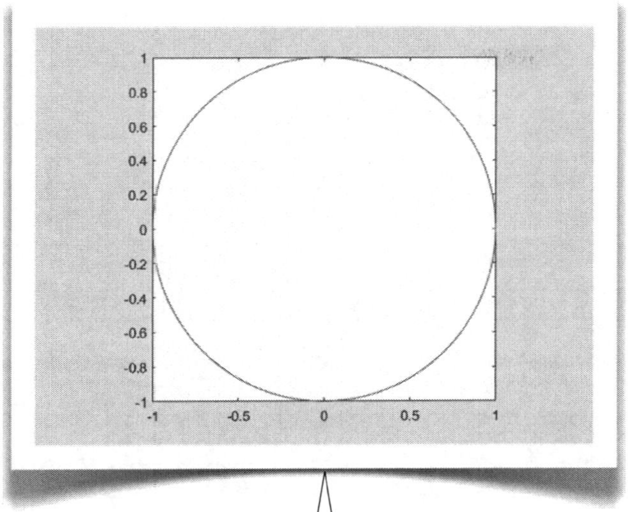

[5] Line 6 sets the axes box to become a square. →

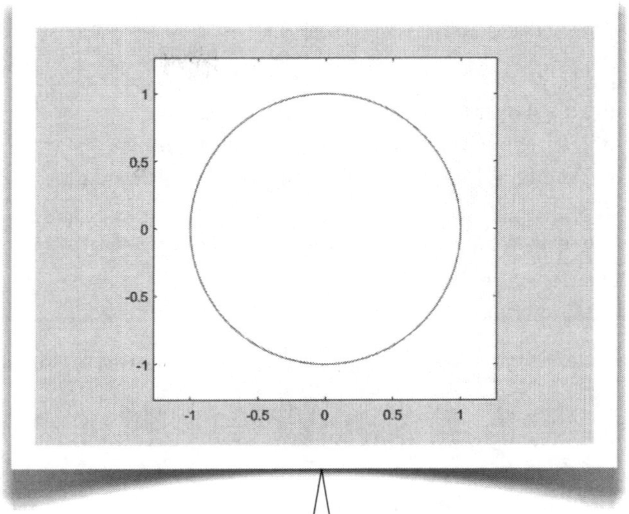

[6] Line 7 extends the axes limits for a better visual effect. #

5.4d Subplots

Example05_04d.m: Subplots

[1] The following commands demonstrate **subplots** in a figure. ↵

```
clear
t = linspace(0,0.1); w = 50;
y = sin(w*t);
v = w*cos(w*t);
a = -w*w*sin(w*t);
h1 = subplot(2,2,1);
plot(t,y), xlabel('Time'), ylabel('Displacement')
h2 = subplot(2,2,2);
plot(t,v), xlabel('Time'), ylabel('Velocity')
h3 = subplot(2,2,3);
plot(t,a), xlabel('Time'), ylabel('Acceleration')
h4 = subplot(2,2,4);
plot(y,a), xlabel('Displacement'), ylabel('Acceleration')
delete(h1)
delete(h2)
delete(h3)
delete(h4)
delete(gcf)
```

About Example05_04d.m

[2] Lines 3-5 create row vectors `y`, `v`, and `a` representing the displacement, velocity, and acceleration, respectively, of a simple harmonic motion of angular frequency `w` (rad/s). We now want to plot four **subplots** in a single **Figure** object.

Line 6 creates an **Axes** object on the upper-left quarter of the figure and returns a handle to the **Axes**. The function

```
subplot(m,n,p)
```

divides the current figure into an *m*-by-*n* grid and creates an **Axes** in the position specified by *p*. MATLAB numbers its subplots by rows; i.e., the first subplot is the first column of the first row (the upper-left subplot in [3]), the second subplot is the second column of the first row (the upper-right subplot in [3]), and so on. Line 7 plots a displacement-versus-time curve on the current **Axes**, the upper-left one.

Similarly, lines 8-9 create an **Axes** on the upper-right quarter and plot a velocity-versus-time curve. Lines 10-11 create an **Axes** on the lower-left quarter and plot an acceleration-versus-time curve. Lines 12-13 create an **Axes** on the lower-right quarter and plot an acceleration-versus-displacement curve. →

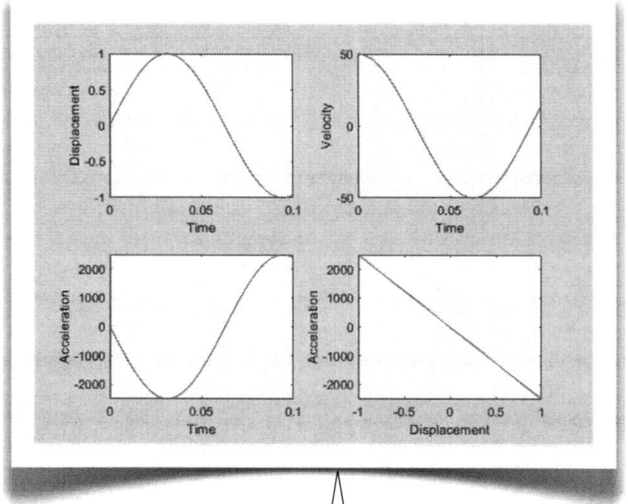

[3] Lines 40-51 create a **Figure** like this. ↓

Use Functions or Set Properties?

[4] Table 5.4a lists some useful functions relating the **Axes** object, and Table 5.4b lists some useful properties of the **Axes** object. Many properties can be set using either way. For example, function

```
axis(0, 20, 0, 10000)
```

has the same effects as

```
h = gca;
h.XLim = [0, 20];
h.YLim = [0, 1000];
```

As a guideline, if a function can achieve desired effects, always use the function rather than setting the property values directly because functions usually provide safeguarding checking to prevent something undesirable. #

Table 5.4a Axes Functions	
Functions	Description
`ha = axes`	Create axes graphics object
`axis(limits)`	Set axis limits
`axis equal`	Use the same length for the data units along each axis
`axis square`	Use the same length for the axis lines
`box on`	Display axes box outline
`ha = gca`	Get current axes
`grid on`	Display of grid lines
`title(text)`	Title for axes
`xlabel(text)`	Label x-axis
`ylabel(text)`	Label y-axis
`yyaxis right`	Specify the active side for the *y*-axis

Table 5.4b Axes Properties	
Properties	Description
`FontSize`	Font size (10 points)
`Position`	Position and size of axes
`Units`	Units of measurement (normalized)
`XLim, YLim, ZLim`	Minimum and maximum axis limits
`XScale, YScale, ZScale`	Scale of values along axis
`XTick, YTick, ZTick`	Tick mark locations
`XTickLabel, YTickLabel, ZTickLabel`	Tick mark labels
Details and More: Help>MATLAB>Graphics>Graphics Objects>Graphics Object Properties>Axes Properties	

5.5 Line Objects

5.5a Line Styles, Colors, and Markers

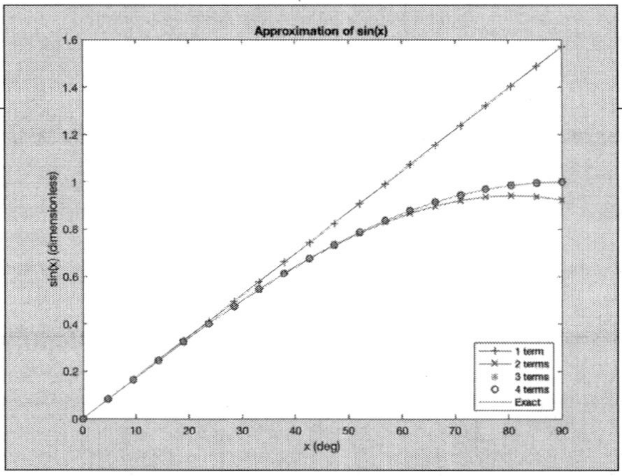

[1] The **Figure** to the right is a copy of that in 2.12e[2], page 112. It demonstrated the plotting of multiple lines in an **Axes**. It also demonstrated how to control the line style and the marker of a **Line** object. Table 5.5a (page 226) lists available line styles, marker types, and their colors.

Plotting functions (e.g., `plot`, `plot3d`) accept string specifier as arguments and modify lines and markers accordingly. For example, `'-r+'` specifies a solid line style (-), red color (`r`), and plus sign (+) marker. ↓

Example05_05a.m

[2] The following commands demonstrate the use of line styles, colors, and marker types. ↓

```
1   clear
2   x1 = [-5 -4 -3 -2 -1 0 1 2 3 4 5];
3   y1 = [23.9, 18.5, 10.7, 4.31, -0.26, -0.87, 0.82, 4.79, 7.67, 13.7, 23.5];
4   p = polyfit(x1, y1, 2)
5   x2 = linspace(-5,5);
6   y2 = polyval(p, x2);
7   h = plot(x1, y1, 'or', x2, y2, '-k');
8   delete(h(1))
9   delete(h(2))
10  delete(gca)
11  delete(gcf)
```

About Example05_05a.m

[3] Lines 2-3 store 11 data points in variables `x1` and `y1`. Line 4 uses the function `polyfit` to find a polynomial of degree 2 that best fits these data points (polynomial curve fittings are discussed in Section 10.6). Its output is

```
p =
      0.9731    -0.2568    -0.0252
```

which means the fitting polynomial is

$$y = 0.9731x^2 - 0.2568x - 0.0252$$

Line 5 creates a row vector of x-values (by default, the function `linspace` creates 100 elements). Line 6 uses the function `polyval` (Section 10.6) to evaluate the polynomial at these x-values. Line 7 plots the 11 data points using circular red markers (`'or'`) and the polynomial using solid black line (`'-k'`). The function `plot` (line 7) returns a vector of two handles pointing to the two **Line** objects, respectively. The **Figure** now looks like [4], next page. ↵

[4] Lines 2-7 create a **Figure** like this. #

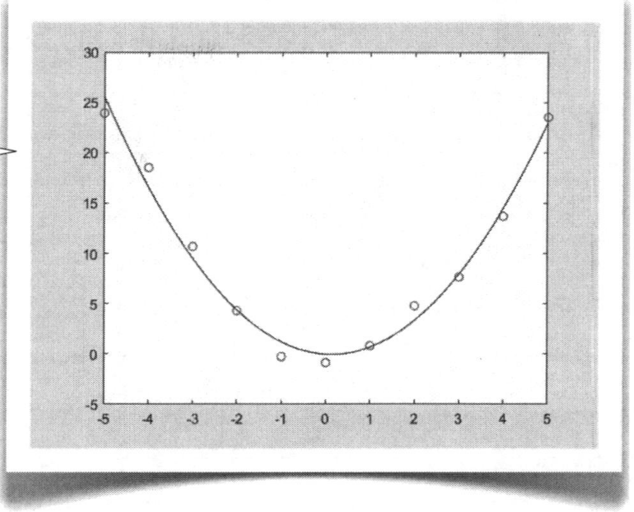

5.5b Change of Line Data

Example05_05b.m

[1] The following commands demonstrate the change of line data. →

```
1   clear
2   x = linspace(0,2*pi);
3   y = sin(x);
4   h = plot(x, y);
5   axis([0, 2*pi, -10, 10])
6   h.YData = 5*sin(x);
7   h.YData = 10*sin(x);
```

About Example05_05b

[2] Line 4 plots a sine curve. Line 5 adjusts the axes limits. The **Figure** is shown in [3]; note that the *y*-values vary between -1 and +1.

Lines 6 and 7 change the *y*-data property of the **Line** object. The graph changes accordingly, but the axes limits are not changed. The **Figure** after the execution of line 7 is shown in [4]; note that the *y*-values vary between -10 and +10. This method can be used to simulate the animation of a vibrating string (Problem06_02, page 275). ↙

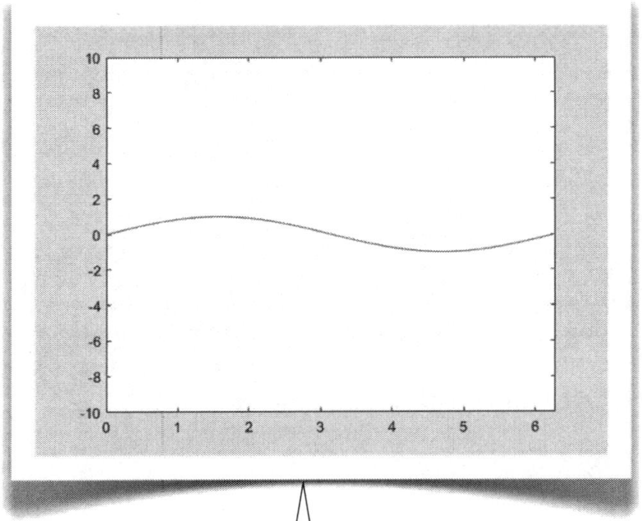

[3] Lines 2-5 create a **Figure** like this. →

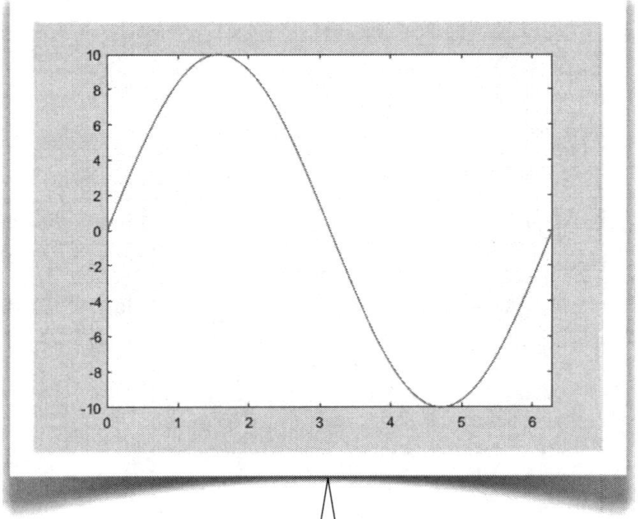

[4] Line 7 redefines the curve like this. #

Table 5.5a Line Styles, Colors, and Marker Types

Line style		Color		Marker Type			
Symbol	Description	Symbol	Description	Symbol	Description	Symbol	Description
`-`	Solid	`r`	Red	`+`	Plus sign	`^`	Up triangle
`--`	Dashed	`g`	Green	`o`	Circle	`v`	Down triangle
`:`	Dotted	`b`	Blue	`*`	Asterisk	`>`	Right triangle
`-.`	Dashed-dot	`c`	Cyan	`.`	Point	`<`	Left triangle
		`m`	Magenta	`x`	Cross	`p`	Pentagram
		`y`	Yellow	`s`	Square	`h`	hexagram
		`k`	Black	`d`	Diamond		
		`w`	White				

Details and More: Help>MATLAB>Graphics>2-D and 3-D Plots>Line Plots>LineSpec (Line Specification)

Table 5.5b Line Functions (2-D)

Functions	Description
`plot(x,y,lineSpec)`	2-D line plot
`loglog(x,y,lineSpec)`	Log-log scale plot
`semilogx(x,y,lineSpec)`	Semilogarithmic plot
`semilogy(x,y,lineSpec)`	Semilogarithmic plot
`fplot(fun,linsSpec)`	Plot expression or function (2-D)
`fimplicit(fun,lineSpec)`	Plot 2-D implicit function

Details and More: Help>MATLAB>Graphics>2-D and 3-D Plots>Line Plots

Table 5.5c Line Properties

Properties	Description
Color	Line color
LineStyle	Line style
LineWidth	Line width (default 0.5)
Marker	Marker symbol
MarkerEdgeColor	Marker outline color
MarkerFaceColor	Marker fill color
MarkerSize	Marker size (default 6)
XData	x values
YData	y values
ZData	z values

Details and More
Help>MATLAB>Graphics>Graphics Objects>Graphics Object Properties>Chart Objects>Chart Line Properties

5.6 Text Objects

5.6a Text Properties

Example05_06a.m

[1] The following commands demonstrate some important properties of **Text** objects. Observe the outcome of each command. ↓

```
1   clear
2   alpha = linspace(0, pi);
3   phi = sin(alpha).*cos(alpha);
4   plot(alpha, phi)
5   axis([0, pi, -1, 1])
6   hx = xlabel('\alpha (rad)');
7   hy = ylabel('\phi(\alpha)');
8   ht = title('\phi = sin(\alpha)\timescos(\alpha)');
9       hx.FontSize = 16;
10      hy.FontSize = 16;
11      ht.FontSize = 18;
12  [value, index] = max(phi);
13  hmax = text(alpha(index), value, ['Max \phi = ', num2str(value)]);
14      hmax.HorizontalAlignment = 'center';
15      hmax.VerticalAlignment = 'bottom';
16  [value, index] = min(phi);
17  hmin = text(alpha(index), value, ['Min \phi = ', num2str(value)]);
18      hmin.HorizontalAlignment = 'center';
19      hmin.VerticalAlignment = 'top';
20  delete(hx)
21  delete(hy)
22  delete(ht)
23  delete(hmax)
24  delete(hmin)
25  delete(gcf)
```

About Example05_06a.m

[2] Lines 2-4 plot a function

$$\phi = \sin(\alpha)\cos(\alpha)$$

Line 5 sets the axes limits. Lines 6-8 add labels and a title to the graph. The syntax for displaying Greek letters and mathematics symbols are summarized in Table 5.6a (page 229; also see 2.13[5], page 114). Lines 9-11 change the font size of the labels to 16 points and that of the title to 18 points. Their default font sizes are 11 points.

In line 12, the function `max` outputs the maximum value and the corresponding index in the vector `phi`. Line 13 writes a string at the maximum of the curve (see [3], next page) and stores a handle of the text in `hmax`. By default, the position is specified in data units (see Table 5.6c, page 230). Lines 14-15 set the text properties such that it aligns horizontally at center and vertically at bottom.

Similarly, line 16 gets the minimum value and the corresponding index in the vector `phi`, line 17 writes a string at the minimum of the curve ([3], next page), and lines 18-19 align the text horizontally at center and vertically at top. ↵

[3] Lines 2-19 create a **Figure** like this. #

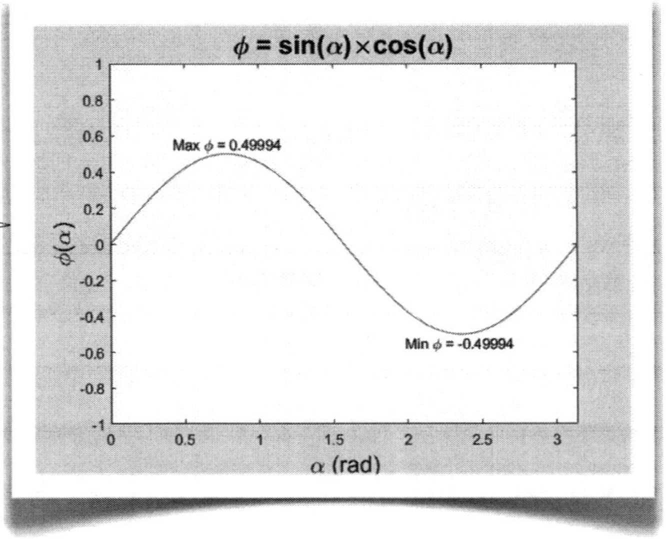

5.6b Example: Displaying Texts

Example05_06b.m

[1] The following commands demonstrate a more sophisticated way of using function `text`. The dimmed lines (lines 1-7) are copied from lines 1-7 of Example05_05a.m (page 224). ↓

```
1   clear
2   x1 = [-5 -4 -3 -2 -1 0 1 2 3 4 5];
3   y1 = [23.9, 18.5, 10.7, 4.31, -0.26, -0.87, 0.82, 4.79, 7.67, 13.7, 23.5];
4   p = polyfit(x1, y1, 2)
5   x2 = linspace(-5,5);
6   y2 = polyval(p, x2);
7   h = plot(x1, y1, 'or', x2, y2, '-k');
8   for k = 1:length(x1)
9       txt{k} = sprintf('(%g,%g)', x1(k), y1(k));
10  end
11  text(x1, y1-0.5, txt, ...
12      'HorizontalAlignment', 'center', 'VerticalAlignment', 'top')
```

About Example05_06b.m

[2] The function `sprintf` (line 9) is similar to `fprintf`; the difference is that `fprintf` writes to the screen or a file, while `sprintf` writes to a string. The use of the format specification `%g` is to avoid trailing zeros (try to use `%f` and see the difference). The string generated by the function `sprintf` is stored as an element of the **cell array** `txt`. Remember (4.2b[3], page 178), this statement can be written in an equivalent form

```
txt(k) = {sprintf('(%g,%g)', x1(k), y1(k))};
```

Lines 11-12 write the cell array of strings at positions specified by `x1` and `y1-0.5`. The *y*-coordinates are lowered by 0.5 data units, to avoid overlapping with the markers. The **Figure** now looks like [3], next page. ↵

[3] Example05_06b.m creates a **Figure** like this. #

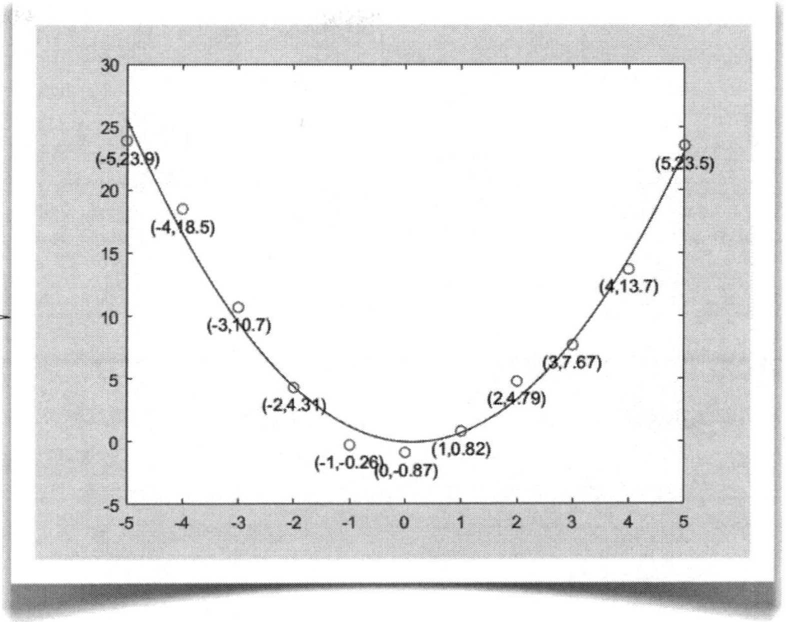

Table 5.6a Greek Letters and Math Symbols

Symbol	Syntax	Symbol	Syntax	Symbol	Syntax
α	\alpha	σ	\sigma	$\times$	\times
β	\beta	τ	\tau	$\div$	\div
γ	\gamma	ϕ	\phi	$\circ$	\circ
δ	\delta	χ	\chi	$\surd$	\surd
ε	\epsilon	ψ	\psi	$\rightarrow$	\rightarrow
ζ	\zeta	ω	\omega	$\leftarrow$	\leftarrow
η	\eta	Γ	\Gamma	$\uparrow$	\uparrow
θ	\theta	Δ	\Delta	$\downarrow$	\downarrow
λ	\lamda	Π	\Pi	(bold face)	\bf
μ	\mu	Σ	\Sigma	(italic)	\it
ν	\nu	Φ	\Phi	(remove)	\rm
ξ	\xi	Ψ	\Psi	(superscript)	^
π	\pi	Ω	\Omega	(subscript)	_
ρ	\rho				

Details and More: Help>MATLAB>Graphics>Graphics Objects>Graphics Object Properties>Primitive Objects>Text Properties>Interpreter

Table 5.6b Text Functions

Functions	Description
`text(x,y,text)`	Create axes graphics object
`title(text)`	Title for axes
`xlabel(text)`	Label *x*-axis
`ylabel(text)`	Label *y*-axis

Details and More: Help>MATLAB>Graphics>Formatting and Annotation>Titles and Labels

Table 5.6c Text Properties

Properties	Description
Color	Text color (black)
FontName	Font name (Helvetica)
FontSize	Font size (10 points)
HorizontalAlignment	Horizontal alignment (left)
Position	Position of text
String	Text to display
Units	Position and extent units (data)
VerticalAlignment	Vertical alignment (middle)

Details and More:
Help>MATLAB>Graphics>Graphics Objects>Graphics Object Properties>Primitive Objects>Text Properties

5.7 Legend Objects

Example05_07.m: Legends

[1] We've shown in Example02_12e.m (page 112) that, when a **Figure** contains multiple curves, adding a **Legend** improves the readability of the **Figure**. The following commands demonstrate the properties of **Legend** objects. The dimmed lines (lines 1-14) are duplicated from lines 1-14 of Example02_12e.m. ✓

```
 1  clear
 2  x = linspace(0,pi/2,20);
 3  n = 4;
 4  k = (1:n);
 5  [X, K] = meshgrid(x, k);
 6  sinx =cumsum(((-1).^(K-1)).*(X .^ (2*K-1))./factorial(2*K-1));
 7  plot(x*180/pi, sinx(1,:), '+-', ...
 8       x*180/pi, sinx(2,:), 'x-', ...
 9       x*180/pi, sinx(3,:), '*', ...
10       x*180/pi, sinx(4,:), 'o', ...
11       x*180/pi, sin(x))
12  title('Approximation of sin(x)')
13  xlabel('x (deg)')
14  ylabel('sin(x) (dimensionless)')
15  h = legend('1 term', '2 terms', '3 terms', '4 terms', 'Exact');
16      h.Position = [0.6, 0.2, 0.25, 0.2];
17      h.FontSize = 16;
18      h.String{5} = 'sin(x)';
19      h.Box = 'off';
```

About Example05_07.m

[2] Line 15 adds a **Legend** containing 5 items to the graph. By default, the **Legend** is located at the "northeast" (i.e., upper-right) of the **Axes**, with a box outline enclosing the **Legend**. Line 16 moves the **Legend** to a new position. Line 17 changes the font size to 16 points (the default is 9 points). Line 18 changes the name of the 5th **Legend** item from `'Exact'` to `'sin(x)'`. Line 19 removes the box outline. The **Figure** now looks like [3]. →

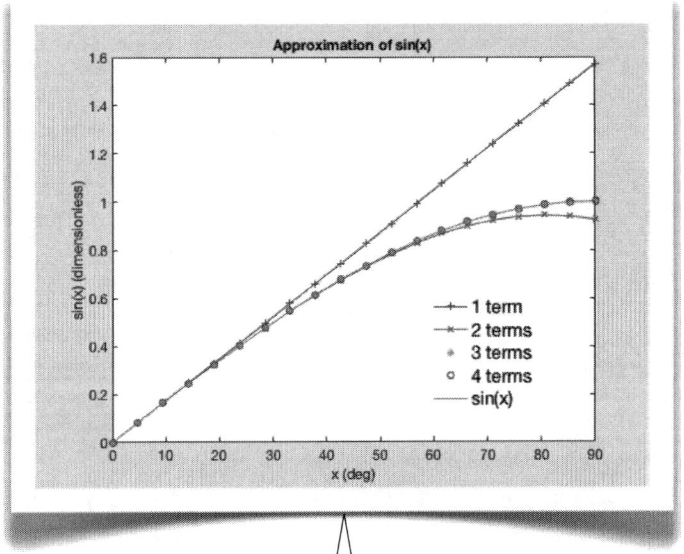

[3] Example05_07.m create a **Figure** like this. #

Table 5.7a Legend Functions

Functions	Description
`legend(labels,name,value)`	Add legend to graph
Details and More: >> `doc legend`	

Table 5.7b Legend Properties

Properties	Description
Box	Box outline (on)
FontSize	Font size (9 points)
Location	Location of legend (northeast)
Position	Custom position and size
String	Legend entry description
Units	Position units (normalized)
Details and More: *Help>MATLAB>Graphics>Graphics Objects>Graphics Object Properties>Illustration Objects>Legend Properties*	

5.8 Bar Plots

Example05_08.m: Bar Plots

[1] The following commands demonstrate the creation of bar plots. Observe the outcome of each command. ↓

```
1   clear
2   USA = [-6.3, -4.3, 0.1, 5.9, 12.1, 17.1, ...
3          19.9, 18.9, 14.4, 7.7, 0.4, -4.8];
4   hb = bar(USA);
5   ha = gca;
6       axis([0, 13, -30, 30])
7       ha.XTickLabel = {'Jan', 'Feb', 'Mar', 'Apr', 'May', 'Jun', ...
8                        'July', 'Aug', 'Sept', 'Oct', 'Nov', 'Dec'};
9   CAN = [-24.6, -23.3, -18.7, -9.8, -0.3, 7.2, ...
10         11.1, 9.5, 3.5, -4.4, -14.5, -21.5];
11  GBR = [3.0, 3.0, 4.7, 6.7, 9.8, 12.8, ...
12         14.4, 14.3, 12.2, 9.5, 5.5, 3.9];
13  y = [USA', CAN', GBR'];
14  delete(hb);
15  hold on
16  hb = bar(y);
17      hb(1).BarWidth = 1.0;
18      hb(2).BarWidth = 1.0;
19      hb(3).BarWidth = 1.0;
20  title('Average Temperature (1961-1999)')
21  ylabel('Temperature (\circC)')
22  legend('United States', 'Canada', 'United Kingdom', 'Location', 'best')
```

About Example05_08.m

[2] Lines 2-3 create a row vector of 12 values, which are the average monthly temperatures (in degrees Celsius) in the USA for the period 1961-1999 (*Data source: http://data.worldbank.org/data-catalog/cckp_historical_data*).

Line 4 plots a **Bar** chart using the data in variable `USA` as the *y*-data. The default value for the *x*-data is

```
x = 1:length(USA)
```

Line 6 adjusts the axes limits. Lines 7-8 change the tick labels (see Table 5.4b, page 223). The **Figure** now looks like [3], next page.

Lines 9-12 create two row vectors storing the average monthly temperatures in Canada and United Kingdom for the period 1961-1999 (*Data source: http://data.worldbank.org/data-catalog/cckp_historical_data*).

Line 13 arranges the three groups of data in 3 columns; each has 12 temperature values. Line 14 deletes the previous **Bar** plot. Line 15 holds on current **Axes** so that the axes limits do not change. Line 16 plots a **Bar** chart using the 3-column matrix `y`, on the existing **Axes**. When the *y*-data is an *m*-by-*n* (in our case 12-by-3) matrix, the function `bar` displays *m* groups of *n* bars and returns an array of *n* handles. Here, `hb` is an array of three handles.

Lines 17-19 set the widths of all the bars to be 1.0; i.e., the three bars in a group touch one another.

Line 22 adds a legend in the graph at the "best" location, selected by MATLAB, where fewest conflicts with other graphic objects occur. In my Mac, MATLAB selects the northeast (i.e., the upper-right) location. ↵

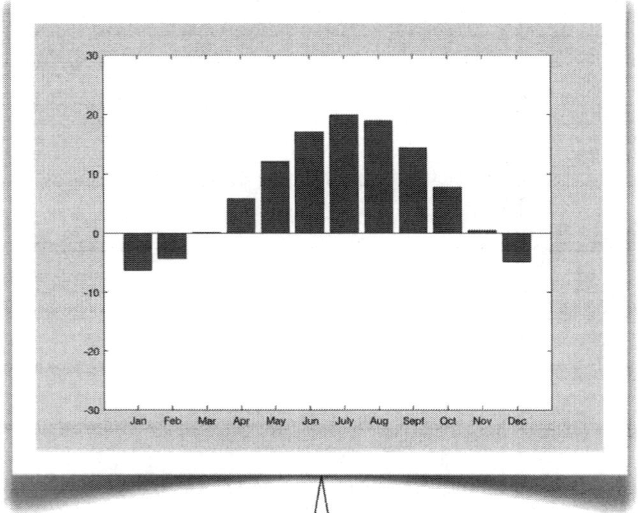

[3] Lines 2-8 create a **Figure** like this. →

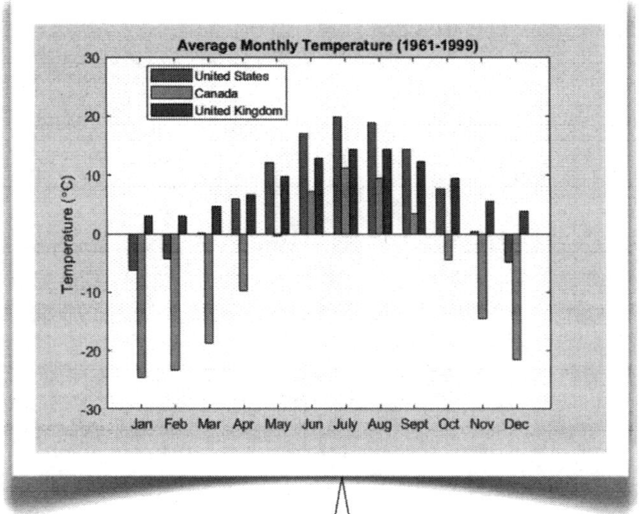

[4] At the end of Example05_08.m, the **Figure** looks like this. #

Table 5.8a Bar Functions

Functions	Description
`bar(y,width)`	Plot bar graph
`bar(y,name,value)`	Plot bar graph
`barh(y,width)`	Plot horizontal bar graph
`bar3(y,width)`	Plot 3-D bar graph
`bar3h(y,width)`	Plot horizontal 3-D bar graph

Details and More: Help>MATLAB>Graphics>2-D and 3-D Plots>Pie Charts, Bar Plots, and Histograms

Table 5.8b Bar Properties

Properties	Description
BarWidth	Relative width of bars (0.8)
BaseValue	Baseline location
EdgeColor	Bar outline color
FaceColor	Bar fill color
XData	Bar locations
YData	Bar length

Details and More:
Help>MATLAB>Graphics>Graphics Objects>Graphics Object Properties>Chart Objects>Bar Properties

5.9 Pie Plots

Example05_09.m: Pie Plots

[1] It is estimated that, in 2008, the total CO_2 emission in the world was 29.85 Bt (billion tons), of which, in descending order, 7.03 Bt was produced by China, 5.46 Bt by United States, 1.74 Bt by India, 1.71 Bt by Russia, 1.21 Bt by Japan, and 0.79 Bt by Germany (*Data source: http://data.worldbank.org/data-catalog/climate-change*). The following script generates a **Pie** plot [2] that shows these data. ↓

```
1   clear
2   world = 29.85;
3   CHN = 7.03; USA = 5.46; IND = 1.74;
4   RUS = 1.71; JPN = 1.21; DEU = 0.79;
5   others = world - CHN - USA - IND - RUS - JPN - DEU;
6   x = [CHN, USA, IND, RUS, JPN, DEU, others];
7   explode = [1, 1, 1, 1, 1, 1, 1];
8   countries = {'China', 'United States', 'India', ...
9       'Russia', 'Japan', 'Germany', 'Other Countries'};
10  for k = 1:7
11      labels{k} = [countries{k}, sprintf(' (%.1f%%)', x(k)/world*100)];
12  end
13  h = pie(x, explode, labels)
14      h(2).FontSize = 12;
15      h(4).FontSize = 12;
16      h(6).FontSize = 12;
17      h(8).FontSize = 12;
18      h(10).FontSize = 12;
19      h(12).FontSize = 12;
20      h(14).FontSize = 12;
```

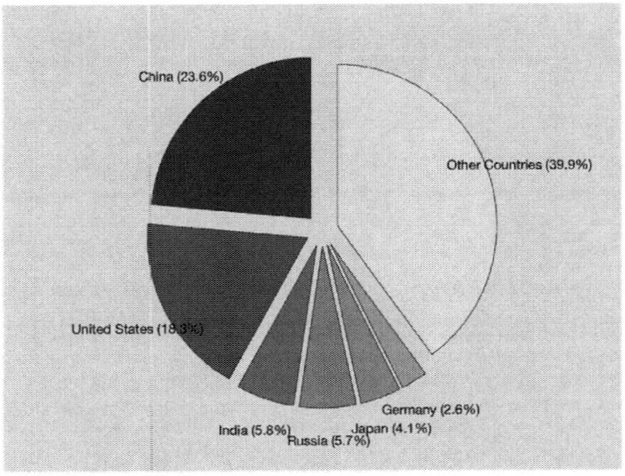

[2] Example05_09.m creates a **Figure** like this. →

About Example05_09.m

[3] Lines 2-6 create a vector **x** storing the CO_2 emissions by the six top countries and by the other countries. Line 7 prepares a vector specifying that all slices need to be exploded (offset). Lines 8-12 prepare a **cell array** containing labels for the slices.

Line 13 plots a **Pie** chart and outputs an array of 14 handles h, which, observed from the **Command Window** output (see [4], next page), contains 7 **Patch** handles and 7 **Text** handles. The properties of **Text** are summarized in Table 5.6c (page 230), while the properties of **Patch** are summarized in Table 5.9b (next page).

Using the 7 **Text** handles, lines 14-20 change the text font sizes to 12 points (the default is 10 points). The **Figure** now looks like [2]. ↵

```
h =
  1×14 graphics array:

  Columns 1 through 8
    Patch    Text     Patch    Text     Patch    Text     Patch    Text
  Columns 9 through 14
    Patch    Text     Patch    Text     Patch    Text
```

[4] Output of line 13. The variable h is an array of 14 handles, 7 **Patch** handles and 7 **Text** handles. #

Table 5.9a Pie Functions	
Functions	Description
`pie(x, explode, labels)`	Pie chart
`pie3(x, explode, labels)`	3-D pie chart
Details and More: Help>MATLAB>Graphics>2-D and 3-D Plots>Pie Charts, Bar Plots, and Histograms	

Table 5.9b Patch Properties	
Properties	Description
FaceColor	Patch fill color
EdgeColor	Patch outline color
Details and More: Help>MATLAB>Graphics>Graphics Objects>Graphics Object Properties>Primitive Objects>Patch Properties	

5.10 3-D Line Plots

Example05_10.m: 3-D Line Plots

[1] The function `plot3(x,y,z)` plots a 3-D line by connecting the following points:

$$(x(k),\ y(k),\ z(k));\ k=1,\ 2,\ ...$$

The following commands create a 3-D line plot (see [3-5], this and next pages) using the following parametric equations

$$x(t)=e^{-t/20}\cos t,\ \ y(t)=e^{-t/20}\sin t,\ \ z(t)=t$$ ↓

```
1   clear
2   z = linspace(0, 8*pi, 200);
3   x = exp(-z/20).*cos(z);
4   y = exp(-z/20).*sin(z);
5   plot3(x,y,z)
6   xlabel x, ylabel y, zlabel z
7   axis([-1, 1, -1, 1, 0, 8*pi])
8   h = gca; h.BoxStyle = 'full'; box on
9   grid on
10  axis vis3d
```

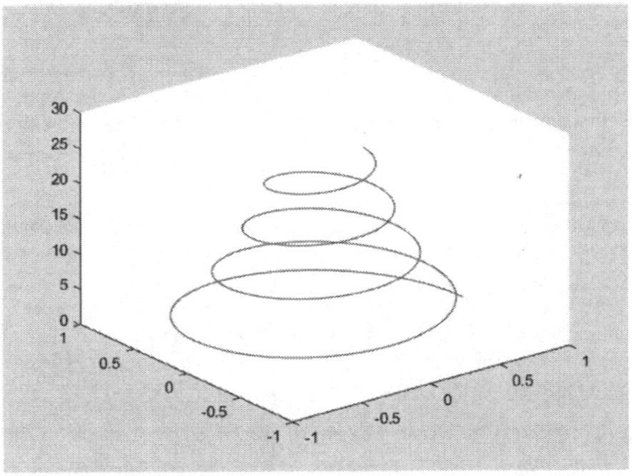

[3] Line 5 creates a 3-D line plot with default settings. ↵

About Example05_10.m

[2] Lines 2-4 prepare the coordinates *x*, *y*, and *z* using the parametric equations in [1]. Line 5 creates a 3-D line plot with default settings (see [3]). Line 6 labels the axes with `x`, `y`, and `z`. Remember that

```
xlabel x, ylabel y, zlabel z
```

is equivalent to

```
xlabel('x'), ylabel('y'), zlabel('z')
```

Line 7 sets the axes limits: `[-1 1]` for *x*-axis, `[-1 1]` for *y*-axis, and `[0 8*pi]` for *z*-axis. In line 8, the axes property **BoxStyle** is set to `full` so that all six edges of the 3-D **box** are displayed when the **box** is turned on. The default **BoxStyle** is `back`, i.e., only the **back planes** of the **box** are displayed when the **box** is on (try it yourself). Line 9 turns on the **grid**. Line 10 freezes the aspect ratio of the axes. Without freezing the aspect ratio, when you manually rotate a 3-D view ([5], next page), the aspect ratio would change accordingly (also see 1.6[19], page 27). ↑

[5] For a 3-D plot, you often need to view from different angles in order to see the details. Move your mouse over the plot (to reveal this toolbar), click **Rotate 3D**, and then drag the graph using your mouse. #

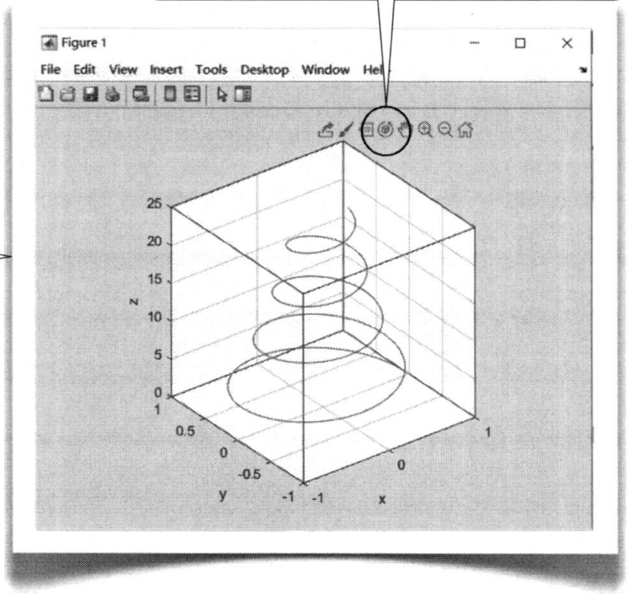

[4] At the end of Example05_10.m, the **Figure** looks like this. ↗

Table 5.10a 3-D Line Plot Functions	
Functions	Description
`plot3(x,y,z,lineSpec)`	Plot 3-D lines
`fplot3(funx,funy,funz,lineSpec)`	3-D parametric curve plotter
`fimplicit3(fun,lineSpec)`	Plot 3-D implicit function
`axis vis3d`	Freeze the aspect ratio
Details and More: Help>MATLAB>Graphics>2-D and 3-D Plots>Line Plots	

Table 5.10b Additional Axes Properties	
Properties	Description
`BoxStyle`	Box style (back)
Details and More: Help>MATLAB>Graphics>Graphics Objects>Graphics Object Properties>Top-Level Objects>Axes Properties	

5.11 Surface and Mesh Plots

5.11a Surface and Mesh Plots

Example05_11a.m: Surface and Mesh Plots

[1] The function `surf(X,Y,Z)` generates a surface mesh in which the grid lines intersect at the following points:

$$(X(i,j),\ Y(i,j),\ Z(i,j));\ i = 1,\ 2,\ ...;\ j = 1,\ 2,\ ...$$

By default, each patch of the mesh is colored according to the current **colormap** (see Table 5.11a, page 243), and the edges are black-colored.

The following commands generate a surface described by

$$z(x,y) = \sin x \cdot \cos y \qquad (a)$$

↓

```
1   clear
2   x = linspace(0,2*pi,100);
3   y = linspace(0,  pi, 50);
4   [X,Y] = meshgrid(x, y);
5   Z = sin(X) .* cos(Y);
6   hs = surf(X, Y, Z)
7   xlabel x, ylabel y, zlabel z
8   h = gca;
9       axis([0, 2*pi, 0, pi, -1, 1])
10      h.XTick = [0, pi/2, pi, 3*pi/2, 2*pi];
11      h.YTick = [0, pi/2, pi];
12      h.XTickLabel = {'0', '\pi/2', '\pi', '3\pi/2', '2\pi'};
13      h.YTickLabel = {'0', '\pi/2', '\pi'};
14      axis vis3d
15      axis equal
16      h.BoxStyle = 'full';
17      box on
18      grid on
19  colorbar
20  colormap hot
21      hs.FaceAlpha = 0.2;
22      hs.EdgeColor = 'none';
```

About Example05_11a.m

[2] In line 4, the matrices `X` and `Y` are generated using the function `meshgrid` (see 2.12d[3], page 111). Line 5 calculates matrix `Z`. Line 6 generates a surface plot. Line 19 displays a **colorbar** showing the color scales of the **current colormap**. So far, we have a figure shown in [3], next page.

Line 20 changes the **current colormap** to `'hot'` (see Table 5.11a, page 243); the face colors change accordingly (see [4]). Line 21 changes the face transparency to 0.2 (see [5]). Line 22 removes the edges (see [6]).

If the function `mesh` is used in place of `surf` in line 6, i.e.,

```
mesh(X, Y, Z)
```

then the mesh plot is shown in [7], page 241, in which the faces are not colored, but the edges are colored instead. ↵

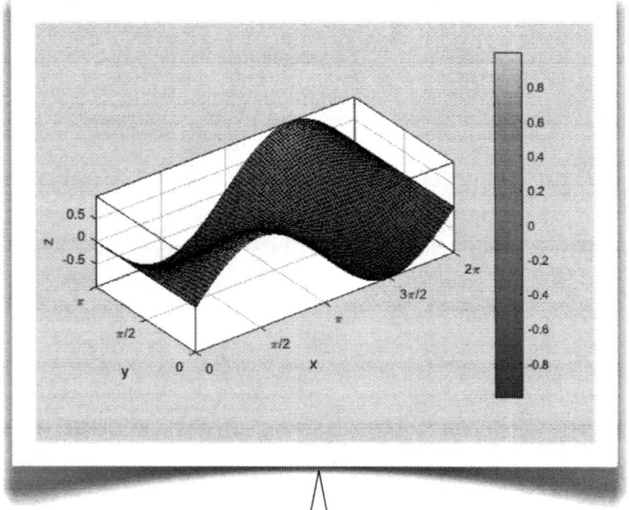

[3] Lines 2-19 create a **Figure** like this. →

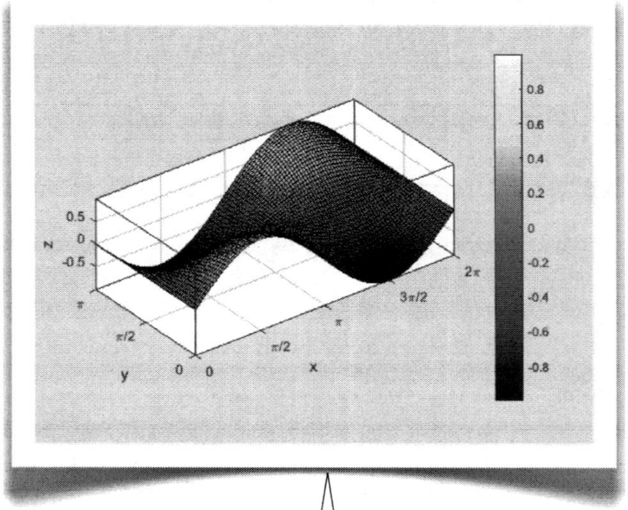

Colormap: `hot`

[4] When the **current colormap** changes (line 20), the **colorbar** and the face colors change accordingly. ↙

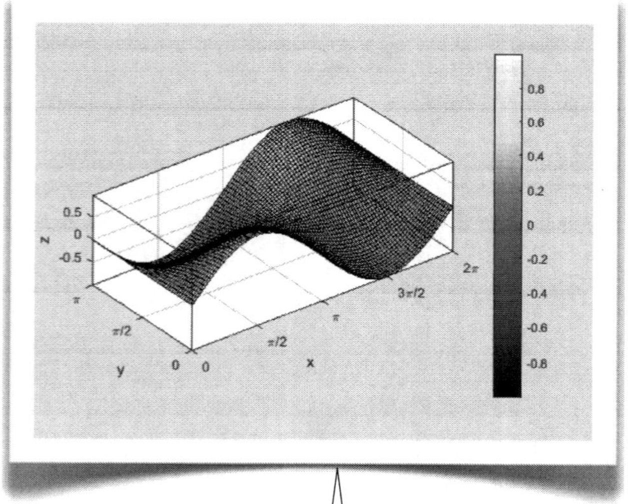

Face Transparency

[5] When the face transparency is set to 0.2 (line 21), you can see through the surface. →

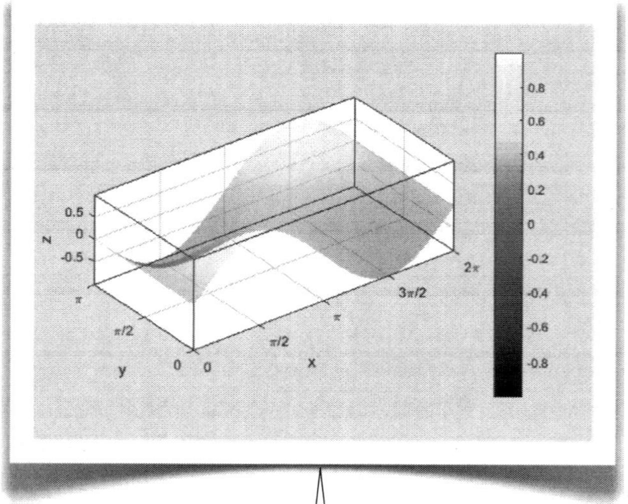

Edge Removed

[6] This is a surface plot with the edges removed (line 22). ↵

Mesh Plots

[7] The function `mesh` is similar to `surf`, except that `mesh` generates a **mesh** instead of a **surface**. To see this, replace line 6 by

```
mesh(X, Y, Z)
```

and lines 2-19 would generate a mesh plot like this. Note that the faces are not colored, but the edges are colored according to the **current colormap**. ↓

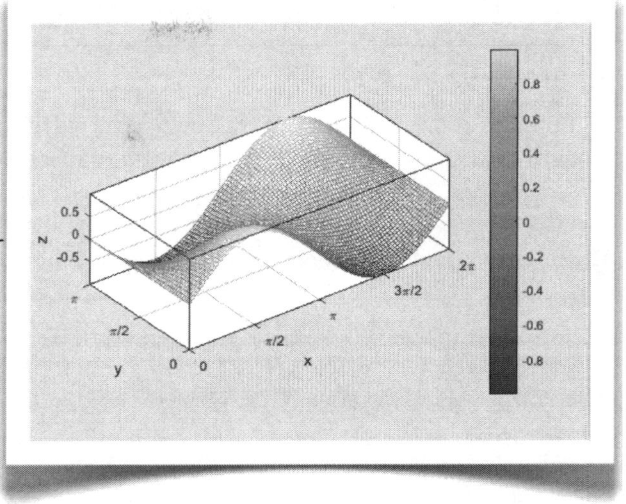

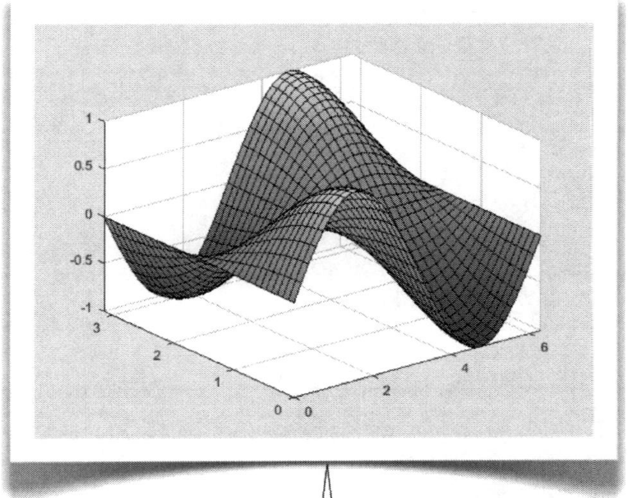

Function `fsurf`

[8] The function `fsurf(fun,xy_interval)` allows you to plot a surface by specifying a function handle `fun` and the interval in *x*-axis and *y*-axis. For example, the following commands plot a surface defined by Eq. (a), page 239.

```
fun = @(x,y) sin(x).*cos(y);
fsurf(fun, [0,2*pi,0,pi])
```

The graphics output is basically the same as that in [3], last page.

Note that, when defining a function that is to be used as an input argument of a built-in function such as `fsurf`, element-wise operators (here, `.*`) are usually used to allow the vectorization in the built-in function. #

5.11b Example: Intersection of Two Surfaces

Example05_11b.m

[1] Consider a spherical surface of radius $2a$ centered at the origin and a cylindrical surface of radius a and length $4a$, centered at $(a, 0, 0)$. The intersection of the two surfaces is a curve given by the following parametric equations:

$$x = a(1+\cos t),\quad y = a\sin t,\quad z = 2a\sin(t/2) \tag{a}$$

The following commands plot the two surfaces and the intersecting curve (see [3], next page). ↓

```
1   clear
2   a = 1;
3   [X,Y,Z] = sphere;
4   surf(2*a*X,2*a*Y,2*a*Z)
5   hold on
6   [X,Y,Z] = cylinder;
7   surf(a*X+a,a*Y,4*a*Z-2*a)
8   shading interp
9   t = linspace(0,4*pi);
10  x = a*(1+cos(t));
11  y = a*sin(t);
12  z = 2*a*sin(t/2);
13  plot3(x,y,z)
14  axis equal
15  axis vis3d
16  xlabel x, ylabel y, zlabel z
17  view(45,30)
```

Functions `sphere` and `cylinder`

[2] The built-in function `sphere` (line 3) generates three matrices, `X`, `Y`, and `Z`, containing points on a spherical surface of unit radius centered at the origin. Line 4 plots a spherical surface by scaling the unit spherical surface by $2a$ in x-, y-, and z-directions.

Similarly, the built-in function `cylinder` (line 6) generates three matrices, `X`, `Y`, and `Z`, representing an upright cylindrical surface of unit radius and unit length with its bottom centered at the origin. Line 7 plots a cylindrical surface by scaling the unit cylindrical surface by $(a, a, 4a)$ and translating it by $(a, 0, -2a)$.

Interpolating Colors

Line 8 sets the shading to `interp` (interpolating) mode, in which the edges are removed and the colors are continuous across the faces. Lines 9-12 prepare data according to Eq. (a). Line 13 plots the intersecting curve in 3-D space. Line 14 sets the three axes to be the same length for the data units. Line 15 freezes the aspect ratio of the axes. Line 16 labels the three axes.

View Angles

Function `view(az,el)` (line 17) sets the viewing angle in a three-dimensional plot. The azimuth (also called the polar angle), `az`, is the horizontal rotation about the z-axis as measured in degrees from the negative y-axis. Positive values indicate counterclockwise rotation of the viewpoint. `el` is the vertical elevation angle of the viewpoint in degrees. Positive values of the elevation angle correspond to moving above the object; negative values correspond to moving below the object. The **Figure** now looks like [3], next page. ↵

[3] Example05_11b.m creates a **Figure** like this. ↓

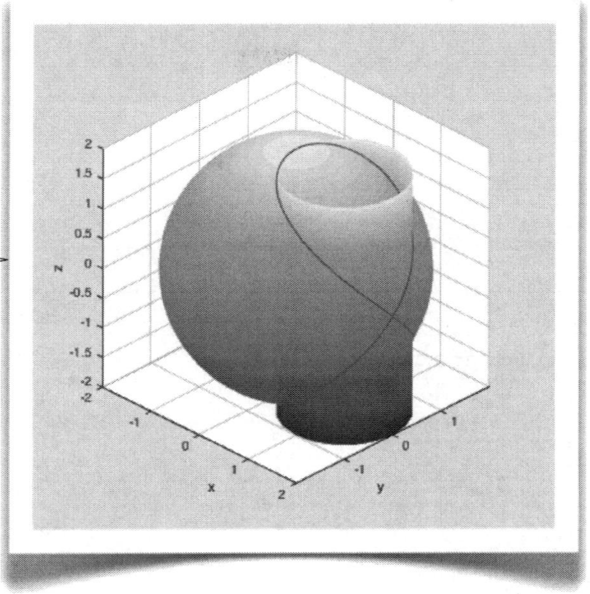

Built-in Colormaps

[4] A colormap is an *n*-by-3 matrix, where *n* is the number of colors in the colormap. Each row defines a color using an **RGB triplet**. An RGB triplet is a row vector of 3 numbers specifying intensities of the **red**, **green**, and **blue** components of a color. The intensities must be in the range [0,1]. A value of 0 indicates no color and a value of 1 indicates full intensity; thus [0 0 0] is black and [1 1 1] is white.

Table 5.11a lists the built-in colormaps; each is a 64-by-3 matrix. You can use the function `colormap` to load a colormap (e.g., line 20, page 239). The default colormap is `parula`. (Versions prior to R2014b use `jet` as the default colormap.)

When plotting a surface, the range of *Z* values (in Example05_11a.m, the range of *Z* values is from -1 to +1; in Example05_11b.m, the range of *Z* values is from -2 to +2) is divided into *n* (in this section, 64) scales and then mapped to the *n* colors of the colormap.

The coloring method using colormaps is called the **indexed coloring**. Another coloring method, called **true coloring**, is to directly specify RGB intensities. The image in Section 1.13[4], page 45, is a **true-color image**; we will discuss both methods in detail in Sections 6.4 and 6.5, respectively. #

Table 5.11a Colormaps

Colormap Name	Color Scale
`parula`	
`jet`	
`hsv`	
`hot`	
`cool`	
`spring`	
`summer`	
`autumn`	
`winter`	
`gray`	
`bone`	
`copper`	
`pink`	
`lines`	
`colorcube`	
`prism`	
`flag`	
`white`	

Details and More: Type >> `doc colormap`

Table 5.11b Surface Functions	
Functions	Description
`surf(X,Y,Z)`	Shaded surface plot
`mesh(X,Y,Z)`	Mesh plot
`fsurf(funx,funy,funz)`	Surface plotter
`colorbar`	Display color scale
`colormap map`	Set current colormap
`[X,Y,Z] = cylinder`	Generate cylinder
`[X,Y,Z] = sphere`	Generate sphere
`[X,Y,Z] = ellipsoid`	Generate ellipsoid
`[X,Y,Z] = peaks`	Generate a surface of "peaks"
`shading mode`	Set color shading properties
`view(az,el)`	View point specification
Details and More: *Help>MATLAB>Graphics>2-D and 3-D Plots>Surface, Volumes, and Polygons>Surface and Mesh Plots*	

Table 5.11c Surface Properties	
Properties	Description
`EdgeColor`	Edge line color
`FaceAlpha`	Face transparency
`FaceColor`	Face color
Details and More: *Help>MATLAB>Graphics>Graphics Objects>Graphics Object Properties>Chart Objects>Chart Surface Properties*	

5.12 Contour Plots

Example05_12.m: Contour Plots

[1] The following commands generate a surface plot shown in [3], next page, and its contour plots shown in [4-8]. ↓

```
1   clear
2   [X,Y,Z] = peaks;
3   surf(X,Y,Z)
4   [C,h] = contour(X,Y,Z, [-6:8]);
5   colorbar
6       h.ShowText = 'on';
7       h.TextList = [-6:2:8];
8   [C,h] = contourf(X,Y,Z, [-6:8]);
9   clabel(C,h, [-6:2:8])
10  [C,h] = contour3(X,Y,Z, [-6:8]);
11  clabel(C,h, [-6:2:8])
```

Function `peaks`

[2] The function `peaks` (line 2) is a demo surface provided by MATLAB for demonstrating functions such as `surf`, `mesh`, `contour`, etc. It returns 3 matrices, `X`, `Y`, and `Z`, representing a surface of mountain. Line 3 generates the surface plot (see [3], next page). Note that the elevations range from about -6 to 8.

Contour Plots

A **contour plot** presents 3-D data in a 2-D space. In line 4, the function `contour` generates a contour plot using the data `X`, `Y`, and `Z`. The contour lines are specified using a vector [-6:8]; one contour line for each elevation unit. The function `contour` returns a **contour matrix** `C` and a contour handle `h`. You don't have to know the details of `C`; it stores the contour lines information and can be input to other functions (e.g., lines 9 and 11) for additional processing. Line 5 adds a **colorbar** to the graph (see [4], next page). Note that the contour lines are colored according to their *Z*-values.

Contour-Line Labels

A way to show the contour-line labels is to turn on the contour property **ShowText** (line 6; see [5], next page). Now, each contour line is labeled with its *Z*-value. By setting the contour property **TextList** (line 7; see [6], next page), the contour lines to be labeled can be specified. Here, only the contour lines with even *Z*-values are labeled.

Filled Contour Plots

The function contourf (line 8) is similar to contour, except that the areas between contour lines are filled with colors according to their *Z*-values. Using the function clabel (line 9) is a more convenient way to show the contour line labels (than setting properties **ShowText** and **TextList**). Now the figure looks like [7], page 247.

3-D Contour Plots

The function contour3 (line 10) is similar to `contour`, except that it generated contour lines in a 3-D space. Function `clabel` can be used in a usual way (line 11; see [8], page 247). ↵

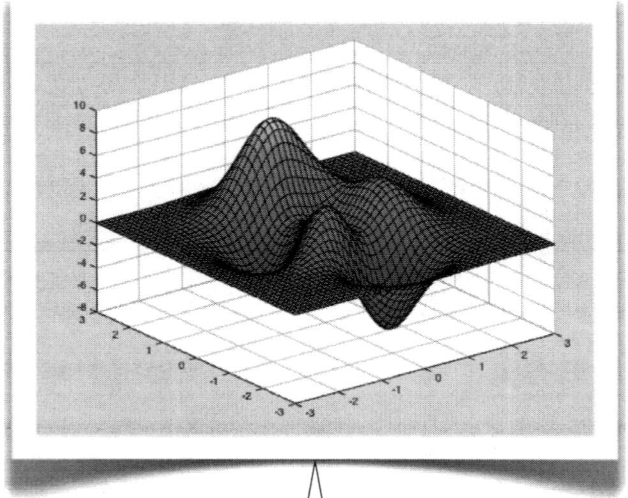

[3] Line 3 creates a **Figure** like this. →

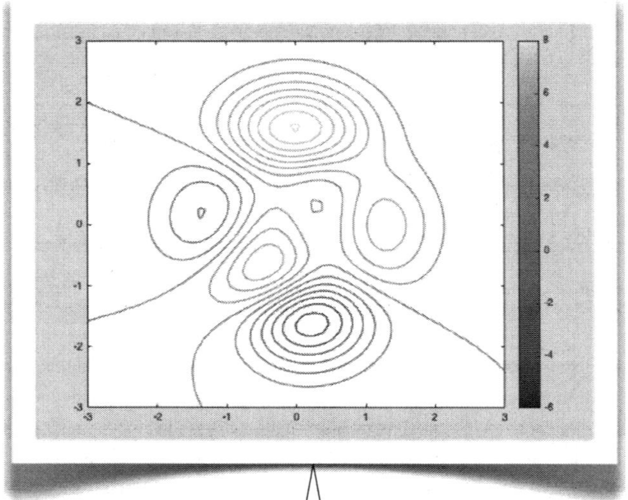

[4] Lines 4-5 re-generate the **Figure** like this. ↙

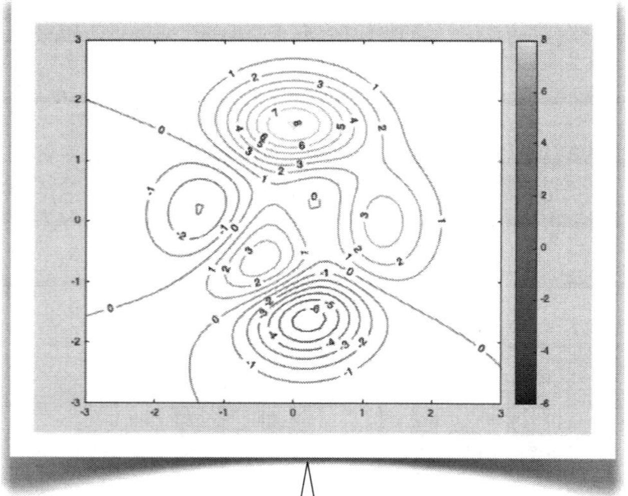

[5] Line 6 turns on contour-line labels. →

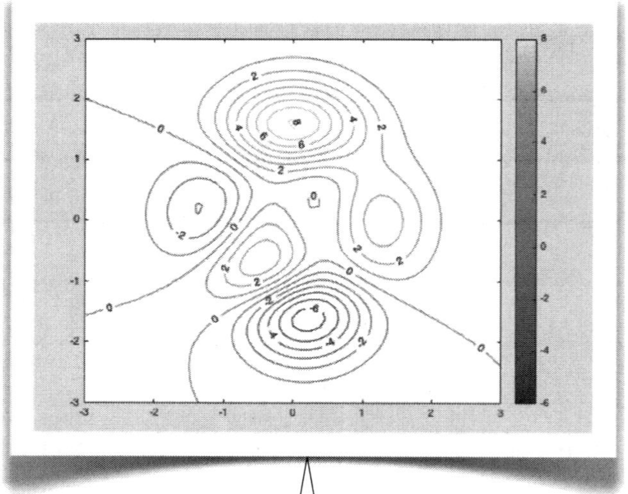

[6] After the execution of line 7, only the contour lines with even Z-values are labeled. ↵

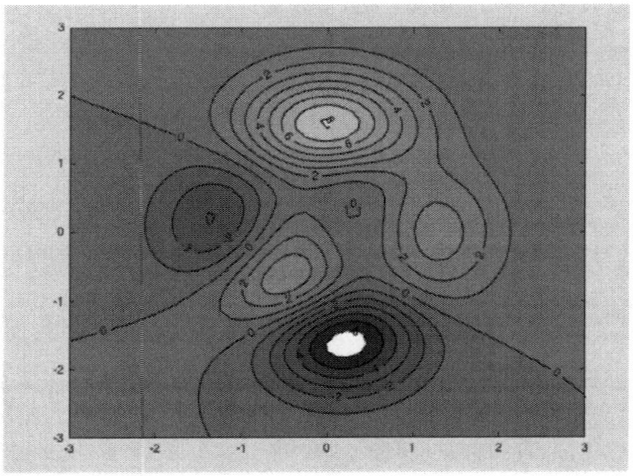

[7] This is a filled contour plot after the execution of lines 8-9. →

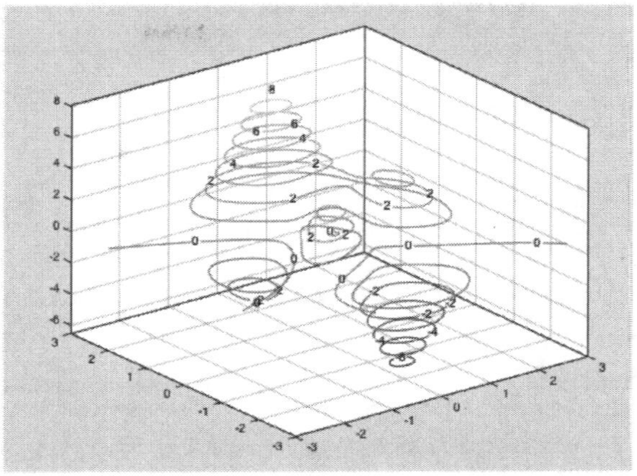

[8] This is a 3-D contour plot after the execution of lines 10-11. #

Table 5.12a Contour Functions	
Functions	Description
`[C,h] = contour(X,Y,Z,values)`	Contour plot
`[C,h] = contourf(X,Y,Z,values)`	Filled contour plot
`[c,h] = contour3(X,Y,Z,values)`	3-D contour plot
`clabel(C,h,values)`	Label contour plot
Details and More: Help>MATLAB>Graphics>2-D and 3-D Plots>Contour Plots	

Table 5.12b Contour Properties	
Properties	Description
`ShowText`	Show contour line labels
`TextList`	Contour lines to label
Details and More: Help>MATLAB>Graphics>Graphics Objects>Graphics Object Properties>Chart Objects>Contour Properties	

5.13 Vector Plots

5.13a 2-D Vector Plots

Example05_13a.m: 2-D Vector Plots

[1] The following commands generate a vector plot as shown in [2]. ↓

```
1   clear
2   [X,Y,Z] = peaks;
3   contour(X,Y,Z);
4   hold on
5   [U,V] = gradient(Z,0.125,0.125);
6   quiver(X,Y,U,V,3)
```

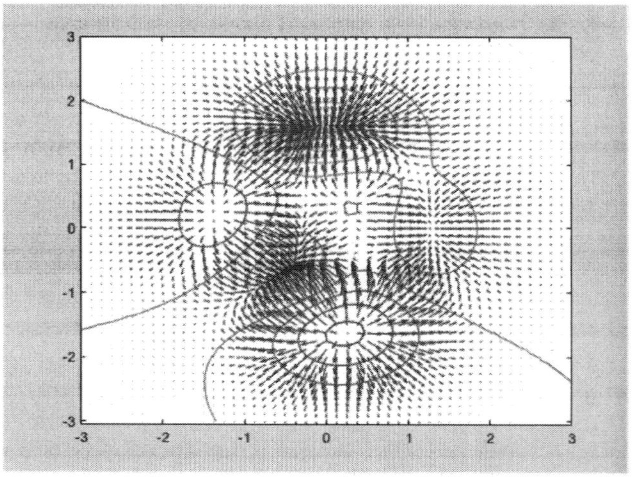

[2] Example05_13a.m creates a 2-D vector plot like this. ↓

About Example05_13a.m

[3] Lines 2-4 generate a 2-D contour plot similar to that in 5.12[4], page 246. Line 4 holds the graphics, so the subsequent graphics will add to the plot.

Function `gradients`

In line 5, the function `gradient(Z,dx,dy)` calculates the gradients (u, v) of `Z` as follows

$$u(x,y)=\frac{\partial z(x,y)}{\partial x},\quad v(x,y)=\frac{\partial z(x,y)}{\partial y}$$

2-D Vector Plots

In line 6, the function `quiver(X,Y,U,V,scale)` plots the vectors

$$(u(x,y),\ v(x,y))$$

as arrows in the x-y space; each arrow starts at the position (x, y). The optional argument `scale` is used to scale the default length of the arrows. Note that `X`, `Y`, `Z`, `U`, and `V` have the same sizes. #

5.13b 3-D Vector Plots

Example05_13b.m: 3-D Vector Plots

[1] The following commands generate a 3-D vector plot as shown in [2]. ↓

```
1  clear
2  [X,Y,Z] = peaks;
3  surf(X,Y,Z);
4  limits = axis
5  hold on
6  [U,V,W] = surfnorm(X,Y,Z);
7  quiver3(X,Y,Z,U,V,W)
8  axis(limits)
```

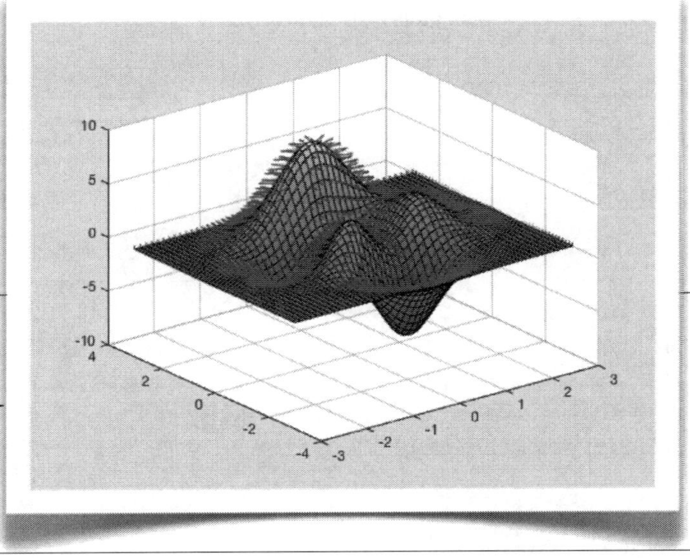

[2] Example05_13b.m creates a 3-D vector plot like this. ↓

About Example05_13b.m

[3] Lines 2-3 produce a surface plot as shown in 5.12[3], page 246. Line 4 saves the axes limits for use later (since line 7 automatically adjusts the axes limits, and we want to keep the axes limits unchanged). Line 5 holds the graphics, so the subsequent graphics will add to the plot.

3-D Vector Plots

In line 6, the function `surfnorm(X,Y,Z)` calculates the surface normal vectors (`U`, `V`, `W`) of `Z`. In line 7, the function `quiver3(X,Y,Z,U,V,W)` plots the 3-D vectors

$$(u(x,y),\ v(x,y),\ w(x,y))$$

as arrows in the *x-y-z* space; each arrow starts at the position (x, y, z).

Line 8 restores the axes limits. #

Table 5.13 Vector Plots Functions

Functions	Description
`quiver(X,Y,U,V,scale)`	2-D Vector plot
`quiver3(X,Y,Z,U,V,W,scale)`	3-D vector plot
`[U,V] = gradient(Z)`	Compute gradient
`[U,V,W] = surfnorm(X,Y,Z)`	Compute surface normals
Details and More: Help>MATLAB>Graphics>2-D and 3-D Plots>Vector Fields	

5.14 Streamline Plots

5.14a 2-D Streamline Plots

Example05_14a.m: 2-D Streamlines

[1] The script below generates a streamline plot for the flow described by a velocity field (u, v),

$$u(x,y) = 0.3 + x$$

$$v(x,y) = 0.4 - y$$

↓

```
1  clear
2  x = 0:0.1:1; y = 0:0.1:1;
3  [X,Y] = meshgrid(x,y);
4  U = 0.3+X; V = 0.4-Y;
5  quiver(X,Y,U,V)
6  sx = [0:0.1:1, zeros(1,11), 0:0.1:1];
7  sy = [zeros(1,11), 0:0.1:1, ones(1,11)];
8  SL = stream2(X,Y, U,V, sx,sy);
9  streamline(SL)
```

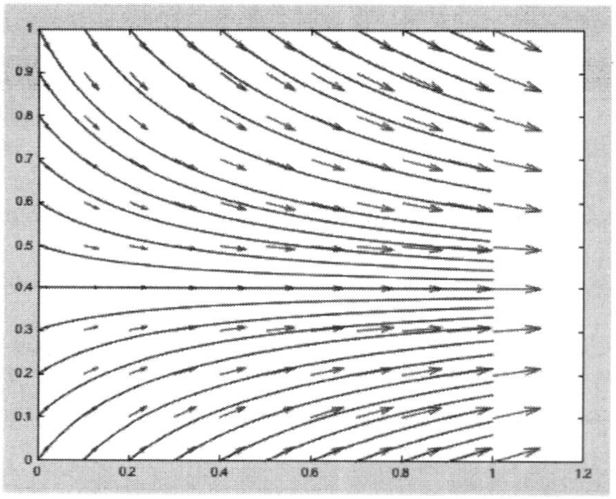

[2] Example05_14a.m creates a 2-D streamline plot like this. ←

About Example05_14a.m

[3] Lines 2-3 generate a 2-D grid in the *x-y* space. Line 4 calculates the velocity field according to the equations in [1]. The function `quiver(X,Y,U,V)` in line 5 plots the velocity field (u, v) as arrows; each arrow locates at (x, y).

The function `stream2(X,Y,U,V,sx,sy)` in line 8 calculates the streamlines `SL`, a cell array. The coordinates of the starting positions of the streamlines are specified in `sx` and `sy`, which are prepared in lines 6-7. The function `streamline(SL)` (line 9) then plots the streamlines `SL`, as shown in [3]. We'll demonstrate the animation of the flow using the function `streamparticles` in Example06_02a.m, page 258. #

Table 5.14 Streamline Plots Functions

Functions	Description
`streamline(SL)`	Streamline plot
`SL = stream2(X,Y, U,V, Sx,Sy)`	Calculate 2-D streamlines
`SL = stream3(X,Y,Z, U,V,W, Sx,Sy,Sz)`	Calculate 3-D streamlines

Details and More: Help>MATLAB>Graphics>2-D and 3-D Plots>Surfaces, Volumes, and Polygons>Volume Visualization>Vector Volume Data

5.14b 3-D Streamline Plots

Example05_14b.m: 3-D Streamlines

[1] The script below generates a 3-D streamline plot for the flow described by a 3-D velocity field (u, v, w),

$$u(x,y) = 0.3 + x$$

$$v(x,y) = 0.4 - y$$

$$w = 0.5 - z$$

↓

```
1   clear
2   x = 0:0.1:1; y = 0:0.1:1; z = 0:0.1:1;
3   [X,Y,Z] = meshgrid(x,y,z);
4   U = 0.3+X; V = 0.4-Y; W = 0.5-Z;
5   % quiver3(X,Y,Z,U,V,W)
6   sx = 0;
7   sy = 0:0.1:1;
8   sz = 0:0.1:1;
9   [Sx, Sy, Sz] = meshgrid(sx,sy,sz);
10  SL = stream3(X,Y,Z, U,V,W, Sx,Sy,Sz);
11  streamline(SL)
12  view(3), axis vis3d, box on
13  xlabel('x'), ylabel('y'), zlabel('z')
```

About Example05_14b.m

[3] Lines 2-3 generate a 3-D grid in the x-y-z space. Line 4 calculates the velocity field according to the equations in [1].

The function `quiver3(X,Y,Z,U,V,W)` in line 5 would plot the velocity field (u, v, w) as arrows. We comment out this line so that the graph is not too congested. The function stream3`(X,Y,W,U,V,W,Sx,Sy,Sz)` in line 10 calculates the 3-D streamlines SL, which is a cell array. The coordinates of the starting positions of the streamlines are specified in `Sx`, `Sy`, and `Sz`, which are prepared in lines 6-9. Note that we plot only those streamlines that start at y-z plane. In line 12, the function `view(3)` switches to a 3-D view, and `axis vis3d` freezes the aspect ratio of the axes. We'll demonstrate the animation of the flow using the function `streamparticles` in Example06_02b.m, page 259. #

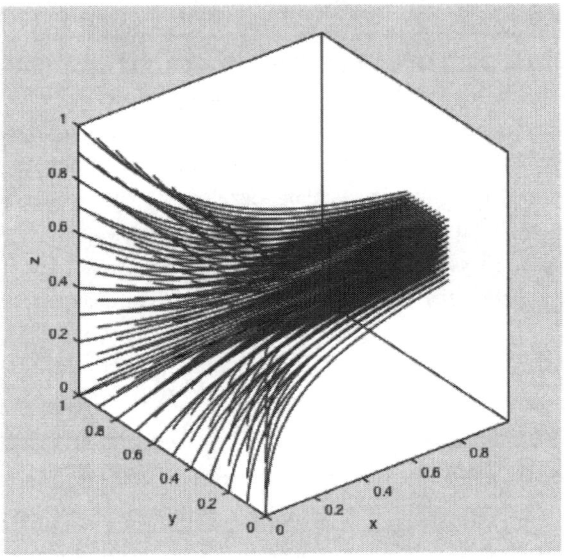

[2] Example05_14b.m creates a 3-D streamline plot like this. ←

5.15 Isosurface Plots

Example05_15.m: Isosurface Plots

[1] Imagine a potential function V in 3-D space,

$$V(x,y,z)=0.2+0.3x+0.4y+0.5z+0.5x^2-0.5y^2-0.5z^2$$

where $0 \le x \le 1$, $0 \le y \le 1$, and $0 \le z \le 1$. An isosurface is a surface on which a function has a specific common value. The following commands generate an isosurface plot for the potential function V. ↓

```
 1  clear
 2  x = 0:0.05:1; y = 0:0.05:1; z = 0:0.05:1;
 3  [X,Y,Z] = meshgrid(x,y,z);
 4  V = 0.3*X+0.4*Y+0.5*Z+0.5*X.^2-0.5*Y.^2-0.5*Z.^2;
 6  colorbar
 7  hold on
 8  for isovalue = 0.4:0.1:0.8
 9      isosurface(X,Y,Z,V, isovalue)
10  end
11  view(3), axis vis3d
12  xlabel('x'), ylabel('y'), zlabel('z')
```

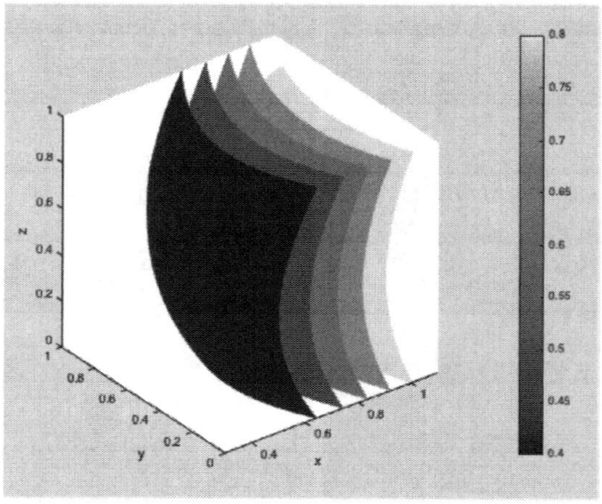

[2] Example05_15.m creates an isosurface plot like this. ←

About Example05_15.m

[3] Lines 2-3 generate a 3-D grid in the *x-y-z* space. Line 4 calculates the potential according to the equation in [1]. Line 6 displays the colorbar; a **Figure** and an **Axes** is also created. Line 7 holds the **Axes**. In line 9, the function `isosurface(X,Y,Z,V,isovalue)` plots an isosurface, on which `V` has a value of `isovalue`. The argument `isovalue` must be a scalar; therefore, we use a `for`-loop (line 8-10) to plot multiple isosurfaces. In line 11, `view(3)` switches to a 3-D view, and `axis vis3d` freezes the aspect ratio of the axes. Line 12 labels the axes. #

Table 5.15 Isosurface Plots Functions

Functions	Description
`isosurface(X,Y,Z,V,isovalue)`	Isosurface plot

Details and More: Help>MATLAB>Graphics>2-D and 3-D Plots>Surfaces, Volumes, and Polygons>Volume Visualization>Scalar Volume Data

5.16 Additional Exercise Problems

Problem05_01: 3-D Curve

Plot a 3-D curve defined by

$$x = (1 - r\cos\varphi)\cdot\cos\eta$$
$$y = (1 - r\cos\varphi)\cdot\sin\eta$$
$$z = r\cdot(\sin\varphi + \frac{P\eta}{\pi})$$

where $r = 0.3$, $P = 3$, $0 \le \eta \le 2n\pi$, $0 \le \varphi \le 2\pi$, and $n = 5$.

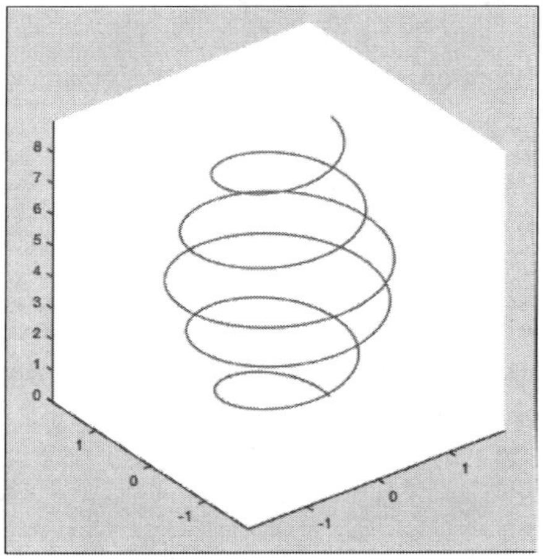

Problem05_02: Polar Plot

The function `polar(theta,r)` generates a 2-D plot in polar coordinates. For example, the following commands produce a polar plot shown right:

```
clear, clc
theta = linspace(0, 2*pi);
r = 1 + cos(theta);
polar(theta, r)
```

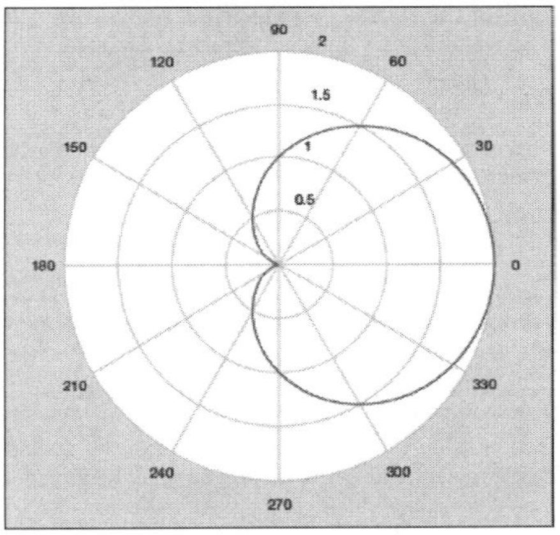

As an exercise, write a script to generate a polar plot using the following equation:

$$r^2 = \cos^2\theta(a\sin^2\theta + b)$$

where $0 \le \theta \le 2\pi$, $a = 7$, $b = 2$.

Problem05_03: Apple

The "apple" shown right is generated by the following equations:

$$x = \cos u \cdot (4 + 5.5\cos v)$$

$$y = \sin u \cdot (4 + 5.5\cos v)$$

$$z = (\cos v + \sin v - 1)\cdot(1 + \sin v)\cdot\log\left(1 - \frac{\pi v}{10}\right) + 7.5\sin v$$

where $0 \le u \le 2\pi$ and $-\pi \le v \le \pi$.

Write a script to produce a surface plot as shown right.

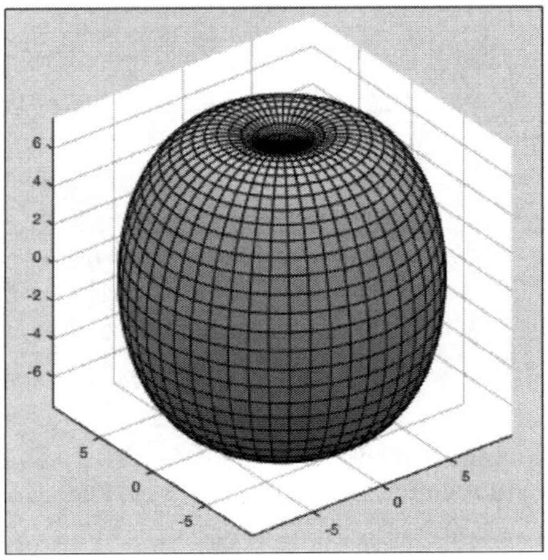

Problem05_04: Histogram Plot

The function `normrnd` samples an array of data which are randomly sampled from a population of normal distribution. For example, the following commands sample 200 data from a population of normal distribution of which the mean is 500 and the standard deviation is 20 (also see 13.1a[3-4], page 485):

```
clear, clc
rng(0)
data = normrnd(500, 20, 1, 200);
```

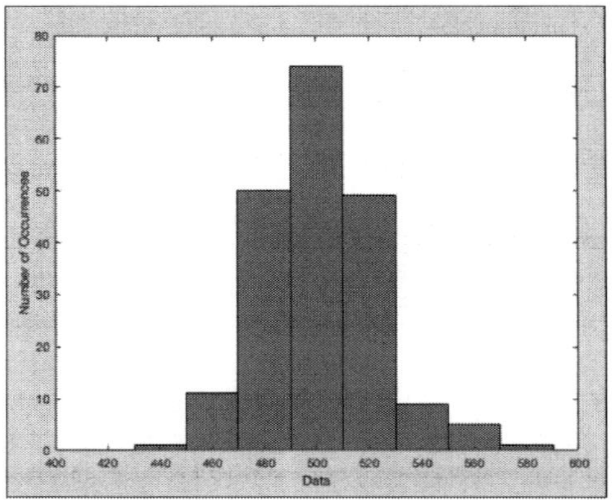

The line `rng(0)` sets the "seed" to a fixed number so that every time you execute these commands, the same sequence of 200 data (listed in 13.1a[1], page 484) is generated.

A histogram is a special type of bar plot showing the distribution of a set of data. Use the function `histogram` to produce a bar plot shown right.

Problem05_05: 3-D Bar Plot

Use the function `bar3` to generate a 3-D bar plot shown right, which contains the same information as that in 5.8[4], page 234.

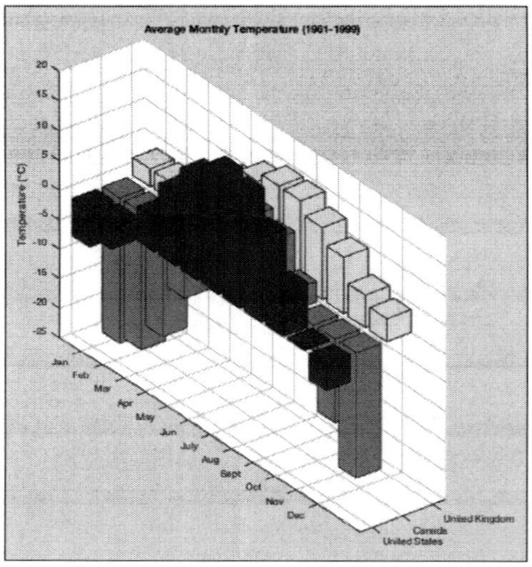

Problem05_06: Field Lines

The field lines shown right are generated by the following equations (*P. Moon and D. E. Spencer, Field Theory Handbook, Springer-Verlag, p. 89*):

$$x = \frac{a \sinh \eta}{\cosh \eta - \cos \varphi}$$

$$y = \frac{a \sin \varphi}{\cosh \eta - \cos \varphi}$$

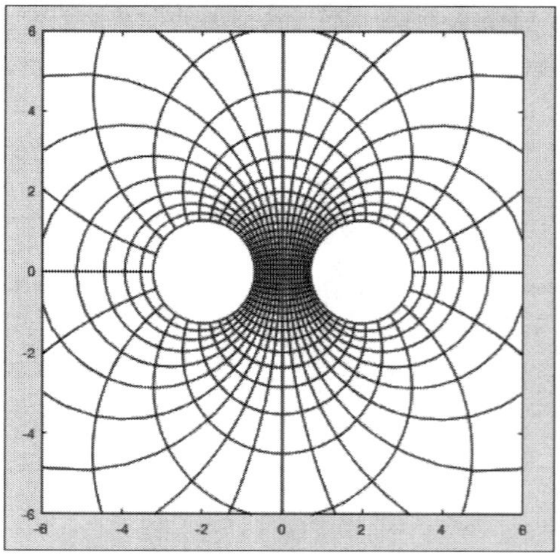

where $-1 \le \eta \le 1$, $0 \le \varphi \le 2\pi$, and a = 1.5. Each line is generated by a constant value of η or a constant value of φ.

Write a script to produce a 2-D plot as shown right.

Problem05_07: MRI of Human Skull

In the Command Window, type

```
>> doc isocaps
```

and find an example script in the on-line documentation. Run the script. It generates a cutaway volume of a human skull as shown. The script uses many functions that are not mentioned in the book. Study each statement, looking up the on-line documentation whenever necessary.

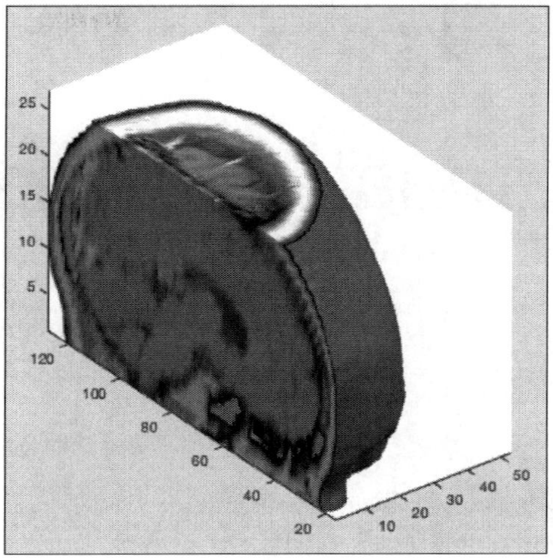

Chapter 6

Animations, Images, Audios, and Videos

Animation, rather than a static picture, is often the best way to present time-dependent data. An engineer often needs to deal with an image file, an audio file, or a video file. MATLAB provides many functions that can open and operate on various formats of image files, audio files, and video files.

6.1 Animation of Line Plots: Comet

Example06_01.m

[1] We've demonstrated an animation of a 2-D line plot in line 37, Example01_18.m, page 55. The following commands demonstrate an animation of a 3-D line plot, which was defined in 5.10[1], page 237. ↙

```
1   clear
2   view(3)
3   axis([-1, 1, -1, 1, 0, 8*pi])
4   xlabel x, ylabel y, zlabel z
5   h = gca; h.BoxStyle = 'full'; box on
6   grid on
7   axis vis3d
8   hold on
9   z = linspace(0, 8*pi, 200);
10  x = exp(-z/20).*cos(z);
11  y = exp(-z/20).*sin(z);
12  comet3(x,y,z)
```

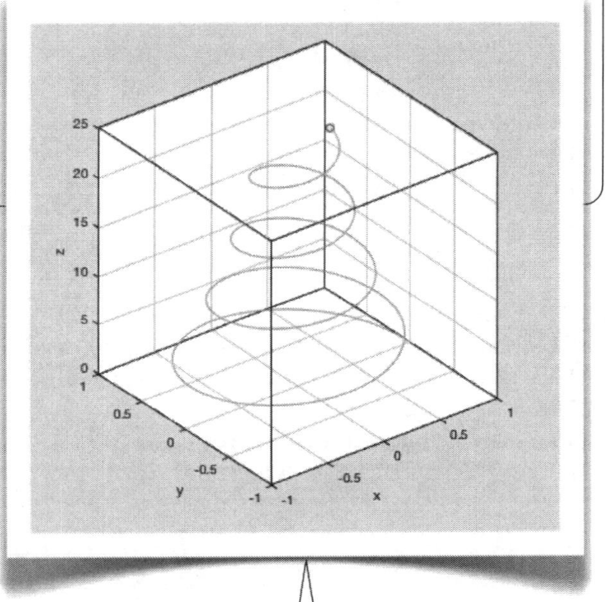

[3] This is the last frame of the animation. #

About Example06_01.m

[2] The function `view(3)` (line 2) creates an **Axes** and displays it in a 3-D view. Line 3 sets axes limits. Line 4 labels the three axes. In line 5, the box style of the **Axes** is set to `full`, so when the box is displayed, all six edges are shown. Line 6 displays the grid. Line 7 freezes the aspect ratio of the axes. Line 8 holds the **Axes**.

Lines 9-11 calculate the coordinates according to the equations defined in 5.10[1], page 237. Line 12 animates a 3-D line defined by the coordinates. →

Table 6.1 Animated Line Plots Functions

Functions	Description
`comet(x,y)`	Animate 2-D line plots
`comet3(x,y,z)`	Animate 3-D line plots
`animatedline(x,y)`	Create animated line (2-D)
`animatedline(x,y,z)`	Create animated line (3-D)

Details and More: Help>MATLAB>Graphics>2-D and 3-D Plots>Animation

6.2 Stream Particles Animations

6.2a Animation of 2-D Streamlines

Example06_02a.m: Animation of 2-D Streamlines

[1] The following commands perform an animation of the flow described in 5.14a[1], page 250. The dimmed lines (lines 1-9) are copied from Example05_14a.m, page 250. →

```
1   clear
2   x = 0:0.1:1; y = 0:0.1:1;
3   [X,Y] = meshgrid(x,y);
4   U = 0.3+X; V = 0.4-Y;
5   quiver(X,Y,U,V)
6   sx = [0:0.1:1, zeros(1,11), 0:0.1:1];
7   sy = [zeros(1,11), 0:0.1:1, ones(1,11)];
8   SL = stream2(X,Y, U,V, sx,sy);
9   streamline(SL)
10  streamparticles(SL, ...
11      'Animate', 5, ...
12      'FrameRate', 30, ...
13      'ParticleAlignment', 'on')
14  sx = zeros(1,11);
15  sy = 0:0.1:1;
16  SL = stream2(X,Y, U, V, sx, sy);
17  streamparticles(SL, ...
18      'Animate', 5, ...
19      'FrameRate', 30, ...
20      'ParticleAlignment', 'on')
```

About Example06_02a.m

[2] Lines 2-9 produce a 2-D streamline plot shown in 5.14a[2], page 250.

In lines 10-13, the function `streamparticles` animates the movement of flow particles using the streamline data `SL` generated by `stream2` in line 8, where the starting positions are specified at $y = 0$, $x = 0$, and $y = 1$ (also see lines 6-7). The property **Animate** (line 11) is the number of times of animation. **FrameRate** (line 12) is the number of frames per second. Line 13 sets **ParticleAlignment** to **on** to draw particles at the beginning of each streamline. A snapshot of the animation is shown in [3].

Lines 14-16 re-specify the starting positions at $x = 0$ and regenerate streamlines `SL` using the new starting positions. And lines 17-20 animate the movement of particles along the streamlines. A snapshot of the animation is shown in [4]. ✓

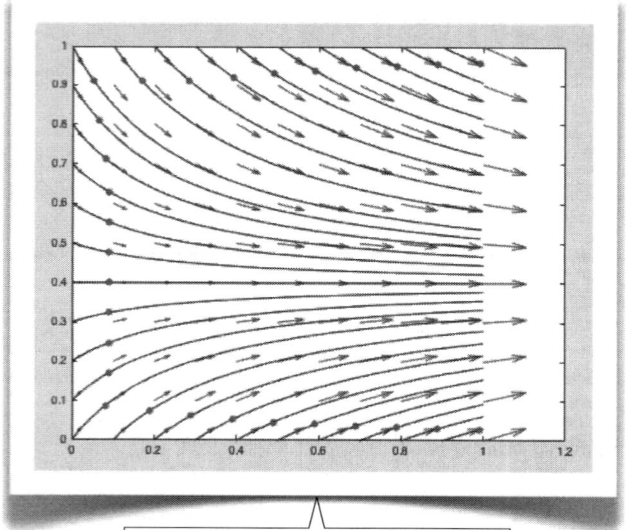

[3] Lines 10-13 produce a stream particles animation like this. →

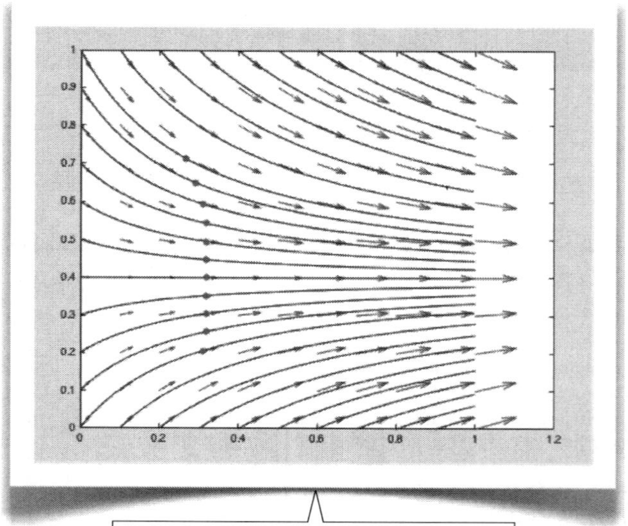

[4] Lines 17-20 produce a stream particles animation like this. #

6.2b Animation of 3-D Streamlines

Example06_02b.m: Animation of 3-D Streamlines

[1] The following commands perform an animation of the flow described in 5.14b[1], page 251. The dimmed lines (lines 1-13) are copied from Example05_14b.m, page 251. ↓

```
1   clear
2   x = 0:0.1:1; y = 0:0.1:1; z = 0:0.1:1;
3   [X,Y,Z] = meshgrid(x,y,z);
4   U = 0.3+X; V = 0.4-Y; W = 0.5-Z;
5   % quiver3(X,Y,Z,U,V,W)
6   sx = 0;
7   sy = 0:0.1:1;
8   sz = 0:0.1:1;
9   [Sx, Sy, Sz] = meshgrid(sx,sy,sz);
10  SL = stream3(X,Y,Z, U,V,W, Sx,Sy,Sz);
11  streamline(SL)
12  view(3), axis vis3d, box on
13  xlabel('x'), ylabel('y'), zlabel('z')
14  streamparticles(SL, ...
15      'Animate', 5, ...
16      'FrameRate', 30, ...
17      'ParticleAlignment', 'on')
```

About Example06_02b.m

[2] Lines 2-13 produce a 3-D streamline plot as shown in 5.14b[2], page 251.

Lines 14-17 animate the movement of flow particles along the streamlines. Note that the starting positions are specified at $x = 0$ (lines 6-8). ↓

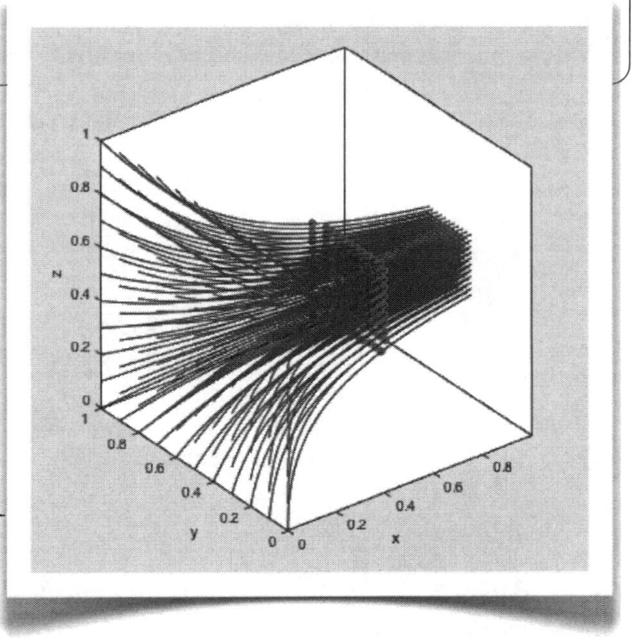

[3] Lines 14-17 produce a 3-D stream particles animation like this. #

Table 6.2 Stream Particles Functions	
Functions	Description
`streamparticles(SL,name,value)`	Plot stream particles
Details and More: Help>MATLAB>Graphics>2-D and 3-D Plots>Surfaces, Volumes, and Polygons>Volume Visualization>Vector Volume Data	

6.3 Movies: Animation of an Engine

Example06_03.m: Animation of an Engine

[1] This program creates a movie that animates the motion of an engine cylinder as shown in [3-7] (next page) and saves the movie as a video file, in AVI format by default. Observe the outcome of each command. ↓

```
 1  clear
 2  n = 50; theta = linspace(0,2*pi,n);
 3  a = 1.1; b = 2.7; c = 0.6; d = 0.4;
 4  aX = a*cos(theta); aY = a*sin(theta);
 5  p = aX+sqrt(b^2-aY.^2);
 6  limits = [-a, a+b+d, -a, a];
 7  cmap = colormap; nc = length(colormap)-1;
 8  for k = 1:n
 9      plot(aX, aY, 'k:')
10      hold on
11          cylinderX = [a, a+b+d, a+b+d, a];
12          cylinderY = [-c, -c, c, c];
13      plot(cylinderX, cylinderY, 'k')
14          pistonX = [p(k)-d, p(k)+d, p(k)+d, p(k)-d, p(k)-d];
15          pistonY = [-c, -c, c, c, -c];
16      fill(pistonX, pistonY, 'c')
17          fuelX = [p(k)+d, a+b+d, a+b+d, p(k)+d, p(k)+d];
18          fuelY = [-c, -c, c, c, -c];
19          color = cmap(ceil((p(k)-b+a)/(2*a)*(nc-1)),:);
20      fill(fuelX, fuelY, color)
21          crankX = [0, aX(k)];
22          crankY = [0, aY(k)];
23      plot(crankX, crankY,'ko-', 'LineWidth', 4)
24          linkX = [aX(k), p(k)];
25          linkY = [aY(k), 0];
26      plot(linkX, linkY,'ko-', 'LineWidth', 4)
27      axis(limits)
28      axis off equal
29      Frames(k) = getframe;
30      hold off
31  end
32  movie(Frames, 5, 30)
33  videoObj = VideoWriter('Engine');
34  open(videoObj);
35  writeVideo(videoObj, Frames);
36  close(videoObj);
```

Structure of Example06_03.m

[2] In each pass of the `for`-loop (lines 8-31), an image is generated (lines 9-28) and the image is captured using the function `getframe` (line 29) and stored as a **frame** in an array `Frames`. Each frame is a **structure** representing an image. At the completion of the `for`-loop, we have an array of 50 frames. In line 32, the frames are played using the function `movie`.

To save the frames as a video file, a video object is created using the function `VideoWriter` (line 33), which supports **AVI** (default), Motion **JPEG 2000**, and **MPEG-4** file formats. A video file is opened (line 34), the frames are written to the file (line 35), and finally the file is closed (line 36). ↵

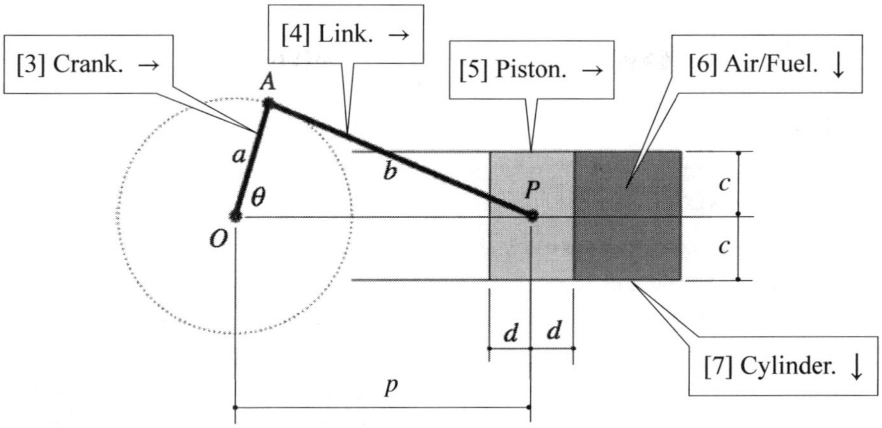

Details of Example06_03.m

[8] An engine cycle is divided into 50 frames (line 2). Line 3 sets the parameters shown in [3-7]. Line 4 calculates the coordinates of point *A* (see [3]); the origin is at *O*, a fixed point in space. Line 5 calculates the distance *p* (see [5]). Line 6 determines the axes limits. Line 7 retrieves the current colormap, `parula` (Table 5.11a page 243), which contains 64 colors.

In the beginning of the `for`-loop (lines 8-31), a dotted circle representing the trace path of *A* is drawn (line 9). The current axes are held (line 10) so the subsequent plotting would not erase the existing drawing. Lines 11-13 draw the cylinder [7]. Lines 14-16 draw the piston and fill with cyan color [5]. Lines 17-20 draw the cylindrical space with compressive fuel [6] and fill with a color according to the volume of the space, smaller space mapping to the higher color in the colormap (line 19); this mimics the effect of air/fuel compression. Lines 21-23 draw the crank [3]. Lines 24-26 draw the link [4]. Line 28 removes the **Axes** and sets the lengths of units equal in both *x*-axis and *y*-axis, so the graphics are not distorted. In line 29, the image is captured using the function `getframe`; it outputs a **structure** containing the image; the **structure** is stored as an element of the array `Frames`. (*See: >> doc getframe*)

At the completion of the `for`-loop, we have an array of 50 frames. In line 32, the frames are played 5 times, 30 frames per second. To save the frames as a video file, a **video object** is created with the name `Engine` using the function `VideoWriter` (line 33). The frames are then written into a video file (lines 34-36). By default, the file extension `.avi` is used. At the completion of the program, you may re-play the AVI file by double-clicking the file **Engine.avi** from your operation system (i.e., outside the MATLAB desktop; do not double-click in the MATLAB desktop). #

Table 6.3 Animated Line Plots Functions

Functions	Description
`movie(Frames,n,fps)`	Play movie frames
`frame = getframe`	Capture axes or figure as movie frame
`videoObj = VideoWriter(filename)`	Create object to write video files
`writeVideo(videoObj,Frames)`	Write video data to file

Details and More: Help>MATLAB>Graphics>2-D and 3-D Plots>Animation

6.4 Indexed Images

6.4a Indexed Images

Example06_04a.m: Indexed Images

[1] MATLAB supports two types of images: **indexed** and **true-color**. The following commands demonstrate the display of an indexed image. We'll discuss **true-color** images in the next section. ↓

```
1  clear
2  load earth
3  image(X)
4  colormap(map)
5  axis image
```

About Example06_04a.m

[2] Line 2 loads a file **earth.mat**, a tutorial file provided by MATLAB, containing two variables `X` and `map` (see [3]). The file extension `.mat` is the default extension for a MATLAB data file saved using the function `save` (Section 7.4). Variable `X` is a 257-by-250 matrix, representing an image of 257-by-250 pixels. Each element is an index number to `map`, a colormap storing 64 colors.

Line 3 displays the image data `X` using the current colormap, `parula` (Table 5.11a, page 243). It is odd with the current colormap (see [4]). Note that, when displaying the 257-by-250 pixels, the 257 pixels are arranged vertically **from top to bottom**, and the 250 pixels are arranged horizontally from **left to right**.

In line 4, the current colormap is changed to `map`, which is included in the image file **earth.mat**. Line 5 sets the axes style to `image`, using the same length for the data units along each axis (i.e., `axis equal`) and fitting the axes box tightly around the data (please try to replace line 5 by `axis equal`, and tell the difference). Now the earth looks pretty (see [5]).

Other Tutorial Indexed Image Files

Other tutorial indexed image files provided by MATLAB include `spine.mat`, `mandrill.mat`, and `clown.mat`. Please try to display these image files yourself. Remember that you may find out where a file is stored by typing `>> which spine.mat` ↑

[3] The **Workspace**. ↓

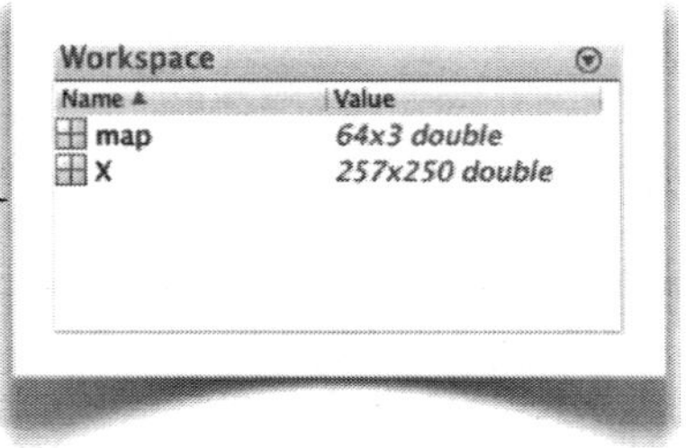

[4] Line 3 displays an image like this. ↓

[5] Lines 4-5 change the image to this. ↲

Indexed Image

[6] The image introduced in Example06_04a.m is called an **indexed image**, since its image data (`X`) contains index numbers to a colormap. Change of the colormap will in turn change the appearance of the image. An indexed image is always accompanied with a colormap; the default colormap is `parula` (Table 5.11a, page 243). #

6.4b Colormaps

Example06_04b.m: Colormaps

[1] The following script demonstrates the creation of a colormap of 4 colors, the creation of a 2-by-4 indexed image, and some operations of the image. Observe the outcome of each command. ↓

```
1   clear
2   MyMap = [1, 0, 0;   % 1. Red
3            0, 1, 0;   % 2. Green
4            0, 0, 1;   % 3. Blue
5            1, 1, 1];  % 4. White
6   MyImage = [1, 2, 3, 4;
7              4, 3, 2, 1];
8   image(MyImage)
9   colormap(MyMap)
10  axis image
11  delete(gcf)
12  save('Datafile06_04b','MyImage','MyMap')
13  clear
14  load('Datafile06_04b')
15  image(MyImage)
16  colormap(MyMap)
17  axis image
```

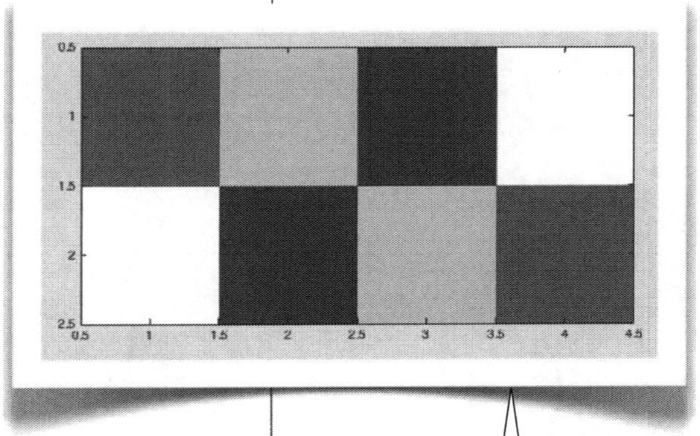

[3] This is the image after the execution of line 15 or line 22. #

About Example06_04b.m

[2] Lines 2-5 create a 4-by-3 matrix `MyMap` representing 4 colors, each described by an RGB triplet (5.11b[4], page 243). Here, the 4 colors we created are red [1 0 0], green [0 1 0], blue [0 0 1], and white [1 1 1]. Lines 6-7 create a 2-by-4 matrix `MyImage` representing an image; each value of the matrix is an index to the colormap `MyMap`. Line 8 displays the image with the default colormap (`parula`). Line 9 loads the colormap `MyMap`, which replaces the previous colormap and becomes the current colormap. Line 10 sets the axes style to `image`. The image now looks like [3]. Note that the image has 2-by-4 pixels; each pixel is centered at a position that has coordinates defined by the indices of the image data `MyImage`. For example, the pixel `MyImage(2,1)` (lower-left pixel; white color) is displayed and centered at the coordinates $y = 2$ and $x = 1$. The vertical coordinate (y) runs from top to bottom and the horizontal coordinate (x) from left to right.

Lines 11-17 demonstrate the saving and loading of the image file. Line 11 deletes the current figure window. Line 12 saves the variables `MyImage` and `MyMap` in the file `Datafile06_04b.mat`. Line 13 clears the **Workspace**. Line 14 loads the variables from the file `Datafile06_04b.mat`. Now, the two variables `MyImage` and `MyMap` are restored in the **Workspace**. Lines 15-17 display the image again. Section 7.4 will discuss more on **.mat** files. ↑

6.5 True-Color Images

6.5a True-Color Images

Example06_05a.m: True Color Images

[1] We saw the following commands in Section 1.13, page 45. They display a true-color image like [2]. Now we look into details of a true-color image. ↘

```
1   clear
2   Photo = imread('peppers.png');
3   image(Photo)
4   axis image
```

[2] Example06_05a.m displays an image like this. ↓

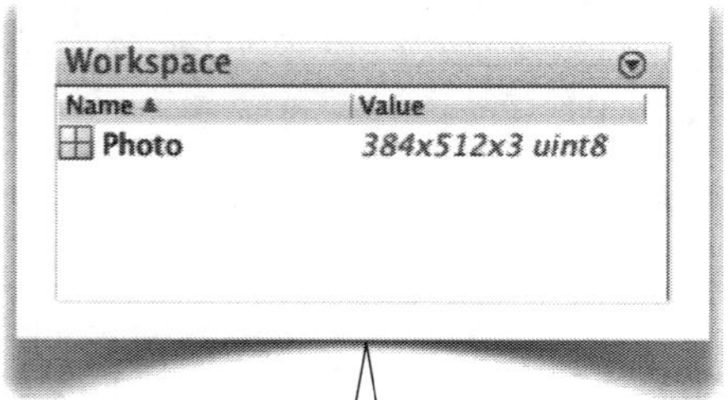

[4] The **Workspace**. #

About Example06_05a.m

[3] The function `imread` (line 2) reads an image file `peppers.png` and returns a 384-by-512-by-3 array of `uint8` (see [4]), representing an image of 384-by-512 pixels. Each pixel is described by an RGB triplet. The RGB triplet is similar to the one used in a colormap (5.11b[4], page 243) except that it can be any data type (the colormap uses `double`). When storing an image in a file, MATLAB uses one of the following three data types: `double`, `uint16`, or `uint8` (*Help>MATLAB>Graphics>Images>Working with Images in MATLAB Graphics*). Data type `uint8` is often used since it is the most storage-efficient data type.

The three values in an RGB triplet represent the intensities of the red, green, and blue colors, respectively. If `double` is used, the intensities range from 0 to 1; if `uint16` is used, the intensities range from 0 to 32767; if `uint8` is used, the intensities range from 0 to 255.

Supported Image Formats

The PNG is one of the graphics file formats supported by MATLAB. Table 6.5a (page 266) lists the graphics file formats supported by MATLAB. ↑

6.5b RGB Triplets

Example06_05b.m: RGB Triplets

[1] The following script demonstrates the creation of a 2-by-4 true-color image and some operations of the image. ↙

```
 1  clear
 2  A = zeros(2,4,3);
 3  A(1,1,1:3) = [1 0 0];  % Red
 4  A(1,2,1:3) = [0 1 0];  % Green
 5  A(1,3,1:3) = [0 0 1];  % Blue
 6  A(1,4,1:3) = [1 1 1];  % White
 7  A(2,1,1:3) = [1 1 1];  % White
 8  A(2,2,1:3) = [0 0 1];  % Blue
 9  A(2,3,1:3) = [0 1 0];  % Green
10  A(2,4,1:3) = [1 0 0];  % Red
11  image(A), axis image
12  imwrite(A, 'Datafile06_05b.png')
13  delete(gcf), clear
14  B = imread('Datafile06_05b.png');
15  image(B), axis image
```

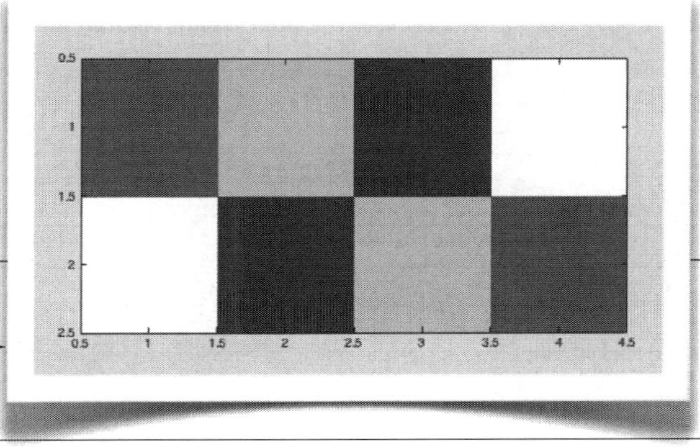

[2] Line 11 (or line 15) displays an image of 2-by-4 pixels. ↓

About Example06_05b.m

[3] Lines 2-10 create an image data of 2-by-4 pixels. Note that we use `double` (see [4]) for the RGB color intensities, which range from 0 to 1.

Line 11 displays the image data [2]. Line 12 stores the image in a file `Datafile06_05b.png`. By default, the image data are converted to `uint8`, which ranges from 0 to 255. Therefore, the red color becomes [255, 0, 0], green [0, 255, 0], blue [0, 0, 255], white [255, 255, 255]. Line 13 deletes the **Figure** and clears the **Workspace**.

After an image is stored in a standard file format such as PNG, you may open it (outside the MATLAB desktop; not within the MATLAB desktop). If you open it (by double-clicking the file), it is a tiny 4-by-2-pixel image.

Line 14 reads the file Datafile06_05b.png, and it outputs an image data of `uint8` (see [5]). Line 15 displays the image data again [2]. ↓

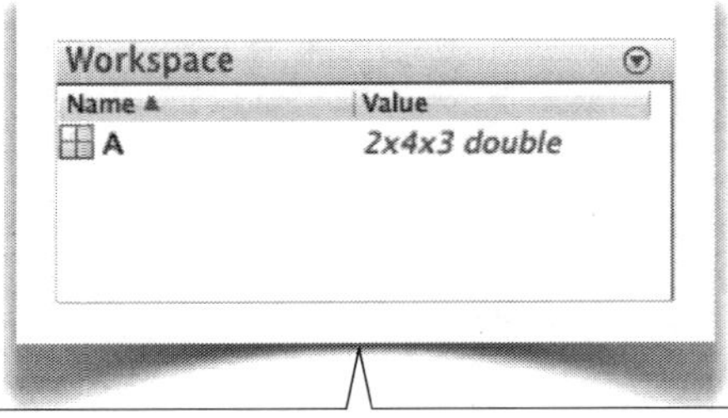

[4] Lines 6-14 create an image data of 2-by-4 pixels; each described by an RGB triplet using three `doubles`. →

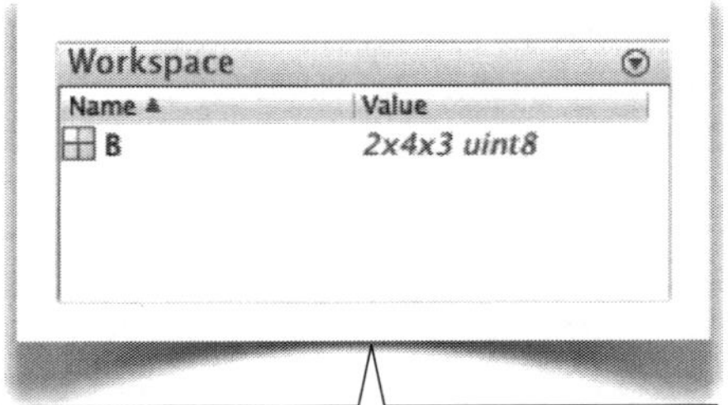

[5] Line 18 reads an image data of 2-by-4 pixels; each described by an RGB triplet using three `uint8s`. ↵

True-Color Image

[6] The colors in an indexed image are usually not smooth; the transition of colors is usually perceivable by ordinary human eyes, since the number of colors it can express is limited by the size of the colormap, which is usually much fewer than the color resolution of human eyes.

On the other hand, in a true-color image, even when three `uint8` integers are used to represent a color, the number of colors they can express is 255^3, which is much more than the color resolution of ordinary human eyes. This is the reason it is called a **true-color** image.

Table 6.5a Supported Image File Formats

Format	Description
BMP	Microsoft Windows Bitmap
GIF	Graphics Interchange Files
HDF	Hierarchical Data Format
JPEG	Joint Photographic Experts Group
PCX	Paintbrush
PNG	Portable Network Graphics
TIFF	Tagged Image File Format
XWD	X Window Dump

Details and More: Help>MATLAB>Graphics>Images> Working with Images in MATLAB Graphics.

Table 6.5b Image Functions

Functions	Description
`colormap map`	Set current colormap
`image(A)`	Display image (indexed or true-color)
`[A,map] = imread(filename)`	Read image (indexed or true-color) from file
`imwrite(A,filename)`	Write true-color image to file
`imwrite(A,map,filename)`	Write indexed image to file
`info = imfinfo(filename)`	Get image information
`B = ind2rgb(A,map)`	Convert indexed image to true-color image

Details and More: Help>MATLAB>Graphics>Images

6.6 Audios

6.6a Audio Data

Example06_06a.m: Audios Data

[1] The following commands demonstrate the play of an audio data and some operations of the audio data. Observe the outcome of each command. ↓

```
1   clear
2   load handel
3   sound(y, Fs)
4   plot(y)
5   audiowrite('handel.wav', y, Fs)
6   delete(gcf), clear
7   [y, Fs] = audioread('handel.wav');
8   plot(y)
9   sound(y, Fs)
```

About Example06_06a.m

[2] Line 2 loads a MATLAB tutorial data file `handel.mat`. This file consists of two variables `Fs` and `y`, where `Fs` is a scalar specifying sample rate and `y` is a vector containing audio signals (see [3]).

The audio signals are a series of samples that capture the amplitude of sound over time. Each sample is a value between -1 and 1. The sample rate is the number of samples taken per second, i.e., in hertz.

Line 3 plays the audio signals `y` with the sample rate `Fs`. If your computer has a speaker, you can hear Handel's *Messiah*. Line 4 plots the audio signals `y` as shown in [4].

Audio File Formats

Lines 5-9 demonstrate the saving and loading of audio signals in a standard audio file format, WAVE.

The function `audiowrite` in line 5 saves the audio signals in a file with the extension `.wav`, a WAVE format. Table 6.6a (page 269) lists audio file formats supported by the function `audiowrite`.

After the audio signals are saved, the **Figure** is deleted and the **Workspace** is cleared (line 6). The function `audioread` in line 7 reads the file and outputs the audio signals `y` and the sample rate `Fs`. Lines 8-9 plot (see [4]) and play the audio signals again. ↗

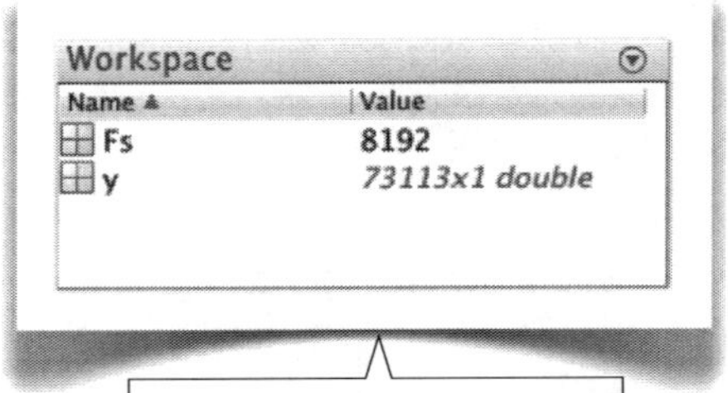

[3] The Workspace after the execution of line 2. ↓

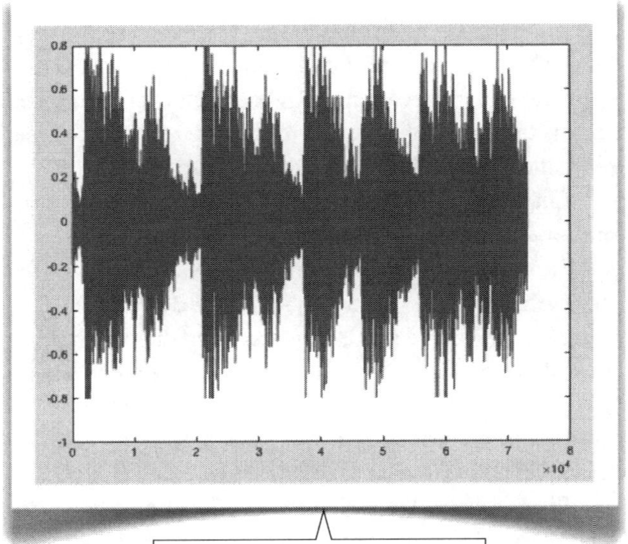

[4] Line 4 (or line 8) produces a plot like this. #

6.6b Example: Voice Recorder

Example06_06b.m: Voice Recorder

[1] Assuming your computer has an audio input device, this script records your voice, plays back the voice, saves it in a file, reads it from the file, plays back again, and plots the signals of the voice. ↙

```
 1  clear
 2  recObj = audiorecorder;
 3  menu('Start Recording', 'OK');
 4  record(recObj)
 5  menu('End recording', 'OK');
 6  stop(recObj)
 7  play(recObj);
 8  y = getaudiodata(recObj);
 9  Fs = recObj.SampleRate;
10  audiowrite('myvoice.wav', y, Fs)
11  clear
12  [y, Fs] = audioread('myvoice.wav');
13  sound(y, Fs)
14  plot(y)
```

About Example06_06b.m

[2] Line 2 creates an **audiorecorder** object `recObj`. Line 3 displays a menu shown in [3], waiting for your clicking at the **OK** button. After clicking, line 4 signals your audio input device (such as a microphone connected to your computer) to start the recording and saves the audio signals to `recObj`. Note that the function `record` in line 4 is to initiate the recording; as soon as the recording starts, the execution immediately goes to line 5, which displays a menu shown in [4], waiting for your clicking at the **OK** button to end the recording. Right after it is clicked, line 6 signals the audio input device to stop the recording. Line 7 plays the recorded audio stored in `recObj`.

Lines 8-14 demonstrate how to convert an **audiorecorder** object to an audio file format such as WAVE. Line 8 retrieves the audio signals `y` from `recObj`, using the function `getaudiodata`. Line 9 retrieves the sample rate `Fs` by accessing the property **SampleRate** of `recObj`. Line 10 saves the audio signals `y` and the sample rate `Fs` as a WAVE file using the function `audiowrite` (also see line 5 of Example06_06a.m, last page).

Line 11 clears the variables. The function `audioread` in line 12 reads the audio file and outputs the audio signals `y` and the sample rate `Fs`. Line 13 plays the audio signals and line 14 plots the audio signals [5]. ↗

[3] Line 3 displays a menu like this and waits. →

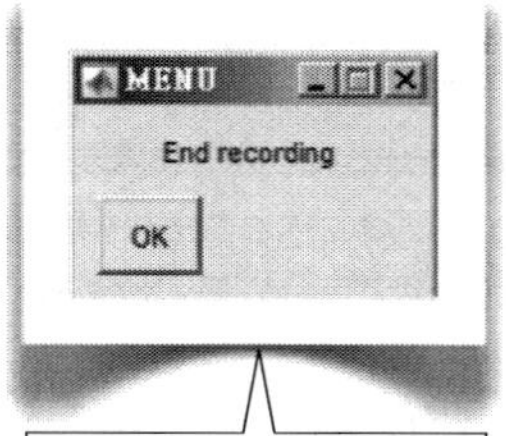

[4] Line 5 displays a menu like this and waits. ↓

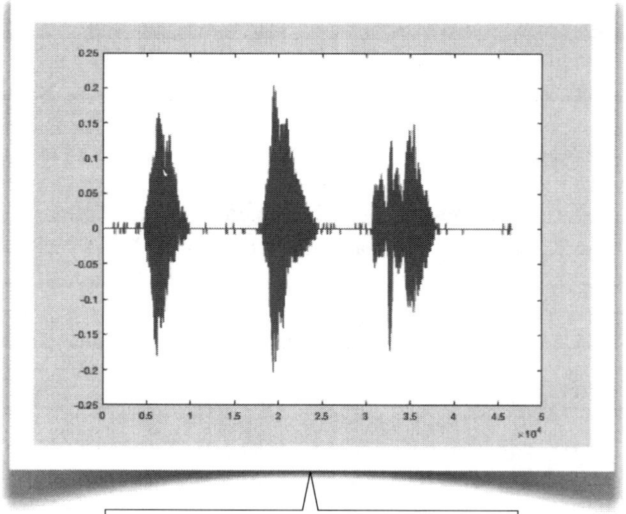

[5] Line 14 plots the audio signals. #

Table 6.6a Supported Audio File Formats

File Extension	Format
`.wav`	WAVE
`.ogg`	OGG
`.flac`	FLAC
`.mp4`	MPEG-4
`.m4a`	AAC
Details and More: >> `doc audiowrite`	

Table 6.6b Audio Functions

Functions	Description
`[y,Fs] = audioread(filename)`	Read audio file
`audiowrite(filename,y,Fs)`	Write audio file
`recObj = audiorecorder`	Create **audiorecorder** object
`y = getaudiodata(recObj)`	Retrieve recorded data
`record(recObj)`	Record to **audiorecorder** object
`play(recObj)`	Play **audiorecorder** object
`stop(recObj)`	Stop recording
`pause(recObj)`	Pause recording
`resume(recObj)`	Resume recording from paused position
`sound(y,Fs)`	Play sound
Details and More: *Help>MATLAB>Data Import and Analysis>Data Import and Export>Standard File Formats>Audio and Video*	

6.7 Videos

Example06_07.m: Videos

[1] The following commands demonstrate the reading of a video file in **mp4** format and the playing of the video using the function `movie` (Section 6.3). A snapshot of the video is shown in [3], next page. (*This example is adapted from the example in Help>MATLAB>Data Import and Analysis>Data Import and Export>Standard File Formats>Audio and Video>Reading and Writing Files>Read Video Files.*) ↓

```
1   clear
2   vidObj = VideoReader('xylophone.mp4');
3   height = vidObj.Height;
4   width  = vidObj.Width;
5   rate   = vidObj.FrameRate;
6   Frames.cdata = zeros(height, width, 3, 'uint8');
7   Frames.colormap = [];
8   k = 1;
9   while hasFrame(vidObj)
10      Frames(k).cdata = readFrame(vidObj);
11      k = k+1;
12  end
13  set(gcf, 'Position', [150, 150, width, height])
14  set(gca, 'Units', 'pixels')
15  set(gca, 'Position', [0, 0, width, height])
16  movie(Frames, 1, rate)
```

About Example06_07.m

[2] Line 2 creates a **VideoReader** object `vidObj`, ready to read the video data in the file `xylophone.mp4`. You may think of `vidObj` as a file pointer pointing to the beginning of the video file. Through `vidObj`, the sizes of the video frames can be retrieved (lines 3-4): `height` is the number of pixels in the vertical direction, and `width` is the number of pixels in the horizontal direction. Line 5 retrieves the frame rate. In this case, the frame size is 240-by-320 and the frame rate is 30 frames per second (see [4], next page).

The first input argument of the function `movie` (line 16) requires a **structure array** storing frames of the video (see >> *doc getframe*). In lines 6-7, a structure of two fields is created. The field `cdata` (line 6) is to store the image data as true-color system of `uint8`. For true-color systems, the field `colormap` (line 7) is not used, hence it is empty.

In lines 8-12, the video frames are read one frame at a time using function `readFrame` (line 10) and stored in **structure array** `Frames`. The function `hasFrame` in line 9 outputs `false` if end-of-file is reached, otherwise it outputs `true`. At the end of the `while`-loop, `Frames` stores all frames of the video. You may display a frame using the function `image`; for example

```
>> image(Frames(5).cdata)
```

displays the 5th frame (see [5], next page).

Line 13 sets the position and size of a new **Figure**. Lines 14-15 set the position and size of an **Axes** in the **Figure**. Line 16 plays the video frames once with the specified frame rate. ↵

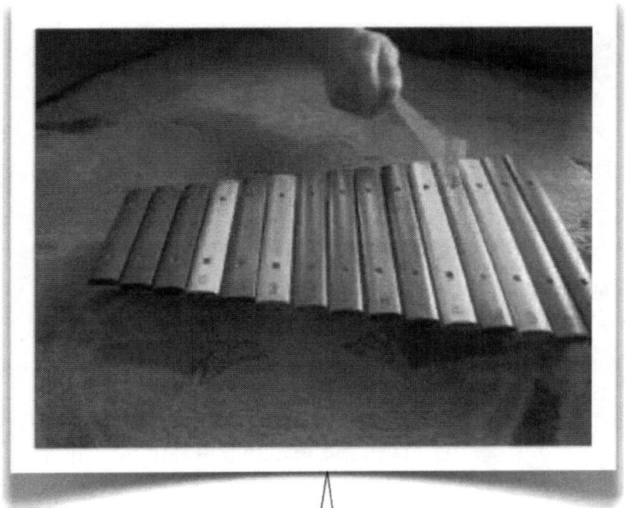

[3] A snapshot of the video. ↓

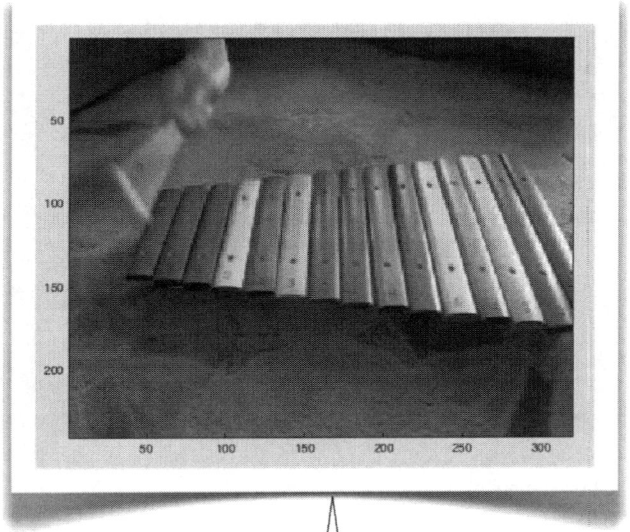

[5] The 5th frame displayed using the function `image`. #

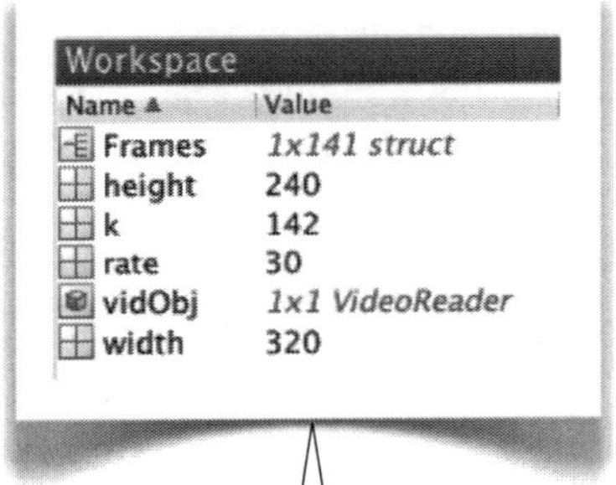

[4] The **Workspace**. ↗

Table 6.7 Video Functions

Functions	Description
`vidObj = VideoReader(filename)`	Create **VideoReader** object
`vidObj = VideoWriter(filename)`	Create **VideoWriter** objcct
`open(vidObj)`	Open file for writing video data
`close(vidObj)`	Close file after writing video data
`frameData = readFrame(vidObj)`	Read video frame from video file
`writeVideo(vidObj,Frames)`	Write frames to video file
`tf = hasFrame(vidObj)`	Determine if end-of-file reached
`movie(Frames,n,fps)`	Play movie frames

Details and More:
Help>MATLAB>Data Import and Analysis>Data Import and Export>Standard File Formats>Audio and Video

6.8 Example: Statically Determinate Trusses (Version 4.0)

Example06_08.m: Truss 4.0

```
1   clear
2   Nodes= struct; Members = struct;
3   disp(' 1. Input nodal coordinates')
4   disp(' 2. Input connecting nodes of members')
5   disp(' 3. Input three supports')
6   disp(' 4. Input loads')
7   disp(' 5. Print truss')
8   disp(' 6. Solve truss')
9   disp(' 7. Print results')
10  disp(' 8. Save data')
11  disp(' 9. Load data')
12  disp('10. Quit')
13  disp('11. Plot truss')
14  while 1
15      task = input('Enter the task number: ');
16      switch task
17          case 1
18              Nodes = inputNodes(Nodes);
19          case 2
20              Members = inputMembers(Members);
21          case 3
22              Nodes = inputSupports(Nodes);
23          case 4
24              Nodes = inputLoads(Nodes);
25          case 5
26              printTruss(Nodes, Members)
27          case 6
28              [Nodes, Members] = solveTruss(Nodes, Members);
29          case 7
30              printResults(Nodes, Members)
31          case 8
32             saveAll(Nodes, Members)
33          case 9
34              [Nodes, Members] = loadAll;
35          case 10
36              break
37          case 11
38              plotTruss(Nodes, Members)
39      end
40  end
41
    ...
209 end
```

[1] In this example, we modify the program Example04_04.m (pages 182-186) to include an option that plots a truss.

First, duplicate Example04_04.m and save as Example06_08.m. Modify the main program by adding 3 lines as shown in lines 13, and 37-38.

You don't need to make any changes for any user-defined functions in Example04_04.m. However, add a function `plotTruss` to the end of the file Example06_08.m (see [2], next page). ↵

[2] Add these lines to the end of Example06_08.m. These lines define the function `plotTruss`. ↵

```

function plotTruss(Nodes, Members)
if (size(fieldnames(Nodes),1)<6 || size(fieldnames(Members),1)<2)
    disp('Truss data not complete'); return
end
n = length(Nodes); m = length(Members);
minX = Nodes(1).x; maxX = Nodes(1).x;
minY = Nodes(1).y; maxY = Nodes(1).y;
for k = 2:n
    if (Nodes(k).x < minX) minX = Nodes(k).x; end
    if (Nodes(k).x > maxX) maxX = Nodes(k).x; end
    if (Nodes(k).y < minY) minY = Nodes(k).y; end
    if (Nodes(k).y > maxY) maxY = Nodes(k).y; end
end
rangeX = maxX-minX; rangeY = maxY-minY;
axis([minX-rangeX/5, maxX+rangeX/5, minY-rangeY/5, maxY+rangeY/5])
ha = gca; delete(ha.Children)
axis equal off
hold on
for k = 1:m
    n1 = Members(k).node1; n2 = Members(k).node2;
    x = [Nodes(n1).x, Nodes(n2).x];
    y = [Nodes(n1).y, Nodes(n2).y];
    plot(x,y,'k-o', 'MarkerFaceColor', 'k')
end
for k = 1:n
    if Nodes(k).supportx
        x = [Nodes(k).x, Nodes(k).x-rangeX/20, Nodes(k).x-rangeX/20, Nodes(k).x];
        y = [Nodes(k).y, Nodes(k).y+rangeX/40, Nodes(k).y-rangeX/40, Nodes(k).y];
        plot(x,y,'k-')
    end
    if Nodes(k).supporty
        x = [Nodes(k).x, Nodes(k).x-rangeX/40, Nodes(k).x+rangeX/40, Nodes(k).x];
        y = [Nodes(k).y, Nodes(k).y-rangeX/20, Nodes(k).y-rangeX/20, Nodes(k).y];
        plot(x,y,'k-')
    end
end
end
```

```
>> Example06_08
 1. Input nodal coordinates
 2. Input connecting nodes of members
 3. Input three supports
 4. Input loads
 5. Print truss
 6. Solve truss
 7. Print results
 8. Save data
 9. Load data
10. Quit
11. Plot truss
Enter the task number: 9
Enter file name (default Datafile): Datafile04_04a
Enter the task number: 11
Enter the task number: 9
Enter file name (default Datafile): Datafile04_04b
Enter the task number: 11
Enter the task number: 10
>>
```

[3] Copy the data files `Datafile04_04a.mat` and `Datafile04_04b.mat` (which were created in Section 4.4) to the **Current Folder** and run the program Example06_08.m like this. Input data are **boldfaced**. The graphics output for the 3-bar truss is shown in [4] and the graphics output for the 21-bar truss is shown in [5]. →

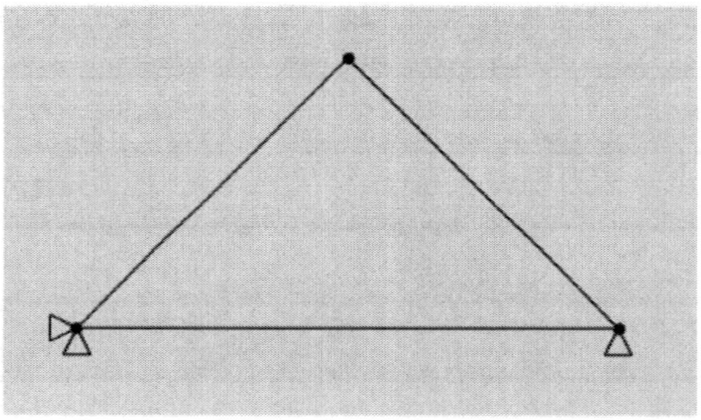

[4] This is the plotting of the 3-bar truss. ↙

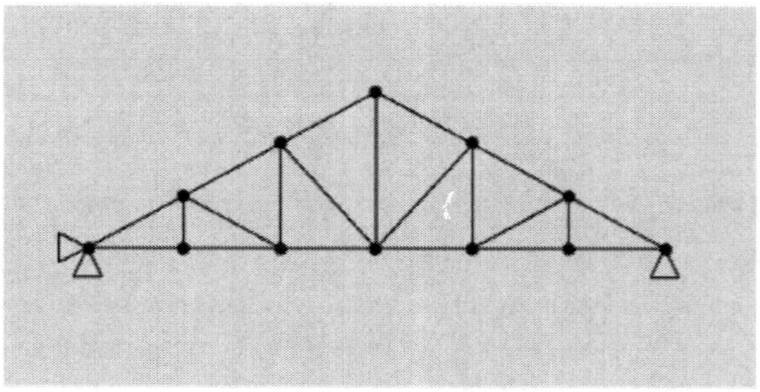

[5] This is the plotting of the 21-bar truss. #

6.9 Additional Exercise Problems

Problem06_01: Moving Sine Curve

Write a script that animates a sine curve moving from left to right; i.e., animate the function

$$y = \sin(x - \theta)$$

using θ as the animation variable.

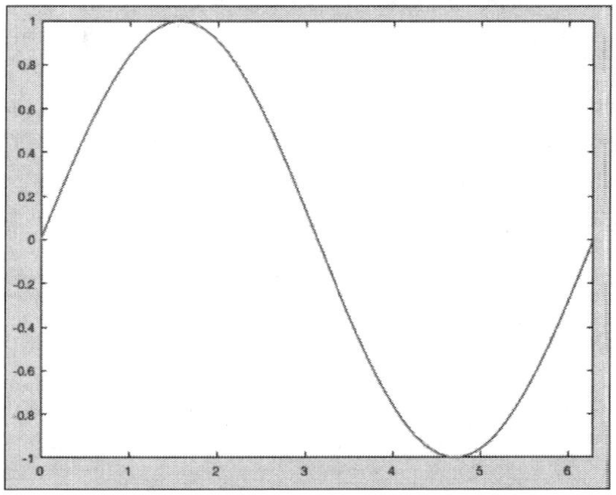

Problem06_02: Vibrating String

Write a script to simulate the vibrations of a string fixed at both ends. You may use a harmonic function, e.g., $\sin(x)$, to represent the vibrating mode.

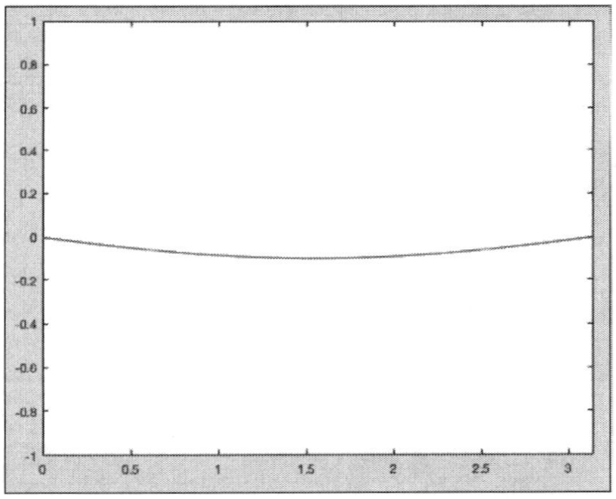

Problem06_03: Vibrating Circular Membrane

Write a script to simulate the vibrations of a membrane supported along a circle as shown.

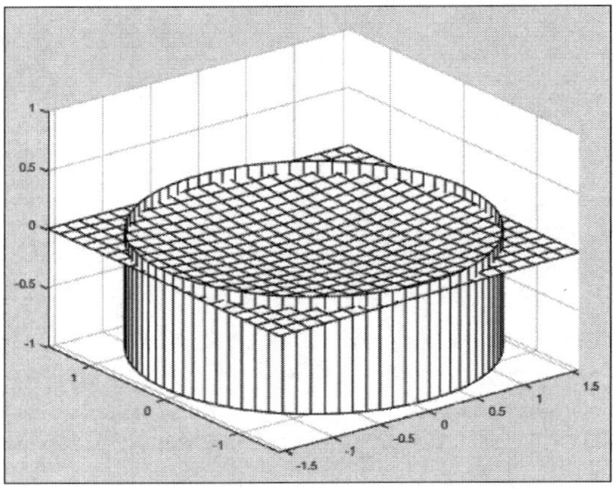

Problem06_04: Stream Particles

In the **Command Window**, type

```
>> doc streamparticles
```

and find an example script in the documentation. Run the script. It animates a flow without displaying streamlines. The script uses many functions that are not mentioned in the book. Study each statement, looking up the on-line documentation whenever necessary.

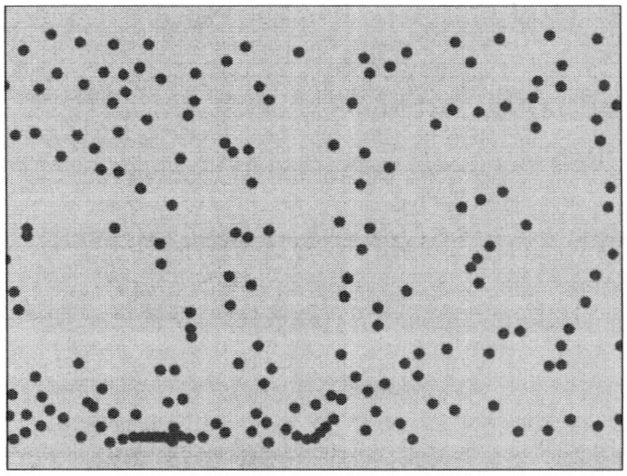

Chapter 7

Data Import and Export

A program can be viewed as a data processing system. Data can be exported to or imported from a device (e.g., keyboard) or a disk file. We've seen many examples in which data are input from the keyboard and output to the computer screen. We've also seen many examples in which data are read from and written to files. In this chapter, we'll discuss details and more about data import and export.

7.1 Screen Text I/O

7.1a Screen Text I/O

Example07_01a.m: `input` and `disp`

[1] The function `input` reads data from your computer screen and the function `disp` writes data to the computer screen. Run this script and enter data as shown in [2]. ↓

```
1   clear
2   while 1
3       a = input('Enter anything: ');
4       if strcmp(a, 'stop') break, end
5       disp(class(a))
6       disp(a)
7   end
```

```
8    >> Example07_01a
9    Enter anything: 56
10   double
11       56
12   Enter anything: 3+11
13   double
14       14
15   Enter anything: 5*sin(pi/5)^2
16   double
17       1.7275
18   Enter anything: int16(56)
19   int16
20      56
21   Enter anything: 'b'
22   char
23   b
24   Enter anything: 'bcdef'
25   char
26   bcdef
27   Enter anything: b
28   Error using input
29   Undefined function or variable 'b'.
30   Error in Example07_01a (line 3)
31       a = input('Enter anything: ');
32   Enter anything: bcdef
33   Error using input
34   Undefined function or variable 'bcdef'.
35   Error in Example07_01a (line 3)
36       a = input('Enter anything: ');
37   Enter anything: 'stop'
38   >>
```

[2] This is a test-run of Example07_01a.m. ↗

Function `input`

[3] A syntax for the function `input` is

`var = input(prompt)`

It displays the string *`prompt`*, waits for the user to input a data, reads the data, and stores it in *`var`*. The user can enter expressions (lines 12, 15). All numerical data are treated as `double`, unless converted into other types (line 18). To input a string, you need to include single quotes (lines 21, 24). A string without single quotes is an error (lines 27, 32).

Another syntax for the function `input` is

`var = input(prompt, 's')`

It reads the entire data as a string; you don't need to include single quotes, as demonstrated in line 6 of Example02_10a.m, page 102.

To stop the program, enter `'stop'` (line 37). Or, although not recommendable, you always can break a program by pressing Control-C. ↓

Function `disp`

[4] A syntax for the function `disp` is

`disp(var)`

It displays the value of *`var`*, which can be any type (class) of data. Actually, each class of data has its definition of `disp`. We've demonstrated this in Section 4.9 (also see 4.9[10], page 203).

These are some more examples:

```
39   >> a = [3, 6, 7, 2];
40   >> disp(a)
41        3     6     7     2
42   >> c = 6; d = 5;
43   >> disp(c>d)
44        1
```

In line 43, the result of `c>d` is of class `logical`, hence it displays a logical value 1 (line 44). #

7.1b Formatted Text Output

Formatted Text Output: Functions `fprintf` and `sprintf`

[1] The syntax for the function `fprintf`, which formats data and displays the result on the screen, is

```
fprintf(formatSpec, a1, a2, ...)
```

where *a1*, *a2*, ... are data to be formatted according to the format specification, *formatSpec*.

The syntax for the function `sprintf` (also see 5.6b[2], page 228), which formats data and stores the result in a string variable *str*, is

```
str = sprintf(formatSpec, a1, a2, ...)
```

Format Specifications

A format specification starts with a percent sign (%) and ends with a conversion character; for example, `%f`. The % and the conversion character are required. Optionally, you can specify identifier, flags, field width, precision, and subtype between % and the conversion character. (see Table 7.1a, next page.) ↓

```
>> clear
>> a = pi*10000; b = -314;
>> fprintf('%f %f\n', a, b)
31415.926536 -314.000000
>> fprintf('%.4f %.4f\n', a, b)
31415.9265 -314.0000
>> fprintf('%12f %12f\n', a, b)
31415.926536  -314.000000
>> fprintf('%12.4f %12.4f\n', a, b)
  31415.9265    -314.0000
>> fprintf('%8.4f %8.4f\n', a, b)
31415.9265 -314.0000
>> fprintf('%-12.4f %-12.4f\n', a, b)
31415.9265   -314.0000
>> fprintf('%+12.4f %+12.4f\n', a, b)
 +31415.9265    -314.0000
>> fprintf('%e %e\n', a, b)
3.141593e+04 -3.140000e+02
>> fprintf('%.4e %.4e\n', a, b)
3.1416e+04 -3.1400e+02
>> fprintf('%12.4e %12.4e\n', a, b)
  3.1416e+04  -3.1400e+02
>> fprintf('%g %g\n', a, b)
31415.9 -314
>> fprintf('%.4g %.4g\n', a, b)
3.142e+04 -314
>> fprintf('%12.4g %12.4g\n', a, b)
   3.142e+04         -314
>> fprintf('%d %d\n', b, b)
-314 -314
>> fprintf('%5d %5d\n', b, b)
 -314  -314
>> fprintf('%c %c\n', 'A', 'B')
A B
>> fprintf('%c %c\n', 65, 66)
A B
>> fprintf('%5c %5c\n', 'A', 'B')
    A     B
>> fprintf('%s %s\n','A','string')
A string
>> fprintf('%8s %15s\n','A','string')
       A          string
>> fprintf('%3s %3s\n','A','string')
  A string
```

Example07_01b.m: `fprintf`

[2] The function `fprintf` writes data according to specified format. These are some examples. ↵

About Example07_01b.m

[3] Line 2 creates two numbers. Lines 3-16 demonstrate the fixed-point notation, `%f`. Without any options (line 3), a format specification `%f` displays data with 6 digits after the decimal point (line 4). You may specify the number of digits after the decimal point (line 5). If you specify only the total width (line 7), 6 digits after the decimal point are displayed (line 8). You may specify both the total width and the number of digits after the decimal point (line 9). If the total width is not enough (line 11), a minimum required width is automatically used (line 12). A minus sign signifies left-justification (lines 13-14). A plus sign signifies the display of sign character (+ or –, lines 15-16).

Lines 17-22 demonstrate the exponential notation, `%e`. Without any options (line 17), the format specification `%e` displays data with 6 digits after the decimal point (line 18). You may specify the number of digits after the decimal point (lines 19-20), or both the total width and the number of digits after the decimal point (lines 21-22). Remember, if the total width is not enough, a minimum required width is automatically used.

Lines 23-28 demonstrate the general format, `%g`, which uses either `%f` or `%e`, depending on which one is more compact. Note that the number after a decimal point (e.g., `%.4g` in line 25) specifies the number of significant digits (instead of number of digits after the decimal point as in `%f` or `%e` formats).

Lines 29-32 demonstrate the display of signed integers, using `%d`. Use `%u` to display unsigned integers.

Lines 33-38 demonstrate the display of characters.

Lines 39-44 demonstrate the display of strings. #

Table 7.1a Examples of Format Specifications

Format	Description
`%8.4f`	Fixed-point notation
`%8.4e`	Exponential notation
`%8.4g`	The more compact of %f or %e
`%8d`	Signed integer
`%8u`	Unsigned integer
`%8c`	Character
`%8s`	String

Details and More: Help>MATLAB>Data Import and Analysis>Data Import and Export>Lower-Level File I/O>fprintf>Input Arguments>formatSpec

Table 7.1b Screen Text I/O

Functions	Description
`x = input(prompt, 's')`	Request user input
`disp(x)`	Display value of variable
`fprintf(format,a,b,...)`	Write text data to screen or file
`s = sprintf(format,a,b,...)`	Format text data into string

7.2 Low-Level Text File I/O

Example07_02.m: Text-File Explorer

[1] This program, a "text-file explorer," is designed to demonstrate many text-file I/O functions (see Table 7.2, page 285). We'll use the file Example07_01a.m (page 278, which is a text file of 124 characters; see a copy in [3], next page) as the target to test this program. Before looking into each statement, test run this program as shown in [4], page 283.

```
clear
fileName = input('Enter the file name: ', 's');
fileID = fopen(fileName);
disp('0. stop')
disp('1. Read the file once for all')
disp('2. Read the file one line at a time')
disp('3. Read a line')
disp('4. Read a character')
disp('5. Rewind to the beginning')
disp('6. Move forward a character')
disp('7. Move backward a character')
while 1
    task = input('Enter task number: ');
    switch task
        case 0
            fclose(fileID);
            break
        case 1
            text = fileread(fileName);
            disp(text)
            characters = length(text);
            disp([num2str(characters), ' characters read'])
        case 2
            frewind(fileID), lines = 0; characters = 0;
            while ~feof(fileID)
                text = fgetl(fileID);
                disp(text)
                lines = lines+1;
                characters = characters + length(text);
            end
            disp([num2str(lines), ' lines read'])
            disp([num2str(characters), ' characters read'])
        case 3
            if feof(fileID)
                disp('End of file!')
            else
                text = fgetl(fileID);
                disp(text);
            end
```

(Continued at [2], next page) ↵

[2] Example07_02.m (Continued). ↓

```
        case 4
            if feof(fileID)
                disp('End of file!')
            else
                text = fscanf(fileID, '%c', 1);
                disp(text);
            end
        case 5
            frewind(fileID)
        case 6
            if feof(fileID)
                disp('End of file!')
            else
                fseek(fileID, 1, 'cof');
            end
        case 7
            if ftell(fileID) == 0
                disp('Beginning of file!')
            else
                fseek(fileID, -1, 'cof');
            end
    end
    position = ftell(fileID);
    disp(['File pointer at ', num2str(position)])
end
```

```
clear
while 1
    a = input('Enter anything: ');
    if strcmp(a, 'stop') break, end
    disp(class(a))
    disp(a)
end
```

[3] The text file Example07_01a.m (page 278) is used as the target to test the program Example07_02.m. ↵

```
65  >> Example07_02
66  Enter the file name: Example07_01a.m
67  0. stop
68  1. Read the file once for all
69  2. Read the file one line at a time
70  3. Read a line
71  4. Read a character
72  5. Rewind to the beginning
73  6. Move forward a character
74  7. Move backward a character
75  Enter task number: 1
76  clear
77  while 1
78      a = input('Enter anything: ');
79      if strcmp(a, 'stop') break, end
80      disp(class(a))
81      disp(a)
82  end
83  119 characters read
84  File pointer at 0
85  Enter task number: 2
86  clear
87  while 1
88      a = input('Enter anything: ');
89      if strcmp(a, 'stop') break, end
90      disp(class(a))
91      disp(a)
92  end
93  7 lines read
94  113 characters read
95  File pointer at 119
96  Enter task number: 5
97  File pointer at 0
98  Enter task number: 3
99  clear
100 File pointer at 6
101 Enter task number: 3
102 while 1
103 File pointer at 14
104 Enter task number: 5
105 File pointer at 0
106 Enter task number: 4
107 c
108 File pointer at 1
109 Enter task number: 6
110 File pointer at 2
111 Enter task number: 4
112 e
113 File pointer at 3
114 Enter task number: 4
115 a
116 File pointer at 4
117 Enter task number: 7
118 File pointer at 3
119 Enter task number: 4
120 a
121 File pointer at 4
122 Enter task number: 3
123 r
124 File pointer at 6
125 Enter task number: 0
126 >>
```

A Test-Run of Example07_02.m

[4] Start to run the program (line 65) and enter the file name Example07_01a.m (line 66), which is used as the target to be explored. It displays a menu of 7 tasks to be chosen (lines 67-74).

Task 1 (line 75) reads the entire target file (Example07_01a.m), displays the contents (lines 76-82), and reports number of characters read (line 83) and the current position of the file pointer (line 84). There are 119 characters (line 83) in the file, including 6 newline characters (in this file, each line ends with a newline character except the last line; see 1.9[9], page 35). The file pointer doesn't move; it remains at the beginning (line 84), right before the first character.

Task 2 (line 85) does a similar job (lines 86-95). The difference is that task 1 reads the entire file using the function `fileread` (line 19), while task 2 reads the file one line at a time using the function `fgetl` (line 26). Remember that each text line ends with a newline character. It reports that 7 lines (line 93) and 113 characters (line 94; not including the 6 newline characters) are read. The file pointer points to the end of the file (line 95), i.e., the last character (the 119th character).

Task 5 (line 96) rewinds the pointer to the beginning, i.e., right before the first character (line 97), ready to read the first character. (Continued at [5], next page.) ↵

A Test-Run of Example07_02.m (Continued)

[5] Task 3 (line 98) reads a line and displays the line (line 99). After reading, the file pointer moves forward and points to the 6th character (line 100), which is the newline character at the end of the first line. Line 101 reads a line again (line 102) and the file pointer is at the 14th character (line 103), which is the newline character at the end of the second line.

Line 104 rewinds the pointer to the beginning again (line 105). Task 4 (line 106) reads a single character and displays the character (line 107) and the position of the file pointer (line 108).

Task 6 (line 109) moves the file pointer forward one character (line 110).

In lines 111-116, two characters are read sequentially.

Task 7 (line 117) moves the file pointer backward one character (line 118). Line 119 reads a character again (lines 120-121). Now the file pointer is at the 4th character (`a`). Line 122 reads a line; it reads the rest of the line (line 123) and the file pointer is right after the newline character of the first line (line 124).

Task 0 stops the program. ↓

About Example07_02.m

[6] In the beginning of the program, the target file name is requested (line 2) and the file is opened (line 3); the program then displays a menu of 8 tasks to be chosen (lines 4-11). The main body of the program is a `while`-loop (lines 12-64). According to the user's choice of task (line 13), it switches to a `case`-block (line 14).

Task 0 (lines 15-17) closes the file and breaks the `while`-loop, i.e., jumping out of the `while`-loop; since there are no statements after the `while`-loop, it essentially quits the program.

Task 1 (lines 18-22) reads the entire file using the function `fileread` (line 19), which reads the entire file without moving the file pointer and outputs the text of the entire file. The text is then displayed (line 20) and the number of characters, including newline characters, are reported (lines 21-22). The position of the file pointer is reported in lines 62-63, which are executed after each `case`-block.

Task 2 (lines 23-32) does a similar job as task 1, except that it uses the function `fgetl` (line 26) to read the text file one line at a time. First, it rewinds the file pointer to the beginning (line 24), ready to read. In each pass of the `while`-loop in lines 25-30, it reads a line using the function `fgetl` (line 26). The line is displayed (line 27) and the number of lines and number of characters are counted (lines 28-29). The `while`-loop continues as long as the end of the file is not encountered (line 25), i.e., unless the file pointer is at the last character. By the completion of the `while`-loop, the number of lines and number of characters are reported (lines 31-32).

Task 3 (lines 33-39) reads a single line. If the file pointer is at the end of the file (line 34), it reports a message (line 35) and does nothing more. Otherwise (line 36) it reads a line using the function `fgetl` (line 37) and displays the line (line 38).

Task 4 (lines 40-46) reads a single character. If the file pointer is at the end of the file (line 41), it reports a message (line 42) and does nothing more. Otherwise (line 43) it reads a character using the function `fscanf` (line 44) and displays the character (line 45). Note that, when using the function `fscanf` (line 44), the length of the data must be specified as the 3rd input argument, otherwise it would read the entire file.

Task 5 (lines 47-48) simply rewinds the file pointer to the beginning of the file (line 48), i.e., before the first character.

Task 6 (lines 49-54) moves the file pointer forward one byte. If the file pointer is at the end of the file (line 50), it reports a message (line 51) and does nothing more. Otherwise (line 52) it moves the file pointer forward a character using the function `fseek` (line 53), in which the second input argument specifies that the number of character is +1, and the third argument specifies that the reference position is the current position of the file (`'cof'`). (Continued at [7], next page.) ↵

About Example07_02.m (Continued)

[7] Task 7 (lines 55-60) moves the file pointer backward one character. If the file pointer is at the beginning (line 56), it reports a message (line 57) and does nothing more. Otherwise (line 58) it moves the file pointer backward a character using the function `fseek` (line 59), in which the second input argument specifies that the number of bytes is -1 (i.e., one character backward), and the third argument specifies that the reference position is the current position of the file (`'cof'`).

At the end of the `while`-loop (lines 62-63), the current position of the file pointer is retrieved using the function `ftell` (line 62), and the position is displayed (line 63). #

Table 7.2 Low-Level Text File I/O

Functions	Description
`fileID = fopen(filename,permission)`	Open file
`fclose(fileID)`	Close one or all open files
`tf = feof(fileID)`	Test for end-of-file
`[message,errnum] = ferror(fileID)`	Information about file I/O errors
`s = fgetl(fileID)`	Read line from file, removing newline character
`s = fgets(fileID)`	Read line from file, keeping newline character
`s = fileread(filename)`	Read contents of file into string
`fprintf(fileID,format,a,b,...)`	Write data to text file
`frewind(fileID)`	Move file position indicator to beginning of open file
`a = fscanf(fileID,format)`	Read formatted data from text file
`fseek(fileID,offset,origin)`	Move to specified position in file
`position = ftell(fileID)`	Position in open file
`type filename`	Display contents of file

Details and More: Help>MATLAB>Data Import and Analysis>Data Import and Export>Low-Level File I/O

7.3 Low-Level Binary File I/O

What are Binary Files?

[1] Data may be stored in a file in two forms: **text form** or **binary form**. The text form is also called a **formatted form**, and the binary form is called an **unformatted form**. We've introduced text file in Sections 7.1 and 7.2. When stored in a text file, data are represented in ASCII codes; the file stores the ASCII codes. For example `'3.14159265'` is represented in ten ASCII codes. On the other hand, when stored in a binary file, data are stored in their machine codes. For example, in 2.3a[1] (page 74), we showed that a number 28 of `double` type is internally stored as a 64-bit pattern

`0100000000111100000000000000000000000000000000000000000000000000`

The rightmost bit is the 0th bit, and the leftmost bit is the 63rd bit. To ease the visual difficulty, we tabulate the bit pattern as shown below (remember that the 0th bit is the rightmost bit). The last column shows each byte's value when interpreted as 8-bit unsigned integer (`uint8`).

Byte	Bits	Bit Pattern 7654 3210	uint8 Value
1	0-7	0000 0000	0
2	8-15	0000 0000	0
3	16-23	0000 0000	0
4	24-31	0000 0000	0
5	32-39	0000 0000	0
6	40-47	0000 0000	0
7	48-55	0011 1100	60
8	56-63	0100 0000	64

Why Binary Files?

An advantage of using text files is that they can be read by human eyes. On the other hand, an advantage of using binary files over text files is that binary files are usually more efficient: they usually require less disk space and less computer processing time. ↓

Example07_03.m: Bit Pattern

[2] This script confirms the concepts presented in [1]. ↵

```
clear
a = 28;
fileID = fopen('tmp.dat','w+');
fwrite(fileID, a, 'double');
frewind(fileID)
b = fread(fileID, 8, 'uint8');
disp(b')
fclose(fileID);
delete('tmp.dat')
```

About Example07_03.m

[3] Line 3 opens a file for writing and reading. Line 4 writes the number 28, a 64-bit `double` number, to the file using the function `fwrite`, which stores all 64 bits in the file. Line 5 rewinds the file pointer (to the beginning). Line 6 reads the contents of the file as eight `uint8` numbers. The result `b` is a column vector of eight `uint8` numbers. Line 7 displays the transpose of the column vector:

```
0     0     0     0     0     0    60    64
```

Line 8 closes the file and line 9 deletes the file.

Example07_03.m demonstrates writing/reading data in binary form using low-level functions such as `fwrite` and `fread`. In the next section, we'll introduce a more convenient way of writing/reading binary files, **MAT-files**. #

Table 7.3 Low-Level Binary File I/O

Functions	Description
`fileID = fopen(filename,permission)`	Open file
`fclose(fileID)`	Close one or all open files
`a = fread(fileID,size)`	Read data from binary file
`fwrite(fileID,a)`	Write data to binary file
`tf = feof(fileID)`	Test for end-of-file
`[message,errnum] = ferror(fileID)`	Information about file I/O errors
`frewind(fileID)`	Move file position indicator to beginning of open file
`fseek(fileID,offset,origin)`	Move to specified position in file
`position = ftell(fileID)`	Position in open file

Details and More: Help>MATLAB>Data Import and Analysis>Data Import and Export>Low-Level File I/O

7.4 MAT-Files

[1] MATLAB provides functions that save variables to a binary file (`save`) and read variables from a binary file (`load`). These files are called **MAT-files** because the extension of the filename is `.mat`. A MAT-file not only stores values of variables but also their names, dimensions, etc.

We've shown many times the use of `save` and `load` (e.g., Example01_12.m, page 44; Example03_13.m, page 151; Example 03_15.m, page 161), so we assume that you're quite familiar with the functions `save` and `load` and won't reiterate the use of these two functions. We now introduce a feature of MAT-Files, namely, out-of-core variables.

Consider a situation that you're dealing with a very large-size data. For example, in engineering applications, it is not uncommon that you are dealing with a matrix of size 100,000-by-100,000! It takes 80 GB of disk space to store this matrix of `double` type. The problem is that you usually don't have so much in-core memory space available. The function `matfile` allows you to access variables in MAT-files, without the need to load the variables into the in-core memory. ↓

Example07_04.m: Out-of-Core Matrices

[2] This script demonstrates the ideas in [1]. ↓

```
clear
M = matfile('tmp');
n = 10;
for i = 1:n
    for j = 1:n
        M.A(i,j) = i+(j-1)*n;
    end
end
clear
load('tmp')
delete('tmp.mat')
disp(A)
```

```
     1    11    21    31    41    51    61    71    81    91
     2    12    22    32    42    52    62    72    82    92
     3    13    23    33    43    53    63    73    83    93
     4    14    24    34    44    54    64    74    84    94
     5    15    25    35    45    55    65    75    85    95
     6    16    26    36    46    56    66    76    86    96
     7    17    27    37    47    57    67    77    87    97
     8    18    28    38    48    58    68    78    88    98
     9    19    29    39    49    59    69    79    89    99
    10    20    30    40    50    60    70    80    90   100
```

[3] This is the screen output. ↵

About Example07_04.m

[4] Line 2 creates a MAT-file object `M`, which connects to a MAT-file `tmp.mat`. Now you may treat `M` as an ordinary **Workspace** variable; any changes of `M` will cause corresponding changes in the MAT-file.

For demonstration purposes, we consider a 10-by-10 matrix `A`; you may extend the ideas to a huge-size matrix. Lines 4-8 assign values to matrix `A`. Here, we use arbitrary values to demonstrate the ideas. In a real application, the calculated values are assigned to matrix `A`.

At the end of the nested `for`-loop (lines 4-8), the MAT-file contains a matrix `A` with the values. Lines 9-12 confirm this. Line 9 clears the **Workspace**. Line 10 loads the variable (i.e., `A`) in the MAT-file. Line 11 deletes the MAT-file. Line 12 displays the variable `A`. #

Table 7.4 MAT-Files

Functions	Description
`load(filename)`	Load variables from file into Workspace
`save(filename,v1,v2,...)`	Save variables to file
`save filename`	Save all variables to file
`M = matfile(filename)`	Access variables in MAT-files, without loading into memory

Details and More:
Help>MATLAB>Data Import and Analysis>Data Import and Export>Workspace Variables and MAT-Files

7.5 ASCII-Delimited Files

Example07_05.m

[1] An ASCII-delimited file is a text file containing data separated by delimiters such as space, comma, tab, semicolon, newline, etc. This script demonstrates the reading and writing of ASCII-delimited files. ↓

```
 1  clear
 2  type count.dat
 3  A = dlmread('count.dat');
 4  dlmwrite('tmp.dat', A)
 5  type tmp.dat
 6  clear
 7  B = csvread('tmp.dat');
 8  delete tmp.dat
 9  csvwrite('tmp1.dat', B)
10  type tmp1.dat
11  delete tmp1.dat
```

```
>> type count.dat

    11    11     9
     7    13    11
    14    17    20
    11    13     9
    43    51    69
    38    46    76
    61   132   186
    75   135   180
    38    88   115
    28    36    55
    12    12    14
    18    27    30
    18    19    29
    17    15    18
    19    36    48
    32    47    10
    42    65    92
    57    66   151
    44    55    90
   114   145   257
    35    58    68
    11    12    15
    13     9    15
    10     9     7
```

[2] The output of line 2. →

```
>> type tmp.dat

11,11,9
7,13,11
14,17,20
11,13,9
43,51,69
38,46,76
61,132,186
75,135,180
38,88,115
28,36,55
12,12,14
18,27,30
18,19,29
17,15,18
19,36,48
32,47,10
42,65,92
57,66,151
44,55,90
114,145,257
35,58,68
11,12,15
13,9,15
10,9,7
```

[3] The output of line 5 (and 10). ↵

About Example07_05.m

[4] In this example, we use a tutorial sample file `count.dat` to demonstrate the manipulation of an ASCII-delimited file. Remember, to see the location of the file, type

```
>> which count.dat
```

Line 2 lists the contents of the file `count.dat` (see [2], last page), using the function `type`. The file contains data separated by spaces and newline characters.

Line 3 reads the contents of the file into an array `A`, using the function `dlmread`. The **Workspace** shows that `A` is a 24-by-3 matrix of `double`. An ASCII-delimited file is a text file containing data separated by delimiters. By default, the following characters are treated as delimiters: space, comma (`,`), tab (`\t`), semicolon (`;`), and newline (`\n`). Multiple spaces are treated as a single space. When read and stored in a matrix, the **space**, **comma**, and **tab** are treated as the delimiters between values in a row, while the **semicolon** and **newline** are treated as the delimiters between rows. According to these rules, the data in `count.dat` are read as a 24-by-3 matrix of `double`,

Line 4 writes the matrix `A` to an ASCII-delimited file `tmp.dat`, using the function `dlmwrite`. By default, **commas** are used as the delimiters between values in a row, and **newlines** are used as the delimiters between rows. Line 5 lists the contents of the file (see [3]) to confirm this.

CSV Files

The file `tmp.dat` (see [3]) is also called a CSV (comma-separated value) file. A CSV file is a special type of ASCII-delimited file in which **commas** are used as the delimiters between values in a row, and **newlines** are used as the delimiters between rows.

Line 6 clears the **Workspace**. Line 7 reads the contents of the file `tmp.dat` into an array `B`, using the function `csvread`. The **Workspace** shows that `B` is a 24-by-3 matrix of `double`. Line 8 deletes the file. Line 9 writes the contents of matrix `B` to another CSV file `tmp1.dat`, using the function `csvwrite`. Line 10 displays the contents of the file (see [3]). Line 11 deletes the file. #

Table 7.5 ASCII-Delimited Files

Functions	Description
`M = dlmread(filename)`	Read ASCII-delimited file into matrix
`dlmwrite(filename,M)`	Write matrix to ASCII-delimited file
`M = csvread(filename)`	Read comma-separated value file (CSV)
`csvwrite(filename,M)`	Write comma-separated value file (CSV)

Details and More:
Help>MATLAB>Data Import and Analysis>Data Import and Export>Standard File Formats>Text Files

7.6 Excel Spreadsheet Files

Example07_06.m: Excel Files

[1] MATLAB provides functions that write to (`xlswrite`) and read from (`xlsread`) **Microsoft Excel** spreadsheet files (`.xls` or `.xlsx` files). To use these functions, you need to have Microsoft Excel installed in your computer. This script demonstrates the use of these functions. ↓

```
1  clear
2  A = reshape(1:15, 5, 3);
3  xlswrite('tmp', A, 'Sheet1', 'A2')
4  title = {'First', 'Second', 'Third'};
5  xlswrite('tmp', title, 'Sheet1', 'A1:C1')
6  clear
7  [num, txt] = xlsread('tmp', 'Sheet1')
8  delete('tmp.xls')
```

```
num =
     1     6    11
     2     7    12
     3     8    13
     4     9    14
     5    10    15
txt =
  1×3 cell array
    {'First'}    {'Second'}    {'Third'}
```

[3] The output of line 7. ↓

About Example07_06.m

[2] Line 2 creates a 5-by-3 matrix `A`. Line 3 creates an Excel file `tmp.xls` and writes the matrix `A` to the worksheet `Sheet1`, in a rectangular region, the upper-left corner located at A2 cell. Line 4 creates a cell array containing three strings of characters. Line 5 writes the three strings to the worksheet `Sheet1` (of the file `tmp.xls`) in A1:C1. Lines 2-5 demonstrate that both matrices and cell arrays can be written. Note that, if a worksheet name is not specified, data will be written to the first worksheet. However, in that case, a full range must be specified instead of just specifying the upper-left corner. Thus, line 3 can be re-written as follows:

```
xlswrite('tmp', A, 'A2:C6')
```

The reason for a full range is that, without a colon (`:`), MATLAB has no way to distinguish between a worksheet name and a cell name.

Line 6 clears the **Workspace**. Line 7 reads the entire worksheet, using the function `xlsread`; it returns a matrix of 5-by-3 `double` and a cell array of three strings (see [3-4]). Line 8 deletes the file. ↗

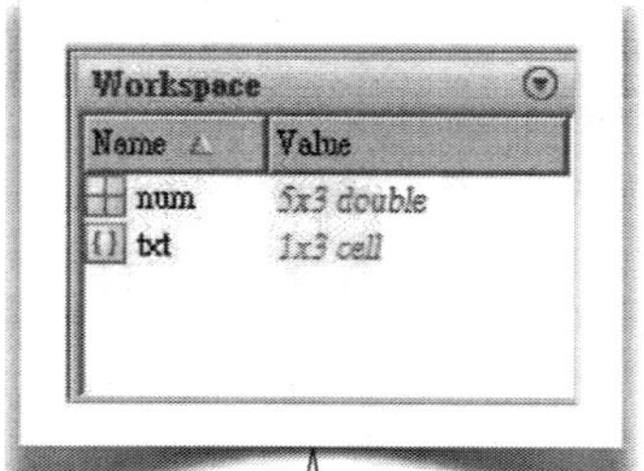

[4] The **Workspace**. #

Table 7.6 Excel Spreadsheet Files	
Functions	Description
`[num,txt] = xlsread(filename,sheet,range)`	Read Microsoft Excel spreadsheet file
`xlswrite(filename,M,sheet,range)`	Write Microsoft Excel spreadsheet file

Details and More:
Help>MATLAB>Data Import and Analysis>Data Import and Export>Standard File Formats>Spreadsheets

7.7 Additional Exercise Problems

Problem07_01: Read Data from an Excel File

This exercise is to plot a bar graph the same as that in 5.8[4], page 234. Instead of being given the data as in lines 2-3 and 9-12 of Example05_08.m, page 233, you are asked to read data from an Excel file.

Go to the webpage

http://data.worldbank.org/data-catalog/cckp_historical_data

and download a file shown in the figure below and save it in your working folder. The temperature data is in the worksheet **Country_temperatureCRU**. The data for USA, CAN, and GBR are stored in rows 169, 27, and 58, respectively.

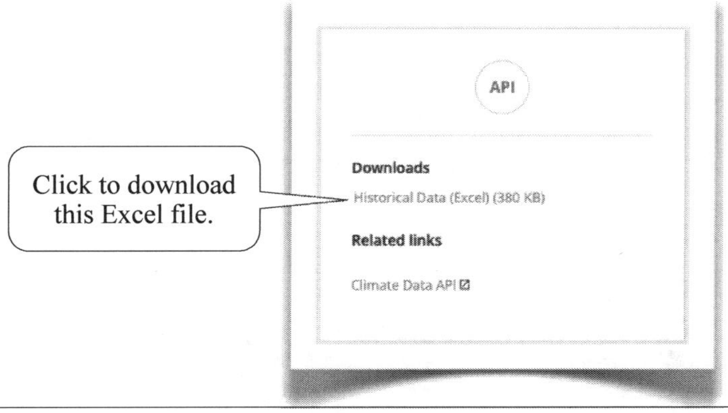

Problem07_02: Read a Webpage

The webpage

http://heritage.stsci.edu/2007/14/images/p0714aa.jpg

contains an image of Jupiter. The function `webread` can read the contents of a webpage, given the **url** of the webpage. Write a script to read and display the picture.

Problem07_03: Read a Webpage

Function `webread` can read data in a webpage; for example, the webpage

http://climatedataapi.worldbank.org/climateweb/rest/v1/country/cru/tas/year/USA

contains the average temperatures in USA from the years 1901 to 2012. Write a script to read the data and generate a temperature-versus-year plot.

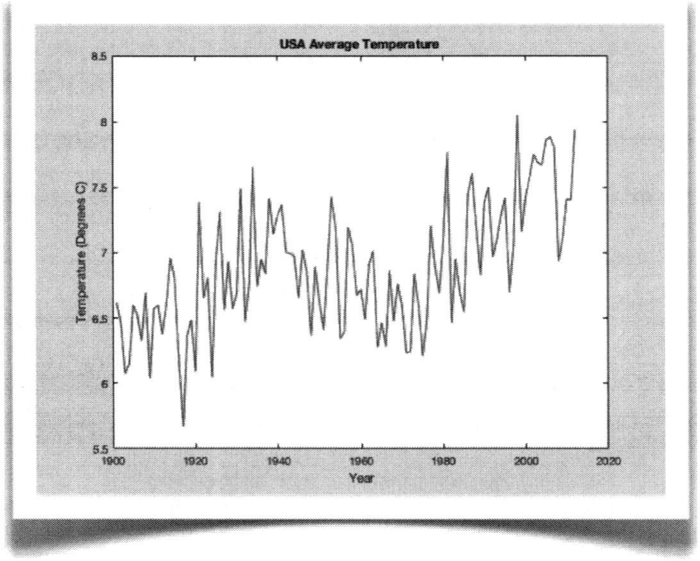

Chapter 8
Graphical User Interfaces

User interface design is a crucial part of programming activities. It is not uncommon that a programmer spends a majority of programming time designing the graphical user interface of a program. It is also not uncommon that a software package fails in the market just because it has a poor user interface design, even if it has excellent functionalities.

8.1 Predefined Dialog Boxes

8.1a Predefined Dialog Boxes

Example08_01a.m: Triangle

[1] MATLAB provides many predefined dialog boxes (Table 8.1, page 299). The following script demonstrates some of these predefined dialog boxes. This script requests the user input three sides of a triangle as shown in [2], calculates the three angles according to the Law of Cosine (2.11b[1], page 106), and displays the result as shown in [3]. If the three sides do not satisfy the **triangle inequality** (explained in [4], next page), an **error dialog box** as shown in [5] (next page) is displayed. ↓

```
clear
answer = inputdlg({'Side-1', 'Side-2', 'Side-3'}, ...
    'Input data', 1, {'5', '6', '7'});
s = str2double(answer);
s = sort(s); a = s(1); b = s(2); c = s(3);
if (a+b) <= c
    errordlg('Triangle does not exsist', 'Error!', 'modal')
else
    alpha = acosd((b^2+c^2-a^2)/(2*b*c));
    beta  = acosd((c^2+a^2-b^2)/(2*c*a));
    gamma = acosd((a^2+b^2-c^2)/(2*a*b));
    message = sprintf('Three angles are %.2f, %.2f, and %.2f degrees.', ...
        alpha, beta, gamma);
    msgbox(message, 'Output data', 'modal')
end
```

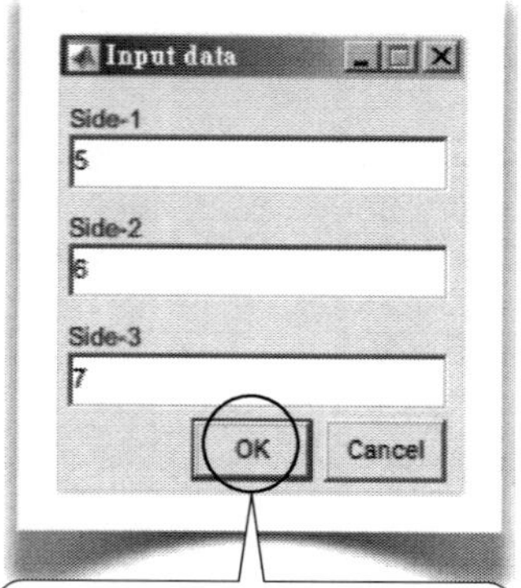

[2] Click **OK** after typing three sides of a triangle. →

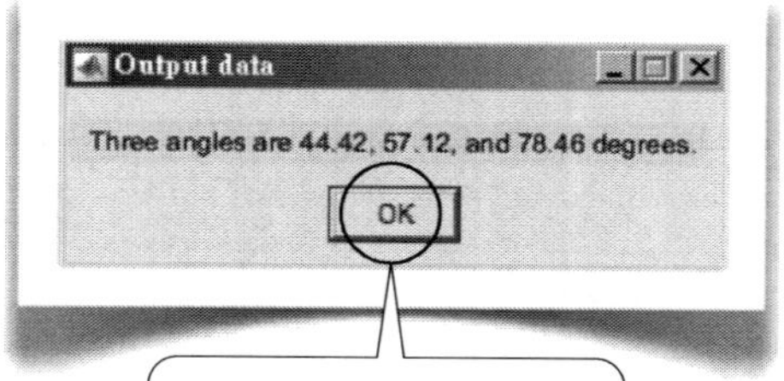

[3] Click **OK** to dismiss this window. ↵

About Example08_01a.m

Function `inputdlg`

[4] Line 2 displays an **input dialog box** as shown in [2], last page, using the function `inputdlg`, of which a syntax is

```
answer = inputdlg(prompt, title, lines, default)
```

where *`prompt`* is a cell array of strings; the number of elements of the cell array determines the number of input areas in the dialog box; *`title`* is a string used as the title of the dialog box; *`lines`* determines the height of the input areas; *`default`*, a cell array of strings, contains the default values to be displayed on the input areas. The output argument *`answer`* is a cell array of strings, containing the input strings from the user.

Line 4 converts the cell array of strings into a vector of `double` values, using the function `str2double`. The function `str2double` is similar to `str2num` but more robust; the documentation suggests that, in most cases, `str2double` should be used in place of `str2num` (see >> *`doc str2num`*). Note that the result `s` is a numeric vector, not a cell array.

Line 5 sorts the vector `s` in ascending order, using the built-in function `sort`, and assigns the smallest value to `a`, the medium value to `b`, and the largest value to `c`.

Functions `errordlg` and `msgbox`

If the three sides do not satisfy the **triangle inequality** (line 6), which states that *the sum of the lengths of any two sides of a triangle must be greater than the length of the third side* (*Wikipedia>Triangle*), then an **error dialog box** as shown in [5] is displayed using the function `errordlg` (line 7); a syntax for the function `errordlg` is

```
errordlg(message, title, mode)
```

where *`message`*, a string, is an error message to be displayed as the contents of the dialog box; *`title`* is a string to be displayed as the title of the dialog box; *`mode`* can be `modal`, `nonmodal` (default), or `replace`. A `modal` dialog box prevents the user from interacting with other windows in the MATLAB desktop before responding. A `replace` mode replaces the error dialog box having the specified *`title`*.

If the **triangle inequality** is satisfied (line 8), then the three angles are calculated (lines 9-11) using the Law of Cosines (2.11b[1], page 106). The calculated result is written to a string using the function `sprintf` (lines 12-13) and displayed on a message dialog box (line 14) using the function `msgbox` as shown in [3], last page; a syntax for the function `msgbox` is similar to that of `errordlg`:

```
msgbox(message, title, mode)
```

↓

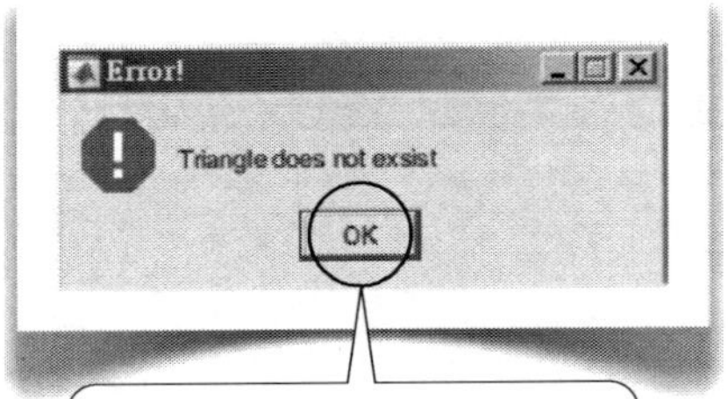

[5] Line 7 produces an error dialog box. Click **OK** to dismiss this window. #

8.1b Example: Voice Recorder

Example08_01b.m: Voice Recorder

[1] This script, an enhanced version of Example06_06b.m (page 268), uses additional predefined dialog boxes. It displays a menu of 5 tasks for you to choose [2-3]: start the recording, end the recording, play the voice, save the voice as a sound file, and load a sound file. ↓

```
clear
y = [];
while 1
    choice = menu('Voice Recorder', ...
        'Start', 'End', 'Play', 'Save', 'Load');
    switch choice
        case 0   % The user clicks the close button
            break
        case 1   % Start recording
            recObj = audiorecorder;
            record(recObj)
        case 2   % End recording
            stop(recObj)
            y = getaudiodata(recObj);
            Fs = recObj.SampleRate;
        case 3   % Play
            if isempty(y)
                errordlg('Empty!','Error!','modal')
            else
                sound(y, Fs);
            end
        case 4   % Save
            if isempty(y)
                errordlg('Empty!','Error!','modal')
            else
                [file, path] = uiputfile('*.wav');
                if file
                    audiowrite([path, file], y, Fs)
                end
            end
        case 5   % Load
            [file, path] = uigetfile('*.wav');
            if file
                [y, Fs] = audioread([path, file]);
            end
    end
end
```

[3] To quit the program, click **Close** button. ↵

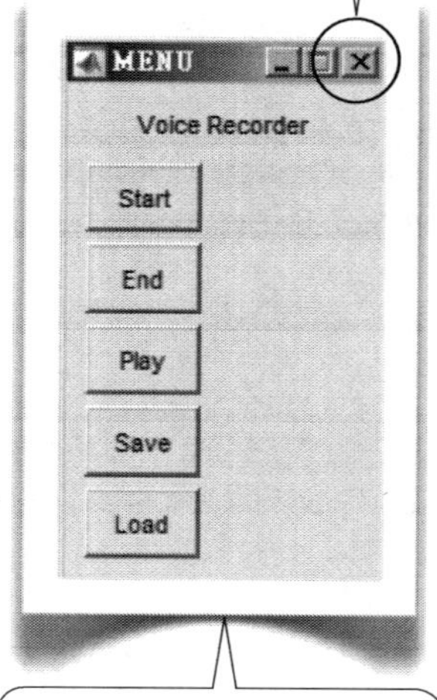

[2] Example08_01b.m displays a menu of 5 tasks. Test-run this program by choosing each task one after another. This program assumes that your system has a microphone and a sound card. ↑

About Example08_01b.m

[4] In the beginning of the `while`-loop (lines 3-37), the program displays a **menu dialog box** of 5 push-down buttons (lines 4-5) as shown in [2-3] (last page), using the function `menu`; a syntax for the function `menu` is

```
choice = menu(message, op1, op2, ...)
```

where `message` is a string to be displayed on the dialog box; the rest of the input arguments (*`op1`*, *`op2`*, ...) are strings to be displayed on the push-down buttons; the output argument *`choice`* is an integer number indicating which button is clicked by the user: 1 for the first button, 2 for the second button, and so on.

If the user clicks the **Close** button at the right of the title bar [3], the function `menu` returns zero (line 7) and the `while`-loop breaks (line 8), causing the program to end (line 37).

If the user clicks the **Start** button (line 9), an object of `audiorecorder` class is created (line 10), which is then passed to the function `record` (line 11) to initiate a recording session. The recording continues until the user clicks the **End** button (line 12), at which the recording stops (line 13) and the sound data and its sample rate are retrieved (lines 14-15).

If the user clicks the **Play** button (line 16), and if the sound data is empty (line 17), then an error message (similar to 8.1a[5], page 297) is displayed (line 18), otherwise the sound data is played using the function `sound` (lines 19-20).

If the user clicks the **Save** button (line 22), and if the sound data is empty (line 23), then an error message is displayed (line 24), otherwise (line 25) a standard **save-file dialog box** is displayed (line 26). The function `uiputfile` (line 26) normally returns a selected file name and its path; in case the user clicks the **Cancel** button in the **save-file dialog box**, it outputs a zero as the first output argument. If the first output value is not a zero (line 27), the sound data `y` and the sample rate `Fs` are saved in the file using the function `audiowrite` (line 28).

If the user clicks the **Load** button (line 31), then a standard **open-file dialog box** (line 32) is displayed. The function `uigetfile` (line 32) normally returns a selected file name and its path; in case the user clicks the **Cancel** button in the **open-file dialog box**, it outputs a zero as the first input argument. If the first output value is not a zero (line 33), then the sound data `y` and the sample rate `Fs` are read from the file using the function `audioread` (line 34).

This GUI has to be improved in many aspects. For example, the **menu dialog box** ([2-3], last page) should not disappear and reappear after each clicking of a button. In the next section, we'll present an improvement of the Voice Recorder using more sophisticated UI-controls. #

Table 8.1 Predefined Dialog Boxes

Functions	Description
`errordlg(message,title,mode)`	Create error dialog box
`warndlg(message,title,mode)`	Create warning dialog box
`msgbox(message,title,mode)`	Create message dialog box
`waitbar(x,message)`	Open or update wait bar dialog box
`button = questdlg(message,title)`	Create yes-no-cancel dialog box
`answer = inputdlg(prompt,title,n,default)`	Create dialog box that gathers user input
`choice = listdlg(name,value)`	Create list-selection dialog box
`[file,path] = uigetfile(filterSpec)`	Open file-selection dialog box
`[file,path] = uiputfile(filterSpec)`	Open dialog box for saving files
`choice = menu(message,op1,op2,...)`	Create multiple-choice dialog box

Details and More: Help>MATLAB>App Building>GUIDE or Programmatic Workflow>Dialog Boxes

8.2 UI-Controls: Pushbuttons

Example08_02.m: Voice Recorder

[1] MATLAB provides many **UI-controls** that allow a more flexible design of a GUI. We start with a simple UI-control, namely the **pushbutton**.

This is another version of the Voice Recorder. Its functionalities are the same as those of Example08_01b.m, page 298, but it uses **UI-controls**. (Continued at [2], next page.) ↵

```
function Example08_02
y = []; Fs = 0; recObj = [];
figure('Position', [300, 300, 200, 300], ...
    'Name', 'Voice Recorder', ...
    'MenuBar', 'none', ...
    'NumberTitle', 'off');
uicontrol('Style', 'pushbutton', ...
    'String', 'Start', ...
    'Position', [50, 250, 100, 20], ...
    'Callback', @cbStart)
uicontrol('Style', 'pushbutton', ...
    'String', 'End', ...
    'Position', [50, 210, 100, 20], ...
    'Callback', @cbEnd)
uicontrol('Style', 'pushbutton', ...
    'String', 'Play', ...
    'Position', [50, 170, 100, 20], ...
    'Callback', @cbPlay)
uicontrol('Style', 'pushbutton', ...
    'String', 'Save', ...
    'Position', [50, 130, 100, 20], ...
    'Callback', @cbSave)
uicontrol('Style', 'pushbutton', ...
    'String', 'Load', ...
    'Position', [50, 90, 100, 20], ...
    'Callback', @cbLoad)
uicontrol('Style', 'pushbutton', ...
    'String', 'Quit', ...
    'Position', [50, 50, 100, 20], ...
    'Callback', @cbQuit)

    function cbStart(~, ~)
        recObj = audiorecorder;
        record(recObj)
    end

    function cbEnd(~, ~)
        stop(recObj)
        y = getaudiodata(recObj);
        Fs = recObj.SampleRate;
    end

    function cbPlay(~, ~)
        if isempty(y)
            errordlg('Empty voice!', 'modal')
        else
            sound(y, Fs);
        end
    end

```

[2] Example08_02.m (continued). ↓

```
    function cbSave(~, ~)
        if isempty(y)
            errordlg('Empty voice!', 'modal')
        else
            [file, path] = uiputfile('*.wav');
            if file
                audiowrite([path, file], y, Fs)
            end
        end
    end

    function cbLoad(~, ~)
        [file, path] = uigetfile('*.wav');
        if file
            [y, Fs] = audioread([path, file]);
        end
    end

    function cbQuit(~, ~)
        close
    end
end
```

Test-Run the Program

[3] Program Example08_02.m displays 6 **pushbuttons**. Test-run this program by clicking a **pushbutton** one after another. This program assumes that your system has a microphone and a sound card. The functionalities of this program are the same as those of Example08_01b.m (page 298). However, here, the GUI remains (rather than disappearing and reappearing) when a button is clicked. Also note that we added a **Quit** button, which simply quits the program as though the user clicks the **Close** button at the title bar. ↵

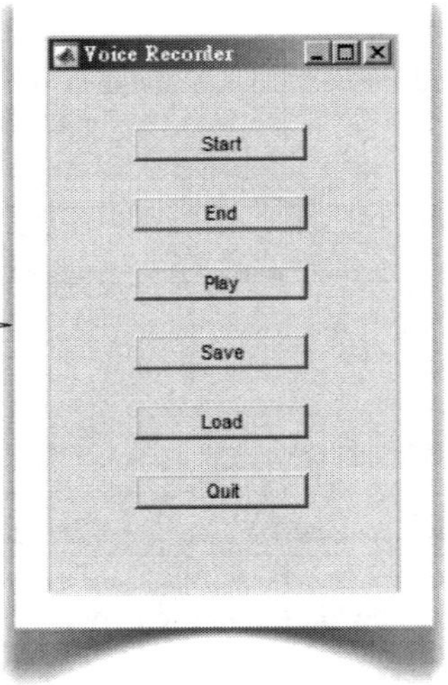

Use of Nested Functions

[4] The program consists of a **main function** (lines 1-72), under which six **nested functions** are defined: `cbStart` (lines 32-35), `cbEnd` (lines 37-41), `cbPlay` (lines 43-49), `cbSave` (lines 51-60), `cbLoad` (lines 62-67), and `cbQuit` (lines 69-71). Remember that nested functions can be defined only WITHIN a function; they cannot be defined AFTER a main program. Using nested functions is convenient because variables in the parent function (specifically `y`, `Fs`, and `recObj` in line 2) are visible to the nested functions. This approach has become a standard practice when implementing callback functions. It simplifies the communication of data to the callback functions. Another approach is to explicitly declare variables as **global**; e.g., Example01_18.m (lines 2 and 29, page 55).

If we delete lines 1 and 72 and lines 2-30 become a **main program**, that would be syntactically correct; however, the 6 **nested functions** would become **subfunctions** and the variables in the main program would be no longer visible to the **subfunctions**. ↓

About Example08_02.m

[5] Six **pushbuttons** are defined (lines 7-30) and the six nested functions serve as the callback functions for the six pushbuttons, respectively. Here, a callback function is called when its associated pushbutton is clicked. By protocol, a callback function must have two input arguments and no output arguments. The first input argument is a handle to the associated UI-control, here a pushbutton; the handle can be used to access the pushbutton properties. In all of the six callback functions, since we don't need to use the handle, we replace the first input argument with a tilde (~), a **placeholder**. The second input argument is reserved for the future versions of MATLAB and has no use in the current version, so we also fill the second input argument with a placeholder (~).

Line 2 creates variables with empty data for the sound data `y`, the sample rate `Fs`, and an **audiorecorder** object `recObj`. Lines 3-6 create a **Figure**, removing the menubar and the number title (lines 5-6). The toolbar is automatically removed when the menubar is removed.

Lines 7-10 create the **Start** button shown in [3] (last page) and specify its callback function (line 10). The syntax we used here for the function `uicontrol` is

```
uicontrol(name, value, ...)
```

Where both arguments are case-insensitive strings.

Similarly, lines 11-30 create the **End, Play**, **Save**, **Load**, and **Quit** buttons, respectively, and specify their callback functions.

For a short callback function like `cbQuit` (lines 69-71), you may provide the statements directly in the function `uicontrol`; e.g., you may delete lines 69-71 and replace line 30 by

```
'Callback', 'close')
```

Positions and Sizes of UI-Controls

Positioning and sizing a UI-control usually involves much trial-and-error. It is not practical to calculate the exact positions and sizes before writing your codes. A common practice is that you use approximate positions and sizes as an initial design of the GUI, and then adjust them iteratively after each test-run. #

Table 8.2a UI Control Properties

Property	Description
`Style`	Style of UI control. (See Table 8.2b)
`Parent`	Parent of uicontrol
`Position`	Location and size of UI control, [left, bottom, width, height]
`Units`	Units of measurement. (Default: pixels)
`FontSize`	Font size for text, a positive number
`String`	Text to display
`BackgroundColor`	Background color of uicontrol
`HorizontalAlignment`	Alignment of text
`Callback`	Callback function when user interacts with uicontrol
`ButtonDownFcn`	Button-press callback function
`UIContextMenu`	Uicontrol context menu
`Value`	Current value of uicontrol
`Max`	Maximum value of uicontrol
`Min`	Minimum value of uicontrol
`SliderStep`	Slider step size
`Enable`	Operational state of uicontrol

Details and More: Help>MATLAB>App Building>GUIDE or Programmatic Workflow> Components and Layout>Interactive Components>Uicontrol Properties

Table 8.2b Style of UI Control

Style	Description
`pushbutton`	Button that appears to depress until you release the mouse button
`togglebutton`	The state of a toggle button changes every time you click it
`checkbox`	The state of a toggle button changes every time you click it
`radiobutton`	Radio buttons are intended to be mutually exclusive within a group of buttons
`edit`	Editable text field
`text`	Static text field
`slider`	The position of a slider button indicates a value within a range
`listbox`	List of items from which the user can select one or more items
`popupmenu`	Menu that expands to display a list of choices

Details and More: Help>MATLAB>App Building>GUIDE or Programmatic Workflow> Components and Layout>Interactive Components>Uicontrol Properties>Type of Control>Style

8.3 Example: Image Viewer

Example08_03.m: Image Viewer

[1] This program opens an image file and displays it on a **Figure** window ([4-6], next page). It also can save the file as another file name. This program demonstrates a more sophisticated use of functions `uigetfile` and `uiputfile` ([5], page 306), which we used in Example08_01b.m, page 298. Locations and sizes of the **Axes** and the **pushbuttons** are specified in normalized units, so the **Figure** window can be resized without twisting the components in the **Figure** window [6]. (Continued at [2], next page.) ↵

```
function Example08_03
Photo = [];
figure('Position', [30, 30, 600, 400], ...
    'Name', 'Image Viewer', ...
    'MenuBar', 'none', ...
    'NumberTitle', 'off');
axes('Position', [.1 .1 .7 .8]);
uicontrol('Style', 'pushbutton', ...
    'String', 'Open...', ...
    'Callback', @cbOpen, ...
    'Units', 'normalized', ...
    'Position', [.825, .6, .15, .1])
hSaveAs = uicontrol('Style', 'pushbutton', ...
    'String', 'Save As...', ...
    'Callback', @cbSaveAs, ...
    'Enable', 'off', ...
    'Units', 'normalized', ...
    'Position', [.825, .4, .15, .1]);
uicontrol('Style', 'pushbutton', ...
    'String', 'Quit', ...
    'Callback', 'close', ...
    'Units', 'normalized', ...
    'Position', [.825, .2, .15, .1])

    function cbOpen(~, ~)
        [file, path] = uigetfile( ...
        {'*.png', 'Portable Network Graphics (*.png)'; ...
         '*.jpg;*.jpeg', 'Joint Photographic Experts Group (*.jpg;*.jpeg)'; ...
         '*.tif;*.tiff', 'Tagged Image File Format (*.tif;*.tiff)'});
        if file
            Photo = imread([path, file]);
            image(Photo);
            axis off image
            hSaveAs.Enable = 'on';
        end
    end

```

[2] Example08_03.m (continued). ↓

```
38        function cbSaveAs(~, ~)
39            [file, path] = uiputfile( ...
40            {'*.png', 'Portable Network Graphics (*.png)'; ...
41             '*.jpg', 'Joint Photographic Experts Group (*.jpg)'; ...
42             '*.tif', 'Tagged Image File Format (*.tif)'});
43            if file
44                imwrite(Photo, [path, file])
45            end
46        end
47    end
```

Test-Run

[3] We need an image file to test the program. Now, copy the image file `peppers.png` (1.13[4], page 45) to the **Current Folder** by typing:

```
>> copyfile(which('peppers.png'),'test.png')
```

Remember that the function `which` returns the full name of a file (1.13[7], page 46). Now run the program [4-7]. ↙

[5] Click the **Open** button to open the image file `test.png`. After it is opened, the image file is displayed on the **Figure** window. ↓

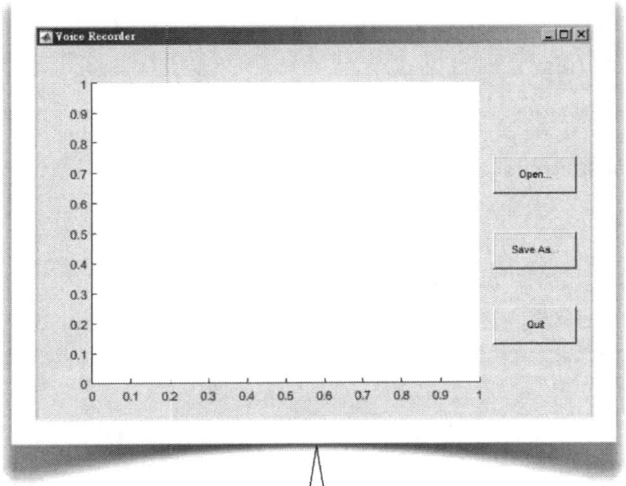

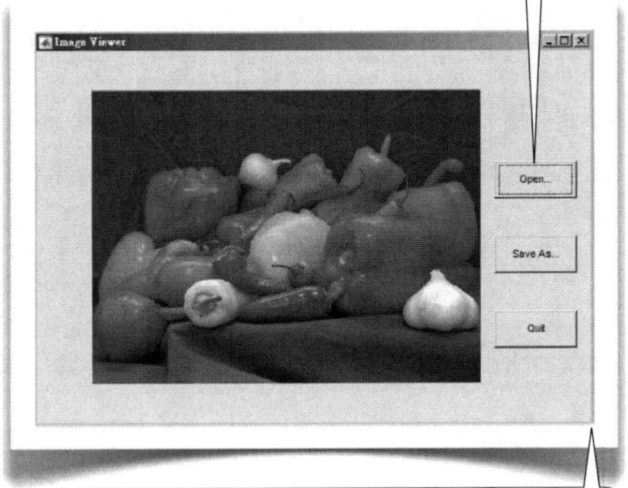

[4] The initial GUI has three **pushbuttons** and an **Axes**. ↗

[6] Try to resize the **Figure** window by dragging the corners or the edges. The **pushbuttons** and the **Axes** are resized accordingly, because of the use of normalized units (lines 11, 17, and 22). ↵

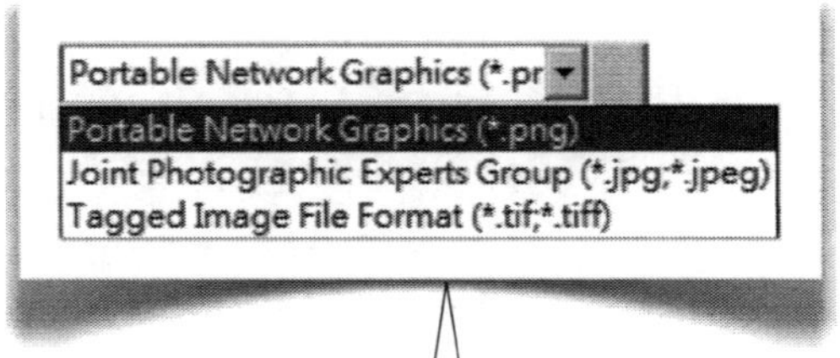

[7] Click the **Save As...** button. This is the popup menu in the standard **Open-File** dialog. ↓

About Example08_03.m

[8] This program consists of a function (lines 1-47), within which two nested functions are defined (lines 25-36 and 38-46), which serve as the callback functions of the **Open** and **Save As** buttons, respectively. As mentioned (8.2[4], page 302), using nested functions has become a standard practice when implementing callback functions, because variables in the parent function (specifically `Photo` in line 2 and `hSaveAs` in line 13) are visible to the nested functions.

Line 2 creates an empty image data `Photo`. Lines 3-6 create a **Figure** window, removing the menubar and the number title (lines 5-6). Line 7 creates an **Axes**. Note that, by default, the function `axes` uses normalized units, with which the entire **Figure** window has a size of 1-by-1.

Lines 8-23 create 3 **pushbuttons** as shown in [4], using normalized units, specifying the callback functions. Note that we initially disable the **Save As** button (line 16), because there is no image data to be saved at the beginning.

The callback function `cbOpen` (lines 25-36) uses the function `uigetfile` (lines 26-29) to request an image file name, including its path. The syntax used here for `uigetfile` is

```
[file, path] = uigetfile(FilterSpec)
```

We use a 3-by-2 cell array (lines 27-29) for *`FilterSpec`* to specify a list of file types and give them descriptions (see [7]). Each row of the cell array specifies a file type and gives a description. The first string of a row specifies the file type, while the second string of the row is the description. If the user clicks **Cancel** in the dialog, both `file` and `path` become zeros. If `file` is not zero (line 30), the image file is read (line 31) and displayed (lines 32-33), and the **Save As** button is enabled (line 34).

The callback function `cbSaveAs` (lines 38-46) uses the function `uiputfile` (lines 39-42) to request an image file name. If the returned value of `file` is not zero (line 43), the image is saved to the file (line 44). #

8.4 UI-Menus: Image Viewer

Example08_04.m: Image Viewer (UI-Menus)

[1] Another way to implement a GUI for the Imager Viewer is using pulldown menus. This program, modified from Example08_03.m (pages 304-305), demonstrates the use of UI-menus, including nested menus (submenus) shown in [2], next page. Note that the callback function `cbOpen` (lines 16-27) is the same as that in Example08_03.m. ↵

```
 1  function Example08_04
 2  Photo = [];
 3  figure('Position', [30, 30, 600, 400], ...
 4      'Name', 'Image Viewer', ...
 5      'ToolBar', 'none', ...
 6      'NumberTitle', 'off');
 7  axes('Position', [.15 .1 .7 .8]);
 8  hImage = uimenu('Label', 'Image');
 9      uimenu(hImage, 'Label', 'Open...', 'Callback', @cbOpen)
10      hSaveAs = uimenu(hImage, 'Label', 'Save As', 'Enable', 'off');
11          hPNG = uimenu(hSaveAs, 'Label', 'PNG', 'Callback', @cbSaveAs);
12          hJPG = uimenu(hSaveAs, 'Label', 'JPG', 'Callback', @cbSaveAs);
13          hTIF = uimenu(hSaveAs, 'Label', 'TIF', 'Callback', @cbSaveAs);
14      uimenu(hImage, 'Label', 'Quit', 'Callback', 'close')
15
16      function cbOpen(~, ~)
17          [file, path] = uigetfile( ...
18          {'*.png', 'Portable Network Graphics (*.png)'; ...
19           '*.jpg;*.jpeg', 'Joint Photographic Experts Group (*.jpg;*.jpeg)'; ...
20           '*.tif;*.tiff', 'Tagged Image File Format (*.tif;*.tiff)'});
21          if file
22              Photo = imread([path, file]);
23              image(Photo);
24              axis off image
25              hSaveAs.Enable = 'on';
26          end
27      end
28
29      function cbSaveAs(h, ~)
30          if h == hPNG
31              [file,path] = uiputfile({'*.png','Portable Network Graphics (*.png)'});
32          elseif h == hJPG
33              [file,path] = uiputfile({'*.jpg','Joint Photographic Experts Group (*.jpg)'});
34          else
35              [file,path] = uiputfile({'*.tif','Tagged Image File Format (*.tif)'});
36          end
37          if file
38              imwrite(Photo, [path, file])
39          end
40      end
41  end
```

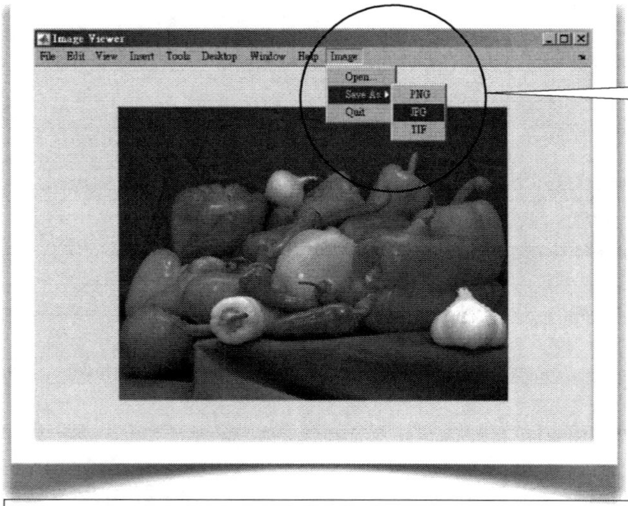

[2] This program demonstrates the use of UI-menus, including nested menus (submenus). ↓

About Example08_04.m

[3] This program has the same structure as that of Example08_03.m. The function `cbOpen` (lines 16-27) serves as a callback function for the **Open** menu, and the function `cbSaveAs` (lines 29-40) is the common callback function for the submenus **PNG**, **JPG**, and **TIF**.

Lines 3-6 create a **Figure** window, removing the toolbar and the number title (lines 7-8). Note that the menubar is not removed. Lines 8-14 create the menus shown in [2]. Line 8 inserts a menu with the label **Image**. Lines 9-10, and 14 create three menus (with labels **Open**, **SaveAs**, and **Quit**, respectively) as submenus of the **Image** menu. Their syntax is

```
handle = uimenu(parent, name, value, ...)
```

Lines 11-13 create three submenus (**PNG**, **JPG**, and **TIF**) under the **Save As** menu. Note that the three menus share the same callback function `cbSaveAs` (see the last input arguments in lines 11-13). Also note that we initially disable the **Save As** menu (line 10); its submenus are in turn automatically disabled.

In the callback function `cbSaveAs` (lines 29-40), the first input argument (`h` in line 29) is the handle of the menu triggering the event. If the event is triggered by the **PNG** menu (see lines 11 and 30), then only the PNG file type is allowed (line 31). If the event is triggered by the **JPG** menu (see lines 12 and 32), then only the JPG file type is allowed (line 33). Otherwise, the event must be triggered by the **TIF** menu (see lines 13 and 34), and only the TIF file type is allowed (line 35). #

Table 8.4 UI-Menus Properties

Property	Description
`Label`	Menu label
`Callback`	Callback function when the user selects the ui-menu
`Separator`	Separator line mode (off)
`Enable`	Operational state of ui-menu (on)
`Accelerator`	Keyboard equivalent
`Parent`	Parent of ui-menu

Details and More: Help>MATLAB>App Building>GUIDE or Programmatic Workflow>Components and Layout>Properties>Interactive Components>Uimenu Properties

8.5 Panels, Button Groups, and More UI-Controls

Example08_05.m: Sorting and Searching

[1] This program is a GUI version of Example03_13.m (pages 151-152). The GUI is shown in [5-10], page 312. Note that the functions `sort` and search (lines 132-161) are the same as those in Example03_13.m (page 152).
(Continued at [2], next page.) ↵

```
 1  function Example08_05
 2  figure('Position', [30, 30, 400, 400], ...
 3      'Name', 'Sorting and Searching', ...
 4      'MenuBar', 'none', ...
 5      'NumberTitle', 'off', ...
 6      'Resize', 'off')
 7  uicontrol('Style', 'text', ...
 8      'String', 'List of Numbers', ...
 9      'Units', 'normalized', ...
10      'Position', [.1 .8 .25 .1])
11  hList = uicontrol('Style', 'listbox', ...
12      'Units', 'normalized', ...
13      'Position', [.1 .1 .25 .75]);
14  hPanel1 = uipanel('Position', [.4 .725 .55 .2]);
15      uicontrol(hPanel1, 'Style', 'text', ...
16          'String', 'Enter a Number', ...
17          'Units', 'normalized', ...
18          'Position', [.1 .6 .35 .2])
19      uicontrol(hPanel1, 'Style', 'edit', ...
20          'Callback', @cbEnter, ...
21          'Units', 'normalized', ...
22          'Position', [.1 .1 .35 .4])
23      hSort = uicontrol(hPanel1, 'Style', 'checkbox', ...
24          'String', 'Sort', ...
25          'Callback', @cbSort, ...
26          'Value', true, ...
27          'Units', 'Normalized', ...
28          'Position', [.6 .4 .35 .2]);
29  hPanel2 = uipanel('Position', [.4 .4 .55 .3]);
30      uicontrol(hPanel2, 'Style', 'text', ...
31          'String', 'Find a Number', ...
32          'Units', 'Normalized', ...
33          'Position', [.1 .6 .35 .2])
34      hFind = uicontrol(hPanel2, 'Style', 'edit', ...
35          'Callback', @cbFind, ...
36          'Enable', 'off', ...
37          'Units', 'normalized', ...
38          'Position', [.1 .35 .35 .25]);
```

[2] Example08_05.m (Continued). (Continued at [3], next page.) ↵

```
    hGroup = uibuttongroup(hPanel2, ...
        'Position', [.5, .2, .45, .6]);
        uicontrol(hGroup, 'Style', 'radiobutton', ...
            'String', 'Keep', ...
            'Value', true, ...
            'Units', 'normalized', ...
            'Position', [.2 .6 .7 .3])
        hRemove = uicontrol(hGroup, 'Style', 'radiobutton', ...
            'String', 'Remove', ...
            'Units', 'normalized', ...
            'Position', [.2 .1 .7 .3]);
uicontrol('Style', 'pushbutton', ...
    'String', 'Open...', ...
    'Callback', @cbOpen, ...
    'Units', 'normalized', ...
    'Position', [.45 .3 .2 .075])
hSaveAs = uicontrol('Style', 'pushbutton', ...
    'String', 'Save As...', ...
    'Callback', @cbSaveAs, ...
    'Enable', 'off', ...
    'Units', 'normalized', ...
    'Position', [.45 .2 .2 .075]);
uicontrol('Style', 'pushbutton', ...
    'String', 'Quit', ...
    'Callback', 'close', ...
    'Units', 'Normalized', ...
    'Position', [.45 .1 .2 .075]);

    function cbEnter(h, ~)
        number = str2double(h.String);
        h.String = [];
        if isempty(hList.String)
            a = [];
        else
            a = str2double(hList.String);
        end
        if search(a, number) > 0
            errordlg('The number exists!')
        else
            a(length(a)+1) = number;
            if hSort.Value
                a = sort(a);
            end
            hList.String = num2cell(a);
        end
        hSaveAs.Enable = 'on';
        hFind.Enable = 'on';
    end

```

[3] Example08_05.m (Continued). (Continued at [4], next page.) ↵

```
    function cbSort(~, ~)
        a = str2double(hList.String);
        if hSort.Value && ~isempty(a)
            a = sort(a);
            hList.String = num2cell(a);
        end
    end

    function cbFind(h, ~)
        number = str2double(h.String);
        h.String = [];
        a = str2double(hList.String);
        k = search(a, number);
        if k == 0
            errordlg('The number not exist!')
        else
            hList.Value = k;
            if hRemove.Value
                n = length(a);
                b(1:n-1,1) = [a(1:k-1);a(k+1:n)];
                hList.String = num2cell(b);
            end
        end
    end

    function cbOpen(~, ~)
        [file, path] = uigetfile('*.mat');
        if file
            load([path, file], 'a');
            hList.String = num2cell(a);
            hSaveAs.Enable = 'on';
            hFind.Enable = 'on';
        end
    end

    function cbSaveAs(~, ~)
        [file, path] = uiputfile('*.mat');
        if file
            a = str2double(hList.String);
            save([path, file], 'a');
        end
    end
end
```

[4] Example08_05.m (Continued). →

```
function out = sort(a)
n = length(a);
for i = n-1:-1:1
    for j = 1:i
        if a(j) > a(j+1)
            tmp = a(j);
            a(j) = a(j+1);
            a(j+1) = tmp;
        end
    end
end
out = a;
end

function found = search(a, key)
n = length(a);
low = 1;
high = n;
found = 0;
while low <= high && ~found
    mid = floor((low+high)/2);
    if key == a(mid)
        found = mid;
    elseif key < a(mid)
        high = mid-1;
    else
        low = mid+1;
    end
end
end
```

[5] This is the initial GUI. ↙

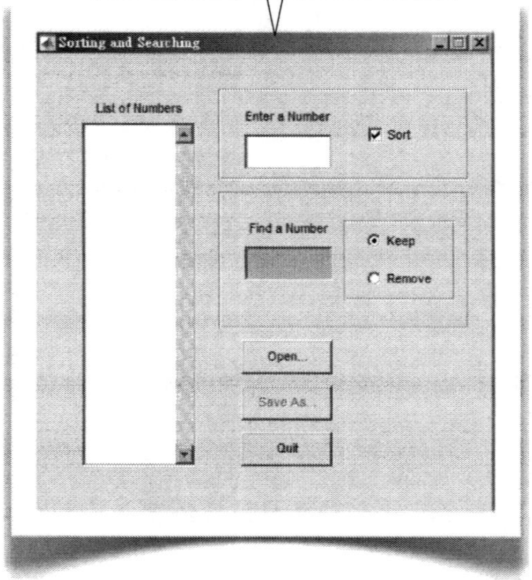

[6] The user enters numbers in this **editable text box**. ↓

[8] If this **check box** is checked, the list is sorted each time the user enters a number. Otherwise, the number is simply appended to the list. ↙

[7] The numbers are shown in the **list box**. ↗

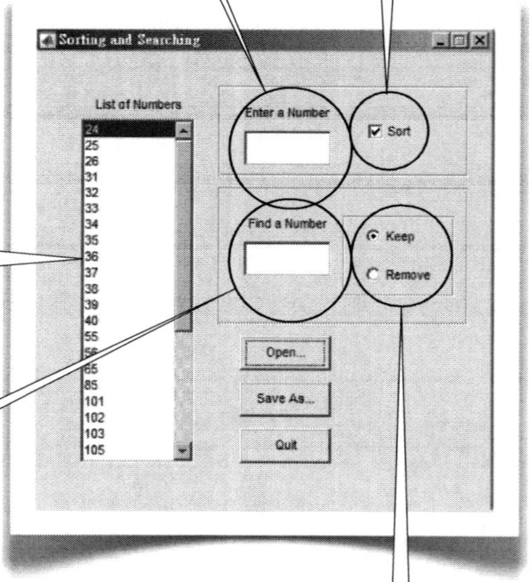

[9] The user may search a number by entering a number in this **editable text box**. →

[10] States of **radio buttons** within a group are mutually exclusive. When **Keep** is selected, the found number is highlighted. When **Remove** is selected, the found number is removed from the list. ↵

About Example08_05.m

[11] This program consists of a main function (lines 1-130) and 2 local functions (subfunctions): `sort` (lines 132-144) and `search` (lines 146-161). Within the main function, five nested functions are defined: `cbEnter` (lines 67-86), `cbSort` (lines 88-94), `cbFind` (lines 96-111), `cbOpen` (lines 113-121), and cbSaveAs (lines 123-129). The 5 nested functions serve as callback functions for five UI components, respectively, and the local functions `sort` and `search` are used in some callback functions (lines 75, 80, 91, and 100).

Function sortSearch

Lines 2-6 create an un-resizable (line 6) **Figure** window. Lines 7-10 create a static text **List of Numbers**. Lines 11-13 create a **list box** [7]. Line 14 creates a **panel** that will enclose a **static text**, an **editable text box** [6], and a **check box** [8]; lines 15-18 create the **static text**; lines 19-22 create the **editable text box** [6]; lines 23-28 create the **check box** [8]. Note that the **Value** of the **check box** is initially set to `true` (line 26); i.e., it is initially checked.

Line 29 creates another **panel** that will enclose a **static text**, an **editable text box** [9], and two **radio buttons** [10]; lines 30-33 create the **static text**; lines 34-38 create the **editable text box** [9], which is initially disabled (line 36; also see [5]); lines 39-49 create two **radio buttons** [10]. Each **radio button** can have two states: selected or deselected. States of **radio buttons** are mutually exclusive within a group of radio buttons. To create a group of radio buttons, a **button group panel** has to be created first (lines 39-40) and the **radio buttons** are then created as children of the **button group panel** (lines 41-49). Note that the **Value** of the **Keep** radio button is initially set to `true` (line 43); i.e., it is initially selected and the **Remove** radio button is thus deselected, due to the mutual exclusiveness.

Lines 50-65 create three pushbuttons: **Open** (lines 50-54), **Save As** (lines 55-60), and **Quit** (lines 61-65). Note that the **Save As** button is initially disabled (line 58; also see [5]).

Callback Functions

The callback function `cbEnter` (lines 67-86) is called when a number is entered into the **editable text box** shown in [6] (see line 20). The number, stored as a string, is converted to a numeric type (line 68) and erased from the text box (line 69). The list of numbers [7], stored as a cell array of strings, is converted to a column vector `a` of numeric values (lines 71, 73). If the number is in the vector `a` (line 75), an error message is displayed (line 76), otherwise the number is appended to the end of the vector `a` (line 78). If the **Sort** check box [8] is checked (line 79), then the vector `a` is sorted (line 80). The numeric values in `a` are converted to a cell array and stored in the list (line 82). Before ending the function, the **SaveAs** button and the **editable text box** in [9] are enabled (lines 84-85).

The callback function `cbSort` (lines 88-94) is called when the **Sort** check box [8] is clicked (see line 25). The list of numbers [7] is converted to a column vector `a` of numeric values (line 89). If the **Sort** check box [8] is checked and the vector `a` is not empty (line 90), the vector `a` is sorted (line 91), converted to a cell array of strings, and stored in the list box (line 92).

The callback function `cbFind` (lines 96-111) is called when a number is entered into the **editable text box** in [9] (see line 35). The number, stored as a string, is converted to numeric type (line 97) and erased from the text box (line 98). The list of numbers [7] is converted to a column vector `a` of numeric values (line 99). If the number is not in the vector `a` (lines 100-101), an error message is displayed (line 102), otherwise (line 103) the number becomes the current selected number in the list (line 104). If the **Remove** radio button [10] is active (line 105), the number is removed from the list (lines 106-108).

The callback function `cbOpen` (lines 113-121) is called when the **Open** pushbutton is clicked (line 52). A get-file dialog is displayed for the user to select a file (line 114). If the dialog is not canceled by the user and a file name is returned (line 115), the variable `a` is loaded from the file (line 116), converted to a cell array of strings, and stored in the list box (line 117). The **SaveAs** button and the **editable text box** in [9] are enabled (lines 118-119).

The callback function `cbSaveAs` is similar to `cbOpen`. #

Table 8.5 UI-Controls and Indicators	
Function	Description
`hf = figure`	Create figure window
`ha = axes`	Create axes object
`h = uicontrol(parent,name,value)`	Create UI-control
`h = uitable(parent,name,value)`	Create table UI component
`h = uipanel(parent,name,value)`	Create panel container object
`h = uibuttongroup(parent,name,value)`	Create button group to manage radio buttons and toggle buttons
`h = uitab(parent,name,value)`	Create tabbed panel
`h = uitabgroup(parent,name,value)`	Create container for tabbed panels
Details and More: *Help>MATLAB>App Building>GUIDE or Programmatic Workflow>Components and Layout>UI Components*	

8.6 UI-Controls: Sliders

Example08_06.m: Sliders

[1] This program demonstrates the use of a **slider** to change the value of an input data (see [2-6], next page). ↵

```
function Example08_06
figure('Position', [50, 50, 400, 400], ...
    'Name', 'Slider Demo', ...
    'MenuBar', 'none', ...
    'NumberTitle', 'off')
axes('Position', [.1 .5 .8 .4])
omega = 1;
sinewave(omega);
hEdit = uicontrol('Style', 'edit', ...
    'String', num2str(omega), ...
    'Callback', @cbEdit, ...
    'Units', 'normalized', ...
    'Position', [.4 .3 .2 .05]);
hSlider = uicontrol('Style', 'slider', ...
    'Callback', @cbSlider, ...
    'Units', 'normalized', ...
    'Position', [.2 .1 .6 .05], ...
    'Value', 1, ...
    'Min', 0, ...
    'Max', 10, ...
    'SliderStep', [0.01, 0.1]);

    function cbEdit(h, ~)
        omega = str2double(h.String);
        hSlider.Value = omega;
        sinewave(omega);
    end

    function cbSlider(h, ~)
        omega = h.Value;
        hEdit.String = num2str(omega);
        sinewave(omega);
    end

    function sinewave(omega)
        t = linspace(0, 2*pi);
        y = sin(omega*t);
        plot(t, y)
        axis([0, 2*pi, -1, 1])
    end
end
```

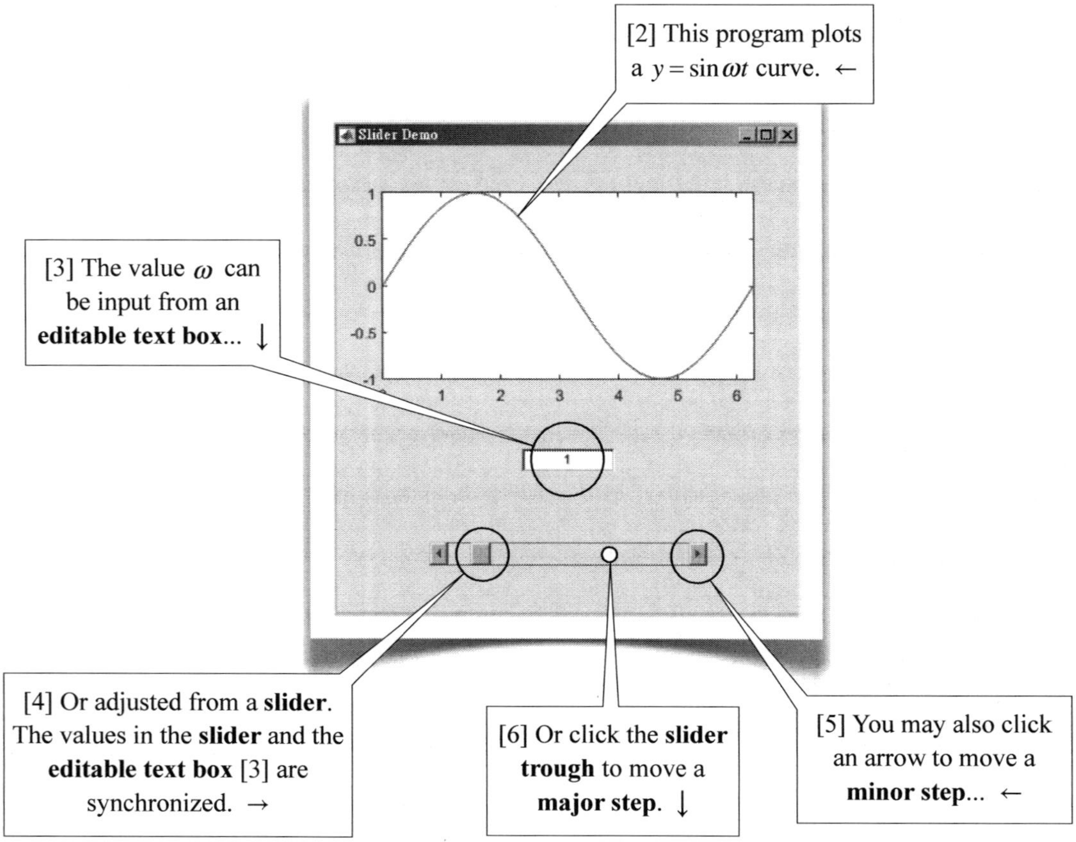

About Example08_06.m

[7] This program consists of a main function (lines 1-41), within which three nested functions are defined: `cbEdit` (lines 23-27), `cbSlider` (lines 29-33), and `sinewave` (lines 35-40). The function `cbEdit` (lines 23-27) serves as the callback function for the **editable text box** (see [3] and line 11). The function `cbSlider` (lines 29-33) serves as the callback function for the **slider** (see [4-6] and line 15). Both the callback functions use function `sinewave` (lines 35-40), which plots a sine wave (see [2]).

Lines 2-5 create a **Figure** window. Line 6 creates an **Axes** in the **Figure**. Lines 7-8 plot a sine wave with an angular frequency `omega`, which has an initial value of 1 (line 7). Lines 9-13 create an **editable text box** [3]. Lines 14-21 create a **slider** [4-6]; lines 19-20 specify the range (0-10) for the slider value; line 21 specifies a **minor step** (0.01; also see [5]) and a **major step** (0.1; also see [6]). These step sizes (0.01 and 0.1) are the fraction of the slider range (10).

In the callback function `cbEdit` (lines 23-27), the data in the **editable text box** [3] is retrieved (line 24), the slider value is synchronized (line 25), and the sine wave is plotted (line 26).

In the callback function `cbSlider` (lines 29-33), the slider value [4] is retrieved (line 30), the data in the **editable text box** is synchronized (line 31), and the sine wave is plotted (line 32). #

8.7 UI-Tables: Truss Data

8.7a Example: Truss Nodal Data

Example08_07a.m: Truss Nodal Data

[1] This program demonstrates the use of a **UI-table** to input the truss nodal data such as those listed in Table3.14a (page 157). Run the program and experience the operations of the **UI-table** as shown in [2-5], next page. The **UI-tables** created in this section will be integrated into the Statically Determinate Trusses program in the next section. ↵

```
function Example08_07a
Nodes = struct('x', 0, 'y', 0, ...
    'supportx', false, 'supporty', false, ...
    'loadx', 0, 'loady', 0, ...
    'reactionx', 0, 'reaction', 0);
figure('Position', [30, 30, 590, 200], ...
    'Name', 'Nodal Data', ...
    'MenuBar', 'none', ...
    'NumberTitle', 'off')
data = struct2cell(Nodes)';
columnName = {'X', 'Y', 'SupportX', 'SupportY', ...
    'LoadX', 'LoadY', 'ReactionX', 'ReactionY'};
columnFormat = {'numeric', 'numeric', ...
    'logical', 'logical', ...
    'numeric', 'numeric', 'numeric', 'numeric'};
columnEditable = logical([1 1 1 1 1 1 0 0]);
uitable('Data', data, ...
    'KeyPressFcn', @cbKeyPressNodes, ...
    'ColumnName', columnName, ...
    'ColumnFormat', columnFormat, ...
    'ColumnEditable', columnEditable, ...
    'ColumnWidth', {60}, ...
    'Units', 'normalized', ...
    'Position', [.05 .1 .9 .8]);

    function cbKeyPressNodes(hTable, hKey)
        if strcmpi(hKey.Key, 'downarrow')
            n = size(hTable.Data, 1);
            hTable.Data(n+1,:) = {0 0 false false 0 0 0 0};
        end
    end
end
```

[2] Example08_07a.m creates a **UI-table** of eight fields: six numeric and two logical. Initially it has only one row. Each time you press the **down-arrow** key (↓), a row is added to the **UI-table**. Before typing data, click an editable cell and press the **down-arrow** *n*-1 times to add enough rows, where *n* is the number of nodes. ↓

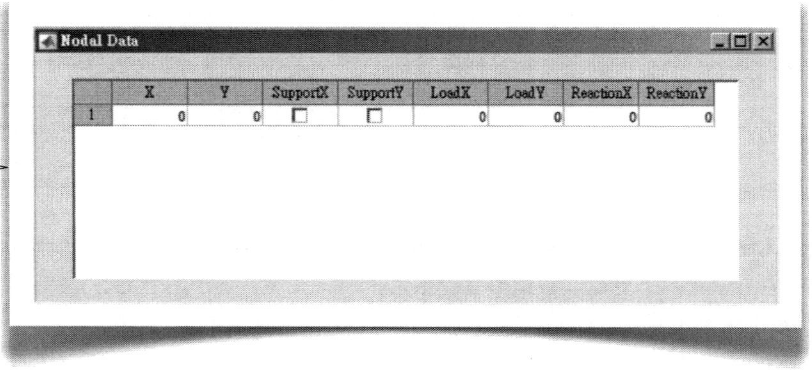

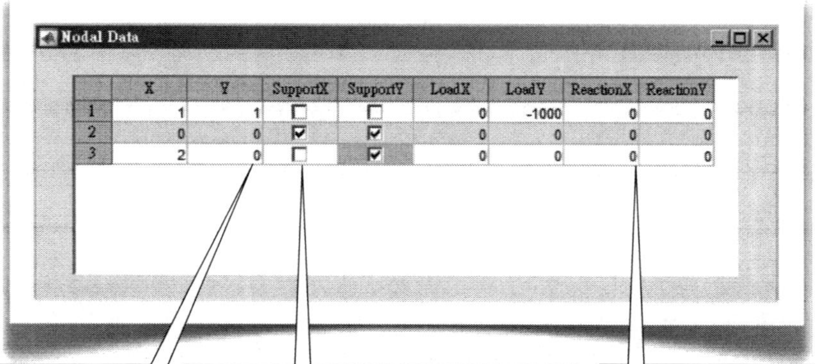

[3] The 1st, 2nd, 5th, and 6th fields are editable numeric fields; you can enter data directly. →

[4] The 3rd and 4th fields are logical fields; you simply check (true) or uncheck (false) a box. →

[5] The 7th and 8th fields are non-editable numeric fields. They store calculated data. ↓

About Example08_07a.m

[6] The program consists of a main function (lines 1-32), within which a nested function `cbKeyPressNodes` (lines 26-31) is defined, which serves as a callback function for the **UI-table** (see line 18); the callback function is triggered each time a key is pressed. The purpose of this callback function is to intercept a **down-arrow** key (↓), to add a row to the **UI-table**.

Lines 2-5 create a row of nodal data, a **structure** of eight fields as shown in [2]. Lines 6-9 create a **Figure** window.

Lines 10-16 prepare input data to the function `uitable` in lines 17-24. Line 10 converts the structure data `Nodes` to a **cell array** `data` because the input argument `data` in line 17 is required to be in cell array form. Lines 17-24 create a **UI-table** and specify the associated data (see lines 10 and 17), column names (see lines 11-12 and 19), column formats (lines 13-15 and 20), column editabilities (lines 16 and 21), and the callback function for the event when a key is pressed (line 18).

As the user enters data in the **UI-table**, the data (`data` in line 17) is automatically updated, and a callback function seems unnecessary. However, to allow the user to add a row to the **UI-table** by pressing the **down-arrow**, a callback function is triggered whenever a key is pressed (lines 18 and 26-31), to intercept a **down-arrow** key (↓).

By protocol, two arguments are passed to the callback function (line 26): a handle to the **UI-table** (`hTable`) and a handle to the pressed key (`hKey`). If the key is the **down-arrow** (line 27; also see Table 5.6a, page 229), a row is added to the **UI-table** (lines 28-29). #

8.7b Example: Truss Member Data

Example08_07b.m: Truss Member Data

[1] This program uses a **UI-table** to input the truss member data such as those listed in Table3.14b (page 157), as shown in [2]. This program is similar to Example08_07a.m and you should be able to read it by yourself. ↓

```
function Example08_07b
Members = struct('node1', 0, 'node2', 0, 'force', 0);
figure('Position', [30, 30, 260, 200], ...
    'Name', 'Member Data', ...
    'MenuBar', 'none', ...
    'NumberTitle', 'off')
uitable('Data', struct2cell(Members)', ...
    'KeyPressFcn', @cbKeyPressMembers, ...
    'ColumnName', {'Node1', 'Node2', 'Force'}, ...
    'ColumnEditable', logical([1 1 0]), ...
    'ColumnWidth', {60}, ...
    'Units', 'normalized', ...
    'Position', [.05 .1 .9 .8]);

    function cbKeyPressMembers(hTable, hKey)
        if strcmpi(hKey.Key, 'downarrow')
            n = size(hTable.Data, 1);
            hTable.Data(n+1,:) = {0 0 0};
        end
    end
end
```

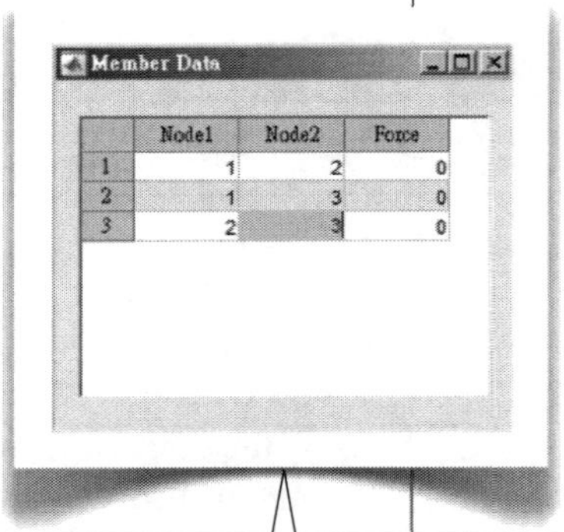

[2] Example08_07b.m creates a **UI-table** which has three numeric fields; the 3rd field is non-editable. Initially the **UI-table** has only one row. Each time you press the **down-arrow** key (↓), a row is added to the **UI-table**. Before typing data, click an editable cell and press the **down-arrow** m-1 times to add enough rows, where m is the number of truss members. #

Table 8.7 UI-Table Properties

Property	Description
`Position`	Location and size of uitable
`Data`	Table content, a cell array
`CellEditCallback`	Cell edit callback function
`KeyPressFcn`	Key press callback function
`ColumnName`	Column heading names
`ColumnFormat`	Cell display format
`ColumnEditable`	Ability to edit column cells
`ColumnWidth`	Width of table columns
`RowName`	Row heading names
`Parent`	Parent of uitable
`FontSize`	Font size

Details and More: Help>MATLAB>App Building>GUIDE or Programmatic Workflow>Components and Layout>Interactive Components>Uitable Properties

8.8 Example: Statically Determinate Trusses (Version 5.0)

Example08_08.m: Truss 5.0

[1] This is a GUI version of the program to solve statically determinate trusses, an improved version of Example06_08.m (pages 272-273). With the GUI, you can input truss data, plot the truss, solve the truss, and so on, in a much more intuitive way, reducing human mistakes (see [6-15], pages 325-326). (Continued at [2], next page.) ↵

```
function Example08_08
Nodes = struct('x', 0, 'y', 0, ...
    'supportx', false, 'supporty', false, ...
    'loadx', 0, 'loady', 0, ...
    'reactionx', 0, 'reactiony', 0);
Members = struct('node1',0, 'node2',0, 'force',0);
hf = figure('Position', [40, 20, 590, 450], ...
    'Name', 'Planar Truss: Untitled', ...
    'MenuBar', 'none', ...
    'NumberTitle', 'off')
axes('Position', [.05 .05 .475 .575]), axis off
data = struct2cell(Nodes)';
columnName = {'X', 'Y', 'SupportX', 'SupportY', ...
    'LoadX', 'LoadY', 'ReactionX', 'ReactionY'};
columnFormat = {'numeric', 'numeric', ...
    'logical', 'logical', ...
    'numeric', 'numeric', 'numeric', 'numeric'};
columnEditable = logical([1 1 1 1 1 1 0 0]);
hNodes = uitable('Data', data, ...
    'KeyPressFcn', @cbKeyPressNodes, ...
    'ColumnName', columnName, ...
    'ColumnFormat', columnFormat, ...
    'ColumnEditable', columnEditable, ...
    'ColumnWidth', {45 45 60 60 60 60 72 72}, ...
    'Units', 'normalized', ...
    'Position', [.05 .65 .9 .275]);
hMembers = uitable('Data', struct2cell(Members)', ...
    'KeyPressFcn', @cbKeyPressMembers, ...
    'ColumnName', {'Node1', 'Node2', 'Force'}, ...
    'ColumnEditable', logical([1 1 0]), ...
    'ColumnWidth', {54, 54, 72}, ...
    'Units', 'normalized', ...
    'Position', [.55 .325 .4 .275]);
```

[2] Example08_08.m (Continued). (Continued at [3], next page.) ↵

```
uicontrol('Style', 'pushbutton', ...
    'String', 'Plot', ...
    'Callback', @cbPlot, ...
    'Units', 'normalized', ...
    'Position', [.55 .225 .175 .075])
uicontrol('Style', 'pushbutton', ...
    'String', 'Solve', ...
    'Callback', @cbSolve, ...
    'Units', 'normalized', ...
    'Position', [.55 .135 .175 .075])
uicontrol('Style', 'pushbutton', ...
    'String', 'Open', ...
    'Callback', @cbOpen, ...
    'Units', 'normalized', ...
    'Position', [.775 .225 .175 .075])
uicontrol('Style', 'pushbutton', ...
    'String', 'Save As', ...
    'Callback', @cbSaveAs, ...
    'Units', 'normalized', ...
    'Position', [.775 .135 .175 .075])
uicontrol('Style', 'pushbutton', ...
    'String', 'Quit', ...
    'Callback', 'close', ...
    'Units', 'normalized', ...
    'Position', [.775 .05 .175 .075])
uicontrol('Style', 'text', ...
    'String', 'Nodal Data', ...
    'Units', 'normalized', ...
    'Position', [.425 .925 .2 .04])
uicontrol('Style', 'text', ...
    'String', 'Member Data', ...
    'Units', 'normalized', ...
    'Position', [.65 .6 .2 .04])

```

[3] Example08_08.m (Continued). (Continued at [4], next page.) ↵

```
    function cbPlot(~, ~)
        Nodes = cell2struct(hNodes.Data, fieldnames(Nodes), 2)';
        Members = cell2struct(hMembers.Data, fieldnames(Members), 2)';
        plotTruss(Nodes, Members)
    end

    function cbSolve(~, ~)
        Nodes = cell2struct(hNodes.Data, fieldnames(Nodes), 2)';
        Members = cell2struct(hMembers.Data, fieldnames(Members), 2)';
        [Nodes, Members] = solveTruss(Nodes, Members);
        hNodes.Data = permute(struct2cell(Nodes), [1 3 2])';
        hMembers.Data = permute(struct2cell(Members), [1 3 2])';
    end

    function cbOpen(~, ~)
        [file, path] = uigetfile('*.mat');
        if file
            Nodes = []; Members = [];
            load([path, file])
            hNodes.Data = permute(struct2cell(Nodes), [1 3 2])';
            hMembers.Data = permute(struct2cell(Members), [1 3 2])';
            hf.Name = ['Planar Truss: ', file];
        end
    end

    function cbSaveAs(~, ~)
        [file, path] = uiputfile('*.mat');
        if file
            Nodes = cell2struct(hNodes.Data, fieldnames(Nodes), 2)';
            Members = cell2struct(hMembers.Data, fieldnames(Members), 2)';
            save([path, file], 'Nodes', 'Members')
            hf.Name = ['Planar Truss: ', file];
        end
    end

    function cbKeyPressNodes(hTable, hKey)
        if strcmpi(hKey.Key, 'downarrow')
            n = size(hTable.Data, 1);
            hTable.Data(n+1,:) = {0 0 false false 0 0 0 0};
        end
    end

    function cbKeyPressMembers(hTable, hKey)
        if strcmpi(hKey.Key, 'downarrow')
            n = size(hTable.Data, 1);
            hTable.Data(n+1,:) = {0 0 0};
        end
    end
end

```

[4] Example08_08.m (Continued). (Continued at [5], next page.) ↵

```
function [outNodes, outMembers] = solveTruss(Nodes, Members)
n = size(Nodes,2); m = size(Members,2);
if (m+3) < 2*n
    disp('Unstable!')
    outNodes = 0; outMembers = 0; return
elseif (m+3) > 2*n
    disp('Statically indeterminate!')
    outNodes = 0; outMembers = 0; return
end
A = zeros(2*n, 2*n); loads = zeros(2*n,1); nsupport = 0;
for i = 1:n
    for j = 1:m
        if Members(j).node1 == i || Members(j).node2 == i
            if Members(j).node1 == i
                n1 = i; n2 = Members(j).node2;
            elseif Members(j).node2 == i
                n1 = i; n2 = Members(j).node1;
            end
            x1 = Nodes(n1).x; y1 = Nodes(n1).y;
            x2 = Nodes(n2).x; y2 = Nodes(n2).y;
            L = sqrt((x2-x1)^2+(y2-y1)^2);
            A(2*i-1,j) = (x2-x1)/L;
            A(2*i,  j) = (y2-y1)/L;
        end
    end
    if (Nodes(i).supportx == 1)
        nsupport = nsupport+1;
        A(2*i-1,m+nsupport) = 1;
    end
    if (Nodes(i).supporty == 1)
        nsupport = nsupport+1;
        A(2*i, m+nsupport) = 1;
    end
    loads(2*i-1) = -Nodes(i).loadx;
    loads(2*i)   = -Nodes(i).loady;
end
forces = A\loads;
for j = 1:m
    Members(j).force = forces(j);
end
nsupport = 0;
for i = 1:n
    Nodes(i).reactionx = 0;
    Nodes(i).reactiony = 0;
    if (Nodes(i).supportx == 1)
        nsupport = nsupport+1;
        Nodes(i).reactionx = forces(m+nsupport);
    end
    if (Nodes(i).supporty == 1)
        nsupport = nsupport+1;
        Nodes(i).reactiony = forces(m+nsupport);
    end
end
outNodes = Nodes; outMembers = Members;
disp('Solved successfully.')
end

```

[5] Example08_08.m (Continued). ↵

```
function plotTruss(Nodes, Members)
if (size(fieldnames(Nodes),1)<6 || size(fieldnames(Members),1)<2)
    disp('Truss data not complete'); return
end
n = length(Nodes); m = length(Members);
minX = Nodes(1).x; maxX = Nodes(1).x;
minY = Nodes(1).y; maxY = Nodes(1).y;
for k = 2:n
    if (Nodes(k).x < minX) minX = Nodes(k).x; end
    if (Nodes(k).x > maxX) maxX = Nodes(k).x; end
    if (Nodes(k).y < minY) minY = Nodes(k).y; end
    if (Nodes(k).y > maxY) maxY = Nodes(k).y; end
end
rangeX = maxX-minX; rangeY = maxY-minY;
axis([minX-rangeX/5, maxX+rangeX/5, minY-rangeY/5, maxY+rangeY/5])
ha = gca; delete(ha.Children)
axis equal off
hold on
for k = 1:m
    n1 = Members(k).node1; n2 = Members(k).node2;
    x = [Nodes(n1).x, Nodes(n2).x];
    y = [Nodes(n1).y, Nodes(n2).y];
    plot(x,y,'k-o', 'MarkerFaceColor', 'k')
end
for k = 1:n
    if Nodes(k).supportx
        x = [Nodes(k).x, Nodes(k).x-rangeX/20, Nodes(k).x-rangeX/20, Nodes(k).x];
        y = [Nodes(k).y, Nodes(k).y+rangeX/40, Nodes(k).y-rangeX/40, Nodes(k).y];
        plot(x,y,'k-')
    end
    if Nodes(k).supporty
        x = [Nodes(k).x, Nodes(k).x-rangeX/40, Nodes(k).x+rangeX/40, Nodes(k).x];
        y = [Nodes(k).y, Nodes(k).y-rangeX/20, Nodes(k).y-rangeX/20, Nodes(k).y];
        plot(x,y,'k-')
    end
end
end
```

[6] Run the program. This is the initial GUI, which has two UI-tables (**Nodal Data** and **Member Data**), 5 pushbuttons (**Plot**, **Solve**, **Open**, **Save As**, and **Quit**), and an invisible **Axes**. ↙

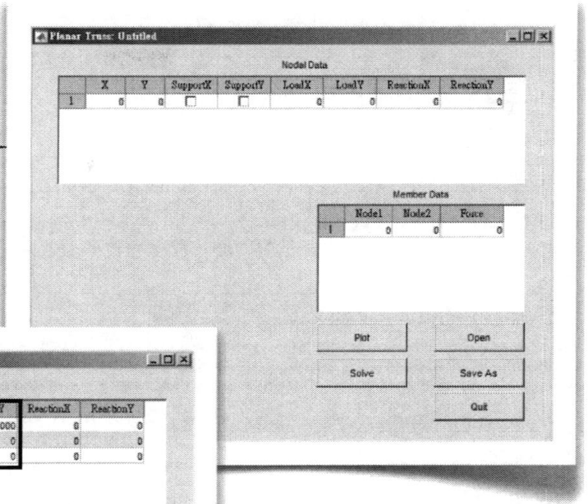

[7] Nodal data are input here (see 8.7a[2-5], page 318). Remember, before typing the data, click an editable cell and press the **down-arrow** n-1 times to add enough rows, where n is the number of nodes. →

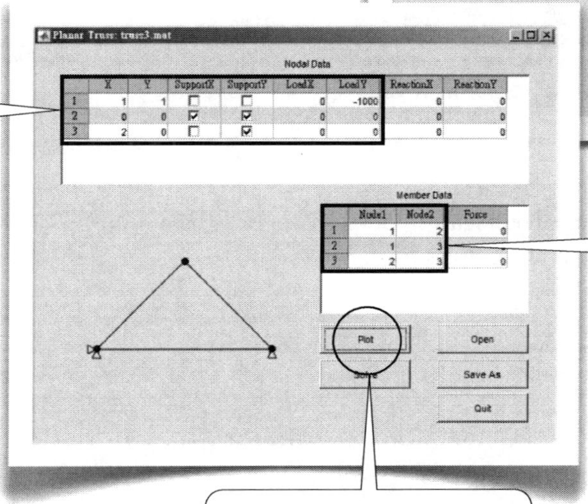

[8] Member data are input here (see 8.7b[2], page 319). Remember, before typing the data, click an editable cell and press the **down-arrow** m-1 times to add enough rows, where m is the number of truss members. ←

[9] Click **Plot** button to plot the truss on the **axes**. ↙

[11] The reaction forces are displayed here. ↘

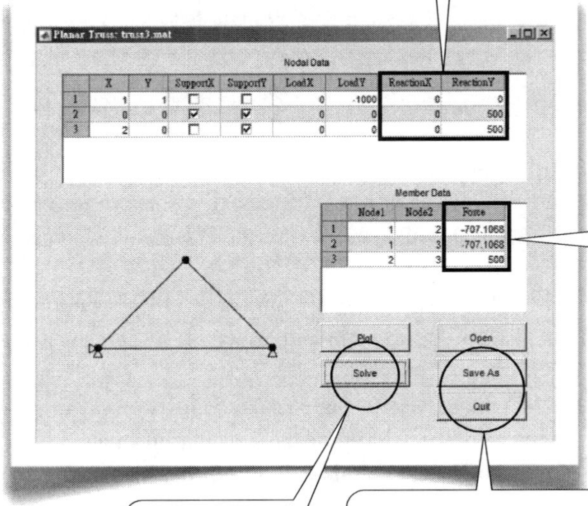

[12] The member forces are displayed here. ↙

[10] Click **Solve** button. ↑

[13] Save the file and quit the program. ↲

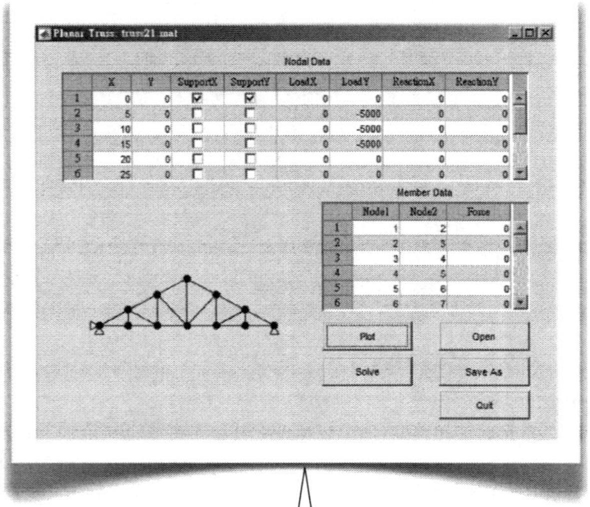

[14] As a second example, input nodal data and member data for the 21-bar truss (the shaded areas in Table 3.15a and Table 3.15b, page 168). →

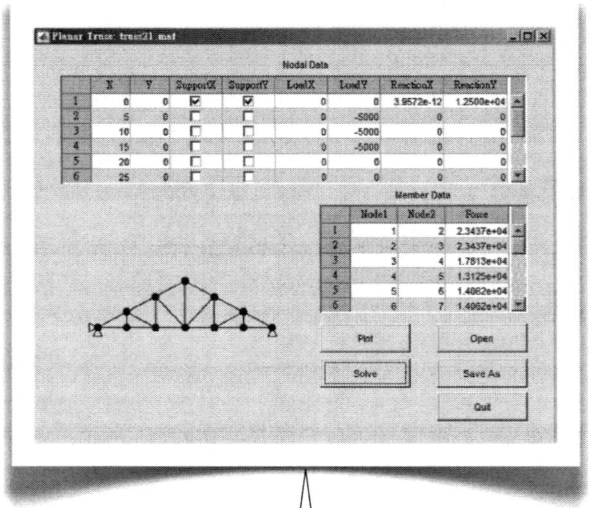

[15] And solve the truss. ↓

Program Structure

[16] This program consists of a main function (lines 1-116) and 2 local functions: `solveTruss` (lines 118-173) and `plotTruss` (lines 175-211). Within the main function (lines 1-116), 6 nested functions are defined: `cbPlot` (lines 68-72), `cbSolve` (lines 74-80), `cbOpen` (lines 82-91), `cbSaveAs` (lines 93-101), `cbKeyPressNodes` (lines 103-108), and `cbKeyPressMembers` (lines 110-115).

The local functions, `solveTruss` (lines 118-173) and `plotTruss` (lines 175-211) are the same as those in the previous versions (see the function `solveTruss` in pages 185-186 and the function `plotTruss` in page 273).

Two of the nested functions, `cbKeyPressNodes` (lines 103-108) and `cbKeyPressMembers` (lines 110-115) are the same as those in Section 8.7 (see lines 26-31 in Example08_07a.m, page 317; and lines 15-20 in Example08_07b.m, page 319).

The GUI

Lines 2-66 create an initial GUI as shown in [6], last page.

Lines 2-6 create initial truss data, a row of nodal data (lines 2-5) and a row of member data (line 6). Lines 7-10 create a **Figure** window. Line 11 creates an **Axes** on the lower-left of the **Figure** window and turns the **Axes** off, so the **Axes** is initially invisible [6].

Lines 12-26, almost the same as lines 10-24 of Example08_07a.m, page 317, create a **UI-table** for the input of nodal data. Lines 27-33, almost the same as lines 7-13 of Example08_07b.m, page 319, create a **UI-table** for the input of member data.

Lines 34-58 create five pushbuttons (**Plot**, **Solve**, **Open**, **Save As**, and **Quit**) on the lower-right of the **Figure** window (see [6], last page). A callback function is specified for each pushbutton (lines 36, 41, 46, 51, and 56).

Lines 59-66 create two static texts, **Nodal Data** and **Member Data**, as the titles of the two **UI-tables**, respectively.

↵

Callback Functions

[17] When the user clicks the **Plot** pushbutton, the callback function `cbPlot` (lines 68-72; also see line 36) is called. Its main task is to call the function `plotTruss` (lines 175-211; also see line 71). Before calling `plotTruss` in line 71, we need to prepare data for the function `plotTruss`, which uses two structure arrays `Nodes` and `Members`. The truss data stored in the UI-tables are cell arrays (see lines 12, 19 and 27). Before being passed to the function `plotTruss`, the truss data need to be converted from **cell arrays** to **structure arrays**, using the function `cell2struct` (lines 69-70), which has a syntax

```
s = cell2struct(c, fields, dim)
```

where the cell array *c* is converted to the structure array *s*. The argument *fields* can be a cell array of strings specifying the field names of *s*. The argument *dim* specifies which dimension of the cell array *c* is to be used as the fields in creating the structure array *s*. To explain the argument *dim*, we now use line 69 and the data in [7] (page 325) as an example. Set up a break point (Section 1.11) at line 69 and run the program. Complete steps [7-9] (pages 325). When the program stops at line 69, type

```
K>> size(hNodes.Data)
ans =
     3     8
```

The output shows that the cell array is of dimensions 3-by-8. That's why we specify the 2nd dimension in line 69 as the fields in creating the structure array. The function `cell2struct` outputs a 3-by-1 structure array of 8 fields. It, after the transpose, becomes a 1-by-3 structure array of 8 fields, which is what we need. Stepping through line 69 (1.11[19], page 42), you may confirm this by typing

```
K>> size(Nodes)
ans =
     1     3
```

The output is 1-by-3. In general it is a 1-by-*n* structure array, where *n* is the number of nodes. Similarly, line 70 converts the cell array `hMembers.Data` to a structure array `Members`, a 1-by-*m* structure array, where *m* is the number of truss members.

When the user clicks the **Solve** pushbutton, the callback function `cbSolve` (lines 74-80) is called. Its main task is to call the function `solveTruss` (lines 118-173; also see line 77). Before calling, the cell arrays need to be converted to structure arrays (lines 75-76) as before. And, after solving, the structure arrays need to be converted back to cell arrays (lines 78-79). The conversion of the **structure arrays** to **cell arrays** is done by using the function `struct2cell`, which has a syntax

```
c = struct2cell(s)
```

In line 78, the structure array `Nodes`, which is a 1-by-3 structure array of 8 fields, is first converted to an 8-by-1-by-3 cell array. Then the function `permute` is used to rearrange the dimensions: switching the 2nd and 3rd dimensions. It becomes an 8-by-3-by-1 cell array, equivalent to an 8-by-3 cell array (remember that if the last dimension size is one, it can be simply neglected). After the transpose, it becomes a 3-by-8 cell array, which is what we need. Similarly, line 79 converts the structure array `Members` to a cell array `hMembers.Data`.

When the user clicks the **Open** pushbutton, the callback function `cbOpen` (lines 82-91) is called. It requests a file name (line 83), loads the variables (`Nodes` and `Members`) from the file (line 86), converts the structure arrays to cell arrays (lines 87-88), and changes the title of the **Figure** window (line 89).

When the user clicks the **Save As** pushbutton, the callback function `cbSaveAs` (lines 93-101) is called. It requests a file name (line 94), converts the cell arrays to structure arrays (lines 96-97), saves the variables (`Nodes` and `Members`) to the file (line 98), and changes the title of the **Figure** window (line 99). #

8.9 GUIDE: Graphical User Interface Development Environment

Three Ways to Build a GUI

[1] You can create a GUI for a program in three ways: First, create the GUI programmatically, as demonstrated in Sections 8-1 through 8-8. Second, create the GUI using GUIDE, as demonstrated in Section 1.19. You may create a GUI with GUIDE first and then modify it programmatically, but you cannot create a GUI programmatically and then modify it with GUIDE. Third, create the GUI using **App Designer**, new in R2016a, as demonstrated in Section 1.20.

The approach you choose depends on your experience, your preferences, and your goals (*Details and More: Help>MATLAB>App Building>Ways to Build Apps*). An advantage of using GUIDE or **App Designer** is that you can visually arrange the UI components. With the programmatic approach, you usually guess an approximate location and size for a UI component, and then adjust it later with several trials.

This section implements the same functionalities as demonstrated in 8.8[6-15] (pages 325-326) using GUIDE. In the next section, we'll create the same functionalities using **App Designer**. ↙

[2] To start **GUIDE**, on **Command Window**, type →

```
>> guide
```

[3] A **Blank GUI** is displayed. ↓

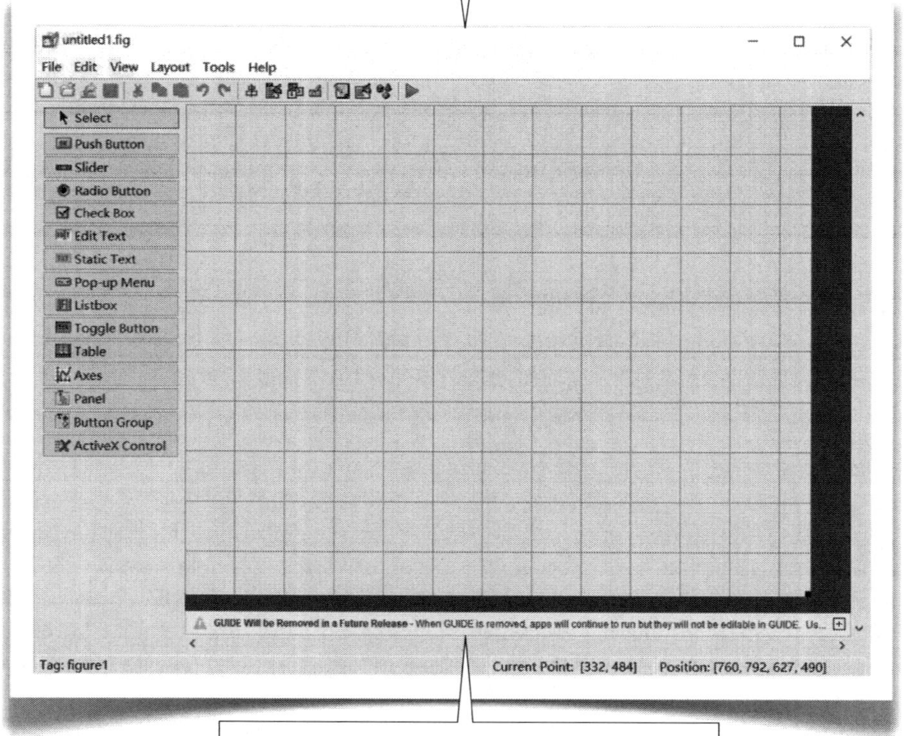

[4] A warning message says that the GUIDE will be removed in a future release. ↲

[5] A **Figure** object is created. ↓

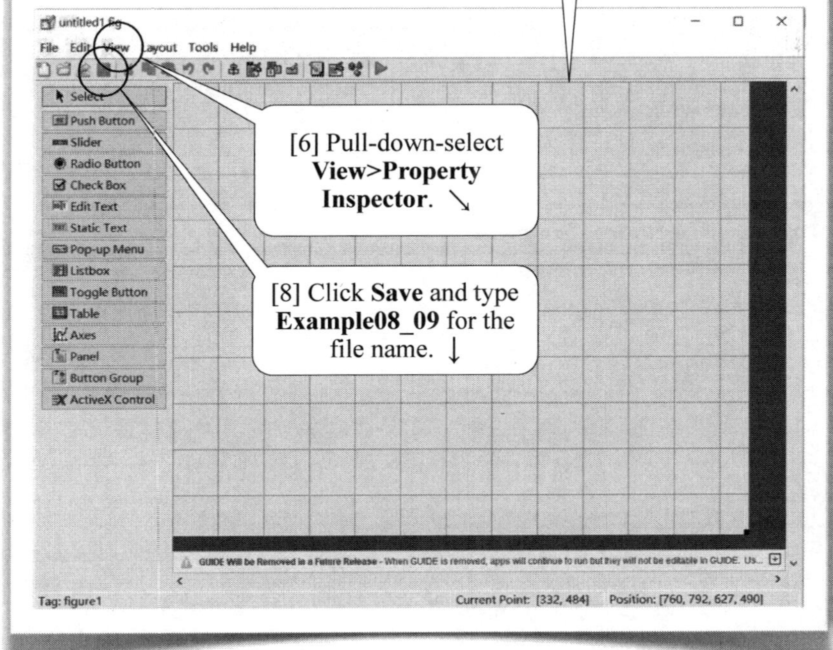

[6] Pull-down-select **View>Property Inspector**. ↘

[8] Click **Save** and type **Example08_09** for the file name. ↓

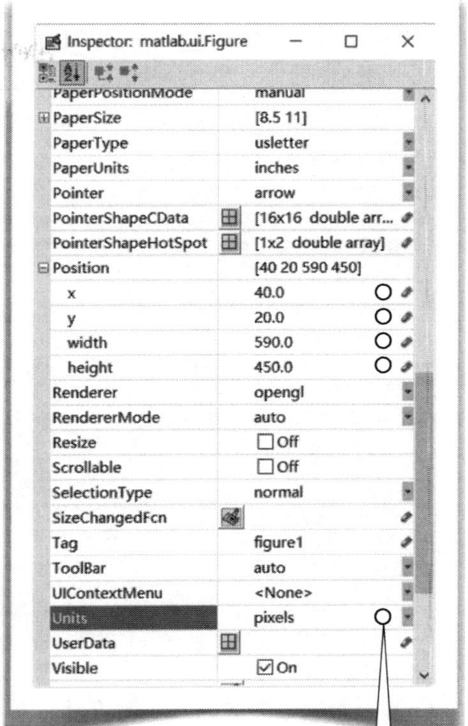

[7] In the **Property Inspector**, the properties are arranged in alphabetical order. Set **Units** to **pixels** and **Position** (click + to expand it if needed) to [40 20 590 450] as shown. Don't close the **Property Inspector**. ↖

[9] Two files are created in the **Current Folder**: Example08_09.fig and Example08_09.m. The **.fig** file contains GUI components and the **.m** file is a program, which is opened in the **Editor** window like this. We'll add statements to this file as we create GUI components. ↵

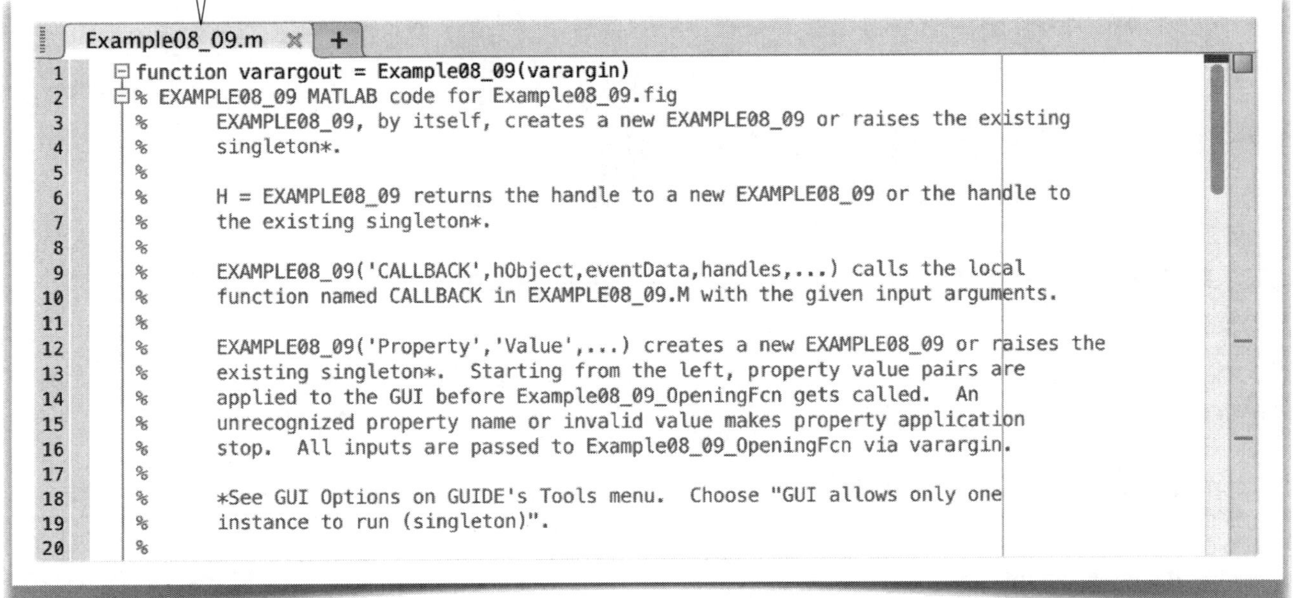

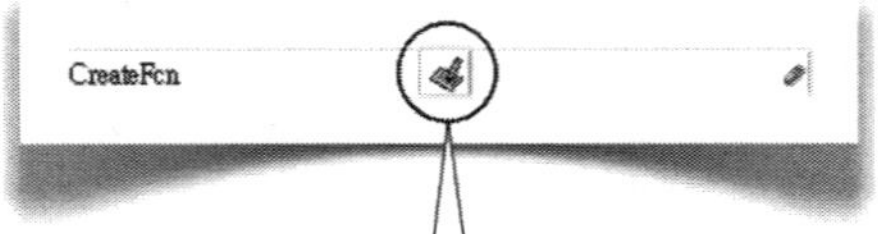

[10] Note that the only graphic object now is the **Figure** ([5], last page) and it is highlighted. In the **Property Inspector**, click the button next to **CreateFcn**. We now define a callback function that is executed when the **Figure** object is created. →

[11] On the **Editor** window, a function **figure1_CreateFcn** is created. Append these statements to the end of the function (don't include the statement numbers). Lines 3-7 are duplicated from lines 2-6, Example08_08, page 320. The `global` statement allows variables to pass to other functions. We mentioned (3.5a[6-7], pages 135-136) that if an `end` statement is omitted, a function closes at the end of the file or another function is encountered. We'll follow this practice; i.e., every function in Example08_09.m will not have an `end` statement at the end of the function. ↙

```
1   global hf Nodes Members
2   hf = hObject;
3   Nodes = struct('x', 0, 'y', 0, ...
4       'supportx', false, 'supporty', false, ...
5       'loadx', 0, 'loady', 0, ...
6       'reactionx', 0, 'reactiony', 0);
7   Members = struct('node1', 0, 'node2', 0, 'force', 0);
```

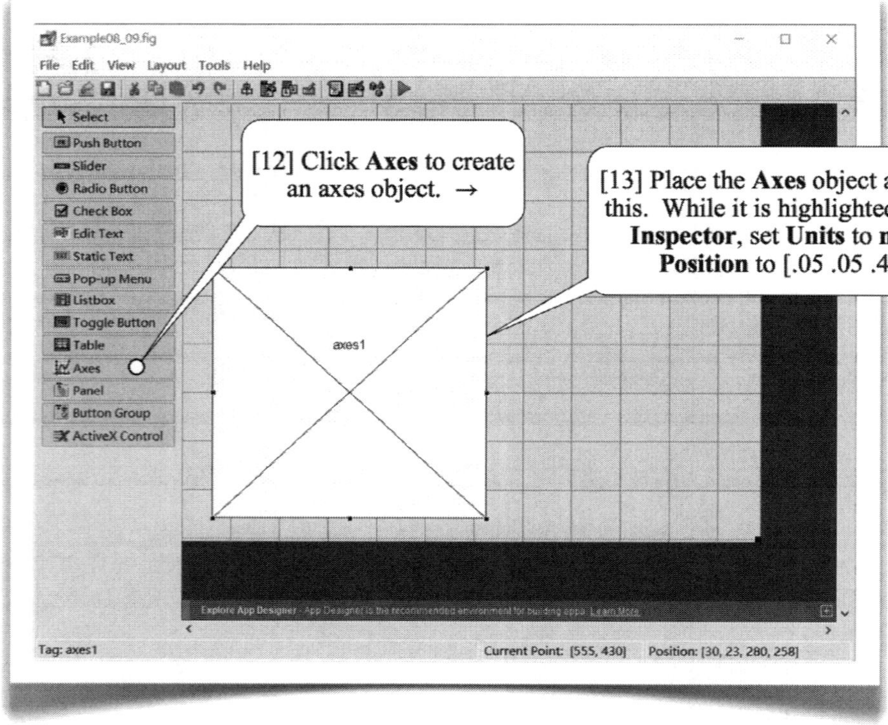

[12] Click **Axes** to create an axes object. →

[13] Place the **Axes** object approximately like this. While it is highlighted, in the **Property Inspector**, set **Units** to **normalized** and **Position** to [.05 .05 .475 .575]. ↙

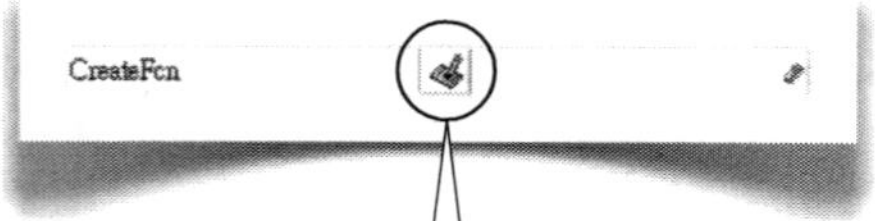

[14] In the **Property Inspector**, click the button next to **CreateFcn**. We now define a callback function that is executed when the **Axes** object is created. →

```
8   axis off
```

[15] On the **Editor** window, a function **axes1_CreateFcn** is created. Append this statement to the end of the function (don't include the statement number). ↵

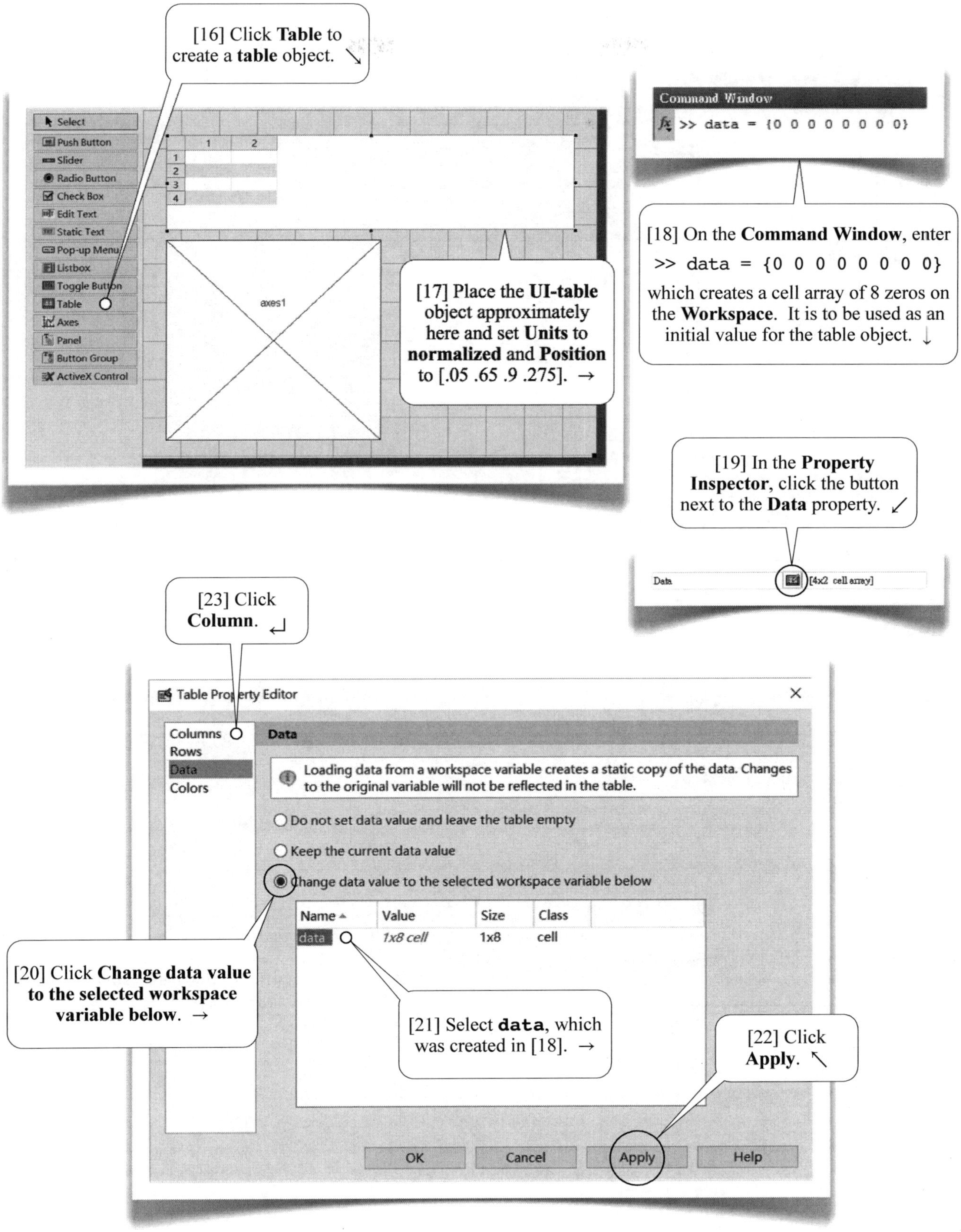

[16] Click **Table** to create a **table** object. ↘
Select
Push Button
Slider
Radio Button
Check Box
Edit Text
Static Text
Pop-up Menu
Listbox
Toggle Button
Table
Axes
Panel
Button Group
ActiveX Control
axes1
[17] Place the **UI-table** object approximately here and set **Units** to **normalized** and **Position** to [.05 .65 .9 .275]. →
Command Window
>> data = {0 0 0 0 0 0 0 0}
[18] On the **Command Window**, enter
>> data = {0 0 0 0 0 0 0 0}
which creates a cell array of 8 zeros on the **Workspace**. It is to be used as an initial value for the table object. ↓
[19] In the **Property Inspector**, click the button next to the **Data** property. ↙
Data
[4x2 cell array]
[23] Click **Column**. ↵
Table Property Editor
Columns
Rows
Data
Colors
Data
Loading data from a workspace variable creates a static copy of the data. Changes to the original variable will not be reflected in the table.
Do not set data value and leave the table empty
Keep the current data value
Change data value to the selected workspace variable below
Name
Value
Size
Class
data
1x8 cell
1x8
cell
[20] Click **Change data value to the selected workspace variable below**. →
[21] Select **data**, which was created in [18]. →
[22] Click **Apply**. ↖
OK
Cancel
Apply
Help

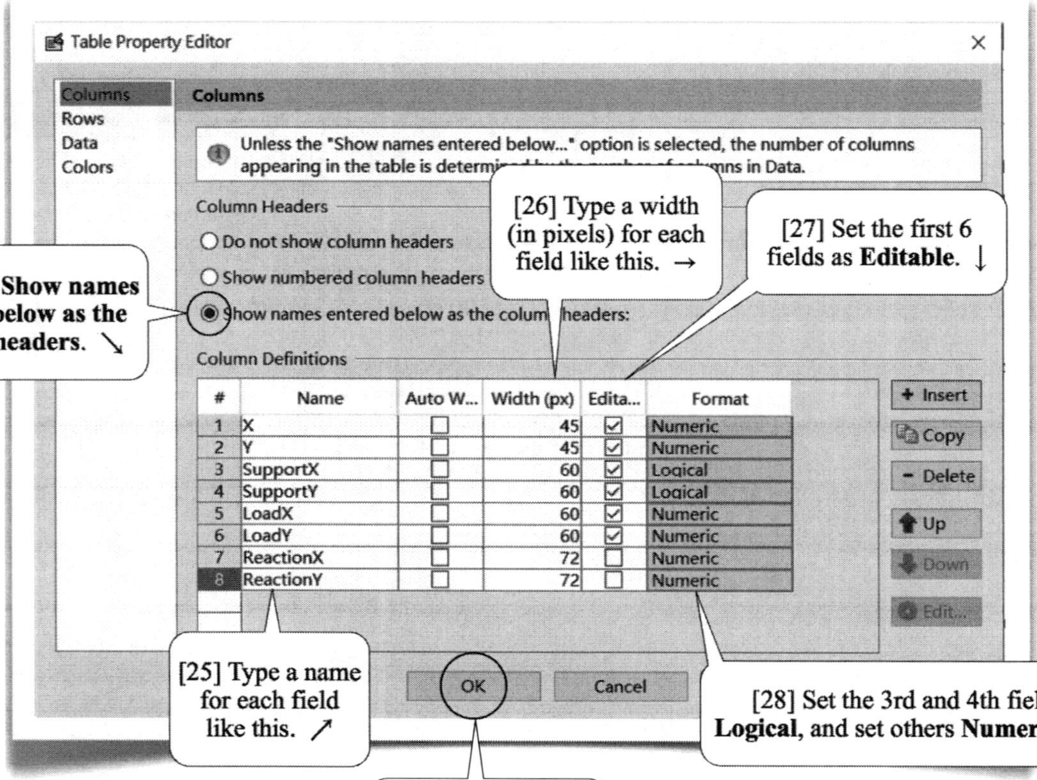

[24] Click **Show names entered below as the column headers.** ↘

[25] Type a name for each field like this. ↗

[26] Type a width (in pixels) for each field like this. →

[27] Set the first 6 fields as **Editable.** ↓

[28] Set the 3rd and 4th fields **Logical**, and set others **Numeric**. ↙

[29] Click **OK**. ←

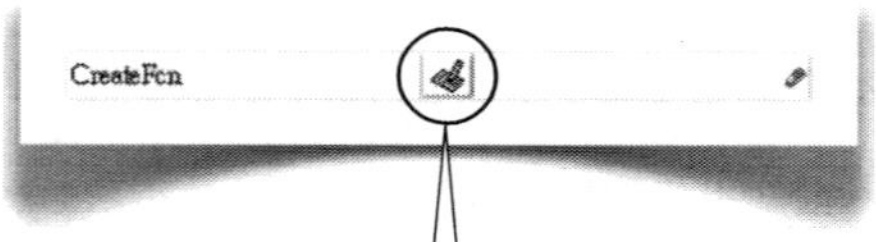

[30] Click the button next to **CreateFcn**. →

[31] On the **Editor** window, a function **uitable1_CreateFcn** is created. Append these two statements to the end of the function. ↙

```
global hNodes
hNodes = hObject;
```

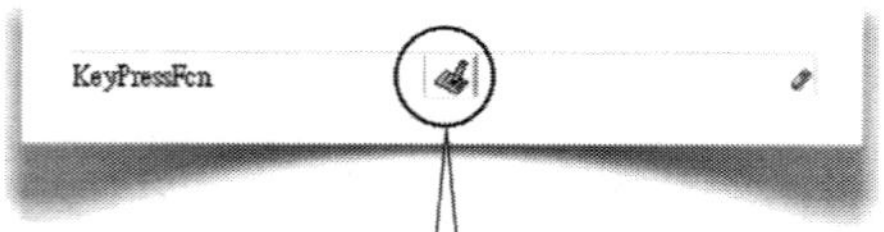

[32] Click the button next to **KeyPressFcn**. We now define a callback function that will be executed when a key is pressed. →

[33] On the **Editor** window, a function **uitable1_KeyPressFcn** is created. Append these statements to the end of the function, which are adapted from lines 104-107, Example08_08.m, page 322. The variable `hObject` is a handle to the **table** object, and `eventdata` is a handle to the pressed key. ↵

```
if strcmpi(eventdata.Key, 'downarrow')
    n = size(hObject.Data, 1);
    hObject.Data(n+1,:) = {0 0 false false 0 0 0 0};
end
```

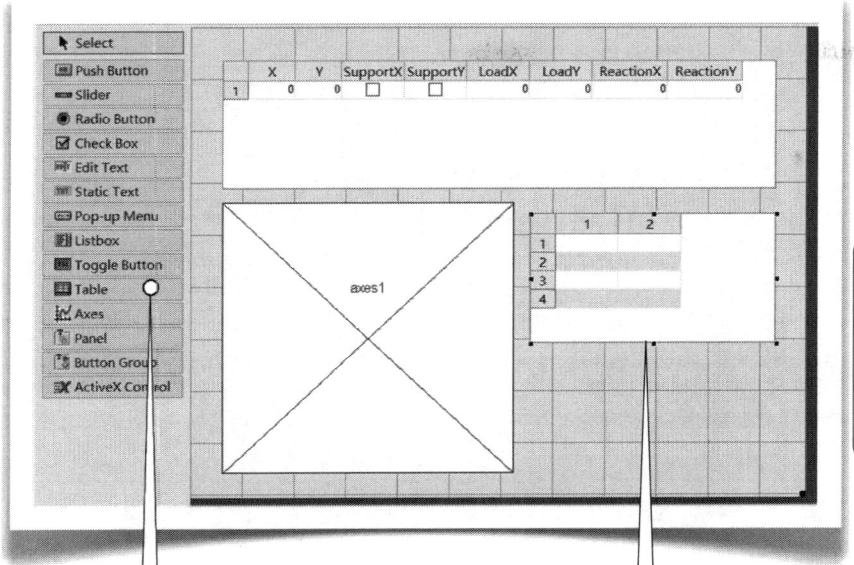

[34] Click **Table** to create a **table** object. →

[35] Place the **UI-table** object approximately here and set **Units** to **normalized** and **Position** to [.55 .325 .4 .275]. ↑

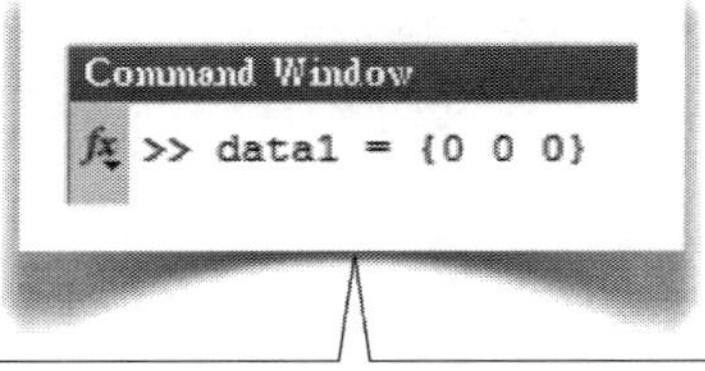

[36] On the **Command Window**, enter

```
>> data1 = {0 0 0}
```

which creates a cell array of three zeros on the **Workspace**. It is to be used as the initial data values for the newly created **table** object. ↓

[37] Click the button next to the **Data** property. ↙

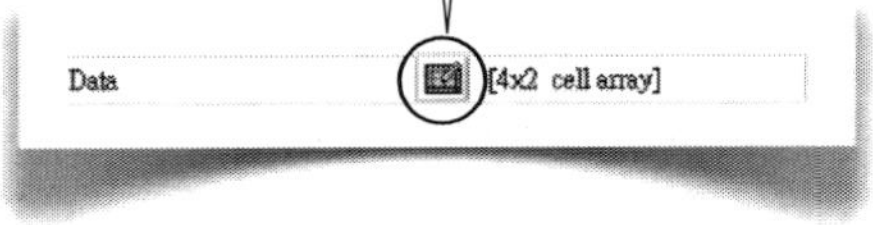

[41] Click **Column**. ↵

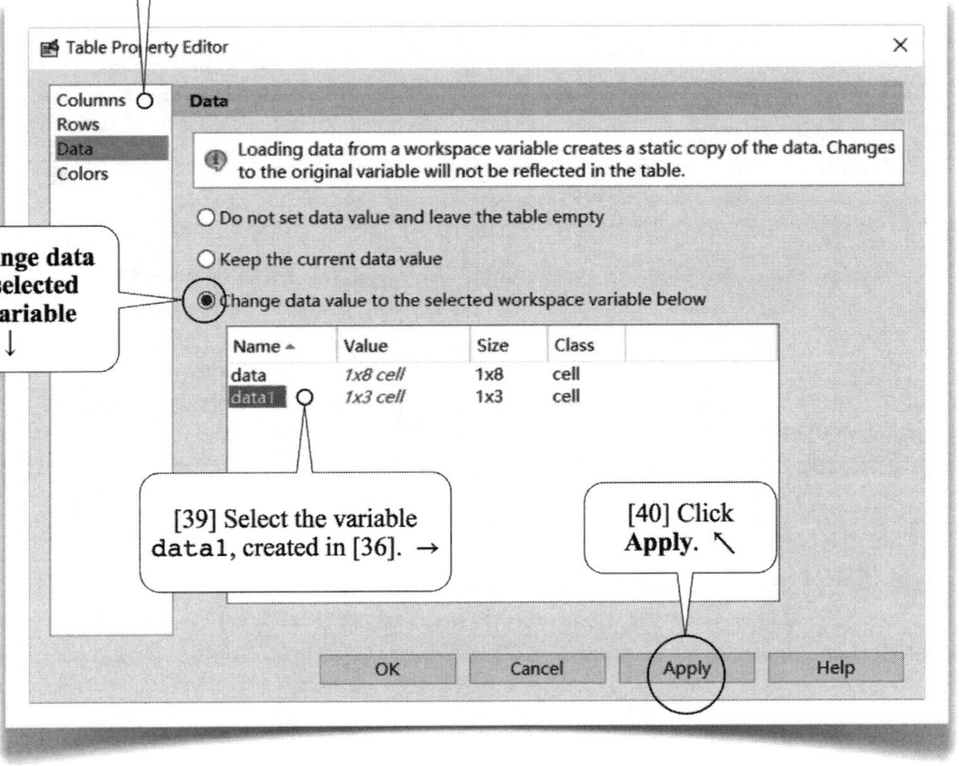

[38] Click **Change data value to the selected workspace variable below**. ↓

[39] Select the variable `data1`, created in [36]. →

[40] Click **Apply**. ↖

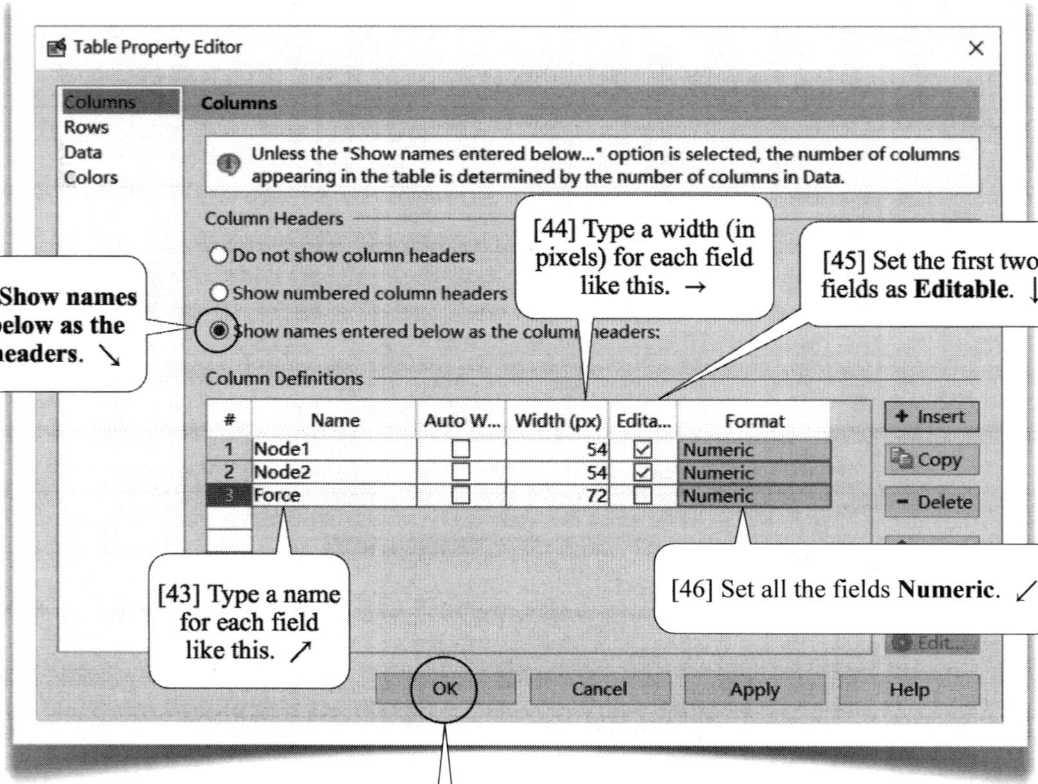

[42] Click **Show names entered below as the column headers.** ↘

[43] Type a name for each field like this. ↗

[44] Type a width (in pixels) for each field like this. →

[45] Set the first two fields as **Editable**. ↓

[46] Set all the fields **Numeric**. ↙

[47] Click **OK**. ↙

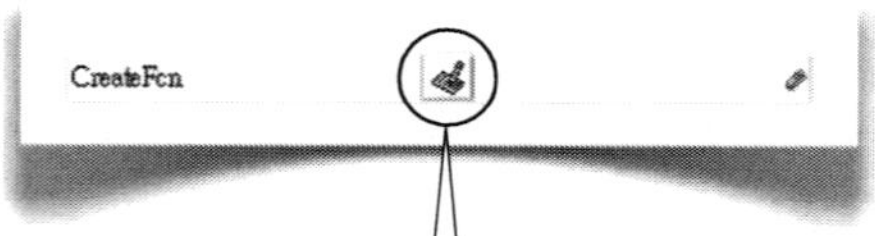

[48] Click the button next to **CreateFcn**. →

[49] On the **Editor** window, a function **uitable2_CreateFcn** is created. Append these two statements to the end of the function. ↙

```
global hMembers
hMembers = hObject;
```

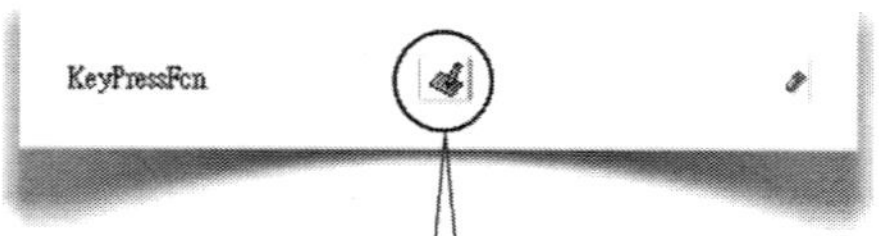

[50] Click the button next to **KeyPressFcn**. →

[51] On the **Editor** window, a function **uitable2_KeyPressFcn** is created. Append these statements to the end of the function. These statements are adapted from lines 111-114, Example08_08.m, page 322. The variable `hObject` is a handle to the **table** object, and `eventdata` is a handle to the pressed key. ↵

```
if strcmpi(eventdata.Key, 'downarrow')
    n = size(hObject.Data, 1);
    hObject.Data(n+1,:) = {0 0 0};
end
```

[52, 54, 56, 58, 60] Click **Push Button** to create a pushbutton object. ↘

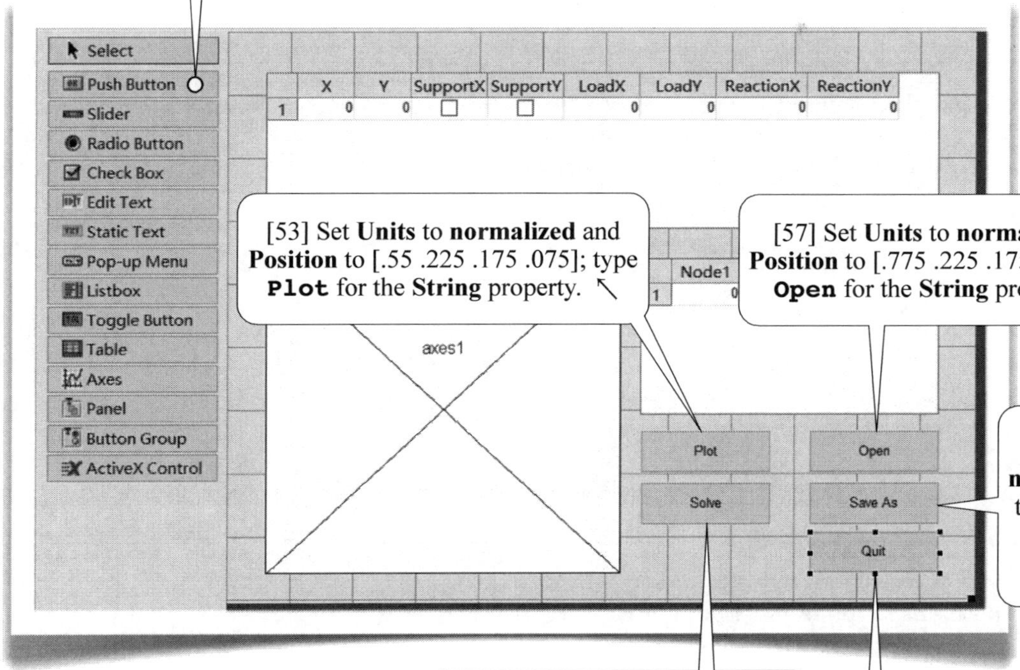

[53] Set **Units** to **normalized** and **Position** to [.55 .225 .175 .075]; type **`Plot`** for the **String** property. ↖

[57] Set **Units** to **normalized** and **Position** to [.775 .225 .175 .075]; type **`Open`** for the **String** property. ↖

[59] Set **Units** to **normalized** and **Position** to [.775 .135 .175 .075]; type **`Save As`** for the **String** property. ↖

[55] Set **Units** to **normalized** and **Position** to [.55 .135 .175 .075]; type **`Solve`** for the **String** property. ↖

[61] Set **Units** to **normalized** and **Position** to [.775 .05 .175 .075]; type **`Quit`** for the **String** property and **type `'close'`** (with or without the quotes) for the **Callback** property. A single-line callback function can be defined in this way. ↙

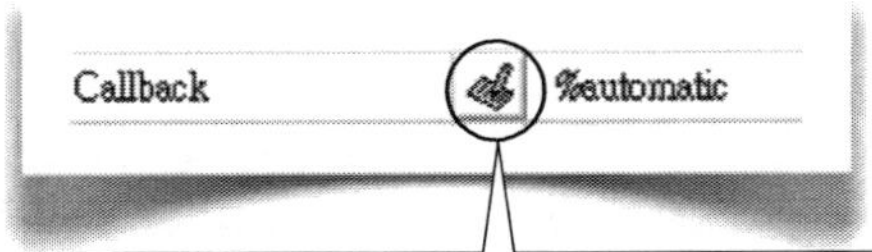

[62] Highlight any **Push Button** other than the **Quit** button and click the button next to **Callback**. On the **Editor** window, four callback functions are created: **pushbutton1_Callback**, **pushbutton2_Callback**, **pushbutton3_Callback**, and **pushbutton4_Callback**. ↓

[63] Append these statements to **pushbutton1_Callback**. The last three lines are duplicated from lines 69-71, Example08_08.m, page 322. ↵

```
global Nodes Members hNodes hMembers
Nodes = cell2struct(hNodes.Data, fieldnames(Nodes), 2)';
Members = cell2struct(hMembers.Data, fieldnames(Members), 2)';
plotTruss(Nodes, Members)
```

[64] Append these statements to **pushbutton2_Callback**. The last five lines are duplicated from lines 75-79, Example08_08.m, page 322. ↓

```
global Nodes Members hNodes hMembers
Nodes = cell2struct(hNodes.Data, fieldnames(Nodes), 2)';
Members = cell2struct(hMembers.Data, fieldnames(Members), 2)';
[Nodes, Members] = solveTruss(Nodes, Members);
hNodes.Data = permute(struct2cell(Nodes), [1 3 2])';
hMembers.Data = permute(struct2cell(Members), [1 3 2])';
```

[65] Append these statements to **pushbutton3_Callback**. The last eight lines are duplicates of lines 83-90, Example08_08.m, page 322. ↓

```
global Nodes Members hNodes hMembers hf
[file, path] = uigetfile('*.mat');
if file
    Nodes = []; Members = [];
    load([path, file])
    hNodes.Data = permute(struct2cell(Nodes), [1 3 2])';
    hMembers.Data = permute(struct2cell(Members), [1 3 2])';
    hf.Name = ['Planar Truss: ', file];
end
```

[66] Append these statements to **pushbutton4_Callback**. The last seven lines are duplicates of lines 94-100, Example08_08.m, page 322. ↵

```
global Nodes Members hNodes hMembers hf
[file, path] = uiputfile('*.mat');
if file
    Nodes = cell2struct(hNodes.Data, fieldnames(Nodes), 2)';
    Members = cell2struct(hMembers.Data, fieldnames(Members), 2)';
    save([path, file], 'Nodes', 'Members')
    hf.Name = ['Planar Truss: ', file];
end
```

[67, 69] Click **Static Text** to create a text object. →

[68] Set **Units** to **normalized** and **Position** to [.425 .925 .2 .04]; type **`Nodal Data`** for the **String** property. ←

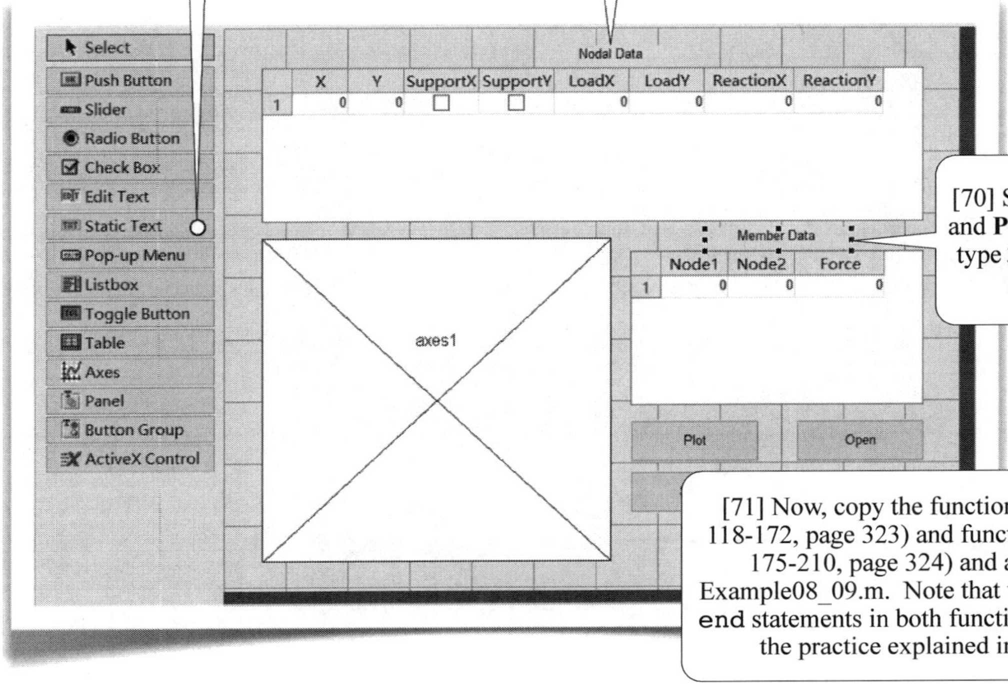

[70] Set **Units** to **normalized** and **Position** to [.65 .6 .2 .04]; type **`Member Data`** for the **String** property. ↓

[71] Now, copy the function `solveTruss` (lines 118-172, page 323) and function `plotTruss` (lines 175-210, page 324) and append to the end of Example08_09.m. Note that we didn't include the last `end` statements in both functions to be consistent with the practice explained in [11], page 330. ↓

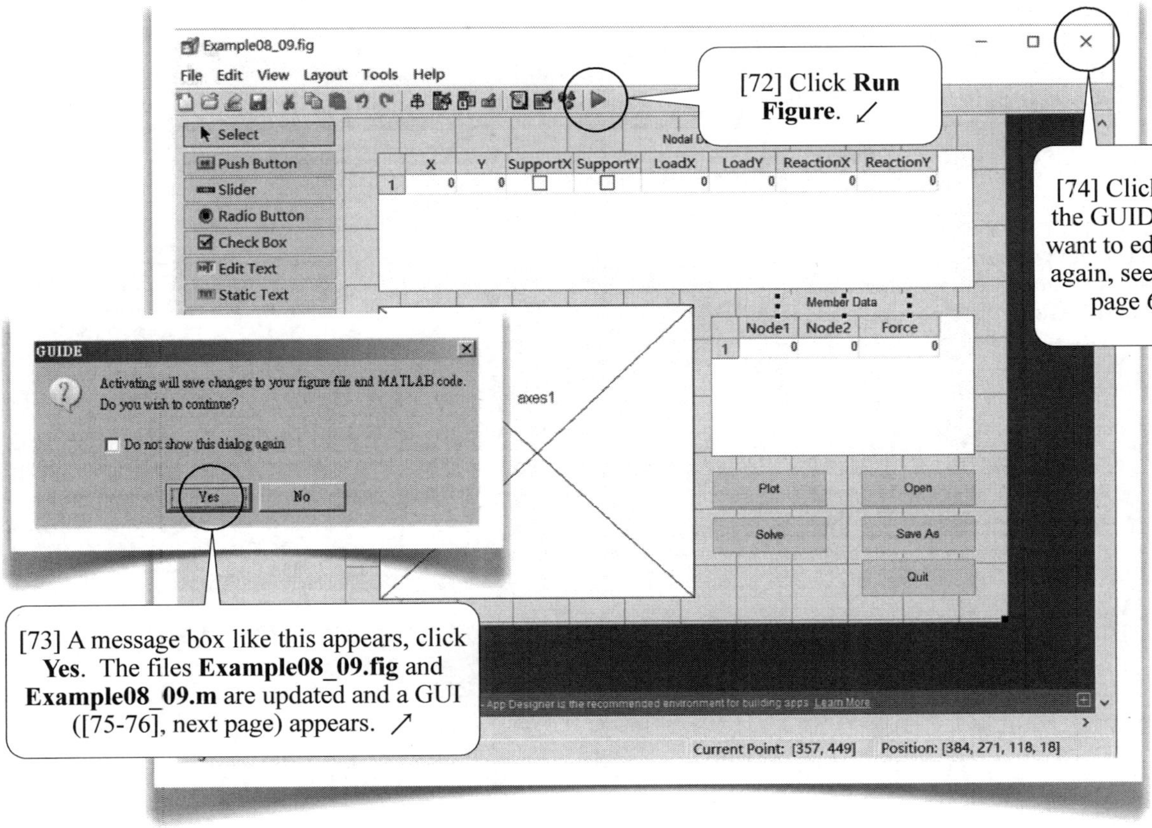

[72] Click **Run Figure**. ↙

[73] A message box like this appears, click **Yes**. The files **Example08_09.fig** and **Example08_09.m** are updated and a GUI ([75-76], next page) appears. ↗

[74] Click to close the GUIDE. If you want to edit the GUI again, see 1.19[37], page 62. ↲

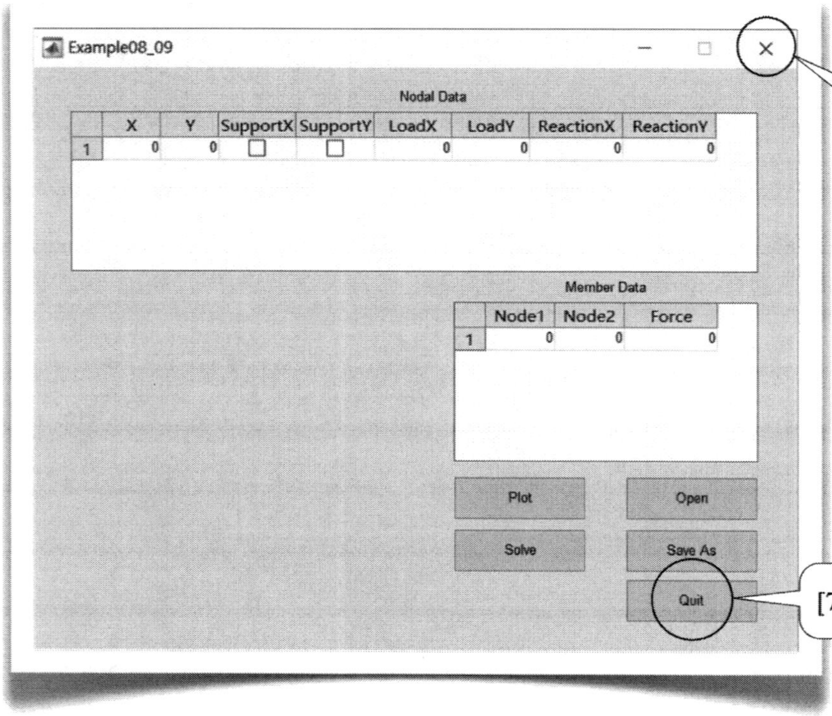

[76] You also may click here to close the GUI. ↙

[75] Click **Quit**. ↑

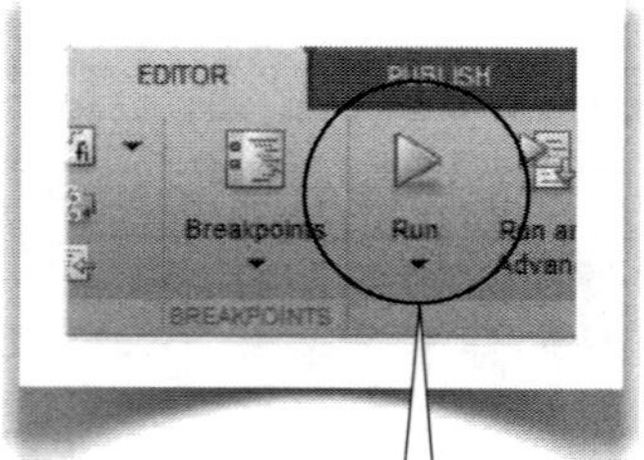

[77] To run the program, click the **Run** button in the **Script Editor**. ↘

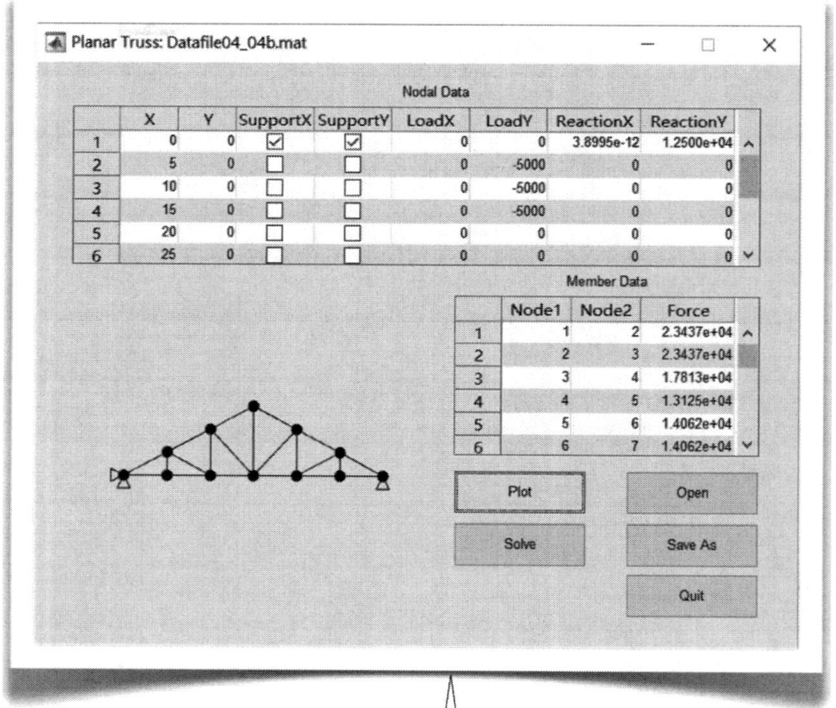

[78] Now, you can test-run the program, following the steps in 8.8[6-15], pages 325-326. #

8.10 App Designer

[1] Introduced in R2016a, **App Designer** provides more interactive components and a more intuitive way of building **apps** (see *Help>MATLAB>App Building>App Designer*) than **GUIDE**. As mentioned in 1.20[36] (page 67), for a small program, I personally prefer the programmatic approach (Sections 8.1-8.8); for a medium to large-scaled program, the newest introduced **App Designer** is usually recommended. This section demonstrates the use of **App Designer** to create an **app** that has the same functionality as the ones created in the last two sections. Some of the concepts that were already introduced in Section 1.20 are reiterated here, as a review of **App Designer**. →

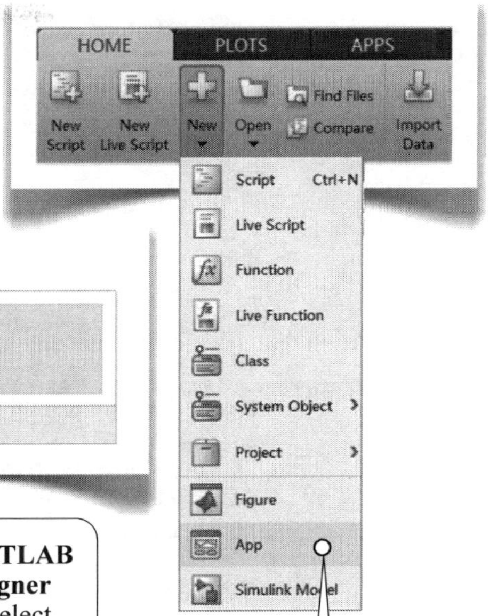

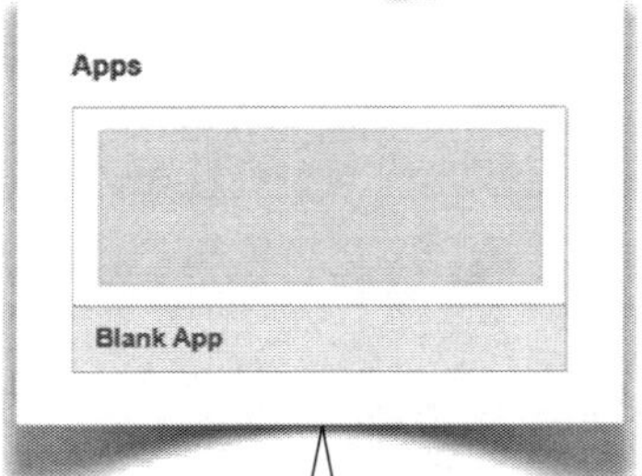

[2] Pull-down-select **New>App**. Or type ↖

>> appdesigner

[3] In a **MATLAB App Designer** window, select **Blank App**. ←

[4] An **App Designer** window appears. All the **app**-building tasks will be done within this environment. →

[5] The default name for the new **app** is **app1.mlapp**. An **app** created by **App Designer** has a file extension **.mlapp**. ↓

[6] You may switch between **Design View** and **Code View**. The **Design View** lets you arrange components in a **Figure**, while the **Code View** lets you work on functions (e.g., callback functions). Initially, we're in **Design View**. ↓

[9] The **COMPONENT BROWSER** displays the names of existing components. A **Figure** with the name **app.UIFigure** is preexisting. Click the name (or the **Figure** in [7]) to highlight it. ↓

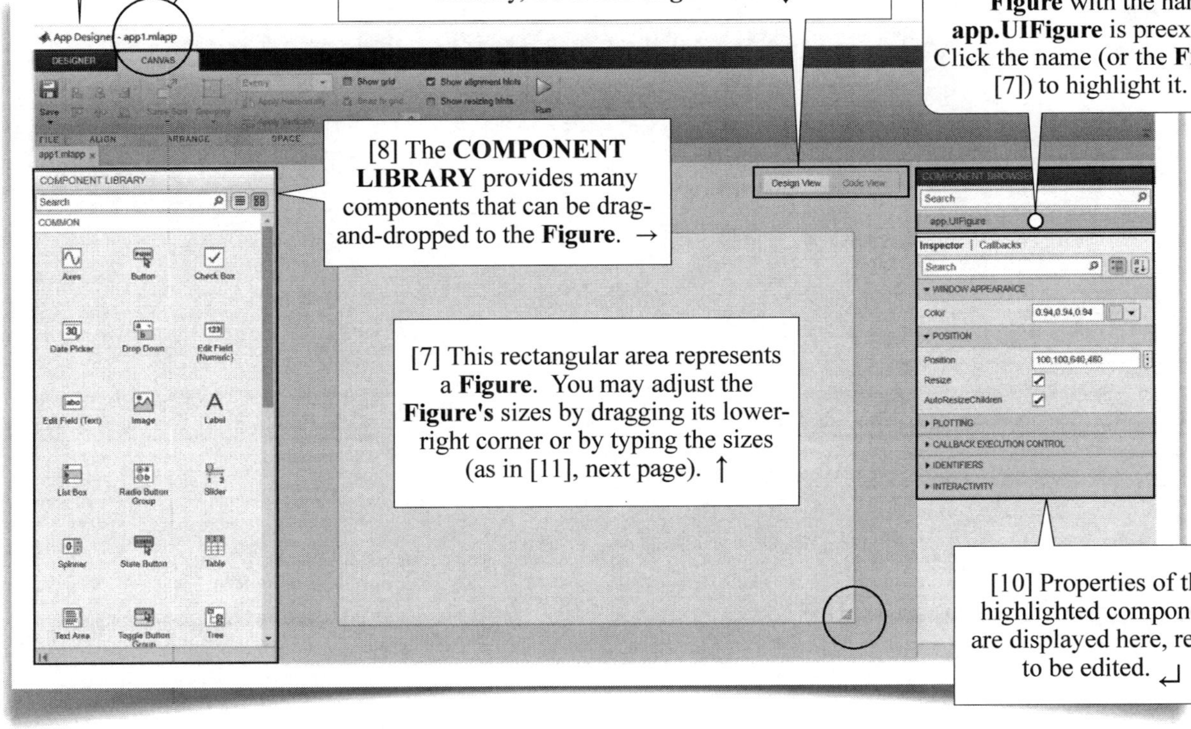

[8] The **COMPONENT LIBRARY** provides many components that can be drag-and-dropped to the **Figure**. →

[7] This rectangular area represents a **Figure**. You may adjust the **Figure's** sizes by dragging its lower-right corner or by typing the sizes (as in [11], next page). ↑

[10] Properties of the highlighted component are displayed here, ready to be edited. ↵

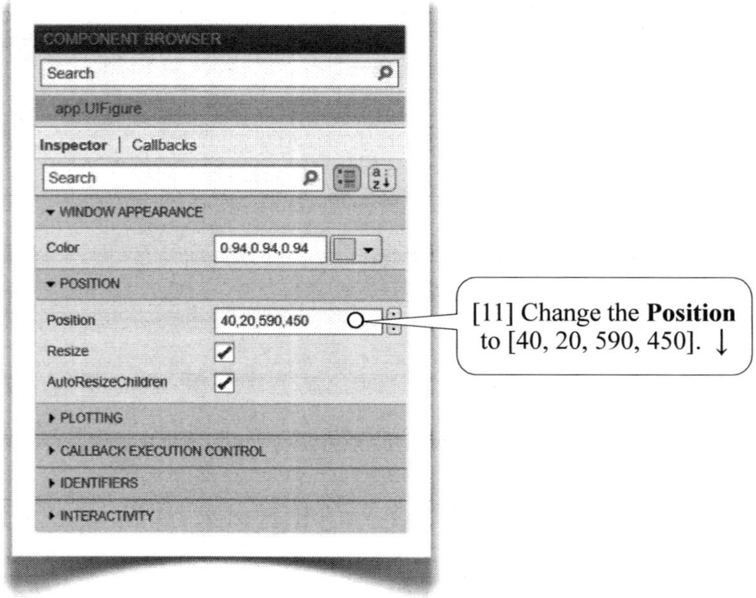
COMPONENT BROWSER
app.UIFigure
Inspector | Callbacks
WINDOW APPEARANCE
Color 0.94,0.94,0.94
POSITION
Position 40,20,590,450
Resize
AutoResizeChildren
PLOTTING
CALLBACK EXECUTION CONTROL
IDENTIFIERS
INTERACTIVITY
[11] Change the **Position** to [40, 20, 590, 450]. ↓

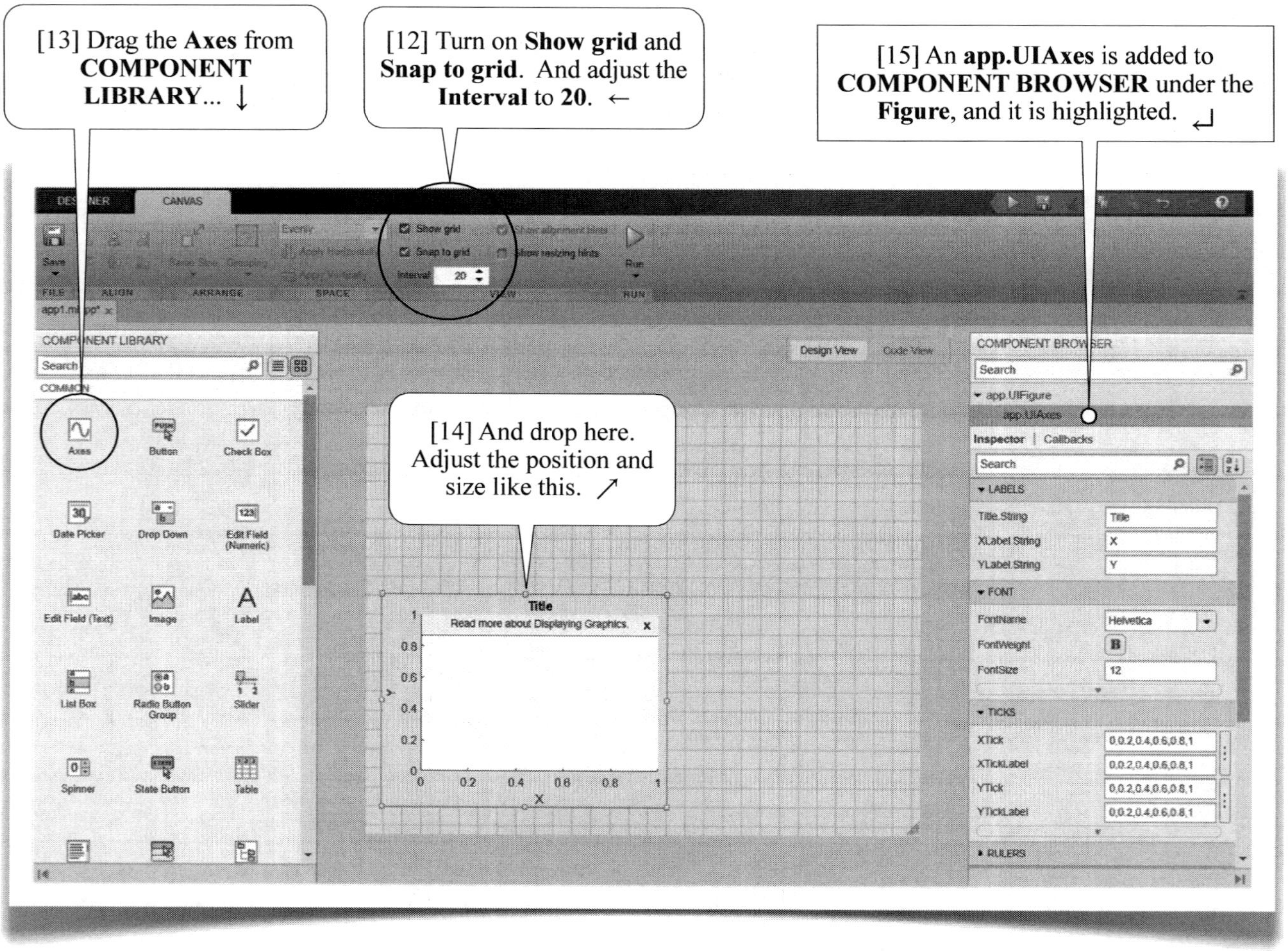
[13] Drag the **Axes** from **COMPONENT LIBRARY**... ↓
[12] Turn on **Show grid** and **Snap to grid**. And adjust the **Interval** to **20**. ←
[15] An **app.UIAxes** is added to **COMPONENT BROWSER** under the **Figure**, and it is highlighted. ↲
[14] And drop here. Adjust the position and size like this. ↗

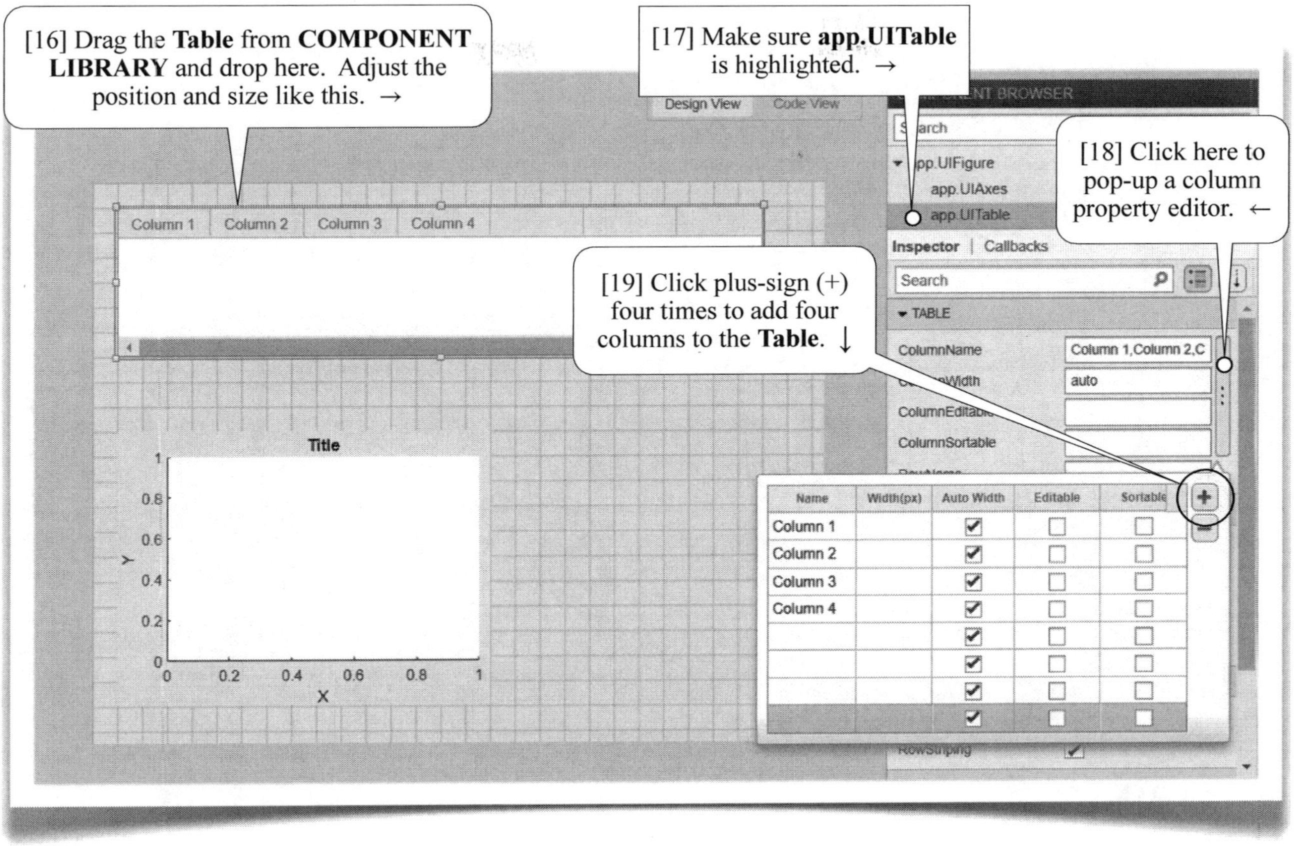
[16] Drag the Table from COMPONENT LIBRARY and drop here. Adjust the position and size like this. →
[17] Make sure app.UITable is highlighted. →
[18] Click here to pop-up a column property editor. ←
[19] Click plus-sign (+) four times to add four columns to the Table. ↓
Design View
Code View
app.UIFigure
app.UIAxes
app.UITable
Inspector
Callbacks
Search
TABLE
ColumnName
Column 1,Column 2,C
auto
ColumnSortable
Column 1
Column 2
Column 3
Column 4
Name
Width(px)
Auto Width
Editable
Sortable
Title
X
Y

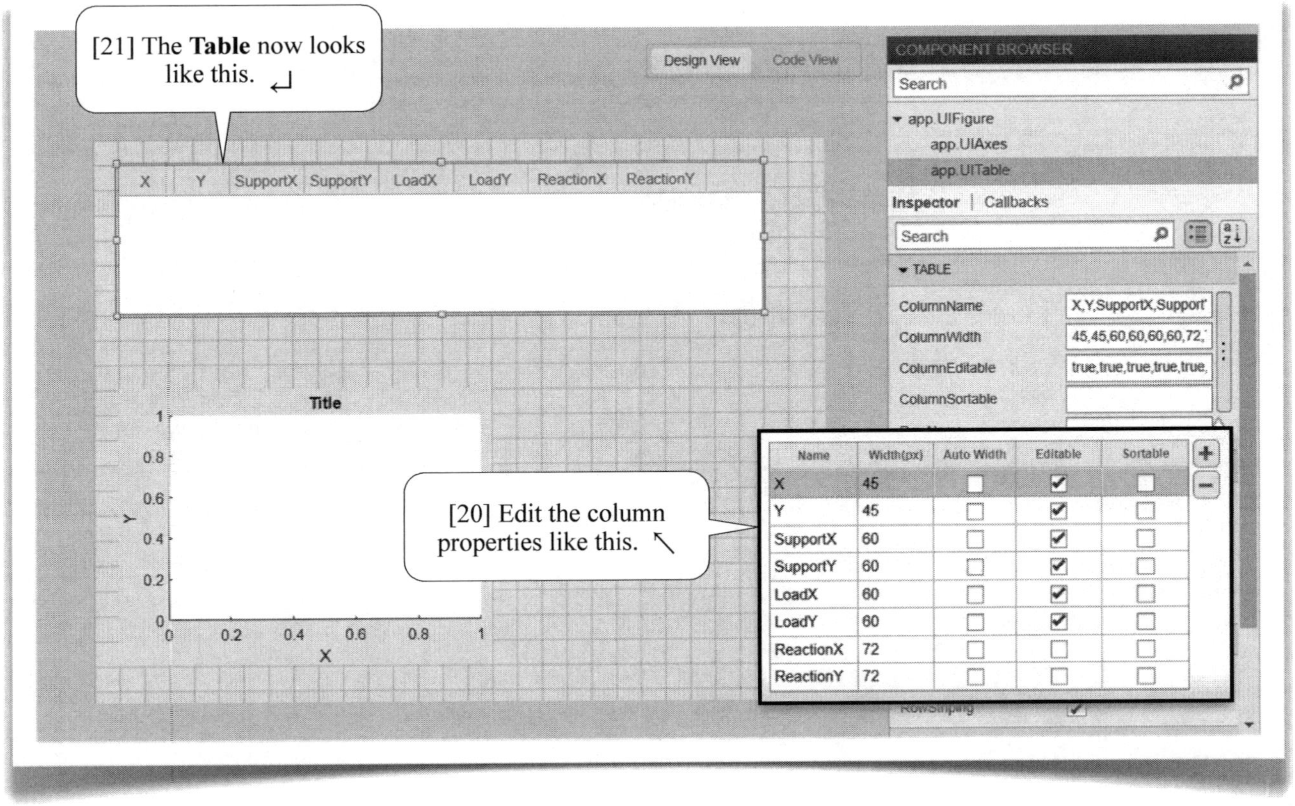
[21] The Table now looks like this. ↵
[20] Edit the column properties like this. ↖
Design View
Code View
COMPONENT BROWSER
Search
app.UIFigure
app.UIAxes
app.UITable
Inspector
Callbacks
TABLE
ColumnName
ColumnWidth
ColumnEditable
ColumnSortable
X,Y,SupportX,Support
45,45,60,60,60,60,72,
true,true,true,true,true,
X
Y
SupportX
SupportY
LoadX
LoadY
ReactionX
ReactionY
Name
Width(px)
Auto Width
Editable
Sortable
45
60
72
Title

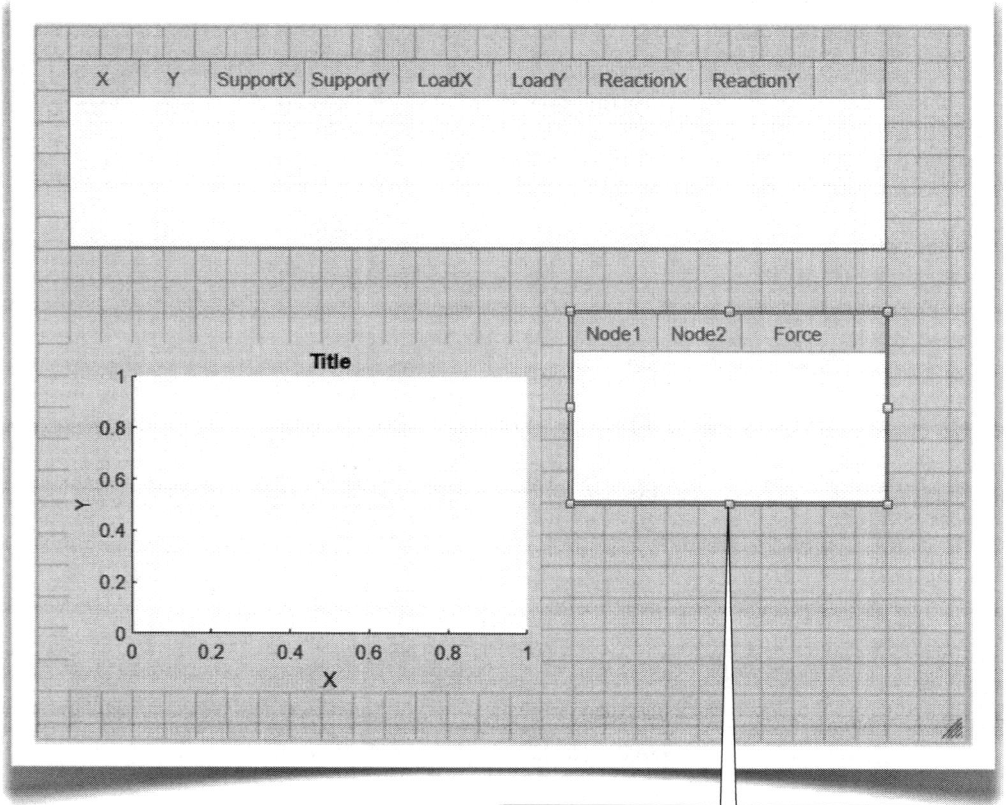

[22] Repeat a similar procedure in [16-20] (last page) to add another **Table** like this (see [23, 24]). ↓

[24] Edit the column properties like this. ↵

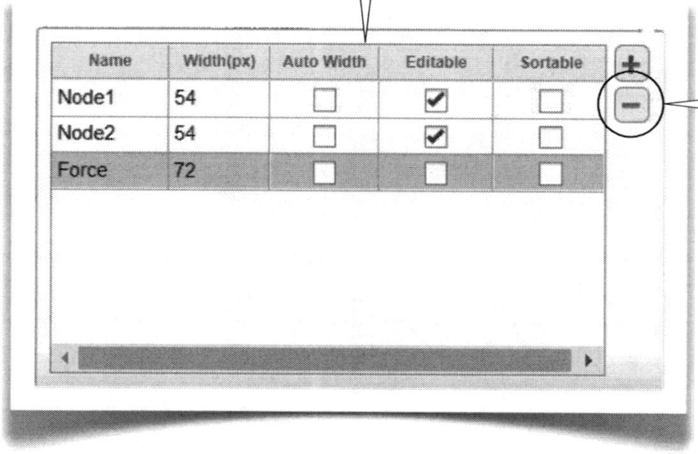

[23] Remember, a four-column **Table** is initially created. Click minus-sign (-) once so that it reduces to three columns. ←

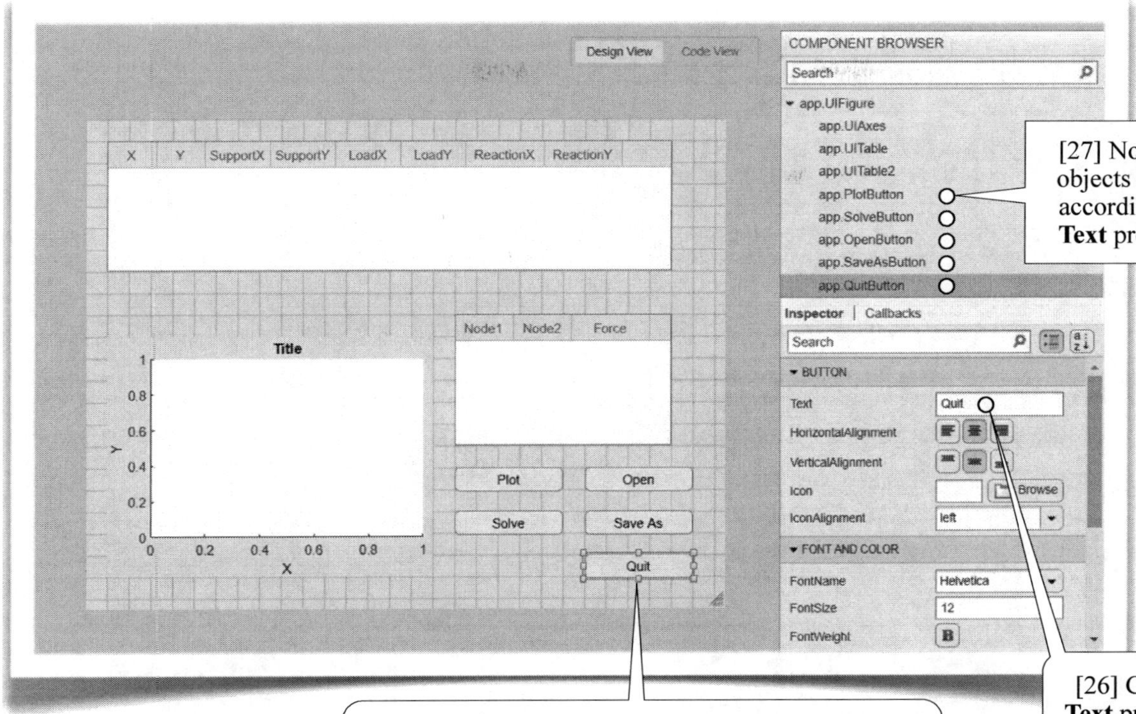

[27] Note that the objects are named according to their **Text** property. ↙

[26] Change the **Text** property of a **Button** like this. ↑

[25] Create 5 **Buttons** like this by dragging the **Button** from **COMPONENT LIBRARY**. Change the **Text** property of the **Buttons** to **Plot**, **Solve**, **Open**, **Save As**, and **Quit**, respectively (also see [26, 27]). →

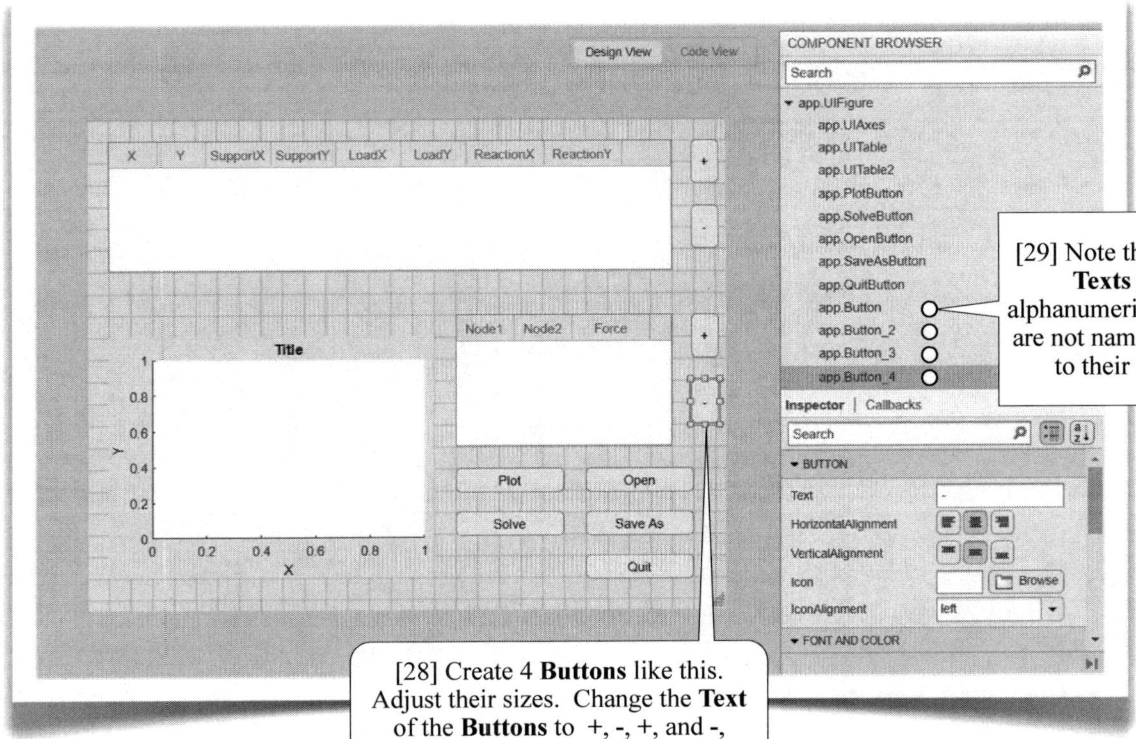

[29] Note that, since the **Texts** are not alphanumeric, the objects are not named according to their **Text**. ↵

[28] Create 4 **Buttons** like this. Adjust their sizes. Change the **Text** of the **Buttons** to +, -, +, and -, respectively, like this. ↗

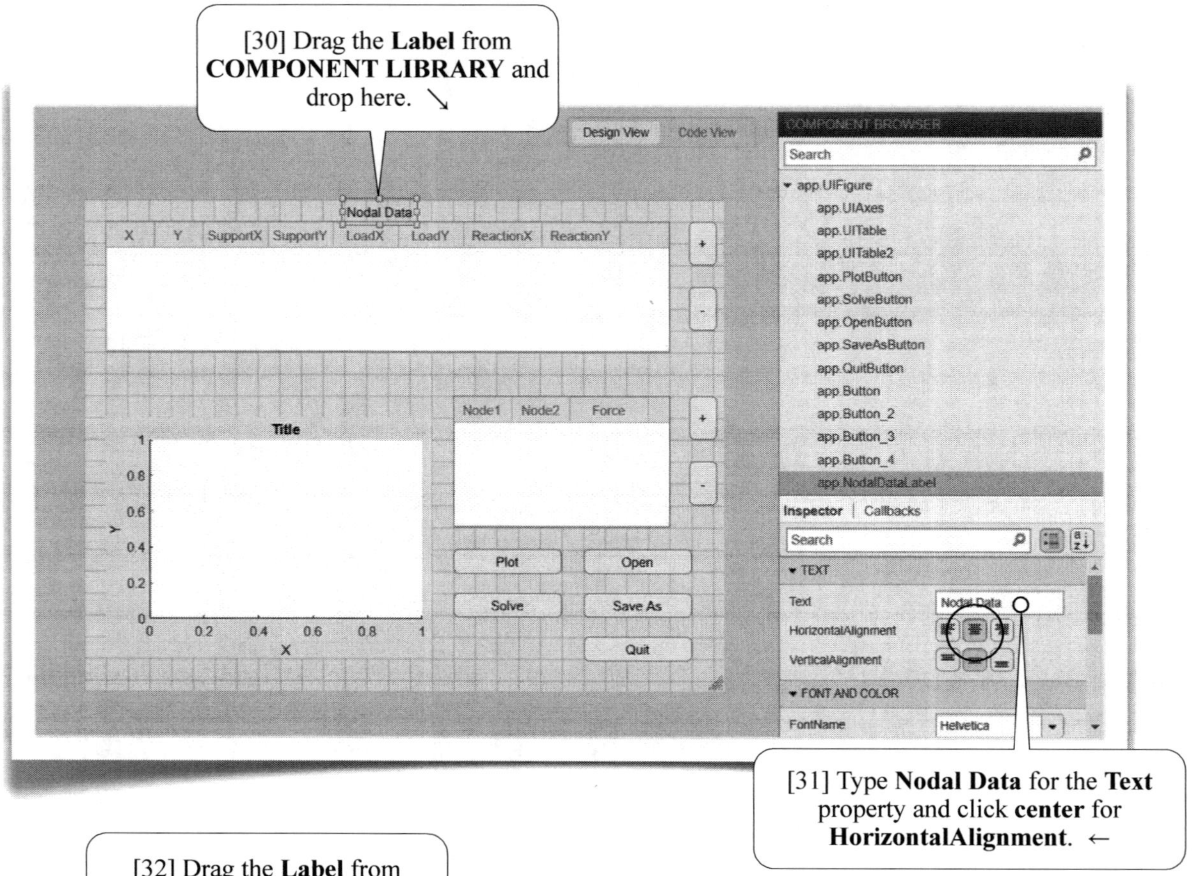
[30] Drag the **Label** from **COMPONENT LIBRARY** and drop here. ↘
[31] Type **Nodal Data** for the **Text** property and click **center** for **HorizontalAlignment**. ←

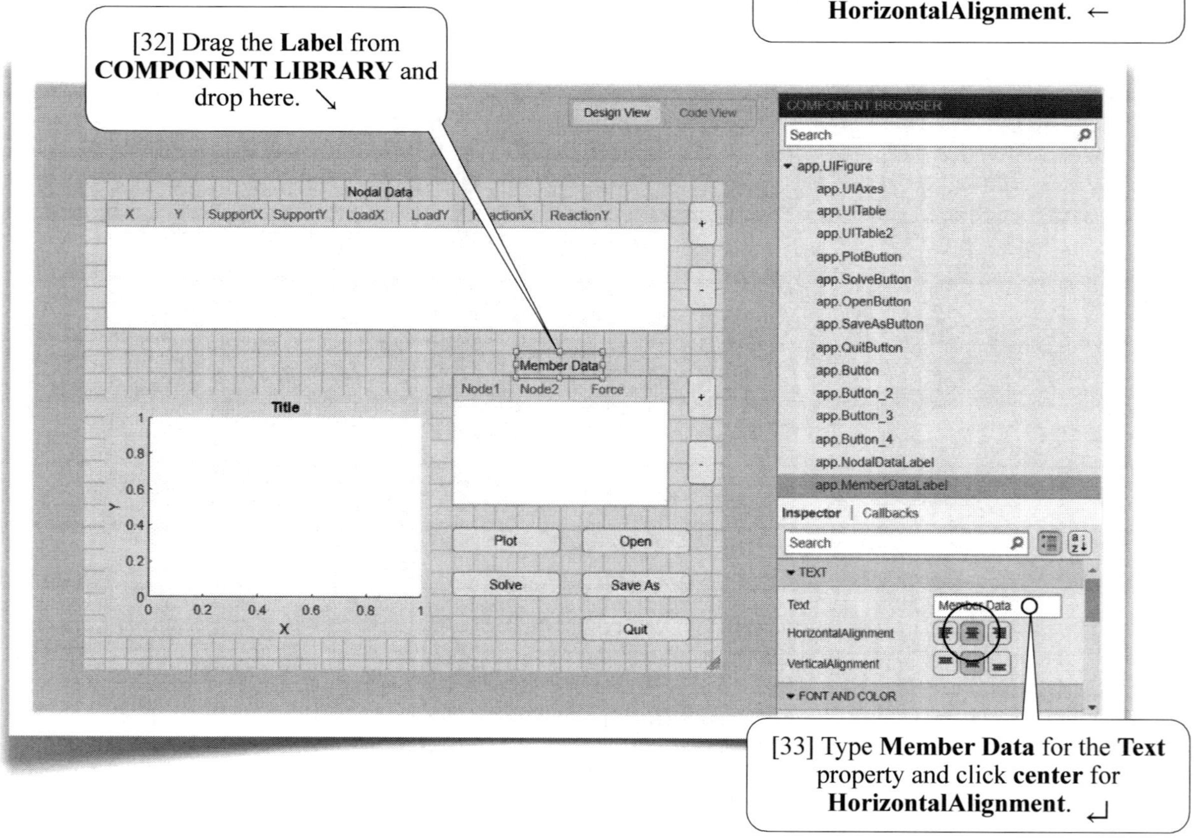
[32] Drag the **Label** from **COMPONENT LIBRARY** and drop here. ↘
[33] Type **Member Data** for the **Text** property and click **center** for **HorizontalAlignment**. ↵

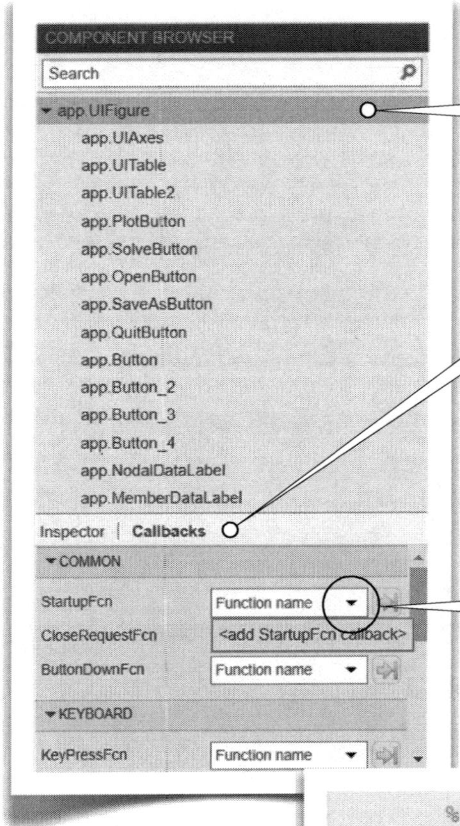

[34] Now we want to add functions. First we create a **startup** function, which is executed after all components are created. Highlight **app.UIFigure**. ↓

[35] Click **Callbacks**. ↓

[36] Pull-down-select **<Add StartupFcn callback>**. The **App Designer** switches to **Code View**; a function `startupFcn` is created, ready for you to type statements. ↓

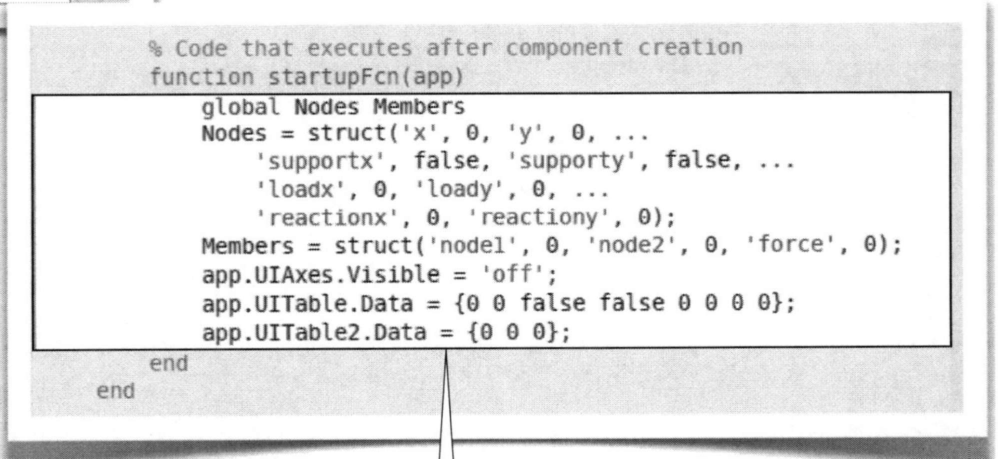

```
% Code that executes after component creation
function startupFcn(app)
    global Nodes Members
    Nodes = struct('x', 0, 'y', 0, ...
        'supportx', false, 'supporty', false, ...
        'loadx', 0, 'loady', 0, ...
        'reactionx', 0, 'reactiony', 0);
    Members = struct('node1', 0, 'node2', 0, 'force', 0);
    app.UIAxes.Visible = 'off';
    app.UITable.Data = {0 0 false false 0 0 0 0};
    app.UITable2.Data = {0 0 0};
end
end
```

Function `startupFcn`

[37] Type these statements. The first 6 lines are almost the same as lines 1 and 3-7 of page 330. The last two lines are to assign the initial values for the two **Tables**, respectively. A **Table** has a **ColumnFormat** property, which determines the format of each column (see 8.9[28], page 332). The **App Designer** can automatically detect the format of each column according to the initially assigned values. According to the last two lines, the following two statements are implicitly established by **App Designer**:

```
app.UITable.ColumnFormat = {'numeric','numeric','logical','logical',...
                            'numeric','numeric','numeric','numeric'};
app.UITable2.ColumnFormat = {'numeric','numeric', 'numeric'};
```

↵

[38] You may test-run the program any time by clicking the **Run** button in the **App Designer**. Now click **Run**. When a **Save File** dialog appears, asking for a file name, type **Example08_10**. The **app** is saved as **Example08_10.mlapp** in the **Current Folder**. ↓

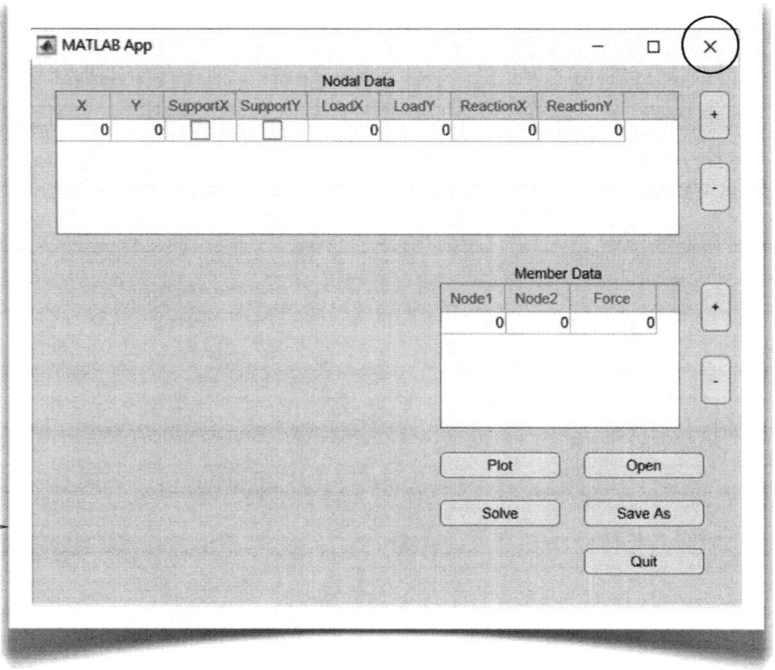

[39] This is the GUI we've created. Close the testing window. ↓

[40] Switch to **Design View**, highlight this **Button**. →

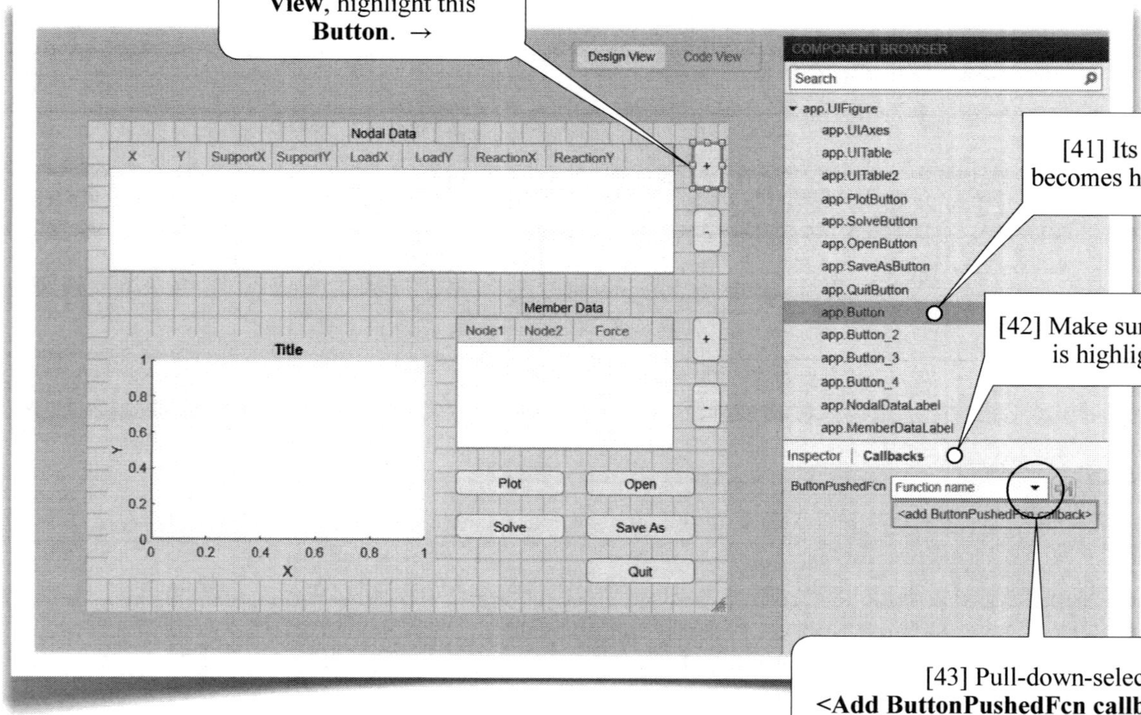

[41] Its name also becomes highlighted. ↓

[42] Make sure **Callbacks** is highlighted ↓

[43] Pull-down-select **<Add ButtonPushedFcn callback>**. The **App Designer** switches to **Code View**; a function `ButtonPushed` is created, ready for you to type statements. ↵

```
    % Button pushed function: Button
    function ButtonPushed(app, event)
        n = size(app.UITable.Data, 1);
        app.UITable.Data(n+1,:) = {0 0 false false 0 0 0 0};
    end
end
```

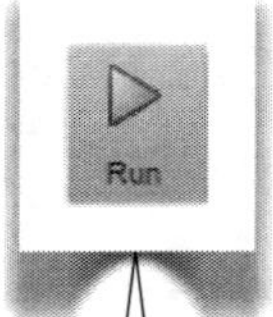

Function `ButtonPushed`

[44] Type these two statements; they are modified from lines 12-13 of page 332. Each time this **Button** is pushed, a row is added to the end of the **Table**. →

[45] Remember that you may test-run the program any time. Now click **Run**. ↓

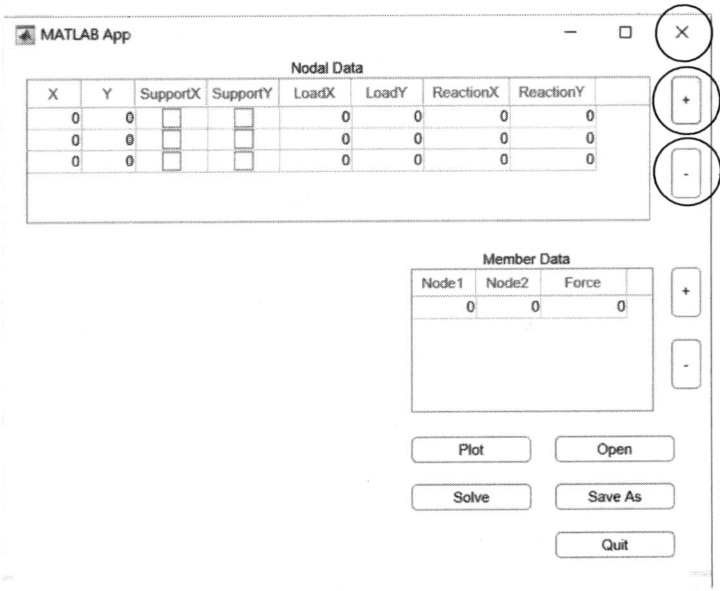

[46] Test this **Button** by clicking twice. Two rows are added to the **Table**. Close the **Figure**. ↓

[47] Close the window. Repeat a similar procedure in [40-45] to add a callback function `Button_2Pushed` for this **Button** (its name is **app.Button_2**; [44] is replaced by [48]). ↓

```
    % Button pushed function: Button_2
    function Button_2Pushed(app, event)
        n = size(app.UITable.Data, 1);
        if n > 1
            app.UITable.Data(n,:) = [];
        end
    end
end
```

Function `Button_2Pushed`

[48] Type these statements. Each time this **Button** is pushed, the last row is removed from the **Table**, unless there is only one row in the **Table**. ↵

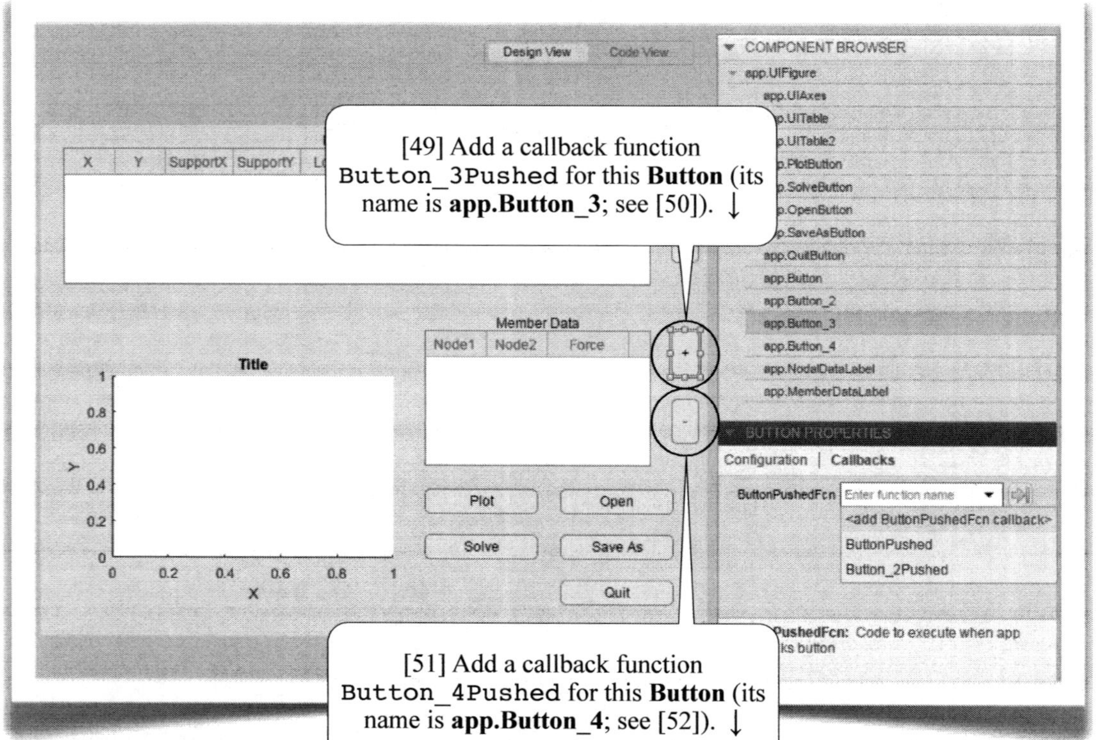

[49] Add a callback function `Button_3Pushed` for this **Button** (its name is **app.Button_3**; see [50]). ↓

[51] Add a callback function `Button_4Pushed` for this **Button** (its name is **app.Button_4**; see [52]). ↓

```
    % Button pushed function: Button_3
    function Button_3Pushed(app, event)
        m = size(app.UITable2.Data, 1);
        app.UITable2.Data(m+1,:) = {0 0 0};
    end
end
```

Function `Button_3Pushed`

[50] Type these statements. Each time this **Button** is pushed, the last row is removed from the **Table**, unless there is only one row in the **Table**. ↑

```
    % Button pushed function: Button_4
    function Button_4Pushed(app, event)
        m = size(app.UITable2.Data, 1);
        if m > 1
            app.UITable2.Data(m,:) = [];
        end
    end
end
```

Function `Button_4Pushed`

[52] Type these statements. Each time this **Button** is pushed, the last row is removed from the **Table**, unless there is only one row in the **Table**. ↵

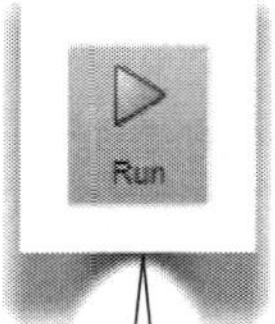

[53] Test-run the program. Remember to close the window. ↘

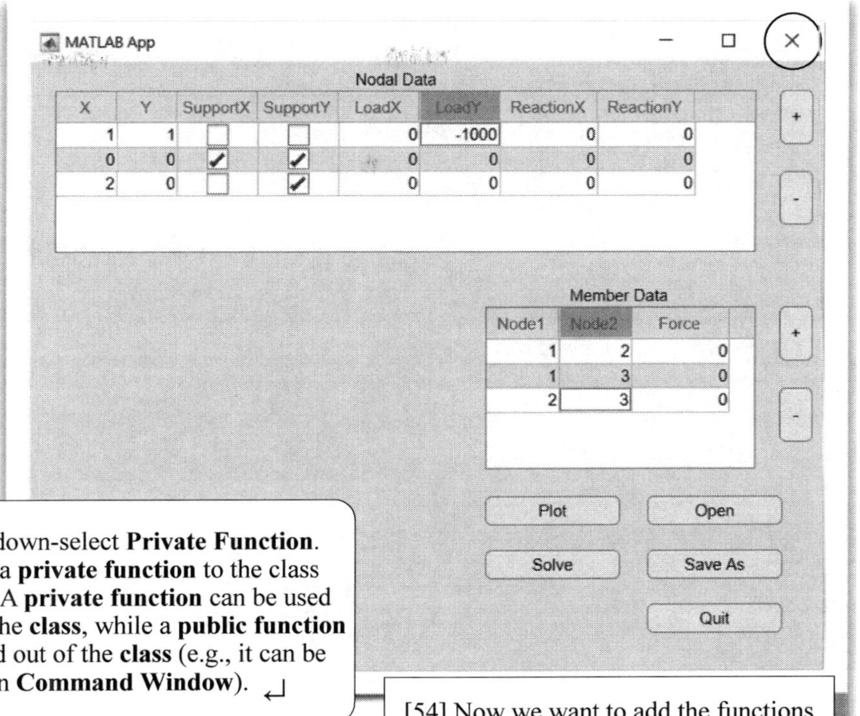

[56] Pull-down-select **Private Function**. This adds a **private function** to the class definition. A **private function** can be used only within the **class**, while a **public function** can be used out of the **class** (e.g., it can be typed in **Command Window**). ↵

[55] In **CODE BROWSER**, click **Functions**. ↗

[54] Now we want to add the functions `solveTruss` (page 323) and `plotTruss` (page 324) to the program. Make sure you are in **Code View**. ←

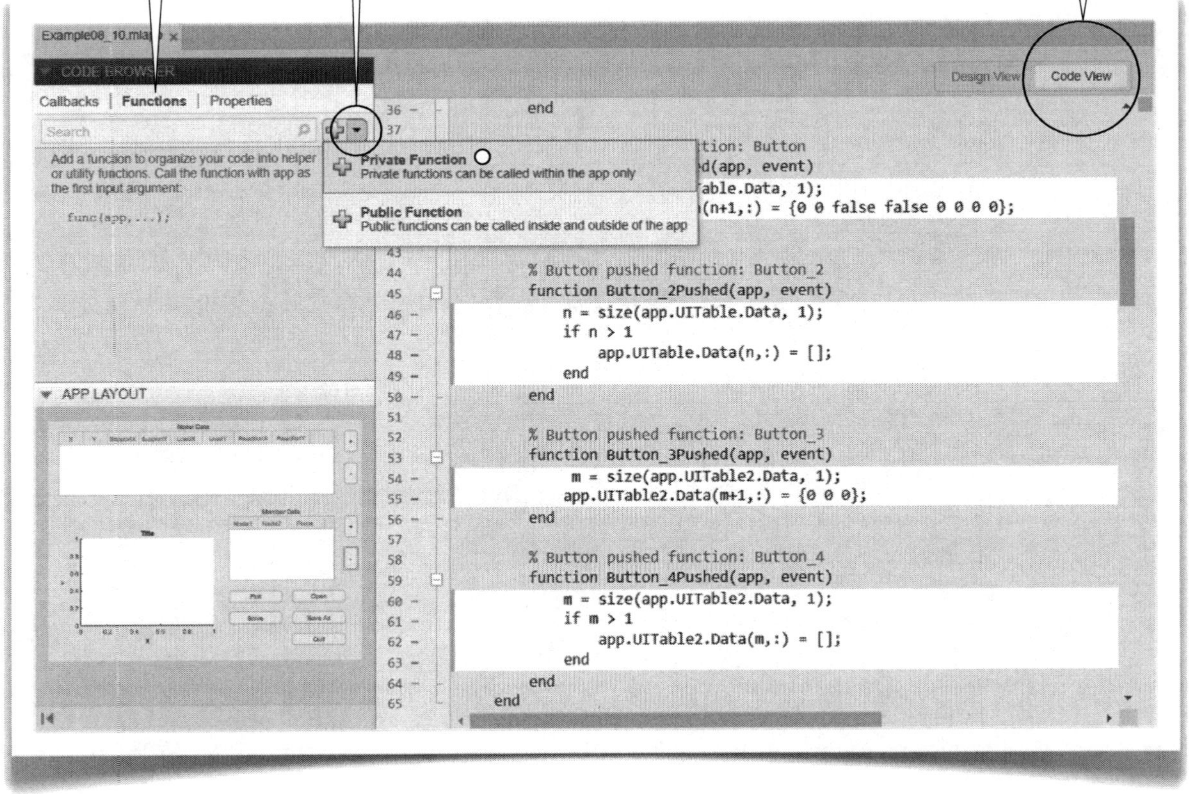

[57] An empty function is created. Replace these three lines with the functions `solveTruss` and `plotTruss` (lines 118-211, pages 323-324). ↓

```
methods (Access = private)

    function results = func(app)

    end
end
```

```
function plotTruss(app, Nodes, Members)
if (size(fieldnames(Nodes),1)<6 || size(fieldnames(Members),1)<2)
    disp('Truss data not complete'); return
end
n = length(Nodes); m = length(Members);
minX = Nodes(1).x; maxX = Nodes(1).x;
minY = Nodes(1).y; maxY = Nodes(1).y;
for k = 2:n
    if (Nodes(k).x < minX) minX = Nodes(k).x; end
    if (Nodes(k).x > maxX) maxX = Nodes(k).x; end
    if (Nodes(k).y < minY) minY = Nodes(k).y; end
    if (Nodes(k).y > maxY) maxY = Nodes(k).y; end
end
rangeX = maxX-minX; rangeY = maxY-minY;
axis(app.UIAxes, [minX-rangeX/5, maxX+rangeX/5, minY-rangeY/5, maxY+rangeY/5])
delete(app.UIAxes.Children)
axis(app.UIAxes, 'equal', 'off'), title(app.UIAxes, ' ')
hold(app.UIAxes, 'on')
for k = 1:m
    n1 = Members(k).node1; n2 = Members(k).node2;
    x = [Nodes(n1).x, Nodes(n2).x];
    y = [Nodes(n1).y, Nodes(n2).y];
    plot(app.UIAxes, x,y,'k-o', 'MarkerFaceColor', 'k')
end
for k = 1:n
    if Nodes(k).supportx
        x = [Nodes(k).x, Nodes(k).x-rangeX/20, Nodes(k).x-rangeX/20, Nodes(k).x];
        y = [Nodes(k).y, Nodes(k).y+rangeX/40, Nodes(k).y-rangeX/40, Nodes(k).y];
        plot(app.UIAxes, x,y,'k-')
    end
    if Nodes(k).supporty
        x = [Nodes(k).x, Nodes(k).x-rangeX/40, Nodes(k).x+rangeX/40, Nodes(k).x];
        y = [Nodes(k).y, Nodes(k).y-rangeX/20, Nodes(k).y-rangeX/20, Nodes(k).y];
        plot(app.UIAxes, x,y,'k-')
    end
end
end
```

[58] Modify the function `plotTruss` like this. Modification of the first line is necessary because `app` must be the first input argument for all functions in the class. The rest of the modifications are to direct the graphics output to **app.UIAxes**, instead of the "current" **Axes**. ↵

[59] For the function `solveTruss`, modify the first line like this. It is required that `app` is always the first input argument for all functions in the class. ↵

```
function [outNodes, outMembers] = solveTruss(app, Nodes, Members)
n = size(Nodes,2); m = size(Members,2);
if (m+3) < 2*n
    disp('Unstable!')
    outNodes = 0; outMembers = 0; return
elseif (m+3) > 2*n
    disp('Statically indeterminate!')
    outNodes = 0; outMembers = 0; return
end
A = zeros(2*n, 2*n); loads = zeros(2*n,1); nsupport = 0;
for i = 1:n
    for j = 1:m
        if Members(j).node1 == i || Members(j).node2 == i
            if Members(j).node1 == i
                n1 = i; n2 = Members(j).node2;
            elseif Members(j).node2 == i
                n1 = i; n2 = Members(j).node1;
            end
            x1 = Nodes(n1).x; y1 = Nodes(n1).y;
            x2 = Nodes(n2).x; y2 = Nodes(n2).y;
            L = sqrt((x2-x1)^2+(y2-y1)^2);
            A(2*i-1,j) = (x2-x1)/L;
            A(2*i,  j) = (y2-y1)/L;
        end
    end
    if (Nodes(i).supportx == 1)
        nsupport = nsupport+1;
        A(2*i-1,m+nsupport) = 1;
    end
    if (Nodes(i).supporty == 1)
        nsupport = nsupport+1;
        A(2*i, m+nsupport) = 1;
    end
    loads(2*i-1) = -Nodes(i).loadx;
    loads(2*i)   = -Nodes(i).loady;
end
forces = A\loads;
for j = 1:m
    Members(j).force = forces(j);
end
nsupport = 0;
for i = 1:n
    Nodes(i).reactionx = 0;
    Nodes(i).reactiony = 0;
    if (Nodes(i).supportx == 1)
        nsupport = nsupport+1;
        Nodes(i).reactionx = forces(m+nsupport);
    end
    if (Nodes(i).supporty == 1)
        nsupport = nsupport+1;
        Nodes(i).reactiony = forces(m+nsupport);
    end
end
outNodes = Nodes; outMembers = Members;
disp('Solved successfully.')
end
```

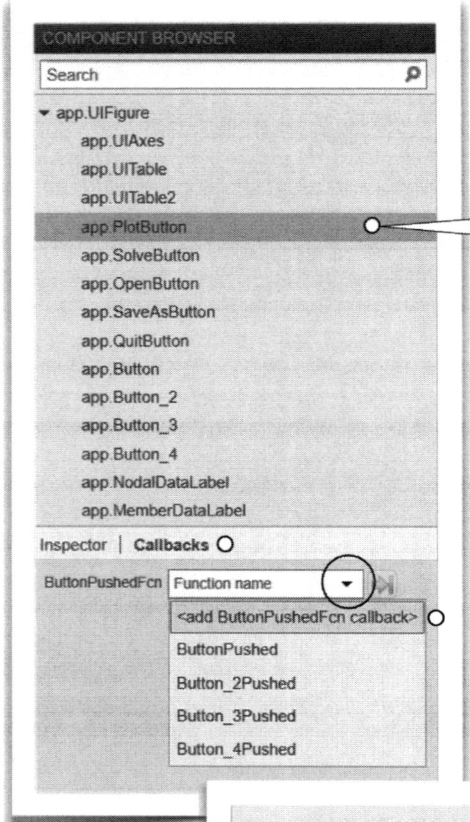

[60] Now we want to add callback functions for **Plot**, **Solve**, **Open**, **SaveAs**, and **Quit** buttons, respectively. For each **Button**, highlight it (either in **Design View** or in **Component Browser**), make sure **Callback** is highlighted, and pull-down-select **<add ButtonPushedFcn callback>**. ↓

[61] Add these statements to the function **PlotButtonPushed**. They are adapted from 8.9[63], page 335. The function converts the nodal data and member data from **cell arrays** to **structure arrays** and calls the function `plotTruss`. ↓

```
        % Button pushed function: PlotButton
        function PlotButtonPushed(app, event)
            global Nodes Members
            Nodes = cell2struct(app.UITable.Data, fieldnames(Nodes), 2)';
            Members = cell2struct(app.UITable2.Data, fieldnames(Members), 2)';
            plotTruss(app, Nodes, Members)
        end
    end
```

[62] Add these statements to the function **SolveButtonPushed**. They are adapted from 8.9[64], page 336. The function converts the nodal data and member data from **cell arrays** to **structure arrays**, calls the function `solveTruss`, and converts the updated nodal data and member data from **structure arrays** to **cell arrays**. ↵

```
        % Button pushed function: SolveButton
        function SolveButtonPushed(app, event)
            global Nodes Members
            Nodes = cell2struct(app.UITable.Data, fieldnames(Nodes), 2)';
            Members = cell2struct(app.UITable2.Data, fieldnames(Members), 2)';
            [Nodes, Members] = solveTruss(app, Nodes, Members);
            app.UITable.Data = permute(struct2cell(Nodes), [1 3 2])';
            app.UITable2.Data = permute(struct2cell(Members), [1 3 2])';
        end
    end
```

[63] Add these statements to the function **OpenButtonPushed**. They are adapted from 8.9[65], page 336. The function requests a file name, loads the variables `Nodes` and `Members` from the file, converts the **structure arrays** to **cell arrays**, and changes the title of the **Figure** window. ↓

```
        % Button pushed function: OpenButton
        function OpenButtonPushed(app, event)
            global Nodes Members
            [file, path] = uigetfile('*.mat');
            if file
                Nodes = []; Members = [];
                load([path, file])
                app.UITable.Data = permute(struct2cell(Nodes), [1 3 2])';
                app.UITable2.Data = permute(struct2cell(Members), [1 3 2])';
                app.UIFigure.Name = ['Planar Truss: ', file];
            end
        end
    end
```

[64] Add these statements to the function **SaveAsButtonPushed**. They are adapted from 8.9[66], page 336. The function requests a file name, converts the **cell arrays** to **structure arrays**, saves the variables `Nodes` and `Members` to the file, and changes the title of the **Figure** window. ↓

```
        % Button pushed function: SaveAsButton
        function SaveAsButtonPushed(app, event)
            global Nodes Members
            [file, path] = uiputfile('*.mat');
            if file
                Nodes = cell2struct(app.UITable.Data, fieldnames(Nodes), 2)';
                Members = cell2struct(app.UITable2.Data, fieldnames(Members), 2)';
                save([path, file], 'Nodes', 'Members')
                app.UIFigure.Name = ['Planar Truss: ', file];
            end
        end
```

[65] Add this statement to the function **QuitButtonPushed**. It simply closes the **Figure** window. ↵

```
        % Button pushed function: QuitButton
        function QuitButtonPushed(app, event)
            close(app.UIFigure)
        end
    end
```

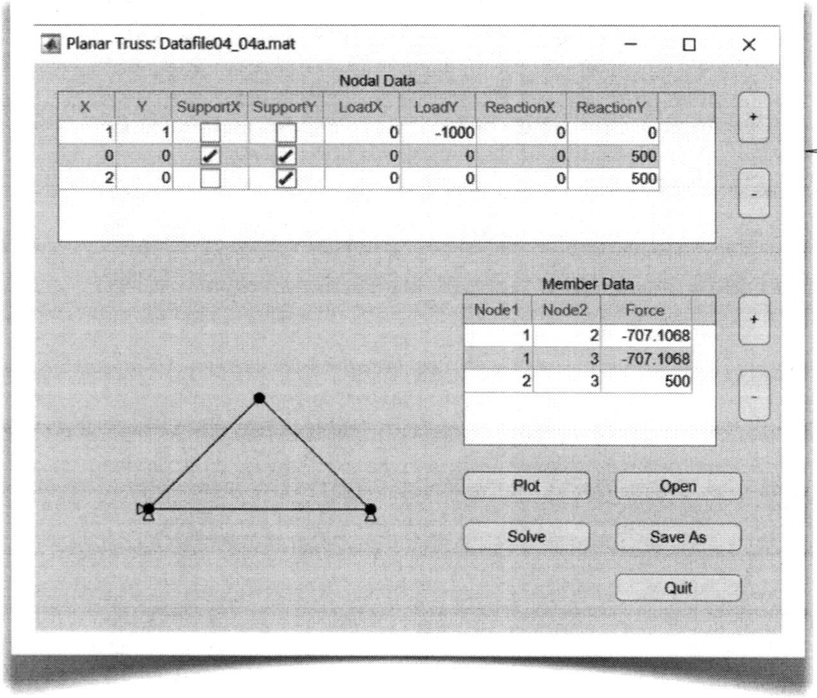

[66] Now, you may test-run the program by solving the three-bar example, following the steps in 8.8[6-13], page 325. ↓

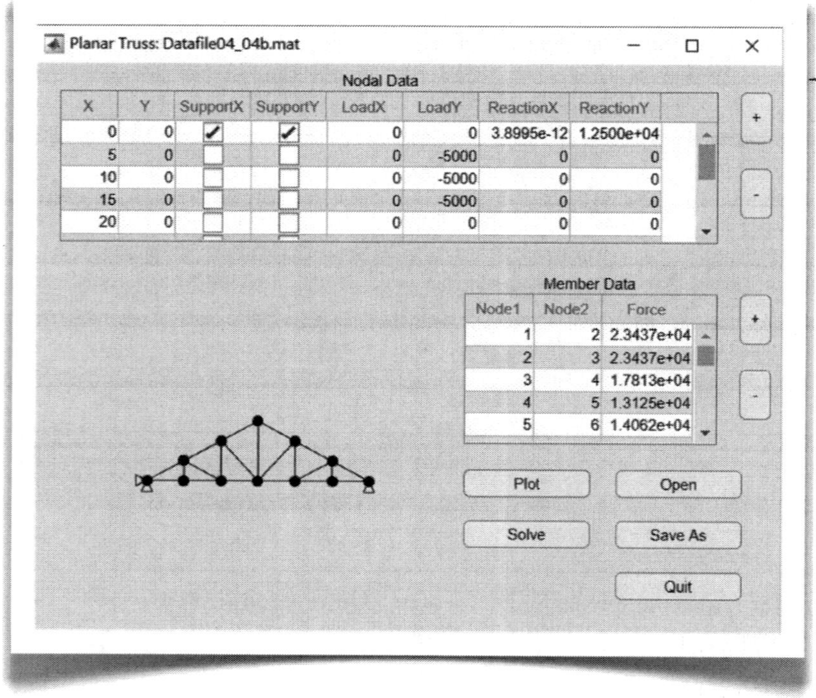

[67] And you may also test-run the program by solving the 21-bar example, following the steps in 8.8[14-15], page 326. ↓

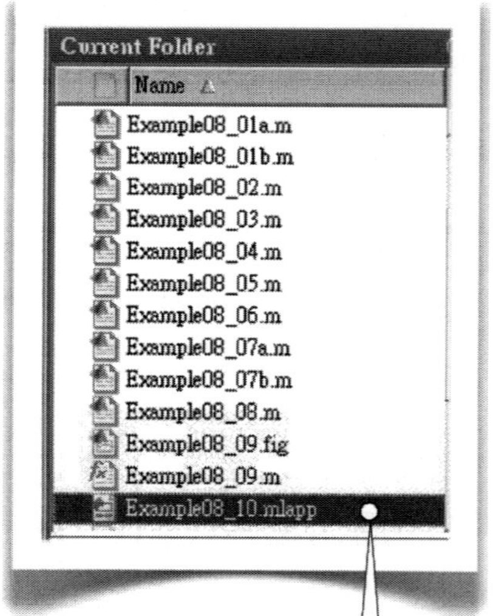

[68] Close **App Designer**. To run the **app** again, right-click-select **Run** (or double-click it). To modify the **app**, right-click-select **Open**. Now right-click **Example08_10.mlapp** and select **Open**. We want to examine the program structure. ↵

```
classdef Example08_10
    properties (Access = public)
        UIFigure    ...
        ...
    end

    methods (Access = private)
        function solveTruss
        ...

        function plotTruss
        ...
    end

    methods (Access = private)
        function startupFcn
        ...

        function ButtonPushed
        ...

        function Button_2Pushed
        ...

        function Button_3Pushed
        ...

        function Button_4Pushed
        ...

        function OpenButtonPushed
        ...

        function PlotButtonPushed
        ...

        function QuitButtonPushed
        ...

        function SaveAsQuitButtonPushed
        ...

        function SolveButtonPushed
        ...
    end

    methods (Access = private)
        function createComponents(app)
        ...
    end

    methods (Access = public)
        function app = Example08_10
        ...

        function delete
        ...
    end
end
```

Program Structure

[69] This is a schematic representation of the program. MATLAB uses the **object-oriented programming paradigm** (see Section 4.9) when using the **App Designer**. It defined a class with the name Example08_10.

As mentioned in Section 4.9, a class definition consists of **properties** sections and **methods** sections. In this case, there is one **properties** section and three **methods** sections. The **properties** section and the last **methods** section are **public**. The other methods sections are **private**.

Public Properties and Methods

A `public` section can be accessed from the **Command Window**; for example, you can use the public method Example08_10 (the second last function) to create an object

```
>> myApp = Example08_10
```

The variable `myApp` is a **handle** to the created **object**; the initial configuration of the object is like [39], page 346. You may access the public properties with the handle; for example,

```
>> myApp.UIFigure.Color = 'red'
```

changes the background color to red. You may delete the object by using the public method `delete` (the last function):

```
>> delete(myApp)
```

You may clear the handle in a usual way:

```
>> clear myApp
```

You don't have to create the handle; you may simply create an object by entering the class name:

```
>> Example08_10
```

Private Methods

The first **methods** section contains two functions: `solveTruss` and `plotTruss`. The second **methods** section contains all callback functions. The third **methods** section contains a function `createComponents`, which creates all the components as shown in [39] (page 346) when the **method** Example08_10 (the second last function) is executed. #

8.11 Additional Exercise Problems

Problem08_01: Voice Recorder

Modify Example08_02.m (page 300-301) to include a **Plot** button in the GUI. When the user clicks the **Plot** button, the program plots an audio signal like the one in 6.6b[5] (page 268).

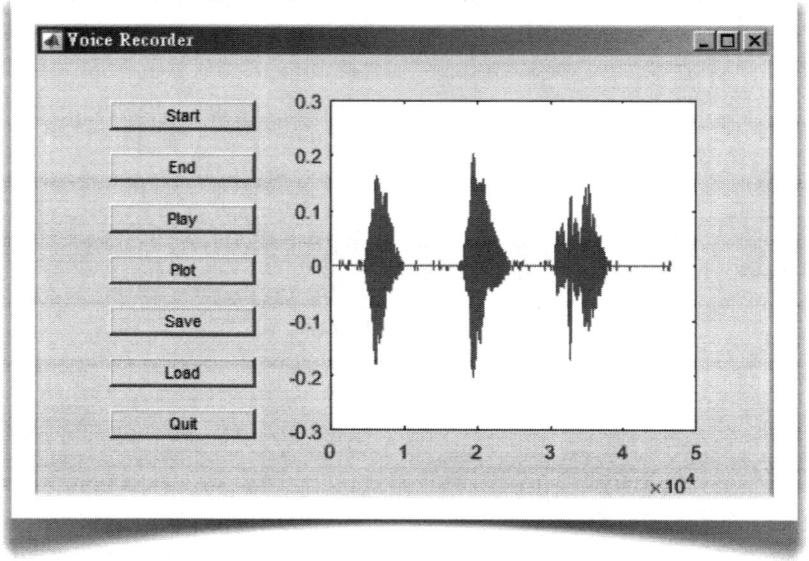

Problem08_02: Voice Recorder Using GUIDE

Implement the voice recorder in Problem08_01, using **GUIDE**. Add a **Pause** button and a **Resume** button. (See the functions `pause` and `resume` in Table 6.6b, page 269).

Problem08_03: Voice Recorder Using App Designer

Implement the voice recorder in Problem08_01, using **App Designer**. Add a **Pause** button and a **Resume** button. (See the functions `pause` and `resume` in Table 6.6b, page 269).

Problem08_04: Sorting and Searching Using GUIDE

Implement the **Sorting and Searching** program in Section 8.5, using **GUIDE**.

Problem08_05: Sorting and Searching Using App Designer

Implement the **Sorting and Searching** program in Section 8.5, using **App Designer**.

Chapter 9
Symbolic Mathematics

MATLAB can process not only numeric data but also symbolic expressions. To use symbolic mathematics, you need a license that includes Symbolic Math Toolbox. This chapter assumes that you have a license that includes Symbolic Math Toolbox.

9.1 Symbolic Numbers, Variables, Functions, and Expressions

9.1a Basic Concepts

Symbolic Expressions

[1] Recall that a numeric expression is a syntactic combination of numeric constants, variables, and functions. Similarly, a **symbolic expression** is a syntactic combination of **symbolic numbers**, **symbolic variables**, and **symbolic functions**. A numeric variable must have a numeric value before it can be used in an expression. Similarly, a symbolic variable must have a symbolic value before it can be used in a symbolic expression.

Live Script

As mentioned in Section 1.8, a feature of **Live Editor** is that it outputs textbook-quality equations when using Symbolic Mathematics. All the scripts in this book are saved as plane scripts (**.m** files) and can be opened as **Live Scripts (.mlx** files) and executed in the **Live Editor**. In this chapter, we'll save the scripts as plane scripts but open them as **Live Scripts** (see [3]) and execute them in the **Live Editor**. This arrangement is to make sure that all the scripts in this book can be executed in either the plane **Script Editor** or the **Live Editor**. It is not certain whether or not the plane **Script Editor** would become obsolete in the future and the **Live Editor** would become the primary editor. For the time being, I suggest that you be familiar with both the plane **Script Editor** and the **Live Editor**. ⁄

Example09_01a.m: Basic Concepts

[2] Type the following commands and save as Example09_01a.m. These commands demonstrate the creation of symbolic numbers, symbolic variables, and symbolic expressions, using the functions sym. →

```
clear
a = sym(2/3)
b = sym('2/3')
isequal(a, b)
sym(pi)
x = sym('y')
x^2
x = sym('c')+sym('y')
x^2
x = sym('x')
p = x^2+2*x+3
q = diff(p)
```

[3] Right-click Example09_01a.m and select **Open as Live Script**. ↵

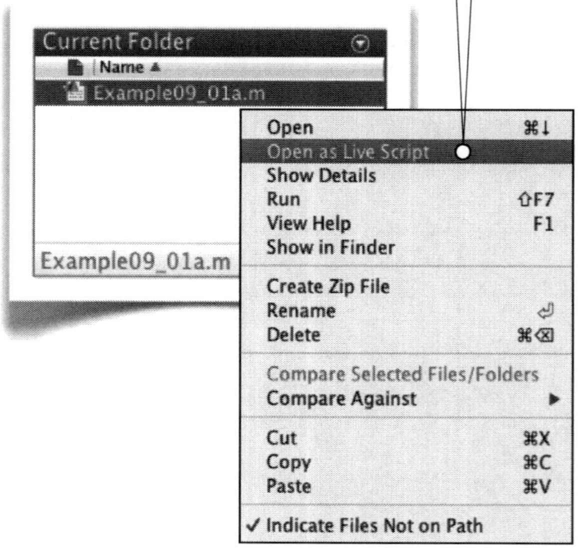

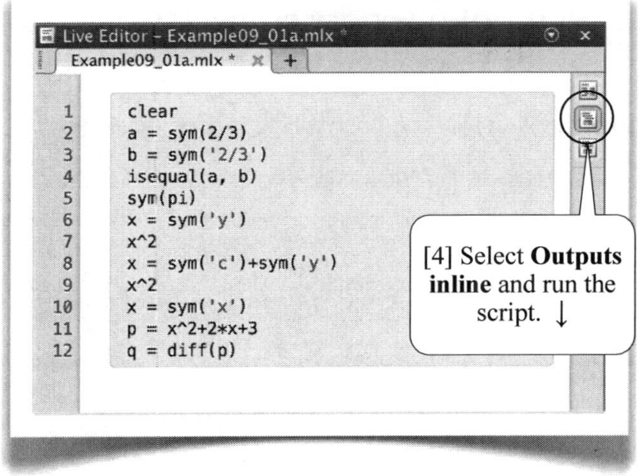

[4] Select **Outputs inline** and run the script. ↓

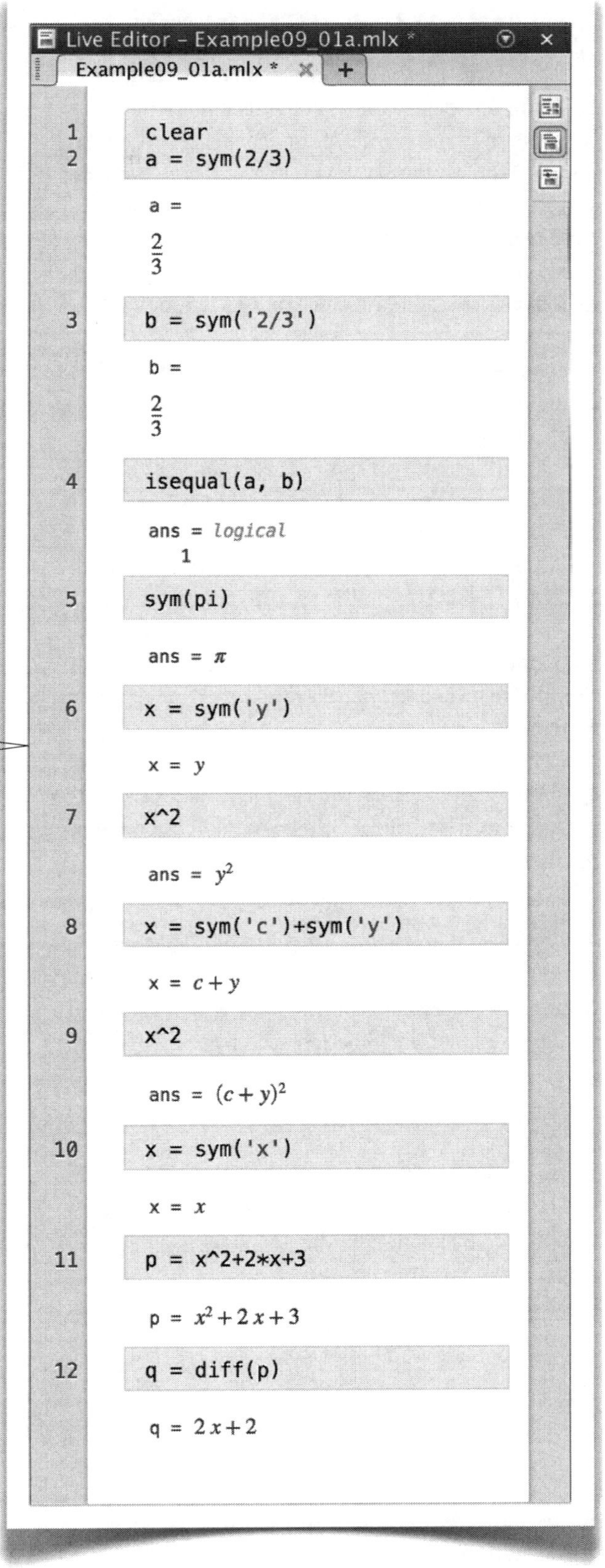

[5] The textbook-quality mathematical expressions are inserted between the command lines; the command lines are highlighted with gray color. ↓

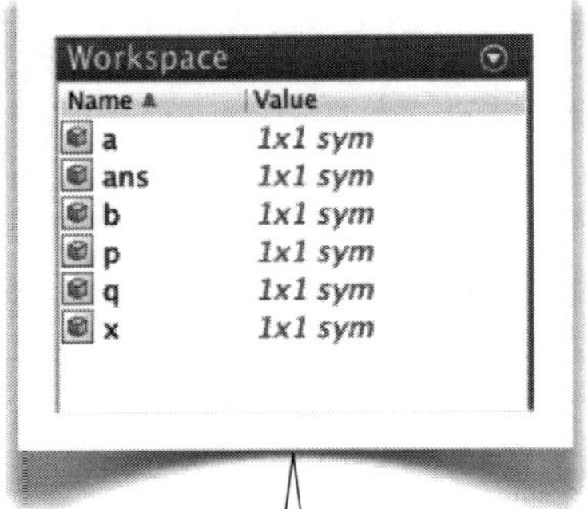

[6] All the variables created are symbolic variables, i.e., of class `sym`. ↵

About Example09_01a.m

[7] The function `sym` converts a non-symbolic data to a symbolic data. Line 2 converts a numeric constant 2/3 to a symbolic number, which is then assigned to `a`, a symbolic variable. Line 3 converts a string `'2/3'` to a symbolic number. `b` is also of class `sym`. There is no difference between `a` and `b`; this is confirmed in line 4. Line 5 is another example of converting a numeric constant to a symbolic number.

Line 6 converts a string `'y'` (the quotes MUST be included) to a **symbol** `y` and assigns to the symbolic variable `x`. Note that `y` is not a symbolic variable; it is simply a **symbol**; you don't see a `y` created in the **Workspace** (see [4], last page). `x` is a symbolic variable containing the symbol `y`.

Line 7 squares the variable `x`, and the output is y^2 (see [5], last page). Line 8 converts strings `'c'` and `'y'` to symbols `c` and `y`, creates an expression by adding them together, and assigns the expression to `x`. Line 9 squares the variable `x` and the output is $(c+y)^2$.

Line 10 demonstrates that, in practice, a symbolic variable is often assigned a symbol with the same name. Here, the symbolic variable `x` contains a symbol `x`. A shorthand for line 10 is

```
>> syms x
```

The above statement, equivalent to line 10, creates a symbolic variable `x` containing a symbol of the same name. The style such as lines 6 and 8 is obsolete. It is suggested that line 8 be replaced by

```
>> syms c y
>> x = c + y
```

Expressions constructed with this practice (a symbolic variable contains a symbol with the same name) are consistent with the mathematical expressions in textbooks. For example, line 11 creates an expression:

$$p = x^2 + 2x + 3$$

Line 12 differentiates p with respect to `x`

$$q = \frac{dp}{dx} = 2x + 2$$

The function `diff` in line 12 performs a symbolic differentiation. #

9.1b Symbolic Expressions

Example09_01b.m: Symbolic Expressions

[1] As exercises, let's create the following expressions: ↵

$$f = \frac{8\cos\theta}{\sin\left(\dfrac{3\theta}{\theta+1}\right)} \quad \text{(a)}$$

$$g = ax^3 + bx + c \quad \text{(b)}$$

$$h = \frac{d}{dx}\sqrt{5x^2+3x+7} = \frac{10x+3}{2\sqrt{5x^2+3x+7}} \quad \text{(c)}$$

$$M = \begin{bmatrix} 5\sin t & -\cos t^2 \\ \cos 2t & -\sin t \end{bmatrix} \quad \text{(d)}$$

```
clear
syms theta
f = 8*cos(theta)/sin((3*theta)/(theta+1))
syms a b c x
g = a*x^3+b*x+c
h = diff(sqrt(5*x^2+3*x+7))
syms t
M = [5*sin(t),-cos(t^2);cos(2*t),-sin(t)]
class(M)
size(M)
det(M)
```

[2] Open Example09_01b.m as a **Live Script** and run the script. Remember to select **Outputs inline**. →

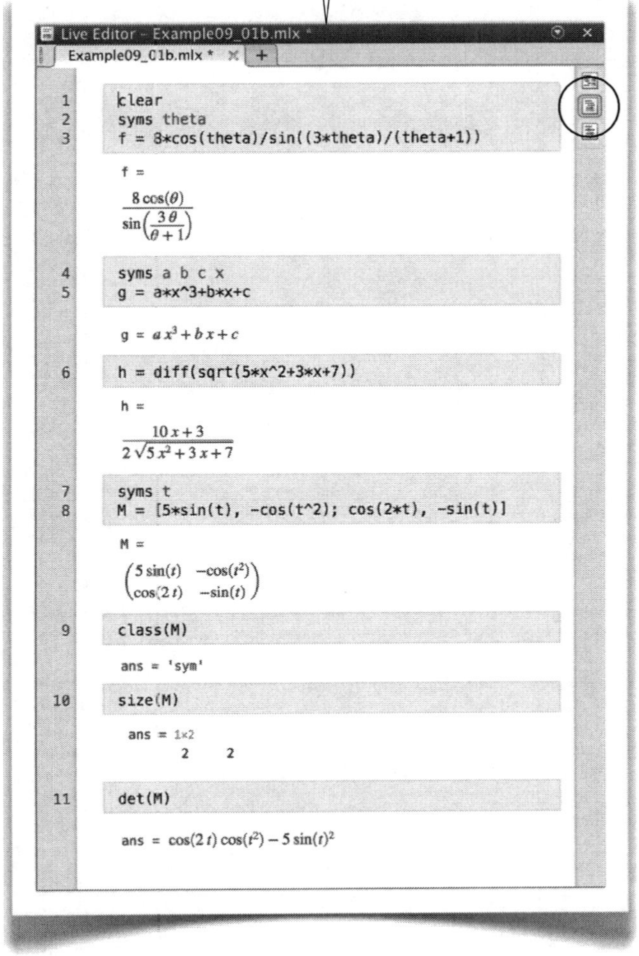

About Example09_01b.m

[3] Line 2 declares that `theta` is a symbolic variable containing the symbol `theta`. Remember, it is shorthand for

```
theta = sym('theta')
```

We'll stick to the shorthand for the rest of the book.

Line 3 creates the expression (a) using the variable `theta` (see [2]).

Line 4 creates four symbolic variables, `a`, `b`, `c`, and `x`, each containing a symbol of the same name. Using the function `syms`, several symbolic variables can be conveniently created in a single statement. Line 5 creates the expression (b).

Line 6 creates the expression (c). Note that the function `diff` differentiates an expression with respect to the default variable `x`. If an expression doesn't contain the variable `x`, the default variable is the one that is alphabetically closest to `x` (to be discussed further below).

Line 7 creates a symbolic variable `t`. Line 8 creates the expression (d), a 2-by-2 symbolic matrix. Line 9 confirms that `M` is of class `sym`. Line 10 confirms that `M` is a 2-by-2 matrix.

MATLAB provides many functions that operate on symbolic expressions. For example, the function `det` (line 11) calculates the determinant of a matrix symbolically. The function `diff` (line 6) is another example. We'll introduce more in this chapter.

Use `symvar` to determine default variables

When you are working on Calculus, it is always safer to explicitly specify the independent variable. For example, in line 6, you may instead write

```
h = diff(sqrt(5*x^2+3*x+7), x)
```

If you don't specify a variable, then MATLAB internally determines the independent variables by using the function `symvar`. The function

```
symvar(expr, n)
```

returns a vector of *n* symbolic variables in *`expr`* in an order that is alphabetically closer to `x`. For example, `symvar(g,1)` returns `x`, and `symvar(g,2)` returns a row vector `[x,c]`. #

9.1c Symbolic Functions

Example09_01c.m: Symbolic Functions

[1] The following commands demonstrate the creation and the use of symbolic functions. ↓

```
clear
syms x y
f(x,y) = x^3*y^2
class(f)
f(2,3)
clear
syms f(x,y)
f(x,y) = x^3*y^2
diff(f)
diff(f,y)
syms a b
g = f(a+1,b+1)/(a+b)
h = f + x^2 + y
f(x,y) = sin(x*y)
f = sin(x*y)
class(f)
```

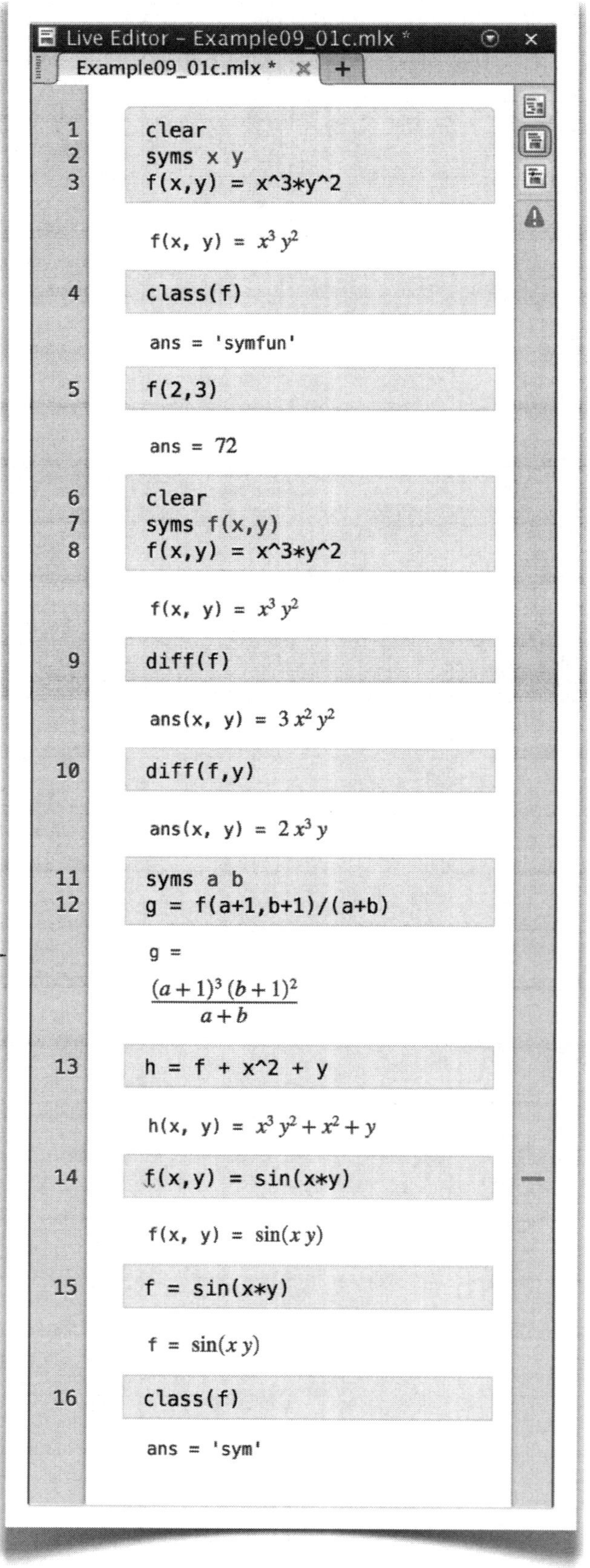

[2] Open Example09_01c.m as a **Live Script** and run the script in the **Live Editor**. (Ignore the warning messages.) ↓

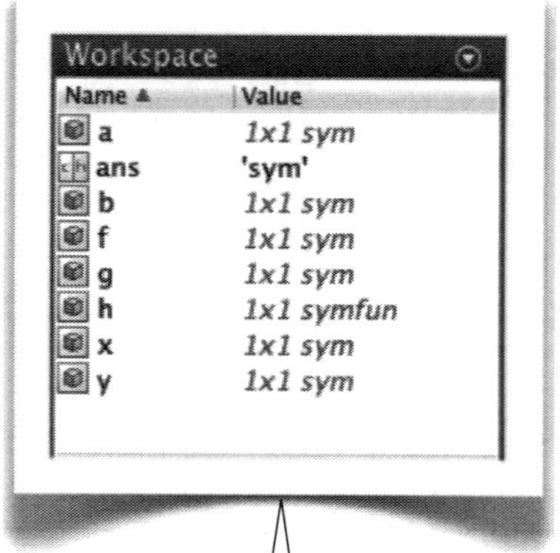

[3] The **Workspace**. ↵

About Example09_01c.m

[4] Line 2 creates two symbolic variables, `x` and `y`. Line 3 defines a **symbolic function** `f`; its class is `symfun` (line 4). A symbolic function can be evaluated by providing symbolic values as arguments (line 5). Note that, in line 5, the numeric values 2 and 3 are automatically converted to symbolic numbers.

Line 6 clears the **Workspace**. Lines 7-8 demonstrate an equivalent way as lines 2-3 to create the symbolic function `f`. With a single statement, line 7 creates a symbolic function `f` and two symbolic variables `x` and `y`. Line 8 then gives the definition of the function.

A **symbolic function** can be used like a symbolic variable. For example, line 9 differentiates the function `f` with respect to `x`. Remember that if you don't specify an independent variable for a built-in function such as `diff`, the default is the one alphabetically closest to `x`. To differentiate with respect to the variable `y`, line 10 explicitly specifies the independent variable `y` for the function `diff`.

The function value of a symbolic function can be used in an expression (line 12), and the result (here, `g`) is a symbolic variable, not a symbolic function.

A symbolic function itself can be used in an expression (line 13), and the result (here, `h`) is a symbolic function, not a symbolic variable. Note that, since the arguments are omitted in `h` (line 13), the default variables (`x` and `y`) are used (see the output in [2], last page).

You may redefine a symbolic function (line 14). When doing so, don't leave out the arguments. If you leave out arguments (line 15), it will be treated as a symbolic variable rather than a symbolic function. Line 16 and its output in [2] confirm this. #

Table 9.1 Creation of Symbolic Constants, Variables, and Functions

Functions	Description
`syms v1 v2 ...`	Create symbolic variables and functions.
`s = sym(string)`	Create symbolic constants, variables, and functions.
`s = sym(number)`	Create symbolic constants, variables, and functions.
`v = symvar(s,n)`	Return n variables closest to x.

Details and More: Help>Symbolic Math Toolbox>Symbolic Computations in MATLAB>Symbolic Variables, Expressions, Functions, and Preferences>Create Symbolic Variables, Expressions, and Functions

9.2 Simplification of Expressions

9.2a Simplification of Expressions

Different Forms of Expressions

[1] Most symbolic expressions can be represented in many forms, and there is no universal idea as to which form is the simplest. For example, the following two expressions represent the same polynomial in different forms:

$$expr1 = (x+2)(x+3)\text{, } expr2 = x^2 + 5x + 6$$

The first form shows the zeros of the polynomial, while the second form serves best when you want to see the coefficients of the polynomial. If you need a particular form of an expression, the best approach is to choose an appropriate simplification function. If you do not need a particular form of expression, the function `simplify` usually gives the shortest form. ↓

Example09_02a.m: Simplification of Expressions

[2] The following commands demonstrate the use of some simplification functions. ↓

```
clear
syms x y a b
f = (x+a)^2*(y+b)
g = expand(f)
h = factor(g)
prod(h)
collect(g)
collect(g, y)
collect(g, [a b])
simplify(g)
simplify(sin(x)^2+cos(x)^2)
simplify((x^2+2*x+1)/(x+1))
```

[3] Open Example09_02a.m as a **Live Script** and run the script in the **Live Editor**. ↵

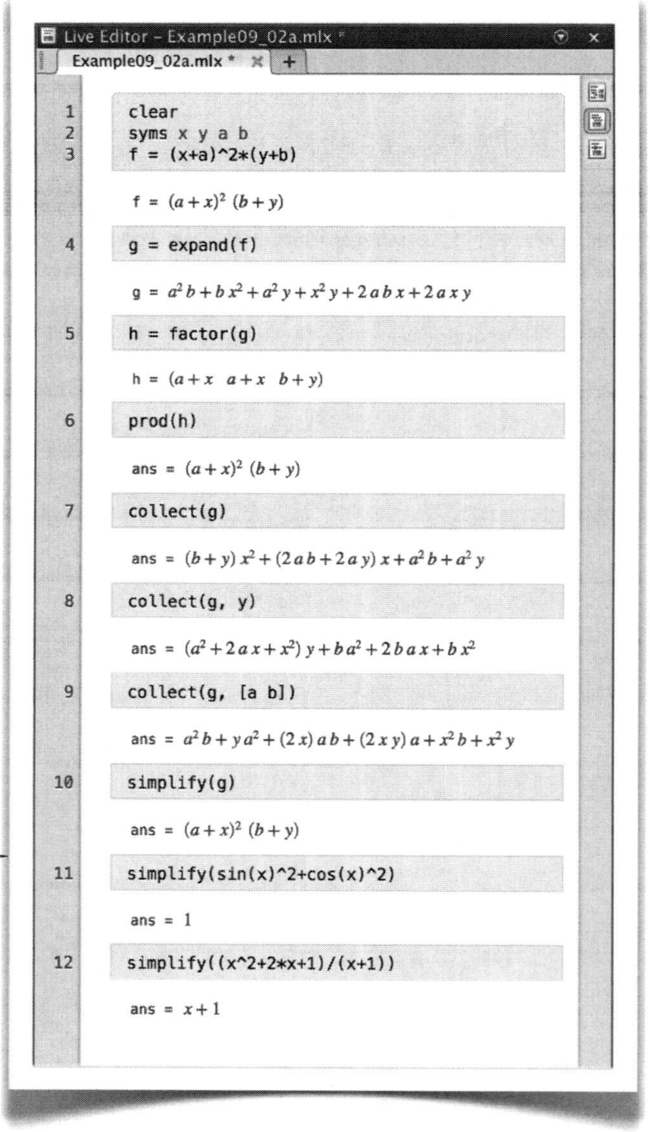

About Example09_02a.m

[4] Line 2 creates four symbolic variables: `x`, `y`, `a`, and `b`. Line 3 creates an expression

$$f = (x+a)^2(y+b)$$

Line 4 expands the expression using the function `expand` (see the output in [3], last page). In line 5, the expanded form is factorized using the function `factor`; the result is a vector of three symbolic expressions (see [3]), of which the product (line 6) is the original expression.

Line 7 rearranges the expression `g` in terms of the powers of the default variable `x`. Remember that, if a variable is not specified, the default variable is the one that is closest to `x`. Line 8 rearranges the expression in terms of the powers of the variable `y`. Line 9 rearranges the expression in terms of the powers of the two variables `a` and `b`.

Lines 10, 11, and 12 provide three simple examples to demonstrate the use of the function `simplify`, which usually gives the shortest form of an expression. #

9.2b Assumptions

Example09_02b.m: Assumptions

[1] The following commands demonstrate the use of the function `combine` to simplify expressions. They also show the use of the function `assume` to set assumptions on symbolic variables. ↘

```
clear
syms x y
combine(sqrt(3)*sqrt(x))
combine(sqrt(x)*sqrt(y))
assume(x, 'positive')
combine(sqrt(x)*sqrt(y))
clear
syms x y
combine(sqrt(x)*sqrt(y))
assumptions(x)
```

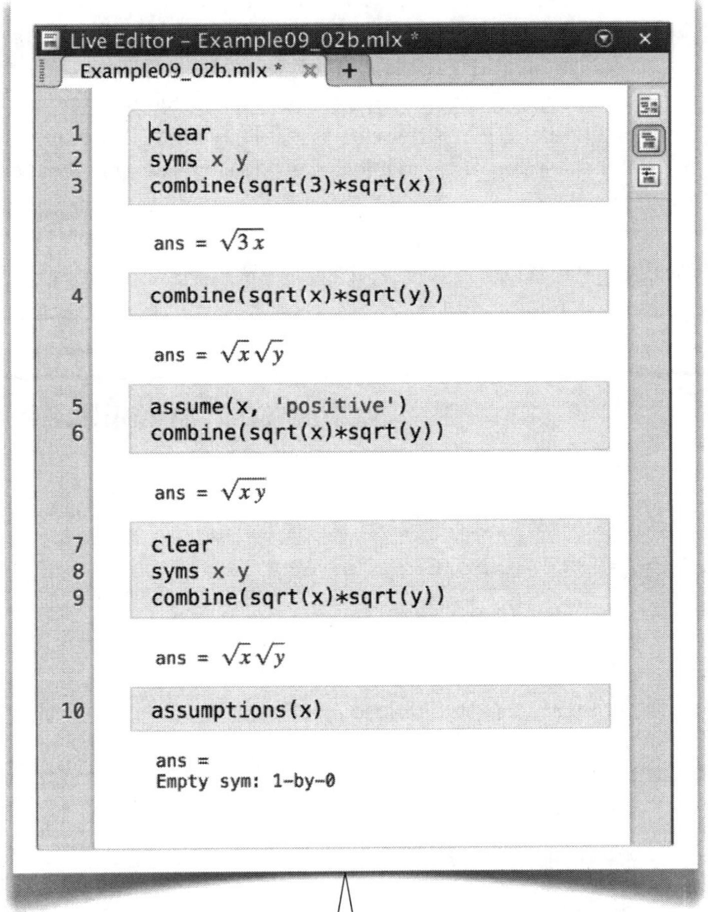

[2] Open Example09_02b.m as a **Live Script** and run the script in the **Live Editor**. ↵

About Example09_02b.m

[3] The function `combine` combines terms of the same algebraic structures. For example, it uses the following rules for powers when these identities are valid:

$$x^a x^b = x^{a+b},\ x^a y^a = (xy)^a,\ (x^a)^b = x^{ab}$$

Line 3 provides a simple example (see [2], last page)

$$\sqrt{3}\sqrt{x} = \sqrt{3x}$$

Note that even though x is a negative number, the above identity is still valid. However, the identity

$$\sqrt{x}\sqrt{y} = \sqrt{xy} \qquad \text{(a)}$$

is not always true. In fact, when both x and y are negative,

$$\sqrt{x}\sqrt{y} = -\sqrt{xy}$$

That's why, in line 4, the two square roots are not combined (see [2]). If the variable x is assumed to be positive (line 5), then the identity (a) becomes true and the square roots are combined (see line 6 and its output in [2]).

The deletion of a variable also deletes its assumptions. This is demonstrated in lines 7-9, in which we clear all the variables (line 7), re-create `x` and `y` (line 8), and combine the square roots (line 9). The result (see [2]) shows that the assumption (that `x` is positive) is not valid any more. We emphasize this because in the earlier versions (2018a and before) the deletion of a variable doesn't delete its assumptions; hence the result of line 9 remains $\sqrt{xy}$ for the earlier versions.

The function `assumptions` is used in line 10 to ask the assumption of `x`; the answer is that the positive assumption no longer holds for the variable `x`. #

Table 9.2 Simplification of Expressions

Functions	Description
`s = expand(expr,name,value)`	Expand expressions
`f = factor(expr,name,value)`	Factor expressions
`s = collect(expr,var)`	Collect terms with same powers
`s = combine(expr,name,value)`	Combine terms of same algebraic structures
`s = simplify(expr,name,value)`	General simplification
`s = simplifyFraction(expr,name,value)`	Compute normal forms of rational expressions
`assume(expr,set)`	Set assumption on symbolic variables
`assumptions(var)`	Show assumptions of symbolic variables

Details and More: Help>Symbolic Math Toolbox>Mathematics>Formula Manipulation and Simplification

9.3 Symbolic Differentiation: Curvature of a Curve

[1] The curvature κ of a planar curve described by the Cartesian parametric equations $x = x(t)$ and $y = y(t)$ is given by

$$\kappa = \frac{\dot{x}\ddot{y} - \dot{y}\ddot{x}}{(\dot{x}^2 + \dot{y}^2)^{3/2}} \qquad \text{(a)}$$

where the dot denotes the derivative with respect to t. In this section, we'll demonstrate the use of some symbolic functions by determining the curvature of a curve described by

$$x = \cos 2t + \cos t,\ y = -\sin 2t + \sin t,\ \text{where } 0 \le t \le 2\pi \qquad \text{(b)}$$

Example09_03.m: Curvature of a Planar Curve

[2] The following commands calculate the curvature of a curve given in [1]. →

```
clear
syms t
x =  cos(2*t) + cos(t);
y = -sin(2*t) + sin(t);
fplot(x, [0, 2*pi]), hold on
fplot(y, [0, 2*pi]), hold off
fplot(x, y, [0,2*pi])
x1 = diff(x)
x2 = diff(x1)
y1 = diff(y)
y2 = diff(y1)
n = x1*y2 - y1*x2
d = (x1^2 + y1^2)^(3/2)
n = simplify(n)
d = simplify(d)
k = n / d
fplot(k, [0, 2*pi])
k = subs(k, cos(3*t), 'C')
```

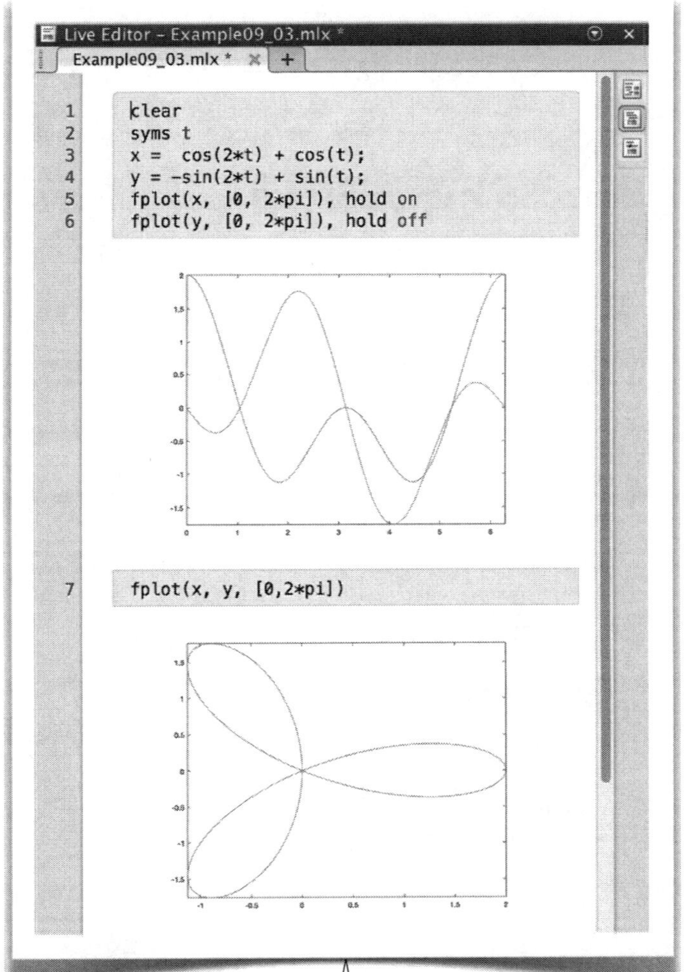

[3] The output with **Live Editor** (Continued at [4], Next page).

```
x1 = diff(x)
```

x1 = $-2\sin(2\,t)-\sin(t)$

```
x2 = diff(x1)
```

x2 = $-4\cos(2\,t)-\cos(t)$

```
y1 = diff(y)
```

y1 = $\cos(t)-2\cos(2\,t)$

```
y2 = diff(y1)
```

y2 = $4\sin(2\,t)-\sin(t)$

```
n = x1*y2 - y1*x2
```

n = $-(2\cos(2\,t)-\cos(t))\,(4\cos(2\,t)+\cos(t))-(4\sin(2\,t)-\sin(t))\,(2\sin(2\,t)+\sin(t))$

```
d = (x1^2 + y1^2)^(3/2)
```

d = $((2\sin(2\,t)+\sin(t))^2+(2\cos(2\,t)-\cos(t))^2)^{3/2}$

```
n = simplify(n)
```

n = $2\cos(3\,t)-7$

```
d = simplify(d)
```

d = $(5-4\cos(3\,t))^{3/2}$

```
k = n / d
```

k =

$$\frac{2\cos(3\,t)-7}{(5-4\cos(3\,t))^{3/2}}$$

[4] (Continued.) The output with **Live Editor** (Continued at [5]). ↓

```
fplot(k, [0, 2*pi])
```

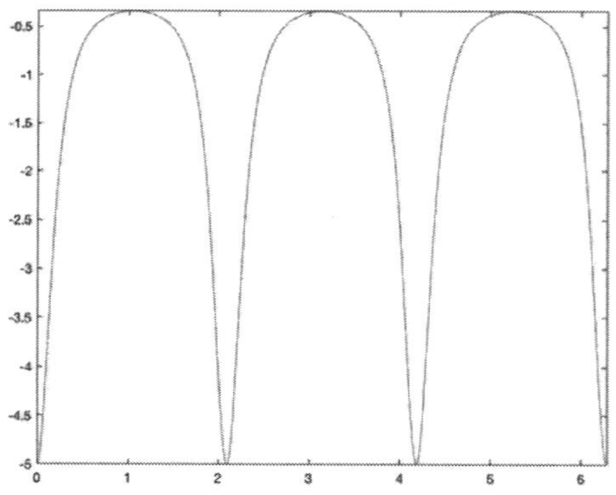

```
k = subs(k, cos(3*t), 'C')
```

k =

$$\frac{2\,C-7}{(5-4\,C)^{3/2}}$$

[5] (Continued.) The output with **Live Editor**. ↵

About Example09_03.m

[6] Lines 3-4 create parametric expressions x and y representing the curve defined in Eq. (b), page 367. Using the function `fplot`, which plots an expression over a specified domain, lines 5-6 plot an x-versus-t curve and a y-versus-t curve in the same **Axes** (see the graph in [3], page 367). Line 7 plots a y-versus-x curve. Note that the curve we want to determine is the y-versus-x curve.

Lines 8-11 calculate the first derivatives and the second derivatives of the expressions x and y, respectively (see the output in [4], last page):

$$\dot{x} = -2\sin 2t - \sin t$$
$$\ddot{x} = -4\cos 2t - \cos t$$
$$\dot{y} = -2\cos 2t + \cos t$$
$$\ddot{y} = 4\sin 2t - \sin t$$

Note that we use `x1` to represent $\dot{x}$, `x2` to represent $\ddot{x}$, `y1` to represent $\dot{y}$, and `y2` to represent $\ddot{y}$.

Lines 12-13 calculate the numerator and the denominator, respectively, in Eq. (a), page 367 (see [4]).

$$\begin{aligned} n &= \dot{x}\ddot{y} - \dot{y}\ddot{x} \\ &= (-2\sin 2t - \sin t)(4\sin 2t - \sin t) - (-2\cos 2t + \cos t)(-4\cos 2t - \cos t) \\ &= -(2\cos 2t - \cos t)(4\cos 2t + \cos t) - (4\sin 2t - \sin t)(2\sin 2t + \sin t) \end{aligned}$$

$$\begin{aligned} d &= (\dot{x}^2 + \dot{y}^2)^{3/2} \\ &= \left[(2\sin 2t + \sin t)^2 + (2\cos 2t - \cos t)^2\right]^{3/2} \end{aligned}$$

Lines 14-15 use the function `simplify` to simplify the above two expressions (see [4]),

$$n = 2\cos 3t - 7, \; d = (5 - 4\cos 3t)^{3/2}$$

It is left to you, as an exercise, to prove the two identities above.

Finally, line 16 calculates the curvature by dividing the numerator with the denominator (see [4]),

$$k = \frac{2\cos 3t - 7}{(5 - 4\cos 3t)^{3/2}}$$

Line 17 plots the curvature-versus-t curve (see the graph in [5], last page).

The function `subs` can be used to replace a part of an expression with a symbol. For example, line 18 replaces $\cos 3t$ with a symbol C, and the result is (see [5])

$$k = \frac{2C - 7}{(5 - 4C)^{3/2}}$$

#

Table 9.3 Line Plots

Functions	Description
`fplot(fun,lineSpec)`	Plot expression or function
`fplot3(funx,funy,funz,lineSpec)`	3-D parametric curve plotter
`fimplicit(fun,lineSpec)`	Plot implicit function
`fimplicit3(fun,lineSpec)`	Plot 3-D implicit function

Details and More: Help>MATLAB>Graphics>2-D and 3-D Plots>Line Plots

9.4 Symbolic Integration: Normal Distributions

[1] German mathematician Carl Friedrich Gauss (1777-1855) proposed a model to describe **normal distributions**, in which the **probability density function** (p.d.f.) is given by

$$f(x) = \frac{1}{\sqrt{2\pi}\sigma} \exp\left[-\frac{(x-\mu)^2}{2\sigma^2} \right] \qquad \text{(a)}$$

The model contains two parameters: a mean μ and a standard deviation σ. The probability that a sampling data, its population distributed normally, is less than x can be calculated by integrating the p.d.f. from $-\infty$ to x,

$$p(x) = \int_{-\infty}^{x} f(x)dx \qquad \text{(b)}$$

The above function is called the **cumulative distribution function** (c.d.f.).

The **standard normal distribution** is a normal distribution in which $\mu = 0$ and $\sigma = 1$. ↓

Example09_04.m: Normal Distribution Curves

[2] This script plots a p.d.f. curve, Eq. (a), for the standard normal distribution. It also integrates the p.d.f. using the function `int` to obtain a c.d.f., Eq. (b), and plots a c.d.f. curve. ↵

```
clear
mu = 0; sigma = 1;
syms x
f = exp(-(x-mu)^2/(2*sigma^2))/(sqrt(2*pi)*sigma);
fplot(f, [-3, 3]), hold on
p = int(f, x, -inf, x);
fplot(p, [-3, 3])
axis([-3, 3, 0, 1])
xlabel('x')
title('Standard Normal Distribution')
legend('Probability Density Function', ...
        'Cumulative Distribution Function', ...
        'Location', 'northwest')
```

[3] Open Example09_04.m as a **Live Script** and run the script in **Live Editor**. ↓

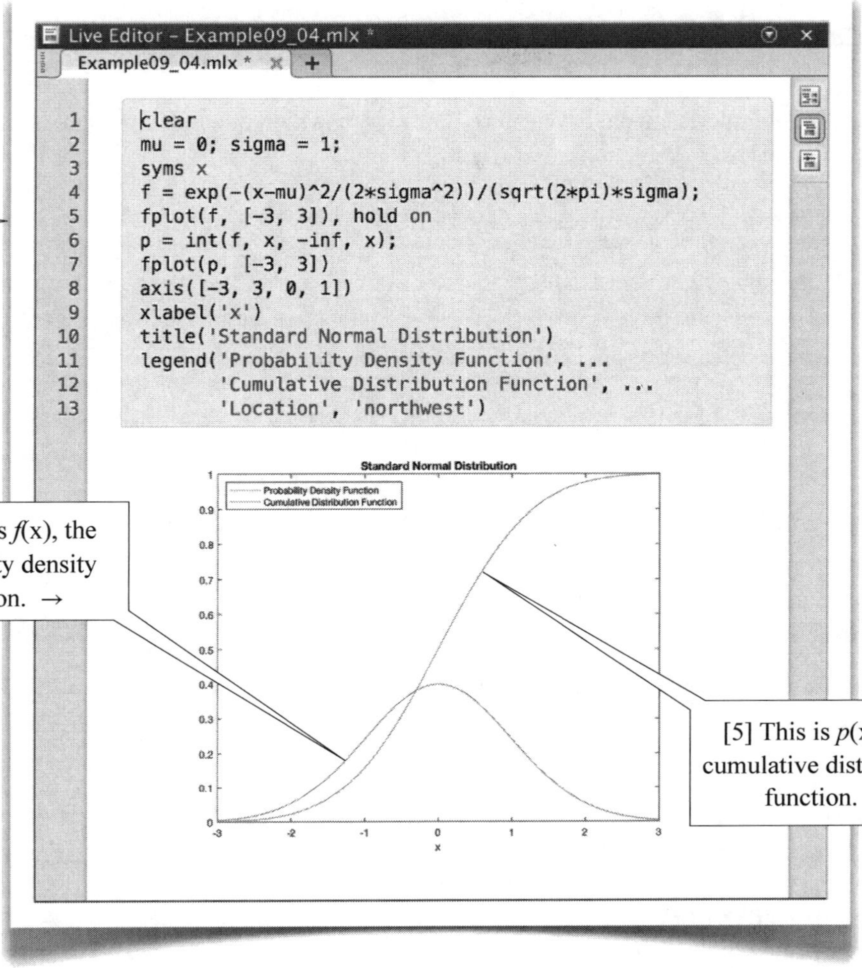

[4] This is $f(x)$, the probability density function. →

[5] This is $p(x)$, the cumulative distribution function. ↓

About Example09_04.m

[6] Line 2 sets up parameters for a standard normal distribution: $\mu = 0$ and $\sigma = 1$. Line 3 creates the independent variable x. Line 4 defines the p.d.f. $f(x)$, Eq. (a), for the standard normal distribution. Line 5 plots $f(x)$ within a specified range (see [4]). Line 6 integrates $f(x)$ with respect to x from $-\infty$ to x, and the result is the c.d.f., Eq. (b), of the standard normal distribution. The built-in constant `inf` represents infinity. Line 7 plots the c.d.f. curve (see [5]). The meaning of $p(x)$ is the area under the curve $f(x)$ and less than x. In particular, $p(0) = 0.5$ and $p(\infty) = 1$. Line 8 sets the axes limits. Lines 11-13 add legends at the upper-left corner of the graphics area.

To see the form of the c.d.f. $p(x)$, type

```
>> p
```

You will see lengthy constants in the expression. To help with legibility, type

```
>> vpa(p,5)
ans =
0.5*erf(0.70711*x) + 0.5
```

The function `vpa` evaluates constants in an expression to a specified number of significant digits. The error function `erf` is defined by $erf(x) = \frac{2}{\sqrt{\pi}} \int_0^x e^{-t^2} \, dt$. #

9.5 Limits

[1] The concept of limits is crucial in Calculus. The differentiation of a function $f(x)$ with respect to its independent variable x is defined as

$$f'(x) = \frac{df(x)}{dx} = \lim_{h \to 0} \frac{f(x+h) - f(x)}{h}$$

For example, if $f(x) = \sin x$,

$$f'(x) = \lim_{h \to 0} \frac{\sin(x+h) - \sin x}{h} = \cos x$$

And if $f(x) = x^n$,

$$f'(x) = \lim_{h \to 0} \frac{x^{x+h} - x^n}{h} = nx^{n-1}$$

The function `limit` allows you to study the limits of an expression. ↙

Example09_05.m: Limits

[2] The following commands demonstrate the use of the function `limit`. ↘

```
clear
syms x h n
f(x) = sin(x);
g(x) = limit((f(x+h)-f(x))/h, h, 0)
g(x) = diff(f)
f(x) = x^n;
g(x) = limit((f(x+h)-f(x))/h, h, 0)
g(x) = diff(f)
limit(sin(x)/x, x, 0)
f(x) = limit((1+x/n)^n, n, inf)
vpa(f(1))
```

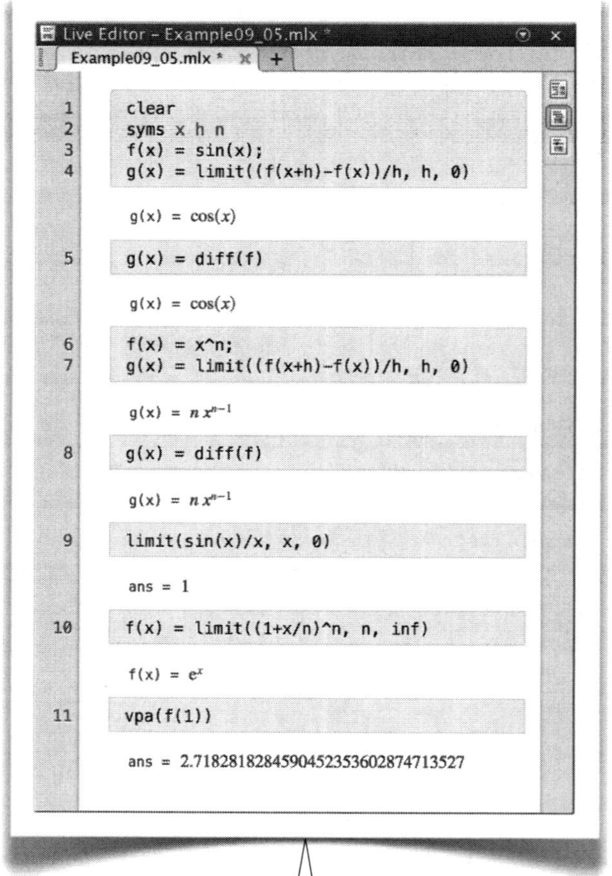

[3] Open Example09_05.m as a **Live Script** and run the script in the **Live Editor**. ↵

About Example09_05.m

[4] Line 2 creates three symbolic variables: x, h, and n. Line 3 defines a symbolic function $f(x)=\sin x$. Line 4 calculates its derivative using the definition,

$$g(x)=f'(x)=\lim_{h\to 0}\frac{\sin(x+h)-\sin x}{h}=\cos x$$

Line 5 verifies this using the function `diff`.

Line 6 defines a function $f(x)=x^n$. Line 7 calculates its derivative using the definition,

$$g(x)=f'(x)=\lim_{h\to 0}\frac{x^{x+h}-x^n}{h}=nx^{n-1}$$

Line 8 verifies this using the function `diff`.

Line 9 shows that

$$\lim_{x\to 0}\frac{\sin x}{x}=1$$

Line 10 shows that

$$\lim_{n\to\infty}\left(1+\frac{x}{n}\right)^n=e^x$$

Line 11 calculates the numeric value of e. Note that, by default, the function `vpa` evaluates a constant to 32 significant digits. #

Table 9.5 Limits

Functions	Description
`limit(expr,x,a)`	Compute limit of symbolic expression
Details and More: Help>Symbolic Math Toolbox>Mathematics>Calculus>Limits	

9.6 Taylor Series

[1] Theory of Taylor series can be stated as follows: A function $f(x)$ can be approached by a series of polynomials:

$$f(x)=\sum_{k=0}^{\infty}\frac{f^{(k)}(a)}{k!}(x-a)^k \quad \text{(a)}$$

where $f^{(k)}(x)$ is the kth derivative of the function and a is called an expansion point. Using Taylor series, you can evaluate a function value (e.g., $\sin x$) using basic arithmetic operations (+, -, *, /). That is how a digital computer calculates the value of a function such as sin(x). In theory, infinite number of terms ($k=0,\ 1,\ 2,\ \ldots\ \infty$) is needed to obtain a value equal to the analytical function value; in practice, finite number of terms (i.e., $k=0,\ 1,\ 2,\ \ldots\ n$) is used. Also, the closer the evaluated point to the expansion point, the more accurate the function value. Another way to obtain a more accurate function value is to use more terms in the series. For $\sin x$, when expanded at $a=0$, its Taylor series is shown as Eq. (a) of 2.12a, page 108. And when expanded at $a=\pi/4$, the Taylor series is

$$\sin x=\frac{\sqrt{2}}{2}\left[1+(x-\pi/4)-\frac{(x-\pi/4)^2}{2}-\frac{(x-\pi/4)^3}{6}+\frac{(x-\pi/4)^4}{24}+\frac{(x-\pi/4)^5}{120}-\ldots\right] \quad \text{(b)}$$

↓

Example09_06.m: Taylor Series

[2] The following commands evaluate sin($\pi/4$) using three forms of Taylor series: First, expand at $a=0$ to the 5th order; second, expand at $a=0$ to the 7th order; third, expand at $a=\pi/4$ to the 5th order. ↵

```
clear
syms x
f(x) = sin(x);
T1(x) = taylor(f)
T2(x) = taylor(f, x, 'Order', 8)
T3(x) = taylor(f, x, pi/4)
vpa(f(pi/4))
vpa(T1(pi/4))
vpa(T2(pi/4))
vpa(T3(pi/4))
```

Table 9.6 Taylor Series

Functions	Description
`expr = taylor(fun)`	Taylor series
`expr = taylor(fun,var,a)`	Taylor series
`expr = taylor(fun,var,name,value)`	Taylor series

Details and More: Help>Symbolic Math Toolbox>Mathematics>Calculus>Series

[3] Open Example09_06.m as a **Live Script** and run the script in the **Live Editor**. ↓

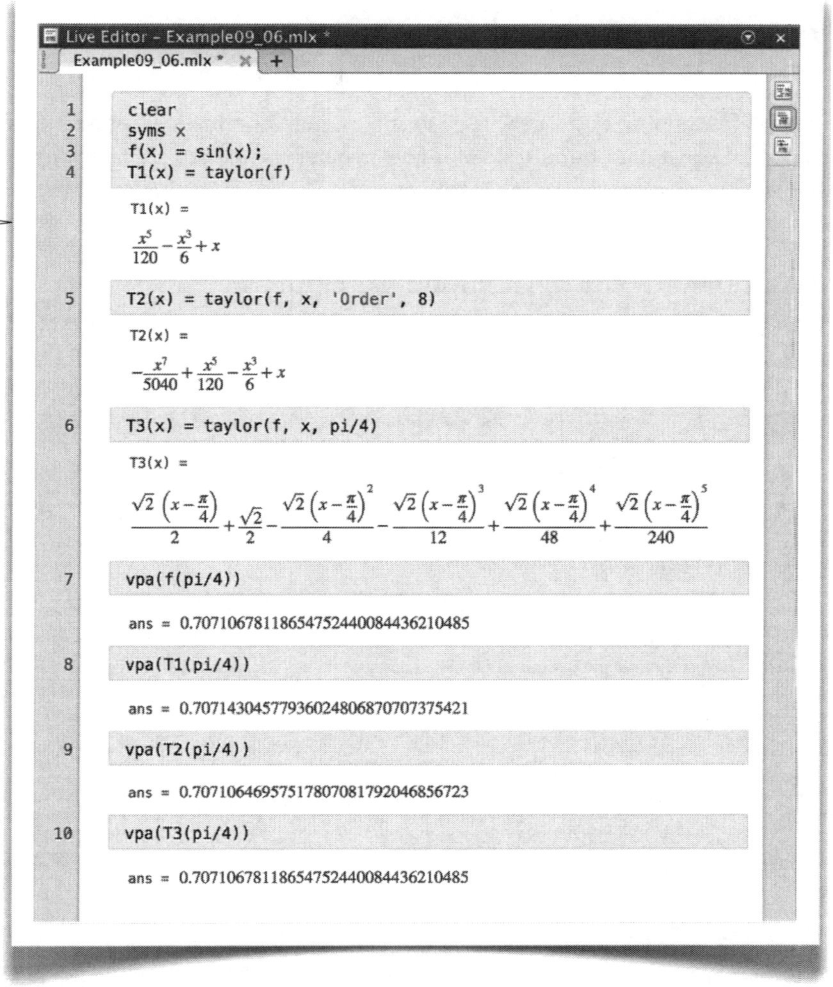

About Example09_06.m

[4] Line 2 creates a symbolic variable x. Line 3 defines a symbolic function $f(x)=\sin x$. Line 4 uses the function `taylor` to obtain a Taylor series for $\sin x$. By default, it expands at $a=0$ to the 5th order (see [3]).

$$\sin x \approx x-\frac{x^3}{3!}+\frac{x^5}{5!}$$

Line 5 uses `taylor` again, specifying an order of 8. It expands at $a=0$ to the 7th order (see [3]).

$$\sin x \approx x-\frac{x^3}{3!}+\frac{x^5}{5!}-\frac{x^7}{7!}$$

Note that the function `taylor(f,x,'Order',n)` outputs the Taylor series to the (n-1)th order; by default, $n=6$.

Line 6 uses `taylor` again, specifying an expansion point at $a=\pi/4$; by default, it expands to the 5th order.

Lines 7-10 compare the numerical results. Line 7 uses the original function ($\sin x$) to calculate an "exact" value at $x=\pi/4$. Remember, by default, the function vpa outputs numbers with 32 significant digits.

Lines 8, 9, and 10 evaluate $\sin(\pi/4)$ using the three forms of Taylor series, respectively. By comparing their output numbers (see [3]), we conclude that T3 is the best approximation (it is accurate up to the 32nd digit after the decimal point), T1 is the poorest (accurate up to the 4th digit), and T2 has the medium accuracy (6th digit). #

9.7 Algebraic Equations

[1] The function `solve` can be used to solve algebraic equations, either linear or nonlinear, either a single equation or a system of equations. For a system of linear equations, a more efficient way is to solve it in matrix form using the function `linsolve` or the **backslash** operator (\). This section demonstrates the use of these functions. ↓

Example09_07.m: Algebraic Equations

[2] The following commands demonstrate the symbolic solution of algebraic equations. ↓

```
clear
syms x a b c
eq = a*x^2+b*x+c;
solve(eq)
eq = (cos(x)==1);
solve(eq)
[sol, param, cond] = solve(eq, 'ReturnConditions', true)
syms y d e f
eq1 = a*x+b*y==c;
eq2 = d*x+e*y==f;
sol = solve(eq1, eq2)
[sol.x, sol.y]
[A, b] = equationsToMatrix(eq1, eq2, x, y)
sol = linsolve(A, b)
sol = A\b
sol = inv(A)*b
```

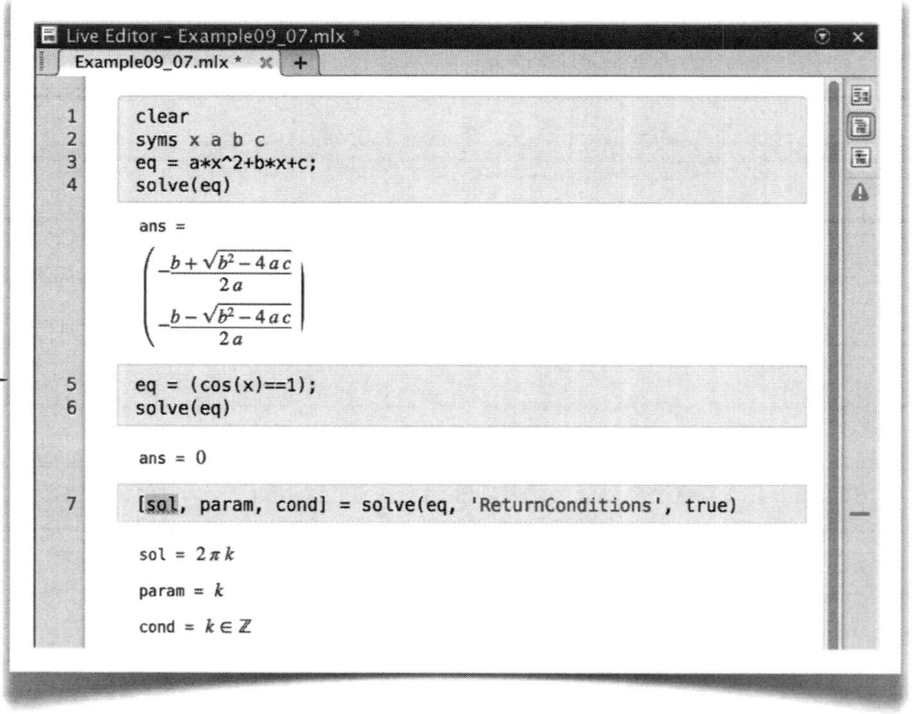

[3] Open Example09_07.m as a **Live Script** and run the script in the **Live Editor**. (Ignore the warning messages. Continued at [4], next page) ↵

[4] Continued from [3], last page. ↵

```
syms y d e f
eq1 = a*x+b*y==c;
eq2 = d*x+e*y==f;
sol = solve(eq1, eq2)
```

```
sol = struct with fields:
    x: [1×1 sym]
    y: [1×1 sym]
```

```
[sol.x, sol.y]
```

ans =

$$\begin{pmatrix} -\frac{b\,f-c\,e}{a\,e-b\,d} & \frac{a\,f-c\,d}{a\,e-b\,d} \end{pmatrix}$$

```
[A, b] = equationsToMatrix(eq1, eq2, x, y)
```

A =

$$\begin{pmatrix} a & b \\ d & e \end{pmatrix}$$

b =

$$\begin{pmatrix} c \\ f \end{pmatrix}$$

```
sol = linsolve(A, b)
```

sol =

$$\begin{pmatrix} -\frac{b\,f-c\,e}{a\,e-b\,d} \\ \frac{a\,f-c\,d}{a\,e-b\,d} \end{pmatrix}$$

```
sol = A\b
```

sol =

$$\begin{pmatrix} -\frac{b\,f-c\,e}{a\,e-b\,d} \\ \frac{a\,f-c\,d}{a\,e-b\,d} \end{pmatrix}$$

```
sol = inv(A)*b
```

sol =

$$\begin{pmatrix} \frac{c\,e}{a\,e-b\,d} - \frac{b\,f}{a\,e-b\,d} \\ \frac{a\,f}{a\,e-b\,d} - \frac{c\,d}{a\,e-b\,d} \end{pmatrix}$$

Table 9.7 Algebraic Equations

Functions	Description
`sol = solve(eqn,var)`	Solve algebraic equations
`[A,b] = equationsToMatrix(eqns,vars)`	Convert linear system of equations to matrix form
`sol = linsolve(A,b)`	Solve linear system of equations in matrix form
`x = A\b`	Solve linear system of equations Ax = b
`B = inv(A)`	Inverse of a matrix

Details and More:
Help>Symbolic Math Toolbox>Mathematics>Equation Solving>Linear and Nonlinear Equations and systems

About Example09_07.m

[5] Line 2 creates four symbolic variables. Line 3 creates a symbolic variable `eq` containing an expression ax^2+bx+c, which is then input to the function `solve` (line 4). If the right-hand side of an equation is not specified, the function `solve` assumes a zero for the right-hand side; i.e., it solves the equation

$$ax^2+bx+c=0$$

for the default variable, which is x. The result is a column vector of two symbolic expressions (see [3], page 376):

$$x=\frac{-b\pm\sqrt{b^2-4ac}}{2a}$$

Line 5 defines an equation

$$\cos x=1$$

Note that we explicitly include an equal sign (==). Also note that the assignment operator = has the lowest precedence (see 2.8[1], page 92); therefore, the outer parentheses in line 5 is not really necessary; they are included for clarity. Line 6 solves the equation for x. A trivial solution (0) is output (see [3]). For this equation, a general form of solutions is

$$x=2k\pi\,,\ k\in \text{integer}$$

Line 7 uses the function `solve` again and sets **ReturnConditions** option to `true`. It then returns all solutions along with the parameters in the solutions and the conditions of the parameters (see [3]). Note that the Z in the condition

$$k\in Z$$

is the set of all integer numbers.

Lines 8-10 create two equations.

$$\begin{aligned} ax+by&=c\\ dx+ey&=f \end{aligned}$$

Line 11 solves the system of equations. For a system of two equations, the function `solve` assumes that the two variables closest to x are the unknown variables to be solved (see 9.1b[3], page 361). Thus, line 11 solves the system of equations for x and y. The result `sol` is a structure of two fields: x and y (see [4]). Line 12 displays the two fields (see [4]),

$$x=-\frac{bf-ce}{ae-bd},\ y=\frac{af-cd}{ae-bd} \qquad \text{(a)}$$

As mentioned, to solve a system of linear equations, a more efficient way is using the function `linsolve` or the backslash operator (\). The system of equations needs to be in a matrix form. The function `equationsToMatrix` (line 13) converts a system of linear equations to a matrix form

$$\mathbf{Ax}=\mathbf{b}$$

It outputs a matrix **A** and a column vector **b**.

Line 14 solves the system of linear equations using the function `linsolve`, which outputs solutions in a column vector of two expressions the same as those in Eq. (a).

Lines 15 and 16 demonstrate two other ways of solving a system of linear equations in matrix form: using the **backslash** operator (line 15; also see 3.14[2], page 155) and using the function `inv` (line 16; inverse of a matrix). In general, using `inv` to solve a system of linear equations is not recommended, since it is usually much less efficient than using the **backslash**. #

9.8 Inverse of Matrix: Hooke's Law

[1] In Mechanics of Materials, we often assume that the stress σ and strain ε has a linear relationship and they follow the Hooke's law. Let $\sigma = [\sigma_x \ \sigma_y \ \sigma_z \ \tau_{xy} \ \tau_{yz} \ \tau_{zx}]^T$ be the stress components and $\varepsilon = [\varepsilon_x \ \varepsilon_y \ \varepsilon_z \ \gamma_{xy} \ \gamma_{yz} \ \gamma_{zx}]^T$ be the strain components at a certain point in a solid body. Hooke's law states that

$$\varepsilon = \mathbf{K}\sigma$$

where

$$\mathbf{K} = \begin{bmatrix} 1/E & -v/E & -v/E & 0 & 0 & 0 \\ -v/E & 1/E & -v/E & 0 & 0 & 0 \\ -v/E & -v/E & 1/E & 0 & 0 & 0 \\ 0 & 0 & 0 & 1/G & 0 & 0 \\ 0 & 0 & 0 & 0 & 1/G & 0 \\ 0 & 0 & 0 & 0 & 0 & 1/G \end{bmatrix}$$

in which E is called the Young's modulus, v the Poisson's ratio, and G the shear modulus.

It is possible to rewrite Hooke's law in an inverse form:

$$\sigma = \mathbf{F}\varepsilon$$

where $\mathbf{F} = \mathbf{K}^{-1}$.

The function `inv` finds the inverse of a matrix symbolically (the function `inv` also can be used to inverse a matrix numerically). ↓

Example09_08.m: Inverse of Matrix

[2] The following commands calculate **F** defined in [1]. ↵

```
clear
syms E v G
K = [1/E, -v/E, -v/E,    0,    0    0;
     -v/E,  1/E, -v/E,    0,    0,    0;
     -v/E, -v/E,  1/E,    0,    0,    0;
        0,    0,    0, 1/G,    0,    0;
        0,    0,    0,    0, 1/G,    0;
        0,    0,    0,    0,    0, 1/G]
F = inv(K)
```

[3] Open Example09_08.m as a **Live Script** and run the script in **Live Editor**. ↓

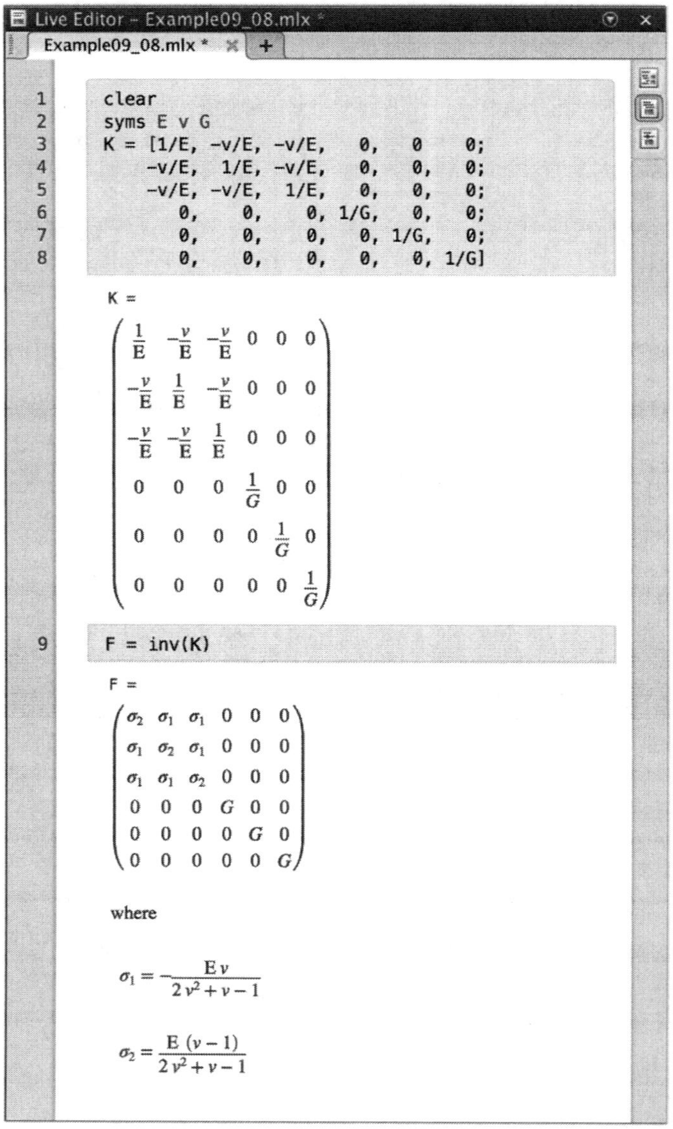

$$K = \begin{pmatrix} \frac{1}{E} & -\frac{v}{E} & -\frac{v}{E} & 0 & 0 & 0 \\ -\frac{v}{E} & \frac{1}{E} & -\frac{v}{E} & 0 & 0 & 0 \\ -\frac{v}{E} & -\frac{v}{E} & \frac{1}{E} & 0 & 0 & 0 \\ 0 & 0 & 0 & \frac{1}{G} & 0 & 0 \\ 0 & 0 & 0 & 0 & \frac{1}{G} & 0 \\ 0 & 0 & 0 & 0 & 0 & \frac{1}{G} \end{pmatrix}$$

$$F = \begin{pmatrix} \sigma_2 & \sigma_1 & \sigma_1 & 0 & 0 & 0 \\ \sigma_1 & \sigma_2 & \sigma_1 & 0 & 0 & 0 \\ \sigma_1 & \sigma_1 & \sigma_2 & 0 & 0 & 0 \\ 0 & 0 & 0 & G & 0 & 0 \\ 0 & 0 & 0 & 0 & G & 0 \\ 0 & 0 & 0 & 0 & 0 & G \end{pmatrix}$$

where

$$\sigma_1 = -\frac{E\,v}{2v^2 + v - 1}$$

$$\sigma_2 = \frac{E\,(v-1)}{2v^2 + v - 1}$$

[4] Note that the result of the inverse can be further rearranged as follows.

$$\mathbf{F} = \begin{bmatrix} \frac{(1-v)E}{(1+v)(1-2v)} & \frac{vE}{(1+v)(1-2v)} & \frac{vE}{(1+v)(1-2v)} & 0 & 0 & 0 \\ \frac{vE}{(1+v)(1-2v)} & \frac{(1-v)E}{(1+v)(1-2v)} & \frac{vE}{(1+v)(1-2v)} & 0 & 0 & 0 \\ \frac{vE}{(1+v)(1-2v)} & \frac{vE}{(1+v)(1-2v)} & \frac{(1-v)E}{(1+v)(1-2v)} & 0 & 0 & 0 \\ 0 & 0 & 0 & G & 0 & 0 \\ 0 & 0 & 0 & 0 & G & 0 \\ 0 & 0 & 0 & 0 & 0 & G \end{bmatrix}$$

#

9.9 Ordinary Differential Equations (ODE): Vibrations of Supported Machines

9.9a Example: Undamped Free Vibrations

[1] Consider again the supported machine in 2.15a[2], page 117. For the undamped free vibration case (2.15a[3], page 117), the equation and the initial conditions are

$$m\ddot{x} + kx = 0 \quad \text{(a)}$$

$$x(0) = \delta \text{ and } \dot{x}(0) = 0 \quad \text{(b)}$$

The solution of the above ODE is

$$x(t) = \delta \cos \omega t \quad \text{(c)}$$

$$\omega = \sqrt{\frac{k}{m}} \quad \text{(d)}$$

For the damped free vibration case (2.15b[1], page 118), the equation and the initial conditions are

$$m\ddot{x} + c\dot{x} + kx = 0 \quad \text{(e)}$$

$$x(0) = \delta \text{ and } \dot{x}(0) = 0 \quad \text{(f)}$$

The solution of the above ODE is

$$x(t) = \delta e^{-\frac{ct}{2m}}\left(\cos \omega_d t + \frac{c}{2m\omega_d} \sin \omega_d t\right), \quad \text{(g)}$$

$$\omega_d = \omega\sqrt{1 - \left(\frac{c}{c_c}\right)^2} \quad \text{(h)}$$

In Section 2.15, we left you to prove the solutions by substituting them to the equations. In this section, we'll solve for these solutions using the function `dsolve`, which solves an ODE (or a system of ODEs) symbolically. ↓

Example09_09a.m: Undamped Free Vibrations

[2] The following commands successfully obtain a general solution for the undamped case, Eq. (a); however, they fail to obtain a solution that satisfies the initial conditions, Eq. (b). ↵

```
clear
syms t m k delta omega
syms x(t)
x1(t) = diff(x);
x2(t) = diff(x1);
ode = m*x2+k*x==0;
x(t) = dsolve(ode)
assume([m, k], 'positive')
x(t) = dsolve(ode)
x(t) = combine(x)
x(t) = subs(x, (k/m)^(1/2), omega)
x(t) = dsolve(ode, x(0)==delta, x1(0)==0)
```

[3] Open Example09_09a.m as a **Live Script** and run the script. →

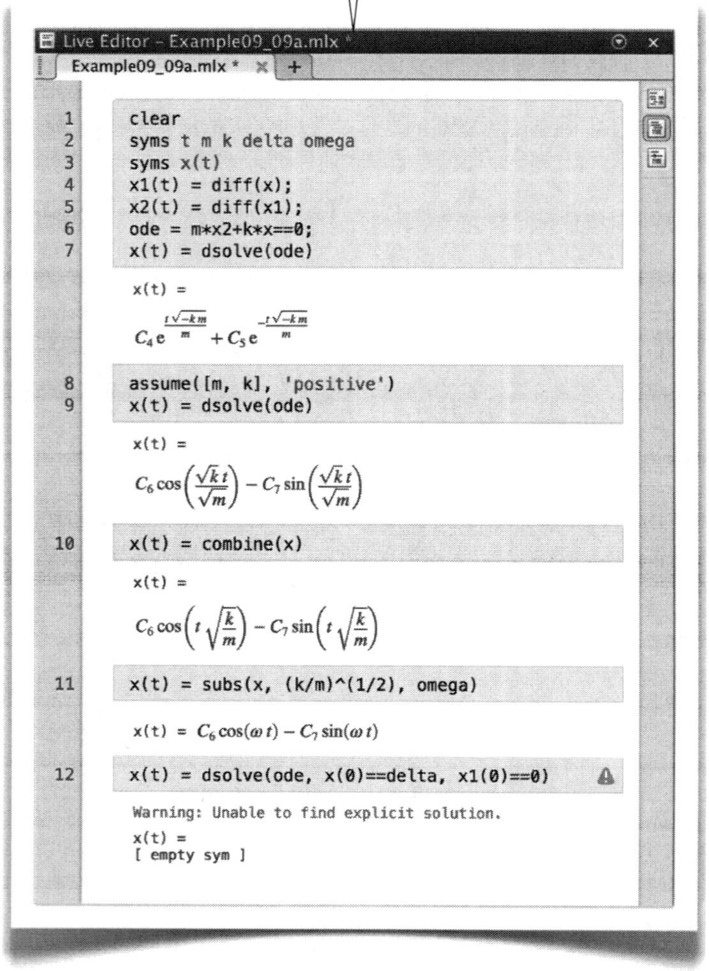

About Example09_09a.m

[4] Line 2 creates symbolic variables used in this script. We use `x1` to represent the first derivative of $x(t)$ (line 4) and `x2` to represent the second derivative of $x(t)$ (line 5). Line 6 defines the ODE, Eq. (a), without initial conditions; that is, it finds a general solution for the undamped free vibration case. The output (see [3]) involves $\sqrt{-km}$, which is an imaginary number because both the spring constant k and the mass m are positive numbers. However, MATLAB has no way to know that they are positive.

Line 8 adds an assumption that both k and m are positive; line 9 solves the ODE again. This time, it gives a solution involving trigonometric functions (see [3]). After the use of the function `combine` (line 10), a general solution is obtained:

$$x(t) = C_6 \cos\left(t\sqrt{k/m}\right) + C_7 \sin\left(t\sqrt{k/m}\right)$$

The quantity $\sqrt{k/m}$ is the natural frequency ω (see Eq. (d)). Line 11 substitutes this quantity with the variable `omega` and the general solution has a more compact form:

$$x(t) = C_6 \cos(\omega t) + C_7 \sin(\omega t)$$

Next, line 12 tries to obtain a solution for the specified initial conditions, Eq. (b). But the function `dsolve` fails to give a solution, and it gives a warning message (see the red-colored message in [3]).

If you keep struggling over this problem, using all kinds of tricks, it is possible that you would eventually obtain a solution. But more likely, the solution would never be obtained. There is a general way to ease the problem: reducing a high-order ODE to a system of first-order ODEs, discussed next. #

9.9b Systems of First-Order ODEs

[1] If we introduce a second dependent variable

$$v(t) = \dot{x}(t) \qquad \text{(a)}$$

Then the second-order ODE, Eq. 9.9a(a), becomes

$$m\dot{v} + kx = 0 \qquad \text{(b)}$$

We now solve the system of **first-order** ODEs, Eqs. (a, b), for $x(t)$ and $v(t)$ with the initial conditions:

$$x(0) = \delta \qquad \text{(c)}$$

$$v(0) = 0 \qquad \text{(d)}$$

↓

Example09_09b.m: Undamped Free Vibrations

[2] The following commands successfully obtain a solution by solving the system of first-order ODEs, Eqs. (a, b), along with the initial conditions, Eqs. (c, d). ↵

```
clear
syms t m k delta omega
syms x(t) v(t)
x1(t) = diff(x);
v1(t) = diff(v);
ode1 = m*v1+k*x==0;
ode2 = x1==v;
assume([m, k], 'positive')
sol = dsolve(ode1, ode2, x(0)==delta, v(0)==0)
x(t) = sol.x
v(t) = sol.v
x(t) = combine(x)
x(t) = subs(x, (k/m)^(1/2), omega)
v(t) = combine(v)
v(t) = subs(v, (k/m)^(1/2), omega)
```

[3] Open Example09_09b.m as a **Live Script** and run the script. ↓

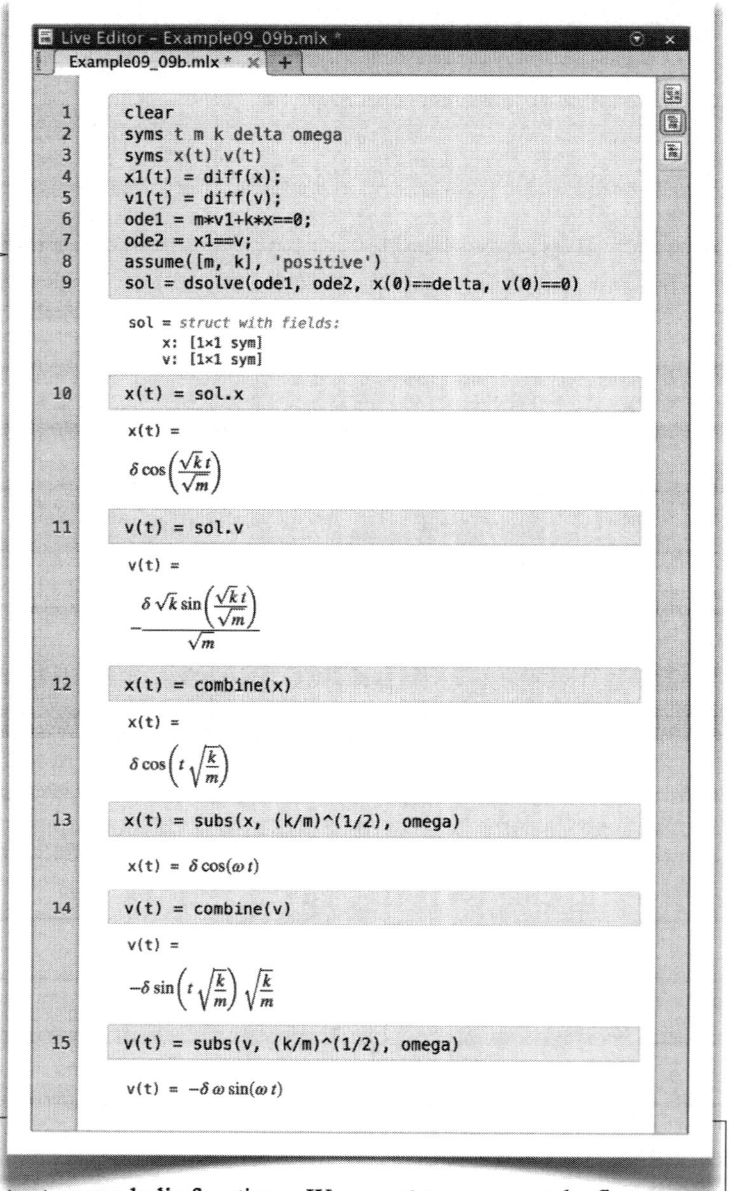

About Example09_09b.m

[4] Line 2 creates five symbolic variables; line 3 creates two symbolic functions. We use `x1` to represent the first derivative of $x(t)$ (line 4) and `v1` to represent the first derivative of $v(t)$ (line 5). Lines 6-7 define the two first-order ODEs, Eqs. (b, a), respectively. Line 8 adds an assumption that m and k are positive. Line 9 solves the system of ODEs using the function `dsolve`, in which the two ODEs and the two initial conditions, Eqs. (c, d), are input as four arguments; they can also be input in a vector form as follows:

```
sol = dsolve([ode1, ode2], [x(0)==delta, v(0)==0)]
```

The result `sol` is a structure of two fields: `x` and `v` (see [3], last page). Lines 10-11 display `x` and `v` (see [4]). After the use of the functions `combine` (line 12) and `subs` (line 13), we have the solutions in compact forms (see [4]):

$$x(t) = \delta \cos \omega t$$
$$v(t) = -\delta\omega \sin \omega t$$

which are consistent with that in Eq 9.9a(c), page 381. #

9.9c Example: Damped Free Vibrations

[1] For the damped case, the ODE, Eq. 9.9a(e), can be reduced to a system of two first-order ODEs

$$m\dot{v} + cv + kx = 0 \qquad \text{(a)}$$

$$v(t) = \dot{x}(t) \qquad \text{(b)}$$

with the initial conditions:

$$x(0) = \delta \qquad \text{(c)}$$

$$v(0) = 0 \qquad \text{(d)}$$

↓

Example09_09c.m: Damped Free Vibrations

[2] The following commands solve the system of ODEs, Eqs. (a, b), along with the initial conditions, Eqs. (c, d). ↓

```
clear
syms t x(t) v(t)
m = 1; c = 1; k = 100; delta = 0.2;
x1(t) = diff(x);
v1(t) = diff(v);
ode1 = m*v1+c*v+k*x==0;
ode2 = x1==v;
sol = dsolve(ode1, ode2, x(0)==delta, v(0)==0)
x(t) = sol.x
v(t) = sol.v
fplot(x, [0,2])
fplot(v, [0,2])
vpa(x, 5)
vpa(v, 5)
```

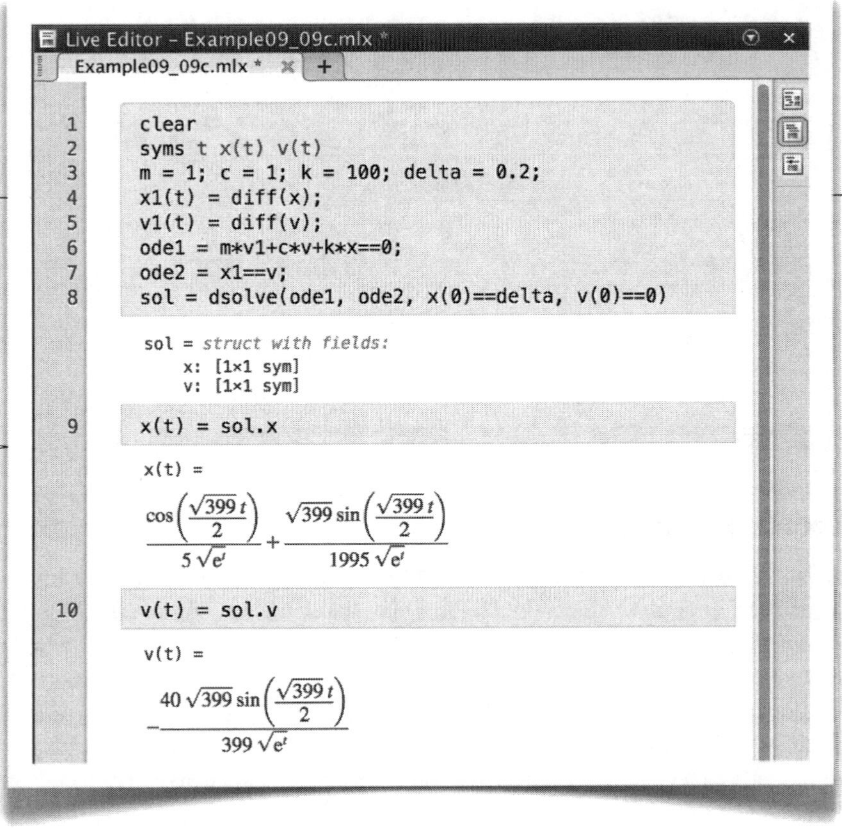

[3] Open Example09_09c.m as a **Live Script** and run the script. (Continued at [4], next page.) ↵

```
11  fplot(x, [0,2])
```

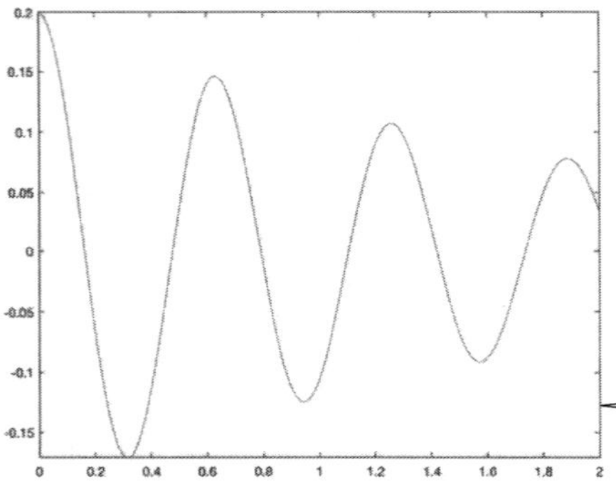


```
12  fplot(v, [0,2])
```

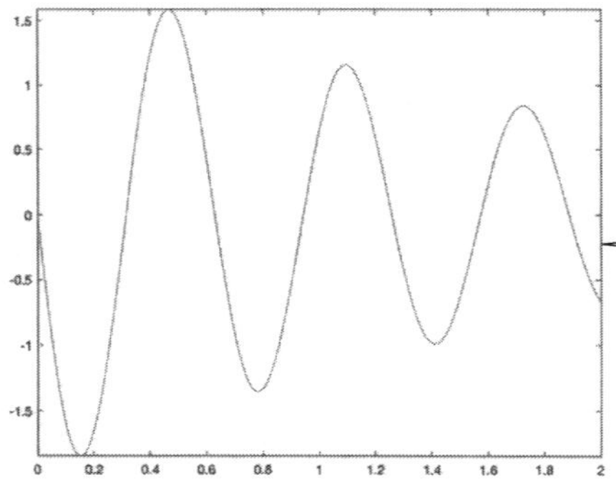


```
13  vpa(x, 5)
```

ans(t) =

$$\frac{0.2\cos(9.9875\,t)}{\sqrt{e^t}}+\frac{0.010013\sin(9.9875\,t)}{\sqrt{e^t}}$$

```
14  vpa(v, 5)
```

ans(t) =

$$-\frac{2.0025\sin(9.9875\,t)}{\sqrt{e^t}}$$

[4] Continued from [3], last page. ↓

[5] Line 11 plots the displacement (also see Eq. 9.9a(g), page 381):

$$x(t) = \delta e^{-\frac{ct}{2m}}\left(\cos\omega_d t+\frac{c}{2m\omega_d}\sin\omega_d t\right)$$

$$= 0.2e^{-t/2}\cos 9.9875t + 0.010013e^{-t/2}\sin 9.9875t$$

↓

[6] Line 12 plots the velocity:

$$v(t) = -\delta\left(\omega_d+\frac{c^2}{4m^2\omega_d}\right)e^{-\frac{ct}{2m}}\sin\omega_d t$$

$$= -2.0025e^{-t/2}\sin 9.9875t$$

↓

About Example09_09c.m

[7] Line 2 creates a symbolic variable and two symbolic functions. In line 3, we substitute m, c, k, and δ with their respective values given in Section 2.15. This usually makes the solving of the problem much easier. As usual, we use `x1` to represent the first derivative of $x(t)$ (line 4) and `v1` to represent the first derivative of $v(t)$ (line 5). Lines 6-7 define the two first-order ODEs, Eqs. (a, b), respectively. Line 8 solves the system of ODEs with the initial conditions, Eqs. (c, d), using the function `dsolve`. As usual, the result `sol` is a structure of two fields: `x` and `v` (lines 9-10). Line 11 plots the displacement $x(t)$ (see [5]) and line 12 plots the velocity $v(t)$ (see [6]). In lines 13-14, to further simplify the functions $x(t)$ and $v(t)$, we use the function `vpa` to calculate values to the 5th significant digit. #

9.10 Additional Exercise Problems

Problem09_01: Indefinite Integrals

Find each indefinite integral.

a. $\int \frac{xe^x + 1}{x} dx$ b. $\int \frac{x^3}{\sqrt{1-x^2}} dx$ c. $\int x^2 \cos x \, dx$

Problem09_02: Definite Integrals

Evaluate each definite integral.

a. $\int_0^2 \frac{1}{x^2+1} dx$ b. $\int_0^4 \sqrt{x} e^x dx$ c. $\int_{-1}^1 e^{x^2} dx$

Problem09_03: Limits

Find the following limits.

a. $\lim_{x \to 2} \frac{\frac{1}{x} - \frac{1}{2}}{x-2}$ b. $\lim_{x \to 0} (1+2x)^{1/x}$ c. $\lim_{x \to 0} (1 - \sin 2x)^{1/x}$

Problem09_04: Taylor Polynomials

Find the fifth Taylor polynomial at $x = 0$ for each function.

a. $f(x) = e^x$ b. $f(x) = \ln(x+1)$ c. $f(x) = \sqrt{x+2}$

Problem09_05: Systems of Linear Equations

Solve x, y, and z for the following system of linear equations.

$$\begin{cases} ax + 2y + z = 3 \\ x + y + bz = 2 \\ 4x + 2y + 5z = 6 \end{cases}$$

Problem09_06: Systems of Nonlinear Equations

Solve x and y for the following system of nonlinear equations. Find the numeric solutions for the case $a = 3$ and $b = 2$.

$$\begin{cases} \frac{x^2}{a^2} + \frac{y^2}{b^2} = 1 \\ y = x^2 - 4 \end{cases}$$

Chapter 10

Linear Algebra, Polynomial, Curve Fitting, and Interpolation

So far, we've introduced the core functionalities of MATLAB. Starting from this chapter, we'll introduce topics that are useful for junior engineering college students. We'll use either symbolic approach or numeric approach whenever it is more instructional and practical.

10.1 Products of Vectors

10.1a Products of Vectors

[1] The **dot product** of two vectors **a** and **b** in the 3-D space is defined by

$$\mathbf{a}\cdot\mathbf{b} = |\mathbf{a}||\mathbf{b}|\cos\theta \qquad \text{(a)}$$

where θ is the angle between the two vectors. Let $\mathbf{a} = [a_1\ a_2\ a_3]$ and $\mathbf{b} = [b_1\ b_2\ b_3]$, where a_1, a_2, a_3, b_1, b_2, and b_3 are real numbers; then it can be proved that

$$\mathbf{a}\cdot\mathbf{b} = a_1b_1 + a_2b_2 + a_3b_3 \qquad \text{(b)}$$

The **cross product** of the two vectors **a** and **b** is denoted by $\mathbf{a}\times\mathbf{b}$. Its direction is perpendicular to the plane containing **a** and **b**, following the right-hand rule. Its magnitude is defined by

$$|\mathbf{a}\times\mathbf{b}| = |\mathbf{a}||\mathbf{b}|\sin\theta \qquad \text{(c)}$$

It can be proved that

$$\mathbf{a}\times\mathbf{b} = [a_2b_3 - a_3b_2,\ a_3b_1 - a_1b_3,\ a_1b_2 - a_2b_1] \qquad \text{(d)}$$ ✓

Example10_01a.m: Products of Vectors

[2] These commands calculate the **dot product** and **cross product** expressed in Eqs. (b) and (d), using a symbolic approach. ↓

```
1  clear
2  syms a1 a2 a3 b1 b2 b3 real
3  a = [a1, a2, a3];
4  b = [b1, b2, b3];
5  d = dot(a,b)
6  c = cross(a,b)
```

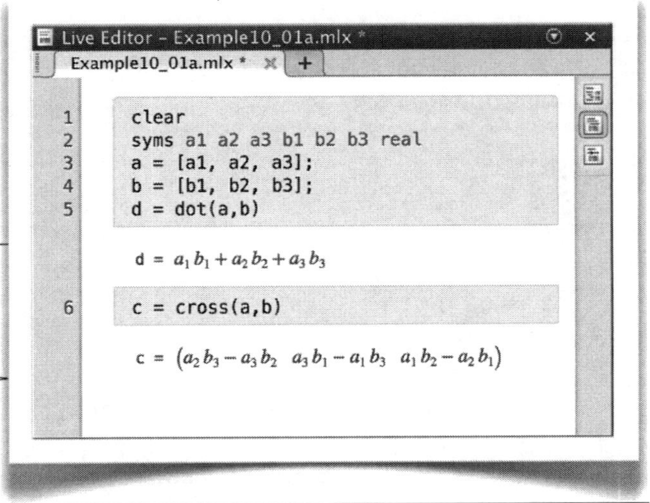

[3] Open Example10_01a.m as a **Live Script** and run the script in the **Live Editor**. ↓

About Example10_01a.m

[4] Line 2 creates 6 symbolic variables, assuming they are real numbers. The keyword `real` at the end of line 2 imposes an assumption that the variables are real numbers. Remember that the discussion in [1] assumes that a_1, a_2, a_3, b_1, b_2, and b_3 are real numbers. Without the assumption of real numbers, in this case, the result remains the same. However, some of the equations in [1] may not be valid when complex numbers are involved (see *Wikipedia>Dot product;* and *Wikipedia>Cross product*).

Lines 3-4 create two vectors. Line 5 performs the dot product of the two vectors. Line 6 performs the cross product of the two vectors. #

10.1b Example: Angles and Normal of a Triangle

[1] Three points in the 3D space can define a triangle. Let $\mathbf{p}_1$, $\mathbf{p}_2$, and $\mathbf{p}_3$ be three vertices of a triangle in the 3D space. We can calculate any of the three angles as follows.

The angle θ at $\mathbf{p}_1$ is the angle between the vectors **a** and **b**, where

$$\mathbf{a} = \mathbf{p}_2 - \mathbf{p}_1,\ \mathbf{b} = \mathbf{p}_3 - \mathbf{p}_1 \tag{a}$$

From Eqs. 10.1a(a, c), last page, the angle can be calculated in two ways

$$\theta = \cos^{-1} \frac{\mathbf{a} \cdot \mathbf{b}}{|\mathbf{a}||\mathbf{b}|} \tag{b}$$

or

$$\theta = \sin^{-1} \frac{|\mathbf{a} \times \mathbf{b}|}{|\mathbf{a}||\mathbf{b}|} \tag{c}$$

The unit normal **n** to the plane defined by the three vertices can be calculated as follows

$$\mathbf{n} = \frac{\mathbf{a} \times \mathbf{b}}{|\mathbf{a} \times \mathbf{b}|} \tag{d}$$ ↙

Example10_01b.m: Angle and Normal

[2] Given three points, these commands calculate an angle and a unit normal according to [1], using a numerical approach. →

```
1   clear
2   p1 = [3, 5, 2];
3   p2 = [1, 0 ,0];
4   p3 = [3, -1, 0];
5   a = p2-p1;
6   b = p3-p1;
7   d = dot(a,b)
8   theta = acosd(d/(norm(a)*norm(b)))
9   c = cross(a,b)
10  theta = asind(norm(c)/(norm(a)*norm(b)))
11  n = c/norm(c)
```

```
12  >> Example10_01b
13  d =
14      34
15  theta =
16     20.6391
17  c =
18     -2    -4    12
19  theta =
20     20.6391
21  n =
22     -0.1562   -0.3123    0.9370
23  >>
```

[3] Run the script in the plane **Script Editor**. This is the **Command Window** output. ↓

About Example10_01b.m

[4] Lines 2-4 give three points in the 3D space. Lines 5-6 calculate **a** and **b** vectors as in Eq. (a). Lines 7-8 calculate the angle (in degrees) using Eq. (b); lines 13-16 are their outputs. Lines 9-10 calculate the angle again using Eq. (c); lines 17-20 are their outputs. Note that, Eqs. (b, c) output the same result (lines 16 and 20). Line 11 calculates the unit normal using Eq. (d); the outputs are shown in lines 21-22. #

10.1c Example: Plane Defined by 3 Points

[1] Three points $\mathbf{p}_1$, $\mathbf{p}_2$, and $\mathbf{p}_3$ in the 3D space can define a plane. We can find the equation of the plane as follows. Let

$$\mathbf{a} = \mathbf{p}_2 - \mathbf{p}_1 \text{ and } \mathbf{b} = \mathbf{p}_3 - \mathbf{p}_1 \qquad \text{(a)}$$

then $\mathbf{a} \times \mathbf{b}$ is normal to the pane. Let $\mathbf{r} = [x\ y\ z]$ be an arbitrary point in the plane; then $\mathbf{r} - \mathbf{p}_1$ (or $\mathbf{r} - \mathbf{p}_2$ or $\mathbf{r} - \mathbf{p}_3$) is parallel to the plane. Therefore,

$$(\mathbf{a} \times \mathbf{b}) \cdot (\mathbf{r} - \mathbf{p}_1) = 0 \qquad \text{(b)}$$

Any point $\mathbf{r} = [x\ y\ z]$ satisfying Eq. (j) must be on the plane; therefore, Eq. (j) represents the equation of the plane. ✓

Example10_01c.m: Plane Defined by 3 Points

[2] Given three points, these commands find the equation of the plane defined by the three points, according to Eq. (j). Knowing the equation, this script then plots the plane. →

```
1   clear
2   p1 = sym([3,5,2]);
3   p2 = sym([1,0,0]);
4   p3 = sym([3,-1,0]);
5   a = p2-p1;
6   b = p3-p1;
7   syms x y z
8   r = [x, y, z];
9   eq = dot(cross(a,b),r-p1)==0
10  fimplicit3(eq, [0 10])
11  axis vis3d
```

[3] Open Example10_01c.m as a **Live Script** and run the script in the **Live Editor**. ✓

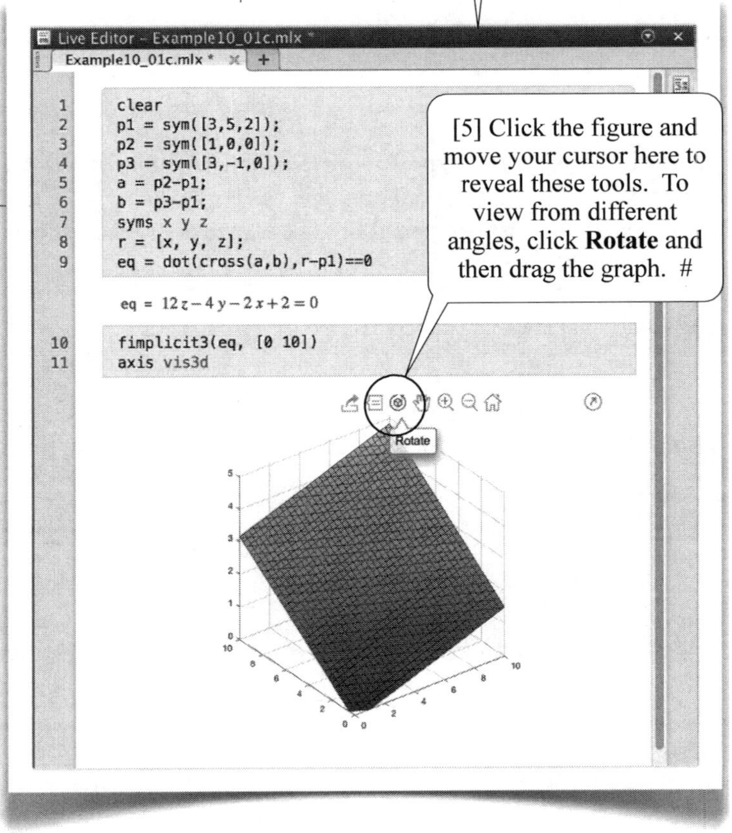

[5] Click the figure and move your cursor here to reveal these tools. To view from different angles, click **Rotate** and then drag the graph. #

About Example10_01c.m

[4] Lines 2-4 create three symbolic vectors representing three points. Note that, because of the use of the function `sym`, the variables `p1`, `p2`, and `p3` are automatically of type `sym`. Lines 5-6 calculate **a** and **b** vectors as in Eq. (a). Lines 7-8 create a vector `r` representing an arbitrary point in the space. Line 9 establishes the symbolic equation representing the plane as in Eq. (j) (see the output in [3]). Line 10 plots the plane in the interval [0 10] for the three axes (see [3]), using the 3-D implicit function plotter `fimplicit3`. Line 11 freezes the aspect ratio so that, when you rotate the graph (see [5]), the aspect ratio won't change. →

10.1d Converting a Symbolic Expression to a Numerical Function

Example10_01d.m

[1] Often, we need to convert a symbolic expression to a MATLAB function, so we may process the data numerically. We now demonstrate the use of the function `matlabFunction` to convert a symbolic expression to a numerical function. And the plane is plotted using the function `mesh`.

Now, while the symbolic expression `eq` is still in the Workspace, execute the following commands:

```
1  z = solve(eq, z)
2  z = matlabFunction(z)
3  [X,Y] = meshgrid(0:10,0:10);
4  Z = z(X,Y);
5  mesh(X,Y,Z)
```

Line 1 converts the equation to the form $z = z(x,y)$; the result is

$$z = \frac{x}{6} + \frac{y}{3} - \frac{1}{6} \tag{a}$$

Line 2 converts the symbolic expression $z(x,y)$ into a MATLAB function using `matlabFunction` (see [2]). Note that the variable `z` before the conversion is of type `sym`.; after the conversion, it is a function handle.

Line 3 creates a mesh grid in the *X*-*Y* space, each axis ranging from 0 to 10. Line 4 calculates *z*-values using the plane equation, Eq. (a). Line 5 plots the plane. ↓

Function `matlabFunction`

[2] Line 2

```
z = matlabFunction(z)
```

transforms the symbolic expression `z` to a MATLAB function. Now, `z` can be used as a usual MATLAB function; for example, `z(5,6)` calculates the *z*-value when $x = 5$ and $y = 6$.

As mentioned in 3.9a (page 144), one way to define a function is using the following syntax

```
handle = @(input-args) statement
```

The function then can be called using

```
handle(input-args)
```

The function `matlabFunction(expr)` transforms a symbolic expression *`expr`* to a function using the syntax shown above. In our case, line 2 is equivalent to the following statement:

```
z = @(x,y) x/6+y/3-1/6
```

An example of using the function `z` is shown in line 4:

```
Z = z(X,Y)
```

in which, since `X` and `Y` are matrices of `double`, the result `Z` is also a matrix of `double`. #

Table 10.1 Summary of Functions

Functions	Description
`syms v1 v2 ... real`	Symbolic variables
`dot(a, b)`	Dot product
`cross(a, b)`	Cross product
`norm(a)`	Vector and matrix norm
`asind(x)`	Inverse sine in degrees
`acosd(x)`	Inverse cosine in degrees
`fimplicit3(f, interval)`	Plot 3-D surface in implicit function form
`fsurf(f, interval)`	Plot 3-D surface in explicit function form
`fplot3(funx, funy, funz)`	Plot 3-D parametric curve
`solve(eq, z)`	Solve equations
`matlabFunction(expr)`	Convert symbolic expression to MATLAB function
`meshgrid(x,y)`	Generate 2D grid
`mesh(X,Y,Z)`	Mesh plot
`axis vis3d`	Freeze aspect ratio of axes

10.2 Systems of Linear Equations

10.2a Systems of Linear Equations

[1] In 9.7[5] (page 378), we showed that for a system of two linear equations

$$\begin{cases} ax_1 + bx_2 = c \\ dx_1 + ex_2 = f \end{cases} \quad \text{or } \mathbf{Ax} = \mathbf{b}$$

where

$$\mathbf{A} = \begin{bmatrix} a & b \\ d & e \end{bmatrix}, \ \mathbf{b} = \begin{pmatrix} c \\ f \end{pmatrix}$$

the solutions are

$$x_1 = -\frac{bf - ce}{ae - bd}, \ x_2 = \frac{af - cd}{ae - bd} \qquad \text{(a)}$$

where the denominator $ae - bd$ is the determinant of the matrix **A**, denoted by $|\mathbf{A}|$. Obviously, when $|\mathbf{A}| = 0$, there is no solution satisfying the system of equations, unless the numerators are also zeros (i.e., $bf - ce = af - cd = 0$); in that case there is an infinite number of solutions satisfying the system of equations.

In this section, we will use graphs to illustrate the above concepts and extend the concepts to a system of n linear equations involving n unknown variables.

$$\begin{aligned} &a_{11}x_1 + a_{12}x_2 + ... + a_{1n}x_n = b_1 \\ &a_{21}x_1 + a_{22}x_2 + ... + a_{2n}x_n = b_2 \\ &... \\ &a_{n1}x_1 + a_{n2}x_2 + ... + a_{nn}x_n = b_n \end{aligned}$$

↓

Solving a System of Linear Equations with `linsolve` or Backslash Operator (\)

[2] Consider a system of two linear equations

$$\begin{cases} x_1 + 2x_2 = 5 \\ 3x_1 + 4x_2 = 6 \end{cases} \quad \text{or } \mathbf{Ax} = \mathbf{b}$$

where

$$\mathbf{A} = \begin{bmatrix} 1 & 2 \\ 3 & 4 \end{bmatrix}, \ \mathbf{x} = \begin{pmatrix} x_1 \\ x_2 \end{pmatrix}, \ \mathbf{b} = \begin{pmatrix} 5 \\ 6 \end{pmatrix}$$

The determinant of matrix **A** is

$$|\mathbf{A}| = 1 \times 4 - 2 \times 3 = -2$$

the solutions are, from Eq. (a),

$$x_1 = -\frac{2 \times 6 - 5 \times 4}{-2} = -4$$

$$x_2 = \frac{1 \times 6 - 5 \times 3}{-2} = 4.5$$

If we draw the two equations in the x_1x_2-space, then the solution is the intersection point of the two lines, as illustrated in [3-5], next page. The system of equations can be solved using the function `linsolve` (line 4, next page) or the backslash operator (line 5, next page). ↵

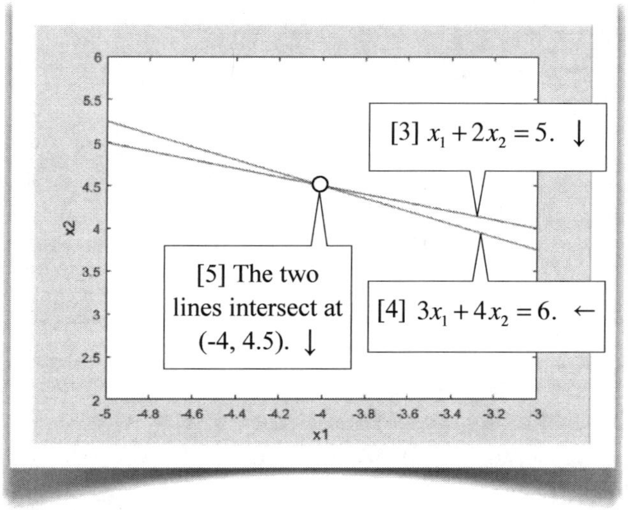

Solving a System of Linear Equations with Slash Operator (/)

[6] The system of equations

$$x_1 + 2x_2 = 5$$
$$3x_1 + 4x_2 = 6$$

can be written in another matrix form

$$\mathbf{xA} = \mathbf{b}$$

where

$$\mathbf{x} = [x_1 \;\; x_2],\ \mathbf{A} = \begin{bmatrix} 1 & 3 \\ 2 & 4 \end{bmatrix},\ \mathbf{b} = [5 \;\; 6]$$

With this form, the system of equations can be solved using the slash operator (/, line 8). Note that the matrix **A** and the vector **b** here are the transpose of those in [2], last page. ↓

Example10_02a.m: A System of Two Linear Equations

[7] These commands solve a system of linear equations, using the methods described in [2] (last page) and [6]. ↵

```
1   clear
2   A = [1 2; 3 4]; b = [5; 6];
3   det(A)
4   x = linsolve(A, b)
5   x = A\b
6   A = A'; b = b';
7   det(A)
8   x = b/A
9   A = [1 2; 3 6]; b = [5; 6];
10  det(A)
11  x = A\b
12  b = [5; 15];
13  x = A\b
```

```
14    >> Example10_02a
15    ans =
16        -2
17    x =
18       -4.0000
19        4.5000
20    x =
21       -4.0000
22        4.5000
23    ans =
24        -2
25    x =
26       -4.0000    4.5000
27    ans =
28         0
29    Warning: Matrix is close to singular or badly scaled. Results may be inaccurate.
30    RCOND =   3.700743e-17.
31    > In Example10_02a (line 11)
32    x =
33      1.0e+16 *
34      -5.4043
35       2.7022
36    Warning: Matrix is close to singular or badly scaled. Results may be inaccurate.
37    RCOND =   3.700743e-17.
38    > In Example10_02a (line 13)
39    x =
40             0
41        2.5000
```

[8] Run the script in the plane **Script Editor**. This is the output. ↓

About Example10_02a.m

[9] Line 2 creates the matrix **A** and vector **b** as in [2], page 393. The determinant of **A** is not zero (lines 3 and 15-16), hence there must exist a unique solution. Line 4 solves the system using `linsolve`. Note that the solution **x** (lines 4 and 17-19) has the same size as **b**, 2-by-1. Another way is using the backslash operator (\; see lines 5 and 20-22).

To solve the equations using the slash operator (/), matrix **A** and vector **b** are transposed (line 6). The determinant of **A** remains the same (lines 7 and 23-24). Line 8 solves the equations using the slash operator. Note that the solution **x** (lines 25-26) has the same size as **b**, 1-by-2.

We now consider the case (line 9)

$$x_1 + 2x_2 = 5$$
$$3x_1 + 6x_2 = 6$$

Its determinant is zero, $|\mathbf{A}| = 1\times 6 - 2\times 3 = 0$ (lines 27-28). In this case, the two lines are parallel to each other (see [10-11], next page); there is no intersection between the two lines, thus no solution for the system of equations. If you try to solve the equations (line 11), a warning appears (lines 29-31) and the numbers reported (lines 32-35) are essentially infinities.

For the case (line 12)

$$x_1 + 2x_2 = 5$$
$$3x_1 + 6x_2 = 15$$

The determinant remains zero and the two lines coincide with each other ([12], next page). In this case, there is an infinite number of intersection points, thus an infinite number of solutions exist. If you try to solve the equations (line 13), a warning appears (lines 36-38) and an arbitrary solution is reported (lines 39-41). ↵

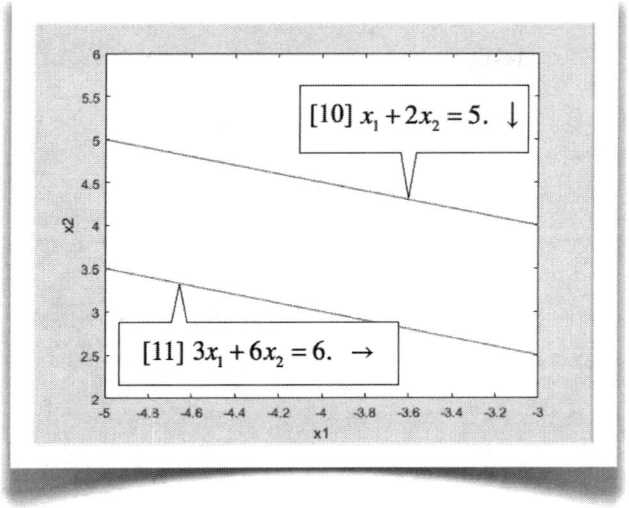

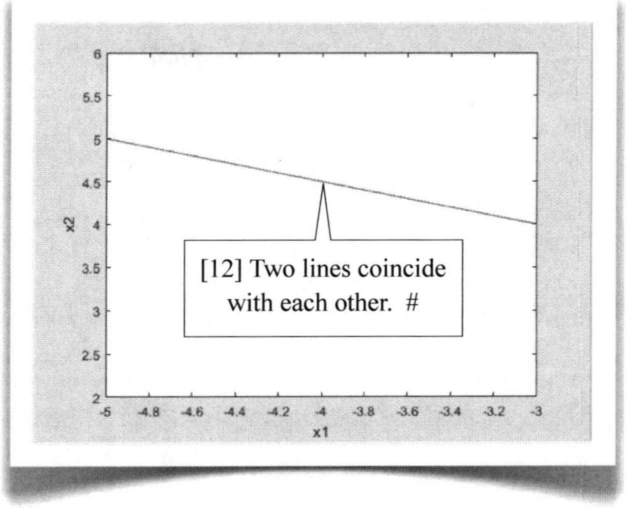

10.2b Example: Three-Bar Truss

Example10_02b.m: Three-Bar Truss

[1] These commands solve the system of linear equations given in Eq. 3.14(b), page 154. ↵

```
clear
a = sqrt(2)/2;
A = [-a   a   0   0   0   0;
      -a  -a   0   0   0   0;
       a   0   1   1   0   0;
       a   0   0   0   1   0;
       0  -a  -1   0   0   0;
       0   a   0   0   0   1];
b = [0, 1000, 0, 0, 0, 0]';
x = A\b
x = linsolve(A,b)
det(A)
A = A';
b = b';
x = b/A
```

[2] This is the **Command Window** output of Example10_02b.m. ↓

```
16   >> Example10_02b
17   x =
18     -707.1068
19     -707.1068
20      500.0000
21             0
22      500.0000
23      500.0000
24   x =
25     -707.1068
26     -707.1068
27      500.0000
28             0
29      500.0000
30      500.0000
31   ans =
32       -1.0000
33   x =
34     -707.1068 -707.1068   500.0000           0  500.0000  500.0000
```

About Example10_02b.m

[3] Lines 2-10 are the same as the commands in 3.14[2], page 155; lines 17-23 are the output. Line 11 solves the system of equations again using the function `linsolve`. The same solution is obtained (lines 24-30). Lines 12 and 31-32 show that the determinant of matrix **A** is indeed nonzero.

To be solved using the slash operator (`/`), the system of equations must be written in a form shown in 10.2a[6] (page 394). Matrix **A** and vector **b** are transposed (lines 13-14). Line 15 solves the system using the slash operator (`/`). The solution is the same, except that **x** is now a 1-by-6 vector (lines 33-34). #

Table 10.2 Summary of Functions

Functions	Description
`det(A)`	Matrix determinant
`linsolve(A, b)`	Solve linear system of equations
`x = A\b`	Solve linear system of equations
`x = b/A`	Solve linear system of equations
`[L, U] = lu(A)`	LU matrix factorization

10.3 Backslash Operator (\)

[1] It is fair to say that the algorithms to solve systems of linear equations are the most important ones among all numerical algorithms in engineering applications. Further, many algorithms for solving nonlinear equations involve subsequently solving a series of subproblems, each itself a system of linear equations. In these nonlinear algorithms, linear equation solvers are the core of the software and the efficiency of the linear solver becomes extremely crucial when the problems are large or highly nonlinear.

MATLAB provides many functions to solve systems of linear equations; some of them are shown in the last section. In general, you should use the backslash operator (\, or called **left divide operator**) to solve a system of linear equations, **Ax** = **b**, as demonstrated in Sections 9.7 (symbolic approach) and Section 10.2 (numeric approach):

$$\mathbf{x} = \mathbf{A} \backslash \mathbf{b}$$

The backslash operator takes advantage of the shape and sparsity of matrix **A** and dispatches to an appropriate solver (algorithm), minimizing computation time, as shown in [2] (*Details and More: >> doc mldivide*). ↓

[2] This is how MATLAB solves **Ax** = **b** using backslash operators; i.e., **x** = **A** \ **b** . Some terminologies are further explained in [3], next page. ↵

```
If A is not sparse
    If A is square
        if A is triangular
            Use triangular solver
        else if A is permuted triangular
            Use permuted triangular solver
        else if A is Hermitian
            If the diagonals of A are real and positive
                Use Cholesky solver
                if Cholesky failed
                    Use LDL solver
                end
            else
                Use LDL solver
            end
        else if A is upper Hessenberg
            Use Hessenberg solver
        else
            Use LU solver
        end
    else (A is not square)
        Use QR solver
    end
else (A is sparse)
    If A is square
        Compute the bandwidth of A
        If A is diagonal
            Use diagonal solver
        else if A is tridiagonal
            Use tridiagonal solver
        else if A is banded
            Use banded solver
        else if A is triangular
            Use triangular solver
        else if A is permuted triangular
            Use permuted triangular solver
        else if A is Hermitian
            if the diagonals of A are real and positive
                Use Cholesky solver
                if Cholesky failed
                    Use LDL solver
                end
            else if A is real
                Use LDL solver
            else
                Use LU solver
            end
        else
            Use LU solver
        end
    else (A is not square)
        Use QR solver
    end
end
```

Classification of Matrices

[3] Some terminologies in [2] need to be clarified. According to its shape and sparsity, a matrix can be classified as follows.

Sparse. Matrix **A** is sparse when most of its elements are zeros. The sparsity can be defined as the fraction of the nonzero elements in the matrix. We then can define a matrix as sparse when its sparsity is less than a threshold. (*Wikipedia>Sparse matrix*)

Square. A matrix is square when the row size is the same as the column size. (*Wikipedia>Square matrix*)

Triangular. A matrix is triangular when its elements above or below the diagonal are all zeros. When the elements below the diagonal are zeros, it is an **upper triangular**; When the elements above the diagonal are zeros, it is a **lower triangular**. (*Wikipedia>Triangular matrix*)

Permuted Triangular. A matrix is permuted triangular if, after permutations of rows or columns, it becomes a triangular. For example, the matrix `L` in lines 14-20, next page, is a permuted lower triangular matrix, since, after the exchange of columns 4 and 5 (or rows 4 and 5), it becomes a lower triangular matrix.

Symmetric. A matrix **A** is symmetric if $a_{ij} = a_{ji}$, where a_{ij} is an element of **A** at row *i*, column *j*. A symmetric matrix must be a square matrix. (*Wikipedia>Symmetric matrix*)

Hermitian. If the elements are all real numbers, a symmetric matrix is also called a Hermitian matrix. In general cases, when involving complex numbers, a matrix is called Hermitian if those pairs of elements that are symmetric are complex conjugates. (*Wikipedia>Hermitian matrix*)

Upper Hessenberg. A Hessenberg matrix is a square matrix that is "almost" triangular. An upper Hessenberg matrix has zero elements below the first subdiagonal. (*Wikipedia>Hessenberg matrix*)

Diagonal. A matrix is diagonal if its elements outside the diagonal are all zero. (*Wikipedia>Diagonal matrix*)

Tridiagonal. A matrix is tridiagonal if it has nonzero elements only on the main diagonal, the first diagonal below, and the first diagonal above. (*Wikipedia>Tridiagonal matrix*)

Banded. A matrix is banded if its nonzero elements are confined to a diagonal band. A tridiagonal matrix is also a banded matrix. (*Wikipedia>Band matrix*) ↗

Example: LU Factorization

[4] To illustrate the algorithm in [2], let's consider the system of linear equations in Example10_02b.m (page 396) again,

$$\mathbf{Ax} = \mathbf{b} \qquad \text{(a)}$$

Since, in this case, **A** is square but not symmetric or triangular, **LU** solver is used, according to [2].

In the **LU solver**, the matrix **A** is decomposed into a lower triangular matrix **L** and an upper triangular matrix **U**,

$$\mathbf{A} = \mathbf{LU}$$

And the system of equations (a) becomes

$$\mathbf{LUx} = \mathbf{b}$$

Let

$$\mathbf{Ux} = \mathbf{y} \qquad \text{(b)}$$

Then the system of equations can be written as

$$\mathbf{Ly} = \mathbf{b} \qquad \text{(c)}$$

Now the system of equations can be solved in two steps: first, Eq. (c) is solved for **y**, and then Eq. (b) is solved for **x**. Both steps take advantage of the fact that **L** and **U** are triangular matrices.

Example10_03.m gives details of these ideas.

Details and More: Help>MATLAB>Mathematics>Linear Algebra>Matrix Decomposition>Factorization
↓

Example10_03.m: LU Factorization

[5] These commands illustrate the method in [4]. ↵

```
 1  clear
 2  a = sqrt(2)/2;
 3  A = [-a   a   0   0   0   0;
 4       -a  -a   0   0   0   0;
 5        a   0   1   1   0   0;
 6        a   0   0   0   1   0;
 7        0  -a  -1   0   0   0;
 8        0   a   0   0   0   1];
 9  b = [0, 1000, 0, 0, 0, 0]';
10  [L,U] = lu(A)
11  y = L\b
12  x = U\y
```

```
13  >> Example10_03
14  L =
15        1.0000         0         0         0         0         0
16        1.0000    1.0000         0         0         0         0
17       -1.0000   -0.5000    1.0000         0         0         0
18       -1.0000   -0.5000         0         0    1.0000         0
19             0    0.5000   -1.0000    1.0000         0         0
20             0   -0.5000         0         0         0    1.0000
21  U =
22       -0.7071    0.7071         0         0         0         0
23             0   -1.4142         0         0         0         0
24             0         0    1.0000    1.0000         0         0
25             0         0         0    1.0000         0         0
26             0         0         0         0    1.0000         0
27             0         0         0         0         0    1.0000
28  y =
29             0
30          1000
31           500
32             0
33           500
34           500
35  x =
36     -707.1068
37     -707.1068
38      500.0000
39             0
40      500.0000
41      500.0000
```

[6] This is the **Command Window** output of Example10_03.m. ↓

About Example10_03.m

[7] Lines 2-9 are the same as lines 2-9 of Example10_02b.m, page 396. Line 10 decomposes the matrix **A** into **L** and **U**, using the function `lu`. The matrix **L** is a permuted lower triangular matrix (lines 14-20); the name comes from the fact that, after the exchange of columns 4 and 5 (or the exchange of rows 4 and 5), it becomes a lower triangular matrix. The matrix **U** is an upper triangular matrix (lines 21-27).

Line 11 solves Eq. (c) for **y** (also see lines 28-34). Line 12 solves Eq. (b) for **x** (also see lines 35-41), which is consistent with the solution before (see 10.2b[2], page 397, lines 24-30). #

10.4 Eigenvalue Problems

[1] The eigenvalue problem can be defined as follows: Knowing two n-by-n square matrices **A** and **B**, we want to find eigenvalues λ (a scalar) and the eigenvectors $\mathbf{x}$ (an n-by-1 vector) that satisfy

$$\mathbf{Ax} = \lambda \mathbf{Bx} \tag{a}$$

There exist at most n eigenvalues that satisfy Eq. (a); each eigenvalue has a corresponding eigenvector.

The problem can be viewed as finding vectors **x** such that, after applying linear transformations using **A** and **B**, their directions remain the same and their magnitudes are different by a scale of λ.

Many applications can be formulated as eigenvalue problems. For example, in structural analyses, if **A** and **B** represent the stiffness matrix and the mass matrix, respectively, then the eigenvalues are the squares of the natural frequencies of the structure and the eigenvectors are the corresponding vibration modes.

To illustrate this, consider again the undamped free vibrations for the single degree of freedom (SDOF) problem described in 2.15a[3], page 117,

$$m\ddot{x} + kx = 0$$

The equation suggests a solution form of sinusoidal function; i.e.,

$$x(t) = C\cos\omega t$$

where ω is the natural frequency and C is a coefficient to be determined. Substitution of $x(t)$ into the equation yields

$$kx = \lambda mx \tag{b}$$

where

$$\lambda = \omega^2 \tag{c}$$

For multiple degrees of freedom (MDOF) problems, k and m are in matrix form, denoted by **K** and **M**, respectively, and Eq. (b) becomes

$$\mathbf{Kx} = \lambda \mathbf{Mx} \tag{d}$$

In this section, we will determine the frequencies (rad/s) of a three-DOF structural system as follows:

$$\mathbf{K} = \begin{bmatrix} 40 & -25 & 0 \\ -25 & 50 & -30 \\ 0 & -30 & 60 \end{bmatrix} \text{(N/m)} \tag{e}$$

$$\mathbf{M} = \begin{bmatrix} 3 & 0 & 0 \\ 0 & 4 & 0 \\ 0 & 0 & 5 \end{bmatrix} \text{(kg)} \tag{f}$$

↵

Example10_04.m: Eigenvalue Problems

[2] These commands solve the eigenvalue problem described in Eqs. (d-f), last page. ↓

```
1   clear
2   K = [40, -25,    0;
3        -25,  50, -30;
4          0, -30,  60]
5   M = diag([3, 4, 5])
6   [X, Lamda] = eig(K, M)
7   Omega = sqrt(Lamda)
```

[3] This is the **Command Window** output of Example10_04.m. ↓

```
8   >> Example10_04
9   K =
10      40   -25     0
11     -25    50   -30
12       0   -30    60
13  M =
14       3     0     0
15       0     4     0
16       0     0     5
17  X =
18     -0.2788    0.3918   -0.3195
19     -0.3547    0.0337    0.3508
20     -0.2296   -0.3271   -0.2008
21  Lamda =
22      2.7318         0         0
23           0   12.6175         0
24           0         0   22.4840
25  Omega =
26      1.6528         0         0
27           0    3.5521         0
28           0         0    4.7417
```

About Example10_04.m

[4] Lines 2-5 prepare the matrices as shown in Eqs. (e, f); lines 9-16 are the output. Note that, since **M** is a diagonal matrix, we use the function `diag` to create the matrix (line 5).

Line 6 uses the function `eig` to solve the eigenvalue problem, Eq. (d). It outputs eigenvectors `X` (lines 17-20) and eigenvalues `Lamda` (see lines 21-24). Each diagonal element in the matrix `Lamda` is an eigenvalue, and each column in the matrix `X` is the corresponding eigenvector.

The natural frequencies are the square roots of the eigenvalues; see Eq. (c). Line 7 calculates the natural frequencies `Omega` (lines 25-28) from `Lamda`. It leaves you to verify Eq. (d), using these eigenvalues and eigenvectors. #

10.5 Polynomials

10.5a Polynomials (Numeric Approach)

[1] In Section 4.9, we implemented a class `Poly`, in which a polynomial is represented as a row vector. MATLAB actually implements this idea in a more extensive, useful fashion.

MATLAB also represents polynomials as row vectors containing coefficients ordered by descending powers. For example

```
p = [1, -2, -1, 2]
```

represents the polynomial

$$p(x) = x^3 - 2x^2 - x + 2$$

↓

Example10_05a.m: Numeric Polynomials

[2] These commands demonstrate some basic functions that manipulate MATLAB polynomials. ↓

```
clear
p = [1, -2, -1, 2];
polyval(p, 3)
x = linspace(-2,3);
plot(x, polyval(p,x)), grid on
r = roots(p)
poly(r)
p1 = polyint(p)
polyder(p1)
a = [1, 3, 5];
b = [2, 4, 6];
c = polyder(a,b)
[n,d] = polyder(a,b)
```

[3] This is the **Command Window** output of Example10_05a.m. ↵

```
>> Example10_05a
ans =
     8
r =
   -1.0000
    2.0000
    1.0000
ans =
    1.0000   -2.0000   -1.0000    2.0000
p1 =
    0.2500   -0.6667   -0.5000    2.0000         0
ans =
     1    -2    -1     2
c =
     8    30    56    38
n =
    -2    -8    -2
d =
     4    16    40    48    36
```

[4] Line 5 produces this plot (the horizontal line and the three circular points are added by the author). The polynomial has zeros at x = -1, 2, and 1. ↓

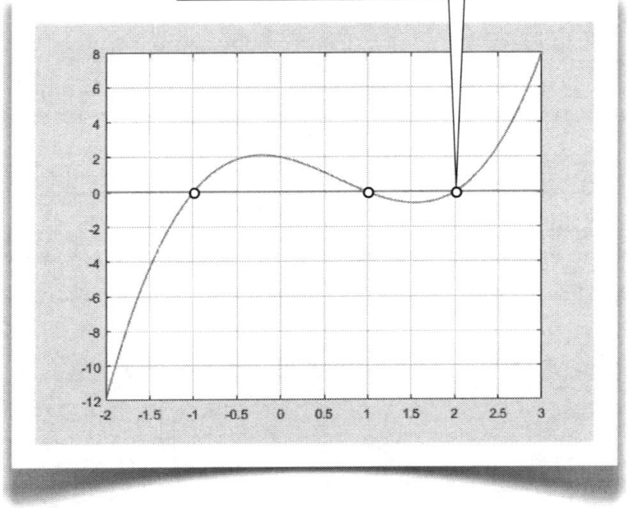

About Example10_05a.m

[5] Line 2 creates a row vector `p`. In line 3, the function `polyval` treats the vector `p` as a polynomial, $p(x) = x^3 - 2x^2 - x + 2$, and evaluates the polynomial at $x = 3$; the result is 8 (lines 15-16). Lines 4-5 plot the polynomial [4]; by visual inspection, it has zero values at x = -1, 2, and 1. Line 6 finds the roots using the function `roots`. The result (lines 17-20) is stored as a column vector. The root finding procedure can be thought of as a factorization process: $p(x) = (x+1)(x-2)(x-1)$. Knowing the roots, or the factors, the original polynomial can be recovered by using the function `poly` (line 7); the output is in row vector form (lines 21-22), the same as that in line 2. A polynomial can be integrated using the function `polyint`; for example (lines 8 and 23-24),

$$p_1(x) = \int p(x)dx = \frac{x^4}{4} - \frac{2x^3}{3} - \frac{x^2}{2} + 2x$$

Note that the integration constant is assumed zero. Differentiation of p_1 using the function `polyder` (line 9) results in the original polynomial (lines 25-26).

Lines 10-11 create two polynomials. With two input arguments and one output argument, the function `polyder` in line 12 differentiates the product of the two polynomials; i.e., it calculates (see output in lines 27-28)

$$\frac{d}{dx}\left[(x^2+3x+5)(2x^2+4x+6)\right] = 8x^3 + 30x^2 + 56x + 38$$

With two input arguments and two output arguments, the function `polyder` in line 13 differentiates the division of the two input polynomials and returns the numerator and the denominator; i.e., it calculates (see output in lines 29-32)

$$\frac{d}{dx}\frac{x^2+3x+5}{2x^2+4x+6} = \frac{-2x^2-8x-2}{4x^5+16x^4+40x^2+48x+36}$$

#

10.5b Polynomials (Symbolic Approach)

Example10_05b.m: Symbolic Polynomials

[1] These commands do the same tasks as those in Example10_05a.m (page 403), but using symbolic approach. ↓

```
clear
syms x
p(x) = poly2sym([1, -2, -1, 2])
p(3)
fplot(p), axis([-2,3,-12,8]), grid on
r = solve(p)
p1 = int(p)
diff(p1)
a = poly2sym([1, 3, 5])
b = poly2sym([2, 4, 6])
c = diff(a*b)
[n,d] = numden(diff(a/b))
```

[2] Open Example10_05b.m as a **Live Script** and run the script in the **Live Editor**. (Continued at [3], next page.) ↵

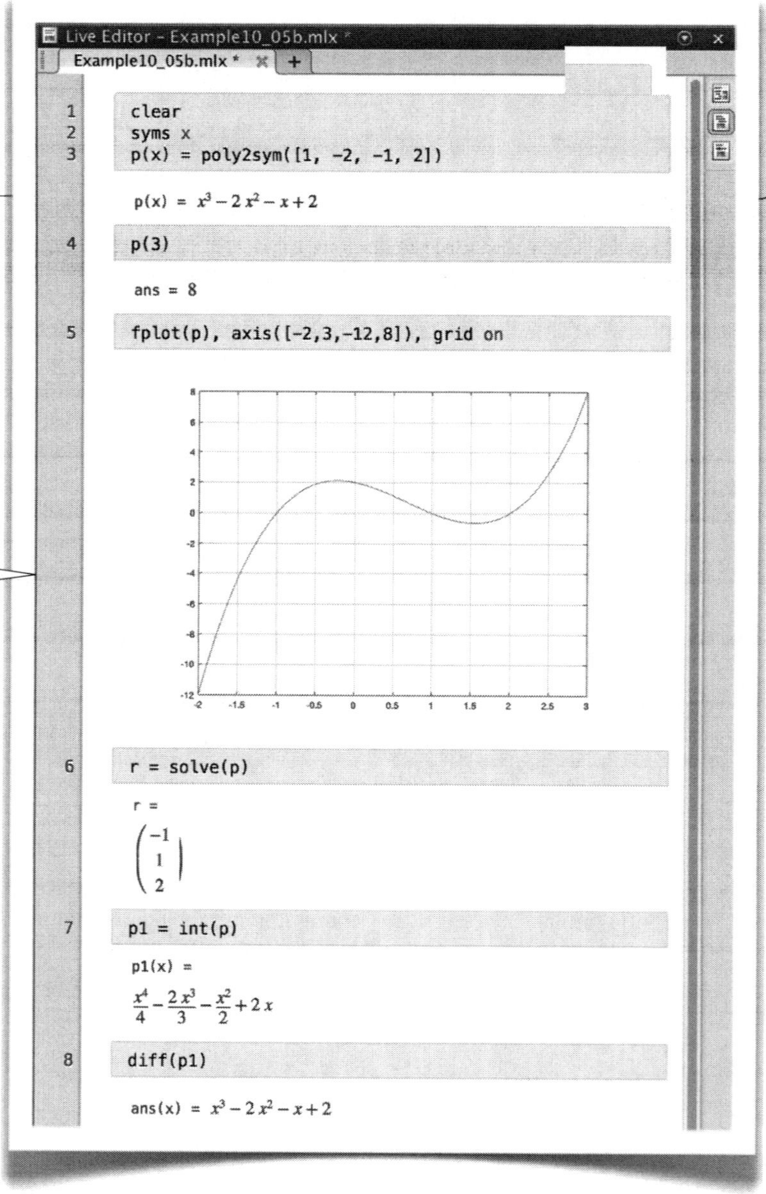

```
9   a = poly2sym([1, 3, 5])
    a = x^2+3 x+5
10  b = poly2sym([2, 4, 6])
    b = 2 x^2+4 x+6
11  c = diff(a*b)
    c = (2 x+3) (2 x^2+4 x+6)+(4 x+4) (x^2+3 x+5)
12  [n,d] = numden(diff(a/b))
    n = -x^2-4 x-1
    d = 2 (x^2+2 x+3)^2
```

[3] Continued from [2], last page. →

About Example10_05b.m

[4] Lines 2-3 demonstrate a way to create a symbolic polynomial using the function `poly2sym`, which converts a polynomial from a row vector form to a symbolic form. Line 3 is equivalent to

```
p(x) = x^3-2*x^2-x+2
```

On the other hand, the function `sym2poly` (not used in this example; see Table 10.5 below) converts a polynomial from a symbolic form to a row vector form.

Line 4 evaluates the polynomial at 3; the result is 8. Line 5 plots the polynomial. Line 6 finds the zeros of the polynomial. Line 7 integrates the polynomial. Line 8 differentiates the integrated polynomial, recovering the original polynomial.

Lines 9-10 create two symbolic polynomials. Line 11 differentiates the product of the two polynomials.

In line 12, the rational polynomial `a/b` (`a` and `b` are created in lines 9-10, respectively) are differentiated using the function `diff`, and then the function `numden` is used to extract the numerator and the denominator. #

Table 10.5 Summary of Functions

Functions	Description
`polyval(p, x)`	Evaluates a polynomial p at x
`roots(p)`	Finds the roots of the equation p = 0
`poly(r)`	Returns a polynomial of specified roots r
`polyint(p)`	Integrates a polynomial p
`polyder(p)`	Differentiates a polynomial p
`p = polyder(p1,p2)`	Differentiates the product of polynomials p1 and p2
`[n,d] = polyder(p1,p2)`	Differentiates the division of polynomials p1 and p2
`s = poly2sym(p)`	Converts a polynomial from numeric form to symbolic form
`sym2poly(expr)`	Converts a polynomial from symbolic form to numeric form
`int(expr)`	Integrates a symbolic expression
`diff(expr)`	Differentiates a symbolic expression
`[n,d] = numden(expr)`	Extracts numerator and denominator of a symbolic expression

10.6 Polynomial Curve Fittings

Young's Modulus vs. Temperature

[1] In Mechanics of Materials, the Young's modulus (also see 9.8[1], page 379) is an important property of a material. The Young's modulus E usually decreases as temperature T increases. The table below lists the Young's moduli of a metal under various temperatures, measured in a series of uniaxial tensile tests.

Temperature T (K)	33	144	255	366	477	589	700	811	922
Young's Modulus E (GPa)	220	213	206	199	192	185	167	141	105

In computer simulations of stress analysis, engineers are often asked to input the Young's modulus as a polynomial function of temperature; i.e.,

$$E(T) = c_0 + c_1 T + c_2 T^2 + ...$$

In this section, we want to find a polynomial to represent the Young's modulus; the procedure is called a curve fitting. ↓

Example10_06.m: Polynomial Curve Fittings

[2] This script finds the polynomials of degrees one, two, and three that best-fit the data points in [1]. ↵

```
clear
T = [ 33, 144, 255, 366, 477, 589, 700, 811, 922];
E = [220, 213, 206, 199, 192, 185, 167, 141, 105];
temp = 0:50:1000;
format shortG
for k = 1:3
    P = polyfit(T, E, k)
    young = polyval(P, temp);
    subplot(2,2,k)
    plot(T, E, 'o', temp, young)
    axis([0,1000,100,250])
    xlabel('Temperature (K)')
    ylabel('Young''s Modulus (GPa)')
    title(['Polynomial of Degree ', num2str(k)])
    residual = E - polyval(P, T);
    error = norm(residual)
    R = sqrt(1-error^2/norm(E)^2)
end
```

[3] This is the text output in the **Command Window**. ↓

```
>> Example10_06
P =
      -0.11514        235.86
error =
        37.055
R =
       0.99775
P =
    -0.00015541      0.033291       213.23
error =
        15.469
R =
       0.99961
P =
    -2.9124e-07    0.00026175      -0.12346        224.67
error =
        3.3894
R =
       0.99998
```

[4] This is the graphic output. ↵

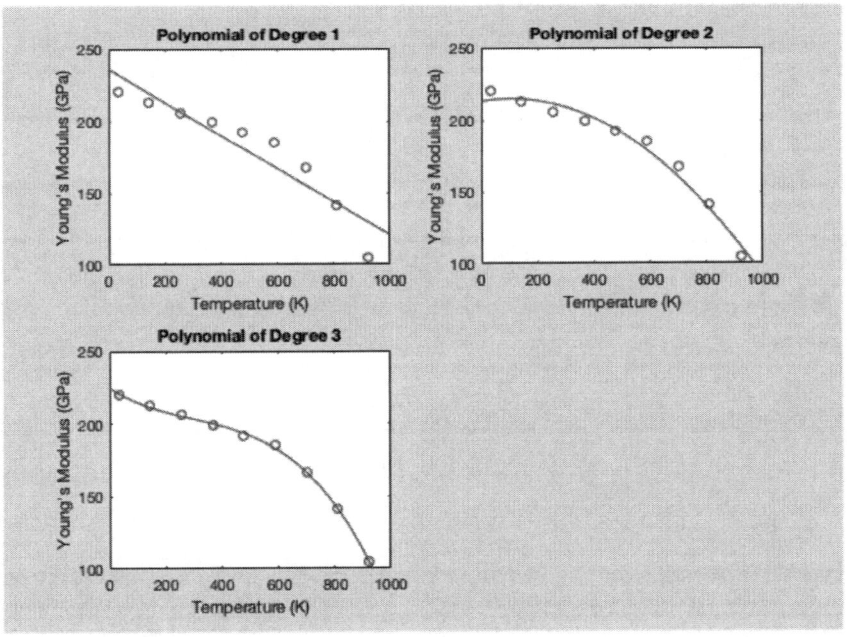

About Example10_06.m

[5] Lines 2-3 prepare the temperature data `T` and the Young's moduli `E` listed in [1], page 407. Line 4 creates a grid of temperature points that will be used to plot curves. Line 5 sets the output format to `shortG` (without this setting the first number in line 33 would be displayed as zero). Line 6 starts a `for`-loop with the counter `k` running from 1 to 3. In each pass, it finds a polynomial of degree `k` that best-fits the data points; it also generates a subplot (5.4d[2]. page 222).

Within the `for`-loop (lines 6-18), line 7 uses the function `polyfit` to find a polynomial of degree `k` that best-fits the data points (`T`, `E`). The returned polynomial `P` is of vector form. Line 8 uses the polynomial `P` to calculate the Young's modulus at temperatures in `temp`. Using the data points and the fitting polynomial, lines 9-14 create a subplot on the **Figure** window (see [4], last page), in which the data points (`T`, `E`) are plotted as circular points and the fitting polynomial (`temp`, `young`) is plotted as a smooth curve.

The three fitting polynomials (see lines 20-21, 26-27, and 32-33) are, respectively,

$$E_1(T) = -0.11514\ T + 235.86$$

$$E_2(T) = -0.00015541\ T^2 + 0.033291\ T + 213.23$$

$$E_3(T) = -2.9124 \times 10^{-7}\ T^3 + 0.00026175\ T^2 - 0.12346\ T + 224.67$$

To see how well a curve fits to the data points, line 15 calculates the **residual**, the distances between the data points and the fitting curve. The norm of the residual (line 16; also see lines 22-23, 28-29, and 34-35) is called the **error** of the curve fitting. The **error** can be thought of as the "average" distance between the data points and the fitting curve. The smaller the **error** is, the better the curve fits the data points.

$$error = \|residual\|$$

In statistics textbooks, a dimensionless quantity R is often used as an index of the degree of fitness,

$$R = \sqrt{1 - \frac{error^2}{\|E\|^2}}$$

Line 17 calculates the R values. The outputs show that $R_1 = 0.99775$ (lines 24-25), $R_2 = 0.99961$ (lines 30-31), and $R_3 = 0.99998$ (lines 36-37). It is obvious, the closer to 1.00 the R is, the better the curve fits the data points.

In the next section, we'll demonstrate the use of an interactive curve-fitting tool to perform the same tasks in this section. #

Table 10.6 Summary of Functions

Functions	Description
`format shortG`	Uses `short` or `shortE`, whichever is more compact
`polyfit(x,y,n)`	Finds a polynomial of degree n that is a best fit for the data points (x, y)
`polyval(p,x)`	Evaluates a polynomial p at x
`subplot(m,n,k)`	Creates axes in tiled positions
`norm(a)`	Calculates vector/matrix norm

10.7 Interactive Curve-Fitting Tools

[1] In this section, we'll demonstrate the use of an interactive curve-fitting tool built in MATLAB to perform the tasks covered in the last section. First, prepare the data points and create a figure: ↙

```
>> clear
>> T = [ 33, 144, 255, 366, 477, 589, 700, 811, 922];
>> E = [220, 213, 206, 199, 192, 185, 167, 141, 105];
>> plot(T, E, 'o')
>> axis([0, 1000, 100, 250])
```

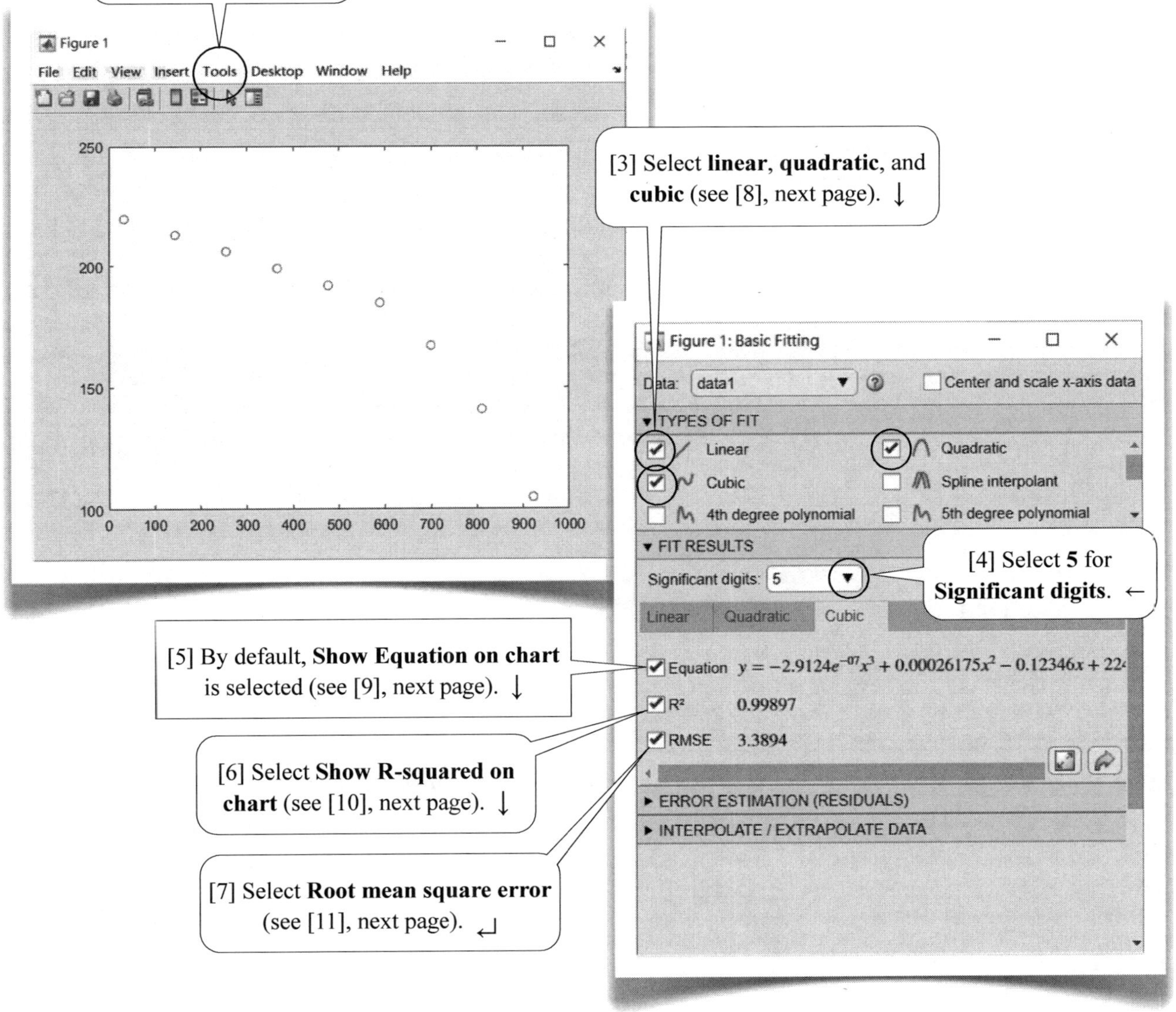

[2] Pull-down-select **Tools>Basic Fitting**. ↘

[3] Select **linear**, **quadratic**, and **cubic** (see [8], next page). ↓

[4] Select **5** for **Significant digits**. ←

[5] By default, **Show Equation on chart** is selected (see [9], next page). ↓

[6] Select **Show R-squared on chart** (see [10], next page). ↓

[7] Select **Root mean square error** (see [11], next page). ↵

[9] Mathematical forms of the fitting polynomials are shown on the chart. Note that these are consistent with those obtained in Section 10.6. ↙

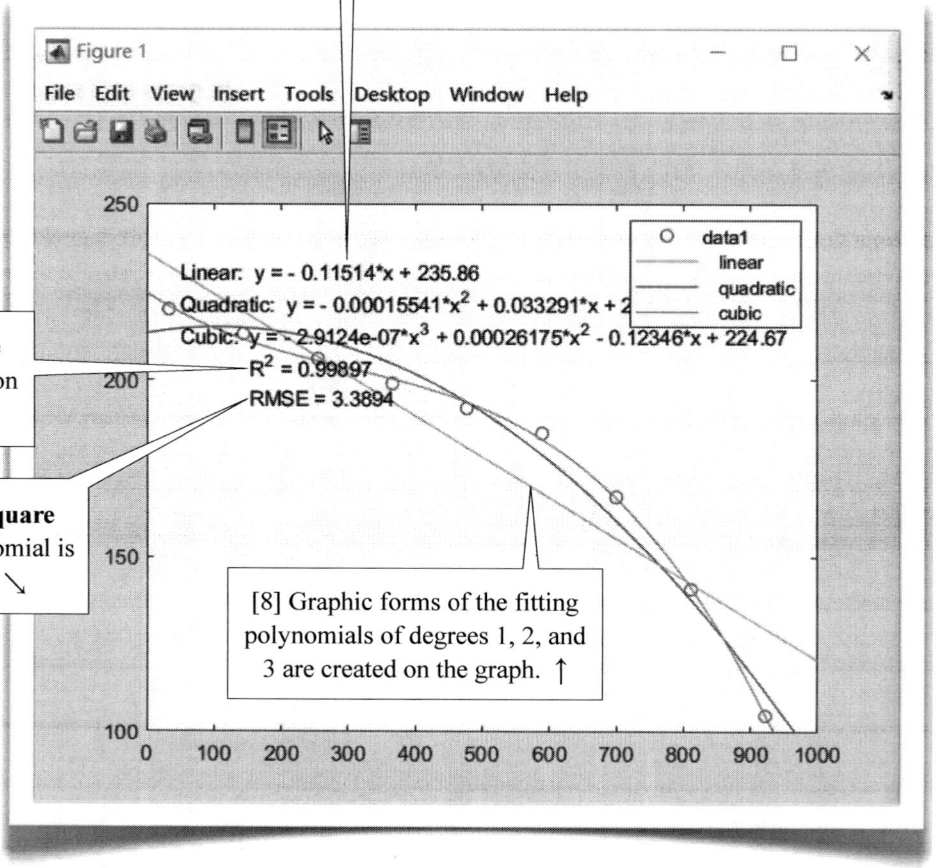

[10] The **R-squared** of the cubic polynomial is shown on the chart. ↓

[11] The **Root mean square error** of the cubic polynomial is shown on the chart. ↘

[8] Graphic forms of the fitting polynomials of degrees 1, 2, and 3 are created on the graph. ↑

Curve-Fitting Toolbox

[12] MATLAB provides a **Curve-Fitting Toolbox** which allows you to fit curves with more than just polynomials. However, you need a license that includes the Curve-Fitting Toolbox. #

10.8 Linear Fit Through Origin: Brake Assembly

10.8a Example: Brake Assembly (Original Design)

[1] An automobile company wants to improve a brake assembly, for which a schematic diagram is shown below: As the driver applies a force on the brake, the brake fluid pressure increases, moving the caliper and forcing the brake pads to grip the brake disk which rotates about an axis.

The brake fluid pressure x can be viewed as the input of the brake system, and the braking torque as the output of the brake system. The following are measured data in a series of tests for the original design of the brake assembly. For a specific input pressure, different braking torques are measured under various noises, e.g., humidity, temperature, etc.

Brake fluid pressure x (kgf/mm^2)	0.008	0.016	0.032	0.064
Braking torque y (kgf-mm)	4.8	11.1	23.1	42.0
	1.2	8.6	18.1	36.0
	5.7	13.0	25.1	43.2
	4.4	11.8	21.4	37.6

Example10_08a.m (page 414) produces a graph shown in [2]. Note that, when the input pressure is zero ($x = 0$), the output torque must be zero ($y = 0$); therefore, it is reasonable to require that the regression line passes through the origin. The pressure-versus-torque plot in [2] reveals some problems of the original design.

First, the **robustness** of the brake must be improved. For a good design of the brake system, the measure data points for a specific input pressure must be as close to the regression line as possible. The deviation of the measured data points from the regression line reflects the fact that the original design is susceptible to the noises.

Second, the **sensitivity** of the brake assembly must be improved. The slope of the regression line (i.e., y/x, the ratio between the output torque and the input pressure) is called the **sensitivity** of the brake system and also represents the mechanical **efficiency**. The sensitivity must be as large as possible. The calculated value here (634.6691 in [2]) is not satisfying, according to the engineers' experiences. ↵

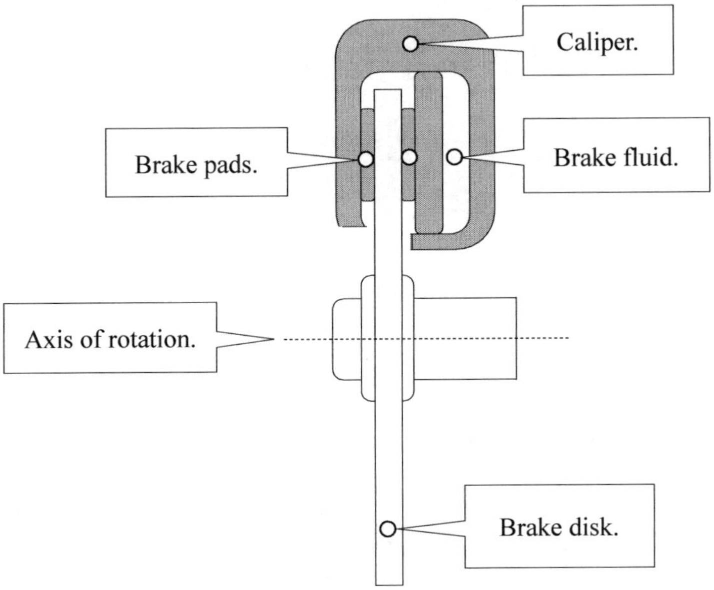

[2] Example10_08a.m (next page) produces a graph like this. The circular marks are measured data in [1], and the solid line is the regression line (i.e., best-fit line) through the origin. ↓

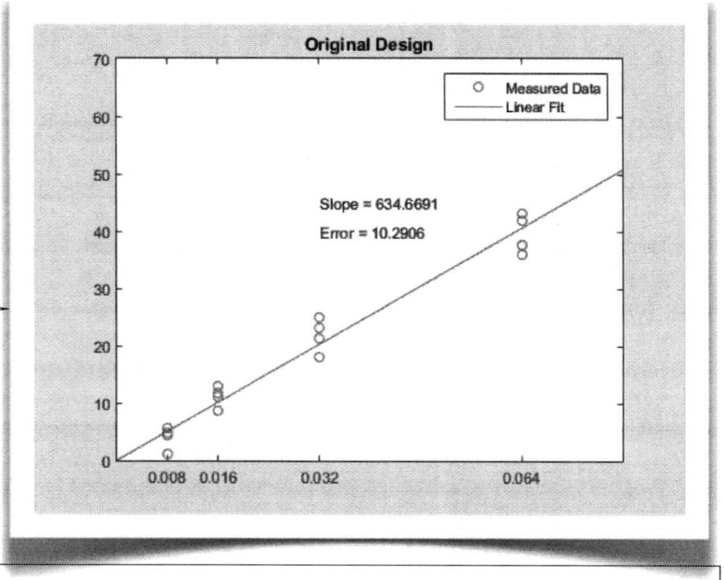

Linear Fit Through Origin

[3] Consider n points $(x_k, y_k), k = 1, 2, \ldots n,$ in the xy-space. We want to find a line $y = bx$ that best-fits (in the sense of least squared errors) the n points. Note that the line $y = bx$ passes through the origin.

The **residuals** (10.6[5], page 409) are

$$y_k - bx_k,\ k = 1,\ 2,\ \ldots n \tag{a}$$

and the sum of squared residuals is

$$S = \sum_{k=1}^{n} (y_k - bx_k)^2 \tag{b}$$

Among all possible b's, the least of S must satisfy $dS/db = 0$, i.e.,

$$\begin{aligned} \frac{dS}{db} &= \frac{d}{db}\sum_{k=1}^{n}(y_k - bx_k)^2 \\ &= -2\sum_{k=1}^{n} x_k (y_k - bx_k) \\ &= -2\left(\sum_{k=1}^{n} x_k y_k - b\sum_{k=1}^{n} x_k^2\right) \\ &= 0 \end{aligned}$$

The slope b is

$$b = \frac{\sum_{k=1}^{n} x_k y_k}{\sum_{k=1}^{n} x_k^2} \tag{c}$$

And the **error** (10.6[5], page 409) is the square root of S.

$$Error = \sqrt{\sum_{k=1}^{n} (y_k - bx_k)^2} \tag{d}$$

↵

Example10_08a.m: The Original Design

[4] This script finds a line through origin that best-fits the data points in [1] and calculates the **error**, Eq. (d). ↓

```
 1  clear
 2  x = [0.008, 0.008, 0.008, 0.008, ...
 3       0.016, 0.016, 0.016, 0.016, ...
 4       0.032, 0.032, 0.032, 0.032, ...
 5       0.064, 0.064, 0.064, 0.064];
 6  y = [4.8,  1.2,  5.7,  4.4, ...
 7      11.1,  8.6, 13.0, 11.8, ...
 8      23.1, 18.1, 25.1, 21.4, ...
 9      42.0, 36.0, 43.2, 37.6];
10  slope = sum(x.*y)/sum(x.^2);
11  residual = y-slope*x;
12  error = norm(residual);
13  plot(x,y,'o'), hold on
14  hAxes = gca;
15  hAxes.XTick = [0.008,0.016,0.032,0.064];
16  axis([0,0.08,0,70]);
17  plot([0,0.08],[0,slope*0.08])
18  text(0.032, 45, ['Slope = ', num2str(slope)])
19  text(0.032, 40, ['Error = ', num2str(error)])
20  legend('Measured Data', 'Linear Fit')
21  title('Original Design')
```

About Example10_08a.m

[5] Lines 2-9 create vectors x and y representing the 16 data points. Line 10 calculates the slope of the regression line according to Eq. (c), last page. Line 11 calculates the residuals, Eq. (a), and line 12 calculates the **error**, Eq. (d). Lines 13-21 produce the graph shown in [2], last page. #

10.8b An Improved Design of the Brake Assembly

[1] The engineers of the brake company, after days of brain-storming and many trials, finally came up with a much better design. The following are measured data in a series of tests for the improved design of the brake assembly:

Brake fluid pressure x (kgf/mm^2)	0.008	0.016	0.032	0.064
	5.3	12.2	24.6	49.3
Braking torque y (kgf-mm)	4.6	10.1	23.1	47.1
	5.8	13.2	25.0	50.1
	5.4	11.9	24.3	48.2

Example10_08b.m produces a graph shown in [3], next page. Comparing the improved design [3] with the original design (10.8a[2], page 413), we see that the error is reduced significantly (from 10.2906 to 3.975). This can be visually observed since the data points now are much closer to the regression line, implying that the new design is much more robust, not affected by noises such as the temperature or humidity changes. The sensitivity is also enhanced significantly (from 634.6691 to 757.9044). ↓

Example10_08b.m: An Improved Design

[2] This script finds a line through origin that best-fits the data points listed in [1], and calculates the **error**. The dimmed lines are copied from Example10_08a.m, last page; the other statements are self-explanatory. ↵

```
clear
x = [0.008, 0.008, 0.008, 0.008, ...
     0.016, 0.016, 0.016, 0.016, ...
     0.032, 0.032, 0.032, 0.032, ...
     0.064, 0.064, 0.064, 0.064];
y = [5.3,  4.6,  5.8,  5.4, ...
    12.2, 10.1, 13.2, 11.9, ...
    24.6, 23.1, 25.0, 24.3, ...
    49.3, 47.1, 50.1, 48.2];
slope = sum(x.*y)/sum(x.^2);
residual = y-slope*x;
error = norm(residual);
plot(x,y,'o'), hold on
hAxes = gca;
hAxes.XTick = [0.008,0.016,0.032,0.064];
axis([0,0.08,0,70]);
plot([0,0.08],[0,slope*0.08])
text(0.032, 45, ['Slope = ', num2str(slope)])
text(0.032, 40, ['Error = ', num2str(error)])
legend('Measured Data', 'Linear Fit')
title('Improved Design')
```

[3] Example10_08b.m produces a graph like this. ↓

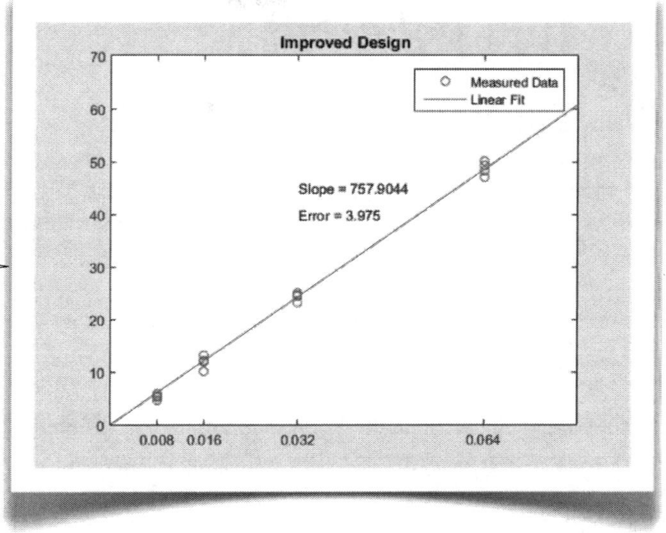

Using Backslash Operator for Least Squares Linear Fit

[4] In Section 10.3, when discussing systems of linear equations

$$\mathbf{Ax} = \mathbf{b}$$

We assumed that **A** is an *n*-by-*n* square matrix, **x** is an *n*-by-1 vector, and **b** is also an *n*-by-1 vector. (We also assume the determinant of **A** is nonzero.)

What if the system of equations is over-specified; i.e., the number of equations is more than the number of unknown variables? Assume that **A** is an *m*-by-*n* matrix (**x** is *n*-by-1 and **b** is *m*-by-1), where *m*>*n*. In such cases, the backslash operator **A\b** will use a least-squares fit algorithm similar to that used by `polyfit`, discussed in Section 10.6.

Now, returning to our problem of finding a line $y = bx$ that best fits *n* points (x_k, y_k), $k = 1, 2, \ldots n$, we may treat the problem as

$$\mathbf{x}'b = \mathbf{y}'$$

where $\mathbf{x}'$ is *n*-by-1, *b* is 1-by-1, and $\mathbf{y}'$ is *n*-by-1. The least squares solution of *b* can be calculated with

```
b = x'\y'
```

To confirm these concepts, at the end of Example10_08b.m, type

```
>> format short
>> b = x'\y'
b =
  757.9044
```

Which are consistent with that calculated using Eq. (c) (page 413) and displayed in [3].

The built-in function `lsqlin` (least-square linear regression) also does the same job:

```
>> b = lsqlin(x',y')
b =
  757.9044
```

We'll discuss more about `lsqlin` for multivariate linear regression in Section 12.8. #

10.9 Interpolations

10.9a Example: Young's Modulus

[1] We mentioned (in 10.6[1], page 407) that, in stress analysis, some computer programs require the Young's modulus be input as a polynomial function of temperature, so the programs can calculate the Young's modulus at any temperature. Yet other computer programs require the Young's modulus be input as a data table like this:

Temperature T (K)	33	144	255	366	477	589	700	811	922
Young's Modulus E (GPa)	220	213	206	199	192	185	167	141	105

The programs then calculate the Young's modulus at any temperature by means of **interpolation**. ↓

Function `interp1`

[2] The function `interp1` (the last character is the number "1", not the letter "l") performs 1-D interpolation. For example, the following commands find the Young's modulus at 273 K (0° C) with **linear interpolation**:

```
>> T = [ 33, 144, 255, 366, 477, 589, 700, 811, 922];
>> E = [220, 213, 206, 199, 192, 185, 167, 141, 105];
>> interp1(T, E, 273)
ans =
  204.8649
```

A syntax for the function `interp1` is

```
y1 = interp1(x, y, x1, method)
```

where the vectors *x* and *y* contain the coordinates of the data points; the *x1* (a scalar or vector) contains the x-coordinates of the query points; the string *method* specifies the interpolation method, e.g., `'linear'`, `'spline'`, etc. The output argument *y1* contains the y-coordinates of the query points. ↓

Example10_09a.m: Interpolations

[3] This script produces a graph shown in [4], next page. ↵

```
clear
T = [ 33, 144, 255, 366, 477, 589, 700, 811, 922];
E = [220, 213, 206, 199, 192, 185, 167, 141, 105];
plot(T, E, 'o'), hold on
temp = 0:10:1000;
young = interp1(T, E, temp);
plot(temp, young, 'r:')
young = interp1(T, E, temp, 'spline');
plot(temp, young, 'b-')
axis([0,1000,100,250])
xlabel('Temperature (K)')
ylabel('Young''s Modulus (GPa)')
legend('Data Points', 'Linear Interpolation', 'Spline Interpolation')
```

[4] Example10_09a.m produces a graph like this. It contains data points from experiments (circular marks), listed in [1] (last page), a linear interpolating curve (red dotted curve), and a spline interpolating curve (blue solid curve). Note that the two interpolating curves almost coincide with each other. ↓

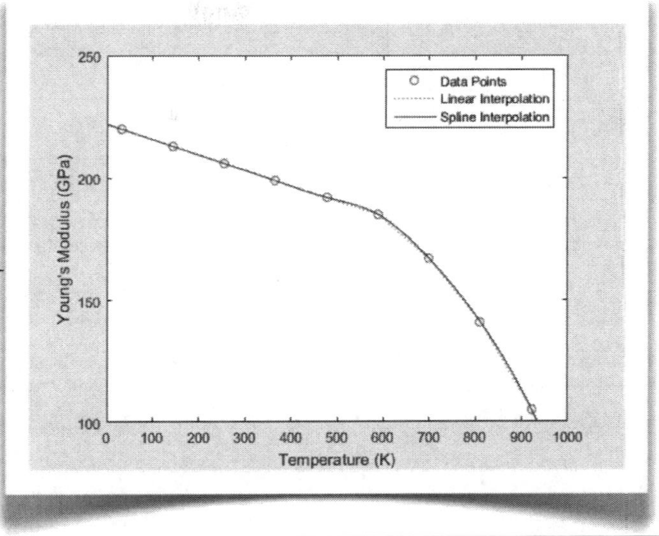

About Example10_09a.m

[5] Lines 2-3 prepare the data points listed in [1], last page. Line 4 plots the 9 data points as circular marks. Line 5 creates temperatures at which the Young's moduli will be calculated. Line 6 calculates the Young's moduli at these temperatures, using the default interpolation method (linear interpolation). Line 7 plots the linearly interpolated points as a red dotted curve. Line 8 calculates the Young's moduli again, using the **spline** interpolation method. Line 9 plots the spline interpolations as a blue solid curve. Line 10 adjusts the axis limits; lines 11-12 add axis labels; line 13 adds legends. #

10.9b Roots Finding by Interpolations

Example10_09b.m: Roots Finding by Interpolations

[1] An application of interpolation is to find the roots of an equation. As an example, this script solves the equation $\sin x + 2\cos x - 0.5 = 0$. The output (see [2]) shows that a solution of the equation is $x = 1.8089$. ↓

```
clear
x = linspace(0,pi);
y = sin(x)+2*cos(x)-0.5;
plot(x,y,[0,pi], [0,0]), hold on
axis([0, pi, -2.5, 2])
x1 = interp1(y,x,0)
plot([x1, x1], [-2.5, 2])
text(x1,0.1,num2str(x1))
```

[2] Example10_09b.m produces this graph. ↓

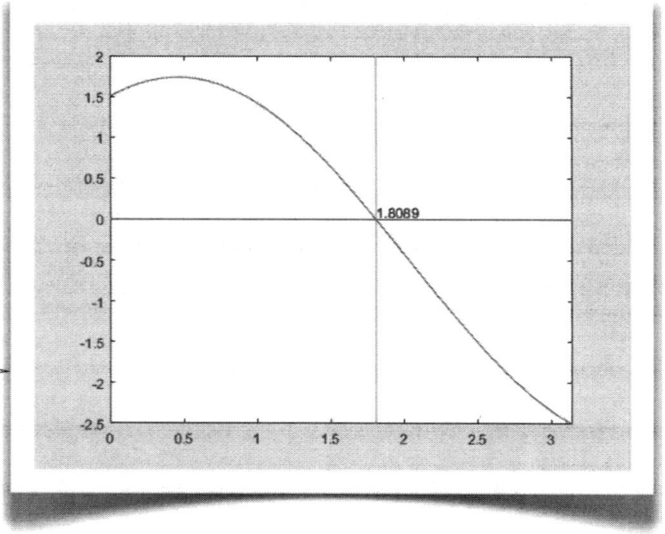

About Example10_09b.m

[3] Line 2 creates 100 x-coordinates ranging from 0 to π. Line 3 calculates the corresponding y-coordinates.

Line 4 plots the curve of the function and a horizontal line $y=0$. The x-coordinate of the intersecting point between the curve and the horizontal line is the root of the equation. Line 5 adjusts the axis limits.

Line 6 uses the function `interp1` to find the x-coordinate of the point that has a zero y-coordinate. The result is $x=1.8089$. Note that, in using the function `interp1`, y is used as the first input argument and x as second input argument, since we want to find an interpolation value of x such that $y=0$.

Line 7 plots a vertical line $x=1.8089$. Line 8 labels the intersection point with the solution. #

10.10 Two-Dimensional Interpolations

Coordinate-Measuring Machines

[1] Coordinate-measuring machines (*Wikipedia>Coordinate-measuring machine*) are used to measure the shape of a real-world object. The measured data can then be used to construct a 3-D model. Example10_10.m illustrates the ideas, in which we use the built-in tutorial function `peaks` to generate a set of "measured data." Please pretend that these data are collected from the measurement of a real-world object. ↓

Example10_10.m: Two-Dimensional Interpolations

[2] This script produces two figures as shown in [3-4]. ↓

```
 1  clear
 2  [X,Y] = meshgrid(-3:3);
 3  Z = peaks(X,Y);
 4  surf(X,Y,Z)
 5  title('Measured Data')
 6  [X1,Y1] = meshgrid(-3:0.1:3);
 7  Z1 = interp2(X,Y,Z,X1,Y1,'spline');
 8  figure
 9  surf(X1,Y1,Z1)
10  title('Spline Interpolation')
```

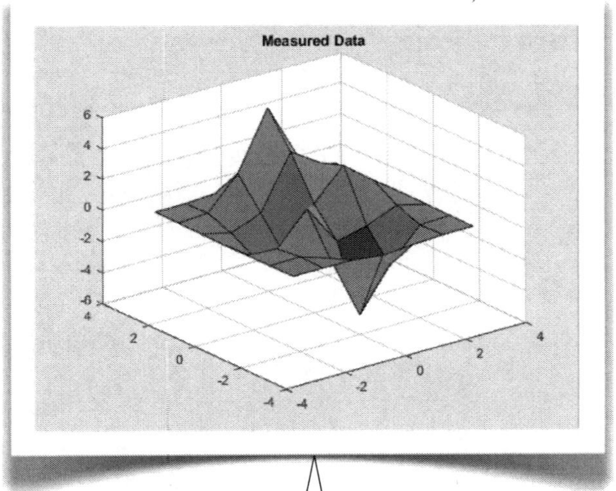

[3] Lines 2-5 produce this 3-D surface plot of "measured data." →

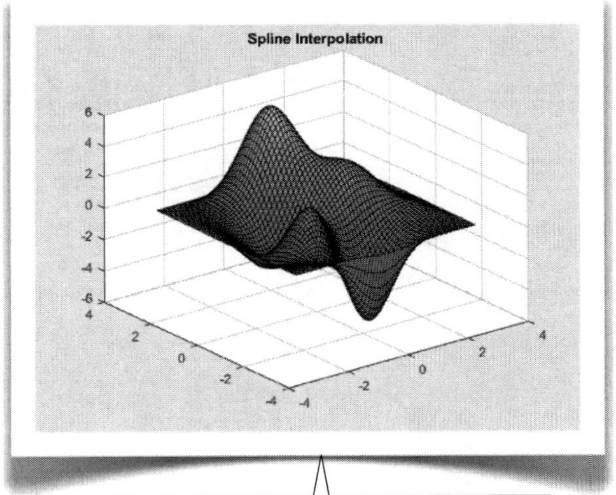

[4] Lines 6-10 produce this spline interpolation of the data. ↓

About Example10_10.m

[5] Line 2 generates 7-by-7 grid points in the *x-y* space. Line 3 generates 7-by-7 "measured data" using the function `peaks`. Line 4 plots these data points as a surface (see [3]). Line 6 generates grid points in the *x-y* space, to be used as interpolating points. Line 7 interpolates the *z*-values at specified points, using the **spline** method. Line 9 plots the interpolated surface (see [4]). #

Chapter 11

Differentiation, Integration, and Differential Equations

Engineering problem-solving often involves three stages: establishing differential equations for the problem, solving the differential equations, and interpreting the solution. Traditional engineering mathematics is abstract and hard for a junior college student. However, through the use of MATLAB, these mathematics become concrete and easy to understand.

11.1 Numerical Differentiation

Review of the Function diff

[1] Consider a vector (either column vector or row vector) of n elements $x = [x_1, x_2, \ldots, x_n]$. The function `diff(x)` returns an $n-1$ vector

$$[x_2 - x_1, x_3 - x_2, \ldots, x_n - x_{n-1}].$$

For example:

```
>> x = [8 5 3 2 2];
>> x1 = diff(x)
x1 =
    -3     -2     -1      0
```

Remember, the function `diff(x)` returns a vector of $n-1$ elements, not n elements. ↓

Numerical Differentiations: Forward, Backward, and Central Differences

[2] Given a function represented by n points

$$(x_i, y_i),\ i = 1, 2, \ldots, n$$

we may approximate the derivative of y with respect to x at a point x_i by a **forward difference** approach:

$$\left(\frac{dy}{dx}\right)_i = \frac{y_{i+1} - y_i}{x_{i+1} - x_i},\ i = 1, 2, \ldots, n-1 \qquad \text{(a)}$$

It is called a **forward difference**, since it calculates the slope over a region $x_{i+1} - x_i$, which is next to the current point x_i. Note that the forward difference approach cannot be applied for $i = n$.

Another approach is **backward difference** approach,

$$\left(\frac{dy}{dx}\right)_i = \frac{y_i - y_{i-1}}{x_i - x_{i-1}},\ i = 2, 3, \ldots, n \qquad \text{(b)}$$

Note that the backward difference approach cannot be applied for $i = 1$.

A third approach is **central difference** approach,

$$\left(\frac{dy}{dx}\right)_i = \frac{y_{i+1} - y_{i-1}}{x_{i+1} - x_{i-1}},\ i = 2, 3, \ldots, n-1 \qquad \text{(c)}$$

Note that the central difference approach cannot be applied for $i = 1$ and $i = n$.

Using $y = \sin(x)$ as an example, Example11_01.m (next page) compares the three approaches. ↵

Example11_01.m: Forward, Backward, and Central Differences

[3] Using $y = \sin(x)$, i.e., $y' = \cos(x)$, as an example, this script compares three numerical differentiation methods introduced in [2], last page. The graphics output is shown in [4-9]. ↓

```
1  clear
2  n = 10;
3  x = linspace(0, pi/2, n);
4  y = sin(x);
5  y1 = cos(x);
6  plot(x, y1, 'b-'), hold on
7  axis([0, pi/2, 0, 1])
8  y1 = diff(y)./diff(x);
9  plot(x(1:n-1), y1, 'kx:')
10 plot(x(2:n), y1, 'k+:')
11 y1 = gradient(y, x);
12 plot(x, y1, 'ko')
13 xlabel('x')
14 ylabel('cos(x)')
15 legend('Exact', 'Forward', 'Backward', 'Central')
```

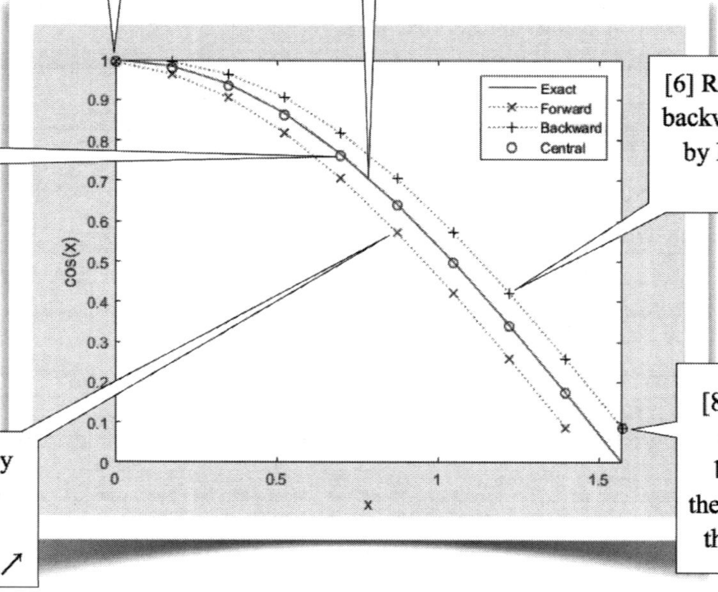

[4] The solid line (plotted by line 6) represents the exact values for the derivative. ↙

[5] Results calculated by the forward difference (plotted by line 9) are below the exact values. ↗

[6] Results calculated by the backward difference (plotted by line 10) are above the exact values. ↖

[7] The circular marks (plotted by line 12) are calculated by the function `gradient` (line 11), in which the first point is calculated using the forward difference; therefore, it is the same as the first point in [5]. ↘

[8] And the last point is calculated using the backward difference; therefore, it is the same as the last point in [6]. ↖

[9] The remaining points are approximated using the central difference, coincident with the exact values (solid line). ↵

About Example11_01.m

[10] To exaggerate the differences among the three approaches, we use $n = 10$ (line 2). Later, we'll show that, as n becomes large, the three approaches converge to the exact values (see [11]).

Line 3 creates an evenly spaced vector of n x-values from 0 to $\pi/2$. Line 4 creates a vector of n y-values, where $y = \sin(x)$. Line 5 creates a vector of n values representing the exact values of the derivative of y with respect to x. Note that we use the notation $y1$ for the first derivative of y. Line 6 then plots these exact values of the derivative (see [4], last page). Line 7 adjusts the axis limits.

Line 8 calculates the derivative using the forward difference approach (see Eq. (a), page 422). Line 9 plots these values (see [5]).

To plot the derivative using the backward differences approach, the same $y1$ calculated in line 8 can be used, but the corresponding x-values need to be shifted backward by one point (see line 10 and [6]).

The function `gradient` (line 11) is used to demonstrate the central differences; it actually calculates the derivative using the forward difference for the first point, the backward difference for the last point, and the central difference for the in-between points. Line 12 plots the results calculated by the function `gradient` (see [7-9]).

Lines 13-14 label the axes. Line 15 adds the legends. ↓

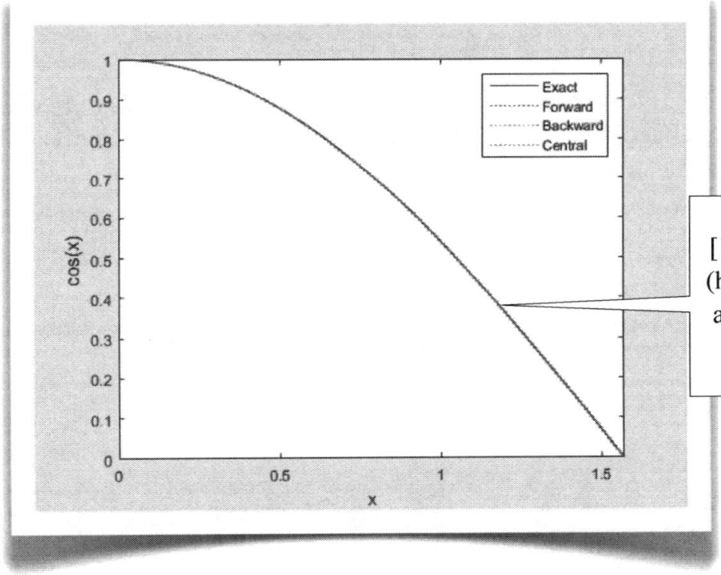

[11] As n becomes large (here, $n = 200$), the three approaches converge to the exact values. ↓

Conclusions

[12] In general, we should use the function `gradient` for numerical differentiations. The function `gradient` also can be used to calculate partial derivatives, as demonstrated in 5.13a[1-3], page 248. #

11.2 Numerical Integration: `trapz`

Trapezoidal Numerical Integrations

[1] Consider that, given a function $y(x)$, we want to evaluate the integration

$$A = \int_a^b y(x)dx$$

Geometric meaning of A is the area bounded by four curves: $x = a$, $x = b$, $y = 0$, and $y = y(x)$.

For example, assuming $y(x) = 20 + x^2$, the integration

$$A = \int_0^{10} y(x)dx$$

is the area below the curve shown in [2]. The symbolic result, $A = 1600/3$, can be obtained by the following commands

```
>> syms x
>> int(20+x^2, [0,10])
ans =
1600/3
```

In many cases, the function is too complicated to be integrated symbolically and needs to be integrated numerically. A simple idea of the numerical integration is to divide the area into many small trapezoidal areas (see [2]). The total area can be approximated by summing up these small areas:

$$A = \sum_{i=1}^{n-1} \frac{(y_i + y_{i+1})(x_{i+1} - x_i)}{2}$$

The function `trapz` performs numerical integration using this simple idea. ↓

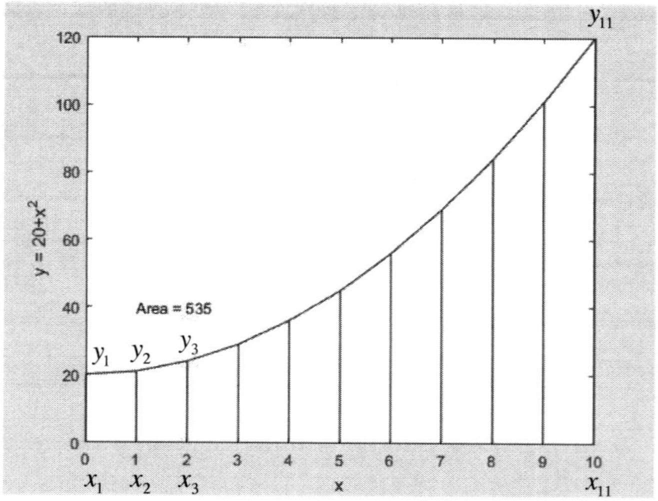

[2] Geometric meaning of $\int_{x_1}^{x_n} y(x)dx$ is the area below the curve $y = y(x)$. ↵

Example11_02.m: Numerical Integration

[3] This script generates a graph as shown in [2], last page, and calculates the area under the curve $y(x) = 20 + x^2$, i.e., performing numerical integration $\int_0^{10} y(x)dx$, using the function `trapz`. ↓

```
1   clear
2   n = 11;
3   x = linspace(0,10,n);
4   y = 20 + x.^2;
5   plot(x, y, 'k'), hold on
6   plot([x;x], [zeros(1,n);y], 'k')
7   axis([0, 10, 0, 120])
8   xlabel('x')
9   ylabel('y = 20+x^2')
10  A = trapz(x, y)
11  text(1, 40, ['Area = ', num2str(A)])
```

About Example11_02.m

[4] We first use $n = 11$ (line 2) to demonstrate that, with coarse grids, the result may deviate from the exact value (1600/3). As n increases, the result becomes closer to the exact value (see [5]).

Line 3 creates a vector of n x-values and line 4 creates a vector of corresponding y-values. Line 5 plots the curve of $y(x)$, and line 6 plots the vertical lines (see [2], last page). Line 7 adjusts the axis limits. Lines 8-9 label the axes.

Line 10, using the function `trapz`, integrates y over the region defined in the vector `x`. Line 11 displays the result on the graphic area. Here, the result is 535 (the exact value is 1600/3). ↓

[5] As n increases (here, $n = 51$), the result (here, 533.4) becomes closer to the exact value. #

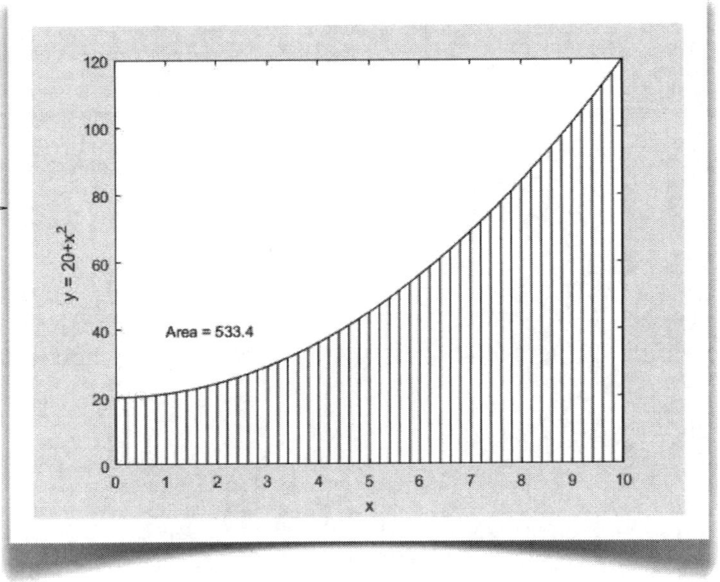

11.3 Length of a Curve

11.3a Example: Length of a Curve

[1] Consider a curve in the 3-D space defined by the parametric equations $x = x(t)$, $y = y(t)$, and $z = z(t)$. The length of the curve L can be calculated by

$$\begin{aligned} L &= \int_{t_1}^{t_2} dL \\ &= \int_{t_1}^{t_2} \sqrt{dx^2 + dy^2 + dz^2} \qquad \text{(a)} \\ &= \int_{t_1}^{t_2} \sqrt{\left(\frac{dx}{dt}\right)^2 + \left(\frac{dy}{dt}\right)^2 + \left(\frac{dz}{dt}\right)^2}\, dt \end{aligned}$$

As an example, Example11_03a.m calculates the length of the following curve from $t = 0$ to $t = 3\pi$:

$$x = \sin 2t,\ y = \cos t,\ z = t \qquad \text{(b)}$$ ↓

Example11_03a.m: Length of a Curve

[2] This script calculates the length of the curve defined by Eq. (b), using the function `trapz`. ↓

```
1   clear
2   n = 500;
3   t = linspace(0,3*pi,n);
4   x = sin(2*t);
5   y = cos(t);
6   z = t;
7   plot3(x, y, z)
8   axis vis3d, box on, grid on
9   xlabel('x'), ylabel('y'), zlabel('z')
10  f = sqrt(gradient(x,t).^2+gradient(y,t).^2+gradient(z,t).^2);
11  L = trapz(t, f)
```

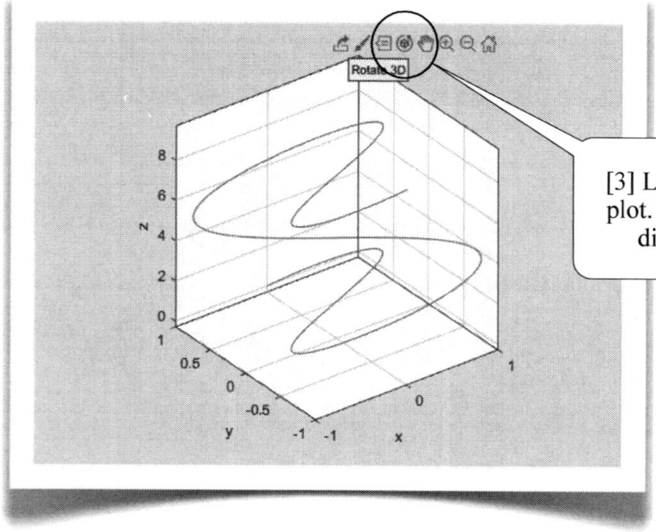

[3] Lines 7-9 produce this plot. Rotate to view from different angles. ↵

About Example11_03a.m

[4] Here, we divide the curve into 500 segments (line 2). In general, the finer the segments, the more accurate the calculated length. Line 3 creates a vector of 500 values for the parameter t, ranging from 0 to 3π. Lines 4-6 create spatial coordinates (see Eq. (b), last page) along the curve. Lines 7-9 plot the curve in the 3-D space, as shown in [3], last page. Line 10 generates a vector of 500 function values of the integrand (see Eq. (a), last page)

$$f = \sqrt{\left(\frac{dx}{dt}\right)^2 + \left(\frac{dy}{dt}\right)^2 + \left(\frac{dz}{dt}\right)^2}$$

Line 11 then integrates f over t. The result (output in the **Command Window**) is 17.2197.

Convergence Study

You might raise a question about the numerical result (17.2197) calculated by Example11_03a.m: How accurate is it? Since the more segments the curve is divided into, the more accurate the calculated result, we may answer this question by conducting a **convergence study**, demonstrated in Example11_03b.m. #

11.3b Convergence Study

Example11_03b.m: Convergence Study

[1] This script repeats the calculation of the length with $n = 100, 200, \ldots, 2000$, and generates a **convergence curve** as shown in [2-3]. ↵

```
clear
k = 0;
for n = 100:100:2000;
     t = linspace(0,3*pi,n);
     x = sin(2*t);
     y = cos(t);
     z = t;
     f = sqrt(gradient(x,t).^2+gradient(y,t).^2+gradient(z,t).^2);
     k = k+1;
     L(k) = trapz(t, f);
end
plot([100:100:2000], L, 'o-'), hold on
plot([0,2000], [L(k), L(k)])
text(1200,L(k)+0.003, ['Length = ', num2str(L(k))])
xlabel('Number of Segments')
ylabel('Calculated Length')
```

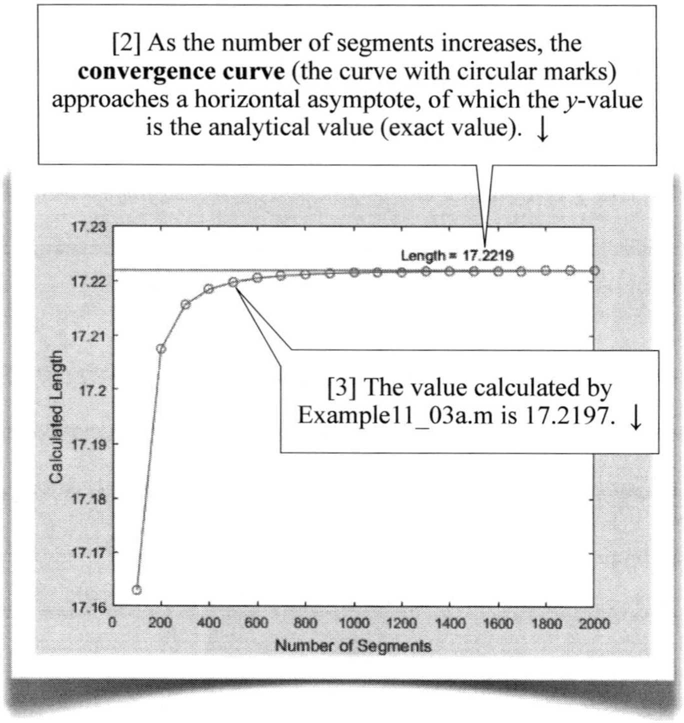

About Example11_03b.m

[4] Lines 3-11 repeatedly calculate the length of the curve by performing the numerical integration with $n = 100, 200, \ldots, 2000$, and store the results in the vector `L`. Lines 4-8 and 10 are basically copied from lines 3-6 and 10-11 in Example11_03a.m, page 427.

Line 12 plots the calculated length `L` versus number of segments `n`. This curve is called a **convergence curve**. As the number of segments increases, the convergence curve approaches a horizontal asymptote. Line 13 plots this horizontal asymptote. Its *y*-value is the analytical value (exact value) of the length. Line 14 displays this analytical value on the graphic area. Lines 15-16 label the axes. #

11.4 User-Defined Function as Input Argument: `integral`

[1] The function `integral` provides a more convenient way for numerical integration: You define the function to be integrated using one of the methods described in Sections 3.5 to 3.9 and then input a function handle as an argument to the function `integral`. It automatically controls the accuracy to a certain number of decimal places. Example11_04.m demonstrates the use of the function `integral`; Sections 11.5 and 11.6 give two more examples. ↓

Example11_04.m: Numerical Integration

[2] This script calculates the length of the curve defined in Eq. (b), page 427, using the function `integral`. ↓

```
1   L = integral(@fun, 0, 3*pi)
2
3   function dL = fun(t)
4   x = sin(2*t);
5   y = cos(t);
6   z = t;
7   dL = sqrt(gradient(x,t).^2+gradient(y,t).^2+gradient(z,t).^2);
8   end
```

About Example11_04.m

[3] Lines 3-8 define the function to be integrated (i.e., the integrand; also see Eq. (a), page 427),

$$f=\sqrt{\left(\frac{dx}{dt}\right)^2+\left(\frac{dy}{dt}\right)^2+\left(\frac{dz}{dt}\right)^2},\quad \text{where } x=\sin 2t,\ y=\cos t,\ z=t$$

The user-defined function may have any name but must allow input and output arguments as vectors; therefore, element-wise operators must be used in the user-defined function when the operands involve the input arguments (e.g., `.^` in line 7). To fully understand this, change line 7 to

```
dL = sqrt(gradient(x,t)^2+gradient(y,t)^2+gradient(z,t)^2);
```

Run the program again and read the error message.

Line 1 integrates the function over t from 0 to 3π. Note that a **function handle** of the user-defined function is used as the first input argument. The calculated length here is 17.2218 (output in the **Command Window**).

Absolute Error Tolerance

You may specify an **absolute error tolerance** when using the function `integral`. For example

```
L = integral(@fun, 0, 3*pi, 'AbsTol', 1e-12)
```

sets the absolute error tolerance to approximately 12 decimal places of accuracy. The default tolerance is 1e-10. *(Details and More >> doc integral)* #

11.5 Area and Centroid

Area Bounded by Two Curves

[1] Consider two curves in the *xy*-space,

$$y = f(x) \text{ and } y = g(x)$$

If the two curves intersect at two points (x_1, y_1) and (x_2, y_2), then the area bounded by the two curves is

$$dA = |f(x) - g(x)|\,dx\,,\ A = \int_{x_1}^{x_2} dA = \int_{x_1}^{x_2} |f(x) - g(x)|\,dx \qquad \text{(a)}$$

And the coordinates (x_c, y_c) of the centroid of the area is

$$x_c = \frac{1}{A}\int_{x_1}^{x_2} x\,dA = \frac{1}{A}\int_{x_1}^{x_2} x|f(x) - g(x)|\,dx \qquad \text{(b)}$$

$$y_c = \frac{1}{A}\int_{x_1}^{x_2} \frac{f(x)+g(x)}{2}\,dA = \frac{1}{A}\int_{x_1}^{x_2} \frac{f(x)+g(x)}{2}|f(x) - g(x)|\,dx = \frac{1}{2A}\int_{x_1}^{x_2} |f^2(x) - g^2(x)|\,dx \qquad \text{(c)}$$

In this section, we'll calculate the area and the centroid of the area bounded by the following two curves:

$$f(x) = x + 2 \text{ and } g(x) = x^2 \qquad \text{(d)}$$

↓

Example11_05.m: Area and Centroid

[2] This script calculates the area and the centroid of the area bounded by two curves defined in Eq. (d). ↵

```
clear
syms x y
fx = x+2;
gx = x^2;
fplot(fx), hold on, fplot(gx)
axis([-3,3,0,6])
legend('y = x+2', 'y = x^2', 'Location', 'southeast')
title('Two Curves')
eq1 = (y == fx);
eq2 = (y == gx);
sol = solve(eq1, eq2);
x1 = double(sol.x(1))
x2 = double(sol.x(2))
y1 = double(sol.y(1))
y2 = double(sol.y(2))
funA = @(x) abs((x+2)-(x.^2));
A = integral(funA,x1,x2)
funXc = @(x) x.*abs((x+2)-(x.^2));
funYc = @(x) abs((x+2).^2-(x.^4));
xc = integral(funXc,x1,x2)/A
yc = integral(funYc,x1,x2)/(2*A)
```

```
22   >> Example11_05
23   x1 =
24          -1
25   x2 =
26           2
27   y1 =
28           1
29   y2 =
30           4
31   A =
32          4.5000
33   xc =
34          0.5000
35   yc =
36          1.6000
```

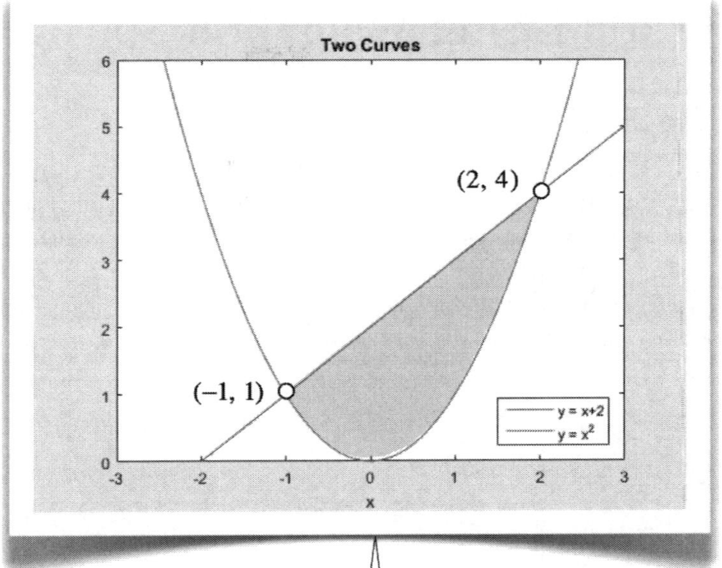

[3] This is the text output on the **Command Window**. →

[4] This is the graphic output. The two curves intersect at (-1,1) and (2,4), as shown in lines 23-30. The circles, coordinates, and shaded area is manually added by the author. ↓

About Example11_05.m

[5] Lines 2-4 define two symbolic expressions representing the two curves, Eq. (d). Lines 5-8 produce a plot of the two curves as shown in [4].

Lines 9-10 define two equations representing the two curves. Line 11 finds the two intersection points by solving the two equations. The result `sol` is a structure of two fields; each is a vector of two symbolic numbers representing the coordinates of the intersection points. Lines 12-15 retrieve these coordinates and convert to `double` (see lines 23-30).

Line 16 defines a function for the integrand in Eq. (a), i.e., $|f(x)-g(x)|$. Line 17 calculates the area using Eq. (a), i.e., $A=\int_{x_1}^{x_2}|f(x)-g(x)|\,dx$; the result is 4.5 (lines 31-32).

Line 18 defines a function for the integrand in Eq. (b), i.e., $x|f(x)-g(x)|$. Line 19 defines a function for the integrand in Eq. (c), i.e., $|f^2(x)-g^2(x)|$. Line 20 calculates the x-coordinate of the centroid using Eq. (b), i.e., $x_c=\frac{1}{A}\int_{x_1}^{x_2}x|f(x)-g(x)|\,dx$; the result is 0.5 (lines 33-34). Line 21 calculates the y-coordinate of the centroid using Eq. (c), i.e., $y_c=\frac{1}{2A}\int_{x_1}^{x_2}|f^2(x)-g^2(x)|\,dx$; the result is 1.6 (lines 35-36). #

11.6 Placing Weight on Spring Scale

The SDOF System Revisit

[1] The single degree of freedom (SDOF) model in 2.15a[2] (page 117; also see the figure below) can be used to represent a spring scale. The mass m represents all translational inertial effects in the mechanical system, and the damping c represents all the energy-dissipation effects. Imagine that we place a weight W on the scale so that the force on the scale ramps linearly from 0 to W in a time duration T_0 (see [2]). The response in terms of a dimensionless time $t = \omega T$ (ω is the natural frequency in rad/s of the mechanical system and T is the real time in seconds) is (*Reference: Vibrations, by B. Balachandran and E. B. Magrab, 2nd Edition, pp. 310-314*):

$$x(t) = \frac{W}{k}\left[h(t)u(t) - h(t-t_0)u(t-t_0)\right] \qquad \text{(a)}$$

where $t_0 = \omega T_0$ and

$$h(t) = \frac{1}{t_0\sqrt{1-\zeta^2}}\int_0^t \tau e^{-\zeta(t-\tau)} \sin\left[(t-\tau)\sqrt{1-\zeta^2}\right] d\tau \qquad \text{(b)}$$

and $u(t)$ is the unit step function,

$$u(t) = \begin{cases} 1 \text{ if } t > 0 \\ 0 \text{ otherwise} \end{cases} \qquad \text{(c)}$$

and ζ is the **damping ratio**: $\zeta = c/c_c$, where $c_c = 2m\omega$, $\omega = \sqrt{k/m}$ (also see 2.15b[1], page 118).

In this section, we'll calculate the response of the system for the force $W = 10$ N and $T_0 = 0.5$ sec. As in Section 2.15, assume the mass $m = 1$ kg, the damping coefficient $c = 1$ N/(m/s), and the spring constant $k = 100$ N/m. These values are arbitrarily chosen for instructional purposes; they may not be practical for a real-world spring scale. ↓

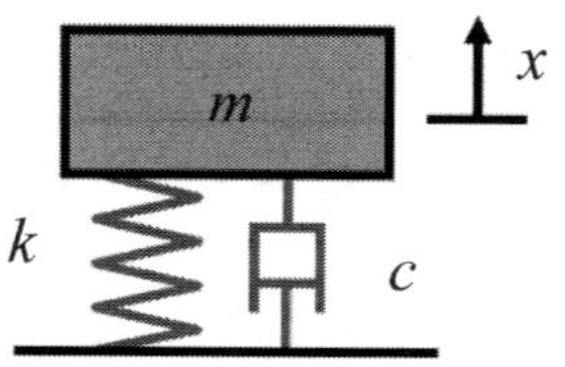

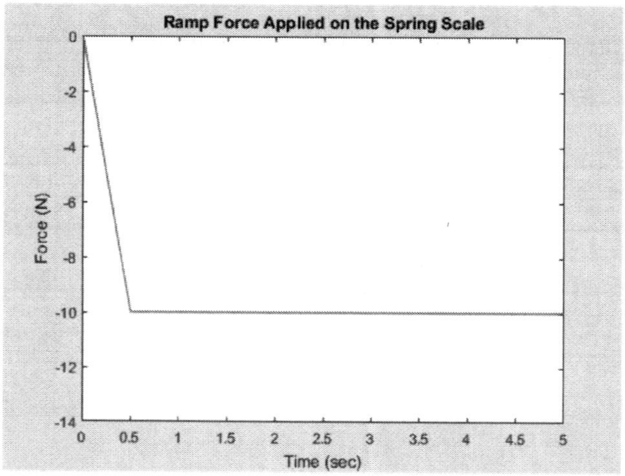

[2] This is the ramp force applied on the spring scale. The downward force increases linearly up to W at time T_0 (here, W = 10 N and $T_0 = 0.5$ sec) and then remains constant. ↵

Example11_06.m: Spring Scale

[3] This program calculates the response of the system described in [1], last page. ↓

```
function Example11_06
m = 1; c = 1; k = 100; W = -10; T0 = 0.5;
omega = sqrt(k/m); cc = 2*m*omega; zeta = c/cc; t0 = omega*T0;
n = 200; t = linspace(0, 50, n);
for i = 1:n
    x(i) = (W/k)*(h(t(i))*(t(i)>0)-h(t(i)-t0)*(t(i)>t0));
end
plot(t/omega, x), grid on
xlabel('Time (sec)'), ylabel('Displacement (m)')
title('Respnse of a SDOF System to a Ramp Force')
[M,I] = min(x);
text(t(I)/omega, M-0.005, ['Max displacement = ', ...
    num2str(M), ' at ', num2str(t(I)/omega), ' sec.'])

    function out = h(t)
        out = (1/(t0*sqrt(1-zeta^2)))*integral(@fun, 0, t);

        function out = fun(tau)
            out = tau.*exp(-zeta*(t-tau)).*sin((t-tau)*sqrt(1-zeta^2));
        end
    end
end
```

[4] This is the output of Example11_06.m. ↵

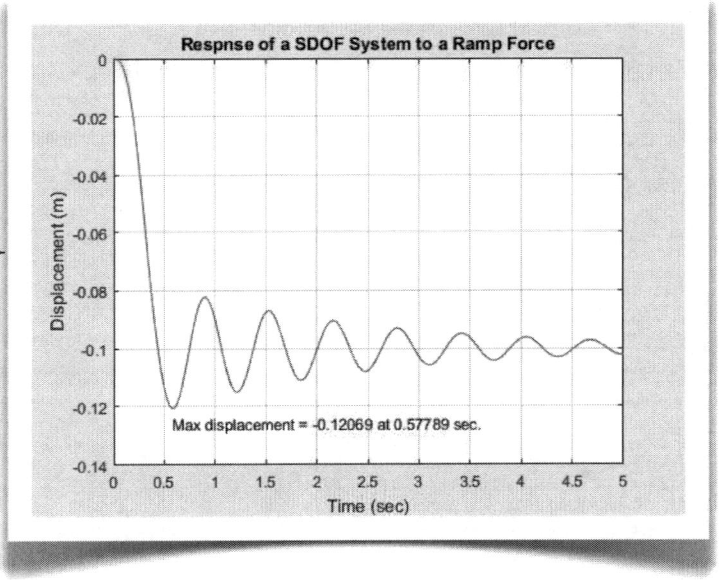

About Example11_06.m

[5] This program consists of a main function (lines 1-22), within which a nested function `h(t)` is defined (lines 15-21); within the function `h(t)` there is yet another nested function `fun(tau)` (lines 18-20). Remember that all variables in a function can be seen by its nested functions. Use of nested functions is a convenient way to pass variables to a function that is not directly called by its parent function. Here, the function `fun(tau)` is not directly called from the function `h(t)` (rather, it is called from the built-in function `integral` in line 16), and passing variables `zeta` and `t` (line 19) to the function `fun(tau)` would need special treatment. One way is to declare them as `global`. In general, using nested functions is more stylish and becoming a standard practice.

Lines 2-3 create parameters for the SDOF system. Line 4 creates a vector `t` storing 200 time points, from 0 to 50 in dimensionless time units (remember: $t = \omega T$; T is the real time in seconds).

Lines 5-7 point-by-point calculate the response using Eq. (a), in which the function `h(t)` is defined in lines 15-21. Note that, in line 6, the unit step function `u(t)` is implemented as `t>0`, which has a result exactly the same as the function defined in Eq. (c), and `u(t-t0)` is implemented as `t>t0`.

Lines 8-10 produce a plot shown in [4], last page. Line 11 retrieves the maximum response value and its corresponding time, and lines 12-13 display them in the graphic area (see [4]). The maximum displacement is 0.12069 m at 0.57789 seconds. Remember that $t = \omega T$; the real time T (in seconds) is obtained by dividing the dimensionless time t with the natural frequency ω (see line 13).

Line 16 calculates `h(t)` according to Eq. (b), in which the integrand is defined in the function `fun(tau)` (lines 18-20). Note that, in line 19, the element-wise multiplication (`.*`) must be used when both operands involve the input argument `tau` (see 11.4[3], page 430). #

11.7 Double Integral: Volume Under Stadium Dome

Double Integral

[1] We mentioned in 11.2[2], page 425, that $\int_{x_1}^{x_2} y(x)dx$ can be viewed as the area below the curve $y = y(x)$. This concept can be extended to double integral: $\int_{y_1}^{y_2}\int_{x_1}^{x_2} z(x,y)dx\,dy$ can be viewed as the volume under the surface $z = z(x,y)$.

Imagine that you are designing the roof of a stadium. The height z of the roof is described by $z = (17200 - x^2 - 2y^2)/200$ where $-100 \le x \le 100$ and $-60 \le y \le 60$. The volume under the stadium dome can be calculated as:

$$V = \int_{y_1}^{y_2}\int_{x_1}^{x_2} z(x,y)dx\,dy = \int_{-60}^{60}\int_{-100}^{100}\left[(17{,}200 - x^2 - 2y^2)/200\right]dx\,dy = 1{,}376{,}000$$

This is simple enough to be calculated manually. In a complicated case, numerical integration may be needed. ↓

Example11_07.m: Volume of Stadium Dome

[2] This script calculates the volume under the stadium dome described in [1]. ↓

```
clear
x = -100:2:100;
y = -60:2:60;
[X, Y] = meshgrid(x, y);
Z = (17200 - X.^2 - 2*Y.^2)/200;
surf(X,Y,Z), axis vis3d equal
A = trapz(x, Z, 2);
V = trapz(y, A)
fun = @(s,t) (17200 - s.^2 - 2*t.^2)/200;
V = integral2(fun, -100, 100, -60, 60)
```

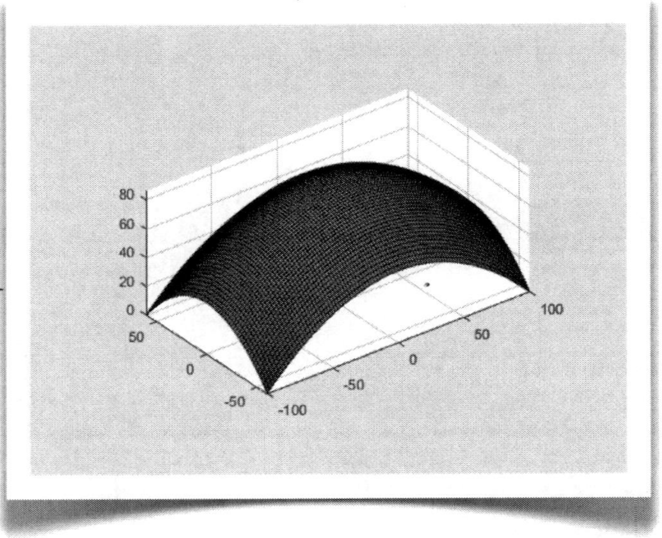

[3] This is the graphic output of Example11_07.m. ↵

About Example11_07.m

[4] Lines 2-8 perform double integral to calculate the volume using the function `trapz`, while lines 9-10 accomplish the same task using the function `integral2`. Like the function `integral`, the function `integral2` (line 10) allows the integrand to be specified with a user-defined function. On the other hand, the function `trapz` (lines 7-8), which operates on arrays of data, is useful when the integrand can not be specified using a user-defined function.

Lines 2-4 prepare a grid in the *xy*-space. Line 5 calculates the *z*-values over the grid, according to the description in [1]. Line 6 generates a surface plot shown in [3].

With the function `trapz`, the double integral needs to be carried out in two steps: first over the *x*-domain and then over the *y*-domain. Line 7 integrates `Z` over the *x*-domain (from -100 to 100; see line 2), which is the 2nd dimension (i.e., column dimension) in the matrix `Z`. The result `A` is a vector; each value is the area that is a cross section running through the *x*-domain and under the surface. Line 8 integrates `A` over the *y*-domain (from -60 to 60; see line 3) and the result is the volume under the surface. The output in the **Command Window** is 1,375,760, consistent with the hand-calculated value in [1].

Integration using the function `integral2` is much simpler (at least for this particular case): you define the integrand in a user-defined function (line 9), and input the function handle to `integral2`, specifying the integration limits. The output in the **Command Window** is 1,376,000, consistent with the hand-calculated value in [1]. #

11.8 Initial Value Problems

Classification of Differential Equations

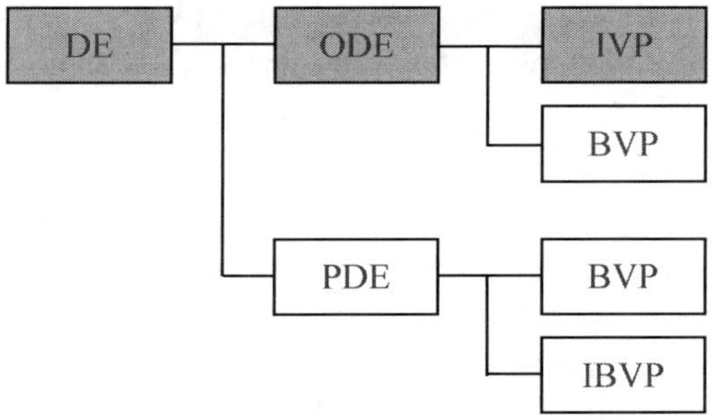

[1] Engineers often deal with differential equations (DE), in which the independent variables are time (t) and/or spatial coordinates (x, y, and z). An ordinary differential equation (ODE) is a DE with only one independent variable, either the time or one of the spatial coordinates. On the other hand, a partial differential equation (PDE) has more than one independent variable.

According to what kind of independent variables (time or spatial coordinates) are involved, DEs can be classified into initial value problems (IVP), boundary value problems (BVP), and initial boundary value problems (IBVP).

If the time t is the only independent variable, then the initial conditions are usually known, but the ending conditions are usually unknown. The problem is called an IVP, of which the initial conditions (IC) are specified.

If the independent variables are one or more of the spatial coordinates (x, y, z), then the conditions in the spatial boundary are usually known. The problem is called a BVP, of which the boundary conditions (BC) are specified.

If the independent variables involve both the time and the spatial coordinates, then the initial conditions and the boundary conditions are usually known. The problem is called an IBVP, of which both the initial conditions and the boundary conditions are specified.

Note that, since an ODE has only one independent variable, an IBVP (which has at least two independent variables) does not belong to the ODE category. On the other hand, a PDE has more than one independent variable; an IVP (which has only time as the independent variable) does not belong to the PDE category.

In this and the next sections, as examples, we present two IVPs (see the shaped blocks in the figure above). ↓

Reducing a DE to a System of First-Order DEs

[2] As we demonstrated in Section 9.9, a DE is usually easier to solve if it is rewritten as a system of first-order DEs. The IVP solvers used in this chapter require that you specify the DE in the form of a system of first-order DEs. Recall that, in 9.9a[1] (page 381), the DE for the damped free vibrations of a SDOF system is

$$m\ddot{x} + c\dot{x} + kx = 0, \text{ with ICs } x(0) = \delta \text{ and } \dot{x}(0) = 0$$

By introducing a second dependent variable $v(t) = \dot{x}$, the IVP can be written as a system of first-order DEs (also see 9.9c[1], page 385):

$$\begin{cases} \dot{x} = v \\ \dot{v} = (-kx - cv)/m \end{cases}, \text{ with ICs } \begin{cases} x(0) = \delta \\ v(0) = 0 \end{cases}$$

To be compatible with the input/output arguments of the IVP solvers in MATLAB, let $y_1(t) = x(t)$ and $y_2(t) = v(t)$, and the IVP becomes

$$\begin{cases} \dot{y}_1 = y_2 \\ \dot{y}_2 = (-ky_1 - cy_2)/m \end{cases}, \text{ with ICs } \begin{cases} y_1(0) = \delta \\ y_2(0) = 0 \end{cases} \quad \text{(a)}$$

In this section, we'll use the same parameters as usual for the system: $m = 1$ kg, $c = 1$ N/(m/s), $k = 100$ N/m, and $\delta = 0.2$ m (see 2.15a[3] and 2.15b[1], pages 117-118). ↵

Function ode45

[3] Table 11.8 (next page) lists some IVP solvers provided by MATLAB. Choice of a solver depends on the nature of the problem. The function `ode23` (second/third order) and `ode45` (fourth/fifth order) use the Runge-Kutta methods (Wikipedia>Runge-Kutta methods). The **order** is the power of integration time steps (Δt) in the error term. In general, the higher the order, the smaller the error.

The simplest syntax is like this:

```
[t, sol] = ode45(@fun, tspan, y0)
```

where `@fun` is a handle to a user-defined function which evaluates the right-hand side of the system of the n first-order DEs (e.g., see Eq. (a), last page), `tspan` is usually a two-element vector specifying the interval of the independent variable, and `y0` is a vector of n elements specifying the right-hand side of the ICs (e.g., see Eq. (a), last page). The first output argument `t` is a column vector of m time points (where m is determined by the solver) spanning the interval specified in `tspan`. The second output argument `sol` is an m-by-n matrix, each column corresponding to a dependent variable. ↓

Example11_08.m: Damped Free Vibrations

[4] This program solves the IVP defined in Eq. (a), last page. ↵

```
function Example11_08
m = 1; c = 1; k = 100; delta = 0.2;
[time, sol] = ode45(@fun, [0,2], [delta, 0]);
plot(time, sol(:,1));
xlabel('Time (sec)')
ylabel('Displacement (m)')
yyaxis right
plot(time, sol(:,2));
ylabel('Velocity (m/s)')
title('Free Vibration of a SDOF Damped System')
grid on

    function ydot = fun(t, y)
        ydot(1) = y(2);
        ydot(2) = (-k*y(1)-c*y(2))/m;
        ydot = ydot';
    end
end
```

[5] This is the output, consistent with the graphs in 9.9c[5-6], page 386. ↓

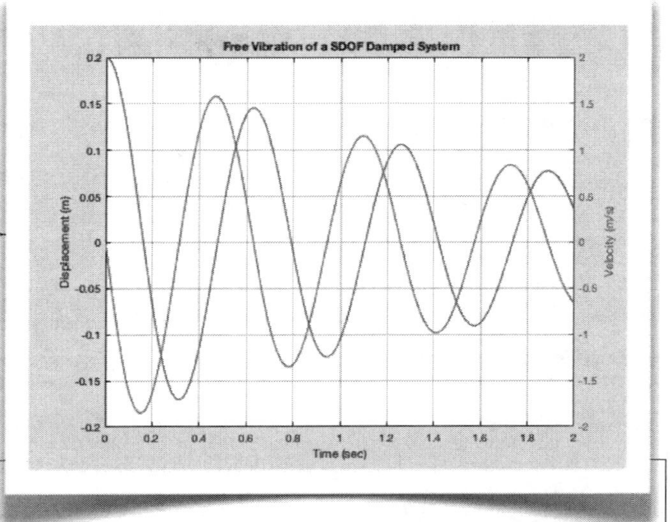

About Example11_08.m

[6] The program consists of a main function (lines 1-18), within which a nested function `fun` (lines 13-17) is defined.

The nested function `fun` (lines 13-17) evaluates the right-hand side of the first-order DEs described in Eq. (a), page 438. The input argument `t` is a scalar and `y` is a column vector of two elements; they provide current values of t, y_1, and y_2. The output argument `ydot` is a column vector of two elements; line 16 transposes a row vector to a column vector.

Line 2 creates parameters for the problem. Line 3 solves the IVP using the function `ode45`. The time span is `[0,2]`, i.e., from 0 to 2 seconds. The ICs are `[delta, 0]`, i.e., $y_1(0) = \delta$ and $y_2(0) = 0$. The first output argument `time` is a column vector of m time points, where m is determined by `ode45`. The second output argument `sol` is an m-by-n matrix (here, $n = 2$), each column corresponding to a dependent variable.

Lines 4-6 plot the displacement (the first column of `sol`) and label the axes. Line 7 activates right y-axis; subsequent graphics commands will target the right side (see 5.4b[2], page 219). Line 8 plots the velocity (the second column of `sol`). Line 9 labels the right y-axis. Line 10 adds a title for the graph. Note that this graphic output is consistent with those in 9.9c[5-6], page 386. #

Table 11.8 Summary of Functions for IVPs

Functions	Description
`[t, sol] = ode45(@fun, tspan, y0)`	Solve nonstiff DEs; medium order method
`[t, sol] = ode15s(@fun, tspan, y0)`	Solve stiff DEs and DAEs; variable order method
`[t, sol] = ode23(@fun, tspan, y0)`	Solve nonstiff DEs; low order method
`[t, sol] = ode113(@fun, tspan, y0)`	Solve nonstiff DEs; variable order method
`[t, sol] = ode23t(@fun, tspan, y0)`	Solve moderately stiff ODEs and DAEs; trapezoidal rule
`[t, sol] = ode23tb(@fun, tspan, y0)`	Solve stiff DEs; low order method
`[t, sol] = ode23s(@fun, tspan, y0)`	Solve stiff DEs; low order method
`[t, sol] = ode15i(@fun, tspan, y0)`	Solve fully implicit DEs, variable order method
`ydot = fun(t, y)`	User-defined function to be input to ODE-IVP solvers

Details and More:
Help>MATLAB>Mathematics>Numerical Integration and Differential Equations>Ordinary Differential Equations

11.9 IVP: Placing Weight on Spring Scale

Problem Description

[1] Consider the problem described in 11.6[1] (page 433) again, in which a weight W is placed on a spring scale so that the force on the scale ramps linearly from 0 to W in a time duration T_0. The DE is

$$m\ddot{x} + c\dot{x} + kx = f(t), \text{ with ICs } x(0) = 0 \text{ and } \dot{x}(0) = 0$$

where $f(t)$ is shown in [3], next page. By introducing a second dependent variable $v(t) = \dot{x}(t)$, the IVP can be rewritten as a system of first-order DEs:

$$\begin{cases} \dot{x} = v \\ \dot{v} = \left[f(t) - kx - cv \right] / m \end{cases} \quad \text{with ICs} \begin{cases} x(0) = 0 \\ v(0) = 0 \end{cases}$$

Further, let $y_1(t) = x(t)$ and $y_2(t) = v(t)$, and the above IVP becomes

$$\begin{cases} \dot{y}_1 = y_2 \\ \dot{y}_2 = (f(t) - ky_1 - cy_2)/m \end{cases} \quad \text{with ICs} \begin{cases} y_1(0) = 0 \\ y_2(0) = 0 \end{cases} \qquad \text{(a)}$$

In this section, we'll use the same parameters as those used in Section 11.6: $m = 1$ kg, $c = 1$ N/(m/s), $k = 100$ N/m, $W = 10$ N, and $T_0 = 0.5$ sec. ↓

Example11_09.m: Spring Scale

[2] This program solves the IVP described in Eq. (a). ↵

```
function Example11_09
m = 1; c = 1; k = 100; W = -10; T0 = 0.5;
[time, sol] = ode45(@fun, [0,5], [0,0]);
plot(time,sol(:,1)), grid on
xlabel('Time (sec)'), ylabel('Displacement (m)')
title('Response of a SDOF System to a Ramp Force')
[M, I] = min(sol(:,1));
text(time(I), M-0.005, ['Max displacement = ', ...
    num2str(M), ' at ', num2str(time(I)), ' sec.'])

    function ydot = fun(t, y)
        force = W*t/T0*(t<T0)+W*(t>=T0);
        ydot(1) = y(2);
        ydot(2) = (1/m)*(force - c*y(2) - k*y(1));
        ydot = ydot';
    end
end
```

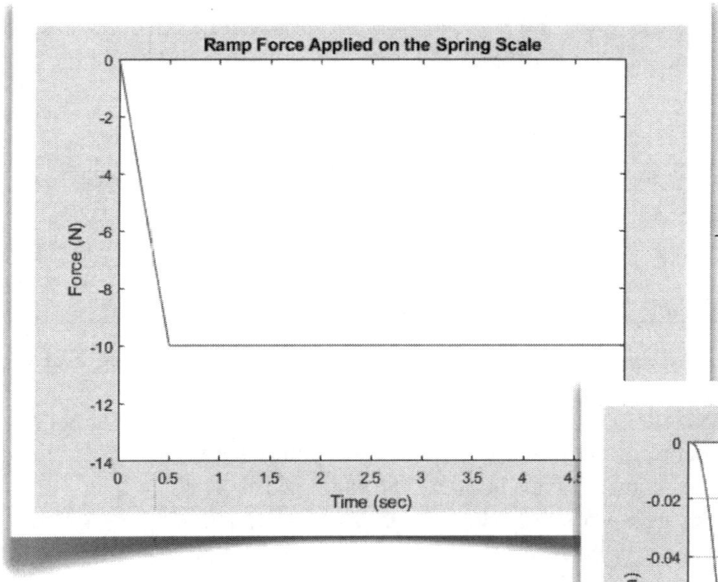

[3] This is the ramp force $f(t)$ applied on the spring scale. The downward force increases linearly up to W at time T_0 (here, $W = 10$ N and $T_0 = 0.5$ sec) and then remains constant. This graph is a duplicate of 11.6[2], page 433. ↙

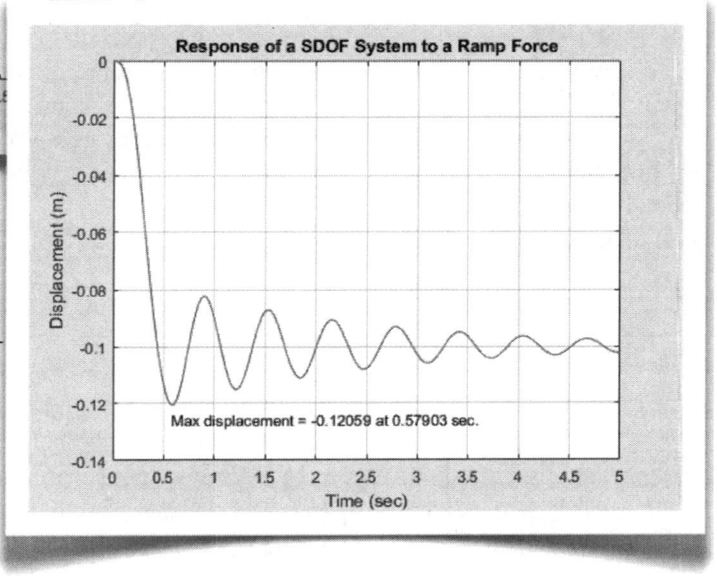

[4] This is the output, consistent with that in 11.6[4], page 434. ↓

About Example11_09.m

[5] The program consists of a main function (lines 1-17), within which a nested function `fun` (lines 11-16) is defined.

The nested function `fun` (lines 11-16) evaluates the right-hand side of the two first-order DEs defined in Eq. (a), last page. Its input argument `t` is a scalar and `y` is a column vector of two elements; they provide current values of t, y_1, and y_2, respectively. The output argument `ydot` is a column vector of two elements. Line 12 defines $f(t)$ (see [3]; also see 11.6[5], page 435). Lines 13-14 evaluate the right-hand side of the two first-order DEs in Eq. (a). Line 15 transposes a row vector to a column vector.

Line 2 creates parameters for the problem. Line 3 solves the IVP using the function `ode45`. The time span is `[0,5]`, i.e., from 0 to 5 seconds. The ICs are `[0,0]`, i.e., $y_1(0) = 0$ and $y_2(0) = 0$. The first output argument `time` is a column vector of m time points, where m is determined by `ode45`. The second output argument `sol` is an m-by-2 matrix, each column corresponding to a dependent variable.

Lines 4-9 plot the displacement (the first column of `sol`; see [4]), which is consistent with that in 11.6[4], page 434, with insignificant difference. #

11.10 ODE-BVP: Deflection of Beams

Problem Description

[1] Consider the problem in Section 3.12 again, in which a simply supported beam of length L is subject to a transversal uniform load q. The deflection $y(x)$ is governed by (*Wikipedia>Deflection (engineering)*)

$$EI\frac{d^4y}{dx^4} = q$$

with boundary conditions (BCs):

$$y(0) = 0,\ y(L) = 0,\ y''(0) = 0, \text{ and } y''(L) = 0$$

The first two equations in the BCs specify that the deflections y are zeros at both ends, while the last two equations specify that the moments are zeros at both ends, since the moment M in a beam can be expressed as $M = EIy''$.

Note that we use prime signs (') to represent the derivatives with respect to x; e.g., $y' = dy/dx$, $y'' = dy'/dx$, and so on. In engineering, we often use dot signs for the derivatives with respect to the time (t), while using prime signs for the derivatives with respect to the spatial coordinate x.

Let $y_1(x) = y(x)$, $y_2(x) = y'(x)$, $y_3(x) = y''(x)$, $y_4(x) = y'''(x)$, and the BVP becomes

$$\begin{cases} y_1' = y_2 \\ y_2' = y_3 \\ y_3' = y_4 \\ y_4' = q/EI \end{cases}, \text{ with BCs } \begin{cases} y_1(0) = 0 \\ y_1(L) = 0 \\ y_3(0) = 0 \\ y_3(L) = 0 \end{cases} \qquad \text{(a)}$$

In this section, we'll use the same parameters for the system as those in Section 3.12: $w = 0.1$ m, $h = 0.1$ m, $L = 8$ m, $E = 210$ GPa, and $q = 500$ N/m. ↓

Functions `bvp4c` and `bvpinit`

[2] Table 11.10 (page 445) lists solvers for ODE-BVPs (BVPs that involve only one independent spatial variable). Choice of a solver (between `bvp4c` and `bvp5c`) depends on the nature of the problem (see *MATLAB Help*). The simplest syntax is

```
sol = bvp4c(@odefun, @bcfun, solinit)
```

where `@odefun` is a handle to a function evaluating the right-hand side of the system of n first-order DEs; e.g., see Eq. (a); `@bcfun` is a handle to a function calculating the **residuals** of the boundary conditions; and `solinit` is a structure containing the initial guess for the solution. You usually create `solinit` using the function `bvpinit` (see Table 11.10, page 445); its simplest syntax is

```
solinit = bvpinit(x, yinit)
```

where `x` is a vector that specifies an initial mesh, and `yinit` is an initial guess for the solution.

The `sol` output by the function `bvp4c` is a structure, in which `sol.x` is the mesh selected by `bvp4c` (and usually the same as `x` you input to `bvpinit`) and `sol.y` is an approximation of $y(x)$.

The details are demonstrated in Example11_10.m, next page. ↵

Example11_10.m: Deflection of Beams

[3] This program solves the BVP defined in Eq. (a), last page. ↓

```
function Example11_10
w = -0.1; h = 0.1; L = 8; E = 2.1e11; q = 500;
I = w*h^3/12;
solinit = bvpinit(linspace(0,L,1000), [1, 1, 1, 1]);
sol = bvp4c(@odefun, @bcfun, solinit);
x = sol.x; y = sol.y(1,:);
plot(x, y*1000)
xlabel('x (m)'), ylabel('y (mm)')
title('Deflection of Uniformly Loaded and Simply Supported Beam')
[M, I] = min(y);
text(x(I), M*1000, ['Maximum deflection = ', num2str(-M*1000)])

    function yprime = odefun(x, y)
        yprime = zeros(4,1);
        yprime(1) = y(2);
        yprime(2) = y(3);
        yprime(3) = y(4);
        yprime(4) = q/(E*I);
    end

    function residual = bcfun(y0, yL)
        residual = zeros(4,1);
        residual(1) = y0(1);
        residual(2) = y0(3);
        residual(3) = yL(1);
        residual(4) = yL(3);
    end
end
```

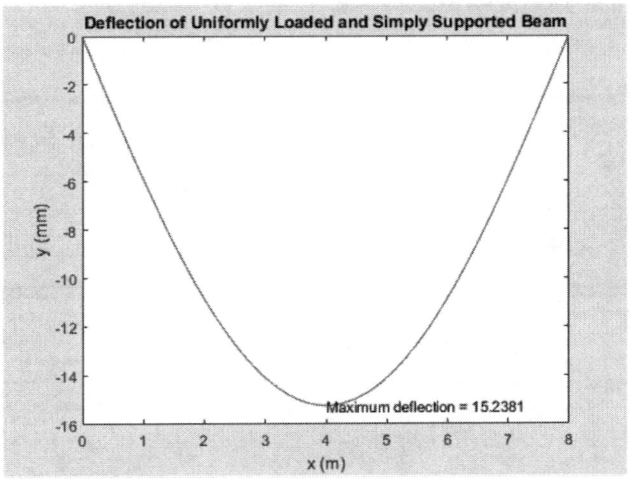

[4] This is the output, consistent with the analytical result in 3.12[5], page 150. ↵

About Example11_10.m

[5] The program consists of a main function (lines 1-28), within which two nested functions, `odefun` (lines 13-19) and `bcfun` (lines 21-27), are defined.

The nested function `odefun` (lines 13-19) evaluates the right-hand side of the four first-order DEs in Eq. (a), page 443. Its input argument `x` is a scalar and `y` is a column vector of four values; they are current values of t, y_1, y_2, y_3, and y_4, respectively. The output argument `yprime` is a column vector of four values. In line 14, `yprime` is created as a column vector, so there is no need to transpose as we did in line 15 of Example11_09.m (page 441) or line 16 of Example11_08.m (page 439).

The nested function `bcfun` (lines 21-27) calculates the **residuals** (to be explained) of the boundary conditions. Both the input arguments `y0` and `yL` are column vectors of four values; `y0` are current values of y_1, y_2, y_3, and y_4 at $x = 0$, and `yL` are current values of y_1, y_2, y_3, and y_4 at $x = L$. The **residuals** are the differences between current values and the values specified in the boundary conditions--here, the BCs in Eq. (a). The output argument `residual` is a column vector of four values. In line 22, `residual` is created as a column vector, so there is no need to transpose at the end of the function.

Line 2 creates parameters for the problems. Line 3 calculates the moment of inertia of the cross-section of the beam. Line 4 prepares a structure `solinit` containing an initial guess for the solution. The first input argument to the function `bvpinit` is a mesh in x-coordinate. Here, we use a very fine mesh (1000 points) because we want to obtain a solution compatible with the analytical solution in 3.12[5], page 150. The second input argument to the function `bvpinit` is a vector containing initial guess values for the solutions $y_1(x)$, $y_2(x)$, $y_3(x)$, and $y_4(x)$. Here, we chose a set of initial guess values that are simply

$$y_1(x) = 1,\ \ y_2(x) = 1,\ \ y_3(x) = 1, \text{ and } y_4(x) = 1$$

Line 5 solves the BVP using the function `bvp4c`, in which the first input argument is a handle to the function `odefun`, the second input argument is a handle to the function `bcfun`, and the third input argument `solinit` is the structure created in line 4. The output argument `sol` is a structure, in which `sol.x` is a row vector of m points representing a mesh of the independent variable `x`, where m is selected by `bvp4c` (here, it has the same size as what you input to `bvpinit` as the first input argument in line 4) and `sol.y` is a 4-by-m matrix, each row containing approximations of $y_1(x)$, $y_2(x)$, $y_3(x)$, and $y_4(x)$, respectively.

Line 6 retrieves the independent variable `x` and the dependent variable $y_1(x)$, which is the deflection of the beam.

Lines 7-11 generates a plot shown in [4], last page. The maximum deflection is consistent with the analytical result calculated in 3.12[5], page 150. #

Table 11.10 Summary of Functions for ODE-BVPs

Functions	Description
`sol = bvp4c(@odefun, @bcfun, solinit)`	Solve BVPs for ODEs
`sol = bvp5c(@odefun, @bcfun, solinit)`	Solve BVPs for ODEs
`solinit = bvpinit(x, yinit)`	Form initial guess for BVP solvers
`yprime = odefun(x, y)`	User-defined function defining the ODE
`residual = bcfun(y0, yL)`	User-defined function defining the BCs

Details and More:
Help>MATLAB>Mathematics>Numerical Integration and Differential Equations>Boundary Value Problems

11.11 IBVP: Heat Conduction in a Wall

Problem Description

[1] Consider the following PDE that describes a one-dimensional heat conduction through the thickness of a wall with heat source (*Reference: E. B. Magrab, et al., An Engineer's Guide to MATLAB, 3rd Ed., page 234*):

$$\frac{\partial T(x,t)}{\partial t} = \frac{\partial}{\partial x}\frac{\partial T(x,t)}{\partial x} + s \tag{a}$$

where all quantities are nondimensional; $0 \le t \le 1$ and $0 \le x \le 1$. The initial condition is

$$T(x,0) = 1 - Ax \tag{b}$$

The boundary conditions are

$$\frac{\partial T(0,t)}{\partial x} = B \cdot T(0,t) \text{ and } T(1,t) = T_1 \tag{c}$$

Where A and B are constants.

We'll solve this problem using the function `pdepe` (see [2] and Table 11.11, page 448), which solves an initial-boundary value problem (IBVP) described by a parabolic-elliptic partial differential equation (PE-PDE) of the form

$$c(x,t,T,\frac{\partial T}{\partial x})\frac{\partial T}{\partial t} = x^{-m}\frac{\partial}{\partial x}\left[x^m f(x,t,T,\frac{\partial T}{\partial x})\right] + s(x,t,T,\frac{\partial T}{\partial x}) \tag{d}$$

where $T = T(x,t)$, $t_0 \le t \le t_f$, and $a \le x \le b$. At $t = t_0$, the initial conditions are of the form:

$$T(x,t) = T_{init}(x) \tag{e}$$

At $x = a$ and $x = b$, the boundary conditions are of the form:

$$p(x,t,T) + q(x,t) f(x,t,T,\frac{\partial T}{\partial x}) = 0 \tag{f}$$

Comparing Eqs. (a, b, c) with the general form in Eqs. (d, e, f), we have $t_0 = 0$, $t_f = 1$, $a = 0$, $b = 1$, and

$$m = 0,\ c = 1,\ f = \frac{\partial T}{\partial x},\ s = 1, \tag{g}$$

$$T_{init} = 1 - Ax, \tag{h}$$

$$p(0,t,T) = -BT(0,t),\ q(0,t) = 1,\ p(1,t,T) = T(1,t) - T_1,\ q(1,t) = 0 \tag{i}$$

In this section, we assume $s = 1$, $A = 0.4$, $B = 0.05$, and $T_1 = 0.6$. ↓

Function pdepe

[2] Table 11.11 (page 448) lists the solver `pdepe`, which solves a PE-PDE in a 1-D space. The simplest syntax is:

```
sol = pdepe(m, @pdefun, @icfun, @bcfun, x, t)
```

where *`m`* is a parameter as in Eq. (d); *`@pdefun`* is a handle to a function calculating the values of *c*, *f*, and *s* as in Eq. (d), given the values of *x*, *t*, *T*, and $\partial T/\partial x$; *`@icfun`* is a handle to a function calculating the value of T_{init} as in Eq. (e), given the value of *x*; *`@bcfun`* is a handle to a function calculating the values of $p(a,t,T)$, $q(a,t)$, $p(b,t,T)$, and $q(a,t)$ as in Eq. (f), given the values of a, T_a, b, T_b, *and t*; *`x`* is a vector specifying the spatial points at which a numerical solution is requested; and *`t`* is a vector specifying the time points at which a numerical solution is requested.

The details are demonstrated in Example11_11.m. ↵

Example11_11.m: Heat Conduction in a Wall

[3] This program solves the problem defined in Eqs. (a, b, c), last page. ↵

```
function Example11_11
A = 0.4; B = 0.05; T1 = 0.6;
x = linspace(0, 1, 21);
t = linspace(0, 1, 101);
T = pdepe(0, @pdefun, @icfun, @bcfun, x, t);
hold on
for k = [1,6,11,16,21]
    plot(t,T(:,k),'k-')
    text(0.05,T(6,k), ['x = ', num2str(x(k))])
end
xlabel('Nondimensional Time')
ylabel('Nondimensional Temperature')
title('Heat Conduction in a Wall, T(t)')

figure, hold on
for k = [1, 51, 101]
    plot(x,T(k,:),'k-')
    text(0.3,T(k,7), ['t = ', num2str(t(k))])
end
xlabel('Nondimensional Distance')
ylabel('Nondimensional Temperature')
title('Heat Conduction in a Wall, T(x)')

    function [c, f, s] = pdefun(x,t,T,Tprime)
        c = 1;
        f = Tprime;
        s = 1;
    end

    function Tinit = icfun(x)
        Tinit = 1-A*x;
    end

    function [pa,qa,pb,qb] = bcfun(a,Ta,b,Tb,t)
        pa = -B*Ta;
        qa = 1;
        pb = Tb-T1;
        qb = 0;
    end
end
```

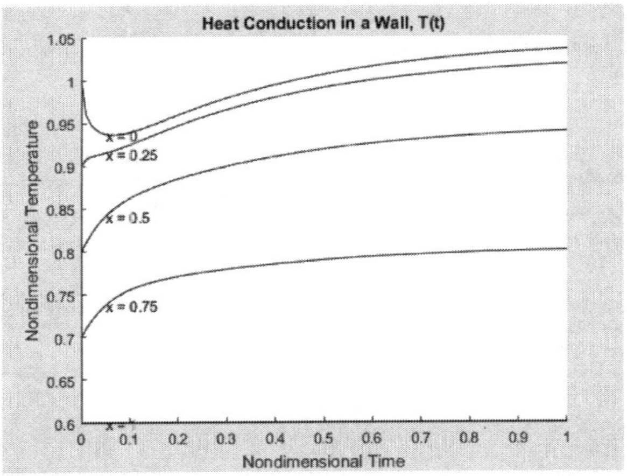

[4] Lines 6-13 produce this temperature-versus-time plot. →

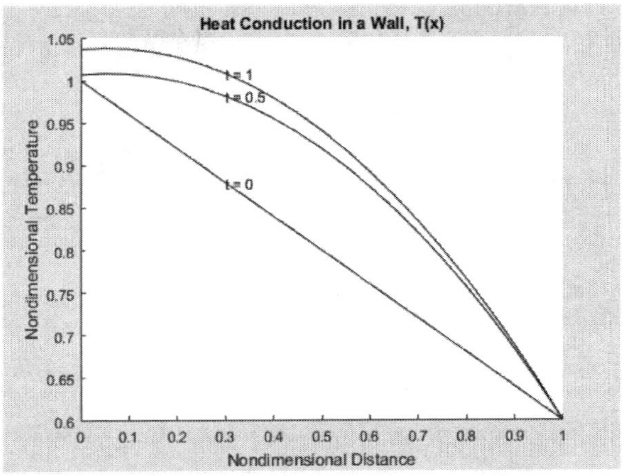

[5] Lines 15-22 produce this temperature-versus-space plot. ↓

About Example11_11.m

[6] The program consists of a main function (lines 1-40), within which three nested functions, `pdefun` (lines 24-28), `icfun` (lines 30-32), and `bcfun` (lines 34-39), are defined.

The function `pdefun` (lines 24-28) evaluates the values of c, f, and s as in Eq. (g). The function `icfun` (lines 30-32) evaluates the value of T_{init} as in Eq. (h). The function `bcfun` (lines 34-39) evaluates the values of p and q at the boundaries $x = a$ and $x = b$ as in Eq. (i).

Line 2 creates parameters for the problem. Line 3 creates a mesh of 21 points along the space x. Line 4 creates a mesh of 101 points along the time t. Line 5 solves the IBVP using the function `pdepe`. Here, the output argument `T` is a 101-by-21 matrix. Each column is a $T(t)$, temperatures varying with the time t, and each row is a $T(x)$, temperatures varying with the space x.

Lines 6-13 produce a plot shown in [4], where each curve is a $T(t)$ for certain x value labeled along with the curve. Lines 15-22 produce a plot shown in [5], where each curve is a $T(x)$ for certain t value labeled along with the curve. #

Table 11.11 Summary of Functions for PE-IBVPs

Functions	Description
`sol = pdepe(m, @pdefun, @icfun, @bcfun, x, t)`	Solve a PE-PDE in 1-D
`[c,f,s] = pdefun(x, t, T, Tprime)`	User-defined function defining the PE-PDE
`T0 = icfun(x)`	User-defined function defining the ICs
`[pl,ql,pr,qr] = bcfun(xl,Tl,xr,Tr,t)`	User-defined function defining the BCs

Details and More: Help>MATLAB>Mathematics>Numerical Integration and Differential Equations>Partial Differential Equations>pdepe

Chapter 12

Systems of Nonlinear Equations and Optimization

Applications of optimization techniques are ubiquitous; e.g., curve fitting. Numerical methods for optimization and nonlinear equations are closely related. Many algorithms for solving nonlinear equations are based on minimization of certain functions. For example, in structural mechanics, an equilibrium state is equivalent to a state in which the system has a minimum potential energy. This chapter uses many functions that are part of the Optimization Toolbox. This chapter assumes that you have a license that includes the Optimization Toolbox.

12.1 Nonlinear Equations: Intersection of Two Curves

Problem Description

[1] The following two equations represent two curves in the *x*-*y* space (see [3], next page):

$$\frac{x^2}{9}+\frac{y^2}{4}=1 \text{ and } y=x^2-4 \tag{a}$$

the first equation is an ellipse and the second equation is a parabola. In this section, we want to find the intersecting points of the two curves; i.e., we want to solve the system of the two nonlinear equations.

In 3.8a[4] (page 141), we introduced the function `fzero`, which is used to find the roots of a single nonlinear equation involving only one variable. It cannot be used to solve a system of nonlinear equations involving multiple variables. The function `fsolve` can be used to solve a system of nonlinear equations.

Function `fsolve`

The function `fsolve` solves a system of nonlinear equations, each equation specified by $f_i(\mathbf{x})=0$, $i=1, 2, \ldots$, where the vector **x** consists of unknown variables. The simplest syntax is:

```
x = fsolve(@fun, x0)
```

where `@fun` is a handle to a function that evaluates the left-hand side of each equation, i.e., $f_i(\mathbf{x})$, $i=1, 2, \ldots$, and `x0` is a vector containing initial guess values of the variables. ↓

Example12_01.m: Intersection of Two Curves

[2] This program solves the system of nonlinear equations defined in Eq. (a). ↵

```
clear, syms x y
fimplicit(x^2/9+y^2/4 == 1, [-4,4]), hold on
fimplicit(y == x^2-4, [-4,4]), axis equal, grid on, box on
legend('x^2/9+y^2/4 = 1', 'y = x^2-4')
title('Intersection of Two Curves')
solveTwoCurves

function solveTwoCurves
xinit = [-1,-1; 1,-1; -1,1; 1, 1];
for k = 1:4
    x = fsolve(@fun, xinit(k,:));
    text(x(1),x(2), ...
        ['x = ', num2str(x(1)), '    y = ', num2str(x(2))], ...
        'HorizontalAlignment', 'center')
end

    function f = fun(x)
        f = zeros(2,1);
        f(1) = x(1)^2/9+x(2)^2/4-1;
        f(2) = x(1)^2-x(2)-4;
    end
end
```

[3] This is the output of Example12_01.m. ↓

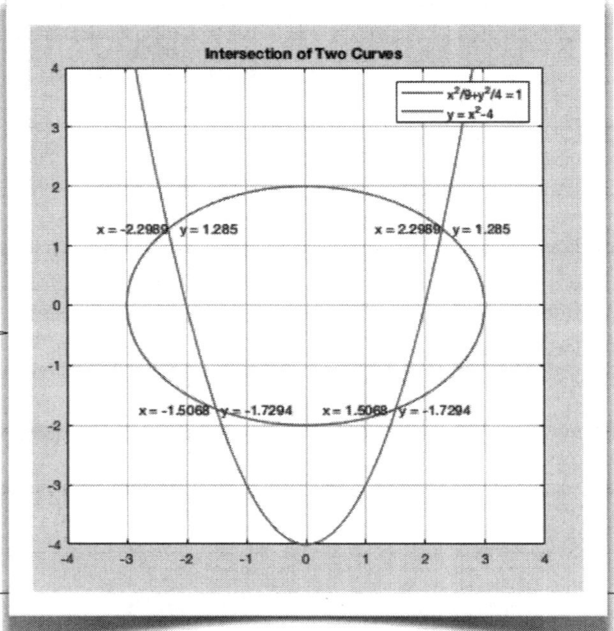

About Example12_01.m

[4] The program consists of a main program (lines 1-6) and a function `solveTwoCurves` (lines 8-22), within which a nested function `fun` (lines 17-21) is defined.

Lines 2-5 plot the two curves in the *x-y* space (see [3]) using `fimplicit` the 2-D implicit function plotter (see Table 9.3, page 369). The numeric solutions are added later in lines 12-14. From the graph, we see that there are four intersection points. Line 6 calls the function `solveTwoCurves`.

The function `fun` (lines 17-21) evaluates the left-hand side of each equation, i.e., $f_i(\mathbf{x})$, $i = 1, 2$. The input argument `x` is a vector containing current values of the two variables; `x(1)` and `x(2)` correspond to x and y, respectively, in Eq. (a). The output argument `f`, a column vector created in line 18, contains the evaluated function values.

If the solution is not unique, then the output values of `fsolve` will depend on the initial guess values: different initial guess values result in different solutions. It is therefore practical to have some preliminary study of the equations. Line 9 sets up four initial points; `xinit` is a 4-by-2 matrix, each row containing an initial point.

Line 10 starts a `for`-loop of four passes. Within the `for`-loop, line 11 solves the system of equations with an initial point. During the execution of `fsolve`, text information is displayed in the **Command Window**. If the text information is annoying to you, you may turn it off by replacing line 11 with the following statements (also see Table 12.4, page 461):

```
options = optimoptions(@fsolve, 'Display', 'off');
x = fsolve(@fun, xinit(k,:), options);
```

Depending on the initial point, a solution near the initial point is obtained; lines 12-14 add the solution to the graph. #

Table 12.1 Summary of Functions for Systems of Nonlinear Equations

Functions	Description
`x = fsolve(@fun, x0)`	Solve system of nonlinear equations
`f = fun(x)`	User-defined function defining the system of nonlinear equations
Details and More: Help>Optimization Toolbox>Systems of Nonlinear Equations	

12.2 Kinematics of Four-Bar Linkage

About Four-Bar Linkage

[1] Consider a four-bar linkage (*Wikipedia>Four-bar linkage*) as shown in the bottom-left figure. Each bar has a known length (*a*, *b*, *c*, or *d*). The points *A* and *D* are fixed in space. The orientation angle (θ_a, θ_b, or θ_c) of each bar is measured counterclockwise from the horizon to the direction defined from its starting point to its ending point. The direction of the bar *AB* is from *A* to *B*; *BC* is from *B* to *C*; *CD* is from *C* to *D*. The orientation angle (θ_a, θ_a, or θ_c) and the angular velocity of each bar (ω_a, ω_b, or ω_c) are time dependent.

Initially, the bar *AB* is upright (i.e., $\theta_a = \pi/2$) and has a constant angular velocity ω (i.e., $\omega_a = \omega$). We want to simulate the motion of this four-bar linkage.

The initial orientation angles θ_b and θ_c can be calculated using the Law of Cosine (2.11b[1], page 106; also see the auxiliary figure at the bottom-right figure):

$$e = \sqrt{a^2 + d^2}\ ,\ \theta_b = \tan^{-1}\frac{d}{a} + \cos^{-1}\frac{b^2 + e^2 - c^2}{2be} - \frac{\pi}{2},\ \theta_c = \theta_b + \cos^{-1}\frac{b^2 + c^2 - e^2}{2bc} - \pi$$

The velocities at *B*, *C*, and *D* can be calculated according to kinematic relation in a rigid body:

$$\begin{aligned}\vec{v}_B &= \vec{\omega} \times \vec{r}_{B/A} \\ &= \omega\vec{k} \times (a\cos\theta_a\vec{i} + a\sin\theta_a\vec{j}), \\ &= -\omega a\sin\theta_a\vec{i} + \omega a\cos\theta_a\vec{j}\end{aligned}$$

$$\begin{aligned}\vec{v}_C &= \vec{v}_B + \vec{\omega}_b \times \vec{r}_{C/B} \\ &= \vec{v}_B + \omega_b\vec{k} \times (b\cos\theta_b\vec{i} + b\sin\theta_b\vec{j}) \\ &= (-\omega a\sin\theta_a - \omega_b b\sin\theta_b)\vec{i} + (\omega a\cos\theta_a + \omega_b b\cos\theta_b)\vec{j}\end{aligned}$$

$$\begin{aligned}\vec{v}_D &= \vec{v}_C + \vec{\omega}_c \times \vec{r}_{D/C} \\ &= \vec{v}_C + \omega_c\vec{k} \times (c\cos\theta_c\vec{i} + c\sin\theta_c\vec{j}) \\ &= (-\omega a\sin\theta_a - \omega_b b\sin\theta_b - \omega_c c\sin\theta_c)\vec{i} + (\omega a\cos\theta_a + \omega_b b\cos\theta_b + \omega_c c\cos\theta_c)\vec{j}\end{aligned}$$

Using the fact that $\vec{v}_D = 0$, we have a system of two equations:

$$\begin{cases}\omega a\sin\theta_a + \omega_b b\sin\theta_b + \omega_c c\sin\theta_c = 0 \\ \omega a\cos\theta_a + \omega_b b\cos\theta_b + \omega_c c\cos\theta_c = 0\end{cases} \qquad \text{(a)}$$

The motion simulation involves solving the system of two equations above in every subsequent small time step. Note that, in Eq. (a), the unknown variables are ω_b and ω_c; this is actually a system of linear equations; it can be solved with the methods discussed in Section 10.2. However, for demonstration purposes, we'll use `fsolve`, which can solve systems of nonlinear equations.

We assume $a = 1.2$ m, $b = 3$ m, $c = 2.6$ m, $d = 3.2$ m, and $\omega = 2\pi$ rad/s (counterclockwise). ↵

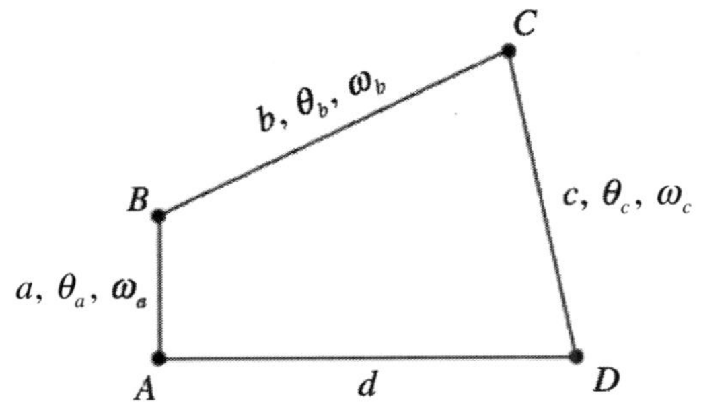

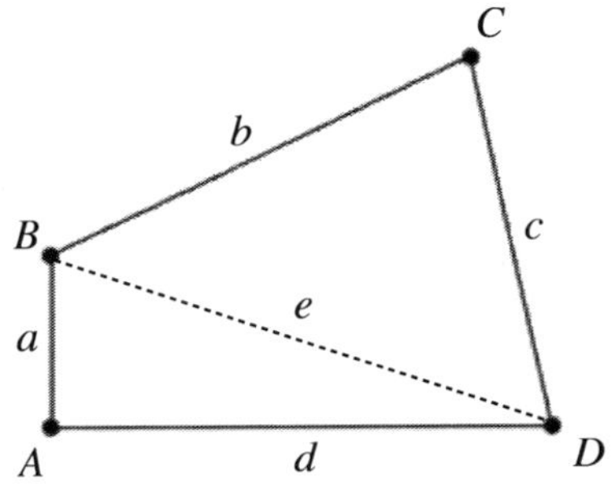

Example12_02.m: Four-Bar Linkage

[2] This program simulates the motion of a four-bar linkage by successively solving Eq. (a), last page. It saves a video in a file (in AVI format), so you can replay the simulation. ↵

```
function Example12_02
a = 1.2; b = 3; c = 2.6; d = 3.2; omega = 2*pi;
ta = pi/2; e = sqrt(a^2+d^2);
tb = atan(d/a)+acos((b^2+e^2-c^2)/(2*b*e))-pi/2;
tc = tb + acos((b^2+c^2-e^2)/(2*b*c)) - pi;
steps = 50; delta = 2*pi/omega/steps;
x = [0, 0];
options = optimoptions(@fsolve, 'Display', 'off');
for k = 1:steps
    xcoord = [0, a*cos(ta), d-c*cos(2*pi-tc), d, 0];
    ycoord = [0, a*sin(ta), c*sin(2*pi-tc), 0, 0];
    plot(xcoord, ycoord, 'k-o', 'MarkerFaceColor', 'k')
    axis([-2, 5, -2, 4]), grid on
    title('Kinematics of Four-Bar Linkage')
    Frames(k) = getframe;
    x = fsolve(@fun, x, options);
    ta = ta + omega*delta;
    tb = tb + x(1)*delta;
    tc = tc + x(2)*delta;
end
movie(Frames, 5, 30)
videoObj = VideoWriter('Linkage');
open(videoObj);
writeVideo(videoObj, Frames);

    function f = fun(x)
        f = zeros(2,1);
        f(1) = omega*a*sin(ta)+x(1)*b*sin(tb)+x(2)*c*sin(tc);
        f(2) = omega*a*cos(ta)+x(1)*b*cos(tb)+x(2)*c*cos(tc);
    end
end
```

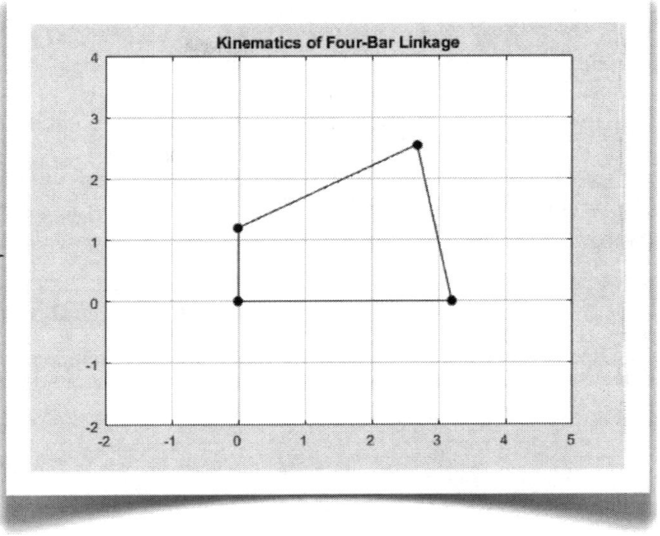

[3] This is the first movie frame generated by Example12_02.m. ↓

About Example12_02.m

[4] The program consists of a main function (lines 1-31), within which a nested function `fun` (lines 26-30) is defined.

The nested function `fun` (lines 26-30) evaluates the left-hand side of Eq. (a), page 452. The input argument `x` is a vector containing current values of the variables ω_b and ω_c; `x(1)` and `x(2)` correspond to ω_b and ω_c, respectively. The output argument `f` is a column vector of two values; `f(1)` and `f(2)` correspond to the function values on the left-hand of Eq. (a).

Line 2 sets up parameters for the four-bar linkage. Lines 3-5 calculate the initial orientations of the bars. Note that we use `ta`, `tb`, and `tc` for θ_a, θ_b, and θ_c, respectively. The simulation proceeds for one cycle, which is divided into 50 time steps (line 6); therefore, each time step is $\Delta t = 2\pi/\omega/steps$.

Line 7 sets up the initial values for ω_b and ω_c, both arbitrarily assuming zeros.

Line 8 sets up `options`, to be used as an input argument of the function `fsolve` in line 18, to turn off the display of the text information (see 12.1[4], page 451).

Line 9 starts a `for`-loop (lines 9-20), starting from $t = 0$; each pass advances the simulation time forward by Δt (`delta` in line 6). Within the `for`-loop, lines 10-14 plot the four bars at the current time (e.g., [3]). Line 15 captures the image using the function `getframe` and stores the output structure as an element of the array `Frame` (also see 6.3[8], page 261).

Line 16 uses `fsolve` to solve the system of equations, Eq. (a), using the values of `x` (ω_b and ω_c) in the current time as the initial gauss values. The output `x` contains new ω_b and ω_c for the next time step. Using the new ω_b and ω_c, lines 17-19 calculate θ_a, θ_b, and θ_c for the next time step:

$$\theta_a^{next} = \theta_a^{current} + \omega\Delta t$$
$$\theta_b^{next} = \theta_b^{current} + \omega_b\Delta t$$
$$\theta_c^{next} = \theta_c^{current} + \omega_c\Delta t$$

At the completion of the `for`-loop, we have an array of video frames. In line 21, the video frames are played 5 times, 30 frames per second.

To save the frames as a video file, a video object is created with the name `Linkage` using the function `VideoWriter` (line 22). The frames are then written into a video file (lines 23-24). The file name `Linkage.avi` is used. At the completion of the program, you may play the AVI file by double-clicking the file `Linkage.avi` from your operation system (e.g., your **Windows** system, not within the MATLAB desktop). #

12.3 Asymmetrical Two-Spring System

Asymmetrical Two-Spring System

[1] Consider a two-spring system as shown below. In addition to a vertical displacement y, a nonzero horizontal displacement x exists, due to the asymmetry of the spring constants k_1 and k_2. The elongated lengths L_1 and L_2 of the springs are, respectively,

$$L_1 = \sqrt{(L+x)^2 + y^2} \text{ and } L_2 = \sqrt{(L-x)^2 + y^2} \tag{a}$$

The elongation ΔL_1 and ΔL_2 of the springs are, respectively,

$$\Delta L_1 = \sqrt{(L+x)^2 + y^2} - L \text{ and } \Delta L_2 = \sqrt{(L-x)^2 + y^2} - L \tag{b}$$

Applying Newton's first law ($\sum \vec{F} = 0$) at the middle node M in the horizontal and vertical directions, respectively, we have two equilibrium equations:

$$\begin{cases} k_1 \Delta L_1 \dfrac{L+x}{L_1} - k_2 \Delta L_2 \dfrac{L-x}{L_2} = 0 \\ k_1 \Delta L_1 \dfrac{y}{L_1} + k_2 \Delta L_2 \dfrac{y}{L_2} - F = 0 \end{cases} \tag{c}$$

Example12_03.m (next page) solves the above system of nonlinear equations for x and y, in which we assume $k_1 = 1.5$ N/cm, $k_2 = 6.8$ N/cm, $L = 12$ cm, and $F = 9.2$ N. ↵

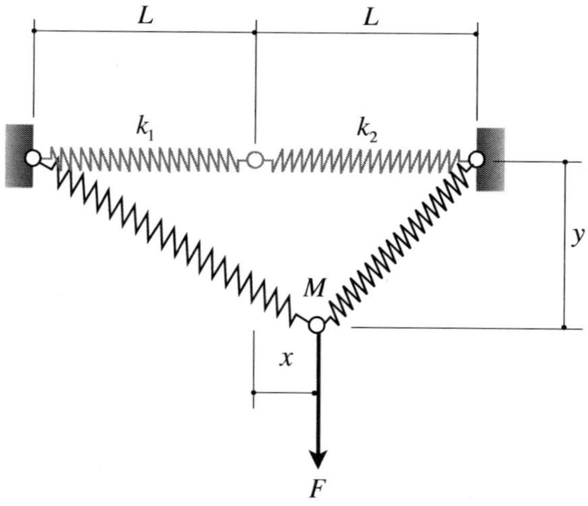

Example12_03.m: Asymmetrical Two-Spring System

[2] This program solves the problem defined in [1] (last page), producing the graph shown in [3-6]. ↙

```
function Example12_03
k1 = 1.5; k2 = 6.8; L = 12; F = 9.2;
L1 = @(x,y) sqrt((L+x).^2+y.^2);
L2 = @(x,y) sqrt((L-x).^2+y.^2);
dL1 = @(x,y) L1(x,y)-L;
dL2 = @(x,y) L2(x,y)-L;
fun1 = @(x,y) k1*dL1(x,y).*(L+x)./L1(x,y)-k2*dL2(x,y).*(L-x)./L2(x,y);
fun2 = @(x,y) k1*dL1(x,y).*y./L1(x,y)+k2*dL2(x,y).*y./L2(x,y)-F;
fimplicit(fun1, [0,5,5,10]), grid on, hold on
fimplicit(fun2, [0,5,5,10])
title('Asymmetrical Two-Spring System')

sol = fsolve(@fun, [5,5]);
text(sol(1),sol(2), ...
    ['x = ', num2str(sol(1)), ', y = ', num2str(sol(2))], ...
    'HorizontalAlignment', 'center')

    function f = fun(z)
        f = zeros(2,1);
        f(1) = fun1(z(1), z(2));
        f(2) = fun2(z(1), z(2));
    end
end
```

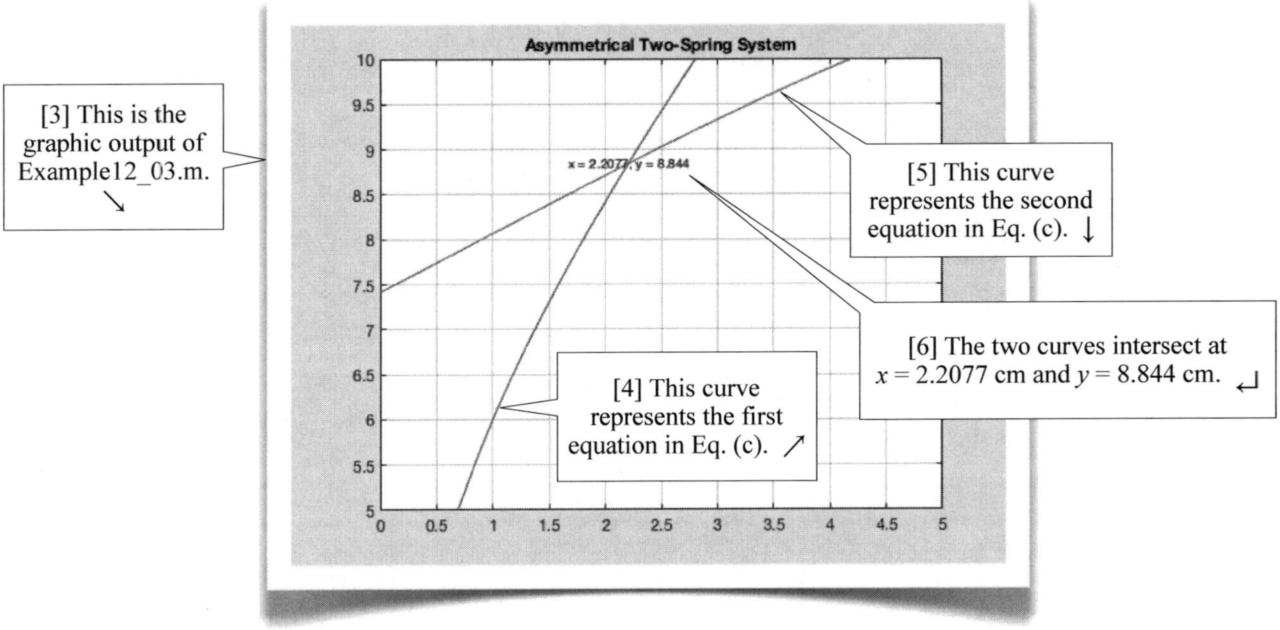

About Example12_03.m

[7] The program consists of a main function (lines 1-23), within which a nested function `fun` (lines 18-22) and 6 anonymous functions: `L1`, `L2`, `dL1`, `dL2`, `fun1`, and `fun2` (lines 3-8) are defined. We use the anonymous functions this way for two reasons: First, for better readability; each anonymous function is a one-to-one transcription of a formula in [1]: Lines 3-4 are the transcriptions of Eq. (a), Lines 5-6 are the transcriptions of Eq. (b), and Lines 7-8 are the transcriptions of Eq. (c). Second, for better reusability; they are used in lines 9-10 for plotting curves and used again in lines 20-21 for defining the system of nonlinear equations.

Line 2 sets up parameters for the problems. Lines 3-8 define 6 anonymous functions. The handles `fun1` and `fun2` point to the functions that evaluate the left-hand side of Eq. (c). Note that the use of element-wise operators (`.^`, `.*`, and `*/`) in lines 3-8 is not really necessary when the functions are used in lines 20-21. However, when used with `fimplicit` in lines 9-10, it would display a warning message if the element-wise operators are not used.

Lines 9-10 plot two curves in Eq. (c) (see [4-5], last page), using `fimplicit`, the 2-D implicit function plotter (Table 9.3, page 369). From the graphic output, we can see the approximate location where the two curves intersect. Line 11 adds a title for the graph.

The nested function `fun` (lines 18-22) evaluates the left-hand side of Eq. (c), using the anonymous functions defined in lines 3-8. The input argument `z` in line 18 is a vector containing the current value of `x` and `y`; `z(1)` and `z(2)` correspond to `x` and `y`, respectively. The output argument `f` in line 18 is a column vector of two values; `f(1)` and `f(2)` correspond to the function values on the left-hand side of Eq. (c).

Line 13 solves the system of equations using `fsolve`. We arbitrarily choose $x = 5$ and $y = 5$ as the initial values. The solver outputs a solution at $x = 2.2077$ and $y = 8.844$. Lines 14-16 write the numerical result on the graphic area (see [6]). #

12.4 Linear Programming: Diet Problem

Linear Programming: `linprog`

[1] Function `linprog` (Table 12.4, page 461) solves a linear programming problem defined as follows: Finding the values of n **variables** $x_1, x_2, \ldots, x_n$ that minimize a linear **objective function**

$$f_1x_1 + f_2x_2 + \ldots + f_nx_n$$

such that the variables satisfy the following m linear **inequality constraints**:

$$\begin{aligned} &a_{11}x_1 + a_{12}x_2 + \ldots + a_{1n}x_n \le b_1 \\ &a_{21}x_1 + a_{22}x_2 + \ldots + a_{2n}x_n \le b_2 \\ &\ldots \\ &a_{m1}x_1 + a_{m2}x_2 + \ldots + a_{mn}x_n \le b_m \end{aligned}$$

and the following p linear **equality constraints**:

$$\begin{aligned} &a_{11}^{eq}x_1 + a_{12}^{eq}x_2 + \ldots + a_{1n}^{eq}x_n = b_1^{eq} \\ &a_{21}^{eq}x_1 + a_{22}^{eq}x_2 + \ldots + a_{2n}^{eq}x_n = b_2^{eq} \\ &\ldots \\ &a_{p1}^{eq}x_1 + a_{p2}^{eq}x_2 + \ldots + a_{pn}^{eq}x_n = b_p^{eq} \end{aligned}$$

and each variable may have a **lower bound** and an **upper bound**:

$$lb_i \le x_i \le ub_i, \; i = 1, 2, \ldots, n$$

The above problem can be written in a matrix form: Finding $\mathbf{x}$ that

$$\text{minimizes a function } \mathbf{f}^T\mathbf{x} \text{ and satisfies } \begin{cases} \mathbf{Ax} \le \mathbf{b} \\ \mathbf{A}_{eq}\mathbf{x} = \mathbf{b}_{eq} \\ \mathbf{lb} \le \mathbf{x} \le \mathbf{ub} \end{cases} \qquad \text{(a)}$$

where $\mathbf{f}$, $\mathbf{x}$, $\mathbf{lb}$, and $\mathbf{ub}$ are column vectors of n elements, $\mathbf{b}$ is a column vector of m elements, $\mathbf{b}_{eq}$ is a column vector of p elements, $\mathbf{A}$ is an m-by-n matrix, and $\mathbf{A}_{eq}$ is a p-by-n matrix.

A syntax for the function `linprog` is

```
[x,fval] = linprog(f,A,b,Aeq,beq,lb,ub,options)
```

where the input arguments *`f`*, *`A`*, *`b`*, *`Aeq`*, *`beq`*, *`lb`*, and *`ub`* are the vectors or matrices in Eq. (a). The last input argument *`options`* is a structure that can be set up using `optimoptions` (Table 12.4, page 461; also see 12.1[4], page 451) or `optimset` (Table 12.4, page 461). To see the options available for `linprog`, you should consult its reference page. The first output argument `x`, a vector of n elements, is the solution of the optimization problem, Eq. (a), and the second output variable `fval`, a scalar, is the corresponding value of the objective function, $\mathbf{f}^T\mathbf{x}$. ↵

Diet Problem Description and Formulation

[2] A school cafeteria is planning a nutritious diet. The goal is to minimize the cost while meeting the following requirements: 2000 kcal, 55-g protein, and 800-mg calcium. The foods considered are listed as follows:

	Food	Serving Size	Calorie	Protein	Calcium	Price per Serving
1	Oatmeal	28 g	110 kcal	4 g	2 mg	US$0.30
2	Chicken	100 g	205 kcal	32 g	12 mg	US$2.40
3	Eggs	2 large	160 kcal	13 g	54 mg	US$1.30
4	Whole Milk	237 cc	160 kcal	8 g	285 mg	US$0.90
5	Cherry pie	170 g	420 kcal	4 g	22 mg	US$2.00
6	Pork and Beans	260 g	260 kcal	14 g	80 mg	US$1.90

Reference: http://resources.mpi-inf.mpg.de/conferences/adfocs-03/Slides/Bixby_1.pdf

Let x_1, x_2, x_3, x_4, x_5, and x_6 be the servings of each food, respectively. Then the problem can be formulated as follows:

$$\text{Minimize } cost = 0.3x_1 + 2.40x_2 + 1.30x_3 + 0.90x_4 + 2.00x_5 + 1.90x_6$$

such that

$$110x_1 + 205x_2 + 160x_3 + 160x_4 + 420x_5 + 260x_6 \geq 2000$$
$$4x_1 + 32x_2 + 13x_3 + 8x_4 + 4x_5 + 14x_6 \geq 55$$
$$2x_1 + 12x_2 + 54x_3 + 285x_4 + 22x_5 + 80x_6 \geq 800$$

and each variable must be positive, i.e.,

$$x_1, x_2, x_3, x_4, x_5, x_6 \geq 0$$

↓

Example12_04.m: Diet Problem

[3] This program solves the linear programming problem defined in [2]. ↵

```
clear
f = [0.3, 2.4, 1.3, 0.9, 2.0, 1.9];
A = -[110, 205, 160, 160, 420, 260;
        4,  32,  13,   8,   4,  14;
        2,  12,  54, 285,  22,  80];
b = -[2000, 55, 800];
lb = [0 0 0 0 0 0];
[x,fval] = linprog(f,A,b,[],[],lb)

[x1,x4] = meshgrid(0:20, 0:14);
cost = 0.3*x1+0.9*x4;
[C, h] = contour(x1, x4, cost, 0:20); clabel(C, h), hold on
syms x1 x4
fimplicit(110*x1+160*x4==2000, [0,20])
fimplicit(4*x1+8*x4==55, [0,20])
fimplicit(2*x1+285*x4==800, [0,20])
axis([0,20,0,14]), xlabel('Oatmeal (x_1)'), ylabel('Whole Milk (x_4)')
title('Minimum Cost Diet Planning')
```

```
19  Optimal solution found.
20
21  x =
22       14.2443
23             0
24             0
25        2.7071
26             0
27             0
28  fval =
29        6.7096
```

[4] Line 8 outputs these texts. The minimum cost is \$6.7096, with 14.2443 servings of oatmeal, 2.7071 servings of whole milk, and none of other foods. ↓

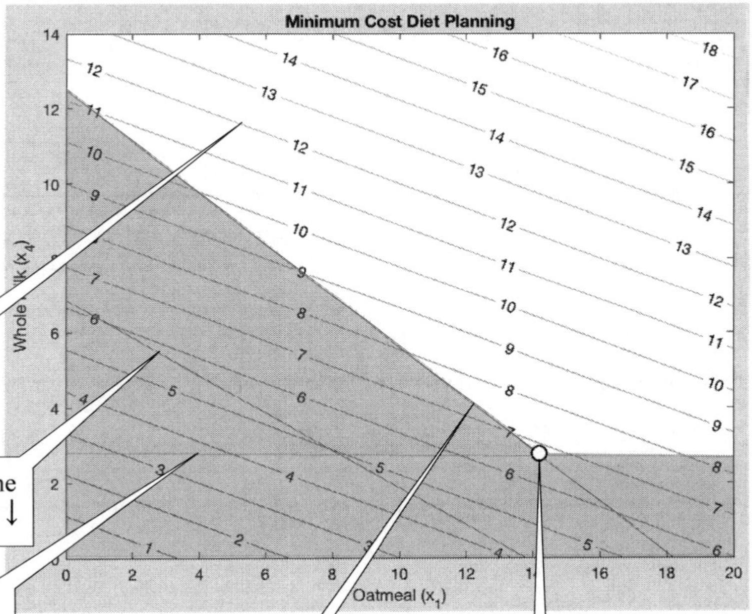

[5] Lines 12-18 produce this graph. It shows contours of the objective function [6] and three inequality constraint functions in the x_1-x_4 space [7-9]. Non-feasible region (area that violates any constraints, see [7]) is shaded. The shading is manually added by the author. ↓

[6] These parallel lines are contours of the objective function. ↓

[8] This line represents the equation $4x_1 + 8x_4 = 55$. ↓

[9] This line represents the equation $2x_1 + 285x_4 = 800$. →

How to Determine the Feasible Region?

[7] This line represents the equation $110x_1 + 160x_4 = 2000$ (x_2, x_3, x_5, and x_6 are zeros), which divides the x_1-x_4 space into two half-spaces. One half-space represents $110x_1 + 160x_4 < 2000$ and the other half-space represents $110x_1 + 160x_4 > 2000$. To determine which half-space represents $110x_1 + 160x_4 > 2000$, one way is to substitute the origin into the left-side of the equation. In this case, since the origin (which is at lower-left) satisfies $110x_1 + 160x_4 < 2000$, the region that satisfies $110x_1 + 160x_4 > 2000$ is the other half-space, i.e., the upper-right. Collection of the points that satisfy all constraints (including bounds) are the feasible region. In this case, the unshaded area is the feasible region (also see [8-9]). ↑

[10] This is the location where $x_1 = 14.2443$, $x_4 = 2.7071$, at which the value of the objective function is 6.7096, the minimum cost. ↵

About Example12_04.m

[11] Lines 2-7 prepare the input for the function `linprog`, according to the formulation in [2], page 459. Line 8 performs linear programming using the function `linprog`. Note that, since there is no equality constraint, we simply input empty arrays for the 4th and 5th input arguments. We also omitted the upper bounds (the 7th input argument); that means no upper bounds, i.e., the upper bounds are infinities. Alternatively, we could input a vector containing elements of `inf`. The output `x` and `fval` (see [4], last page) show that the minimum cost is $6.7096, occurring when $x_1 = 14.2443$ and $x_4 = 2.7071$, and the other variables are zeros.

Lines 10-18 produce a graphic output [5-10], showing contours of the cost function (objective function) and the three inequality constraint functions in the x_1-x_4 space.

Line 10 creates a 15-by-21 rectangular mesh. Line 11 calculates the objective function using the mesh, assuming $x_2 = x_3 = x_5 = x_6 = 0$. Line 12 plots contours of the objective function at $0-$20 [6]. Line 13 creates two symbolic variables `x1` and `x4`. Note that we use the same variables as those used in lines 10-12; therefore, the `x1` and `x4` created in line 10 are cleared. Lines 14-16 plot the three constraint equations [7-9] using the 2-D implicit function plotter `fimplicit`.

In the graphic output, the non-feasible region is shaded [7], so the unshaded area is the **feasible region**. The feasible region is the area in which every point satisfies the constraints and bounds. In [10], we also pointed out the location where the cost reaches a minimum. #

Table 12.4 Summary of `linprog`

Function	Description
`[x,fval] = linprog(f,A,b,Aeq,beq,lb,ub,options)`	Solve linear programming problems
`options = optimoptions(@solver, name, value, ...)`	Create optimization options structure
`options = optimset(name, value, ...)`	Create optimization options structure

Details and More: Help>Optimization Toolbox>Linear Programming and Mixed-Integer Linear Programming

12.5 Mixed-Integer Linear Programming

12.5a Example: Diet Problem

[1] Consider again the diet problem in 12.4[2], page 459. Suppose, for some reason, we have to impose additional constraints that the servings of the eggs (x_3) and the whole milk (x_4) are integer numbers. It is easy to understand the need of these constraints, since a cafeteria usually doesn't serve 0.3 eggs or 2.7071 bottles of milk (assuming each bottle contains a serving of milk). The function `intlinprog` performs mixed-integer linear programming and has an additional input argument *`intcon`* (see Table 12.5, page 464), a vector that specifies which variables are integers; i.e., `x(`*`intcon`*`)` must be integers. ↓

Example12_05a.m

[2] This program solves the diet problem with the additional constraints that the servings of the eggs (x_3) and the whole milk (x_4) are integer numbers. ↓

```
1   clear
2   f = [0.3, 2.4, 1.3, 0.9, 2.0, 1.9];
3   A = -[110, 205, 160, 160, 420, 260;
4           4,  32,  13,   8,   4,  14;
5           2,  12,  54, 285,  22,  80];
6   b = -[2000, 55, 800];
7   lb = [0 0 0 0 0 0];
8   intcon = [3, 4];
9   [x, fval] = intlinprog(f,intcon, A,b,[],[],lb)
```

[3] Line 9 outputs these texts. Note that x_4 is now an integer number. ↓

```
10  x =
11       13.8182
12             0
13             0
14        3.0000
15             0
16             0
17  fval =
18        6.8455
```

About Example12_05a.m

[4] Lines 1-7 are duplicated from lines 1-7 of Example12_04.m, page 459. Line 8 sets up an input argument for the function `intlinprog`, imposing the constraints that the 3rd and 4th variables are integers. Line 9 performs a mixed-integer linear programming using the function `intlinprog`; the text output is shown in [3]. #

12.5b Binary Integer Programming

Maximum Value of a Container

[1] The weight capacity of a container is limited to 280 kg. There are 8 objects that are considered to be placed in the container. Each object has a weight and a value as shown on the right. The container company wants to determine the objects to be placed in the container so that the total value is maximized.

Object	Weight	Value
1	45 kg	US$120
2	30 kg	US$90
3	110 kg	US$200
4	73 kg	US$220
5	20 kg	US$100
6	68 kg	US$150
7	49 kg	US$110
8	150 kg	US$400

Let x_i be a binary number, either 0 or 1, representing the number of ith object placed in the container. The problem can be formulated as follows:

$$\text{Maximize } value = 120x_1 + 90x_2 + 200x_3 + 220x_4 + 100x_5 + 150x_6 + 110x_7 + 400x_8$$

such that

$$45x_1 + 30x_2 + 110x_3 + 73x_4 + 20x_5 + 68x_6 + 49x_7 + 150x_8 \le 280$$

$$x_1, x_2, x_3, x_4, x_5, x_6, x_7, x_8 \text{ are integers, and } 0 \le x_1, x_2, x_3, x_4, x_5, x_6, x_7, x_8 \le 1$$ ↓

Example12_05b.m: Binary Integer Programming

[2] This program solves the problem described in [1]. ↓

```
1  clear
2  f = -[120,90,200,220,100,150,110,400];
3  intcon = 1:8;
4  A = [45,30,110,73,20,68,49,150];
5  b = [280];
6  LB = [0 0 0 0 0 0 0 0];
7  UB = [1 1 1 1 1 1 1 1];
8  [x, fval] = intlinprog(f, intcon, A, b, [], [], LB, UB)
```

[3] Line 8 outputs these texts. The results show that, to maximize the value of the container, the objects 2, 4, 5, and 8 should be placed in the container, and the total value of the container is $810. ↵

```
9   x =
10       0
11       1
12       0
13       1
14       1
15       0
16       0
17       1
18  fval =
19    -810
```

About Example12_05b.m

[4] The function `intlinprog` (and other MATLAB optimization functions) assumes the objective function is to be MINIMIZED. To maximize the *value* defined in [1], we simply take the negative value of the *value* (line 2). Line 3 specifies that all variables are integers. Lines 4-5 prepare the inequality constraints. Line 6 sets the lower bounds and line 7 sets the upper bounds. Lines 3 and 6-7 in effect specify all the variables as binary numbers (either 0 or 1). Line 8 solves the integer linear programming problem using the function `intlinprog`. The text output is shown in [3], last page. We conclude that, to maximize the total value, the objects 2, 4, 5, and 8 (lines 9-17) should be placed in the container, and the total value of the container is $810 (lines 18-19). #

Table 12.5 Summary of Function `intlinprog`

Function	Description
`[x,fval] = intlinprog(f,intcon,A,b,Aeq,beq,lb,ub,options)`	Mixed-integer linear programming
Details and More: Help>Optimization Toolbox>Linear Programming and Mixed-Integer Linear Programming	

12.6 Unconstrained Single-Variable Optimization

12.6a Unconstrained Single-Variable Optimization

[1] The function `fminbnd` (Table 12.6, page 467) solves an unconstrained single-variable optimization problem defined as follows:

Find x that minimizes an **objective function** $f(x)$

where

$$x_1 \le x \le x_2$$

Note that, in some other textbooks, this problem is viewed as a **constrained** single-variable optimization problem, since the bounds for the variable is considered as a constraint.

A syntax for the function `fminbnd` is

```
[x,fval] = fminbnd(@fun,x1,x2,options)
```

where `@fun` is a handle to the function that defines the objective function; for `options`, see Table 12.4, page 461. ↓

Volume of a Paper Container

[2] Given a paper of size $a \times b$, we want to determine the maximum volume of a container made by cutting four squares away from its corners, as shown. The volume of the paper container is

$$volume = x(a-2x)(b-2x)$$

The objective function to be **minimized** can be defined as the negative of the volume:

$$objective = -x(a-2x)(b-2x) \qquad \text{(a)}$$

Given a letter-size paper ($8.5 \text{ in} \times 11 \text{ in}$), Example12_06a.m finds the minimum of the objective function and the corresponding x. ↓

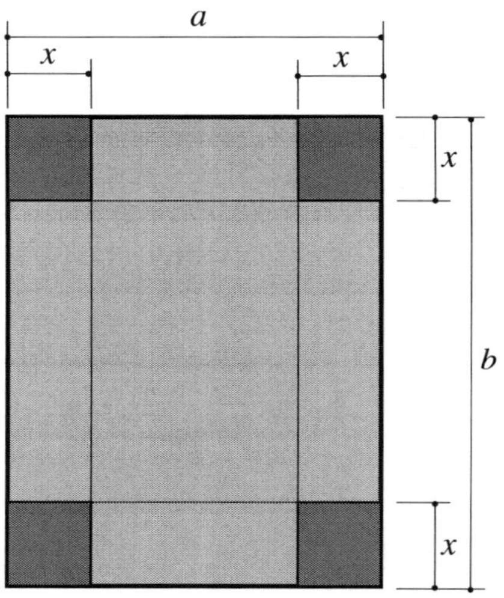

Example12_06a.m: Volume of a Paper Container

[3] This program solves the problem described in [2]. ↵

```
clear
a = 8.5; b = 11;
objective = @(x) (-x.*(a-2*x).*(b-2*x));
LB = 0; UB = min(a,b)/2;
[x, V] = fminbnd(objective, LB, UB);
fplot(objective, [LB, UB]), axis([0 4 -80 0])
text(x, V-2, ...
    ['Volume = ', num2str(-V), ' at x = ', num2str(x)], ...
    'HorizontalAlignment', 'center')
xlabel('x (in)'), ylabel('-Volume (in^3)')
title('Volume of Box')
```

[4] This is the output of Example12_06a.m. The curve represents the objective function, i.e., the negative of the volume. It shows the maximum volume is 66.1482 in^3, when $x = 1.5854$ in. ↓

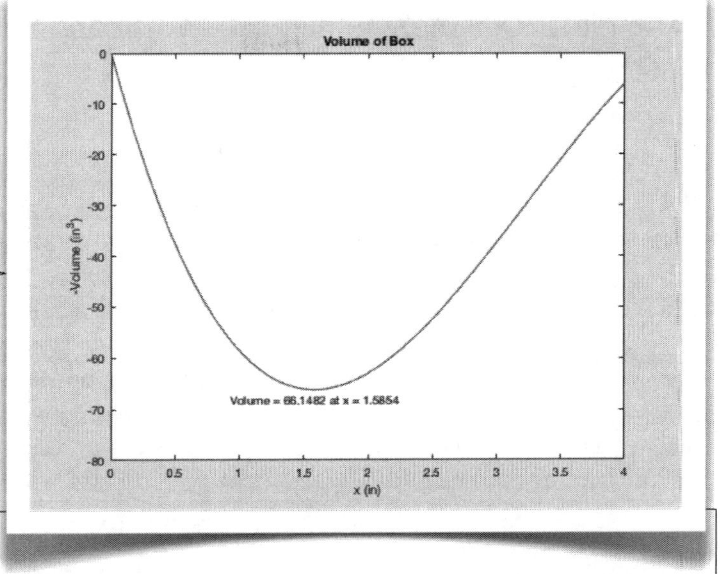

About Example12_06a.m

[5] Line 3 defines the objective function (Eq. (a), last page), using an anonymous function. Note that the use of element-wise operator (`.*` in line 3) is not really necessary when the function is used as an input to `fminbnd` in line 5; you may replace `.*` by `*` to confirm this. The reason we use `.*` is that this function is used again as an input to `fplot` (line 6), which would display a warning message if the element-wise operator is not used.

Line 4 sets the lower bound and upper bound for the variable x. Line 5 solves the problem using `fminbnd`. Note that `objective` itself is a function handle; using `@objective` is not correct.

Line 6 plots the objective function as a curve, using `fplot`; it also adjusts the axis limits. Lines 7-9 add texts in the graphic area. Lines 10-11 label the graph. #

12.6b Example: Symmetrical Two-Spring System

[1] In 3.9b, page 145, we solved the displacement x for a symmetrical two-spring system subject to a force F, using Newton's first law. Another way to solve the problem is by applying the **principle of minimum total potential energy** (*Wikipedia>Potential energy minimization principle*). In this case, the total potential energy is the potential energy stored in the two springs minus the work done by the external force:

$$PE = \frac{1}{2}k\left(\sqrt{L^2 + x^2} - L\right)^2 \times 2 - Fx \qquad \text{(a)}$$

The **principle of minimum total potential energy** states that among all possible configurations (here, all possible x) of a structure system, an equilibrium state is the one that has a minimum total potential energy.

Thus, a second way to solve this problem is to minimize the total potential energy function Eq. (a) over all possible x.

As in 3.9b, page 145, we assume $k = 6.8$ N/cm, $L = 12$ cm, and $F = 9.2$ N. ↵

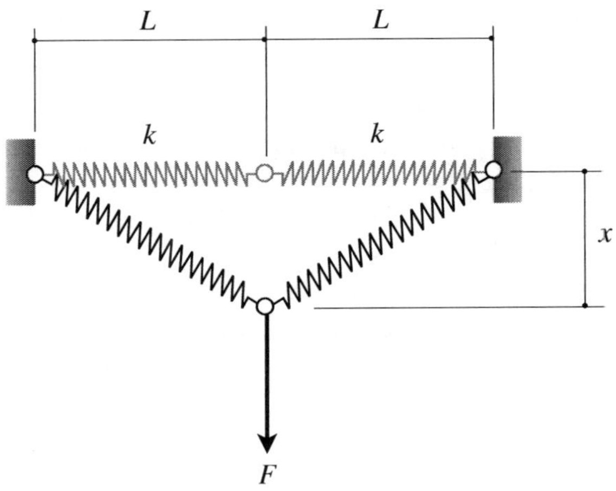

Example12_06b.m: Symmetrical Two-Spring System

[2] This program solves the symmetrical two-spring system described in [1], last page. ↓

```
1  clear
2  k = 6.8; L = 12; F = 9.2;
3  potential = @(x) (0.5*k*(sqrt(L^2+x.^2)-L).^2*2-F*x);
4  LB = 0; UB = 10;
5  [x, PE] = fminbnd(potential, LB, UB);
6  fplot(potential, [LB, UB]), axis([0 10 -50 0])
7  text(x, PE-2, ...
8      ['Total Potential Energy = ', num2str(PE), ' at x = ', num2str(x)], ...
9      'HorizontalAlignment', 'center')
10 xlabel('x (cm)'), ylabel('Total Potential Energy (N-cm)')
11 title('Total Potential Energy of Two-Spring System')
```

[3] This is the output of Example12_06b.m. The curve represents the total potential energy. It shows that the minimum of the total potential energy is -41.6015 N-cm when $x = 6.1485$ cm, which is consistent with that in 3.9b[3], page 145. ↓

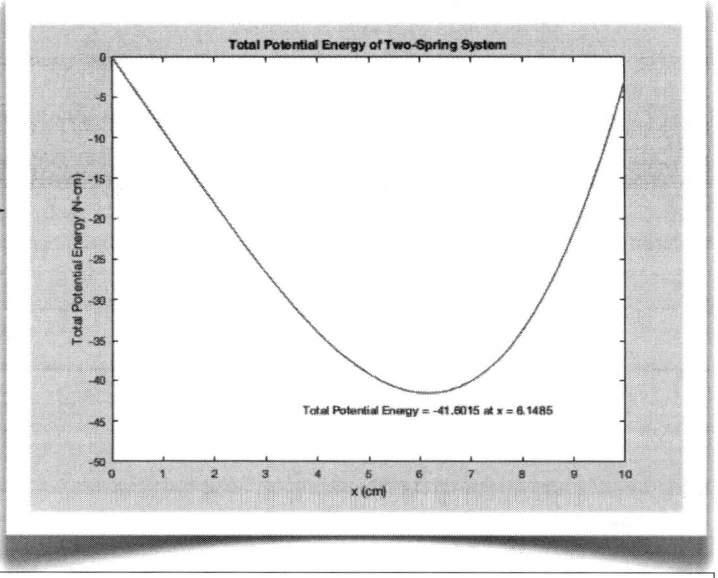

About Example12_06b.m

[4] The structure of this program is almost the same as that of Example12_06a.m, page 465. Let me reiterate that the use of element-wise operator (`.^`) in line 3 is not necessary when the function `potential` is used as an input to `fminbnd` (line 5), but when used as an input to `fplot` in line 6, it would display a warning message if the element-wise operator is not used. #

Table 12.6 Summary of `fminbnd`

Functions	Description
`[x,fval] = fminbnd(@fun,x1,x2,options)`	Find minimum of single-variable function on fixed interval
`f = fun(x)`	Function defining the objective function
Details and More: Help>MATLAB>Mathematics>Optimization>Optimizer	

12.7 Unconstrained Multivariate Optimization

Unconstrained Multivariate Optimization: fminunc and fminsearch

[1] Either the function `fminunc` or the function `fminsearch` (Table 12.7, page 470) solves an unconstrained multivariate optimization problem defined as follows:

Find $\mathbf{x}$ that minimizes an **objective function** $f(\mathbf{x})$

where $\mathbf{x}$ is a vector containing n variables; i.e., $\mathbf{x} = [x_1, x_2, \ldots, x_n]$.

Both `fminunc` and `fminsearch` have the same syntax:

```
[x,fval] = fminunc(@fun,x0,options)
[x,fval] = fminsearch(@fun,x0,options)
```

where `@fun` is a handle to a function that defines the objective function $f(\mathbf{x})$, `x0` is an n-element vector providing a set of initial gauss values; both the functions output the values of $\mathbf{x}$ and the corresponding minimum value of the objective function $f(\mathbf{x})$.

The major difference between `fminunc` and `fminsearch` is that `fminunc` uses a gradient-based method, while `fminsearch` uses a gradient-free method. The gradient-based method requires the evaluations of the gradients (see 5.13a[3], page 248; also see Section 11.1[10], page 424) of the objective function, thus using more computing time but obtaining more accurate results. On the other hand, for many large-scaled engineering applications, the gradient-free method may be more efficient and robust, if accuracy is not crucial. ↓

Asymmetrical Two-Spring System Revisit

[2] Consider the asymmetrical two-spring system in Section 12.3 again. As mentioned in 12.6b[1], page 466, the **principle of minimum total potential energy** states that among all possible configurations (here, all possible x and y) of a structure system, an equilibrium state is the one that has the minimum total potential energy. The total potential energy is the potential energy stored in the two springs minus the work done by the external force:

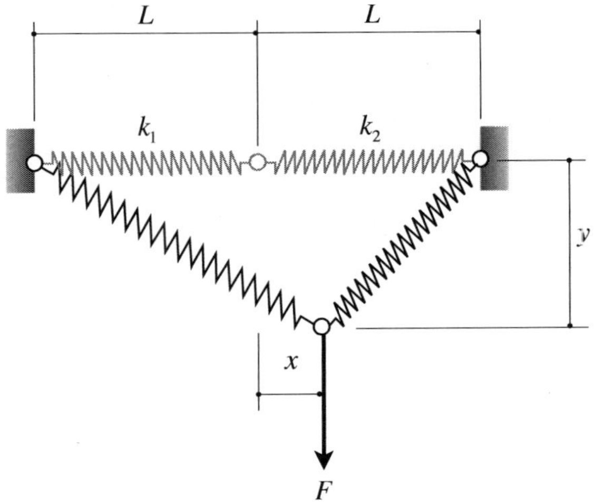

$$PE = \frac{1}{2}k_1\Delta L_1^2 + \frac{1}{2}k_2\Delta L_2^2 - Fy \qquad \text{(a)}$$

where ΔL_1 and ΔL_2 are elongations of the two springs, respectively, and were derived in 12.3[1], page 455,

$$\Delta L_1 = \sqrt{(L+x)^2 + y^2} - L \text{ and } \Delta L_2 = \sqrt{(L-x)^2 + y^2} - L$$

Example12_07.m solves the problem by minimizing the total potential energy function Eq. (a) over all possible x and y. As in 12.3[1], page 455, we assume $k_1 = 1.5$ N/cm, $k_2 = 6.8$ N/cm, $L = 12$ cm, and $F = 9.2$ N. ↵

Example12_07.m: Asymmetrical Two-Spring System

[3] This program solves the problem described in [2] (last page), producing the graph shown in [4]. ↓

```
function Example12_07
k1 = 1.5; k2 = 6.8; L = 12; F = 9.2;
L1 = @(x,y) sqrt((L+x).^2+y.^2);
L2 = @(x,y) sqrt((L-x).^2+y.^2);
dL1 = @(x,y) L1(x,y)-L;
dL2 = @(x,y) L2(x,y)-L;
PE = @(x,y) 0.5*k1*dL1(x,y).^2 + 0.5*k2*dL2(x,y).^2 - F*y;
[X, Y] = meshgrid(linspace(0,5), linspace(5,10));
[C, h] = contour(X, Y, PE(X,Y), -60:5:10);
clabel(C, h), xlabel('x'), ylabel('y'), grid on
title('Asymmetrical Two-Spring System')

[sol, fval] = fminunc(@fun, [5,5]);
text(sol(1),sol(2)+0.1, ['fminunc: ', ...
    'x = ', num2str(sol(1)), ', y = ', num2str(sol(2)), ...
    ' PE = ', num2str(fval)], ...
    'HorizontalAlignment', 'center')

[sol, fval] = fminsearch(@fun, [5,5]);
text(sol(1),sol(2)-0.1, ['fminsearch: ', ...
    'x = ', num2str(sol(1)), ', y = ', num2str(sol(2)), ...
    ' PE = ', num2str(fval)], ...
    'HorizontalAlignment', 'center')

    function f = fun(z)
        f = PE(z(1), z(2));
    end
end
```

[4] This is the graphic output of Example12_07.m. ↵

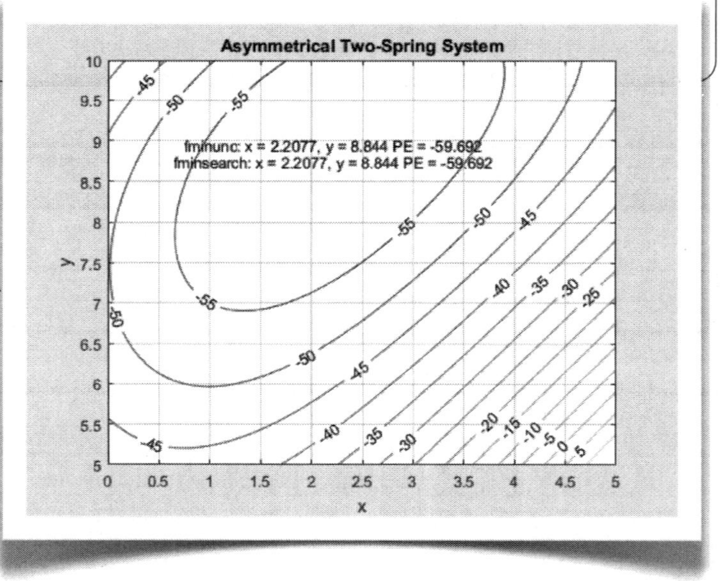

About Example12_07.m

[5] The program consists of a main program (lines 1-28), within which a nested function `fun` (lines 25-27), and 5 anonymous functions: `L1`, `L2`, `dL1`, `dL2`, and `PE` (lines 3-7) are defined. We use the anonymous functions this way for better readability and reusability as explained in 12.3[7], page 457.

Lines 2-6 are duplicated from lines 2-6 of Example12_03.m, page 456. Line 7 defines an anonymous function that evaluates the potential energy function defined in Eq. (a), page 468. Again, the use of the element-wise operator (`.^`) in lines 3-7 is not necessary when used with `fminunc` (line 13) or `fminsearch` (line 19), but when used with `contour` (line 9), it becomes necessary.

Line 8 creates a 2-D mesh: $0 \le x \le 5,\ \ 5 \le y \le 10$. Line 9 plots contours of potential energy at -60, -55, ..., and 10. Line 10 adds contour labels and axis labels and turns the grid on. From the graphic output [4], last page, we can approximately locate where the minimum potential energy occurs.

The function `fun` (lines 25-27) evaluates the potential energy function defined in Eq. (a), page 468, using the anonymous functions in lines 3-7. The input argument `z` in line 25 is a vector containing current values of `x` and `y`; `z(1)` and `z(2)` correspond to `x` and `y`, respectively. The output argument `f` in line 25 is a scalar.

Line 13 finds the minimum potential energy and the corresponding x and y, using the function `fminunc`. We arbitrarily choose $x = 5$ and $y = 5$ as the initial point. The solver finds a minimum value -59.692 N-cm at $x = 2.2077$ cm, $y = 8.844$ cm; lines 14-17 write the result on the graphic area (see [4], last page). As mentioned in [1] (page 468), the function `fminunc` uses a gradient-based method. The gradients of the objective function, by default, are calculated numerically described in Section 11.1. You may also provide gradients in the user-defined function (here, the function `fun` in lines 25-27). (*For details and more, see >> doc fminunc.*)

Lines 19-23 repeat the same tasks as those in lines 13-17 except that `fminsearch`, a gradient-free solver, is used. In this particular case, both `fminnuc` and `fminsearch` have the same numerical result (see [4]). #

Table 12.7 Summary of `fminunc` and `fminsearch`

Functions	Description
`[x,fval] = fminunc(@fun,x0,options)`	Find minimum of an unconstrained multivariable function
`[x,fval] = fminsearch(@fun,x0,options)`	Find minimum of an unconstrained multivariable function
`f = fun(x)`	Function defining the objective function
Details and More: Help>Optimization Toolbox>Nonlinear Optimization>Unconstrained Optimization	

12.8 Multivariate Linear Regression

Problem Description: Injection-Mold Tests

[1] One application of optimization techniques is the least squares line/curve fitting, in which the objective is to minimize the differences between the data points and the fitting line/curve (also see 10.6[5], page 409). In Section 10.8, we've discussed single-variable linear regression. Now, we introduce multivariate linear regression, using an example as follows.

In a series of injection-mold tests, the engineers adjust four process parameters to maximize the strength of a plastic product, measured by uniaxial tensile tests. The table below shows the data obtained from nine mold tests. We want to find a linear equation of the form

$$y = p_0 + p_1x_1 + p_2x_2 + p_3x_3 + p_4x_4 \tag{a}$$

that best fits the test data in the sense of least squared errors.

Let X be a 9-by-5 matrix, which is formed by adding a column of all ones before the four columns shown in the shaded area of the table below; P is a column vector $P = [\,p_0\ p_1\ p_2\ p_3\ p_4\,]^T$; and Y is a column vector containing the values in the last column of the table below. Then XP (matrix multiplication of X and P) represents nine values on the fitting line, Eq. (a). And the column vector $XP - Y$ is the **residual** vector (10.6[5], page 409). Our objective is to minimize the sum of the squares of the values in the residual vector. It is equivalent to minimizing the **error** of the curve fitting (see 10.6[5], page 409),

$$error = \|XP - Y\| \tag{b}$$

Example12_08.m uses three ways to find the coefficients in P; they all have the same result. First, it uses `fminunc` (Section 12.7) to minimize the error defined in Eq. (b). Second, it uses the built-in function `lsqlin` (see Table 12.8, page 473), which implements the multivariate linear regression. Third, it uses the backslash operator (\) to perform the least squares line fit (10.8b[4], page 416). ↵

Test no.	x_1 Melt Temperature (Degrees C)	x_2 Injection Speed (% of Full Speed)	x_3 Packing Pressure (kgf/cm^2)	x_4 Mold Temperature (Degrees C)	y Strength (N)
1	150	50	25	30	65.7
2	150	70	50	40	73.7
3	150	90	75	50	70.0
4	170	50	50	50	82.9
5	170	70	75	30	97.3
6	170	90	25	40	106.1
7	190	50	75	40	119.0
8	190	70	25	50	110.3
9	190	90	50	30	111.4

Example12_08.m: Injection-Mold Tests

[2] This program solves the problem described in [1], last page, producing output shown in [3]. ↓

```
function Example12_08
X = [1, 150, 50, 25, 30;
     1, 150, 70, 50, 40;
     1, 150, 90, 75, 50;
     1, 170, 50, 50, 50;
     1, 170, 70, 75, 30;
     1, 170, 90, 25, 40;
     1, 190, 50, 75, 40;
     1, 190, 70, 25, 50;
     1, 190, 90, 50, 30];

Y = [65.7, 73.7, 70.0, 82.9, 97.3, 106.1, 119.0, 110.3, 111.4]';

P1 = fminunc(@fun, [0,0,0,0,0]')
P2 = lsqlin(X, Y, [],[])
P3 = X\Y

    function error = fun(P)
        error = norm(X*P-Y);
    end
end
```

```
P1 =
   -98.6164
     1.0942
     0.1658
     0.0280
    -0.1867
P2 =
   -98.6167
     1.0942
     0.1658
     0.0280
    -0.1867
P3 =
   -98.6167
     1.0942
     0.1658
     0.0280
    -0.1867
```

[3] This is the output of Example12_08.m. ↵

About Example12_08.m

[4] The program consists of a main function (lines 1-21), within which a nested function `fun` (lines 18-20) is defined.

Lines 2-12 prepare matrix X and column vector Y as described in [1].

The function `fun` (lines 18-20) defines the objective function Eq. (b), page 471.

Line 14 finds the parameters (p_0, p_1, p_2, p_3 and p_4) that minimize the **error**. We arbitrarily use a set of initial values of all zeros. The result is output in lines 22-27: $p_0 = -98.6164$, $p_1 = 1.0942$, $p_2 = 0.1658$, $p_3 = 0.0280$, and $p_4 = -0.1867$.

Line 15 repeats the linear regression using the built-in function `lsqlin`. The result is essentially the same, with negligible differences. Note that `lsqlin` allows the user to specify linear constraints (equality and inequality) and variable bounds (see Table 12.8, below). In our case, there are no constraints and variable bounds.

Line 16 obtains the same result using the backslash operator (\) (10.8b[4], page 416). #

Table 12.8 Summary of Linear Least Squares

Functions	Description
`p = lsqlin(C,d,A,b,Aeq,beq,lb,ub,options)`	Solve constrained linear least-square problems
`x = A\b (mldivide)`	Solve systems of linear equations $\mathbf{Ax} = \mathbf{b}$ for $\mathbf{x}$

Details and More: Help>Optimization Toolbox>Least Squares>Linear Least Squares

12.9 Non-Polynomial Curve Fitting

12.9a Polynomial Curve Fitting

Stress-Strain Relationship

[1] As mentioned in 9.8[1] (page 379), in Mechanics of Materials, if the stress and strain has a linear relationship, then Young's modulus, Poisson's ratio, and shear modulus are used to describe the stress-strain relationship, which is the most important material property in analyzing the mechanical behavior of materials. In other words, these three **material parameters** provide a **material model** for the **linear materials**. When the stress and strain has a nonlinear relationship, then we need a **material model** for describing the nonlinear material. A material model is an expression that describes the relationship between the stress and the strain.

The table below lists the measured stresses under various strains in a set of uniaxial tensile tests.

Strain (Dimensionless)	0	0.0227	0.0557	0.0880	0.1203	0.1524	0.1840	0.2154	0.2475	0.2797
Stress (psi)	0	20.35	38.29	52.12	63.74	73.77	82.80	91.13	99.07	106.58

In this section, we will establish a material model using these data. First, in Example12_09a.m below, we fit the data with polynomials (using `polyfit`, see Section 10.6) of degrees 1, 2, and 3 and observe the **errors** (10.6[5], page 409), which indicate the fitness of the fittings: the smaller, the better. Second, in Example12_09b.m (page 476), we will fit the data with a non-polynomial function using the functions `lsqcurvefit` and `lsqnonlin` (Table 12.9, page 477). We'll show you that a carefully selected form of non-polynomial function may fit the data with fewer material parameters but less errors, compared with the polynomial forms. ↓

Example12_09a.m: Polynomial Curve Fitting

[2] This program fits the data in [1] with polynomials of degrees 1, 2, and 3 and shows the **errors**. ↵

```
clear
strain = [0,0.0227,0.0557,0.0880,0.1203,0.1524,0.1840,0.2154,0.2475,0.2797];
stress = [0, 20.35, 38.29, 52.12, 63.74, 73.77, 82.80, 91.13, 99.07,106.58];

for k = 1:3
    P = polyfit(strain, stress, k);
    x = linspace(0,0.3);
    y = polyval(P, x);
    subplot(2,2,k)
    plot(strain, stress, 'o', x, y)
    axis([0,0.3,0,120])
    xlabel('Strain (Dimensionless)')
    ylabel('Stress (psi)')
    title(['Polynomial of Degree ', num2str(k)])
    error = norm(stress-polyval(P,strain));
    text(0.1, 10, ['Error = ', num2str(error)])
end
```

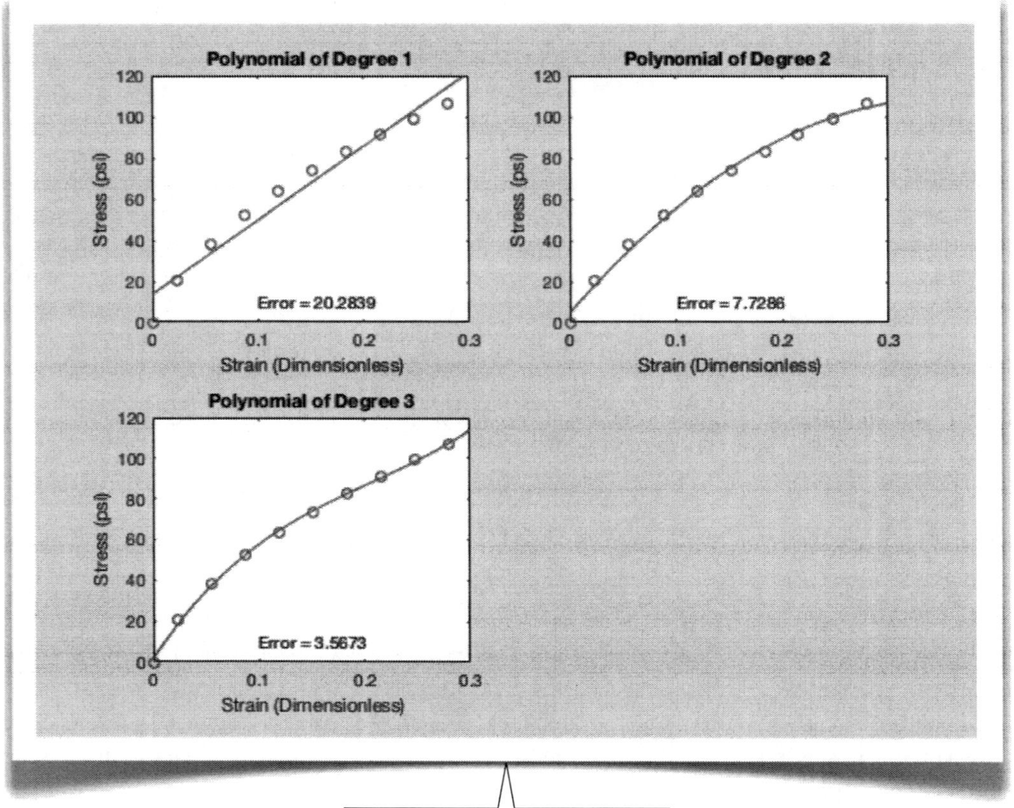

[3] This is the output of Example12_09a.m. ↓

About Example12_09a.m

[4] Lines 2-3 prepare the data listed in [1]. Line 5 starts a `for`-loop (lines 5-17), the counter `k` running from 1 to 3, the degrees of the fitting polynomials.

Line 6 fits the data with a polynomial of degree `k`; the result `P` is a vector of `k`+1 elements containing the coefficients of the fitting polynomial (see 10.5a[1], page 403).

Lines 7-14 plot the data points as well as the fitting polynomial as shown in [3].

Line 15 calculates the error (10.6[5], page 409) and line 16 writes the error on the graphic area.

Note that the polynomial of degree 2 (which has three parameters) fits the data with an error of 7.7286, and the polynomial of degree 3 (which has four parameters) fits the data with an error of 3.5673. We'll compare these values with the result obtained in Example12_09b.m, next page. #

12.9b Non-Polynomial Curve Fitting

Example12_09b.m: Non-Polynomial Curve Fitting

[1] This program fits the data listed in 12.9a[1] (page 474) with a function of the form $\sigma = a\varepsilon^b$, where σ is the stress, ε is the strain, and a and b are parameters to be determined. The functions `lsqcurvefit` and `lsqnonlin` (Table 12.9, next page) are used for the non-polynomial curve fittings. Both functions have the same result; the difference is the way they specify the user-defined functions, explained in [4], next page. ↙

```
clear
strain = [0,0.0227,0.0557,0.0880,0.1203,0.1524,0.1840,0.2154,0.2475,0.2797];
stress = [0, 20.35, 38.29, 52.12, 63.74, 73.77, 82.80, 91.13, 99.07,106.58];

fun1 = @(p, xdata) p(1)*xdata.^p(2);
fun2 = @(p) p(1)*strain.^p(2)-stress;
p0 = [0, 0];
[p1, err1] = lsqcurvefit(fun1, p0, strain, stress)
[p2, err2] = lsqnonlin(fun2, p0)
e = linspace(0, 0.3);
s = p1(1)*e.^p1(2);
plot(strain, stress, 'ko', e, s, 'k-')
xlabel('Strain (\epsilon, Dimensionless)'), ylabel('Stress (\sigma, psi)')
text(0.1, 20, ['\sigma = ', num2str(p1(1)), '\times\epsilon^{', ...
    num2str(p1(2)),'}'])
text(0.1, 10, ['Error = ', num2str(err1)])
legend('Experimental Data', 'Fitting Curve', 'Location', 'southeast')
title('Stress-Strain Relationship')
```

```
...
p1 =
  240.4015    0.6326
err1 =
    4.7698
...
p2 =
  240.4015    0.6326
err2 =
    4.7698
...
```

[2] This is the text output of Example12_09b.m. →

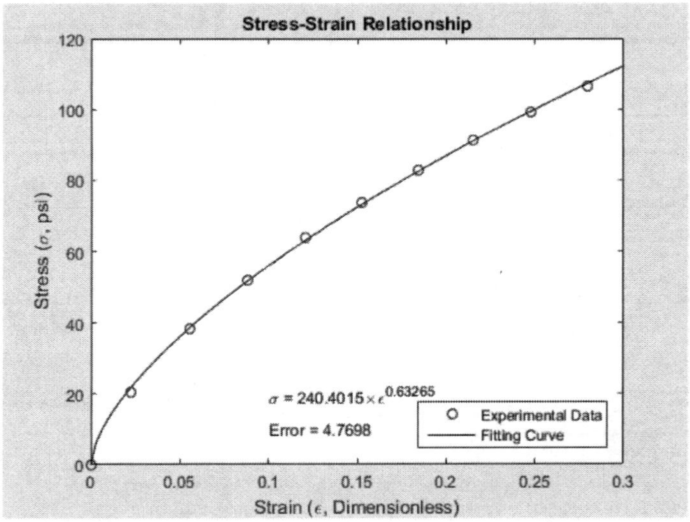

[3] This is the graphic output of Example12_09b.m. ↵

About Example12_09b.m

[4] Lines 1-3 are copied from Example12_09a.m, preparing the data listed in 12.9a[1], page 474.

Lines 5-6 define two anonymous functions to be input to the functions `lsqcurvefit` and `lsqnonlin`, respectively. `fun1` defines the function to fit,

$$f_1 = a\varepsilon^b$$

while `fun2` defines the function whose sum of squares is to be minimized,

$$f_2 = a\varepsilon^b - \sigma$$

Note that the function `fun1` (line 5) has two input arguments: `p` is a vector of parameters (a and b) and `xdata` is the data points along the horizontal axis (here, `strain`). The function `fun2` (line 6) has only one input argument (`p`).

Line 7 prepares a set of initial values for the parameters. We arbitrarily choose zeros for both parameters; i.e., $a = 0$ and $b = 0$.

Lines 8 and 9 fit the data using `lsqcurvefit` and `lsqnonlin`, respectively. Both functions return the parameters (`p1` and `p2`, respectively) and the errors (`err1` and `err2`, respectively). The text output ([2], last page) of lines 8 and 9 show that both have the same numerical result.

Lines 10-13 plot the data points as well as the fitting curve. Lines 14-16 display the fitting equation and the error. Line 17 adds legends to the graph, and line 18 adds a title to the graph.

This model has only two parameters and fits the data pretty well, with an error of 4.7698, substantially less than that of the polynomial of degree 2, which has three parameters and with an error of 7.7286 (see 12.9a[3], page 475).

Why $\sigma = a\varepsilon^b$?

We choose this form for two reasons. First, it passes through the origin (i.e., the stress is zero when the strain is zero). Second, we observed that, as the strain increases, the slope of the curve tends to decrease.

In general, a model should be as simple as possible; the fewer parameters, the better. Of course, the error must be as small as possible. #

Table 12.9 Summary of Functions `lsqcurvefit` and `lsqnonlin`

Functions	Description
`[p,err] = lsqcurvefit(@fun1,p0,x,y,lb,ub,options)`	Solve nonlinear curve-fitting problems
`[p,err] = lsqnonlin(@fun2,p0,lb,ub,options)`	Solve nonlinear curve-fitting problems
`f = fun1(p, xdata)`	Function to fit
`f = fun2(p)`	Function whose sum of squares is minimized

Details and More: Help>Optimization Toolbox>Least Squares>Nonlinear Least Squares (Curve Fitting)

12.10 Constrained Optimization

Constrained Optimization: fmincon

[1] The function `fmincon` (Table 12.10, page 482) solves a constrained nonlinear programming problem defined as follows: Find $\mathbf{x}$ that

$$\text{minimize } f(\mathbf{x}) \text{ such that } \begin{cases} \mathbf{c}(\mathbf{x}) \le 0 \\ \mathbf{c}_{eq}(\mathbf{x}) = 0 \\ \mathbf{A}\mathbf{x} \le \mathbf{b} \\ \mathbf{A}_{eq}\mathbf{x} = \mathbf{b}_{eq} \\ \mathbf{lb} \le \mathbf{x} \le \mathbf{ub} \end{cases} \quad \text{(a)}$$

where $\mathbf{c}(\mathbf{x}) \le 0$ represents nonlinear inequality constraints, $\mathbf{c}_{eq}(\mathbf{x}) = 0$ represents nonlinear equality constraints, $\mathbf{A}\mathbf{x} \le \mathbf{b}$ represents linear inequality constraints, $\mathbf{A}_{eq}\mathbf{x} = \mathbf{b}_{eq}$ represents linear equality constraints, and $\mathbf{lb} \le \mathbf{x} \le \mathbf{ub}$ represents the bounds of the variables.

A syntax for the function `fmincon` is

```
[x,fval] = fmincon(@fun,x0,A,b,Aeq,beq,lb,ub,@nonlcon,options)
```

where the output argument *x* contains the variable values that minimize the objective function, and `fval` is the corresponding value of the objective function. The input argument *@fun* is the handle to a user-defined function that defines the objective function $f(\mathbf{x})$; *x0* is an initial point; *A*, *b*, *Aeq*, *beq*, *lb*, and *ub* are the vectors or matrices as in Eq. (a); *@nonlcon* is the handle to a user-defined function that defines the left-hand side of the nonlinear constraints, i.e., $\mathbf{c}(\mathbf{x})$ and $\mathbf{c}_{eq}(\mathbf{x})$. A syntax for the function *nonlcon* is

```
[c, ceq] = nonlcon(x)
```

where the input argument *x* contains the current values of the design variables $\mathbf{x}$; the output argument *c* is a column vector containing values of the left-hand side of the inequality constraints $\mathbf{c}(\mathbf{x})$; *ceq* is a column vector containing values of the left-hand side of the equality constraints $\mathbf{c}_{eq}(\mathbf{x})$. ↓

Engineering Analysis vs. Engineering Design

[2] Engineering analysis can be viewed as the evaluation of the **response** of an engineering **system** subject to **loads**. For example, in a structural analysis, we are finding the displacement, strain, and stress of the structural system subject to external forces. Most engineering theories or software are developed to deal with engineering analysis problems.

Engineering design, on the other hand, is to the opposite direction: we want to determine the configuration of a system or loads in order to achieve a specific response. For example, we want to determine the sizes of the components of a structure so that the stresses are within a certain limit.

Optimization techniques play an important role in engineering design, as demonstrated in the following example, in which we want to determine forces that deflect a mirror parabolically. The mirror is used in a solar-energy reflecting system. ↵

Forces to Deflect a Beam Parabolically

[3] Consider that we want to determine the forces F_1, F_2, and F_3 that deflect a beam parabolically, as shown below. This situation may happen when we want to design a concave mirror to reflect the incoming light.

We assume the following parameters for the beam: $w = 1$ m, $h = 0.1$ m, $L = 8$ m, and $E = 210$ GPa. The six forces locate at $L/8$, $2L/8$, $3L/8$, $5L/8$, $6L/8$, and $7L/8$, respectively, to the left-end of the beam. It is required that the deflection at the center be $\delta_c = 0.5$ m and the maximum bending stress be limited within $\sigma_{max} = 200$ MPa.

The objective function to be minimized may be defined as the difference between the deflected beam curve and the fitting parabola. Let x_i $(i = 1, 2, \ldots, nx)$ be coordinates along the beam length, δ_i be the corresponding deflections, and $P(x)$ be the second-degree polynomial that best fits the nx points, (x_i, δ_i), $i = 1, 2, \ldots, nx$. Then the problem may be formulated as follows: Find F_1, F_2, and F_3 that

$$\text{minimize } err = \|P(x_i) - \delta_i\| \text{ such that } \begin{cases} \sigma \le \sigma_{max} \\ \delta = \delta_c \\ F_1, F_2, F_3 > 0 \end{cases}$$

where σ is the maximum stress in the beam and δ is the maximum deflection in the beam.

Example12_10.m (next page) solves this constrained optimization problem using `fmincon`. ↵

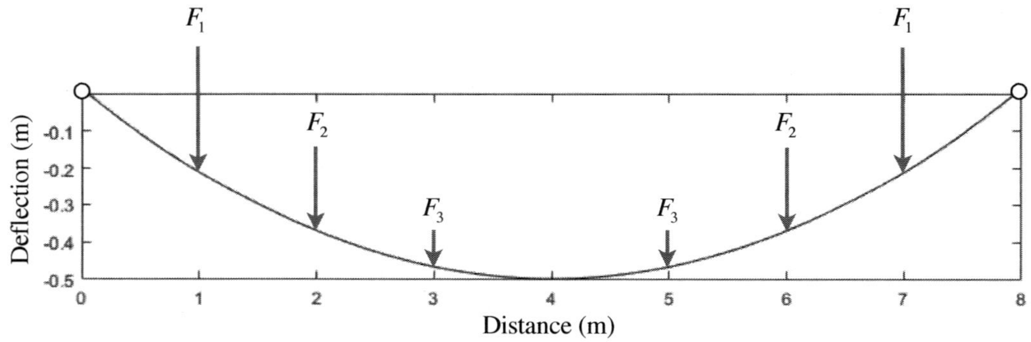

Example12_10.m: Parabolically Deflected Beam

[4] This program solves the problem defined in [3], last page. ↲

```
function Example12_10
w = 1; h = 0.01; L = 8; E = 210e9; maxSigma = 200e6; deltaCenter = 0.5;
nF = 3; a = L/8*[1,2,3]; F0 = [0,0,0]; LB = [0,0,0]; UB = [inf,inf,inf];
nx = 20; x = linspace(0,L,nx); savedDelta = zeros(1,nx); savedP = [0,0,0];
I = w*h^3/12;
[F, err] = fmincon(@fun, F0, [],[],[],[], LB, UB, @nonlcon)
plot(x, -savedDelta, 'ko', x, -polyval(savedP, x), 'k-')
axis([0, L, -deltaCenter, 0])
xlabel('Distance (m)'), ylabel('Deflection (m)')
legend('Beam Deflections', 'Fitting Parabola', 'Location', 'north')
title('Parabolically Deflected Beam')

    function err = fun(F)
        delta = zeros(1,nx);
        for k = 1:nF
            delta = delta + deflection(F(k), a(k), x);
            delta = delta + deflection(F(k), L-a(k), x);
        end
        P = polyfit(x, delta, 2);
        err = norm(delta - polyval(P, x));
        savedDelta = delta; savedP = P;
    end

    function [c,ceq] = nonlcon(F)
        sigma = 0; delta = 0;
        for k = 1:nF
            delta = delta + deflection(F(k), a(k), L/2);
            sigma = sigma + stress(F(k), a(k));
            delta = delta + deflection(F(k), L-a(k), L/2);
            sigma = sigma + stress(F(k), L-a(k));
        end
        c(1) = sigma - maxSigma;
        ceq(1) = delta - deltaCenter;
    end

    function delta = deflection(F, a, x)
        R = F/L*(L-a);
        theta = F*a/(6*E*I*L)*(2*L-a)*(L-a);
        delta = theta*x-R*x.^3/(6*E*I)+F/(6*E*I)*((x>a).*((x-a).^3));
    end

    function sigma = stress(F, a)
        M = F*a/2;
        sigma = M*(h/2)/I;
    end
end
```

```
F =
   508.1211   325.1893     0.0141
err =
     0.0210
```

[5] This is the text output of Example12_10.m. The solution is sensitive to computing platforms. Your output may not be exactly the same as here. →

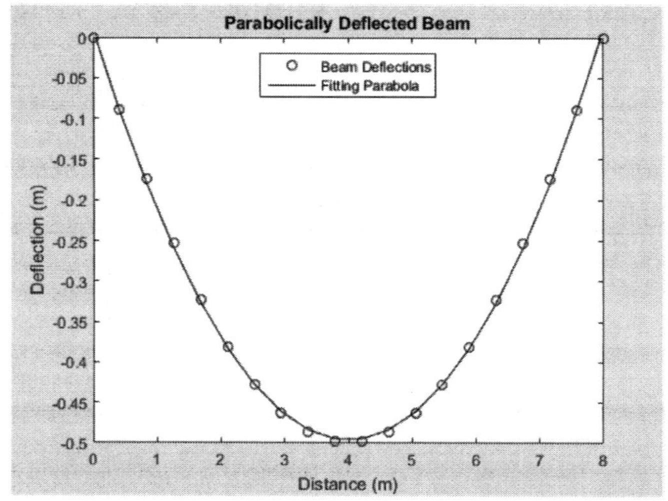

[6] This is the graphic output of Example12_10.m. ↓

About Example12_10.m

[7] This program consists of a main function (lines 1-46), within which four nested functions, `fun` (lines 13-22), `nonlcon` (lines 24-34), `deflection` (lines 36-40), and `stress` (lines 42-45), are defined.

The function `fmincon` in line 6 solves the constrained optimization problem, in which the objective function is specified in the user-defined function `fun` (lines 13-22) and the nonlinear constraints are specified in `nonlcon` (lines 24-34). The function `deflection` (lines 36-40) calculates beam deflections using the formulas in 2.14[1], page 115 (also see lines 10-15 of Example03_12.m, page 149). The function `stress` (lines 42-45) calculates the maximum stress in the beam, using a formula found in any textbooks of Mechanics of Materials,

$$\sigma = \frac{M(h/2)}{I}, \text{ where } M = \frac{Fa}{2}$$

Line 2 prepares beam properties: the beam has a width 1 m, height 0.01 m, length 8 m, Young's modulus 210 GPa, yield stress 200 MPa; the deflection at the mid-span of the beam length must equal to 0.5 m.

Line 3 prepares the forces data: there are three independent forces (F_1, F_2, and F_3), located at first, second, and third eighths of the beam length to the ends. We arbitrarily choose zeros as the initial force values. The lower bounds `LB` are zeros, while the upper bounds `UB` are infinities.

In line 4, twenty x-coordinates are created along the beam length. The variable `savedDelta` and `savedP` are used to store the final values of the beam deflections and the fitting parabola (see line 21).

Line 5 calculates the moment of inertia of the beam cross section.

The function `deflection` (lines 36-40) calculates the deflection at `x` of the beam length, given a force `F` located at `a` to the left-end of the beam. Lines 37-39 are duplicates of lines 12-14 in Example03_12.m, page 149.

The function `stress` (lines 42-45) calculates the maximum stress in the beam, which occurs at the mid-span of the beam length and on the upper/lower extremes of the beam cross section. The bending moment at the mid-span of the beam length is $M = Fa/2$ (line 43), and the bending stress at the upper/lower extremes is $\sigma = M(h/2)/I$ (line 44). (Continued at [8], next page.) ↲

About Example12_10.m (Continued)

[8] The function `fun` (lines 13-22) specifies the objective function defined in [3], page 479. Lines 14-18 calculate the deflections `delta` at x_i $(i = 1, 2, \ldots, nx)$ under the action of the six forces. Line 19 fits the deflected beam curve with a parabola, a second-degree polynomial `P`. Line 20 calculates the error between the fitting polynomial and the deflected beam curve. The variable `err` contains the value of the objective function to be output. Line 21 saves the deflections and the polynomial, of which the final values will be plotted as shown in [6], last page.

The function `nonlcon` (lines 24-34) specifies the nonlinear constraints, consisting of an inequality constraint and an equality constraint defined in [3], page 479. Lines 25-31 calculate the deflection `delta` and the stress `sigma` at the middle of the beam length under the action of the six forces. Note that the nonlinear constraints must be formulated such that the right-hand sides are zeros. Therefore, the constraints should be written as follows:

$$\sigma - \sigma_{\max} \le 0 \text{ and } \delta - \delta_c = 0.$$

Line 32 calculates the left-hand side of the inequality constraint $\sigma - \sigma_{\max}$, and line 33 calculates the left-hand side of the equality constraint $\delta - \delta_c$.

Line 6 solves the constrained optimization problem using `fmincon`. The text output ([5], last page) shows that $F_1 = 508.1194$ N, $F_2 = 325.1898$ N, $F_3 = 0.0144$ N, and the error is 0.0210 m. Note that the solution is sensitive to computing platforms. Your output may not be exactly the same as those in [5].

Lines 7-11 generate a graph shown in [6], last page. #

Table 12.10 Summary of `fmincon`

Functions	Description
`[x,fval] = fmincon(@fun,x0,A,b,Aeq,beq,lb,ub,nonlcon,options)`	Constrained optimization
`f = fun(x)`	Objective function
`[c,ceq] = nonlcon(x)`	Constraints
Details and More: Help>Optimization Toolbox>Nonlinear Optimization>Constrained Optimization	

Chapter 13

Statistics

Statistics is a powerful tool for engineers, but comprehending statistics theories is often challenging for a junior college student. Statistics theories are easier to comprehend by means of statistics experiments, and MATLAB is a perfect tool to conduct statistics experiments, as demonstrated in this chapter. This chapter uses many functions that are part of the Statistics and Machine Learning Toolbox. This chapter assumes that you have a license that includes this toolbox.

13.1 Descriptive Statistics

13.1a Sampling

Thickness of Glass Sheets

[1] The manufacturing process of a type of glass sheets is well controlled such that the thickness of the glass is distributed normally and has a mean value μ of 500 micrometers and a standard deviation σ of 20 micrometers; μ is called the **population mean** and σ the **population standard deviation**. In a particular work day, 200 glass sheets are randomly sampled from the output of the production line and their thicknesses are measured (in micrometers) as follows. This section presents how to describe these sample data. ↓

510.75	536.68	454.82	517.24	506.38	473.85	491.33	506.85	571.57	555.39
473.00	560.70	514.51	498.74	514.29	495.90	497.52	529.79	528.18	528.34
513.43	475.85	514.34	532.60	509.78	520.69	514.54	493.93	505.88	484.25
517.77	477.06	478.62	483.81	441.11	528.77	506.50	484.90	527.41	465.77
497.96	495.17	506.38	506.26	482.70	499.40	496.70	512.55	521.87	522.19
482.73	501.55	475.72	477.73	499.86	530.65	484.61	507.43	495.49	522.35
478.22	500.65	511.05	522.01	530.88	501.72	470.17	485.15	478.77	547.01
487.69	514.96	496.15	517.77	484.70	471.95	471.55	509.76	496.45	496.08
528.39	505.83	503.96	531.75	483.91	513.93	516.70	495.13	504.31	476.68
477.04	502.10	514.45	551.71	486.66	503.75	498.35	461.34	491.22	464.11
516.81	482.24	502.00	489.11	506.07	487.99	509.80	514.79	534.24	496.12
457.23	483.21	527.09	478.56	519.22	502.48	528.73	460.78	496.05	475.84
558.16	516.50	527.58	478.84	490.63	494.55	521.97	494.44	514.03	458.96
492.92	483.53	468.46	510.16	505.64	500.67	473.33	522.55	507.00	494.02
500.46	494.76	465.00	494.29	483.37	480.42	476.87	489.33	459.95	519.28
510.40	499.60	499.30	484.04	520.37	497.34	485.71	527.03	495.50	488.22
494.12	483.04	477.60	550.52	533.11	506.15	474.86	482.69	496.47	515.83
473.36	453.40	471.02	506.67	507.83	509.03	497.39	503.67	490.48	517.24
472.77	509.10	483.03	493.30	511.06	520.78	477.65	525.21	513.20	498.64
496.10	495.65	493.94	500.46	501.03	516.52	530.54	509.34	495.81	512.50

Purposes of Sampling

[2] In this case, the distribution of the population is well established from a long-term observation: it is a normal distribution with a mean μ of 500 micrometers and a standard distribution σ of 20 micrometers. The purpose of the sampling here is to check if the manufacturing process on that particular day is normal. We may calculate the statistics of the sample data, e.g., the sample mean $\bar{x}$ and the sample standard deviation s, and compare them with the population mean μ and the population standard deviation σ. If they are significantly different, then the implication is that the process is abnormal and needs to be fixed immediately. We'll discuss these procedures in the later sections.

In other cases, when the distribution of the population is not known, the purposes of sampling may be to predict how the population is distributed, by calculating the statistics of the sample data, the sample mean $\bar{x}$ and the sample standard deviation s. We often assume that these sample statistics are the best estimates of the population statistics. Knowing the population distribution, we may, for example, calculate the defect rate of the products. We'll discuss the calculation of the defect rate in Section 13.2a. ↵

Example13_01a.m: Random Numbers Generation

[3] The 200 data in [1] is actually generated by the following commands: ↓

```
1   clear
2   rng(0)
3   data = normrnd(500,20,1,200);
```

About Example13_01a.m

[4] Line 3 generates a row vector of 200 data randomly sampled from a population which is **normally distributed** and its **mean** value μ is 500 and its **standard deviation** σ is 20. The sequence of numbers generated depends on a **seed**: the same **seed** produces the same sequence of numbers. Line 2 fixes the seed number (to zero) using the function `rng` (random number generator), to ensure that every time you run this script, the same sequence of the 200 data are generated.

We often use this technique to obtain a series of randomly sampled data representing measured experimental data. #

13.1b Descriptive Statistics

Example13_01b.m: Descriptive Statistics

[1] This script uses the data generated in Example13_01a.m, so please execute this script right after the execution of Example13_01a.m. This script introduces some basic terms in Descriptive Statistics, such as **mean** and **standard deviation**, producing a graphic output shown in [2], next page. ↵

```
mx = max(data)
mn = min(data)
edges = 410:20:590;
counts = histcounts(data, edges);
x = 420:20:580;
bar(x, counts, 0.95)
axis([400,600,0,90])
xlabel('Thickness (Micrometers)'), ylabel('Number of Occurrences')
text(x,counts+3,strsplit(num2str(counts)),'HorizontalAlignment','center')

text(405, 80, ['Number of Samples = ', num2str(length(data))])
text(405, 75, ['Maximum = ', num2str(mx)])
text(405, 70, ['Minimum = ', num2str(mn)])
text(405, 65, ['Mean = ', num2str(mean(data))])
text(405, 60, ['Standard Deviation = ', num2str(std(data))])

cumCounts = cumsum(counts);
yyaxis right
plot(x, cumCounts, 'Marker', 'o')
ylabel('Cumulative Occurrences')
text(x+2, cumCounts, strsplit(num2str(cumCounts)))
legend('Occurences', 'Cumulative Occurrences', 'Location', 'east')
title('Occurrences vs. Thickness')
```

[2] This is the graphic output of Example13_01b.m. The scale on the left vertical-axis (number of occurrences) is used by the bars, and the scale on the right vertical-axis (cumulative occurrences) is used by the line series. ↓

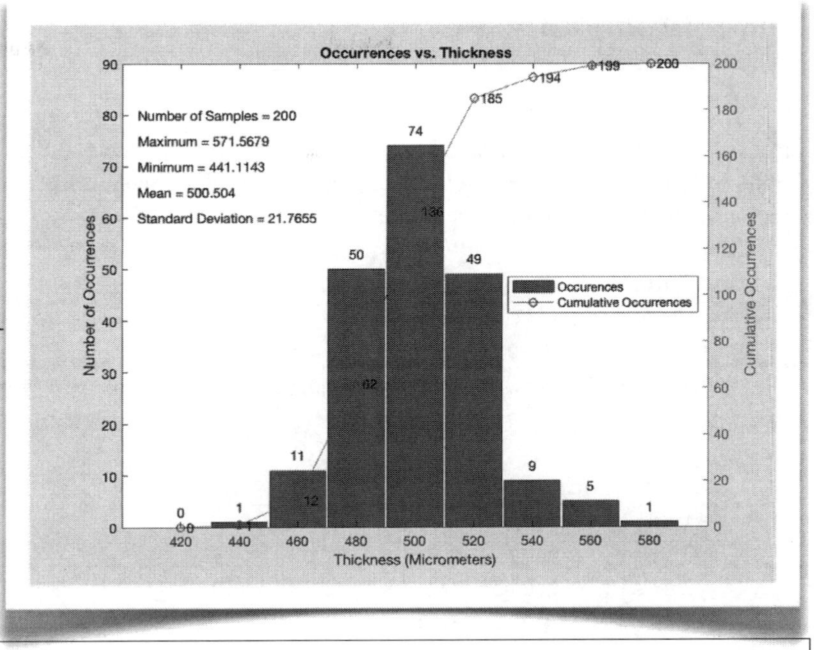

About Example13_01b.m

[3] This script consists of three parts: First, lines 1-9 produce a histogram, the bar graph in [2], including the annotated number of occurrences on the top of each bar; second, lines 11-15 annotate on the upper-left of the graphic area with statistic information; third, lines 17-23 produce a line plot, representing the cumulative sum of the occurences, its y-axis on the right side, overlapping the existing bar graph.

Lines 1-2 find the maximum and minimum of the data, so we can estimate the edges of each bin for the histogram. The text output on the **Command Window** shows that the maximum is 571.5679 and the minimum is 441.1143 (lines 12-13 display them on the upper-left of the graphic area). Line 4 counts the number of occurrences in each bin of the histogram, using `histcounts`. The argument `edges`, a vector [410, 430, 450, ... , 590] created in line 3, specifies the edges of each bin in terms of the horizontal axis: the first bin is 410-430, the second bin 430-450, and so on; there are 9 bins in total. The result `counts` is a row vector of 9 numbers. Line 5 creates a vector [420, 440, ... , 580] specifying the center of each bin: the first bin centers at 420, the second bin at 440, and so on. Line 6 plots the bar graph with 95% of the width (the default is 80%). Line 9 writes the number of occurrences on the top of each bar. Note that, in line 9, `num2str` converts the vector `counts` into a single string containing 9 numbers, and `strsplit` converts the string into a cell array of 9 strings, each containing a number.

Lines 11-15 annotate on the upper-left of the graphic area with statistic information. The functions `mean` (line 14) and `std` (line 15) calculate the mean and standard deviation, respectively, of the sample data. Let x_i, $i = 1, 2, \ldots, n$ be the sample data, then the mean $\bar{x}$ and the standard deviation s of the sample data are calculated, respectively, as follows:

$$\bar{x} = \frac{\sum_{i=1}^{n} x_i}{n}, \quad s = \sqrt{\frac{\sum_{i=1}^{n} (x_i - \bar{x})^2}{n-1}}$$

Line 17 calculates the cumulative sum of the occurrences. For example, `cumCounts(5)` stores the total number of occurrences in the first 5 bins. Obviously, the last number, `cumCounts(9)`, must be the total number of data, 200. Line 18 activates the right y-axis; subsequent graphics commands will target the right side. Line 19 plots the cumulative occurrences as a line series together with circular markers, using the right y-axis. Line 20 labels the right y-axis. Line 21 displays the number of cumulative occurrences along with the line series. Line 22 adds legends. Line 23 adds a title for the graph. #

13.1c Probability

Example13_01c.m: Probability

[1] This script uses data generated in Example13_01b.m, so please execute this script right after the execution of Example13_01b.m. This script introduces the terms such as **probability** and **cumulative probability**, producing a graphics output shown in [2]. ↓

```
1   figure
2   p = counts/length(data);
3   bar(x, p, 0.95)
4   xlabel('Thickness (Micrometers)'), ylabel('Probability')
5   text(x, p+0.015, strsplit(num2str(p)), 'HorizontalAlignment', 'center')
6
7   cumP = cumsum(p);
8   yyaxis right
9   plot(x, cumP, 'Marker', 'o')
10  ylabel('Cumulative Probability')
11  text(x+2, cumP, strsplit(num2str(cumP)))
12  legend('Probability', 'Cumulative Probability', 'Location', 'east')
13  title('Probability vs. Thickness')
```

[2] This is the output of Example13_01c.m. The vertical scales are probability (left; used by the bars) and cumulative probability (right; used by the line series). ↓

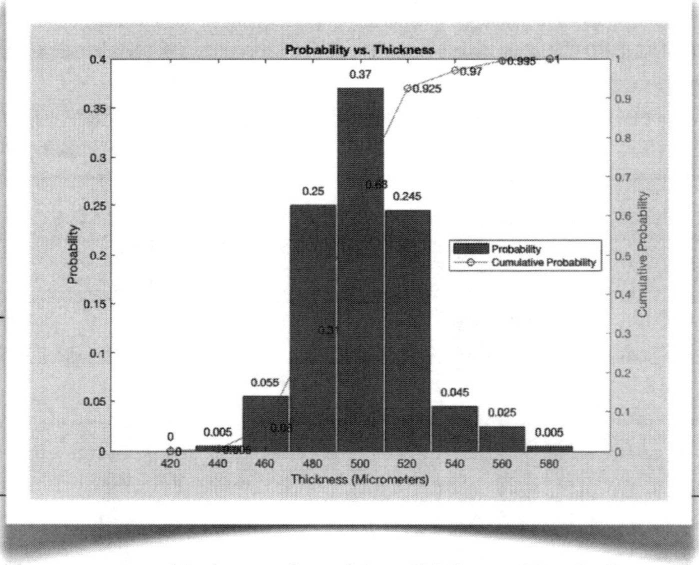

About Example13_01c.m

[3] Line 1 creates a new **Figure** window. Line 2 divides `counts` with the number of data (200), resulting in the **probability**, the fraction of the total number of data in each bin. For example, there are 37% of data in the 5th bin. That is, the sampling suggests that there is a 37% probability that the thickness of a glass sheet in the population is in the range 490-510 micrometers. Line 3 produces a bar plot of probability. Line 4 labels the axes. Line 5 displays the probability at the top of each bar.

Line 7 calculates the cumulative sum of the probability. For example, `cumP(5)` stores the total probability in the first 5 bins, i.e., the probability that the thickness is less than 510 micrometers. Obviously, the last number, `cumP(9)`, must be 100%. Line 8 activates the right *y*-axis. Line 9 plots the cumulative probability as a line series together with circular markers, using the right *y*-axis. Line 10 adds a label to the right y-axis. Line 11 displays the cumulative probability on the circular markers. Line 12 adds legends and line 13 adds a title for the graph. #

13.1d Probability Density

Example13_01d.m: Probability Density

[1] This script uses data generated in Example13_01c.m, so please execute this script right after the execution of Example13_01c.m. This script introduces the term **probability density**; it produces a graphic output shown in [2]. ↓

```
1   figure
2   pd = p/20;
3   bar(x, pd, 0.95)
4   xlabel('Thickness (Micrometers)'), ylabel('Probability Density')
5   text(x, pd+0.00075, strsplit(num2str(pd)), 'HorizontalAlignment','center')
6
7   cumPD = cumsum(pd)*20;
8   yyaxis right
9   plot(x, cumPD, 'Marker', 'o')
10  ylabel('Cumulative Probability')
11  text(x+2, cumPD, strsplit(num2str(cumPD)))
12  legend('Probability Density', 'Cumulative Probability', 'Location','east')
13  title('Probability Density vs. Thickness')
```

[2] This is the output of Example13_01d.m. The vertical scales are probability density (left; used by the bars) and cumulative probability (right; used by the line series). ↓

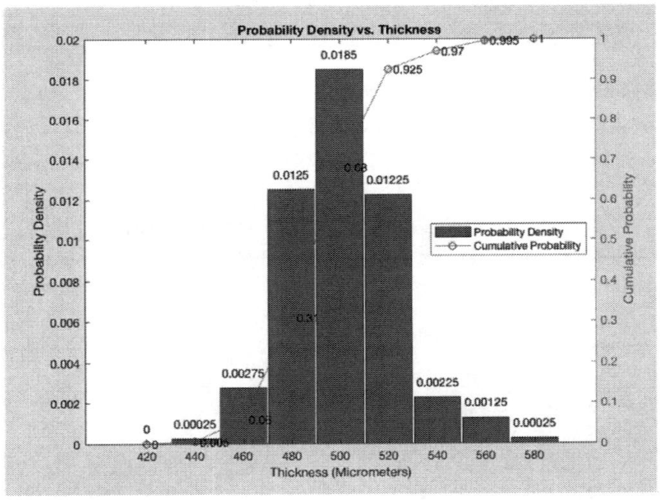

About Example13_01d.m

[13] Line 1 creates a new **Figure** window. Line 2 divides the probability `p` with the width of the bins (20), resulting in the **probability density**. Line 3 produces a bar plot of probability density. Line 4 labels the axes. Line 5 displays the probability density on the top of each bar. The interpretation of the probability density is that, for example, there are 1.85% of data in a unit width around the neighborhood of 500. The area of a bar, i.e., the multiplication of its probability density and its width, is the probability in the bin.

Line 7 calculates the cumulative sum of the probability density and then multiplies it by the width of bins, resulting in the cumulative probability. The variable `cumPD` stores the same numbers as `cumP` (of Example13_01c.m), the cumulative probability. Again, the last number, `cumPD(9)`, must be 100%. Lines 8-13 are similar to the lines 8-13 in Example13_01c.m, last page. #

Table 13.1a Random Number Generation	
Functions	Description
`x = rand(row, col)`	Generates random numbers of uniform distribution
`x = randi(imax, row, col)`	Generates random integer numbers of uniform distribution
`x = randn(row, col)`	Generates random numbers of standard normal distribution
`x = normrnd(mu, sigma, row, col)`	Generates random numbers of normal distribution
`rng(seed)`	Controls random number generation
Details and More: Help>MATLAB>Mathematics>Random Number Generation	

Table 13.1b Descriptive Statistics	
Functions	Description
`m = mean(data)`	Average or mean value of an array of numbers
`s = std(data)`	Standard deviation of an array of numbers
`v = var(data)`	Variance of an array of numbers
`counts = histcounts(data, edges)`	Histogram bin counts
`[counts,edges] = histcounts(data,nbins)`	Histogram bin counts
`histogram(data,edges)`	Histogram plot
`histogram(data,nbins)`	Histogram plot
`histfit(data,nbins)`	Histogram with a distribution fit
Details and More: Help>MATLAB>Data Import and Analysis>Descriptive Statistics	

13.2 Normal Distribution

13.2a Normal Distribution

[1] The Statistics and Machine Learning Toolbox supports many probability distributions; each has a set of functions to work with. In this section, with the normal distribution as an example, we demonstrate the use of these functions. The functions to work with the normal distribution are summarized in Table 13.2, page 493.

A normal distribution has a **probability density function** (pdf; in MATLAB, it is called a **probability distribution function**) of the form

$$\text{pdf} = f(x) = \frac{1}{\sigma\sqrt{2\pi}} e^{\frac{-(x-\mu)^2}{2\sigma^2}} \qquad \text{(a)}$$

where the parameters μ and σ are the mean and the standard deviation, respectively, of the distribution. The geometrical interpretation of the mean and standard deviation are given in 13.2b, pages 492-493. ↓

Example13_02a.m: Normal Distribution

[2] This script produces text output shown in [3] and graphic output shown in [4-6], next page. ↵

```
clear
rng(0)
mu = 500; sigma = 20; n = 200;
data = normrnd(mu, sigma, 1, n);
normplot(data)
[xbar,s] = normfit(data)

x = linspace(mu-5*sigma, mu+5*sigma);
pdf = normpdf(x, mu, sigma);
cdf = normcdf(x, mu, sigma);
figure
plot(x, pdf)
yyaxis right, plot(x, cdf), grid on
legend('Probability Distribution Function', ...
    'Cumulative Distribution Function', ...
    'Location', 'southeast')
title('Normal Distribution: mu = 500, sigma = 20')
defectRate1 = normcdf(440,mu,sigma) + (1-normcdf(560,mu,sigma))

x = linspace(-5, 5);
pdf = normpdf(x);
cdf = normcdf(x);
figure
plot(x, pdf), x, cdf)
yyaxis right, plot(x, cdf), grid on
legend('Probability Distribution Function', ...
    'Cumulative Distribution Function', ...
    'Location', 'southeast')
title('Standard Normal Distribution: mu = 0, sigma = 1')
defectRate2 = normcdf(-3) + (1-normcdf(3))
```

```
xbar =
  500.5040
s =
    21.7655
defectRate1 =
      0.0027
defectRate2 =
      0.0027
```

[3] The text output of Example13_02a.m (lines 6, 18, and 30). ↓

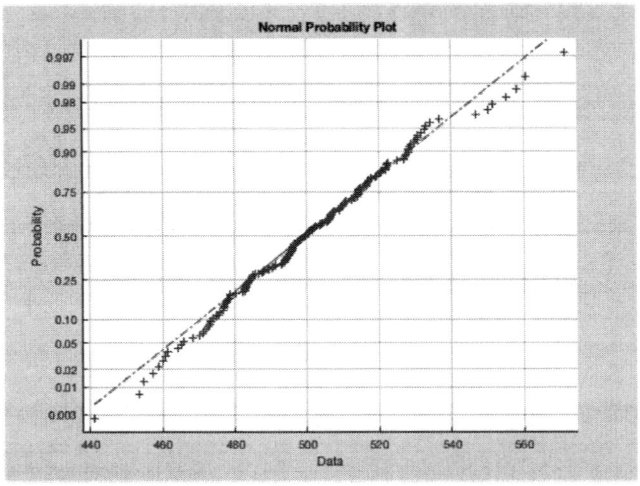

[4] Normality of the data (line 5). ↓

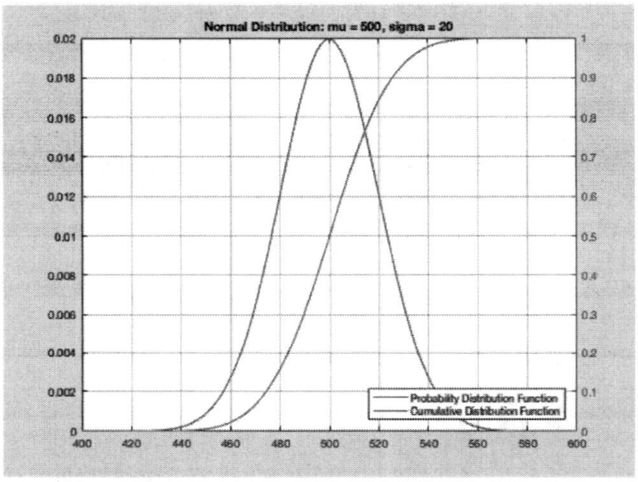

[5] Probability density function (pdf) and cumulative distribution function (cdf) of a normal distribution (line 12). ↓

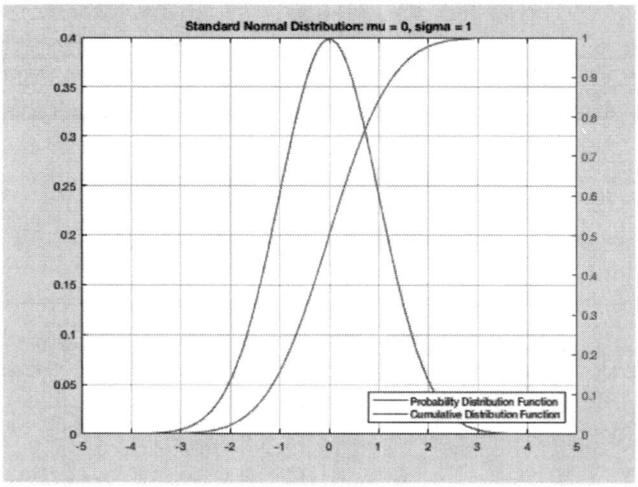

[6] Probability density function (pdf) and cumulative distribution function (cdf) of a standard normal distribution (line 24). ↵

About Example13_02a.m

[7] Lines 2-4 generate the 200 data, listed in 13.1a[1] (page 484) and explained in 13.1a[3-4] (page 485). In line 5, the function `normplot` is used to test if the sample data are indeed distributed normally. It generates a **normal probability plot** (see [4], last page). The straight line in [4] is a special plot of the cumulative distribution function, in which the vertical scale is twisted (transformed) so that the cdf becomes a straight line (the cdf curve in [5] is plotted using an untwisted scale). The 200 data are then marked in the graphic area. The closer to the straight line, the data are more normally distributed. We may conclude that the 200 data are indeed distributed normally.

In line 6, the function `normfit` fits the sample data to the pdf in Eq. (a), page 490, which is a two-parameter model; the output `xbar` and `s` (see lines 31-34, last page) are the parameters that best fit the data; they are called **sample mean** and **sample standard deviation**, respectively. They also can be calculated using the formulas in 13.1b[3], page 486 (see lines 14-15, Example13_01b.m, page 485).

Lines 8-17 produce a graph shown in [5], last page, which represents the population distribution of the glass thickness. The blue-colored curve is the pdf (see [1]) and the orange-colored curve is the cdf (cumulative distribution function), defined as

$$\text{cdf} = F(x) = \int_{-\infty}^{x} f(\tau)d\tau$$

Defect Rate

Assume that the specification for the glass thickness is 500 ± 60 micrometers. That is, a glass sheet of thickness less than 440 micrometers or greater than 560 micrometers is regarded as a defect product. Then the defect rate is the area under the pdf curve in which the thickness is less than 440 or greater than 560. Line 18 calculates the defect rate. The result is 0.0027 (see lines 35-36 in [3], last page).

Lines 20-29 produce a graph shown in [6], which is a **standard normal distribution**, defined as a normal distribution with $\mu = 0$ and $\sigma = 1$. Line 30 demonstrates a second way of calculating the defect rate. Since 440 and 560 in the horizontal axis of [5] correspond to -3 and +3, respectively, in the horizontal axis of [6], the defect rate is the area under the pdf curve of [6] in which the thickness is less than -3 or greater than +3. The output of line 30 is also 0.0027 (see lines 37-38 in [3], last page). #

13.2b Geometrical Interpretation of Mean, Standard Deviation, and Variance

[1] Let $f(x)$ be a probability density function. It can be shown (see Example13_02b.m, next page) that the mean μ is the x-value of the **centroid** of the area under the curve of $f(x)$, i.e.,

$$\mu = \frac{1}{A}\int_{-\infty}^{\infty} x\,dA = \int_{-\infty}^{\infty} xf(x)dx \qquad \text{(a)}$$

where $A = 1$ is the area under the curve of $f(x)$.

The square of the standard deviation, σ^2, is called the **variance**. It can be proved (see Example13_02b,m, next page) that σ^2 is the **moment of inertia** (*See: Wikipedia>Moment of Inertia*) about the vertical line passing through the **centroid**, i.e.,

$$\sigma^2 = \int_{-\infty}^{\infty} (x-\mu)^2\,dA = \int_{-\infty}^{\infty} (x-\mu)^2 f(x)dx \qquad \text{(b)}$$

The **standard deviation** σ is thus the **radius of gyration** (*See: Wikipedia>Radius of Gyration*) about the vertical line passing through the **centroid**.

Using the normal distribution in this section (μ = 500 micrometers, σ = 20 micrometers) as an example, Example13-02b.m (next page) confirms these interpretations. ↵

Example13_02b.m: Mean and Standard Deviation

[2] This script, producing output shown in [3], confirms the interpretations in [1], last page. ↓

```
1   clear
2   mu = 500; sigma = 20;
3   fun1 = @(x) x.*normpdf(x, mu, sigma);
4   fun2 = @(x) (x-mu).^2.*normpdf(x, mu, sigma);
5   mean = integral(fun1, -1000, 1000)
6   stdev = sqrt(integral(fun2, -1000, 1000))
```

[3] The output of Example13-02b.m. ↓

```
7   mean =
8     500.0000
9   stdev =
10     20.0000
```

About Example13_02b.m

[4] Line 3 defines a function for the integrand in Eq. (a), last page, and line 5 performs numerical integrations according to the formulas in Eq. (a), obtaining the **mean**. Line 4 defines a function for the integrand in Eq. (b), last page, and line 6 performs numerical integrations according to the formulas in Eq. (b), obtaining the **standard deviation**. The results [3], the mean and the standard deviation that we used as input arguments (line 2), confirm the interpretations in [1], last page. Note that, in the formulas Eqs. (a, b), the integration is from $-\infty$ to ∞. In lines 5-6, we integrate from -1000 to +1000, resulting in pretty good accuracy. #

Table 13.2 Normal Distribution

Functions	Description
`data = normrnd(mu, sigma, row, col)`	Generates random numbers of normal distribution
`normplot(data)`	Generate a normal probability plot
`[xbar,s] = normfit(data)`	Normal parameter estimates
`pd = normpdf(x, mu, sigma)`	Returns probability density of normal distribution
`p = normcdf(x, mu, sigma)`	Returns probability of normal distribution
`x = norminv(p, mu, sigma)`	Returns x-value of normal distribution

Details and More: Help>Statistics and Machine Learning Toolbox>Probability Distributions> Continuous Distributions>Normal Distribution

13.3 Central Limit Theory

13.3a Dice-Throwing Experiments

[1] Imagine that you are conducting a series of dice-throwing experiments. First, you throw one die at a time ($m = 1$) and record the score. After n trials (n is large, e.g., 50,000), you should have a flat distribution like [3] (next page), in which the horizontal axis is the scores and the vertical axis is the probability density. Since the probabilities for 1, 2, 3, 4, 5, or 6 are equal to 1/6 and the width of each bin is 1.0, the probability density is 1/6. The mean and the variance are also displayed on the graphic area.

Second, you throw two dice at a time ($m = 2$) and record the averaged scores; the resulting distribution is shown in [4]. This process continues for 3, 5, and 10 dice at a time ($m = 3$, 5, and 10), and the resulting distributions of the averaged scores are shown in [5-7], respectively.

Several facts can be observed from the series of experiments: First, as the sample size m increases, the average scores tend to distribute more normally. Second, the mean values remain almost the same. Third, the variances decrease and can be predicted:

$$\sigma_{\bar{x}}^2 \approx \frac{\sigma^2}{m} \text{ (or, equivalently, } \sigma_{\bar{x}} \approx \frac{\sigma}{\sqrt{m}}\text{)} \qquad \text{(a)}$$

where σ^2 is the variance for the original scores ($m = 1$), and $\sigma_{\bar{x}}^2$ is the variance for the averaged scores. In our cases, the variances (see the variances in [3-7]) are, respectively,

$$1.4526 \approx \frac{2.9224}{2},\ 0.9594 \approx \frac{2.9224}{3},\ 0.57982 \approx \frac{2.9224}{5},\ 0.29175 \approx \frac{2.9224}{10}$$

As m increases, Eq. (a) tends to be more accurate (of course, n must be large enough).

The above conclusions drawn from the observation of the dice-throwing experiments is a special case of the *Central Limit Theory*, which we'll present in 13.3b[1] (page 496) in a more formal way. ↓

Example13_03a.m: Dice-Throwing Experiments

[2] This script simulates the series of experiments described in [1], producing the graphs [3-7], next page. ↵

```
clear
n = 50000;
rng(0)
for m = [1,2,3,5,10]
    data = mean(randi(6,m,n),1);
    x = 1:(1/m):6;
    edges = (1-1/m/2):(1/m):(6+1/m/2);
    pd = histcounts(data,edges)/n/(1/m);
    figure
    bar(x, pd, 1.0, 'FaceColor', 'none', 'EdgeColor', 'k')
    axis([0,7,0,0.8])
    text(5, 0.30, ['Mean = ', num2str(mean(data))])
    text(5, 0.25, ['Variance = ', num2str(var(data))])
    xlabel(['Average Scores of ', num2str(m), ' Dice'])
    ylabel('Probability Density')
    title(['Distribution of Average Scores from Throwing ',num2str(m),' Dice'])
end
```

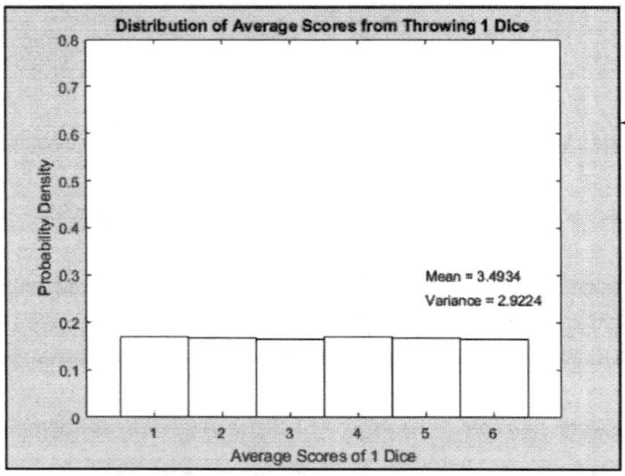

[3] $m = 1$. ↓

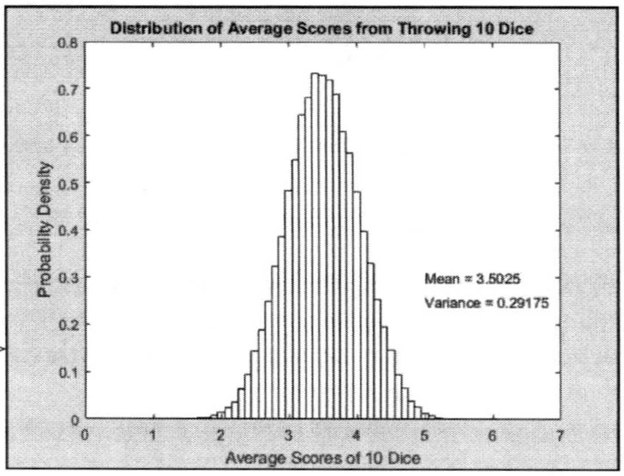

[7] $m = 10$. ↘

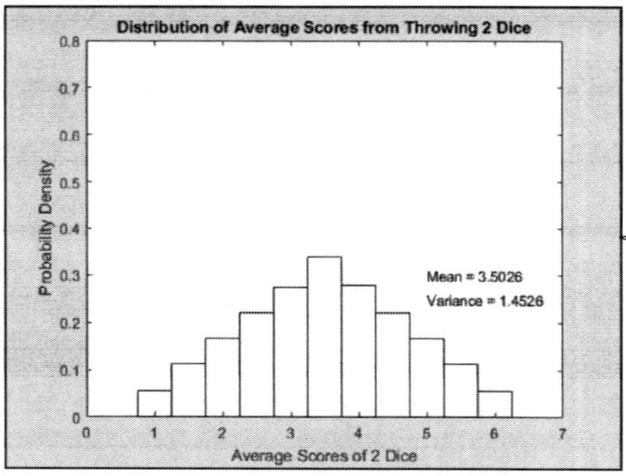

[4] $m = 2$. ↓

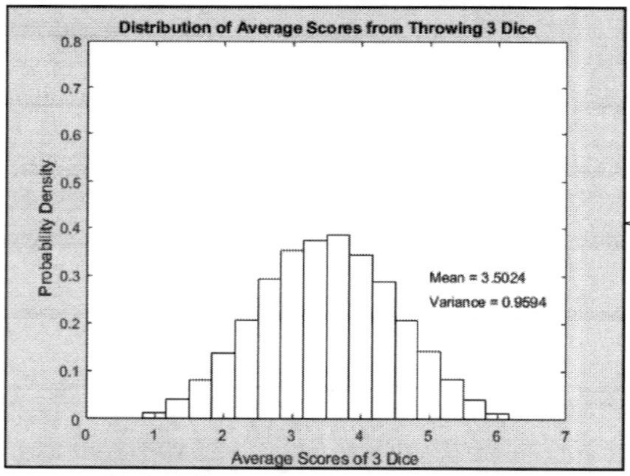

[5] $m = 3$. ↓

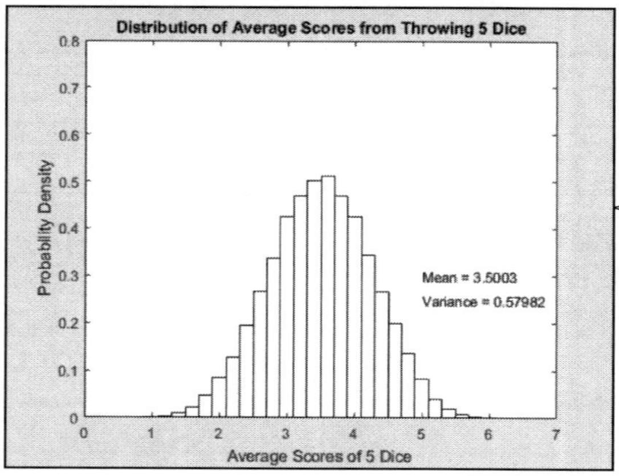

[6] $m = 5$. ↑

About Example13_03a.m

[8] We use $n = 50{,}000$ (line 2) to make sure it is large enough. We also set the seed of the random number generator to zero (line 3) to make sure the results are the same each time you run this program.

Each pass of the `for`-loop (lines 4-17) produces a graph for each m, $m = 1, 2, 3, 5$, and 10 (see [3-7]).

In line 5, the function `randi` generates an m-by-n matrix containing normally distributed integer numbers ranging from 1 to 6. The function `mean` then averages the numbers along the first dimension (row dimension), resulting in a row vector of n numbers, where $n = 50{,}000$ (line 2). Note that the averaged numbers may not be integer numbers; but they fall in a series of specific values. For example, when $m = 2$, the possible values are 1, 1.5, 2, 2.5, 3, 3.5, 4, 4.5, 5, 5.5, or 6. In a bar plot, each bin centers at these numbers, and the width of each bin is $1/m$ (line 6). Line 7 sets up the edges of the bins. Note that there are $(6-1)m+1$ bins in total. The number of edges is one more than the number of bins.

In line 8, the function `histcounts` counts the occurrences in each bin. Each occurrence is divided by n, resulting in a probability. The probability is then divided by the width of the bins ($1/m$), and the final result `pd` is the probability density.

Lines 9-16 then produce a graph ([3-7]). #

13.3b Central Limit Theory

[1] Let x_1, x_2, ... , x_m be randomly sampled data taken from a population whose mean is μ and variance σ^2, and $\overline{x}$ be the average of the sample data (i.e., $\overline{x} = \sum_{i=1}^{m} x_i \Big/ m$), then as m increases, the distribution of z,

$$z = \frac{\overline{x} - \mu}{\sigma/\sqrt{m}} \tag{a}$$

approaches a standard normal distribution.

Note that z is obtained by shifting $\overline{x}$ an amount of the mean $\mu_{\overline{x}}$ (which is equal to μ) and scaling with the standard deviation $\sigma_{\overline{x}}$ (which is equal to $\sigma/\sqrt{m}$). This process is called a standardization, since z has a mean of 0 and a standard deviation of 1, a standard normal distribution (13.2a[7], page 492).

For example, let x_1, x_2, ... , x_{10} be the scores from throwing 10 dice. Each x_i has mean $\mu = 3.5$ and variance $\sigma^2 = 2.9224$ (see 13.3a[3], last page). The distribution of $\overline{x} = \sum_{i=1}^{10} x_i \Big/ 10$ is a normal distribution with mean and variance approximately $\mu_{\overline{x}} = 3.5$ and $\sigma_{\overline{x}}^2 = 2.9224/10 = 0.29224$, respectively (see 13.3a[7], last page), and $z = \dfrac{\overline{x} - 3.5}{\sqrt{0.29224}}$ has a standard normal distribution. ↓

Example13_03b.m: Demonstration of Central Limit Theory

[2] Using the dice-throwing experiments, this script, producing a graphic output shown in [3] (next page), confirms that z, defined in Eq. (a), indeed approaches a standard normal distribution. ↵

```
clear
n = 50000;
rng(0)
data = randi(6,1,n);
mu = mean(data);
sigma = std(data);

m = 10;
data = mean(randi(6,m,n));
data = (data - mu)/(sigma/sqrt(m));
z = ((1:(1/m):6)-mu)/(sigma/sqrt(m));
edges = (((1-1/m/2):(1/m):(6+1/m/2))-mu)/(sigma/sqrt(m));
pd = histcounts(data,edges)/n/(1/m/(sigma/sqrt(m)));
plot(z,pd,'o'), grid on, hold on
axis([-5,5,0,0.5])
x = linspace(-5,5);
plot(x, normpdf(x))
legend('Simulated Data', 'Standard Normal Distribution')
area = trapz(z,pd);
text(0,0.1,['Area = ', num2str(area)], 'HorizontalAlignment', 'center')
xlabel('z = (xbar-\mu)/(\sigma/\surdm)')
ylabel('Probability Density')
title('Demonstration of Central Limit Theory')
```

[3] This is the output of Example13_03b. ↓

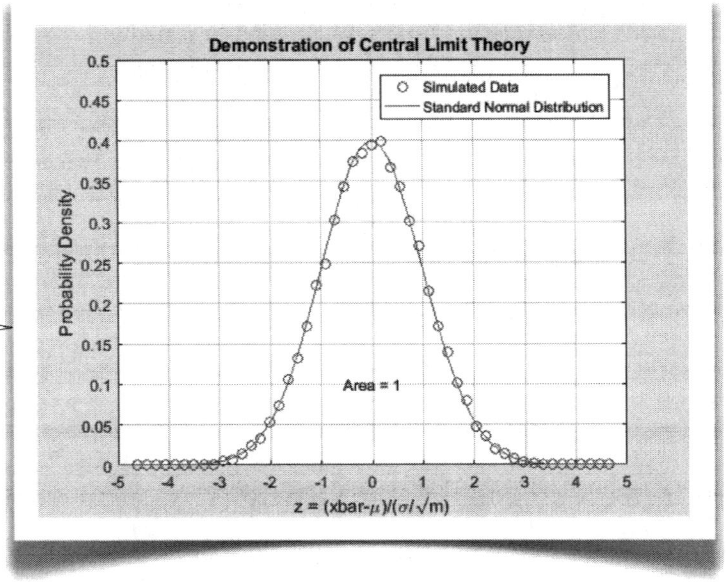

About Example13_03b.m

[4] Example13_03b.m is modified from Example13_03a.m as follows: First, it is a particular case, in which m is set to 10. Second, instead of a bar plot, it produces a line plot. Third, the data are standardized. Fourth, the simulated data are plotted as circular markers and overlapped on a standard normal distribution curve.

Lines 2-6 simulate the throwing of a die 50,000 times and calculate its mean μ and variance σ^2.

Lines 8-9 simulate the throwing of 10 dice 50,000 times and calculate the averages. The vector `data` now contains 50,000 values representing the values of $\bar{x}$. Line 10 standardizes $\bar{x}$ by shifting with the mean μ and scaling with the standard deviation $\sigma_{\bar{x}}$ so that it now has a mean 0 and a variance 1.

Lines 11-14 generate a pdf-versus-z plot with circular markers (see [3]). Before constructing a pdf, occurrences in each bin must be counted. Lines 11 and 12 prepare the centers and the edges of the bins; note that both the centers and the edges need to be standardized by shifting with the mean μ and scaling with the standard deviation $\sigma_{\bar{x}}$. In line 13, occurrences in each bin are counted using `histcounts` and then divided by the width of the bin to obtain the probability density in each bin. Line 14 plots the pdf with circular markers. Line 15 adjusts the axis limits.

Lines 16-17 plot a standard normal distribution curve on top of the simulated data (circular markers). Line 18 adds legends to the graph. Lines 19-20 calculate and display the area under the pdf of the simulated data; it is indeed 100%. Lines 21-22 label the axes. Line 23 adds a title to the graph.

This confirms the Central Limit Theory described in [1], last page. #

13.4 Confidence Interval

Thickness of Glass Sheets

[1] Recall that, in 13.1, the thickness of the glass sheets has a population mean $\mu = 500\ \mu\text{m}$ and a population standard deviation $\sigma = 20\ \mu\text{m}$, and the thickness of the samples of 200 glass sheets taken on a particular day has a sample mean $\bar{x} = 500.504\ \mu\text{m}$ and a sample standard deviation $s = 21.7655\ \mu\text{m}$ (see 13.1b[2], page 486). We want to determine whether the manufacturing process on that particular day is normal or not. We may answer this question by checking if the difference between the two means

$$\bar{x} - \mu = 0.504\ \mu\text{m}$$

is within the error. If so, then we have no reason to say that the manufacturing process on that particular day is abnormal. Now the problem is: what is the error? ↓

Estimation of Errors: Confidence Intervals

[2] Each numerical data (either measured data or calculated data) has an error. For example, each of the 200 measured thicknesses has a standard error $\sigma = 20\ \mu\text{m}$. A standard deviation is also called a **standard error**. The implication of the "standard" error is that, for each x of the 200 measured data, there is a probability of 68.27% (which is calculated by `normcdf(1)-normcdf(-1)`; see the figure below) that its "real" value falls in the interval between $x \pm \sigma$. For example, for the measured data 510.75 (the first data in 13.1a[1], page 484), all we can say is that there is a probability of 68.27% that the "real" value falls in the interval between $510.75 \pm 20\ \mu\text{m}$. The uncertainty is due to the noises, factors that are uncontrollable, e.g., environmental temperature variations, material property variations, etc.

The interval between $x \pm \sigma$ is called a **confidence interval** and the corresponding probability is called a **confidence level**. The two values $x \pm \sigma$ are called the **confidence limits**. A confidence interval is a way to express the error of a data, describing how reliable the data is. The standard error is a particular confidence interval, in which the corresponding confidence level is 68.27%, probability between $x \pm \sigma$. The standard error is also called the one-standard-deviation confidence interval, and 68.27% is called the one-standard-deviation confidence level. Similarly, the two-standard-deviation confidence level is 95.45%, calculated by `normcdf(2)-normcdf(-2)`; the three-standard-deviation confidence level is 99.73%, calculated by `normcdf(3)-normcdf(-3)` (see the figure below). Note that the discussion in this section assumes that the data are distributed normally. The concepts can be extended for data of other distributions.

On the other hand, for a specific confidence level, we may calculate the corresponding confidence interval. For example, for 95% confidence level, the confidence limits are $x \pm 1.96\sigma$, where 1.96 is calculated by `norminv((1-0.95)/2)`. In general, for a confidence level *CL*, the confidence limits are

$$x \pm \text{norminv}\left(\frac{1\text{-}CL}{2}\right) \times \sigma$$

In engineering applications, the most frequently used confidence level is 95%, and the corresponding confidence interval is called the 95% confidence interval. And, while σ is called the standard error, 1.96σ (which is approximately equal to 2σ) is called a 95%-confidence-level error. ↵

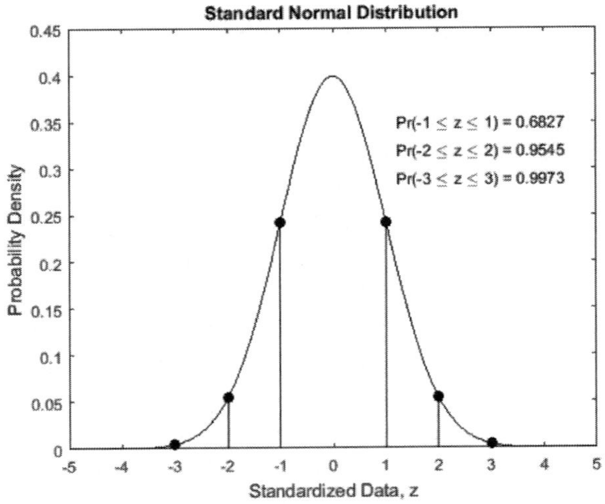

95%-Confidence-Level Error of $(\bar{x}-\mu)$

[3] The sample mean $\bar{x}$ is the average of 200 data ($m = 200$); each data has a standard error $\sigma = 20$ μm. According to Central Limit Theory, the standard error of $\bar{x}$ is $\sigma_{\bar{x}} = \sigma/\sqrt{m} = 20/\sqrt{200} = \sqrt{2}$. The population mean μ can be viewed as an average of large number of data, so the standard error of μ is $\sigma/\sqrt{\infty} = 0$; i.e., μ can be viewed as an exact value. Therefore, the standard error of $(\bar{x}-\mu)$ is the same as that of $\bar{x}$, i.e., $\sigma_{\bar{x}}$. And its 95% confidence-level error is $1.96\sigma_{\bar{x}} = 1.96\sqrt{2} = 2.77$ μm.

Since the difference of the two means, 0.504 μm (see [1]), is within the 95%-confidence-level error 2.77 μm, we may conclude that, with 95% confidence level, the manufacturing process on that particular day is normal. This concept is graphically shown in [4, 5]. The graph is generated by Example13_04.m [6]. ↓

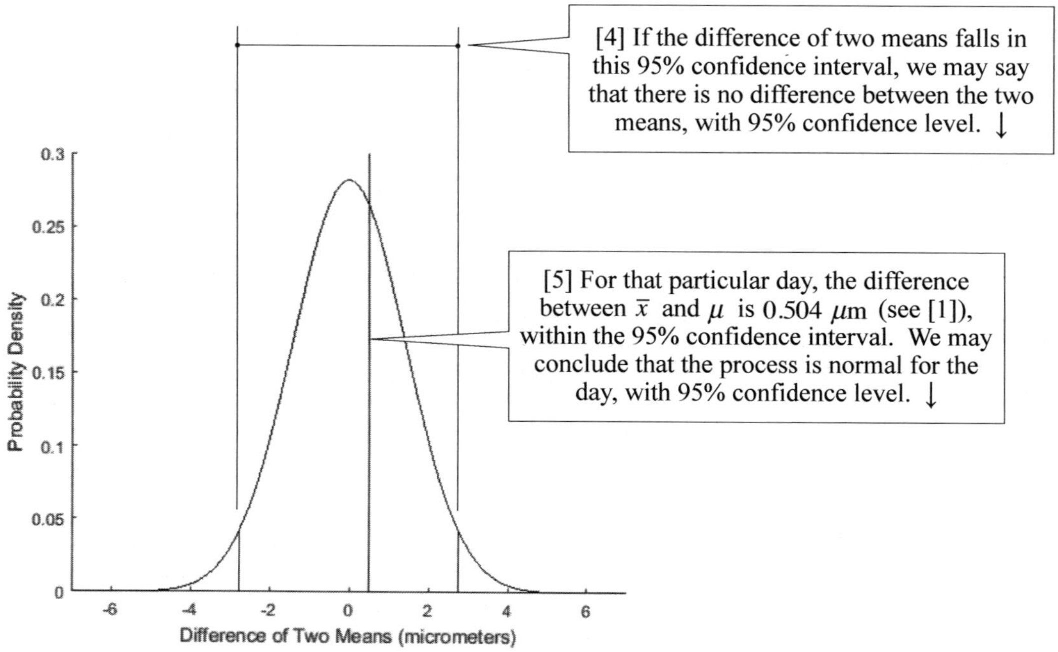

Example13_04.m: Confidence Interval

[6] This script generates the graph shown in [4-5]. #

```
clear
x = linspace(-7,7); sigma = sqrt(2);
plot(x,normpdf(x,0,sigma),'k'), hold on, box off
h = gcf; h.Color = 'w';
axis([-7, 7,0,0.3])
z = norminv(0.025,0,sigma); pd = normpdf(z,0,sigma);
plot([z,z], [0,pd], 'k')
z = norminv(0.975,0,sigma); pd = normpdf(z,0,sigma);
plot([z,z], [0,pd], 'k')
z = 0.504;
plot([z,z], [0,0.3], 'k')
xlabel('Difference of Two Means (micrometers)')
ylabel('Probability Density')
```

13.5 Chi-Square Distribution

13.5a Chi-Square Distribution

[1] In the last section, we determined whether the process is normal by comparing the sample mean and the population mean. Since the difference is within a 95% confidence interval, we conclude that the process is normal with a 95% confidence level.

Another way to test whether the process is normal is by comparing the sample variance and the population variance. If the sample variance is quite different from the population variable, then the implication is that the samples may come from a different population or the population has been "contaminated," and the process is not normal.

To do this, we need to know the relation between the sample variance and the population variance. ↓

[2] Let x_1, x_2, ... , x_m be random samples taken from a population of normal distribution with mean μ and variance σ^2. Let s^2 be the sample variance. Then, the quantity

$$\chi^2 = \frac{(m-1)s^2}{\sigma^2} \tag{a}$$

has a chi-square distribution with $m-1$ degrees of freedom.

We use Example13_05a.m [3] to manifest this theory. ↓

Example13_05a.m: Chi-Square Distribution

[3] This script generates chi-square distributions (see [4-6], next page). If the sample size is 200 (replacing 5 with `200` in line 2, i.e., `m = 200`), the chi-square distributions becomes that shown in [7]. ↵

```
1   clear
2   mu = 500; sigma = 20; m = 5;
3   n = 50000; rng(0)
4   data = normrnd(mu, sigma, m, n);
5   s = std(data);
6   chi2 = (m-1)*s.^2/sigma^2;
7   mx = max(chi2); bins = 40;
8   width = mx/bins;
9   edges = 0:width:mx;
10  pd = histcounts(chi2, edges)/n/width;
11  x = width/2:width:mx-width/2;
12  plot(x, pd, 'ko'), hold on
13  h = gcf; h.Color = 'w';
14  x = linspace(0,mx);
15  pd = chi2pdf(x, m-1);
16  plot(x, pd, 'k-')
17  xlabel('Chi-Square')
18  ylabel('Probability Density')
19  title(['Chi-Square Distribution with ', ...
20      num2str(m-1), ' Degrees of Freedom'])
21  legend('Simulation Data', 'By MATLAB Function')
```

[4] This is the output of Example13_5a.m. →

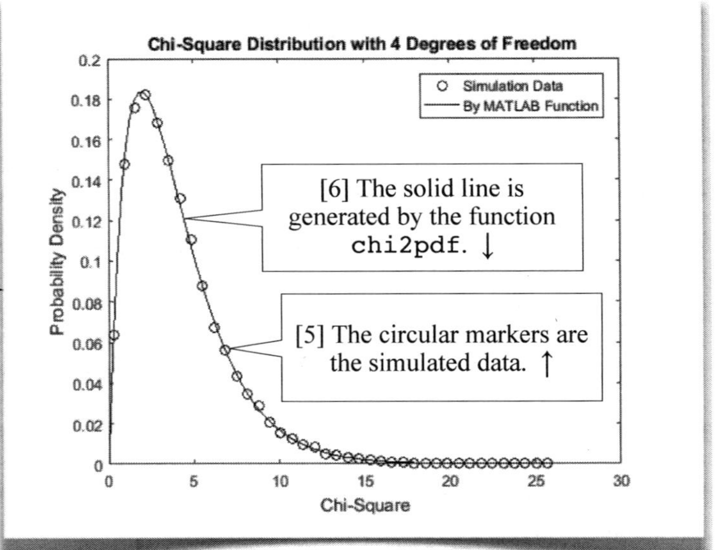

[6] The solid line is generated by the function `chi2pdf`. ↓

[5] The circular markers are the simulated data. ↑

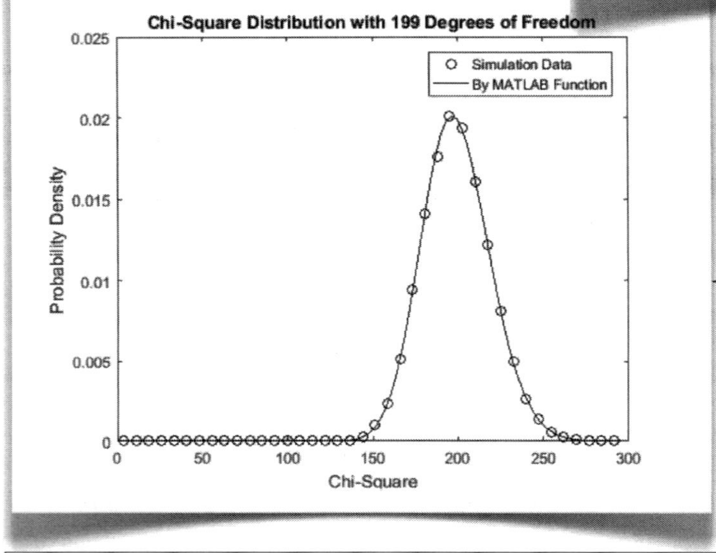

[7] If the sample size is 200 (`m = 200` in line 2), the output of Example13_05a.m is like this, approaching a normal distribution. ↓

About Example13_05a.m

[8] In line 2, we assume a population mean $\mu = 500$, a population standard deviation $\sigma = 20$, and a sample size $m = 5$. We'll generate 50,000 data, using a fixed seed (line 3).

Line 4 generates a set of 5-by-50,000 matrix containing data which are randomly sampled from a population of mean $\mu = 500$ and standard deviation $\sigma = 20$. Line 5 calculates the standard deviation for each column of the data; `s` is a row vector of 50,000 elements. Line 6 calculates the chi-square values from the standard deviations, according to the Eq. (a), page 500; `chi2` is also a row vector of 50,000 elements.

In lines 7-12, the 50,000 chi-square values are divided into 40 bins, the number of occurrences in each bin is counted, and the probability density of each bin is calculated and displayed using circular markers (see [5]).

Lines 14-15 plot a curve of chi-square distribution with m -1 degrees of freedom, using the function `chi2pdf` (see [6]). The chi-square distribution of the simulated data [5] matches the chi-square distribution generated by the function `chi2pdf` [6].

This script can be used to plot chi-square distributions of any sample size. For example, in 13.1a[1] (page 484), the sample size is 200 and the chi-square distributions are shown as [7]. It may be observed that, as the sample size increases, the chi-square distribution approaches a normal distribution. #

13.5b Application of Chi-Square Distribution

[1] Back to the problem posed in 13.5a[1], page 500: how can we determine whether the process is normal by comparing the sample variance with the population variance? We calculate the chi-square value, Eq. 13.5a(a), page 500, and check if it is within the 95% confidence interval. If it is, we may conclude that the process is normal with 95% confidence level.

Recall that $s = 21.7655$ (13.1b[2], page 486) and $\sigma = 20$ (13.1a[4], page 485). The chi-square value is

$$\chi^2 = \frac{(m-1)s^2}{\sigma^2} = \frac{(200-1)21.7655^2}{20^2} = 235.68$$

Knowing the chi-square distribution, we may calculate the 95% confidence interval. The confidence limits are calculated by

```
chi2inv(0.025,199)
chi2inv(0.975,199)
```

which are 161.83 and 239.96, respectively.

Since the chi-square value 235.68 is within the 95% confidence interval as shown in [2-3], we conclude that the process is normal for the day, with 95% confidence level.

The graph [2-3] is generated by Example13_05b.m. ↓

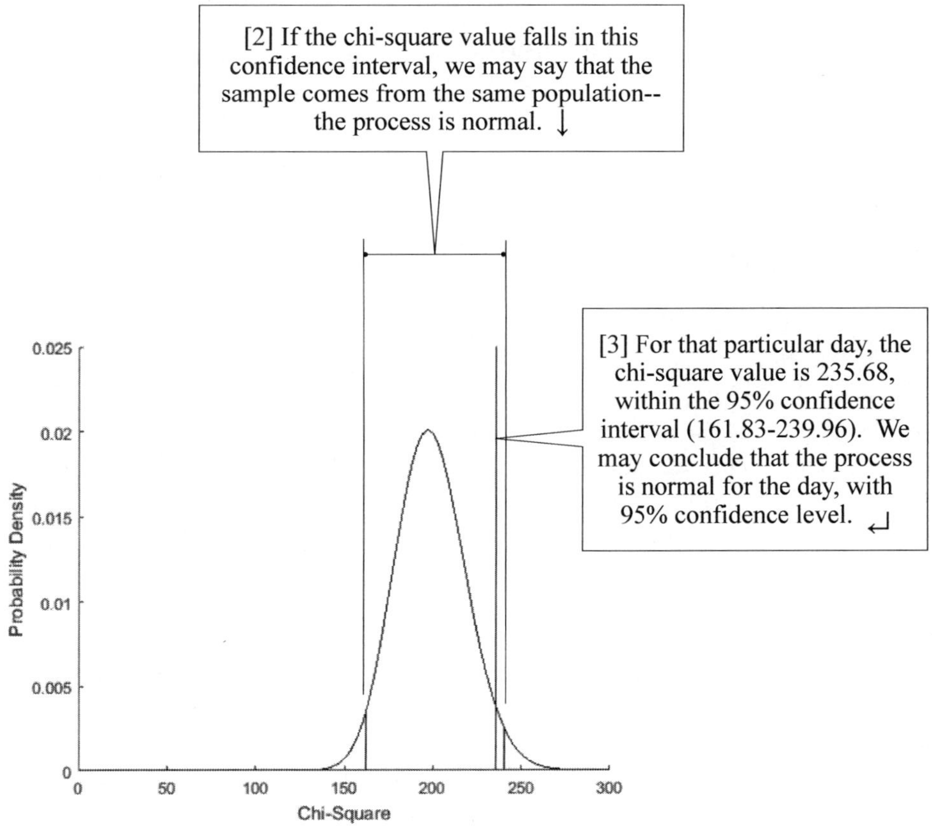

Example13_05b.m: Application of Chi-Square Distribution

[4] This script generates a graph shown in [2-3] (last page) and text output shown in [5]. ↓

```
clear
s = 21.7655; m = 200; sigma = 20;
chi2 = (m-1)*s^2/sigma^2

x = linspace(0,300);
pd = chi2pdf(x, m-1);
plot(x, pd, 'k-'), hold on, box off
h = gcf; h.Color = 'w';
plot([chi2, chi2], [0, 0.025], 'k-')

lower = chi2inv(0.025, m-1)
plot([lower, lower], [0, chi2pdf(lower,m-1)], 'k-')
upper = chi2inv(0.975, m-1)
plot([upper, upper], [0, chi2pdf(upper,m-1)], 'k-')
xlabel('Chi-Square')
ylabel('Probability Density')
```

[5] This is the text output of Example13_05b.m. #

```
chi2 =
  235.6842
lower =
  161.8262
upper =
  239.9597
```

13.5c Chi-Square Test

Hypothesis Tests

[1] The logic behind a test such as that in 13.5b[1] is explained as follows. First, we assume the samples come from a random sampling of the population; i.e., the process is normal. If so, the most probable value of the sample variance s^2 must be the same as the population variance σ^2, and the most probable chi-square value must be m-1 (see Eq. 13.5a(a), page 500). However, in this case, the chi-square value is 235.68. The probability that the chi-square value deviates that much or more is $p = 7.68\%$, calculated by

```
p = chi2cdf(235.68, 199, 'upper')*2
```

If the probability is very small, then we have strong evidence to reject the assumption and conclude that the samples come from a different population, a "contaminated" population; i.e., the process is not normal. Otherwise, we have no reason to reject but to accept the assumption, i.e., the process is normal.

The probability p is called the **significance level**. We usually set up a threshold α for the significance level. In engineering application, we often use $\alpha = 5\%$, which is equivalent to using a confidence level of 95%; i.e., $\alpha = 1 - CL$. ↵

Example13_05c.m: Chi-Square Test

[2] This script calculates the significance level (lines 2-7). It also demonstrates the use of the function `vartest` to perform a chi-square test (line 9). ↓

```
1   clear
2   rng(0)
3   mu = 500; sigma = 20; m = 200;
4   data = normrnd(mu, sigma, 1, m);
5   s = std(data);
6   chi2 = (m-1)*s^2/sigma^2;
7   p1 = chi2cdf(chi2, m-1, 'upper')*2
8
9   [h, p2] = vartest(data, sigma^2)
```

[3] This is the output of Example13_05c.m. ↓

```
10  p1 =
11       0.0768
12  h =
13         0
14  p2 =
15       0.0768
```

About Example13_05c.m

[4] Lines 2-4 generate the 200 sample data as usual (Example13_01a.m, page 485). Lines 5-6 calculate the chi-square value (Eq. 13.5a(a), page 500). Line 7 finds the significance level (also see lines 10-11). If a threshold $\alpha = 5\%$ is used, then, since $7.68\% > \alpha$, we have no strong evidence to reject but to accept the assumption that the process is normal.

Line 9 uses the function `vartest` to perform the chi-square test, i.e., the procedure in lines 5-7. The function `vartest` takes the sample data and the population variance as input and outputs two values. If `h` = 1, it means the assumption is rejected; If `h` = 0, it means the assumption cannot be rejected. By default, a threshold of 5% for the significance level is used. Since 7.68% > 5%, we have no strong evidence to reject the assumption (lines 12-13). As the second output argument, the function `vartest` also outputs the significance level (lines 14-15). #

Table 13.5 Chi-Square Distribution

Functions	Description
`pd = chi2pdf(x, dof)`	Returns probability density of chi-square distribution with specified dof
`p = chi2cdf(x, dof)`	Returns cumulative probability of chi-square distribution with specified dof
`x = chi2inv(p, dof)`	Returns chi-square value, given cumulative probability
`[h,p] = vartest(data, dof)`	Chi-square variance test

Details and More: Help>Statistics and Machine Learning Toolbox>Probability Distributions>Continuous Distributions>Chi-Square Distribution
And: Help>Statistics and Machine Learning Toolbox>Hypothesis Tests

13.6 Student's *t*-Distribution

[1] In 13.1a[1] (page 484), the data are randomly sampled from a normally distributed population which has a known mean μ and a known variance σ^2. Assume that we have *m* samples, $x_1, x_2, \ldots, x_m$, from the population and let $\bar{x}$ be the sample mean and s^2 be the sample variance. Then, according to the Central Limit Theory

$$z = \frac{\bar{x} - \mu}{\sigma/\sqrt{m}}$$

follows the standard normal distribution.

In many other cases, the population variance σ^2 is not known, and the sample variance s^2 is used as an estimation of the population variance σ^2, and the σ in the expression above is replaced by *s*, i.e.,

$$t = \frac{\bar{x} - \mu}{s/\sqrt{m}}$$

Now, the quantity *t* does not follow the standard normal distribution any more. If *m* is large (say 200, as in Section 13.1), *s* would be a good approximation of σ, the difference between *t* and *z* would be negligible, and *t* would follow a distribution much the same as the standard normal distribution. However, if *m* is small, as in many practical situations, the difference is essential and *t* would follow a distribution that is quite different from the standard normal distribution.

It turns out that the distribution of *t* is similar to but different from the standard normal distribution. It is called a *t*-distribution with *m* - 1 degrees of freedom, published by an English statistician William Sealy Gosset (1876-1937) under the pseudonym "A Student." ↓

Student's *t*-Distribution

[2] Let $x_1, x_2, \ldots, x_m$ be random samples taken from a population of normal distribution with a mean μ and a variance σ^2. Let s^2 be the sample variance. Then, the quantity

$$t = \frac{\bar{x} - \mu}{s/\sqrt{m}} \quad \text{(a)}$$

has a *t*-distribution with *m* - 1 degrees of freedom.

We use Example13_06.m ([3], next page) to manifest the meaning of the above statements. We'll show that a *t*-distribution has a mean 0 and a variance 1 (see [4-5], page 507).

Degrees of Freedom

Consider a group of *m* data. If there exist *k* relations among these *m* data, then we said that the group of data has $m-k$ degrees of freedom (DOF). In other words, the DOF is the number of independent pieces of data.

Now, consider a group of *t*-values calculated from Eq. (a). These *t*-values are calculated from the *m* samples, $x_1, x_2, \ldots, x_m$; therefore, we might think that the group of *t*-values has *m* degrees of freedom. However, these data are not totally independent: their mean (μ) is known. Therefore, they have $m-1$ degrees of freedom. ↵

Example13_06.m: Student's *t*-Distribution

[3] This script generates a graphic output shown in [4-5], next page. ↵

```
clear
mu = 500; sigma = 20; m = 5;
n = 50000; rng(0)
data = normrnd(mu, sigma, m, n);
xbar = mean(data);
s = std(data);
t = (xbar-mu)./(s/sqrt(m));

mn = -5; mx = 5; bins = 40;
width = (mx-mn)/bins;
edges = mn:width:mx;
pd = histcounts(t, edges)/n/width;
x = mn+width/2:width:mx-width/2;
plot(x, pd, 'ko'), hold on
h = gcf; h.Color = 'w';

x = linspace(mn,mx);
pd = tpdf(x, m-1);
plot(x, pd, 'k-')

pd = normpdf(x);
plot(x, pd, 'b--')

xlabel('t')
ylabel('Probability Density')
title(['Student''s t-Distribution with ', ...
    num2str(m-1), ' Degrees of Freedom'])
legend('Simulation Data', 'By MATLAB Function')
```

[4] This is the output of Example13_06.m. →

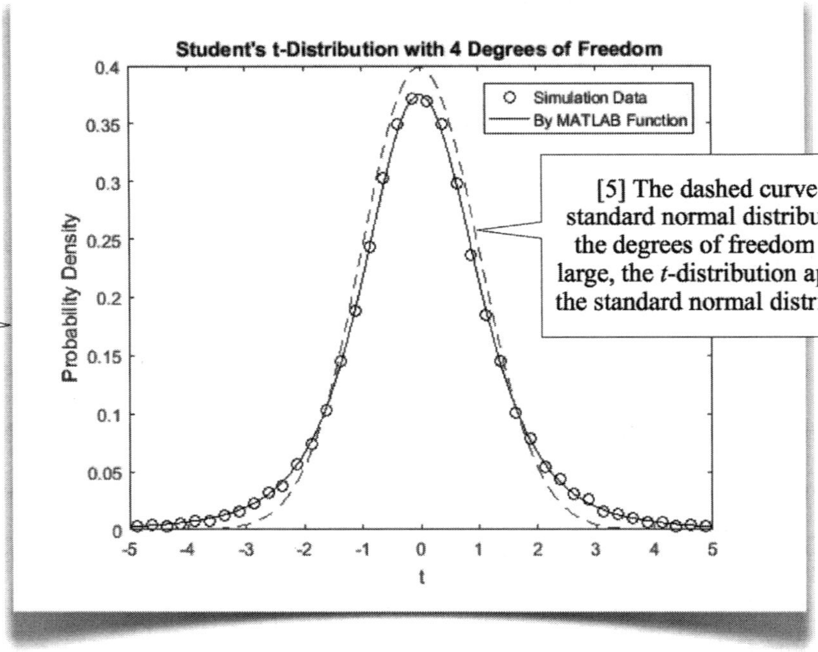

[5] **The dashed curve** is the **standard normal distribution**. As **the degrees of freedom** become **large, the *t*-distribution** approaches **the standard normal distribution**. ↓

About Example13_06.m

[6] Lines 2-4 generate a 5-by-50,000 matrix of normally distributed numbers with $\mu = 500$ and $\sigma = 20$. Lines 5-6 calculate the sample mean and the sample standard deviation, respectively, of the five data in each column. Both `xbar` and `s` are row vectors of 50,000 numbers. Line 7 calculates the *t*-values according to Eq. (a), page 505, resulting in a row vector of 50,000 numbers.

The 50,000 *t*-values are divided into 40 bins (lines 9-11). The number of occurrences in each bin is counted and probability density in each bin is calculated (line 12) and displayed using circular markers (lines 13-14). Line 15 sets the white color as the background color.

Lines 17-19 draw a *t*-distribution curve (solid line) with four degrees of freedom using the function `tpdf`. The simulated *t*-values (circular markers) are consistent with the analytical values calculated with the function `tpdf`.

Lines 21-22 add a dashed blue curve representing the standard normal distribution, to show the difference between a *t*-distribution and a standard normal distribution. As the degrees of freedom become large, the *t*-distribution will approach the standard normal distribution. To show this, you may change the sample size `m` in line 2 to a large number, e.g., 200. The resulting *t*-distribution curve will almost overlap with the standard normal distribution curve. #

Table 13.6 Student's *t*-Distribution

Functions	Description
`pd = tpdf(t, dof)`	Returns probability density of *t*-distribution with specified dof
`p = tcdf(t, dof)`	Returns cumulative probability of *t*-distribution with specified dof
`t = tinv(p, dof)`	Returns *t* value, given cumulative probability

Details and More: Help>Statistics and Machine Learning Toolbox>Probability Distributions>Continuous Distributions>Student's t Distribution

13.7 One-Sample *t*-Test: Voltage of Power Supply

Problem Description

[1] A manufacturer is concerned about the output voltage of a power supply, of which the target is 100 V. The output voltage is reasonably assumed to be normally distributed. The following are voltages sampled from the production line. Does the mean voltage of the samples significantly deviate from the target voltage 100 V, if a threshold of 5% is used as the significance level?

`126, 101, 105, 103, 98, 108, 107, 125, 107, 99`

Example13_07.m answers this question. In this example, the population variance is not known, and we need to approach it using the sample variance. ↓

Example13_07.m: Voltage of Power Supply

[2] This script calculates the significance level (lines 2-8). It also demonstrates the use of the function `ttest` to perform the one-sample *t*-test (line 10). ↓

```
1   clear
2   mu = 100;
3   data = [126, 101, 105, 103, 98, 108, 107, 125, 107, 99];
4   m = length(data);
5   xbar = mean(data);
6   s = std(data);
7   t = (xbar-mu)/(s/sqrt(m))
8   p1 = tcdf(t, m-1, 'upper')*2
9
10  [h, p2] = ttest(data, mu)
```

```
11  t =
12        2.5280
13  p1 =
14        0.0323
15  h =
16          1
17  p2 =
18        0.0323
```

[3] This is the output of Example13_07.m. ↓

About Example13_07.m

[4] Line 2 specifies the target voltage, 100 V. Line 3 creates the sample data. With the data, lines 4-7 calculate the *t*-value according to Eq. (a), page 505, in which, since the population variance is not known, we approach it using the sample variance *s*, calculated in line 6. Line 7 also outputs the *t*-value (lines 11-12), 2.528. Line 8 calculates the significance level (the probability that a *t*-value deviates from zero by more than ± 2.528) and outputs the result, 3.23% (lines 13-14).

Line 10 uses the function `ttest` to perform a one-sample *t*-test, a similar procedure in lines 4-8. The function `ttest` takes the sample data and the population mean as input and outputs two values. If h = 1, it means the assumption (the samples come from a population of normal distribution with mean $\mu = 100$ V; see [5], next page) is rejected; If h = 0, it means the assumption cannot be rejected. By default, a threshold of 5% for the significance level is used. Since 3.23% < 5%, we have strong evidence to reject the assumption (lines 15-16). It also outputs the significance level (17-18), the same as that output in line 8. ↵

One-Sample *t*-Test

[5] The logic behind the foregoing *t*-test is as follows. First, we assume that the sample data come from a population of normal distribution with mean $\mu = 100$ V and unknown variance. Then, according to 13.6[2] (page 505),

$$t = \frac{\bar{x} - \mu}{s/\sqrt{m}}$$

(where $\bar{x}$ is the sample mean, s is the sample standard deviation, and m is the sample size) follows a *t*-distribution with degrees of freedom $m-1$.

In this case, the calculated *t*-value is 2.528 (see [3], last page). The probability that a *t*-value deviates from zero by more than ±2.528 is 3.23% (see [3, 6]), which is the significance level. Since it is so improbable (less than the threshold, 5%), we have strong evidence to reject the assumption and conclude that the voltage of the samples significantly deviates from the target voltage, 100 V. ↓

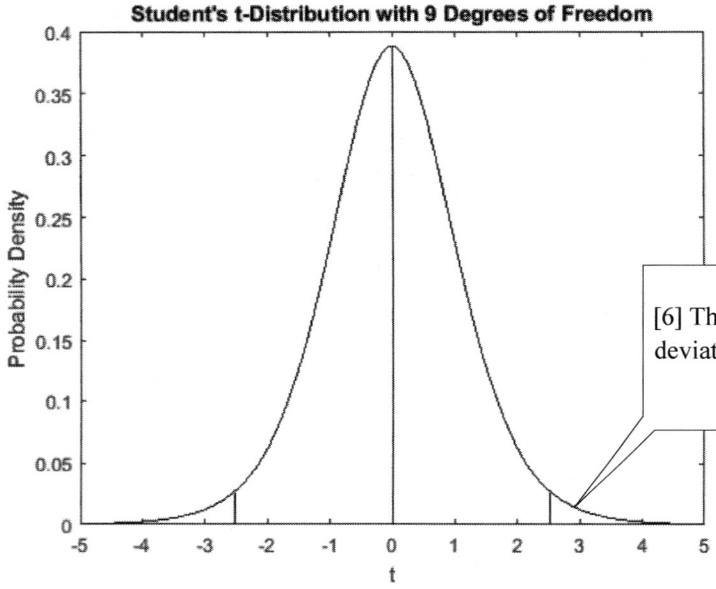

[6] The probability that a *t*-value deviates from zero by more than ±2.528 is 3.23%. #

Table 13.7 One-Sample *t*-Test

Functions	Description
`[h,p] = ttest(data, m)`	One-sample *t*-test
`[h,p] = ttest(data1, data2)`	Paired-sample *t*-test
Details and More: Help>Statistics and Machine Learning Toolbox>Hypothesis Tests	

13.8 Linear Combinations of Random Variables

[1] In many situations, we need to calculate the mean and the variance of a linear combination of random variables. Let x be a random variable with mean μ_x and variance v_x, y be another random variable with mean μ_y and variance v_y, and a and b be two real constant numbers; then

(a) The mean and variance of $(x+y)$ are $(\mu_x+\mu_y)$ and (v_x+v_y), respectively.
(b) The mean and variance of $(x-y)$ are $(\mu_x-\mu_y)$ and (v_x+v_y), respectively.
(c) The mean and variance of ax are $a\mu_x$ and a^2v_x, respectively.
(d) The mean and variance of x/a are μ_x/a and v_x/a^2, respectively.
(e) The mean and variance of $(ax \pm by)$ are $(a\mu_x \pm b\mu_y)$ and $(a^2v_x+b^2v_y)$, respectively. ↓

Example13_08.m: Mean and Variance

[2] This script confirms the properties in [1] by conducting simulations. ↘

```
1   clear
2   muX = 10; muY = 20; varX = 1; varY = 2;
3   n = 50000;
4   rng(0)
5   dataX = normrnd(muX, sqrt(varX), 1, n);
6   dataY = normrnd(muY, sqrt(varY), 1, n);
7   data = dataX + dataY;
8   mu1 = mean(data)
9   var1 = var(data)
10  data = dataX - dataY;
11  mu2 = mean(data)
12  var2 = var(data)
13  data = dataX*3;
14  mu3 = mean(data)
15  var3 = var(data)
16  data = dataX/3;
17  mu4 = mean(data)
18  var4 = var(data)
19  data = dataX*3 + dataY*2;
20  mu5 = mean(data)
21  var5 = var(data)
```

```
22  mu1 =
23      29.9990
24  var1 =
25      2.9874
26  mu2 =
27     -10.0049
28  var2 =
29      2.9795
30  mu3 =
31      29.9911
32  var3 =
33      8.9242
34  mu4 =
35      3.3323
36  var4 =
37      0.1102
38  mu5 =
39      69.9950
40  var5 =
41      16.9154
```

[3] This is the output of Example13_08.m. ↓

About Example13_08.m

[4] The properties in [1] apply to random variables of any distributions, not limited to normal distributions. For demonstration, here, we assume that each random variable has a normal distribution. More specifically, we assume (line 2) $\mu_x = 10$, $\mu_y = 20$, $v_x = 1$, and $v_y = 2$. Line 5 generates 50,000 data for x and line 6 generates another 50,000 data for y.

Lines 7-9, with the output in lines 22-25, confirm the property in (a).
Lines 10-12, with the output in lines 26-29, confirm the property in (b).
Lines 13-15, with the output in lines 30-33, confirm the property in (c).
Lines 16-18, with the output in lines 34-37, confirm the property in (d).
Lines 19-21, with the output in lines 38-41, confirm the property in (e). #

13.9 Two-Sample *t*-Test: Injection Molded Plastic

Problem Description: Injection Molded Plastic

[1] To improve the strength of an injection-molded plastic product, an engineer adds an additive into the material during the molding process. Molding tests are carried out and the strengths are measured by uniaxial tensile tests of the finished products. The table below records the tensile strengths of the sampled products, without and with the additive. The last two columns of the table calculate the sample means and the sample variances, respectively. We may reasonably assume that the tensile strengths distribute normally.

The engineer wants to know if the additive does improve the strength of the product. From the **robust process** point of view, a better process not only increases the mean tensile strength but also lowers the variance. From visual inspection of the table, it looks like, by adding the additive, the mean strength is improved (from 72.1 to 75.1), and so is the variance (from 30.7 to 15.2). However, statistic evidence is needed to conclude this. More specifically, there are two questions to ask: Are the two sample means significantly different? Are the two sample variances significantly different? If a difference is not statistically significant, it might be interpreted as simply the cause of the random sampling.

The first question will be answered in this section, using a two-sample *t*-test (see Example13_09.m). The second question will be answered in Section 13.11, using a two-sample *F*-test. ↓

	Tensile Strength (kgf)								Sample Mean	Sample Variance
Process 1. Without Additive	75	78	65	65	79	77	75	69	72.1	30.7
	74	79	66	67	64	68	76	76		
Process 2. With Additive	79	77	75	70	78	68	71	77	75.1	15.2
	79	74	73	78	72	74	83	74		

Example13_09.m: Injection Molded Plastic

[2] This script calculates the significance level (lines 2-15). It also demonstrates the use of the function `ttest2`, which performs a two-sample *t*-test (line 17), a similar procedure in lines 6-15. ↵

```
1   clear
2   data1 = [75, 78, 65, 65, 79, 77, 75, 69, ...
3            74, 79, 66, 67, 64, 68, 76, 76];
4   data2 = [79, 77, 75, 70, 78, 68, 71, 77, ...
5            79, 74, 73, 78, 82, 74, 83, 74];
6   m1 = length(data1)
7   m2 = length(data2)
8   xbar1 = mean(data1)
9   xbar2 = mean(data2)
10  var1 = var(data1)
11  var2 = var(data2)
12  varPooled = (var1*(m1-1)+var2*(m2-1))/((m1-1)+(m2-1))
13  varDiffAve = varPooled/m1 + varPooled/m2
14  t = (xbar1-xbar2)/sqrt(varDiffAve)
15  p1 = tcdf(t, (m1-1)+(m2-1))*2
16
17  [h, p2] = ttest2(data1, data2)
```

```
18    m1 =
19         16
20    m2 =
21         16
22    xbar1 =
23       72.0625
24    xbar2 =
25       75.7500
26    var1 =
27       30.7292
28    var2 =
29       17.2667
30    varPooled =
31       23.9979
32    varDiffAve =
33        2.9997
34    t =
35       -2.1291
36    p1 =
37        0.0416
38    h =
39         1
40    p2 =
41        0.0416
```

[3] This is the output of Example13_09.m. →

About Example13_09.m

[4] We first assume that both sets of sample data come from the same population (i.e., the additive has no effects on the tensile strength); then

$$t = \frac{\bar{x}_1 - \bar{x}_2}{s} \qquad \text{(a)}$$

follows a *t*-distribution with a degrees of freedom of the data that are used to calculate *s*, which is the standard deviation of $(\bar{x}_1 - \bar{x}_2)$, the difference between the sample means. To calculate *t*-value, we need to calculate *s* first.

Lines 2-5 create the two sets of sample data listed in [1], last page; their sample sizes are `m1` and `m2` (lines 6-7), respectively. Lines 8-9 calculate the respective sample means and lines 10-11 calculate the respective sample variances.

The assumption that both sets of sample data come from the same population implies that they have the same variances. Line 12 calculates the pooled variance (*see Wikipedia>Pooled variance*), using

$$v_{pooled} = \frac{v_1(m_1 - 1) + v_2(m_2 - 1)}{(m_1 - 1) + (m_2 - 1)} \qquad \text{(b)}$$

Line 13 calculates the variance of $(\bar{x}_1 - \bar{x}_2)$, according to 13.8[1], page 510,

$$v_{\bar{x}_1 - \bar{x}_2} = \frac{v_{pooled}}{m_1} + \frac{v_{pooled}}{m_2}$$

Line 14 calculates the *t*-value, using Eq. (a). Line 15 calculates the significance level and outputs the result, a significance level of 4.16%, as shown in lines 36-37.

Line 17 uses the function `ttest2` to perform a two-sample *t*-test, which takes the two sets of sample data as input and outputs two values. If `h` = 1, it means the assumption is rejected; If `h` = 0, it means the assumption cannot be rejected. By default, a threshold of 5% as the significance level is used. Since 4.16% < 5%, we have strong evidence to reject the assumption (lines 38-39). It also outputs the significance level, 4.16% (lines 40-41), which is consistent with the output in lines 36-37. #

Table 13.9 Two-Sample *t*-Test

Functions	Description
`[h,p] = ttest2(data1, data2)`	Two-sample *t*-test

Details and More: Help>Statistics and Machine Learning Toolbox>Hypothesis Tests

13.10 *F*-Distribution

F-Distribution

[1] Let s_1^2 be the variances of a set of samples of size m_1 taken from a population of normal distribution, and s_2^2 be the variance of another set of samples of size m_2 taken from the same population. Then, the ratio

$$F = \frac{s_1^2}{s_2^2} \tag{a}$$

follows an *F*-distribution with $m_1 - 1$ degrees of freedom in the numerator and $m_2 - 1$ degrees of freedom in the denominator.

We use Example13_10.m to manifest the meaning of the above statements. ↓

Example13_10.m: *F*-Distribution

[2] This script generates *F*-distributions as shown in [3-5], next page. ↵

```
clear
mu = 500; sigma = 20; m1 = 6; m2 = 16;
n = 50000; rng(0)
data1 = normrnd(mu, sigma, m1, n);
data2 = normrnd(mu, sigma, m2, n);
v1 = var(data1);
v2 = var(data2);
F = v1./v2;

mx = 6; bins = 40;
width = mx/bins;
edges = 0:width:mx;
pd = histcounts(F, edges)/n/width;
x = width/2:width:mx-width/2;
plot(x, pd, 'ko'), hold on
h = gcf; h.Color = 'w';

x = linspace(0,mx);
pd = fpdf(x, m1-1, m2-1);
plot(x, pd, 'k-')

xlabel('F')
ylabel('Probability Density')
title(['F-Distribution with Degrees of Freedom ', ...
    num2str(m1-1), '/', num2str(m2-1)])
legend('Simulation Data', 'By MATLAB Function')
```

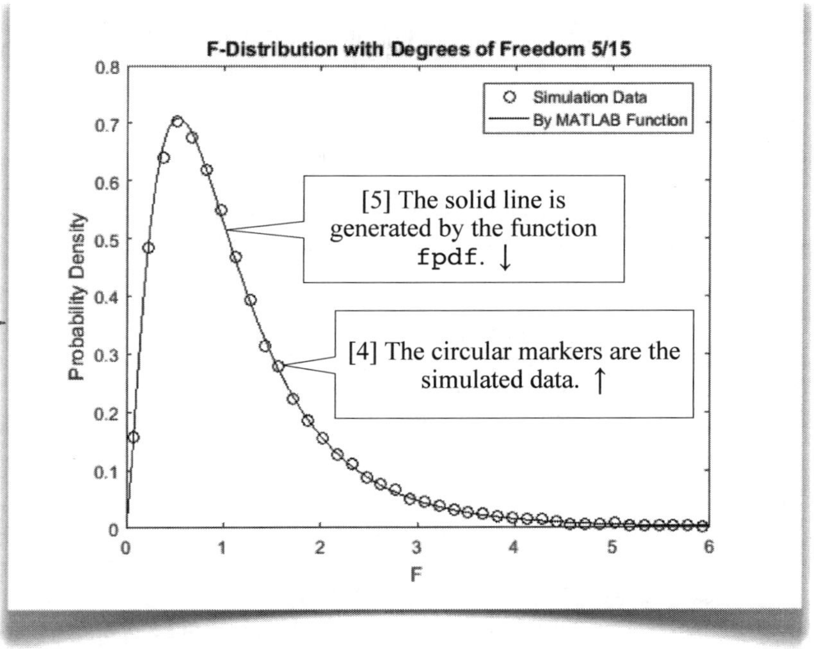

[3] This is the output of Example13_10.m. →

About Example13_10.m

[6] This script is similar to Example13_06.m (page 506), except that two sets of samples are generated (lines 4-5), both sampled from the same population of normal distribution. The common population mean and variance (`mu` and `sigma` in line 2) have no effects on the *F*-distribution; you may try different population mean and variance, and the *F*-distribution curves in [4-5] remain the same. The sample sizes `m1` and `m2` (line 2) are arbitrarily chosen. You may try other sample sizes to obtain different *F*-distribution curves.

Lines 3-5 generate a 6-by-50,000 and a 16-by-50,000 set of numbers, respectively, normally distributed with the specified mean and standard deviation. Lines 6-7 calculate the sample variances of the data in each column. Both `v1` and `v2` are row vectors of 50,000 numbers. Line 8 calculates the *F*-values according to Eq. (a), last page, resulting in a row vector of 50,000 numbers.

The 50,000 *F*-values are divided into 40 bins (lines 10-12). Number of occurrences in each bin is counted and probability density in each bin is calculated (line 13) and displayed using circular markers (lines 14-15; also see [4]).

Lines 18-20 draw an *F*-distribution curve (solid line) with 5 degrees of freedom in the numerator and 15 degrees of freedom in the denominator, using the function `fpdf`. The *F*-values calculated from the simulated data are consistent with those calculated analytically using the function `fpdf`.

Lines 22-26 add annotations to the graph. #

Table 13.10 *F*-Distribution

Functions	Description
`pd = fpdf(F, dof1, dof2)`	Returns probability density of *F*-distribution
`p = fcdf(F, dof1, dof2)`	Returns cumulative probability of *t*-distribution
`F = finv(p, dof1, dof2)`	Returns *F* value, given cumulative probability

Details and More:
Help>Statistics and Machine Learning Toolbox>Probability Distributions>Continuous Distributions>F Distribution

13.11 Two-Sample *F*-Test: Injection Molded Plastic

Problem Description: Injection Molded Plastic

[1] As mentioned in 13.9[1] (page 511), from the **robust process** point of view, we want not only to increase the mean tensile strength but also to decrease the variance of the tensile strength. In this section, we'll verify if the two sample variances (30.7 and 15.2, in 13.9[1], page 511) are significantly different, using a two-sample *F*-test. ↓

Example13_11.m: Injection Molded Plastic

[2] This script calculates the significance level (lines 2-10). It also demonstrates the use of the function `vartest2` to perform a two-sample *F*-test (line 12), a similar procedure in lines 6-10. ↓

```
1   clear
2   data1 = [75, 78, 65, 65, 79, 77, 75, 69, ...
3            74, 79, 66, 67, 64, 68, 76, 76];
4   data2 = [79, 77, 75, 70, 78, 68, 71, 77, ...
5            79, 74, 73, 78, 82, 74, 83, 74];
6   m1 = 16; m2 = 16;
7   var1 = var(data1)
8   var2 = var(data2)
9   F = var1/var2
10  p1 = fcdf(F, m1-1, m2-1, 'upper')*2
11
12  [h, p2] = vartest2(data1, data2)
```

[3] This is the output of Example13_11.m. ↓

```
13  var1 =
14      30.7292
15  var2 =
16      17.2667
17  F =
18      1.7797
19  p1 =
20      0.2755
21  h =
22      0
23  p2 =
24      0.2755
```

About Example13_11.m

[4] We assume the two samples come from the same population. Then

$$F = \frac{s_1^2}{s_2^2}$$

follows an *F*-distribution with the degrees of freedom of `data1` (line 2-3) in the numerator and the degrees of freedom of `data2` (line 4-5) in the denominator.

Lines 2-5 create the two sets of sample data listed in 13.9[1] (page 511), their sample sizes `m1` and `m2` (line 6), respectively. Lines 7-8 calculate the sample variances (also see lines 13-16), respectively. Line 9 calculates the *F*-value (also see lines 17-18), using the formula above. Line 10 calculates the significance level and outputs the result as shown in lines 19-20.

Line 12 uses the function `vartest2` to perform a two-sample *F*-test, which takes the two sets of sample data as input and outputs two values. If `h` = 1, it means the assumption is rejected; if `h` = 0, it means the assumption cannot be rejected. By default, a threshold of 5% for the significance level is used. Since 27.55% > 5%, we have no strong evidence to reject the assumption (lines 21-22). It also outputs the significance level, as shown in lines 23-24.

This is also illustrated in [5-6], next page. ↵

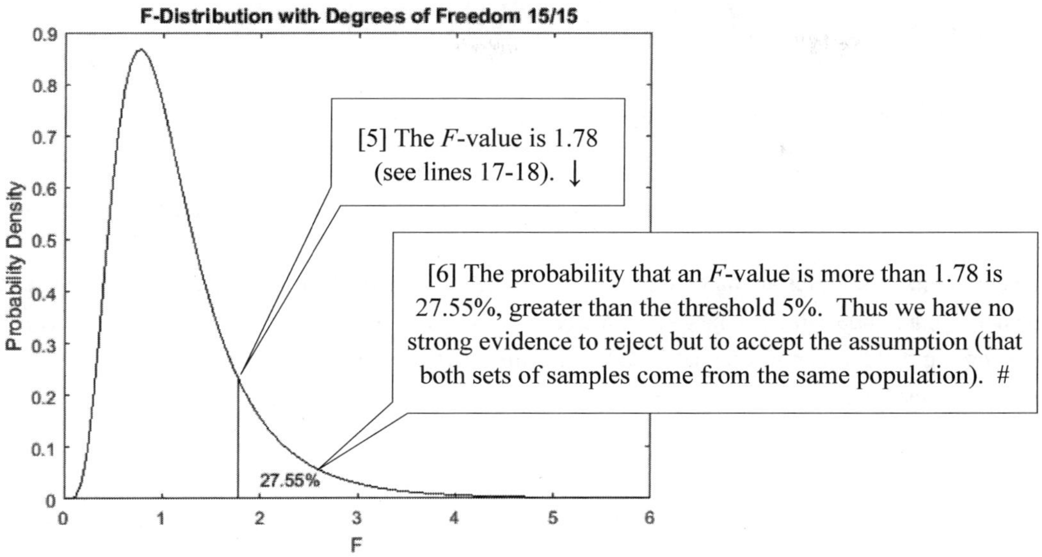

Table 13.11 Two-Sample *F*-Test	
Functions	Description
`[h,p] = vartest2(data1, data2)`	Two-sample *F*-test for equal variances
Details and More: Help>Statistics and Machine Learning Toolbox>Hypothesis Tests	

13.12 Comparison of Means by *F*-Test

Problem Description: Injection Molded Plastic

[1] In Section 13.9, we used a two-sample *t*-test to determine whether the two sample means (72.1 and 75.1) are significantly different. An equivalent way is to see if the **variance** of $\overline{x}_1$ (72.1) and $\overline{x}_2$ (75.1) is significantly larger than it should be.

Again, we assume the two sets of samples are taken from the same population, for which we use a pooled variance s_x^2 (24.0; see line 12 in page 511 and lines 30-31 in page 512) to approach the population variance. According to the Central Limit Theory, and noting that the sample means $\overline{x}_1$ and $\overline{x}_2$ are the averages of every *m* (16) sample data, another way to approach the population variance is

$$s_y^2 = m \times \mathrm{var}(\overline{x}_1, \overline{x}_2) \tag{a}$$

If the two variances (s_x^2 and s_y^2) are significantly different, then we may reject the assumption (that both sets of samples come from the same population) and conclude that the adding of the additive does affect the process.

Example13_12.m finds the significance level using an *F*-distribution. ↓

Example13_12.m: Injection Molded Plastic

[2] This script calculates the significance level using an *F*-distribution. →

```
clear
data1 = [75, 78, 65, 65, 79, 77, 75, 69, ...
          74, 79, 66, 67, 64, 68, 76, 76];
data2 = [79, 77, 75, 70, 78, 68, 71, 77, ...
          79, 74, 73, 78, 82, 74, 83, 74];
m = 16;
xbar1 = mean(data1);
xbar2 = mean(data2);
var1 = var(data1);
var2 = var(data2);
varx = (var1*(m-1)+var2*(m-1))/((m-1)+(m-1))
vary = m*var([xbar1, xbar2])
F = vary/varx
p = fcdf(F, 1, (m-1)+(m-1), 'upper')
```

```
varx =
    23.9979
vary =
   108.7812
F =
     4.5329
p =
     0.0416
```

[3] This is the output of Example13_12.m. ↵

About Example13_12.m

[4] We assume that both sets of samples come from the same population. Then

$$F = \frac{s_y^2}{s_x^2}$$

follows an *F*-distribution with one degrees of freedom in the numerator and 30 degrees of freedom in the denominator.

Lines 2-5 create the two sets of sample data, respectively, as usual. Lines 7-8 calculate the two sample means and lines 9-10 calculate the two sample variances. Line 11 calculates the pooled variance (see Eq. (b), page 512; also see lines 15-16, last page). Applying the Central Limit Theory, line 12 uses Eq. (a), last page, to estimate the population variance (also see lines 17-18). Line 13 calculates the *F*-value (also see lines 19-20), using the formula above. Line 14 calculates the significance level and outputs the result as shown in lines 21-22. Note that the significance level (4.16%) calculated using the *F*-test in this section is the same as that in the two-sample *t*-test (see lines 40-41, page 512). And we reach the same conclusion as that in Section 13.9.

This is also illustrated in [5-6]. ↓

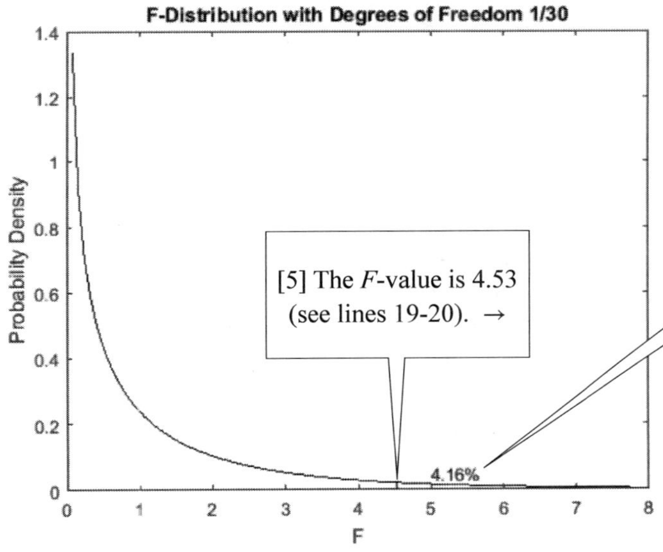

[6] The probability that an *F*-value is more than 4.53 is 4.16% (line 21-22), less than the threshold 5%. Thus we have strong evidence to reject assumption. We conclude that the adding of the additive significantly modifies the population. The additive is a significant factor for the process. ↓

t-Test or *F*-Test?

[7] If you have two means to compare, you may use either a *t*-test, as described in Section 13.9 or an *F*-Test as described in this section. The calculated significance level is the same, as demonstrated in this section. In engineering application, this procedure is extensively used to test if a factor significantly affects the performance of a process or a product.

An advantage of the *F*-test over the *t*-test is that it is applicable when a factor has more than two possible settings. In our example, the factor has only two settings: without or with the additive; both approaches are applicable. If we consider three possible settings--without the additive, with 50% of the additive, and with 100% of the additive--then the *F*-test is much more convenient than the *t*-test. When two or more factors are considered simultaneously, the *F*-test is even much more powerful than the *t*-test. #

Index